STANDING UP FOR JUSTICE

STANDING UP FOR JUSTICE

The Challenges of Trying Atrocity Crimes

THEODOR MERON

OXFORD
UNIVERSITY PRESS

OXFORD
UNIVERSITY PRESS

Great Clarendon Street, Oxford, OX2 6DP,
United Kingdom

Oxford University Press is a department of the University of Oxford.
It furthers the University's objective of excellence in research, scholarship,
and education by publishing worldwide. Oxford is a registered trade mark of
Oxford University Press in the UK and in certain other countries

First Edition published in 2021

Impression: 1

Published in the United States of America by Oxford University Press
198 Madison Avenue, New York, NY 10016, United States of America

British Library Cataloguing in Publication Data

Data available

Library of Congress Control Number: 2020947158

ISBN 978–0–19–886343–4

DOI: 10.1093/oso/9780198863434.001.0001

Printed and bound in
the UK by TJ Books Limited

Contents

Preface xi

PART I: SETTING THE SCENE

I. Roots: The Road to Judgeship 3
The Holocaust 4
And Life Goes On 7
The Palestine Opinions 9
In Academia 16
The International Committee of the Red Cross 17
The Dauchy Case 19
The State Department 20
Judgeships 21
Shakespeare 26
Oxford 29
Looking Back 29

II. From Classroom to a Criminal Courtroom 31

III. Moving from Nuremberg to The Hague 39
The Necessity to Establish a Tribunal for the Former Yugoslavia 39
State of the Law: The Example of Rape 43
Non-International Armed Conflicts 49
Nuremberg Proceedings 50
Moving Forward with the Law and Due Process 53
Justifying International Criminal Tribunals 65

PART II: PRINCIPLES, GOALS, PROCESSES

IV. The Rule of Law, the Principle of Legality and Due Process 69
The Rule of Law 69
Reifying Rule of Law Principles 71

Principle of Legality 73
Selective Accountability 91
Due Process 92

V. Trying Violations of Human Rights in International Criminal Tribunals 103
Post-World War II Changes 104
The Establishment of International Criminal Tribunals 106
Common Article 3 and Crimes Against Humanity 107
Persecution 112

VI. Judicial Independence and Impartiality 116
Why Judicial Independence Matters 118
Ensuring an Independent Judiciary 119
Judicial Selection 121
Should Judges Respond to Outside Criticism? 123
Judicial Assignments and Court Presidents 124
Judicial Bias and Recusal 127
Institutional Design and Management 132
The Presidency and the Prosecution 133
Communicating with the Public 134
Rules and Obstructive Behavior of Defendants 135
The Saga of the Turkish Judge Akay 136

VII. Judicial Decision-Making and Deliberations 143
Decision-Making 143
The uniqueness of the Tribunals 144
Decision-makers 145
Judges and staff—background 146
Judges—processes 148
The Deliberation Process at International Criminal Tribunals 149
Civil Law and Common Law Courts 151
Deliberations at the ICTY/ICTR Appeals Chambers 152
Appeals from Judgements 152
Before the hearing 153
The hearing 154
After the hearing 155
Sentencing deliberations 158
Separate/dissenting opinions 159

Interlocutory appeals, pre-appeal decisions and petitions for review 160
Deliberations at the Trial Chambers 162
Challenges for the Mechanism 163
VIII. Keeping POWs Safe: The Ovčara Massacre **164**
IX. General Gotovina: A Controversial Acquittal **173**
The Background 173
I. Excerpts from the Appeals Chamber Majority Judgement of Acquittal of Gotovina 174
II. A Separate Opinion on Alternate Modes of Liability 177
III. Judgement of the ICJ Supporting the *Gotovina* Majority Decision 179

PART III: SELECTED DECISIONS

X. Fleshing Out Principles of Fairness **185**
Prosecutor v. Ngirabatware 185
Nahimana, Barayagwiza and Ngeze v. The Prosecutor 187
Prosecutor v. Galić 188
Renzaho v. The Prosecutor 189
Prosecutor v. Hadžihasanović and Kubura 190
Prosecutor v. Šešelj 190
Prosecutor v. Mladić 191
Prosecutor v. Mladić 193
Prosecutor v. Šešelj 195
Prosecutor v. Galić 196
Slobodan Milošević v. The Prosecutor 197
Prosecutor v. Slobodan Milošević 199
Zigiranyirazo v. The Prosecutor 200
Prosecutor v. Prlić, Stojić, Praljak, Petković, Ćorić and Pušić 202
Prosecutor v. Karadžić 203
Prosecutor v. Nyiramasuhuko, Ntahobali, Nsabimana, Nteziryayo, Kanyabashi and Ndayambaje 204
Mugenzi and Mugiraneza v. The Prosecutor 206
Prosecutor v. Dragan Nikolić 207
Prosecutor v. Bralo 209
Ntabakuze v. The Prosecutor 210

Prosecutor v. Mrkšić, Šljivančanin 211
Prosecutor v. Karadžić 212

XI. Writing Separately: My Dissenting and Concurring Opinions 215
Nahimana, Barayagwiza and Ngeze v. The Prosecutor 215
Prosecutor v. Galić 225
Bagosora and Nsengiyumva v. The Prosecutor 233
Prosecutor v. Strugar 237
Prosecutor v. Halilović 242
Gacumbitsi v. The Prosecutor 245
Prosecutor v. Gotovina and Markač 250
Prosecutor v. Brđanin 253
Muvunyi v. The Prosecutor 257
Prosecutor v. Stakić 261

XII. Early Release of Prisoners Decisions 263
Background 263
Key Early Release Decisions 268
Prosecutor v. Bisengimana 268
Prosecutor v. Ntakirutimana 272
Prosecutor v. Lazarević 274
Prosecutor v. Galić 276
Prosecutor v. Beara 279
Prosecutor v. Kunarac 286
Prosecutor v. Simba 289
Prosecutor v. Ćorić 298

EPILOGUE

XIII. The Road Ahead: Does International Justice Work? 311
Invigorate the New Era of Accountability 311
Close the Accountability Gap 312
Comply with Existing Obligations 316
Encourage and Invigorate Prosecutions under the Principle of Universal Jurisdiction 318
Review and Revise Laws and Practices to Ensure Due Process, Fair Trials and Judicial Independence 320
Invest in Justice Infrastructure 322
Consider and Support Regional Accountability Initiatives 323

Develop Innovative Solutions to Foster Greater Accountability—
and Revisit or Recycle Past Approaches Where Appropriate 324
Foreswear Amnesties and Targeted Immunities 327
Sustain Support for and Cooperation with Existing Accountability
Mechanisms 329
Tackle Apathy, Intransigence and the Absence of Political Will 332
Measure Success 334
Reflecting on my Personal Journey 345

Index 349

Preface

This book is about fairness, justice and due process of proceedings in international courts and tribunals, principles on which the legitimacy of the project of international criminal justice rests. Standing up for them is vital, now more than ever, when principles of international law and accountability are challenged.

It is not about definitions of crimes and details of procedures. It is about the judicial perspective of trying atrocity crimes, that is the crime of genocide, crimes against humanity and war crimes.

In writing I have benefited from my work over two decades as a Judge of the International Criminal Tribunal for the former Yugoslavia (ICTY), the International Criminal Tribunal for Rwanda (ICTR) and the International Residual Mechanism for Criminal Tribunals (Mechanism), and, in particular, from the experience gained over four terms as President of the ICTY and three terms as President of the Mechanism.

I am grateful to my friends and colleagues for their suggestions and comments, and in particular to Isabelle Lambert, Willow Crystal, Julie Bloch, Professor Jean Galbraith, Professor Miles Jackson, Zoe Flood, Gabrielle McIntyre, Karen Johnson and to the many law clerks who have so greatly enriched my understanding of and commitment to the law.

Many thanks to Merel Alstein for steering the book through the commissioning process and for her insightful comments on early drafts; to Production Editors Lucía Pérez and Matthew Humphrys for guiding and energizing the production of the book; to Jack McNichol and all of Oxford University Press; and to Joy Ruskin-Tompkins for her excellent copy-editing.

I appreciate Dame Hilary Boulding, President of Trinity College, Oxford, and her predecessor Sir Ivor Roberts for giving me a friendly home in Oxford and excellent facilities for writing.

In Chapter III, I drew on an essay co-authored with Jean Galbraith and published in *International Law Stories* (John E. Noyes, Laura A. Dickinson and Mark A. Janis eds, 2007) and in Chapter VII, I drew on an essay co-authored with Christos Ravanides and published in *Collective Judging in Comparative Perspective: Counting Votes and Weighing Opinions* (Birke Hacker and Wolfgang Ernst eds, 2020).

PART I

Setting the Scene

I

Roots

The Road to Judgeship

Why should a book about judging war crimes start with a chapter about one's life, one's childhood, miseries, the ups and downs of a long professional life? One of my close friends, a former law clerk, was among those who suggested a book about judging, arguing that if a Judge's life turns on integrity, independence, ethics, surely, these are not qualities to be acquired at the age of 71 when I first became a Judge. By that age, she said, you either have those qualities or not and your readers will want to know something about your past life to judge your credibility. Others have made similar points. When I gave my last briefing, my swan song to the U.N. Security Council on 11 December 2018 as President of the International Residual Mechanism for Criminal Tribunals, the permanent representative of our host country, the Netherlands, in his generous remarks about my contribution to international criminal law concluded on a personal note. He hoped I would write an autobiography. I have never expected so many members of the Council to give me such a generous personal sendoff.

I decided only to follow these suggestions in part, both because of my reluctance to discuss personal and family matters and because I did not wish to revive controversies in which my presidency of the Tribunals was sometimes involved. Personal or autobiographical aspects will therefore be limited largely to my pre-Judgeship life and to this chapter.

I peaked late in life. I became a full-time academic at the age of 48 and a Judge at the age of 71. And I am completing this book soon after my 90th birthday.

I find it difficult writing this chapter; these personal, rather autobiographical notes. Doing so compels an inquiry into the private domain, the piercing of the veil on essentially private experiences: motivation, achievement,

Standing Up For Justice. Theodor Meron, Oxford University Press (2021). © Theodor Meron.
DOI: 10.1093/oso/9780198863434.003.0001

failure. Striking the right balance between the personal dimension and saying something that may be of interest to readers is challenging. But there is no question that what we write and when we write can only be explained by our own life experiences. I am reminded of a saying attributed to Talmudic sages: "We don't see things as they are, we see things as we are."

The Holocaust

I was born in 1930 in a small town in Poland to a Jewish family, traditionally in the lumber trade, and had a happy but, alas, short childhood. My family leased forests for logging—no one had heard about ecology then—and I spent my summers in villages in the heart of thick, mysterious forests. My fascination for and love of forests has never faded.

By the age of nine, Nazi Germany had invaded Poland, and I was out of school for the duration of World War II. Ghettos and work camps followed, with most of my family falling victim to the Holocaust. When the war ended, I emerged, lucky to be alive, with a hunger for school, for learning, for normality. In 1945, I left Poland for Palestine where I had a wonderful aunt and uncle, who spared no effort in providing me with education and love.

I have to say something about my complex relationship with Poland, the country of my birth. My years in prewar Kalisz, and summers in forests and villages, are largely shrouded in the fog of time. But I still remember kayaking and biking in the summers, skating in the winters and playing hide and seek in my grandfather's lumberyard. Strangely, what survived are the melodies, children's songs and Chopin, often played in school ceremonies.

Next came the war years, largely in Częstochowa, so different and painful. The ghettos, the labor camp, German and Ukrainian SS, most of my family falling victim to the Holocaust. Even during those apocalyptic times, where Poles appeared threatening, hostile and brutally anti-Semitic, there were moments of light, of which I learned only after the war, with many Polish Catholics risking their lives to save Jews, some in my own family. In the threatening sea of anti-Semitism, there were some islands of humanity.

My departure from Poland after the war was followed by a deliberate disconnect, rejection, denial. I did not want to hear of Poland or talk of my wartime experience. I felt embarrassed by my victimhood. I often had nightmares in which I was escaping Germans in black uniforms who were chasing me, not catching me, but chasing and chasing, until I would wake up, sweating. In vain I tried to forget. I could not even think of coming back face to face with places that left such a painful, traumatic imprint on my life. I did not expect to see Poland again. I probably would never have had the courage to go back were it not for an invitation from the International Committee of the Red Cross (ICRC), in 1986, to lecture in their Warsaw Summer Course on International Humanitarian Law. Nor would I have gone without the company and the encouragement of my wife, M. So I decided to confront the past. We travelled to Kalisz, Częstochowa, Treblinka and Auschwitz so closely resonating with the war, and also to Kraków, Kazimierz and Gdynia. It was an incredibly painful trip. I have never believed that a direct confrontation with a traumatic past can liberate a person from the demons of the past. Fortunately, I was proved wrong. The catharsis of returning to my childhood venues exorcised from me the ghosts and nightmares of my childhood. And these have not come back to haunt me ever again. Since then, I have returned to Poland many times, including in 2011 to receive an honorary doctorate from the University of Warsaw. In 2017, Poland made me an Officer of the Order of Merit. I have previously been decorated by France and recently by the United Kingdom but a decoration from Poland was certainly more surprising. I reconciled with the new Poland. I wish it well and hope that its democracy will thrive. I appreciated the fact that Poland invited me to brief the Security Council when it had the Council presidency in 2019.

I was invited to give the Holocaust keynote speech at the United Nations Holocaust Memorial Ceremony marking the 75th anniversary of the liberation of Auschwitz on 27 January 2020. I had never before spoken about the Holocaust in such detail. In my speech I tried to make clear that the German killing machine did not only target Jews, but also the Roma, Poles, Russians and others and I acknowledged those who risked their lives to save Jews:

> It is often forgotten that millions of Poles and Russians also fell victim to the Nazi killing machine. I grieve them all.
>
> The events of the Holocaust may seem far away to many of you, separated as they are from us by decades of progress. But for those who lived through them, as I did as a boy in occupied Poland, they are all too real. By the age of nine when the Nazi Germany invaded, I was overnight a refugee, out of school, out of childhood and constantly in clear and present danger.

What followed was the ghettos, work camps, most of my family falling victim to the Holocaust.

The saving of its entire Jewish population by the people of Denmark will remain forever as a rare epitome of true humanism.

I find it striking that a country which was as anti-Semitic as Poland produced the highest number of righteous gentiles, non-Jews who saved Jews, recognized as such by Yad Vashem in Israel.

And yes, there are stories of bravery and righteousness, of individuals standing up to be counted when the time to do so has come. I think of the young German soldier who found my maternal grandparents in their hiding place and, risking his life, decided not to turn them in. They thus survived for a few more months until caught in the Nazi net.

I think of the Warsaw Catholic baker who sheltered a little girl for all those years, risking her life and that of her own daughter.

I think of Aristides de Sousa Mendes, the Portuguese consul in Bordeaux who in defiance of orders saved thousands of Jews by giving them visas and was, as a result, destroyed by Salazar, or the Pole Jan Karski who infiltrated the Warsaw Ghetto and an extermination camp and then travelled to the West to report to the Allies on the unbelievable destruction that was being inflicted on the Jews. Alas, bombing rail lines to the death camps was not on the Allies' priority list.

It is from acts of humanity that seeds of reconciliation and a shared sense of humanity emerge. Remembrance and acknowledgement of historic crimes, coming clean with the past, is essential to the process of reconciliation.

...

I pay homage to President Chirac who, breaking with a long taboo, accepted the responsibility of France for Vichy's collaboration with the enforcement of the Holocaust, for committing, in the words of Chirac, "the irreparable."

When the war ended I emerged with a hunger for school, for learning, for normality. That I, a child of the Holocaust, was given by fate the honour of presiding over UN War Crimes Tribunals, and of judging the Krstić appeal, the first post-war genocide committed on European soil, the mass killings at Srebrenica, and doing it justly and fairly, is, to myself, one of the wonders of my life.[1]

I ended the speech with the prayer that "neither we nor our children will be victims, or even worse, perpetrators of genocide," and, to paraphrase

1. To view the speech, https://news.un.org/en/story/2020/01/1056122.

Sir Michael Howard's Holocaust speech to the Oxford Chabad Society, that we will not be "those who simply let this happen: thinking the kind of things, tolerating the kind of behavior that ultimately makes genocides possible."

And Life Goes On

In Palestine I faced the daunting task, never quite achieved, of catching up with six lost years. I was catapulted from the age of nine into a difficult young adulthood. Learning Hebrew and English, and mathematics, to pass the high school final exams was hard. I had no time for anything but studying. I attended a high school in Haifa, followed by military service, then studies at the law schools of the University of Jerusalem, Harvard University and the University of Cambridge. In Jerusalem I started focusing on international law. At the two Cambridges I worked on hardly anything else. Jerusalem gave me a solid legal foundation, but I found the old-fashioned educational system, largely based on lectures and memory, to be uninspiring, even boring. It was at Harvard, with its analytical method, that I became comfortable with the law, and knew it was to be my vocation. The imprint of the war made me particularly interested in working in areas that could contribute to making atrocities impossible and eliminate the horrible chaos, the helplessness and the loss of autonomy and normality that I remembered so well.

At Harvard, I was fortunate to become a student of and research assistant to two masters of international law—one specializing in humanitarian law and the law of war, the other in human rights—who became my mentors and models, and with whom I worked on a project of codification/restatement of the law of State responsibility. They were Richard Baxter, later a Judge of the International Court of Justice, and Louis Sohn. As it happened, much of my later scholarship and practice was in these areas. At the University of Cambridge as a Humanitarian Law Scholar, a scholarship which was offered to me by Sir Hersch Lauterpacht on Baxter's recommendation, I was approached by another person to whom I owe a debt of gratitude for contributing so much to my legal education and career: Shabtai Rosenne, the Legal Adviser of the Israeli Foreign Ministry. He offered me a job, which I accepted. I would have preferred an academic job and was exploring British universities, but none was in sight. I stayed in the Israeli foreign service for about 20 years, resigning for personal reasons in 1977 and moving permanently to the United States, where I joined NYU School of Law as a professor of international law.

My diplomatic experience started with the Office of the Legal Adviser of the Ministry for Foreign Affairs in Jerusalem, continued with the Permanent Mission to the U.N. in New York and moved on to Ambassador to Canada and finally to the Permanent Mission to the U.N. in Geneva, which I headed for less than a year before resigning. I became acquainted with NYU Law School when I was in New York for a Rockefeller Foundation Fellowship in 1975–1976 and taught as a visiting professor, upon invitation arranged by my life-long Harvard friend and distinguished internationalist Professor Thomas Franck. I greatly liked its open, friendly, reflective environment, and appreciated its offer to return to teach full time, when after resignation from the Ministry for Foreign Affairs, my future prospects looked quite bleak.

I have, of course, been very, very lucky. After the abyss of the World War II years, life compensated me with so many openings and unusual experiences. My writings grew out of these windows of opportunity. Yet, looking back, I can see something imperfectly resembling an integral whole emerging from the discrete segments. That does not mean that the goal of complete coherence was achievable or even desirable. A combination of chance and seized opportunity sometimes leading in different directions has been critically important. The situation, the circumstances, the needs and the institutional constraints were often the controlling factors. But despite engagement in different activities, when the opportunities arose, I chose those that fitted with my chosen purposes, especially the humanization of the law.

The Israeli Foreign Ministry provided me with an invaluable experience of writing legal opinions, participating in international conferences and litigating cases. It helped me to gain a practical perspective. Soon after my arrival in Jerusalem from the University of Cambridge, I joined the team suing Bulgaria before the International Court of Justice in the case of the Aerial Incident of 27 July 1955 during the height of the Cold War. It was a tragic case in which an El Al passenger plane strayed into Bulgarian air space during a storm and was shot down, causing the death of all the passengers and crew. Bulgaria contested jurisdiction and prevailed, resulting in the dismissal of the claim.

One of the more interesting legal issues was whether in such a case, where the contact with the territorial State was not deliberate and voluntary, there was an obligation for the claimant to exhaust local remedies before suing before the international court. In an article published in the *British Yearbook of International Law* in 1959, I argued that there was no such obligation and suggested parameters for the applicability of the doctrine of local remedies. I had already published law review articles based on my studies at Harvard and my Harvard doctoral dissertation, but the local remedies article was the first in which my practice resulted in a discrete contribution to the theory of international law. I still remember how pleased I was when Professor Roberto Ago, a giant of international law, cited it in his work on State responsibility in the International Law Commission.

In 1961, I joined the Permanent Mission of Israel to the U.N. in New York. As a representative on the Fifth Committee (Administrative and Budgetary), most of my official work was on administrative problems of the U.N. and its Secretariat. I became concerned about the politicization of the Secretariat, its tendency to slide from an international to a multinational institution, the rampant discrimination against women and the inadequacy of due process provisions for the staff of the Secretariat. As Counsellor I also had some political functions and entertained close relations with the officials of the Palestine Conciliation Commission. I fully reported to the Ministry on my meetings and discussions. These discussions involved what appears now to be totally utopian solutions for the Arab refugees from the 1948 war. Naively, I felt such ideas should be discussed and tested and some reasonable solution should be found to end the plight of the refugees. My reports quickly proved to be an embarrassment for Golda Meir, the Minister for Foreign Affairs, who called me to order, instructing me to cease and desist. The question of Arab refugees was placed out of bounds.

The Palestine Opinions

My U.N. period ended with the Six-Day War in June 1967; a traumatic period in which, from the perspective of an Israeli diplomat in New York, the future and the survival of Israel were very much at stake. In June, shortly after the fighting was concluded with a victory for Israel, I was offered the job of the Legal Adviser of the Foreign Ministry in Jerusalem—a significant promotion for a 37 year old—to succeed the great scholar Shabtai Rosenne, who was being moved to New York.

It was in many ways a baptism of fire. Within weeks of my arrival in Jerusalem, I was requested to advise the Prime Minister whether the establishment of Jewish civilian settlements in the occupied West Bank, the Golan Heights and Gaza was allowed by international law. I refer here to a secret legal opinion brought to light many years later by the Israeli journalist Tom Segev,[2] and the historian Gershom Gorenberg in his book *The Accidental Empire* (2006), and reported in *The New York Times*,[3] and by Donald Macintyre in *The Independent*,[4] and subsequently Christiane Amanpour on CNN, and many others. In this Opinion, I wrote that the establishment of civilian settlements in occupied territory violated the Fourth Geneva Convention as well as the private property rights of the Arab inhabitants. The Israeli Government chose to go another way and a wave of settlements followed, making the prospects for a political solution so much more difficult. Although I knew that this was not the opinion that the Prime Minister would have wished me to deliver, I had no doubt that legal advisers of governments must be faithful to the law and call the law as they see it. To the credit of the Israeli government, I must note that there were no repercussions, of which I was aware, from my unpopular opinion. The opinion reflected a commitment to human rights and humanitarian law and it dealt not only with the rights and obligations of States, but with the rights of inhabitants. The following year, on 12 March 1968, I gave another controversial opinion, one in which I stated that the demolition of houses and deportations of Arabs suspected of subversive activities were violations of the Geneva Conventions and constituted collective punishment. The full opinion was later translated into English by the NGO HaMoked.[5]

Oddly, these two opinions have become the best known of all my writings.

The first opinion written in Hebrew bureaucratic language uses expressions I would not use as a scholar or a Judge. But it is clear and concise and does not try to mask the conflict between the establishment of the settlements and international law. Here it is, in part, in translation from the original Hebrew:

Ministry of Foreign Affairs

Jerusalem, 13 Elul 5727
18 September 1967

TOP SECRET

To: Mr Adi Yafeh, Political Secretary to the Prime Minister
From: Legal Adviser, Ministry of Foreign Affairs

2. Tom Segev, Israel in 1967: and the Land Changed its Visage 611 (2005).
3. Gershom Gorenberg, *Israel's Tragedy Foretold*, New York Times, 10 Mar. 2006, Editorials/Op-Ed. Web.
4. Donald Macintyre, *Israelis Were Warned on Illegality of Settlements in 1967 Memo*, The Independent, 11 Mar. 2006, Web.
5. *See* http://www.hamoked.org.

Subject: Settlement in the Administered Territories

At your and Mr Raviv's request, I am enclosing herewith a copy of my memorandum of 14.9.67 on the above subject, which I submitted to the Minister of Foreign Affairs. My conclusion is that civilian settlement in the administered territories contravenes explicit provisions of the Fourth Geneva Convention.

Regards,

[signed]
T. Meron

Copy: Mr A. Shimoni, Director of the Minister's Office

14.9.67
To: Minister of Foreign Affairs
From: Legal Adviser
Most Urgent
TOP SECRET

Subject: Settlement in the Administered Territories

… From the point of view of international law, the key provision is the one that appears in the last paragraph of Article 49 of the Fourth Geneva Convention. Israel, of course, is a party to this Convention. The paragraph stipulates as follows:

> "The occupying power shall not deport or transfer parts of its own civilian population into the territory it occupies".

The Commentary on the Fourth Geneva Convention prepared by the International Committee of the Red Cross in 1958 states:

> This clause was adopted after some hesitation, by the XVIIth International Red Cross Conference. It is intended to prevent a practice adopted during the Second World War by certain Powers, which transferred portions of their own population to occupied territory for political and racial reasons or in order, as they claimed, to colonize those territories. Such transfers worsened the economic situation of the native population and endangered their separate existence as a race.

The paragraph provides protected persons with a valuable safeguard. It should be noted, however, that in this paragraph the meaning of the words "transfer" and "deport" is rather different from that in which they are used in the other paragraphs of Article 49, since they do not refer to the movement of protected persons but to that of nationals of the occupying Power.

The prohibition therefore is categorical and not conditional upon the motives for the transfer or its objectives. Its purpose is to prevent settlement in occupied territory of citizens of the occupying State. If it is decided to go ahead with Jewish settlement in the administered territories, it seems to me vital, therefore, that settlement is carried out by military and not civilian entities. It is also important, in my view, that such settlement is in the framework of camps and is, on the face of it, of a temporary rather than permanent nature.

... we must, from the point of view of international law, have regard to the question of ownership of the land that we are settling.

Article 46 of the Hague Regulations concerning the Laws and Customs of War on Land (Annexes to the Hague Convention (IV) of 1907), regulations that are regarded as a true expression of customary international law that is binding on all countries, states in relation to occupied territory that:

> "private property ... must be respected. Private property cannot be confiscated".

As regards State lands, Article 55 of the Hague Regulations stipulates that an occupying State is permitted to administer the property and enjoy the fruits of the property of the occupied State. Even here there are certain limitations on the occupying State's freedom of action, which derive from the occupying State not being the owner of the property but having merely enjoyment of it.

In relation to the property of charitable, religious or educational institutions or municipalities, they are treated under Article 56 of the Hague Regulations as private property.

Regarding the possibility of engaging in any kind of agricultural activity and settlement on the Golan Heights, it has to be pointed out that the Golan Heights, which lie outside the area of the mandated Land of Israel, are unequivocally "occupied territory" and are subject to the prohibition on settlement. If it is decided to establish any settlements, it is essential that this be done by the army in the form of camps and that it does not point to the establishment of permanent settlements.

In terms of settlement on the [West] Bank, we are trying not to admit that here too it is a matter of "occupied territory". We argue that this area of the Mandate on the Land of Israel was divided in 1949 only according to Armistice Lines, which, under the Armistice agreements themselves, had merely military, not political, significance and were not determinative until the final settlement. We go on to say that the agreements themselves were achieved as a temporary measure according to Security Council action based on Article 40 of the U.N. Charter.

We also argue that Jordan itself unilaterally annexed the West Bank to the Kingdom of Jordan in 1950 and that the Armistice Lines no longer exist because the agreements expired due to the war and Arab aggression.

We must nevertheless be aware that the international community has not accepted our argument that the [West] Bank is not "normal" occupied territory and that certain countries (such as Britain in its speeches at the U.N.) have expressly stated that our status in the [West] Bank is that of an occupying State. In truth, even certain actions by Israel are inconsistent with the claim that the [West] Bank is not occupied territory. For example, Proclamation No. 3 of the IDF Forces Commander in the West Bank of 7.6.67, which brings into force the Order concerning security regulations (in Section 35), states that:

"A military court and the administration of a military court will observe the provisions of the Geneva Convention for the Protection of Civilians in Time of War in everything relating to legal proceedings and where there is conflict between this Order and the aforementioned Convention, the provisions of the Convention will prevail". With regard to Gush Etzion settlement this could to a certain extent be helped by claiming that this is a return to the settlers' homes. I assume that there are no difficulties here with the question of property although the matter requires close examination. With regard to Gush Etzion too, we have to expect, in my view, negative international reaction on the basis of Article 49 of the Geneva Convention. Furthermore, in our settlement in Gush Etzion, evidence of intent to annex the [West] Bank to Israel can be seen.

On the possibility of settlement in the Jordan Valley, the legal situation is even more complicated because we cannot claim to be dealing with people returning to their homes and we have to consider that problems of property will arise in the context of the Hague Regulations ...

Regards,

[signed]
T. Meron

Copy: Director-General

I am often asked whether I stand by those opinions today. I certainly do. My interviews with Donald Macintyre in *The Independent*[6] and others on many occasions since then make this quite clear.

I returned to the question of the settlements in 2017 in an article in the *American Journal of International Law* entitled "The West Bank and International Humanitarian Law on the Eve of the Fiftieth Anniversary of the Six-Day War." In the article I tried to answer the arguments of Professor Yehuda Blum and Justice Meir Shamgar who first developed the thesis of the *sui generis* character of the West Bank and against the

6. The Six-Day War, 26 May 2007.

applicability of the Fourth Geneva Convention. I discussed the legal status of the West Bank and the applicable international humanitarian law and the character of the Fourth Convention as a people-oriented convention and I maintained and developed my thesis on the illegality of the settlements.

I recognize that Israel is, of course, not the only State to challenge or reject the application of the Fourth Geneva Convention to a particular situation. The applicability of the Convention has been contested in other situations as well, including—to mention just a few—in Kuwait by Iraq, and in East Timor by Indonesia. In Iraq, the United States and the United Kingdom recognized the status of occupation, but appear to have taken liberties with both the Fourth Geneva Convention and the Hague Convention No. IV. It has been argued that they failed to establish law, order and safety, and effective law enforcement, and that they have made far-reaching changes in the civil service. Indeed, the elimination of police forces in Iraq has had lasting destabilizing consequences.

Richard Baxter has noted that "[t]he first line of defense against international humanitarian law is to deny that it applies at all." And George H. Aldrich has observed that the refusal to apply the Geneva Conventions in situations where they should be applied is "often based on differences between the conflicts presently encountered and those for which the conventions were supposedly adopted." Such denials or refusals with respect to the application of international humanitarian law in the West Bank cannot, in my view, be accepted. Those of us who are committed to international law, and particularly to respect for international humanitarian law and the principles embodied therein, cannot remain silent when faced with such denials or self-serving interpretations.

But if the continuation of the settlement project on the West Bank has met with practically universal rejection by the international community, it is not just because of its illegality under the Fourth Geneva Convention or under international humanitarian law more generally. Nor is it only because, by preventing the establishment of a contiguous and viable Palestinian territory, the settlement project frustrates any prospect of serious negotiations aimed at a two-State solution, and thus of reconciliation between the Israelis and the Palestinians. It is also because of the growing perception that the human rights of individual Palestinians, as well as their rights under the Fourth Geneva Convention, are being violated and that the colonization of territories populated by other peoples can no longer be accepted in our time.

I appreciated the fact that in his Statement to the Security Council on 23 January 2013, the then Ambassador of Lebanon to the U.N., Nawaf Salam, later a Judge at the International Court of Justice, stated that I was one of the first to recognize the illegality of settlement activity.

In 1971, I became Israel's ambassador to Canada, a position I held until 1975. This was a period in which I had time to write and to teach part time at the University of Ottawa. During this period I wrote my first articles for the *American Journal of International Law*, of which Richard Baxter was editor-in-chief.

Over the years, Oxford University Press became my principal book publisher—and the *American Journal of International Law* became the principal vehicle for publishing my articles; indeed, articles in the journal at times preceded publication of books on the same subjects. I was honored to serve as co-editor-in-chief of the journal in the 1990s. During those years in Ottawa in the early 1970s, I also wrote my first book, *Investment Insurance in International Law* (1976), partly because of my interest in the law of State responsibility and partly to prove to myself that I was capable of writing a technical book on the law.

During that period, the call of academia was becoming irresistible. I was in touch with Hebrew University, which gave me some hopes for an appointment, but which did not materialize. I obtained a year's leave from the Foreign Ministry to go to New York on a grant from the Rockefeller Foundation to write a book about the U.N. Secretariat. One of the great scholars of international law, Professor Oscar Schachter, was head at the time of UNITAR, the U.N. Training and Research Institute, and arranged for my appointment as a visiting fellow at UNITAR. The appointment facilitated my research project enormously. The result was my book *The United Nations Secretariat: The Rules and the Practice* (1977). My research also provided material for articles in law journals. The merit principle, the need to depoliticize, due process and women's rights were among the principal topics covered. Of course, I was building on the experience I had gained as a representative on the General Assembly's Fifth (Administrative and Budgetary) Committee. During that period, I also taught at NYU Law School where my friend Thomas Franck taught.

In Academia

This was a difficult and critical period in my life both personally and professionally. I was looking for ways to leave the foreign service and to enter the academy. NYU was beckoning and soon invited me to join the full-time faculty but I was 48 and still a bit uncertain what I should be doing in my future life. After a short period as Permanent Representative to the U.N. in Geneva, I resigned from the Israeli Foreign Ministry and NYU became my intellectual home. I found the change exciting but also a bit terrifying.

Upon my appointment to the NYU faculty, the question came up about my principal teaching subjects. At that time, human rights were not regularly taught, although the Law School benefited from offerings of human rights by visiting professors. There was clearly student interest in the subject, and the Law School recognized a need for a regular human rights course. I was asked to focus on human rights, and somewhat nervously prepared to teach in what for me was still rather uncharted territory. My background in international law was in State responsibility, treaties and humanitarian law. My knowledge and experience in human rights were, however, thin. (Humanitarian law deals largely with protection by a foreign government of civilians and combatants belonging to the adversary and applicable in times of armed conflict or war. Human rights concern protection of individuals by and from their own authorities or governments primarily in times of peace, although the law has been expanding to times of armed conflicts as well.)

Teaching human rights proved a blessing, offering a natural partner to international humanitarian law. My books *Human Rights Law-Making in the United Nations* (1986), written as a visiting researcher at the Max Planck Institute in Heidelberg, *Human Rights in Internal Strife (Sir Hersch Lauterpacht Memorial Lectures)* (1987), *Human Rights and Humanitarian Norms as Customary Law* (1989), *International Law in the Age of Human Rights* (2004), a general course in the Hague Academy of International Law and its revised version, *Humanization of International Law* (2006), the book that is closest to capturing the core focus of my work, offered an integrated approach to human rights and humanitarian law, grounding both in general international law. It seemed to me clear that repression of human dignity occurs in a continuum of situations of strife, from normality to full-blown international armed conflict, and that all these situations must be covered to provide protection to human beings. I dissented from the tendency in academic quarters and NGOs to treat human rights and humanitarian law as entirely distinct disciplines, and have always viewed them as related aspects of general international law. I am a generalist at heart, resisting overspecialization in segments of international law.

NYU provided me with a friendly, nurturing environment for teaching, research and my more activist or practice-related activities. I continued to write in the fields of international administrative law, human rights and humanitarian law, and, increasingly, international criminal law, as well as on Shakespeare and chivalry, on which I will say a few words later. Apart from Shakespeare, which was love at first sight, my academic interests were closely related to my extracurricular activities. I tried to make them from one cloth, as seamless as possible.

The International Committee of the Red Cross

Once I was established in academia, my work with the ICRC, an organization for which I have always had a great admiration, could begin in earnest. It became a major vehicle for deeper involvement in humanitarian law. I was active in a number of human rights organizations, especially Human Rights Watch, and I owe to its then head, the extraordinary human rights advocate Aryeh Neier, a great deal of my learning of human rights. But my work with the ICRC was continuous and more intensive. With the ICRC, I developed and co-led an annual ICRC/NYU seminar for U.N. diplomats on international humanitarian law; the seminar eventually became an established tradition that recently celebrated its 37th anniversary. The course reflected my belief that teaching should not be limited to the academy in the narrow sense, but should be directed to governmental officials and decision-makers as well.

An appointment as professor at the Graduate Institute of International Law in Geneva for the years 1991–1995 facilitated further work with the ICRC. I began to conduct seminars on humanitarian law in Geneva for young university teachers from all over the world. My involvement in the ICRC groups of experts, including the group on internal strife, on the environment and armed conflicts, on direct participation in hostilities and on customary rules of international humanitarian law (I was a member of the steering committee and one of the rapporteurs of the customary law project) was both demanding and rewarding. The project on customary rules, which required a significant multi-year commitment, fit perfectly with my academic interests, especially as it followed my book *Human Rights and Humanitarian Norms as Customary Law.*

The establishment of the group on internal strife was, in part, triggered by my advocacy for a declaration of minimum humanitarian standards. When I was first settling in at NYU, an invitation arrived to present a paper at a Red Cross conference in Hawaii (February 1983) on the relationship between human rights and humanitarian law. My work on the paper led me to believe that there was a gaping hole in the protections offered by humanitarian and human rights law. In my paper in Hawaii and in follow-up papers for the *American Journal of International Law*, I explained that the conventions on international humanitarian law protect victims of international wars, but offer only very limited protections to victims of internal armed conflicts and disturbances or strife. Moreover, disputes over the characterization of conflicts create opportunities for States to evade the law altogether. Human rights treaties protect individuals from abuses in times of peace, but many of the important protections may be derogated from on grounds of national emergency. In some situations, non-governmental actors exercise control over people while denying that they are bound by international standards. Moreover, most of the rules on permissible weapons and the conduct of hostilities were not considered applicable to non-international armed conflicts. There was thus a significant gap between humanitarian and human rights instruments to the detriment of victims. This was occasionally referred to in the literature as "the Meron gap." As a partial remedy, I proposed the adoption of a declaration of minimum humanitarian standards that would state norms capable of filling that gap for all situations of strife. I was grateful to Oscar Schachter and Louis Henkin, the editors of the journal at the time, for publishing the first of my many articles on this subject,[7] an article that challenged many received wisdoms. I pursued these ideas in my Hersch Lauterpacht Memorial Lectures on "Human Rights in Internal Strife" at the University of Cambridge.

One of the joys of academic law as a discipline is that it allows give and take within the profession—the chance to use the law, which is naturally fluid, to overcome the stark barriers put up by the academic

7. Theodor Meron, *On the Inadequate Reach of Humanitarian and Human Rights Law and the Need for a New Instrument*, 77 AM. J. INT'L L. 589 (1983)

and organizational division of subjects. Fortunately, Alexandre Hay, the President of the ICRC at the time, expressed interest in my ideas and the first consultations of experts started, eventually resulting in the text of the so-called Turku declaration (1990). The proposal encountered opposition, however. Some critics feared that a non-binding declaration would dilute existing legal obligations under the treaties in force; others felt that the declaration went too far in trying to impose additional commitments, albeit of a non-binding character. Eventually the project drifted into a deep coma. Since then, however, the world seems to have moved in the direction envisaged by the project, not through law-making, but through the ICRC project on customary law, treaties and statutes and the jurisprudence of international criminal tribunals, which went beyond the previous rigid distinctions between the law applicable to internal and to international armed conflicts. These developments led to a growing recognition that many rules of international humanitarian law previously applicable only to international wars apply to non-international armed conflicts as well. All of these contributed to expanding the applicability of protective norms to internal armed conflicts and strife. What happened was a kind of bottom-up transition from the field and practice to theory. The net result was that many customary and treaty rules formerly only applicable in international armed conflicts, are now often regarded as non-derogable rules in non-international armed conflicts as well, conflicts which are especially frequent and bloody.

The Dauchy Case

Over the course of my life, I have litigated and advised on only a small number of cases, including two before the International Court of Justice. But following my Rockefeller Foundation Fellowship, international administrative law remained close to my heart. One case I argued before the U.N. Administrative Tribunal arose from my continuing interest in international administrative law and women's rights. In 1990, Jacqueline Dauchy, a French national working for the U.N., asked that I represent her before the U.N. Administrative Tribunal in a case against the U.N. Secretary-General. She had expressed interest in being considered for the post of director of the Codification Division, for which she was fully qualified. That post, however, had been traditionally held by a national of the Soviet Union, and the

Secretary-General in effect restricted eligibility to nationals of that country, tolerating a national preserve.

This was an invitation I could not refuse. I argued that as eligibility for the post was restricted to candidates of Soviet nationality, the inescapable conclusion was that candidates of other nationalities were *ipso facto* excluded irrespective of their qualifications. Thus, in violation of Article 101(3) of the U.N. Charter, which stated that the paramount consideration in the employment of staff was efficiency, competence and integrity, Dauchy was not given consideration despite her unquestionable merit. The respondent, the Secretary-General, insisted that Dauchy had been considered. The United Nations Administrative Tribunal (UNAT) found that "even the most serious consideration of the Applicant given in all good faith, could not have any effect ... The entire exercise therefore proceeded as if the Applicant had not been considered" (1990). The Judgement ordered that Dauchy be paid modest damages. More importantly, she was appointed to the post as soon as the Soviet appointee completed his two-year contract. The Judgement limited the sway of national preserves in U.N. bureaucracy and helped both men and women in the Secretariat to be considered on the basis of individual merit, as required by the Charter.

The State Department

When I moved to the United States in 1978 and joined the faculty of NYU Law School, I had to start my life almost from scratch. I found the opportunities given by NYU, the academic community and the country to be wonderful. In 1984, I became a citizen. I was grateful for the welcome I was given by my adopted country, such as election to the Board of Editors and later as co-editor-in-chief of the *American Journal of International Law*, to the Council on Foreign Relations and to membership of the American Academy of Arts and Sciences. I was looking for an opportunity to serve, to make a contribution. I was therefore particularly pleased when, in 1990, the State Department invited me to become a public member of the US delegation led by Ambassador Max Kampelman to the Conference on the Human Dimension of the OSCE (Organization for Security and Co-operation in Europe), held in Copenhagen. These were exciting, heady times, when the walls of Eastern Europe were crumbling and we, in Copenhagen, believed that we were moving into a period when human rights and the Helsinki

Declaration would soon triumph in the whole of Europe. I was particularly happy to work in Copenhagen with a good friend, Professor Thomas Buergenthal, later a Judge at the International Court of Justice. Max Kampelman had skillfully created a team of professional diplomats partnering with academics to promote a vibrant human rights team.

Additional assignments eventually followed. In 1998, I was invited to join the US delegation to the Rome Conference on the Establishment of an International Criminal Court, where I was involved in negotiating the provisions on war crimes and crimes against humanity. I could not believe my turn of fortune. Here I was discussing, even negotiating, with major countries issues of fundamental importance to international humanitarian and international criminal law and, as a representative of the United States, had some impact on the emerging provisions, especially on crimes against humanity.

A few years later, while visiting the University of California Law School, Berkeley, I was invited to work with the State Department on the *Oil Platforms Case* before the International Court of Justice, which concerned armed incidents between Iran and the United States during the first Gulf War. Soon after, I was appointed Counsellor on International Law in the State Department, a post I held in 2000–2001. The appointment meant a great deal to me as it was one held many years earlier by my Harvard mentors, Louis Sohn and Richard Baxter.

As Counsellor, I was involved in negotiations, litigation and advising. I was impressed by the professionalism and collegiality of the Office of the Legal Adviser, and particularly gratified by the opportunity to work with younger members of the Office who often sought my advice and suggestions. During my counsellorship, I was nominated by the US Government and elected by the U.N. (in 2001) to be a Judge at the U.N. War Crimes Tribunal, the International Criminal Tribunal for the former Yugoslavia (ICTY), in The Hague. Without the experience and the higher profile gained in the State Department I would not, I am sure, have been nominated for such an important and competitive Judgeship.

Judgeships

Being a Judge has proved the most exciting and rewarding assignment in my life. It required a change of instincts, of intuitions, of habits of work. It allowed me to put into practice my commitment to accountability, rule of law and due process. It also meant that my remit was to apply the law and the evidence, not to push the progressive development of the law which I could do as an academic. I know I was terribly fortunate in becoming an international criminal Judge so late in life, when I was 71, when most people would be retired or planning to retire. Again, here I was, a person who had missed a normal education, a survivor of the Holocaust, judging war crimes—something I was committed to doing fairly, justly and without favor or fear.

The departure from the academy was more than rewarded by judicial activity, although my scholarly activity was not entirely abandoned. I wrote occasional articles and books including my general course for the Hague Academy of International Law and two collections of essays for Oxford University Press.

That said, as a Judge, I could put into practice principles which I have always held important, such as the principle of fairness. My position required me to address a myriad of new problems in a focused and precise way. I am grateful to my colleagues, and particularly my wonderful law clerks some of whom had clerked in the US Supreme Court and the D.C. Circuit Court before coming to The Hague, for making my immense task of learning so much easier. This transition allowed me to take part in the most important writing of all: international criminal jurisprudence, such as the seminal Srebrenica Appeal Judgement of General *Krstić*, which established that genocide can be committed even in a circumscribed geographical area; the Appeal Judgement of General *Tolimir* which confirmed that the severe mental suffering of people aware of being sent for execution constituted a separate act of genocide even in cases where they survived; and the *Prosecutor v. Kunarac, Kovač and Vuković* case, which defined rape and sexual slavery as crimes against humanity and violations of international customary law of war crimes.

In 2003, my colleagues, the Judges, elected me President of the Tribunal to fill the post previously occupied by Claude Jorda, a post I held, after reelection, for about three years. Being President required me to preside over most appeal cases, to manage the institution, to provide leadership for the Judges, to represent the Tribunal, to appear before the Security Council and the General Assembly and to meet with the U.N. Secretary-General and with the leaders of the countries of the former Yugoslavia and of other States, to plead for resources, for support of the Tribunal and for the arrest of the fugitives. It was a demanding job from which I could never disengage, day and night, weekend or not, but I found it truly rewarding. I also had the unique privilege of serving at different times a total of four terms as President of the ICTY, and three terms as the first President of the successor tribunal of the ICTY and that of Rwanda (ICTR), the International Residual Mechanism for Criminal Tribunals. I was happy to be involved in the act of the creation of the Mechanism and to end my presidency leaving behind a well-functioning, efficient and fair international court. For a survivor of the Holocaust and a person with my history, to spend nearly two decades judging individuals accused of crimes of atrocity and doing so fairly is something that I can best express by paraphrasing Prospero in *The Tempest*: this is the stuff that dreams are made of.

But some periods on the court were hard. During my years on the Bench, I issued many decisions. A few rulings leading to acquittals received many comments—and much criticism. That criticism was painful. One of the qualities of leadership that I have not acquired is a thick skin. By tradition and custom, Judges do not answer criticism of their judicial work. They take harsh criticism stoically.

Some have suggested that these acquittals demonstrated that international justice is failing. To my mind, nothing is further from the truth. Before I explain why, however, I want to take a moment to sketch out the contours of international criminal justice.

Atrocities are not new to human history. But it was only after World War II that an international criminal tribunal was established, by the victorious powers, in Nuremberg, to try the most serious war crimes and crimes against humanity committed by the Nazi occupiers. The crime of genocide had not yet been recognized and Holocaust crimes were prosecuted as crimes against humanity. Twenty-two leading Nazis were in the dock and, on 1 October 1946, seven received prison terms, twelve were sentenced to hang and three were acquitted. Trials of alleged Japanese war crimes were also held in Tokyo. After the postwar trials there were no international trials for almost half a century.

But in the 1990s, atrocities in the Yugoslav wars and the genocide in Rwanda, perhaps due to the wide publicity they attracted, caused the U.N. to establish two ad hoc Tribunals in 1993 and 1994 respectively. In addition to the Nuremberg crimes (except for crimes against peace), these Tribunals were given explicit jurisdiction over the crime of genocide. Other tribunals followed and, in 1998, the first permanent international criminal court, the

ICC, was established at The Hague and began operations in 2002. After a pause of more than 50 years, international criminal justice had come alive.

In 1946, I hardly knew about the trials going on in Nuremberg. But my life had been formed and forever altered by war. Although my career has followed a circuitous path, the constant theme has been an attempt to grapple with the chaos and pain of war. War shattered my childhood and imbued in me both a craving for education and the desire for the law to right wrongs and bring an end to atrocities. War led me to write my legal opinion against settlement on the West Bank. Later, as a law professor, I taught the law of war. And then, as a Judge of an international criminal tribunal, I heard the appeals of individuals accused of atrocities in times of armed conflict.

International criminal courts, in many ways, resemble criminal courts in national jurisdictions around the world. They weigh evidence, follow due process, ensure the parties are heard and apply and abide by the law and respect human rights. At the same time, international criminal courts—and the cases they hear—are extraordinary. The cases are of tremendous breadth, often involving alleged crimes on a massive scale committed over long periods across many localities. The magnitude of evidence is enormous. This evidence must be obtained without any independent police force—and with the cooperation of sovereign States, which is not always available. The crimes can have complex political dimensions, not least because the individuals charged are frequently a country's top leaders.

Because of their unique role and the nature of the crimes charged, international criminal courts are also often seen as something more than criminal courts. Their judgements are sometimes expected to be definitive histories of the conflict. Their mission is sometimes said to be to foster reconciliation among parties to a conflict or to bring closure to victims through convictions. Indeed, sometimes members of the public, including victims, equate the bringing of heads of State, leaders of political parties and military or paramilitary groups "to justice" with the entering of convictions. Accused who come before international criminal courts thus often come with—in the public mind—an existing narrative of guilt. "Ay, there's the rub," as Shakespeare wrote in his Hamlet soliloquy. Different stakeholders have different expectations or visions of international criminal justice. But for Judges—including myself—bringing someone to justice means simply that the individual charged will be tried: fairly, somberly, in accordance with the law and the evidence, having heard from the parties, preserving the presumption of innocence and observing the time-honored principles of fairness. This is what the rule of law requires on a domestic level and it requires no less on the international level. However, the operation of international criminal courts in this way has often led to criticism and even the claim that international criminal justice is failing. Several judgements of acquittal at the Appeals Chambers of the war crimes tribunal of which I was the President have been decried as evidence of this failing. Nothing is further from the truth. Acquittals in any system cause some level of controversy, and they unquestionably bring victims of crime real pain. This controversy can be magnified at the international level, given the dimensions of the crimes alleged and the political implications of those allegations. Indeed, for victims, an acquittal may feel like a denial of what happened to them, and a betrayal of their hopes and expectations. For others, an acquittal may be seen as rewriting history or a failure of the international court to serve its purpose as part of a broader transitional justice agenda. In my view, a true failure of international criminal justice would be if international courts were to convict an individual where there is an inadequate evidentiary or legal basis to do so. When the law or the evidence do not support a finding that a person is guilty beyond a reasonable doubt of the specific crime for which he or she has been charged, it is the duty of international Judges to rule accordingly. In so doing, Judges are not declaring an individual innocent, they are not redefining history and they are not thinking about the impact on national or transnational reconciliation. They are—or rather we are—carrying out our responsibility to follow the dictates of the law—no more and no less. Judges cannot be swayed by outside sentiment, by popular perceptions or criticisms or by preexisting narratives of guilt. Justice is and must be blind to that. Despite their occasional criticisms, I have frequently met and greatly respected the victims' organizations, especially the Mothers of Srebrenica.

Indeed, although one must be careful not to make sweeping generalizations, acquittals—just like convictions—can be seen as a sign of a mature system of law, an independent system, a system focused on its actual, narrow mandate to try those charged, rather than on trying to satisfy the myriad and sometimes conflicting expectations of victims, observers, civil society groups and others. In my view, criticism of acquittals suggests the importance of strengthening respect for and understanding of the rule of law. Establishing respect for the rule of law is critically important for ensuring protections for human rights and for building and maintaining peaceful and productive societies. And respect for the rule of law requires that we accept not only those judicial decisions with which we agree, but also those decisions with which we disagree. An à la carte approach to accepting court rulings is a denial of the fundamental principles of the rule of law.

My life, in many ways, has come full circle: From World War II to trying war criminals justly and fairly. In doing my work as a Judge in a principled way, come what may in terms of criticism, I have sought to ensure the strength and integrity of international criminal justice. Successfully or not, I have tried to live up to the way in which Shehzad Charania, then Legal Adviser of the British Embassy in The Hague, and now Director at the U.K. Attorney General's Office, entitled his interview with me at The Hague of 27 July 2016: "A Life of Legal Principle, not of Politics."[8]

And in years to come, I trust that others will see these first few decades of international criminal justice for what they are: a time where vital and difficult issues were confronted, and where fledgling courts strove—and succeeded in making profoundly important contributions to the larger shared goals of ending impunity and upholding human rights and dignity.

Shakespeare

I have already mentioned my interest in Shakespeare and would like to elaborate a little on this aspect of my life. If my work on general international law, human rights and humanitarian law represented a commitment or mission, my work on Shakespeare was pure love. Like most things in my life, it resulted from chance. In 1989, I was at All Souls College, Oxford, as a visiting fellow. My wife, M, was also at Oxford and used her time to follow courses on Shakespeare, who had always been her great literary hero. She discovered the law of war in Fluellen's comment to Gower in *Henry V*: "Kill the poys and the luggage! 'Tis expressly against the law of arms."

She suggested I write on the origins of law of war in Shakespeare. After initial resistance, unsurprising for a person whose knowledge of Shakespeare was limited to *Macbeth* in high school, I went to see Laurence Olivier's and Kenneth Branagh's films of *Henry V* and soon became a born-again, if amateur, Shakespearean.

8. Justice in Conflict, 27 July 2016.

A second period as a visiting fellow at All Souls in 1991 allowed me to read intensively medieval history and the chroniclers, essential for understanding the context for Shakespeare's histories. Oxford medieval historians, and especially Maurice Keen of Balliol, generously offered advice and guidance. In 1992, I published my first article on this topic, "Shakespeare's Henry the Fifth and the Law of War," in the *American Journal of International Law*; it was followed in 1993 by my book *Henry's Wars and Shakespeare's Laws* and, in 1998, by another book, *Bloody Constraint: War and Chivalry in Shakespeare*. This work on Shakespeare was helped by the support of NYU Law School, which encouraged involvement of faculty members in humanities and other subjects outside the law *simpliciter*. I also started teaching law and literature at NYU Law School and was pleased by my students' enthusiasm for the subject. There followed articles on Gentili and Grotius and on the authority to make treaties in the Middle Ages, and later on leaders, courtiers and command responsibility in Shakespeare. During the last few years in Oxford, I happily returned to some Shakespearean themes. I gave a seminar and a public lecture in College on Just War in Shakespeare and published another article in the *American Journal of International Law* (2017): "*Shakespeare: A Dove, a Hawk, or Simply a Humanist?*" This was also a subject of another lecture. I felt I could have been a happy medieval historian, had I followed a different path.

In *Henry's Wars*, I tried to provide a humanitarian lawyer's commentary on the law-of-war issues arising in Henry V's French campaigns. My goal was to illustrate the law's evolution and to show how Shakespeare used the law of nations for his dramatic purposes. In *Bloody Constraint*, I moved on from the laws of war to broader issues of chivalry. My task required an exploration of the values of chivalry that sustained and reshaped the customs of war in the Middle Ages and the Renaissance, values that continue to surface in the legal, moral and utilitarian arguments configuring the Geneva and The Hague Conventions and the laws and practices of war today. More than anything else, chivalry meant the duty to act honorably, in peace as in war. Indeed, chivalry's role was not limited to war. It implied an all-important code of behavior for society. Its legacy continues to shape our contemporary law and values.

One of the more gratifying (and serendipitous) results of my interest in Shakespeare came when the director of *Shakespeare in the Park* in New York City took note of my book *Henry's Laws and Shakespeare's Wars*. Although many productions have trod lightly around the horrific slaughter of the

French prisoners of war in Agincourt (*Henry V*), he was persuaded that the atrocity was a central part of the narrative, one that speaks to us even more powerfully today. *The New Yorker* featured an article, "Take No Prisoners" by Lawrence Weschler, about this paradigm shift discussing my work. I was happy to make a contribution towards this reading of Shakespeare.

Not a literary critic, I did not purport to write as one. Rather, I wrote as a scholar of humanitarian law with an interest in history and literature. I focused not on Shakespeare the poet and dramatist, but mostly on Shakespeare the student of the chroniclers, of Plutarch and Homer, a humanist who had an acute understanding of the affairs of State and war. Above all, I wrote about a dramatist whose characters articulate a moving call for civilized behavior, for mercy and quarter, and for moral responsibility, and whose plays are a powerful instrument for illuminating humanism as an ideal for all times.

I tried to show how some of Shakespeare's characters attempt to discourage war through legal, moral and utilitarian arguments, and through irony and sarcasm, as in the famous soliloquy by Canterbury in *Henry V*, where Shakespeare lays bare self-serving and hypocritical assertions of just war. In *Hamlet*, he highlights the futility and emphasizes the inevitable cruelty and cost of war.

Consider the moving exchange on war in *Hamlet*:

CAPTAIN: We go to gain a little patch of ground
That has in it no profit but the name.
To pay five ducats, five, I would not farm it
HAMLET: To my shame I see
The imminent death of twenty thousand men
That, for a fantasy and trick of fame
Go to their graves like beds, fight for a plot
Whereon the numbers cannot try the cause,
Which is not tomb enough and continent
To hide the slain.

I have already disclaimed any competence in literary criticism. I avoided literary methodologies and their consequences for literary interpretation. But I recognized the historicists' concerns and have tried to situate Shakespeare's text in its cultural and political environment, relating it to Tudor and Renaissance societies. I understood that Shakespeare's characters speak with a hundred voices and that there is hardly a text that could not be understood in different, sometimes contradictory, ways. While risking accusations of simplification, I found it worthwhile, nevertheless, to derive from those voices certain themes of chivalry which I dared think were probably Shakespeare's own.

Oxford

I turn to some comments on Oxford. I have written already about my two periods as Visiting Fellow at All Souls. I am so very grateful to Professor Ian Brownlie for recommending me and to the College for electing me. This was an extraordinarily creative period for me. It gave me an introduction to literature and history and humanism and allowed me to meet and talk with some of the world's great intellects. But I did not dare to think I would be able to return to Oxford for longer periods of time and to teach there.

But in 2014, my NYU colleague and friend Philip Alston recommended me to his Oxford colleagues and soon thereafter Professor Catherine Redgwell and Professor Dapo Akande, invited me to introduce a seminar on international criminal law. I gladly accepted and appreciated the privilege of teaching the first Oxford offering on the subject. My honoraria were used to support an internship fund for Oxford students at international criminal tribunals.

Since then I have been Visiting Professor at the law faculty and more recently Honorary Visiting Fellow at Trinity and Visiting Fellow at Mansfield and Bonavero Human Rights Institute. I always dreamt of being an Oxford don and realize how lucky I am to be one at my age and to still continue as a Judge of the Mechanism. I am particularly grateful to the two successive Presidents of Trinity College, Sir Ivor Roberts and Dame Hilary Boulding, who made Trinity such a warm home for me.

Looking Back

As I said at the outset, I am reluctant to view my journey as one that has taken me along a single path to a single goal. I would be profoundly disappointed if that had been the case—so many of the most rewarding experiences are the result of serendipitous diversions. In many ways, the title of my book *Humanization of International Law* could describe the overarching theme of my life's work. My interest in international law evolved from a relatively narrow focus on State responsibility to encompass humanitarian law, human rights law and international criminal law and my desire to integrate these public international law disciplines. I have been blessed to be able to pursue my intellectual passions both in the world of the academy, where we enjoy the luxury of exploring Shakespeare and crafting pristine theories, as well as in the nitty-gritty world of handling cases, negotiating instruments of international law and practicing the law. My time as a Judge on the International Tribunals has been the best of both worlds—shaping doctrines that often have an academic flair but always with an eye toward their impact on the lives of real peoples. My hope is that in some small way, these endeavors have contributed to our thinking critically about how to create a more humane world.

Given my age, it is natural that I would think of Jacques' "seven ages of men" in *As You Like It*. Whatever my present frailties, and age, my Judgeship legitimizes situating me in the fifth age: "the justice, in fair round belly with good capon lined ... full of wise saws and modern instances, and so he plays his part." It is the future, represented by the sixth and the seventh ages, which is more frightening, especially in the age of Coronavirus. For the time being, my intense work, new interests and projects and strong genes may delay somewhat the inevitable coming of the seventh age:

> ... second childishness and mere oblivion,
> Sans teeth, sans eyes, sans taste, sans everything.

II

From Classroom to a Criminal Courtroom

In 2001, I was elected by the United Nations General Assembly to the United Nations International Criminal Tribunal for the former Yugoslavia (ICTY). At the age of 71, I thus found myself starting a new career as an international criminal Judge.

For a person who was catapulted onto an international criminal court after a quarter of a century of teaching at the NYU School of Law, the change was momentous, even existential. Academic habits learned over the years—from obsessing over footnotes on abstruse questions to drawing analogies from across the universe of the law—had rapidly to yield to a new way of thinking and a laser-like focus on the immediate facts and the law of the case. A law teacher must lead the class and keep its attention. He must analyze problems on his feet even when unsure of his answers. In a way, teaching has an element of performing arts, of showmanship, of staying above the radar.

I had to move from the luxury of contemplating theoretical questions and advancing bold ideas about the state of the law to agonizing over the justice of acquitting or convicting a person charged with the gravest crimes known to humanity and heeding principles of judicial restraint and economy in my judicial writing. I had to forsake the comfort gained from circulating drafts to academic peers and learning from their comments, and follow instead quite a solitary decision-making process in which, save in deliberations, a hearing or in a judicial opinion, one may share one's thoughts and concerns only with a few fellow Judges and a law clerk or two,[1] at best. An academic

1. *See* Chapter I.

Standing Up For Justice. Theodor Meron, Oxford University Press (2021). © Theodor Meron.
DOI: 10.1093/oso/9780198863434.003.0002

typically engages in scholarly debates and enjoys responding to critics. Although Judges have some limited latitude with regard to whether or not it would be appropriate for them to respond to criticism of their judicial decisions, many, perhaps most, including myself, would choose not to do so.

How different from academic exchanges is the constant caution and frequent silence required of Judges, who have to watch every word, gesture and ruling, not to prematurely reveal their thinking to the public, to colleagues, to the parties. In other words, not doing anything which might prejudice the Judge's impartiality and independence, and even risk his or her recusal or disqualification. These obligations are even more pronounced for the presiding Judge, which I was during much of my tenure on the court. In deliberations of Judges, the presiding Judge speaks last, not to be suspected of trying to influence his or her colleagues. Even when invited to give even academic lectures, a Judge must be careful when discussing past or present cases, or speculating aloud about future positions. And while following all these *ex abundante cautela* rules, the presiding Judge must know that his or her success, and the success of the court, may depend on his or her ability to lead—albeit cautiously, discreetly—to obtain or to maintain consensus of the Bench. In Chapter VII, I discuss the process of deliberations of Judges.

The life of a Judge is much more circumscribed by rules and traditions than the life of a teacher. Both national and international courts have typically adopted codes of professional and ethical conduct, which often include or are accompanied by disciplinary rules to ensure compliance and accountability. One of such codes is that of the International Residual Mechanism for Criminal Tribunals of May 2015. Its most recent version, which includes disciplinary rules, dates to April 2018. The Code of Professional Conduct for the Judges of the Mechanism sets out core principles to guide Mechanism Judges on issues such as independence, impartiality, integrity and outside activities. Adopting disciplinary provisions is vital to demonstrate that Judges take seriously adherence to the rule of law, and that everyone, including Judges, must be subject to enforcement of legal rules and principles designed to govern their conduct, in short to their accountability.

The 2015 Bologna and Milan Code of Judicial Ethics is particularly detailed and important. It contains separate parts on national and on international Judges and draws on a large variety of judicial codes. I shall revert to it in Chapter VI on judicial independence and impartiality. There are, however, two matters in the commentary which I would like to mention here. First, regarding teaching by Judges, the commentary allows Judges to give lectures and to teach in higher learning institutions, with limitations on their earnings. The second matter concerns involvement of Judges in public debates. I note the comment on the convention of reticence and of not discussing individual cases. However, many aspects of the administration of justice and the functioning of the judiciary are the subject of legitimate public consideration and debate. The commentary recognizes the risk of different Judges expressing conflicting views in the debate.

My experience as an international criminal Judge has been exhausting at times. It has been disquieting, frustrating and, practically always, solitary. It is painful to weather stoically, without responding, even the most hostile and offensive attacks. Yet, my years on the Appeals Bench or as a president (or chief justice) of the court have also been extraordinarily exciting and rewarding. And there is absolutely nothing I would exchange for those years.

The kind of intellectual overhaul I experienced in joining the international judiciary may be common for many of those who become Judges in national courts as well, particularly if they have previously followed a different career path. And indeed, there is much about being a Judge at an international criminal court that is similar to the experience of serving in the criminal courts at the national level. Like Judges in national courts, an international criminal Judge hears arguments, sifts evidence, rules on diverse motions, considers novel questions of law, drafts decisions and judgements and deliberates on verdicts and sentences. Like their counterparts in domestic systems, international criminal Judges must put the fairness of the proceedings at the center of all that they do and be guided by their commitment to judicial independence and impartiality, to the transparent and public nature of the judicial process and to the importance of reasoned judicial decisions.

In other respects, however, the mission and work of an international criminal Judge are unique and different—from that of their national colleagues.

At the most basic level, the cases tried by an international criminal Judge are unparalleled in evidentiary and geographic scope and scale and involve alleged crimes almost never prosecuted on a national level, such as genocide. An international criminal Judge does not have the comfort of applying a penal code of long standing and supported by a gloss of interpretative precedent, but must rely instead on typically skeletal statutes. Hence, to satisfy the principle of legality, international criminal Judges, for instance, have had to ground their rulings in customary international law, the identification of which—due to customary law's often indeterminate nature—requires a

Judge to exercise both discretion and creativity, while resisting any possible drift toward progressive law-making.

An international criminal Judge cannot take for granted that his or her fellow Judges, the advocates who come before them or the public at large, share a common understanding about how the law or legal procedures should be understood or, indeed, how a case should be managed. Judges trained in the common law and those trained in civil law come from different legal and social traditions and cultures, value legal precedents and their import differently, for example, and this difference may impact how the Judges approach each new proposed ruling. Procedural and evidentiary rules, moreover, have to be developed and wielded based on the harmonization of diverse national precedents, legal traditions and a variety of models: no small challenge.

Approaches to judicial precedents vary according to the education and legal culture of Judges and staff. Common law-trained Judges and staff are typically interested in situating proposed decisions in the context of precedents, and they will usually make an effort to distinguish any case that does not follow such precedents. For legal certainty and fear of reversal by higher courts, they try to follow precedents as far as possible and where appropriate.

Civil law-trained Judges and staff tend to follow past precedents as part of the jurisprudence but may be less systematic in canvassing past precedents. They may be more inclined to anchor their decisions in a general theory of law. For all Judges, use of precedents which prioritizes certainty in the law has to be balanced against interests of justice and the need to allow for the evolution of the law.

Even though the accused who come before international criminal courts are always tried as individuals, the work of those courts and the fates of the individuals accused are often taken to be emblematic of broader political considerations. More than anything else, it is this broader political and historical context in which international criminal Judges work—the conditions in which the court was created, the sensitive and often horrifying nature of the allegations at stake, the rank or seniority of those who typically stand accused, the ongoing struggles among ethnic and national groups fighting for the legitimacy of their own historical narratives, the conflicting visions of rights and wrongs and the competing claims of victimhood—that explain the unique nature of an international criminal Judge's professional challenges.

Moreover, the political environment means that decisions involving civil and military leadership may have an impact on a Judge's prospects for renomination or reelection. But to be faithful to the oath, to be impartial and independent, such extraneous or political issues must be pushed outside the judicial agenda and calculus. One of the major changes from academia is that an academic can and typically does take sides. Not so for a Judge, who must not only be independent but impartial and above the fray.

Given this context, it is perhaps inevitable that international criminal courts and their Judges will face criticism for particular rulings. Of course, the right to publicly express disagreement with a judicial decision is an integral part of a free society and a free press. And just as obviously, Judges cannot cave in to pressure or be swayed in any way by public sentiment or criticism. Extrajudicial considerations must remain outside a Judge's decisional ambit, even at the cost of risking non-reelection to judicial posts in courts where such reelection is allowed under their statutes. Yet criticism can nonetheless have a corrosive effect on the credibility of a court, which risks not simply damaging perceptions of the court but undermining its aims, and international justice, more broadly.

Some criticism may simply reflect a lack of understanding of the ruling at issue or be driven by partisan concerns. But other criticism may come from those with the greatest hopes for international criminal justice and expectations from the Judges entrusted with carrying it out. Indeed, international criminal Judges must often carry out their work at the intersection of a myriad of strongly held and sometimes incompatible expectations about what role an international criminal court should play.

As frequent target of fierce criticism, I felt vulnerable, alone, hurt.

Some stakeholders, for instance, look to international criminal courts to establish the "truth" of a particular horrific event or to create a definitive historic record. When the court's judgement fails to agree with an expected narrative of guilt or to find that a specific crime attributed to a particular individual has been committed by him or her, the claim is made that the court itself or the Judges involved have failed in their mission.

There is no doubt that the quantum of evidence collected in relation to a case is often immense and a judgement memorizing such evidence can offer a detailed record of particular events. Moreover, for jurists coming from the civil law tradition with their investigating magistrates, truth-seeking may be seen as an essential component of international criminal justice more, perhaps, than in the common law with its adversarial system.

But we must be careful to recall the core mandate of an international criminal court: it is to try individuals within a governing legal framework and to determine whether—given the specific evidence presented and admitted by the court—the responsibility of an individual accused of international crimes has been established beyond reasonable doubt. The demands of due process, the substantive legal requirements and the precise nature of the evidence necessarily constrain the court's findings in a way that a more free-ranging inquiry outside the judicial process would not. And importantly, these same factors also permit different conclusions to be reached in different cases, meaning that responsibility for a crime may be found beyond reasonable doubt in one case while evidence of the same crime may be found insufficient in another.

Other stakeholders may look to international criminal courts—and to their Judges—to bring about peace and post-conflict reconciliation, as indeed the U.N. Security Council and other bodies have, at times, suggested in establishing such courts. International criminal justice will almost invariably be found wanting by those who believe that international criminal courts are mandated to promote peace and reconciliation, particularly where there is no evidence of any such impact or where rulings are thought to be counter-productive to reconciliatory aims.

Trying those accused of serious violations of international law in a public, fair and careful way may have a beneficial impact on the restoration and maintenance of peace in an area previously shattered by conflict. But these salutary effects should not be confused with the narrow mandate of an international criminal court or its Judges: to try those accused in accordance with the law. Were it otherwise—were international criminal courts responsible, even just in part, for ensuring reconciliation—the fairness of their proceedings would, almost inevitably, be put in doubt, as when the perceived interests of reconciliation would weigh in favor of a particular conviction or acquittal. Legal principle must not be trumped by an extraneous purpose, however desirable that purpose may be.

Finally, one of the most frequently voiced expectations is that international criminal courts should give victims justice. The idea that international criminal justice is done for the victims is popular, just as it is contested. It risks pitting the goal of many victims to ensure punishment of and retribution against those whom they believe to have committed crimes, against the rule of law guarantees of fairness, impartiality and due process. If an individual accused of atrocities, and particularly one who is a political or military leader, is acquitted, or if the Prosecution declines to pursue charges, these decisions are sometimes viewed as a failure of international criminal justice.

But let us be clear. The true failure of international criminal justice would be if convictions or acquittals were issued without the support of law and evidence. If anything, acquittals can be a sign of a mature and independent legal system and of a court focused on the narrow judicial mandate of trying those charged, rather than on attempting to satisfy the often conflicting expectations of diverse stakeholders. Even as we sympathize with the sentiments of victims, the overarching obligation of a criminal Judge—whether at the national or the international level—is to respect the fundamental principles of the rule of law, a concept still more fragile in international jurisdictions than in most domestic settings. It is through affirming the importance of courts and due process—not simply in times of peace but during conflicts and their aftermath—that we ensure that it is the law, and not the rifle and vengeance, that rules. And this, to my mind, is the animating principle at the very heart of international justice, and the principle that has been at the center of my work for two decades as an international criminal Judge.

I conclude this brief chapter with the question I am sometimes asked, whether academics make good criminal Judges. Good question, where the answer turns largely on the qualities of the particular person rather than on a one-size-fits-all approach. Do they have the necessary qualities of experience, knowledge, integrity, impartiality and independence? Of course, judicial experience is particularly important in first instance trials where the evidentiary component of the proceedings is particularly valuable. In appeals courts, academic experience and breadth may, however, be an advantage. I find it interesting that the United Kingdom—where judicial appointments were limited to leading members of the practicing bar—is now making some, though still rare, appointments of academics to the Supreme Court. The United States, in contrast, has been, since the 20th century, appointing academics to the Supreme Court and some other courts, particularly federal courts of appeal.[2]

In international courts where Judges elect presidents of the courts, the election of academics as presidents has been quite frequent. I realize that there is always a danger that an academic may be tempted to use his or her

2. Richard A. Posner, *The Judiciary and the Academy: A Fraught Relationship*, 29 U. QUEENSLAND L.J. 13 (2010).

pulpit for pushing their preferred visions of the law, rather than adhere to judicial economy, neutrality and caution in their decisions. But perhaps the ability to approach difficult issues fairly and with an open mind, with modesty, to resist preconceived ideas, to be able to learn and to listen, may be cardinal. These qualities can be found among academics, as among members of the bar.

Finally, an academic can be much more eclectic than a Judge. He or she can loudly proclaim their own social and political beliefs and practices. They can be a maverick. In contrast, Judges are much more constrained, in their work and even in their private comportment, by accepted principles and traditions of the judiciary, typically reflected by codes of judicial behavior. Like everyone else, Judges may and do make mistakes. I know I did. And at times I could have done things differently and better. But to be a Judge, a person must at least try to live up to the lofty goals of the judiciary. They should try to ensure that the protections offered by the law are respected, equally, for the victims as for the alleged violators. They should remember that procedural fairness and due process are as important as substantive decisions, and that the core judicial norm is that convictions can only be entered or upheld on the basis of the evidence established beyond a reasonable doubt and in accordance with the law. They must at all times protect judicial independence and impartiality, avoiding not only bias, but just as importantly appearance of bias. It is only by respect of such principles that courts, especially international courts, can acquire credibility, authority and legitimacy.

Throughout my nearly two decades on international criminal tribunals, I did my best to ensure the fairness of the judicial process.

Justice is not about achieving any particular outcome. It is about ensuring a principled process that serves to strengthen the rule of law and recognizes the overarching authority of the law. Not surprisingly, commitment to such principles to the exclusion of any extraneous agenda at times resulted in harsh, brutal and personal criticism of some of my decisions, especially those involving acquittals and early release of prisoners who had served two-thirds (ICTY) or three-quarters (ICTR) of their prison sentences. These caused me much pain. But being a target of criticism should perhaps be regarded as part of the job description of an international criminal Judge.

III

Moving from Nuremberg to The Hague

The Necessity to Establish a Tribunal for the Former Yugoslavia

Appalled by the glaring impunity for gross violations of international humanitarian law committed in the course of the Yugoslavia fragmentation wars in early 1990s, I was among those who called for the establishment of a war crimes tribunal for the former Yugoslavia. I was happy to be able to have the *Foreign Affairs Magazine* as my standard bearer, as it carried my 1993 article ('The Case for War Crimes Trials in Yugoslavia').

Here is what I argued:

> The credibility of international humanitarian law demanded a war crimes tribunal to hold accountable those responsible for gross violations in the former Yugoslavia. Opponents in the bitter ethnic and religious conflicts have subjected civilians to summary execution, torture, rape, mass internment, deportation, destruction or confiscation of property and other violations of their rights. Many thousands have died.

A war crimes tribunal, sought by the U.N. Security Council, would be the first since the Nuremberg and Far East trials following World War II. The Security Council's decision, embodied in U.N. Resolution 808 of 22 February 1993, derived its binding authority from the U.N. Charter's Chapter VII provisions regarding threats to peace, breaches of peace and acts of aggression. The Security Council's determination that violations of international humanitarian law constitute a threat to international peace and security and that the establishment of the tribunal would contribute to the restoration and the maintenance of peace was of ground-breaking

Standing Up For Justice. Theodor Meron, Oxford University Press (2021). © Theodor Meron.
DOI: 10.1093/oso/9780198863434.003.0003

importance. Considered from a different perspective, the Security Council's decision to establish a war *crimes* tribunal reflected the failure of the Security Council's primary mission to end the conflict and the atrocities.

Reaffirming the Nuremberg tenets and the principle of accountability should deter those in Yugoslavia and elsewhere who envisaged "final solutions" to their conflicts with ethnic and religious minorities. A war crimes tribunal could also educate the general public not to accept egregious violations of human rights and humanitarian norms. Above all, there was a moral imperative to rigorously prosecute the offenders, given the deliberate, systematic and outrageous nature of the violations in the former Yugoslavia.

I noted that there was nothing new, of course, in prosecuting offenders against the laws and customs of war as reflected in national military codes. For centuries military commanders—from Henry V of England, under his famous ordinances of war of 1419, to the American military prosecutions of soldiers involved in the Mỹ Lai massacre under the U.S. Code of Military Justice—had enforced such laws against violators. In other cases, States had brought to trial captured prisoners of war for offenses committed against the customary laws of war. Thus, both the accused's own State and the captor State had standing to prosecute. Neither system, however, functioned with any degree of efficiency. Except in the case of total defeat or subjugation—for example, Germany after World War II—prosecutions of enemy personnel accused of war crimes had been both rare and difficult. National prosecutions had also been rare because of nationalistic, patriotic or propagandistic considerations.

The Treaty of Versailles after World War I illustrates the case of a defeated but not wholly occupied State. Germany was obligated to hand over to the Allies for trial about 900 persons accused of violating the laws of war. But even a weak and defeated country such as Germany was able to effectively resist compliance. The Allies eventually agreed to trials by German national courts of a significantly reduced number of Germans. The sentences were both few and clement. The Versailles model proved to be clearly disappointing.

On the other hand, after the four principal victorious and occupying powers established an International Military Tribunal (IMT) following World War II, several thousand Nazi war criminals were tried either by national courts under Allied Control Council Law No. 10 or by various States under national decrees. Nuremberg's IMT, before which 22 major offenders were tried, and the national courts functioned reasonably well;

the Allies had supreme authority over Germany and thus could often find and arrest the accused, obtain evidence and make arrangements for extradition.

Despite the revolutionary development of human rights in the U.N. era, no attempts were made to bring to justice such gross perpetrators of crimes against humanity or genocide as Idi Amin or Saddam Hussein perhaps because the atrocities in Uganda and Iraq (against the Kurds) did not occur in the context of international wars. Such trials as were held, were before national not international courts. The same was true of Nazi war criminals arrested many years after Nuremberg, such as Eichmann (tried in Israel) and Papon (tried in France). Internal strife and even civil wars were still largely outside the parameters of war crimes and the grave breaches provisions of the Geneva Conventions.

The Persian Gulf War, as an international war, provided a classic environment for the vindication of the laws of war violated by Iraq by its plunder of Kuwait and its treatment of Kuwait's civilian population and Kuwaiti and Allied prisoners of war. Although the Security Council had invoked the threat of prosecution of Iraqi violators of international humanitarian law, the ceasefire resolution did not contain a single word regarding criminal responsibility. Instead, the U.N. resolution promulgated a system of war reparations and established numerous obligations for Iraq in areas ranging from disarmament to boundary demarcation.

This result is not surprising, for the U.N. Coalition's war objectives were limited, and there was an obvious tension between negotiating a ceasefire with Saddam Hussein and demanding his arrest and trial as a war criminal. A historic opportunity was missed to breathe new life into the critically important concept of individual criminal responsibility for the laws of war violations. At the very least, the Security Council should have issued a warning that Saddam and other responsible Iraqis would be subject to arrest and prosecution under the grave breaches provisions of the Geneva Conventions whenever they set foot abroad.

I made it clear that to be credible, an ad hoc tribunal for the former Yugoslavia must respect impeccable legality and fairness. For better or worse, the precedent of such a tribunal would be invoked in future situations. The tribunal must comply with the basic norms of due process, including the rights of the defendants to counsel, to cross-examine witnesses, to present evidence and, going beyond the procedural guarantees of Nuremberg, to appeal to an appeals court. The defendant's right to participate in their own defense should preclude *in absentia* trials, which are inherently vulnerable to abuse.

The rejection of *in absentia* trials need not, however, lead to the conclusion that nothing should be done. An independent and credible prosecuting authority, acting under the Security Council's mandate, could request arrest warrants from the new tribunal for suspected offenders and call on all States to hand over those persons for trial. Such warrants could clash with the accused's claims of diplomatic or sovereign immunity. Security Council resolutions adopted under Chapter VII must trump such claims.

Atrocities had been committed by all parties. Fairness and credibility required that the Serbs, although reportedly responsible for most violations, not be the only group prosecuted. Muslims and Croats who had committed war crimes—or anyone else for that matter—should thus be equally investigated and prosecuted.

The marshaling of evidence strong enough to support convictions in criminal cases would prove difficult, especially as regards senior ranks. The U.N. Kalshoven Commission of experts charged with providing evidence of violations had negligible resources. In contrast, the prosecution at Nuremberg employed hundreds of lawyers and investigators.

The Kalshoven *interim* report states that while grave breaches had been committed, tangible evidence had yet to be obtained. There is a world of difference between reliable reports on the events and evidence establishing individual guilt. Moreover, proof of command responsibility would be difficult as would be the identification of some obscure militias.

Critics of the Nuremberg trials censured as retroactive the rules of international humanitarian law that formed the basis for the prosecutions. However, the principle of individual criminal responsibility of persons committing or ordering grave breaches of international humanitarian law is now generally accepted, as is the list of treaty and customary provisions defining war crimes. In addition, both Nuremberg and post-Nuremberg international law reject the act of State defense and largely the defense of superior orders. And it was evident that the complaint that Nuremberg was a case of victors' justice was irrelevant to the new tribunal.

Warnings of war crimes trials had been unsuccessful deterrents in past wars and might have proved no more effective in the case of the former Yugoslavia. The precedent and moral considerations required action in any event. Furthermore, several factors could strengthen deterrence. First, modern media ensured that all actors knew of the steps being taken to establish the tribunal and strengthen public support for accountability. Second, the tribunal would probably be established while the war was still being waged. Even the worst war criminals knew that their countries would eventually want to emerge from isolation and be reintegrated into the international community. Moreover, they themselves would want to travel abroad without risking arrest. Normalization of relations and travel could depend on compliance with warrants of arrests.

As I was writing in 1993, I pointed out that one of the difficulties was that most provisions of international humanitarian law still applied to international wars only. Violations of Common Article 3 of the Geneva Conventions which address non-international armed conflicts were not as yet recognized as grave breaches or even war crimes. Were any part of the conflict deemed internal, the perpetrators could argue that they could not be prosecuted for such crimes. Of course, they could be prosecuted for genocide or crimes against humanity, if applicable. The first international tribunal since Nuremberg and Tokyo should apply only generally accepted provisions of international law which establish criminal responsibility of individuals and not only the responsibility of the State. It is helpful that the parties to the conflicts in an accord of 22 May 1992, agreed to apply most provisions of Additional Protocol I to the Geneva Conventions (except grave breaches).

State of the Law: The Example of Rape

I have already mentioned the inadequacy of the law recognized as applicable to non-international armed conflicts. I now turn specifically to rape.

Special difficulties could be encountered with regard to prosecuting ethnic cleansing and rape. Ethnic cleansing is, of course, an amalgam of illegal acts such as harassment, discrimination, beatings, expulsions, summary executions, mass and systematic rape, destruction of secular and religious property, arbitrary arrests and detentions, sieges and cutting off of essential supplies. Many of these considered in isolation constitute war crimes and possibly crimes against humanity. Considered as a cluster of violations, they may constitute crimes against humanity and genocide. The state of law on rape, gender crimes and indeed on the norms applicable to non-international armed conflicts was also unsatisfactory. In an editorial comment in the *American Journal of International Law* in July 1993, "Rape as a

Crime under International Humanitarian Law," I deplored the unsatisfactory state of international law on rape and urged rapid change.

I noted that it took the repeated and massive atrocities in the former Yugoslavia, especially in Bosnia and Herzegovina, to persuade the Security Council that the commission of those atrocities constituted a threat to international peace, and that the creation of an ad hoc international criminal tribunal would contribute to the restoration of peace. Indeed, the Security Council decided to establish such a tribunal under Chapter VII (Resolutions 808 and 827). For the first time since the founding of the U.N., the Security Council became, at least for that moment, a major force for ensuring respect for international humanitarian law.

Today, in contrast to the past, the rapid dissemination of knowledge about the continuing abuses combines with the public's broader sensitivity to human rights to strengthen political will and make some kind of action a moral imperative.

Because the international community failed in the central task of ending the bloodshed and atrocities, the establishment of the tribunal became the preferred means to promote justice and effectiveness of international law.

That the practice of rape was deliberate, massive and egregious, particularly in Bosnia and Herzegovina, was amply demonstrated in reports of the U.N., the European Community as it then was, the Conference on Security and Co-operation in Europe and various non-governmental organizations. The Special Rapporteur appointed by the U.N. Commission on Human Rights, Tadeusz Mazowiecki, highlighted the role of rape both as an attack on the individual victim and as a method of "ethnic cleansing" "intended to humiliate, shame, degrade and terrify the entire ethnic group."[1] Indescribable abuse of thousands of women in the territory of the former Yugoslavia was needed to shock the international community into rethinking the prohibition of rape as a crime under the laws of war.[2] Important as the decision to

1. Tadeusz Mazowiecki, *Report on the Situation of Human Rights in the Territory of the former Yugoslavia*, U.N. Doc. A/48/92-S/25341, Annex, at 20, 57 (1993). *See generally*, Theodor Meron, *Rape as a Crime under International Humanitarian Law*, 87 AM. J. INT'L L. 424 (1993).
2. There has already been considerable recognition that custodial rape, or rape in circumstances for which a government is liable under the law of State responsibility, violates the prohibitions of torture or inhuman treatment in international human rights. The reports of Peter Kooijmans, Special Rapporteur of the U.N. Commission on Human Rights, have greatly contributed to this development. *See also* European Commission of Human Rights, *Cyprus v. Turkey*, Application Nos 6780/74 and 6950/75 (1976); Andrew Byrnes, *The Committee against Torture*, in THE UNITED NATIONS AND HUMAN RIGHTS 509, 519 & n. 38 (Philip Alston ed., 1992).

establish the tribunal was, institutional process must work in tandem with the substantive development of international law. What, then, was the status of rape at that time as a crime under international humanitarian law?

Rape by soldiers has of course been prohibited by the law of war for centuries, and violators have been subjected to capital punishment under national military codes, such as those in England of Richard II (1385) and Henry V (1419).[3] Of more immediate influence on the modern law of war was the prohibition of rape as a capital crime by the Lieber Instructions (1863).[4] Indeed, rape committed on an individual soldier's initiative has frequently been prosecuted in national courts. In many cases, however, rape has been given license, either as an encouragement for soldiers or as an instrument of policy.[5] Nazi and Japanese practices which enforced prostitution and rape on a large scale are among the egregious examples of such policies.[6]

Under a broad construction, Article 46 of the Hague Regulations can be considered to cover rape,[7] but in practice it has seldom been so interpreted. Rape was neither mentioned in the Nuremberg Charter nor prosecuted in Nuremberg. Such a crime constituted "beyond doubt ... part of international customary law, ... applicable in armed conflict, i.e., a war crime under customary international law."[8] It was prosecuted in Tokyo as a war crime.[9]

3. Theodor Meron, HENRY'S WARS AND SHAKESPEARE'S LAWS, chs 6, 8 (1993).
4. Francis Lieber, *Instructions for the Government of Armies of the United States in the Field*, Art. 44, originally published as U.S. War Department, Adjutant General's Office, General Orders No. 100 (24 April 1863), *reprinted in* THE LAWS OF ARMED CONFLICTS 3 (Dietrich Schindler & Jiri Toman eds, 3d rev. ed., 1988).
5. Theodor Meron (n. 3), ch. 6; *see also* Theodor Meron, *Common Rights of Mankind in Gentili, Grotius and Suárez*, 85 AM. J. INT'L L. 110, 115–16 (1991).
6. For another example, *see* Walter Kälin, *Report on the Situation of Human Rights in Kuwait under Iraqi Occupation*, U.N. Doc. E/CN.4/1992/26, at 47–8.
7. "Family honour and rights, the lives of persons, and private property, as well as religious convictions and practice must be respected." Convention Respecting the Laws and Customs of War on Land, with Annex of Regulations, 18 Oct. 1907, 36 Stat. 2277, 1 Bevans 631 [Hague Convention No. IV].
8. *See* Statute of the International Criminal Tribunal for the Former Yugoslavia, U.N. Doc. S/25704, Annex (1993), paras. 34–5; 32 ILM 1192 [hereinafter ICTY Statute]. In some cases, enforced prostitution was prosecuted in national courts outside Germany. 15 United Nations War Crimes Commission, Law Reports of Trials of War Criminals 121 (1949). A Dutch court in Batavia, for example, found some Japanese persons responsible for forced prostitution guilty of violating the laws and usages of war. Philip R. Piccigallo, THE JAPANESE ON TRIAL 179–80 (1979).
9. Charter of the International Military Tribunal for the Far East, 19 Jan. 1946, *amended* 26 Apr. 1946, TIAS No. 1589, 4 Bevans 20. The IMT in Tokyo found some Japanese military and civilian officials guilty of war crimes, including rape, because they failed to carry out their duty to ensure that their subordinates complied with international law. *See* John Alan Appleman, MILITARY TRIBUNALS AND INTERNATIONAL CRIMES 259 (1971). The IMT considered rape a war

Another seed for future normative development was sown in Control Council Law No. 10,[10] adopted by the four occupying powers in Germany as a charter for war crimes trials by their own courts in Germany. It expanded the list of crimes against humanity found in the Nuremberg Charter to include rape. Nevertheless, although both the Fourth Geneva Convention[11] and the Additional Protocols[12] explicitly prohibit rape, these instruments did not follow the precedent of Control Council Law No. 10 and did not list rape among the grave breaches subject to universal jurisdiction.[13]

It was time for a change. Indeed, under the weight of the events in the former Yugoslavia, the hesitation to recognize that rape could be a war crime or a grave breach had already begun to dissipate.[14] The ICRC and various States aided this development by adopting a broad construction of existing law. The ICRC declared that the grave breach of "wilfully causing great suffering or serious injury to body or health" (Article 147 of the Fourth Geneva Convention) covered rape.[15] If so, surely rape—in certain circumstances—could also rise to the level of such other grave breaches as torture or inhuman treatment. I was happy that this view of rape as torture, for which I pleaded in 1993, is now a part of the jurisprudence of international criminal tribunals.

crime. 2 THE TOKYO JUDGMENT: THE INTERNATIONAL MILITARY TRIBUNAL FOR THE FAR EAST 965, 971–2, 988–9 (B.V. A. Röling & C. F. Rüter eds, 1977); 1 *id.* at 385; Gordon Ireland, Uncommon Law in Martial Tokyo, 4 WORLD AFF. Y.B. 54, 61 & n. 14 (1950). Regarding the case of Admiral Toyoda, who was charged with violating laws and customs of war by tolerating various abuses, including rape (he was acquitted of all charges), see William H. Parks, *Command Responsibility for War Crimes*, MIL. L. REV., Fall, 1, 69–73 (1973).

10. Control Council for Germany, Official Gazette, 31 Jan. 1946, at 50, *reprinted in* Naval War College, DOCUMENTS ON PRISONERS OF WAR 304 (International Law Studies vol. 60, Howard S. Levie ed., 1979).
11. Art. 27.
12. Protocol Additional to the Geneva Conventions of 12 August 1949, and Relating to the Protection of Victims of International Armed Conflicts, opened for signature 12 Dec. 1977, Arts 76(1) and 85, 1125 UNTS 3, 16 ILM 1391 (1977) [Protocol I]; Protocol Additional to the Geneva Conventions of 12 August 1949, and Relating to the Protection of Victims of Non-International Armed Conflicts, opened for signature 12 Dec. 1997, Art. 4(2)(e), 1125 UNTS 609, 16 ILM 1442 (1997) [Protocol II].
13. *See generally*, Françoise Krill, *The Protection of Women in International Humanitarian Law*, 25 INT'L REV. RED CROSS 337, 341 (1985).
14. ICRC, Aide-Mémoire (3 Dec. 1992).
15. As early as 1958, the ICRC Commentary on the four Conventions recognized that the grave breach of "inhuman treatment" (Art. 147) should be interpreted in the context of Art. 27, which also prohibits rape. COMMENTARY ON THE GENEVA CONVENTIONS OF 12 AUGUST 1949: GENEVA CONVENTION RELATIVE TO THE PROTECTION OF CIVILIAN PERSONS IN TIME OF WAR 598 (Oscar M. Uhler & Henri Coursier eds, 1958).

Moreover, the massive and systematic practice of rape and its use as a "national" instrument of "ethnic cleansing" provide an additional justification for its prosecution as a crime against humanity.

The U.S. Department of State unequivocally stated that rape was already a war crime or a grave breach under customary international law and the Geneva Conventions and could be prosecuted as such.[16]

This evolution in the approach of the ICRC and the United States was paralleled by the positions and draft charters submitted by several States to the U.N. Secretary-General pursuant to Security Council Resolution 808. The U.S. proposal adapted the definition of crimes against humanity in Control Council Law No. 10 to the Yugoslav circumstances, and listed rape among the punishable crimes.[17] Most important, the Statute of the International Tribunal proposed by the U.N. Secretary-General lists rape among crimes against humanity.[18]

The confirmation of the principle stated in Control Council Law No. 10, that rape can constitute a crime against humanity, was, both morally and legally, of groundbreaking importance. Nevertheless, the possibility of prosecuting rape as war crimes or grave breaches could not be neglected.

16. The Department stated:

> We believe that there is no need to amend the Geneva Conventions to accomplish the objectives stated in your letter, however, because the legal basis for prosecuting troops for rape is well established under the Geneva Conventions and customary international law. As stated in the authoritative Department of the Army Law of War Manual, any violation of the Geneva Conventions is a war crime (FM 27-10, para. 499.). Article 27 of the Geneva Convention Relative to the Protection of Civilian Persons in Time of War provides that women shall be "especially protected ... against rape." Article 13 of the Geneva Convention Relative to the Treatment of Prisoners of War provides that prisoners "must at all times be protected, particularly against acts of violence"; article 14 requires that women "be treated with all the regard due to their sex." Both Conventions list grave breaches, including willful killing, torture or inhuman treatment, and (with regard to civilians) willfully causing great suffering or serious injury to body or health: Under the Geneva Conventions and customary international law, all parties to an international conflict (including all parties to the conflict in the former Yugoslavia) are required either to try persons alleged to have committed grave breaches or to extradite them to a party that will. In our reports to the United Nations on human rights violations in the former Yugoslavia, we have reported sexual assaults as grave breaches. We will continue to do so and will continue to press the international community to respond to the terrible sexual atrocities in the former Yugoslavia.

Letter from Robert A. Bradtke, Acting Assistant Secretary for Legislative Affairs, to Senator Arlen Specter (27 Jan. 1993).

17. "Acts of murder, torture, extrajudicial and summary execution, illegal detention, and rape that are part of a campaign or attack against any civilian population in the former Yugoslavia on national, racial, ethnic, or religious grounds." U.N. Doc. S/25575, Annex II, Art. 10(b)(i) (1993).

18. U.N. Doc. S/25704 (n. 8), Annex, Art. 5. This Statute was approved by S.C. Res. 827.

Although, formally, the law stated by the Security Council under Chapter VII of the U.N. Charter was necessarily contextual and applicable only to the former Yugoslavia, the Tribunal's Statute, like that of Nuremberg, was likely quickly to become a fundamental normative instrument of the general law of war. The Security Council's (Resolution 827), recognition of rape as a punishable offense under international humanitarian law could expedite the recognition of rape, in some circumstances, as torture or inhuman treatment in the international law of human rights as well.[19] Meaningful progress in combating rape could only be made by more vigorous enforcement of the law. The recognition of rape as a crime under international law punishable by the future war crimes tribunal for the former Yugoslavia was a vital step in that direction.

By a strange coincidence, the first appeal case on which I sat in the ICTY was the case of *Kunarac et al.* (2002) in which we, the Judges, made major contributions to the clarification and the development of the international law on rape. We found that the appellants were guilty of sexual enslavement as a crime against humanity. We rejected the defence claim that rape could only occur when the victim showed "continuous resistance" and when physical force was used. Of course, force provides clear evidence of non-consent, but non-consent can be inferred from circumstantial evidence and need not be proved explicitly. We determined that coercive circumstances make impossible the very notion of consent by the victim. And it is the absence of consent that is the determining criterion for the crime of rape. Furthermore, we approved the Trial Chamber's conclusion that the public official requirement under the U.N. Convention against Torture is not a requirement in relation to the criminal responsibility of an individual outside the Torture Convention. And we agreed with the *Furundžija* ICTY Judgement (Trial Judgement in 1998, Appeal Judgement in 2002) that severe pain or suffering, as required by the definition of torture, is caused by rape,

19. The pernicious phenomenon of rape continues unabated in war as in peace. *See*, e.g., Majority Staff of the Senate Judiciary Committee, 102d Cong., 2d Sess., *Violence Against Women: A Week in the Life of America* (1992); Americas Watch, UNTOLD TERROR: VIOLENCE AGAINST WOMEN IN PERU'S ARMED CONFLICT (1992); Middle East Watch, PUNISHING THE VICTIM: RAPE AND MISTREATMENT OF ASIAN MAIDS IN KUWAIT (1992); Americas Watch, CRIMINAL INJUSTICE: VIOLENCE AGAINST WOMEN IN BRAZIL (1991). For efforts by the Committee on the Elimination of Discrimination to combat violence against women, see CEDAW General Recommendation No. 19: Violence against Women, *in* COMPILATION OF GENERAL COMMENTS AND GENERAL RECOMMENDATIONS ADOPTED BY HUMAN RIGHTS TREATY BODIES, U.N. Doc. HRI/GEN/1, at 74 (1992).

which necessarily implies such pain and suffering. Thus rape per se causes the pain and suffering necessary for torture, and constitutes torture. The prosecution therefore did not have to prove pain and suffering by medical evidence. We also accepted that rape constitutes a war crime under customary international law. And in the statutes of international tribunals and courts rape is clearly listed as a crime against humanity.

Moreover, the ICTR's first case, *Akayesu* (1998), decided that rape can constitute a genocidal act when it is carried out with the intent to destroy a protected group in whole or in part. It constitutes an infliction of serious bodily and mental harm within the terms of the Genocide Convention. The jurisprudence of the ICTY and the ICTR thus produced a seismic change in the law on rape as it existed on the eve of the establishment of the Tribunals. The jurisprudence of the Tribunals clearly informed the particularly comprehensive and detailed definition of rape in the Statute and in the Elements of Crimes of the ICC. And the Rules of Procedure and Evidence of the Tribunals provided for easier prosecution of cases of rapes and better protection for the victims.

Non-International Armed Conflicts

I have mentioned already that one of the shortcomings of international humanitarian and criminal law in 1993 was that most of their provisions were regarded as applicable to international armed conflicts and to the obligations of States only, and that violations of Common Article 3 were not necessarily considered to implicate the criminal responsibility of individuals.

Of course this situation was transformed by the *Tadić Interlocutory Decision on Jurisdiction* (1995). That decision determined that many of the rules, previously governing the responsibility of States and not individuals and only in international armed conflicts, were also applicable to non-international armed conflicts and governed individual criminal responsibility as well. The Decision confirmed that Article 3 applied not only to the responsibility of the parties to a non-international armed conflict but also to individual criminal responsibility. I was happy to have contributed to the development of the law with my 1995 article in the *American Journal of International Law* ("The International Criminalization of Internal Atrocities").

These are just a few examples of the critical contributions that U.N. war crimes tribunals made to the development of international humanitarian and criminal law. Their jurisprudence fleshed out and contributed tremendously to the law of genocide, crimes against humanity and war crimes.

Of course, modern international tribunals have been inspired by the model of Nuremberg.

While international humanitarian law saw considerable doctrinal development in the half century preceding the Nuremberg trials, as nations codified many laws of war in treaties, many powers embraced the concepts of crimes against humanity and command responsibility and many nations rejected the notion of head-of-State immunity, enforcement lagged far behind the doctrinal development. Nobody faced an international tribunal after World War I, few faced domestic prosecution in Germany and Turkey and in those cases that were actually brought, the few-and-far-between convictions resulted in light penalties. Indeed, as one commentator observed, "[A]part from helping to lay the legal foundations for international criminal justice in the future, the Allies' experiment in retributive justice following the First World War was a dismal failure."[20]

Nuremberg Proceedings

The Agreement for the Prosecution and Punishment of the Major War Criminals of the European Axis, and Charter of the International Military Tribunal (1945) ("Nuremberg Charter" also known as the "London Charter") set out three types of substantive crimes: first, crimes against peace, which it defined mainly as starting or waging a war of aggression; second, war crimes; and, third, crimes against humanity.[21] Although the United States had opposed the charges both of waging a war of aggression and of "crimes against humanity" in the aftermath of World War I, it now supported their inclusion.[22] Similarly, the Charter rejected head-of-State immunity.[23] The Charter also contained two novel aspects—both

20. M. Cherif Bassiouni, *World War I: The War to End All Wars and the Birth of a Handicapped International Criminal Justice System*, 30 DENV. J. INT'L L. & POL'Y 244 at 290 (2002).
21. London Charter, Annexed to the Agreement for the Prosecution and Punishment of Major War Criminals of the European Axis, Art. 6, 82 UNTS 279.
22. Indeed, the other three Allies were opposed to including the launch of an aggressive war as a crime, and only energetic efforts by Jackson persuaded them otherwise. *See* Robert E. Conot, JUSTICE AT NUREMBERG 21–3 (1983).
23. London Charter (n. 21), Art. 7.

stemming from a memorandum prepared earlier by the U.S. Department of War.[24] First, the Charter included conspiracy as a crime—a decision reached over some objections from France, whose civil law system (like that of the Soviet Union) did not separately criminalize conspiracy.[25] Second, the Charter authorized the International Military Tribunal (IMT) to try Nazi organizations such as the S.S. and the Gestapo and provided that if such organizations were convicted, individuals belonging to those organizations could be tried "for membership therein" without having the right to reopen the question of the criminality of the organization.[26]

Only one article of the Charter was devoted to the rights of the defendants and ensured them: (1) copies of the indictments against them; (2) translations of the indictment, incorporated documents and trial proceedings in their own language; (3) the right to conduct their own defense or have the assistance of counsel; and (4) the right to present evidence and cross-examine the prosecution witnesses.[27] Notably lacking were the right to remain silent, the right to be present[28] and the right of appeal.[29] Nor was there any specification of the burden of proof.

The IMT would "not be bound by technical rules of evidence" and it primarily followed the adversarial system used in common law rather than the inquisitorial system used in civil law—thus the prosecution and the defense were primarily responsible for interrogation and cross-examination of witnesses.[30]

Although brief, the London Charter thus covered important ground. It clearly resolved issues that had proved controversial in the aftermath of World War I, including the nature of the substantive crimes and the question of head-of-State immunity. It also indicated that the IMT would proceed more along common law lines than civil law lines.

24. *See* Norman Silber & Geoffrey Miller, *Toward "Neutral Principles" in the Law: Selections from the Oral History of Herbert Wechsler*, 93 COLUM. L. REV. 854, 893–5, 898–9 (1993).
25. London Charter (n. 21), Art. 6; *see also* Henry T. King, Jr., *Robert Jackson's Vision for Justice and Other Reflections of a Nuremberg Prosecutor*, 88 GEO. L.J. 2421, 2425 (2000).
26. London Charter (n. 21), Arts 9–11.
27. *Id.* at Art. 16.
28. Indeed, the Charter specified that a defendant could be tried *in absentia*. *id.*, Art. 12.
29. The Charter did give the Control Council the power to reduce the sentences entered by the IMT. *See id.*, Art. 29.
30. *See id.* at Arts 19, 24.

The host of topics covered in the proceedings and in the judgements was immense. Yet the trial lasted less than four months,[31] and the number of witnesses was hardly large—only 33 witnesses testified orally for the prosecution.[32]

The prosecution's slim use of witnesses was made possible by the availability of documentary evidence. In Jackson's words, "the defendants had their share of the Teutonic passion for thoroughness in putting things on paper."[33] In the course of their investigations, the prosecution sifted through huge quantities of captured evidence, including 100,000 documents, millions of feet of moving film and 25,000 photographs (many taken by Hitler's personal photographer), of which the prosecution ultimately introduced around 4,000 documents, certain sections of the film and 1,800 photographs into evidence.[34] Finds included a complete set of notes taken by Hitler's interpreter at meetings with foreign officials and official reports on the killing of Jews.[35] There were also many documents produced or signed by the defendants themselves, including the 36-volume official diary of Hans Frank's time in Poland.[36] As the Judgement ultimately stated, "[t]he case ... against the defendants rests in a large measure on documents of their own making, the authenticity of which has not been challenged except in one or two cases."[37]

Herbert Wechsler has remarked that the possibility of acquittals at Nuremberg was inconceivable at the beginning of the process.[38] Certainly the London Charter supports this impression, focusing on "trial and punishment" as though the outcome were not in doubt.[39] The Judgement that came down, however, drew clear distinctions between the different individual defendants and also took a restrictive view of certain substantive crimes.

The 170-page document began with a general overview of the IMT, of the applicable law and of the major offenses committed by Germany over the course of the war—including the planning and waging of aggressive

31. *See* 8 IMT TRIAL (TRIAL OF THE MAJOR WAR CRIMINALS BEFORE THE INTERNATIONAL MILITARY TRIBUNAL, NUREMBERG, 14 NOVEMBER 1945–1 OCTOBER 1946), at 495 (1947).
32. 1 IMT TRIAL (n. 31), at 172.
33. 1 IMT TRIAL (n. 31), at 102.
34. Report to the President by Mr. Justice Jackson, 7 Oct. 1946, *in* INTERNATIONAL CONFERENCE ON MILITARY TRIALS 433 (1949).
35. Conot (n. 22), at 37.
36. *Id.*
37. 1 IMT TRIAL (n. 31), at 173.
38. Silber & Miller (n. 24), at 906–7.
39. London Charter (n. 21), Art. 1.

warfare, the murder and ill-treatment of POWs and civilian populations and the persecution of the Jews.[40] Two aspects of this discussion are particularly noteworthy. First, the IMT discussed and rejected the defendants' claim that the offenses charged were not criminalized under international law at the time of their occurrence.[41] Second, the IMT read the charge of conspiracy narrowly, interpreting the London Charter to permit this charge only with regard to crimes against peace and not with regard to war crimes or crimes against humanity.[42]

As to the organizational defendants, the Judgement upheld the charges against some of the organizations, including the S.S. But while the London Charter had suggested that individual members of these organizations could later be convicted based simply on their membership of the organizations, the IMT ruled that "membership alone is not enough."[43] Instead, in future trials, the prosecution would have to show that those individuals shared in the criminal aims or acts of the organizations.[44]

The Judgement then analyzed the evidence against each defendant. Nineteen were found guilty of various crimes. Of these, 12 were sentenced to hang and the rest received prison terms of various lengths.[45]

Over the dissent of the Soviet Judge, the remaining three defendants were acquitted.

Moving Forward with the Law and Due Process

Prior to the establishment of the IMT, although customary international law existed, it had never been applied in an international criminal court. The challenge for the IMT, then, was to find a way to bring the existing law to bear in an international court.

Each of the crimes listed in the Nuremberg Charter was controversial. Never before had aggression been treated as a legal, rather than a merely political, wrong, and never had senior officials been held criminally liable as individuals. The concept of conspiracy liability was not only novel in

40. 1 IMT TRIAL (n. 31), at 171–254. 41. 1 IMT TRIAL (n. 31), at 219–23.
42. 1 IMT TRIAL (n. 31), at 226. 43. *Id.* at 256. 44. *See id.* 45. *Id.* at 365–6.

international law, but was especially foreign to lawyers from civil law traditions. And although the notion of "crimes against humanity," which defined criminal liability as including citizen-to-citizen acts, seems like second nature to us now, it had never formed the basis for international criminal liability before World War II. Even the charge of war crimes was ambiguous, since the laws of war had not previously delimited the boundaries of lawful military conduct with much precision.[46]

Despite the initial controversy, the IMT's legal legacy was rapidly and broadly established.[47]

That is how matters stood until the establishment of the modern international criminal tribunals at The Hague and Arusha.

Today we take the IMT at Nuremberg for granted. In its time it was, in the words of U.S. Prosecutor Robert Jackson, both "novel and experimental."[48] It consciously broke from the approach taken at the end of World War I, when the prosecution of war crimes was left to the defeated nations with the result that very few individuals were tried and even fewer received meaningful punishments. Instead of leaving prosecutions to the defeated Germany after World War II, the Allied Powers therefore set up their own Tribunal, composed of Judges and Prosecutors from the United Kingdom, the United States, France and the Soviet Union, to try top Nazi leaders. In its single year-long trial, the Tribunal heard evidence in relation to a mind-boggling number of issues: from the planning and waging of aggressive war, to the deportation, forced labor, persecution and annihilation of the Jewish people; to the atrocities committed against civilians and soldiers of the occupied countries; to the plunder of the occupied countries and crimes against culture; and to the inhumane treatment of prisoners of war. Ultimately, the IMT convicted several organizations such as the S.S. and the Gestapo and 19 of 22 individual defendants, with sentences for those individuals ranging from 10 years' imprisonment to death. Three individual defendants were acquitted.

Of course, this was not all that the IMT did. In the course of the trial and the resulting Judgement, it also developed and clarified many important

46. *See* Yoram Dinstein, The Conduct of Hostilities Under the Law of International Armed Conflict 57–105 (2004).

47. *See* Jonathan A. Bush, *Nuremberg: The Modern Law of War and Its Limitations*, 93 Colum. L. Rev. 2022, 2063 (1993) (reviewing Telford Taylor, The Anatomy of the Nuremberg Trials: A Personal Memoir (1992)).

48. 2 IMT Trial (n. 31), at 99 (Opening Statement).

issues of substantive law, and especially crimes against humanity with its citizen-to-citizen criminal liability. In addition, it also had to resolve differences between how the civil law courts of continental Europe and the common law courts of the United States and Britain operated.

Relatedly, the IMT had to grapple with what due process rights defendants should receive—and did a reasonable job in that regard, albeit one that was somewhat rudimentary by today's standards. Unlike the parallel Tokyo trials conducted by the International Military Commission for the Far East, the Nuremberg trial thus provided reassurance that there was some justice to victors' justice. It was generally judged a success.

After the IMT closed its doors in the fall of 1946, there were further trials conducted by individual Allied powers, particularly the United States, within their own zones of occupation in Germany. But there were no more international criminal tribunals. The enforcement of substantive international criminal law became very much a country-by-country affair rather than a matter for the international community more broadly. Although not framed or even intended that way, there was something of a compromise in the international community with regard to international criminal justice. The substance of international criminal law was able to develop through powerful and important treaties, including the Genocide Convention of 1948, the 1949 Geneva Conventions for the Protection of Victims of War and the two Additional Protocols to the Geneva Conventions that were adopted in 1977. The enforcement of international criminal law at an international level, however, went nowhere. While there were calls as early as 1948 for the establishment of an international criminal court, the great powers seemed remarkably content to let the issue stall in committees. This is why international criminal justice was primarily a memory of Nuremberg, at least as far as its international practice was concerned. Back then, I do not think that even the most fervent advocates of the creation of international criminal tribunals could have predicted the explosion of courts that has since occurred with the ICTY, the ICTR and of course the International Criminal Court (ICC). We also had several so-called "hybrid courts" and increased emphasis on domestic prosecution of international war crimes. International criminal law has become one of the more dynamic branches of international law.

How did this happen? How did we get from a dream of Nuremberg to a world where international criminal tribunals seem to be part of the international community's response to every conflict-related crisis that it addresses?

The establishment of the ICTY was crucial in this regard. The ethnically charged conflict in the former Yugoslavia sent shockwaves rippling through Europe, where nothing like it had occurred since World War II. At the same time, the political dynamics that followed the breakdown of the Soviet Union had loosened the Security Council, at least temporarily, from its traditional standoff. As one of the modest measures it put in place in response to the conflict—and at the urging of NGOs, the media and academic commentators—in short, public opinion—the Security Council established the ICTY in 1993. The ICTY had jurisdiction over genocide, war crimes and crimes against humanity—that is, atrocity crimes—that were committed in the former Yugoslavia from 1991 onward.

In summary, in 1993, the Security Council gambled that the answer to the question "Does international criminal justice work?" was "Yes." The gamble, admittedly, was a sensible one. At best, the ICTY would help bring justice, and possibly peace, to the region. At worst, the ICTY would simply be ineffective. This would lead to costs in terms of money and prestige, but those costs would be mitigated by the temporary and experimental nature of the Tribunal. And, however it turned out, the ICTY could be considered a test case for an international criminal court. This gamble was made again in 1994 with the establishment of the ICTR. It would have been awkward, to say the least, for the Security Council to set up a tribunal in relation to atrocities in Europe, but not to do the same with regard to the genocide in African Rwanda.

By 1998, it was clear that both the ICTY and ICTR were functioning institutions, although they had neither conducted many trials nor, in the case of the ICTY, gained custody over any particularly high-level indictees. Since then, however, international pressure has resulted in the arrival at The Hague of many senior accused. Eventually, all 161 indictees of the ICTY were accounted for, an incredible law enforcement success, as well as all but six (after the arrest of Kabuga and information on the death of Bizimana in May 2020) of the ICTR indictees. Five of the ICTR fugitives have been referred to Rwanda for trial; the other two, "the big fish" (one of the two is still a fugitive) are to be tried by the Mechanism. The experiences of the ad hoc Tribunals may have helped to encourage the renewed push for an international criminal court, which culminated in 1998. The ICC was officially established in July 2002, following the 60th ratification of the Rome Statute.

The international community had also been experimenting with hybrid courts, such as the Special Court for Sierra Leone, the Extraordinary

Chambers in the Courts of Cambodia (Khmer Rouge Tribunal), the Special Tribunal for Lebanon (Hariri Tribunal) and the Specialist Chambers for Kosovo. These hybrids use a mix of domestic and international law and personnel. They either have jurisdiction over certain international or domestic crimes that occurred before the ICC came into effect or, as in the case of the Lebanon Tribunal, over particular crimes under the law of Lebanon that do not fall within the categories of crimes over which the ICC can exercise jurisdiction. Finally, there has been an increased emphasis on domestic prosecution of international war crimes, as exemplified by the domestic trials in the States of the former Yugoslavia and in Rwanda, and from time to time in other countries under their legislation reflecting the principle of universality of jurisdiction.

The establishment of the ICC created a mantra that the international community is tired of ad hoc criminal tribunals, which are, it has been argued, expensive, slow and selective. The assumption was that the ICC would be less costly, more effective and practically universal. It is not obvious, however, whether or not these hopes about the ICC have been rather rosy and whether the international criminal tribunals have had their day. States appreciate the work and the jurisprudence of the ad hoc and special Tribunals and the jury is still out on the workload and the efficiency of the ICC. The comparison of the judicial output of the Tribunals with that of the ICC is not flattering for the ICC.

Using the London Charter as a model, the U.N. Security Council, exercising its authority under Chapter VII of the U.N. Charter, enacted the Statutes that created the ICTY and the ICTR.[49] Those Statutes set forth in detail the crimes over which the ad hoc Tribunals would exercise jurisdiction. As at Nuremberg, those crimes include war crimes and crimes against humanity, and the crime of genocide was added. Unlike the London Charter, however, the ICTY and ICTR Statutes do not include crimes against peace.[50] They are also marked by more detailed definitions and a broader scope—encompassing war crimes in internal conflicts; thus, these Statutes manifest the growing humanization of humanitarian law under the

49. *See* U.N. Doc. S/25704 (n. 8), Annex (1993), 32 ILM 1192; Statute of the International Criminal Tribunal for Rwanda, S.C. Res. 955, Annex (8 Nov. 1994), 33 ILM 1602 (1994) [hereinafter ICTR Statute].

50. *Compare* London Charter (n. 21), *with* ICTY Statute (n. 49) *and* ICTR Statute (n. 8).

influence of human rights.[51] And the Statute of the ICC contains even more detailed definitions of crimes.[52]

At the ICTY, although the definitions were more detailed, they still required extensive judicial interpretation. In adding that judicial gloss, the ICTY Judges, like the court at Nuremberg, refer to the customary law underpinnings of the crimes.[53] The ICTY's resort to customary law, however, was more methodical than Nuremberg, partly because of the criticisms leveled against the Nuremberg convictions. Critics of the Nuremberg trials charged that the law that was applied there originated in the London Charter and that it was unlawfully applied *ex post facto* to the German defendants.[54] To forestall similar criticisms, the ad hoc Tribunals took pains to explain the customary and conventional underpinnings of their decisions. Consequently, the ICTY helped to revitalize customary law and to anchor international humanitarian and criminal law not only in codified law, such as treaties and statutes, but also in customary law and judicial decisions.[55] The ICC is different in this respect. Its Statute resembles more of a civil law code and is to be applied as such, though, broadly speaking, the crimes it enumerates are declaratory of customary law.

The London Charter limited its definition of crimes against humanity to offenses that had occurred "in execution of or in connection with any crimes within the jurisdiction of the [IMT]."[56] In other words, although the Charter extended international criminal responsibility to atrocities committed within a single country, even between its own citizens ("against any civilian population, before or during the war"),[57] the scope of that liability was limited, because the offenses were required to be wartime atrocities within the IMT's jurisdiction. As a result, the IMT did not have jurisdiction over atrocities committed within and by Germany in the years leading up to

51. Theodor Meron, *The Humanization of Humanitarian Law*, 94 AM. J. INT'L L. 239 (2000), Theodor Meron, THE HUMANIZATION OF INTERNATIONAL LAW (2006). For a detailed discussion of the substantive law applied at the ICTY and ICTR, *see* Guénaël Mettraux, INTERNATIONAL CRIMES AND THE AD HOC TRIBUNALS (2005).
52. Rome Statute of the International Criminal Court, 17 July 1998, Arts 6–9, 2187 UNTS 3 [hereinafter ICC Statute].
53. *See*, e.g., *Prosecutor v. Hadžihasanović, Alagic and Kubura*, Decision on Interlocutory Appeal Challenging Jurisdiction in Relation to Command Responsibility, ICTY Appeals Chamber, Case no. IT-01-47-AR72 (16 July 2003).
54. *See* Kevin R. Chaney, *Pitfalls and Imperatives: Applying the Lessons of Nuremberg to the Yugoslav War Crimes Trials*, 14 DICK. J. INT'L L. 57, 71–2 (1995).
55. Theodor Meron, *The Revival of Customary Humanitarian Law*, 99 AM. J. INT'L L. 817 (2005).
56. London Charter (n. 21), Art. 6(c).
57. London Charter (n. 21), Art. 6(c).

World War II. Nevertheless, there is no question that crimes against humanity constituted the most revolutionary contribution of the Nuremberg trials to international criminal law, exceeding even crimes against peace, which owed at least a semblance of a foundation to the Treaty of Versailles.

Over time, however, the definition of crimes against humanity lost the required nexus with armed conflict. For instance, the U.N. Convention on the Non-Applicability of Statutory Limitations to War Crimes and Crimes against Humanity of 1968 applies to "crimes against humanity whether committed in time of war or in time of peace."[58] The ICTY Statute, in Article 5, defines crimes against humanity subject to the jurisdiction of the Tribunal as certain crimes "committed in armed conflict, whether international or internal in character."[59] Although this provision appears to require a nexus with armed conflict, the Appeals Chamber has interpreted the requirement of armed conflict as relating only to the Tribunal's subject matter jurisdiction.[60] The case law of ad hoc Tribunals makes clear that a war nexus is not required under customary law.

The ICC Statute confirms that no nexus with armed conflict is required. Under Article 7, crimes against humanity can be committed in all situations—international wars, internal wars of whatever intensity and peacetime.[61]

These changes relate to another significant legal development: the international criminalization of internal atrocities. The Security Council's Statutes for the ad hoc Tribunals have contributed significantly to the extension of international humanitarian law to non-international armed conflicts. The ICTY Statute and jurisprudence treat the conflict in the former Yugoslavia as both international and non-international in scope.[62] The ICTR Statute, however, is predicated on the assumption that the conflict in Rwanda was internal.[63] And the ICC Statute sets forth violations not only of the laws and customs of war applicable in international armed conflicts, but also of the laws and customs applicable in armed conflicts not of an international character—within the established framework of international law.[64]

58. Convention on the Non-Applicability of Statutory Limitations to War Crimes and Crimes Against Humanity, 26 Nov. 1968, Art. 1(b), 754 UNTS 73 (entered into force 11 Nov. 1970).

59. ICTY Statute (n. 49), Art. 5.

60. *Prosecutor v. Tadić*, Decision on the Defence Motion for Interlocutory Appeal on Jurisdiction, ICTY Appeals Chamber, at paras. 78–9, Case no. IT-94-1-AR72 (2 Oct. 1995).

61. ICC Statute (n. 52), Art. 7.

62. *See Prosecutor v. Tadić* (n. 60), paras. 71–93.

63. ICTR Statute (n. 49), Art. 1.

64. ICC Statute (n. 52), Art. 8(2)(c)–(f).

These developments are a natural extension of the Nuremberg principles. Of course, these developments were greatly aided by the ICRC Customary International Humanitarian Law Study of 2005 (I was a member of its steering committee and one of its rapporteurs), and the ICTY Appeals Chamber 1995 *Interlocutory Decision on Jurisdiction* in the *Tadić* case.

Through its ongoing work on the drafting of new commentaries on the Geneva Conventions, the ICRC continues to make major contributions to the development of international humanitarian law. Thus, going beyond *Tadić*, the ICRC Commentary on the First Geneva Convention took the position that as the wording of Common Article 3 makes it applicable to all persons not taking an active part in the hostilities, the article protects even those who are not the power of the enemy. "Examples would include members of armed forces who are tried for alleged crimes—such as war crimes or ordinary crimes in the context of the armed conflict—by their own Party and members of armed forces who are sexually or otherwise abused by their own Party."[65] Such expansion of war crimes to intra-force crimes would be of major importance if consolidated in State practice and jurisprudence.

Of course, the jurisprudence of the ICTY has already departed from the strict interpretation of Article 4 of the Fourth Geneva Convention which required that only a person held by a State of which he is not a national could be protected by that Convention. Instead, the jurisprudence treats a person who is held by an adversary in the conflict, even if of the same nationality as that of the adversary, as a person protected by the Convention.

I turn to due process issues. One of the principal criticisms of Nuremberg was, and is, that it was a victors' court trying the vanquished. That criticism resonates most strongly in the context of due process protections.

Two examples illustrate this point. First, the London Charter expressly provided that trials could be conducted *in absentia* "if [an accused] has not been found or if the Tribunal, for any reason, finds it necessary, in the interests of justice, to conduct the hearing in [the accused's] absence."[66]

65. ICRC, COMMENTARY ON THE FIRST GENEVA CONVENTION, paras. 545–7 (2016) and n. 293 referencing ICC decisions in Ntaganda (2014) and Katanga (2008).
66. London Charter (n. 21), Art. 12.

As it happened, the Allies were unable to locate and arrest Martin Bormann, head of the Nazi Party Chancellery, but the IMT tried, convicted and sentenced him to death anyway.[67] The second example is that the Charter contained no protection against double jeopardy. On the contrary, Article 11 stated that persons convicted by the IMT could be separately charged and punished by a national, military or occupation courts;[68] and some were. Indeed, the three defendants acquitted by the IMT were later prosecuted in German courts.[69]

All the same, the IMT track record on due process protections was not all bad. The Allies agreed to the Nuremberg enterprise largely because they assumed that the trials would be quick, the outcome never in doubt. Frankly, the London Charter was short on due process protections because they were not among the Allies' chief concerns. But fairness norms inevitably crept into the proceedings, in spite of the conciseness of the IMT's Charter. The Charter, for instance, made no reference to the burden of proof.[70] In fact, the Soviets took the view that the burden should rest on the defense rather than the prosecution.[71] Nonetheless, the IMT imposed a rigorous Anglo-American burden of proof on the prosecution—one so rigorous that some of the accused were acquitted.

Due process protections also triumphed over the American plan to focus on trials of Nazi organizations such as the Gestapo.[72] The intention was to convict these organizations at trial and then use the convictions in follow-on proceedings to bring thousands of individual members to justice.[73] The only question in the later trials would be whether the individual defendants knowingly participated in the criminal conspiracy. But the IMT thwarted this plan by interpreting conspiracy narrowly and reading additional elements of specific intent into the conspiracy and aggressive war charges.[74] As a result, many of the individuals who were charged with conspiracy were acquitted of that charge, as were some of the organizational defendants. And as noted earlier, the IMT held that individual members of organizations who were convicted were liable only if their participation or membership was both knowing and willing, and active.[75]

67. Jonathan A. Bush, *Lex Americana: Constitutional Due Process and the Nuremberg Defendants*, 45 St. Louis U. L.J. 515, 536 (2001).
68. London Charter (n. 21), Art. 11.
69. *See* Chaney (n. 54), at 69–70.
70. Bush (n. 67), at 531–2.
71. *Id.*
72 *Id.* at 533.
73. *Id.*
74. *Id.* at 534.
75. *Id.*

One of the enduring lessons of Nuremberg, then, is that due process protections are not an impediment to the administration of international justice; rather, they are indispensable to it. The ad hoc Tribunals at The Hague and Arusha and the permanent ICC are supported by detailed statutes and extensive rules of procedure and evidence—a far cry from the brief London Charter. The ICTY and ICTR Statutes entitle the accused to be present at his trial, and accord primacy to the Tribunals over national courts, preventing concurrent or consecutive convictions by multiple jurisdictions for the same charges. The U.N. Statutes expressly created an Appeals Chamber to which defendants may appeal not only their convictions, but also certain interlocutory issues. Moreover, in general, the modern tribunals adhere to the catalog of human rights protections embodied in the International Covenant on Civil and Political Rights, and, increasingly, those in the European Convention on Human Rights. Therefore, while the IMT was hardly a failure from the perspective of due process rights, its shortcomings inspired its heirs to do better, and the result is a rigorous commitment to due process across the international criminal courts.

Finally, I turn to the discussion of the principle of legality. I will return to it in Chapter IV. The principle of *nullum crimen sine lege*, also known as the legality principle, has been much discussed with respect to the Nuremberg tribunals. Customary law was essential to the ability of the IMT and the later American tribunals under Control Council Law No. 10 to convict Nazi war criminals: the Convention relative to the Treatment of Prisoners of War, Geneva (27 July 1929) was not ratified by the Soviet Union and thus was inapplicable on the Eastern Front, and the Fourth Hague Convention was challenged on the ground that the situation of the belligerents did not conform with its *si omnes* clause, as not all the belligerents were party to it.[76] Moreover, the applicable provisions of the Geneva and Hague Conventions that define the relevant substantive proscriptions and are considered declaratory of customary law did not expressly criminalize their violation.[77] Nuremberg therefore faced the question as to whether, for the purposes of the legality principle, offenders had been sufficiently on notice that their conduct entailed criminal liability. The IMT described the Nuremberg Charter as both the exercise of the sovereign

76. *See* Theodor Meron, Human Rights and Humanitarian Law as Customary Law 41–62 (1989).
77. *See* Theodor Meron, *International Criminalization of Internal Atrocities*, 89 Am. J. Int'l L. 554, 564 (1995).

power of the victorious countries and as "the expression of international law existing at the time of its creation."[78] In dismissing the challenge based on the principle of legality, the IMT noted that the law of war was to be found in treaties, as well as in the customs and practices of States and the general principles of justice.[79]

Addressing this question, the Military Tribunal under Control Council Law No. 10 similarly explained:

> It is not essential that a crime be specifically defined and charged in accordance with a particular ordinance, statute, or treaty if it is made a crime by international convention, recognized customs and usages of war, or the general principles of criminal justice common to civilized nations generally. If the acts charged were in fact crimes under international law when committed, they cannot be said to be *ex post facto* acts or retroactive pronouncements.[80]

Some criticized the Nuremberg tribunals for this relatively loose approach to the legality principle.[81] Nonetheless, the crimes with which the Nuremberg defendants were charged—including murder, torture and enslavement, carried out on an enormous scale—were so clearly criminal under every domestic legal system in the world that it could hardly be said that the prospect of criminal liability for them was unpredictable. Ultimately, the *nullum crimen* principle turns on fairness to the defendant.

The ICTY likewise declined to engage in an overly formalistic assessment of custom in instances where the criminality of conduct was obvious (or, to use the Nuremberg terminology, where it was clearly established under the relevant "general principles" of law). In its seminal *Interlocutory Decision on Jurisdiction* in the *Tadić* case (1995), the ICTY Appeals Chamber stated that to be subject to prosecution by the Tribunal as a violation of laws and customs of war, an offense must violate either customary law or a treaty that was unquestionably binding on the parties at the time of the alleged offense.[82] The Nuremberg trials, of course, serve as a precedent for the principle of legality to be satisfied by reference to treaties that were in force at the time of the offense. However, in the case of the ICTY, such reliance

78. 1 IMT TRIAL (n. 31), at 218. 79. *Id.* at 221.

80. *United States v. List*, in 11 TRIALS OF WAR CRIMINALS BEFORE THE NUERNBERG MILITARY TRIBUNALS UNDER CONTROL COUNCIL LAW NO. 10, at 759, 1239 (1950).

81. Hans-Heinrich Jescheck, *The General Principles of International Criminal Law Set out in Nuremberg, as Mirrored in the ICC Statute*, 2 J. INT'L CRIM. JUSTICE 38, 40–2 (2004).

82. *Prosecutor v. Tadić* (n. 60), paras. 94, 143.

on treaties must be reconciled with the statement in the U.N. Secretary-General's 1993 report to the Security Council that the Tribunal should apply rules of international humanitarian law that beyond any doubt form part of customary law. The *Tadić* Bench found that the purpose of this statement was merely to avoid a conflict with the *nullum crimen* principle when a party to the conflict was not a party to a treaty; the statement therefore does not exclude reliance on treaties in the absence of a potential conflict.[83] If the principle of legality can thus be satisfied by grounding a prosecution in a treaty binding the parties, why did the ICTY not make treaty law the principal foundation of its approach to *ratione materiae* jurisdiction, preferring instead to rely on customary principles (especially since treaties have the added advantage of satisfying the principle of specificity)?[84] One obvious reason was to adhere as closely as possible to the language of the Secretary-General's report. Another may have been to avoid doubts as to succession to treaties, their continuing binding character and reservations and the scope and validity of ad hoc agreements between the belligerents. Reliance on customary law provides additional comfort because of its generality. In addition, where the ICTY showed some readiness to apply treaties, they were, wholly or largely, declaratory of customary law—for example, the Geneva Conventions and Additional Protocol I.[85] This factor only underscores the point that the ICTY found customary law to be a more solid basis for its jurisdiction.

The legality principle likewise governed the other modern international criminal tribunals, the ICTR, the Special Court for Sierra Leone and the International Residual Mechanism for Criminal Tribunals, which is the successor to the ICTY and the ICTR. Since the conflict in Rwanda was non-international in character, and since (as the Secretary-General noted when the ICTR Statute was adopted) Rwanda had been party to the relevant international humanitarian law treaties, which constituted part of its domestic law, the ICTR did not generally need to consider whether a

83. *Id.* at para. 143; *See* Report of the Secretary-General pursuant to Paragraph 2 of Security Council Resolution 808 (1993), U.N. Doc. S/25704, para. 34 (1993).
84. Hans-Heinrich Jescheck (n. 81), at 41.
85. *Cf. Prosecutor v. Galić*, Judgement, ICTY Appeals Chamber, at para. 85, Case no. IT-98-29-A (30 Nov. 2006) (explaining that "while binding conventional law that prohibits conduct and provides for individual criminal responsibility could provide the basis for the International Tribunal's jurisdiction, in practice the International Tribunal always ascertains that the treaty provision in question is also declaratory of custom").

violation of its Statute was also a violation of customary law at the time of the offense; it sufficed that the treaties were violated.[86]

As far as possible, the Rome Conference on the establishment of the ICC sought to formulate the content of customary international law in the language of the Statute. However, for the ICC, its Statute is the primary norm, while customary law is a secondary norm. Subjects on which it diverges from customary law may pose particular difficulties when nationals of non-State parties to the ICC Statute are prosecuted.

Justifying International Criminal Tribunals

The most obvious justification for international criminal tribunals is simply that they provide a forum for dealing with high-level international war criminals. Without international criminal courts, what would we do with alleged war criminals captured at the end of a period of war or turmoil? Leaving them to go free is untenable, as is summary execution or perpetual detainment without trial. That leaves some form of legal process. But while trials in the accuseds' former countries—or in the countries in which they allegedly committed the crimes—may in some instances prove successful, this will not always be the case. Sometimes, as in the post-World War I trials in Leipzig, the former country will prove unjustly lenient. At other times, the new government of the former country may harbor too much vengeance toward its former leaders, even toward the worst of the worst.[87]

International criminal courts may also play some role in deterring international crimes. As Jackson observed in his opening remarks before the IMT, "I am too well aware of the weaknesses of juridical action alone to contend that in itself your decision under this Charter can prevent future wars.... But the ultimate step in avoiding periodic wars, which are inevitable in a system of international lawlessness, is to make statesmen responsible to law."[88] If there is a deterrent effect, though, it is hard to measure, and

86. Report of the Secretary-General Pursuant to Paragraph 5 of Security Council Resolution 955 (1994), U.N. Doc. S/1995/134, paras. 11–12.

87. This may have proved the case with regard to Saddam Hussein, where questions have been raised as to both the manner in which his execution was carried out and the decision to execute him before the conclusion of his trial for abuses of the Kurds (though after his conviction for the murder of 148 Shiites). *See*, e.g., Hendrik Hertzberg, *Desolation Rows*, THE NEW YORKER, 15 Jan. 2006, pp. 21–3.

88. 2 IMT TRIAL (n. 31), at 153–4.

there has sadly been no shortage of international crimes in the years since Nuremberg. This, however, may change if more atrocities are adjudicated in international tribunals and national courts, and if the ICC proves to be a vibrant, robust and effective institution.

International criminal courts may also play some role in assisting the postwar recovery of the nations at issue. Courts provide time for passions to cool and constrain tendencies to resort to a bloodbath against former oppressors by the liberated peoples.[89] By institutionalizing the process of judgement and punishment, international criminal courts may offer some hope of closure to the crimes they adjudicate.

89. Silber & Miller (n. 24), at 914.

PART II

Principles, Goals, Processes

IV

The Rule of Law, the Principle of Legality and Due Process

The creation of the International Criminal Tribunal for the former Yugoslavia in the early 1990s marked the dawn of a new era in international law and opened the way for the founding of a host of international and hybrid criminal tribunals, including the world's first permanent International Criminal Court.

The advent of this new universe of international criminal justice reflects not simply the evolution of international law but a sea-change in attitude. If, for millennia, wartime atrocities were seen as an inevitable by-product of conflict, or at most a moral wrong, and impunity for such brutal acts was allowed to prevail, today the commission of atrocities is no longer met with indifference or resignation—it is met with indignation and calls for accountability and for justice. All of this points to a growing respect for the power of courts and for the importance of enforcing the law: in essence, a growing respect for the rule of law.

International criminal tribunals such as the ICTY and its sister tribunal, the ICTR and their successor, the International Residual Mechanism for Criminal Tribunals (IRMCT), have done a great deal to help to enhance respect for the rule of law. Over nearly three decades, international criminal tribunals have not only demonstrated that just and fair trials of some of the worst crimes imaginable are possible, they have also striven to serve as an embodiment of rule of law ideals—as highly visible examples of rule of law principles put into practice.

The Rule of Law

According to former U.N. Secretary-General Kofi Annan, who proclaimed the concept to be at "the very heart" of the U.N.'s mission, the

Standing Up For Justice. Theodor Meron, Oxford University Press (2021). © Theodor Meron.
DOI: 10.1093/oso/9780198863434.003.0004

rule of law "refers to a principle of governance in which all persons, institutions and entities, public and private, including the State itself, are accountable to laws that are publicly promulgated, equally enforced and independently adjudicated, and which are consistent with international human rights norms and standards."[1] He went on to explain that the rule of law "requires … measures to ensure adherence to the principles of supremacy of law, equality before the law, accountability to the law, fairness in the application of the law, separation of powers, participation in decision-making, legal certainty, avoidance of arbitrariness and procedural and legal transparency."[2]

This is, of course, just one formulation of the rule of law; the academic literature is rife with many more.

It is also worth noting that questions abound in the academic literature as to whether, and how, the concept of the rule of law—traditionally deployed in reference to systems within a nation-State—may be transposed to the international sphere, where many of the features deemed necessary to the operation of the rule of law at a national level—such as a centralized legislative power and a consistent mechanism to ensure equal enforcement of the laws—are lacking.

This is a rich area for debate. Indeed, the very first substantive *Interlocutory Appeal on Jurisdiction* at the ICTY (*Tadić* 1995) raised a challenge as to the application of basic rule of law concepts at the international level and, in particular, the satisfaction of such principles in the context of the establishment of the ICTY. In its 1995 ruling, the ICTY's Appeals Chamber rejected an argument that international legal standards designed to apply in the national context necessarily apply at the international level as well. At the same time, however, the Chamber affirmed that an international criminal court may not be set up at the "mere whim of a group of governments" but instead must be "rooted in the rule of law and offer all guarantees embodied in the relevant international instruments."[3] In other words, such a court "must provide all the guarantees of fairness, justice

1. Report of the Secretary-General on the Rule of Law and Transitional Justice in Conflict and Post-Conflict Societies, U.N. Doc. S/2004/616, at para. 6.
2. *Id.* at para. 6.
3. *Prosecutor v. Dusko Tadić*, Decision on the Defence Motion for Interlocutory Appeal on Jurisdiction, ICTY Appeals Chamber, at para. 42, Case no. IT-94-1-AR72 (2 Oct. 1995).

and even-handedness, in full conformity with internationally recognized human rights instruments."[4]

These are the guiding principles that have been at the heart of the Tribunals' work over the course of the two and a half decades since this ruling in the *Tadić* case, and I would suggest that it is through adherence to these principles that the ICTY—as well as its fellow international criminal tribunals—have made considerable contributions to the strengthening of the rule of law on the global plane. While I recognize that domestic aspects of the rule of law cannot be transferred lock, stock and barrel to the international plane and international courts, I see no difficulty in the applicability to international courts of such core principles as judicial independence and judicial impartiality, protection of Judges from pressure, secure terms of service and conditions of service, fairness, due process, transparency, human rights and conformity of legal procedures with human rights, public promulgation of the law, accessibility and predictability of the law and non-retroactivity of criminal norms. Indeed, the Declaration of the High-level Meeting of the U.N. General Assembly of 30 November 2012, recognized that the rule of law applies to the U.N., especially as regards predictability and legitimacy. In this chapter, I discuss only some rule of law, legality and due process issues. Other components of the rule of law will be addressed in other chapters.

Reifying Rule of Law Principles

It is, perhaps, hardly a surprise that international criminal tribunals would seek to adhere to the same principles of fairness and due process that underlie national conceptions of the rule of law. After all, international criminal tribunals are, in many ways, like criminal courts in national jurisdictions around the world. They weigh evidence, hear the parties and witnesses and provide reasoned opinions for their rulings grounded in the law.

At the same time, international criminal tribunals—and the cases they hear—are extraordinary. They are stand-alone courts, courts that operate without the legal and administrative supportive framework found in national systems and provided by various ministries and particularly ministries of

4. *Id.* at para. 45.

justice, and the development of processes and rules to manage their courtroom activities has required the harmonization of diverse legal traditions and outlooks. The cases these courts hear are of tremendous breadth, often involving alleged crimes on a massive scale committed over long periods across many localities, and these cases can have complex political dimensions, not least because the individuals charged are frequently among a country's top leaders. The magnitude of evidence at stake is enormous, and this evidence must be obtained without any independent police force—and with the cooperation of sovereign States, which is not always available. The relevant substantive law is, in many cases, being applied for the first time in a criminal proceeding. I do not believe I go too far when I suggest that the creation of international criminal tribunals has truly represented a bold experiment, and one that many observers in the early 1990s were not sure would succeed.

Yet, it is perhaps precisely because of the unique (and uniquely challenging) nature of the mandates and work of international criminal tribunals—and because of the impact of the human rights revolution that helped to make these courts possible—that the modern generation of international criminal tribunals has gone to such great lengths to abide by rule of law principles.

Nowhere is this more true than for the ICTY and the ICTR, which were the first two international criminal tribunals of the modern era.

These tribunals, for instance, have not only fleshed out norms governing the prohibitions of genocide, crimes against humanity and war crimes, they have developed rules of procedure and evidence and other regulatory policies to guide their work; they have also produced an extraordinary corpus of rulings on procedural and evidentiary issues—a body of jurisprudence that, by its very existence and repeated application, promotes legal certainty, procedural transparency and the avoidance of arbitrariness. Importantly, in these rulings, the ICTY and ICTR have made frequent recourse and reference to the decisions of human rights courts and other human rights precedents, going to great lengths to ensure consistency with international human rights norms and standards—and, by so doing, helping to strengthen the coherence and consistency of the international legal order.

The ICTY and ICTR routinely adhered to a presumption that proceedings and rulings should be public. They articulated and observed robust theories of legal precedent so as to avoid arbitrariness and increase legal certainty and equality of enforcement.

Principle of Legality

In their application of the substantive law governing their proceedings, the ICTY and ICTR strictly adhered to the principle of *nullum crimen sine lege*, or the legality principle, meaning that a defendant may only be convicted on the basis of legal rules clearly established at the time of the offence.

The legality principle, as enshrined in the principal conventions on human rights, is a basic component of the rule of law and serves as a fundamental check on the ability of courts to push the progressive development of the law, no matter how much the Judges of that court might believe that certain conduct deserves punishment. Only such an approach respects an accused's procedural right to fair notice of the law. By determining whether the relevant substantive legal norm was sufficiently firmly established as custom at the time of the offence (such that the offender could have identified the rule he or she was expected to obey), the Tribunals have been able to ensure that the principle of legality is respected even where the alleged crimes occurred before the Tribunals' Statutes entered into force.

Because of the sometimes indeterminate character of customary international law, ascertaining the existence of a customary international legal norm is not a straightforward task and has frequently entailed close analysis of treaties, State practice and other sources. But this work has been tremendously important. It was by reference to customary law that the ICTY and ICTR articulated the elements of individual crimes and explained the nuances of modes of individual responsibility. It was on the basis of customary law that the ICTY did away, to a large extent, with the distinction in some treaty provisions between international and non-international armed conflicts, making clear that many protections that originally only applied in international armed conflicts apply also in non-international armed conflicts. And it was thanks in great part to this reliance on customary law that the ICTY and ICTR developed a remarkable body of jurisprudence, setting important legal precedents for international and national courts and for militaries and governments around the world—and thereby contributing in a profound way to a process of normative accretion that has strengthened international law and the humanitarian protections provided thereby as well as bolstering adherence to the law at the local level. It is thanks to customary law that the Tribunals have applied some norms initially governing State responsibility as norms governing individual criminal responsibility.

I am not blind, of course, to the ways in which international criminal tribunals have sometimes fallen short of some of the ideals and principles inherent in the rule of law. We all know, for instance, that proceedings at international criminal tribunals often run far longer than many observers, and even many of us within the Tribunals, may like, raising financial concerns and, more importantly, concerns about a defendant's right to a speedy trial. There is more that can and should be done to address internal deficiencies that stand in the way of effective and efficient proceedings.

International criminal tribunals—especially the ICTY—have developed a rich jurisprudence elucidating customary principles of humanitarian law. The approach taken by these tribunals should be and usually is rigorous. Criminal tribunals are bound to respect the principle of *nullum crimen sine lege*: a defendant may only be convicted on the basis of legal rules that were clearly established at the time of the offense. If a criminal conviction for violating uncodified customary law is to be reconciled with this principle—and I argue that it can be—it must be through the use of clear and well-established methods for identifying customary law. The legality principle is, thus, a restraint on the tribunals' ability to be "progressive" in their contributions to the development of customary humanitarian law. The need for a rigorous approach suggests caution toward an overly broad or rapid expansion of customary law offenses, and, thus, a guarantee of due process and the human rights of the accused.

I start from addressing an important threshold question: Why does customary international humanitarian law matter at all, when we have treaties, conventions and other written rules aimed at protecting civilians and others during times of armed conflict?

I will offer three responses to this question.

First, customary international law is binding on all States. This is important because some States may not have ratified certain treaties that offer key protections during armed conflicts or may have lodged reservations or issued declarations of interpretation in relation to these treaties, arguably limiting the treaties' force. As a result, the application of those treaties may be in doubt. Reliance on customary international law rather than on specific conventions also avoids questions concerning the succession to treaties and the validity of ad hoc agreements between belligerents. Simply put, because the rules of customary law are universally binding, they help to address ambiguities in the coverage offered by treaties and other agreements (with the possible exception of those rare instances in which a State that has lodged a reservation to a treaty continues to object to the treaty even after that treaty crystallizes into customary international law).

The second reason that customary international law matters is that it fills substantive gaps left by treaty law, thus strengthening the protections offered. We need only to consider the extraordinary growth of non-international armed conflicts in recent decades—and the paucity of provisions in international conventions explicitly providing protections during such conflicts—to realize the important role that customary international humanitarian law plays in enhancing legal protection in such conflicts.

Finally—and just as importantly—even where there are treaties in force, customary international law plays a critical interpretive role by elucidating the scope and extent of the protections and prohibitions set out in conventional law, thus helping to reinforce the mandatory, binding nature of the obligations at stake.

This is particularly true when it comes to international humanitarian law, since much of the applicable treaty law explicitly addresses State, rather than individual, responsibilities and, with a few exceptions, prohibits but does not explicitly criminalize the behavior in question. However, the existence of widespread and generally consistent State practice and *opinio juris*—together, the essential ingredients of customary international law—can demonstrate the intention of States to treat the violations of certain international rules as criminal offenses, thus providing a basis for concluding that violations may trigger individual criminal responsibility. Indeed, it is as a result of their reliance on customary international law in judgement after judgement that the ICTY and ICTR have been at the forefront of articulating and clarifying the elements of crimes and the various modes of individual criminal responsibility.

Importantly, in doing so, they have strengthened the protections afforded by international humanitarian law by helping to make the parameters of responsibility and the consequences of noncompliance clearer.

Given these important roles played by customary international law, it is astonishing to pause and remember that, only as recently as in the early 1990s, I and many others would have described customary international law primarily as a matter of scholarly inquiry. Today, however, customary law is enjoying a remarkable revival, effectively moving from the domain of academia to the courtroom—and beyond.

The roots of this revival can be traced back to the trials conducted at Nuremberg in the wake of World War II and the debate over which crimes the Nuremberg Tribunal had legal authority to prosecute.

Criminal courts are bound to respect the principle of *nullum crimen nulla poena sine lege*—or the legality principle—which requires that defendants only be convicted on the basis of legal rules that were clearly established at the time the offense occurred.

The London Charter, which established the IMT at Nuremberg, gave that Tribunal explicit jurisdiction over "crimes against peace," "war crimes" and "crimes against humanity." Yet the Charter was issued after the crimes at issue were alleged to have occurred, which led some to suggest that the Charter amounted to an unlawful, *ex post facto* law. This made reliance on the Charter alone a problematic proposition.

As discussed in Chapter III, the Nuremberg Tribunal could not rely heavily on treaties in construing the ambits of the crimes within its jurisdiction. The Convention relative to the Treatment of Prisoners of War, Geneva (27 July 1929) ("Geneva POW Convention") was not applicable on the Eastern Front, as it had not been ratified by the Soviet Union, and the application of the Fourth Hague Convention was challenged because the situation of the belligerents did not conform with its *si omnes* clause, since not all of the belligerents were parties. Moreover, while the relevant provisions of both the Geneva and Hague Conventions defined substantive proscriptions, the Conventions did not explicitly criminalize their violation.

In short, a question arose at Nuremberg as to whether the legality principle had been satisfied—in other words, whether the accused had been sufficiently on notice at the time of the alleged offense that their conduct entailed criminal liability.

In answering this question, the Nuremberg Tribunal reasoned that the law of war was to be found not only in treaties, but also in customary international law and in the general principles of justice. In other words, insofar as the acts in the indictment were in fact crimes under customary international law when committed, charging them could not be said to violate *ex post facto* proscriptions.

This conclusion received some criticism. Nonetheless, by becoming the first international court to look to the customary law underpinnings of international crimes, the Nuremberg Tribunal opened the way for all that followed.

Not surprisingly, when the ICTY was established nearly 50 years after the Nuremberg Tribunal had concluded its work, this new, ad hoc international criminal tribunal faced many of the same challenges as its predecessor.

Although the Tribunal's jurisdiction is defined by a specific statute adopted by the Security Council, it has been recognized from the beginning of its operation that its authority is circumscribed by customary law. The Statute was not yet in effect when some of the relevant crimes were committed, and such acts can only be punished as international crimes if they are so categorized at the time they are committed. Yet there was a lack of certainty whether all the relevant nations were party to treaties that definitively outlined the relevant criminal prohibitions. Accordingly, in his report accompanying the adoption of the Statute, the Secretary-General noted that "the application of the principle of *nullum crimen sine lege* requires that the international tribunal apply rules of international humanitarian law which are beyond any doubt part of customary law so that the problem of adherence of some but not all States to specific conventions does not arise."[5]

It might fairly be asked whether a conviction for violating uncodified customary law can ever meet the *nullem crimen* standard. After all, codification of criminal prohibitions is the modern norm in domestic systems, even in common law countries—in the United States, for example, there are no common law crimes, and in the United Kingdom there are few. Nonetheless, in my view the legality principle does not bar such a conviction. It bears noting that application of the principle always involves some element of legal fiction. It is certainly not much less realistic to expect a would-be offender to be aware of, and conform his or her behavior to, well-established principles of the law of nations than to expect them to learn the details of a long, arcane and often-changing national criminal code. Thus, in my view, customary law can provide a safe basis for a conviction, but only if genuine care is taken in determining that the legal principle was sufficiently firmly established as custom at the time of the offense so that the offender could have identified the rule he or she was expected to obey.

This, in a nutshell, was the approach of the ICTY. In effect, the Tribunal's chambers superimposed on the Statute the test of whether each of the crimes within the Tribunal's jurisdiction reflected customary law. This

5. Report of the Secretary-General Pursuant to Paragraph 2 of Security Council Resolution 808 (1993), at para. 34, U.N. Doc. S/25704 (3 May 1993). *See generally*, Theodor Meron, HUMAN RIGHTS AND HUMANITARIAN NORMS AS CUSTOMARY LAW (1989).

requirement was applied not only to crimes specifically listed as grave breaches of the Geneva Conventions as well as genocide and crimes against humanity, but also to violations of the laws and customs of war, which are mentioned non-exhaustively in Article 3 of the Statute. Specifically, and with rigor that increased over the years, the chambers engaged in a serious search for State practice and *opinio juris*. Inherent in the requirement that criminal prohibitions be clearly established is the notion that a tribunal's methodology in identifying those prohibitions must be predictable, and it must not be vague. Predictability is of course also important in non-criminal areas of the law,[6] but in criminal courts, wherein deprivation of liberty is at stake, there is less freedom than there may be in other institutions to push the legal envelope when it comes to the recognition of customary norms.

It bears noting at the outset that laborious inquiry into the question whether a particular legal principle enjoyed the status of customary international law at a particular time is not *always* required by the *nullum crimen* principle with respect to *every* crime with which an accused is charged in an international criminal tribunal. Rather, it is only required where the unlawfulness of the conduct in question at the time would not have been clear, absent an applicable customary international law rule. The ICTY Appeals Chamber correctly recognized that the point of the legality principle was to protect persons from later prosecution for acts that they reasonably believed to be *lawful*—a belief that cannot be reasonable if the acts in question are obviously barred by domestic law. In the *Čelebići* case, the Appeals Chamber thus affirmed the Trial Chamber's holding that:

> It is undeniable that acts such as murder, torture, rape, and inhuman treatment are criminal according to "general principles of law" recognised by all legal systems… . It strains credibility to contend that the accused would not recognise the criminal nature of the acts alleged in the Indictment. The fact that they could not foresee the creation of an International Tribunal which would be the forum for prosecution is of no consequence.[7]

6. *See Serbia and Montenegro v. Italy* (*Case Concerning Legality of Use of Force*), Joint Declaration of Vice-President Ranjeva, Judges Guillaume, Higgins, Kooijmans, Al-Khasawneh, Buergenthal and El-Araby, ICJ, 15 Dec. 2004, at para. 3 (stating that in discerning principles of law, the ICJ "must ensure consistency with its own past case law in order to provide predictability" and that "[c]onsistency is the essence of judicial reasoning").
7. *Prosecutor v. Delalić et. al.*, Judgement, ICTY Appeals Chamber, at para. 179, Case no. IT-96-21-A (20 Feb. 2001).

Likewise, the Appeals Chamber's decision in the *Kordić and Čerkez* case held that where conduct is criminalized by an applicable treaty to which all the relevant States were clearly party, this could itself satisfy the legality principle, making recourse to customary law unnecessary.[8] The Trial Chamber's Judgement in the *Galić* case raises a related issue. The indictment against General Stanislav Galić (commander of troops besieging Sarajevo) charged him with conduct violating the laws or customs of war, relying not on customary law but on treaty law, namely Additional Protocol I to the Geneva Conventions Relating to the Protection of Victims of War.[9] Specifically, the charge was that Galić acted with the purpose of spreading terror among the civilian population, a crime under Article 51(2) of Additional Protocol I to the Geneva Conventions. While prior Trial Chamber decisions referred to customary international law to determine whether the crimes charged complied with the *nullum crimen* principle, the *Galić* Trial Judgement refrained from deciding whether the pertinent provision of Protocol I was declaratory of customary law and relied exclusively on treaty law. On appeal, however, the ICTY Appeals Chamber, in its Judgement of 30 November 2006, followed the Tribunal's self-imposed norms and grounded its reasoning in customary humanitarian law.[10]

Many of the Tribunal's cases, however, involved conduct of less obvious criminality—to take one example, omissions that support liability under a command responsibility theory—and, notwithstanding the approach taken in the *Kordić and Čerkez* case, the previously mentioned report of the Secretary-General makes clear that it will not always be possible to look to treaties to resolve the matter. In such cases, the relevant customary law must be ascertained, and fair notice to the would-be offender, sufficient to satisfy the *nullum crimen* principle, might be sought through either of two related approaches. The first might be characterized as "methodological conservatism"—that is, the use of only firmly established, traditional methods for identifying the applicable customary norms. Because the requirement that custom be established through widespread (but not perfectly consistent)

8. *Prosecutor v. Kordić and Čerkez*, Judgement, ICTY Appeals Chamber, at paras. 44–6, Case no. IT-95-14/2-A (17 Dec. 2004).
9. *Prosecutor v. Galić*, Indictment, at para. 5, Case no. IT-98-29-I (26 Mar. 1999).
10. *Prosecutor v. Galić*, Judgement, ICTY Appeals Chamber, at paras. 80–5, Case no. IT-98-29-A (30 Nov. 2006).

State practice supported by *opinio juris* has been long established in international law, a methodologically traditional approach would presumably require showing that those criteria were satisfied at the time of the offense in order to support any particular rule's status as customary law. Alternatively, if it could be established that any other method for identifying custom had become so widely accepted at the time of the offense that its use by a later tribunal was foreseeable, then such a method might be used. In either event, the question is whether the offender could, at the time of the offense, reasonably be expected to realize that his conduct conflicted with customary international law.

A second approach might be referred to as "outcome conservatism," pursuant to which doubts regarding the customary status of any particular legal principle are resolved in favor of the defendant (*in dubio pro reo*). This is simply another way of stating the requirement that criminal prohibitions be *clear* in their scope and application. Although the traditional showing of State practice and *opinio juris* is likely to be the easiest way to show that a particular prohibition was clearly established, it might also be possible to point to other factors. For instance, the existence and widespread recognition of legal precedent identifying a particular rule as customary, such as the holding by the International Court of Justice (ICJ) in the *Nicaragua* case concerning the customary status of Common Articles 1 and 3 of the Geneva Conventions, might be sufficient, for the purposes of the legality principle, to establish the rule with the necessary clarity, so that a putative offender could be expected to conform his conduct to it.

The ICTY blended these two approaches, and did so in a way that, I believe, respected the fundamental principle of *nullum crimen*. It emphasized the core requirements of State practice and *opinio juris*, and several times held that a particular legal rule that the prosecution sought to enforce was not sufficiently supported by State practice or *opinio juris* to qualify as customary law. Sometimes, to be sure, the Tribunal recognized a principle as customary law without articulating the specific evidence of State practice and *opinio juris* supporting that finding. But when it did so, it had in my view strong reasons for believing that the customary principle was clearly established at the time of the crime. Notably, these cases typically involved principles that were grounded in provisions of the Geneva Conventions that are nearly universally accepted as customary law, and/or "general principles" of law that have been well recognized since the time of the Nuremberg proceedings.

An example illustrating the Tribunal's approach is the interlocutory appeal in *Prosecutor v. Hadžihasanović, Alagic and Kubura*.[11] The Appeals Chamber in *Hadžihasanović* was confronted with two issues. The first was whether there was a basis in customary international law for applying the doctrine of command responsibility to a conflict that was internal, not international, in character. On that question the five-member panel unanimously agreed, concluding that customary law at all times relevant to the conflict made clear that some war crimes can be committed by a member of an organized military force in the course of an internal armed conflict, and that the doctrine of command responsibility applies to such crimes.[12] In reaching this conclusion, the Appeals Chamber specifically noted that "to hold that a principle was part of customary international law, it has to be satisfied that State practice recognized the principle on the basis of supporting *opinio juris*."[13] Citing decisions of the ICJ, including the *Nicaragua* case as well as the *Corfu Channel* case from 1949, it held that Common Article 3 of the Geneva Conventions had "long been accepted as having customary status", and held that the logic of that Article was fully applicable to internal conflicts.[14] For further elucidation of the command responsibility principle, the *Hadžihasanović* Appeals Chamber turned to Additional Protocols I and II to the Geneva Conventions, the Regulations Respecting the Laws and Customs of War annexed to the Fourth Hague Convention of 1907 and the "authoritative" ICRC Commentary on the Geneva Conventions.[15] In light of these indicia of general acceptance among States of customary law's application of the command responsibility principle to internal conflict, the Appeals Chamber found that it was not necessary to demonstrate that most States had passed domestic legislation codifying that principle.[16]

Notably, although the Appeals Chamber found that it was not necessary for it to set forth anew the evidence supporting findings of State practice and *opinio juris* with regard to that point of law, citing the U.S. Supreme Court

11. *Prosecutor v. Hadžihasanović, Alagic and Kubura*, Decision on Interlocutory Appeal Challenging Jurisdiction in Relation to Command Responsibility, ICTY Appeals Chamber, Case no. IT-01-47-AR72 (16 July 2003).

12. *Id.* at para. 31.

13. *Id.* at para. 12.

14. *Id.* at para. 13. For subsequent developments, *see also* ICRC, COMMENTARY ON THE FIRST GENEVA CONVENTION, paras. 505, 520, n. 255 (2016).

15. *Id.* at paras. 14–15.

16. *Id.* at para. 17.

case of *Yamashita v. Styer*,[17] it specifically affirmed the findings of the Trial Chamber to that effect.[18] The Trial Chamber's findings had encompassed, for instance, the history of the confirmation of the Nuremberg principles by the U.N. General Assembly, the inclusion of command responsibility principles in the military manuals of, for instance, the former Yugoslavia, the United States, the United Kingdom and Germany; and the history surrounding the adoption of the Geneva Conventions' Additional Protocols in the 1970s, including the statements of several national delegates.[19] The Appeals Chamber also followed its own case law that had set forth evidence supporting the customary status of the command responsibility doctrine. Particularly when that evidence is taken together with the codification of the command responsibility principle and with the Appeals Chamber's reasoning concerning that principle's necessary implications, the Appeals Chamber's approach seems clearly consistent with its duty to uphold the legality principle.

The second issue in *Hadžihasanović* proved more contentious. In question was whether a superior could be held responsible for acts that were committed before he became the superior of the persons who committed the offenses. The indictment had alleged that a co-defendant, Amir Kubura, assumed his position as acting commander of a brigade of the Bosnian Army on 1 April 2003.[20] It charged Kubura with criminal responsibility for crimes that were, for the most part, committed by the troops of that brigade more than two months before he took command, including killings and wanton destruction and plunder of property in Dusina.[21]

The Appeals Chamber began its analysis by examining customary law as it was in force at the time the crimes were committed. The Chamber could find no State practice and no *opinio juris* to sustain the proposition that a commander could be held responsible for crimes committed by a subordinate prior to the commander's assumption of command over the subordinate.[22] In fact, the Chamber found evidence militating *against*

17. 327 U.S. 1, 14–15 (1946).
18. *Prosecutor v. Hadžihasanović, Alagic and Kubura* (n. 11), at para. 27.
19. *See Prosecutor v. Hadžihasanović, Alagic and Kubura*, Decision on Joint Challenge to Jurisdiction, ICTY Trial Chamber, at paras. 67–93, Case no. IT-01-47-PT (12 Nov. 2002).
20. *Prosecutor v. Hadžihasanović and Kubura*, Third Amended Indictment, ICTY Trial Chamber, at para. 6, Case no. IT-01-47-PT (26 Sept. 2003).
21. *Id.* at paras. 39, 40, 44, 45.
22. *Prosecutor v. Hadžihasanović and Kubura* (n. 11), at para. 45.

the existence of such a rule in Article 28 of the Rome Statute of the International Criminal Court, Article 86(2) of Additional Protocol I to the Geneva Conventions and in the *Kuntze* case before the Nuremberg Military Tribunals.[23] The Appeals Chamber observed that it was required to rely not merely on a construction of the Statute to establish the applicable law on criminal responsibility, but to ascertain the state of customary law in force at the time the crimes were committed.[24] Moreover, an expansive reading of criminal texts violates the principle of legality, which the Appeals Chamber found was widely recognized as a peremptory norm of international law, and which in any event was essential to the protection of the human rights of the accused.[25] In case of doubt, the Appeals Chamber thus found that criminal responsibility could not be found to exist.

Hadžihasanović is by no means the only case in which the ICTY grappled with the application of the legality principle. In *Prosecutor v. Aleksovski*, for example, the accused argued that a previous decision could not be used as a statement of the governing customary law, since that decision was made after the alleged commission of the crimes, and thus could not meet the requirements of the principle of legality.[26] In its Judgement of 24 March 2000, the ICTY Appeals Chamber distinguished the interpretation and clarification of customary law, which is permissible, from the creation of new law, which would violate the *ex post facto* prohibition.[27] As the Appeals Chamber explained, the *nullum crimen* principle "does not prevent a court, either at the national or international level, from determining an issue through a process of interpretation and clarification as to the elements of a particular crime; nor does it prevent a court from relying on previous decisions which reflect an interpretation as to the meaning to be ascribed to particular ingredients of a crime."[28]

In the *Čelebići* case, the Appeals Chamber applied the principles previously developed in *Tadić* and *Aleksovski*,[29] affirming the applicability of command responsibility theories to internal conflicts, but refusing to hold that a defendant could be liable under such a theory if he had no reason

23. *Id.* at paras. 46–8, 50. 24. *Id.* at para. 51. 25. *Id.* at para. 55.
26. *Prosecutor v. Aleksovski*, Judgement, ICTY Appeals Chamber, at para. 123, Case no. IT-95-14/1-A (24 Mar. 2000).
27. *Id.* at para. 126. 28. *Id.* at para. 127.
29. *Prosecutor v. Delalić et al.* (n. 7), at paras. 158–73.

to know of the criminal conduct in question; as to the latter point, the Appeals Chamber cited examples of contrary State practice and *opinio juris* that could not be reconciled with the rule the prosecution sought.[30] The Trial Chamber in the *Vasiljević* case followed suit.[31] Indeed, venturing further, the *Vasiljević* Trial Chamber confirmed that the prohibition on the creation of new offences extended even to offences stated in the Statute, if they were not recognized by customary law at the time the alleged crime was committed or if they were not defined with sufficient clarity so as to be foreseeable.[32]

The Trial Chamber therefore held in *Vasiljević* that although Common Article 3 of the Geneva Conventions mentions the term "violence to life and person" as a prohibited act, and although the Appeals Chamber had earlier held that customary international law imposed criminal liability for all serious violations of Common Article 3, the Trial Chamber could not convict the accused of "violence to life and person" because that crime was not recognized or defined with sufficient clarity by customary international law.[33] The Trial Chamber therefore acquitted the accused of that charge.[34] I discuss the conformity of Common Article 3 with the principle of legality further in Chapter V. Similarly, in the Interlocutory Appeal in the case of *Milan Milutinović and others*, the Appeals Chamber clarified that the Tribunal's *ratione materiae* jurisdiction was determined both by the Statute and by customary international law.[35]

Other cases, beyond those turning specifically on the *nullum crimen* principle, further illustrate the comparatively rigorous approach the Tribunal took to the ascertainment of customary law. For instance, in one of its earliest decisions, concerning an interlocutory appeal in the *Tadić* case, the Appeals Chamber offered an important methodological observation: because accurate information concerning the conduct of troops in the field of battle is largely inaccessible, conclusions about State practice in the area of humanitarian law must necessarily be based on such sources as "official pronouncements of States, military manuals

30. *Id.* at paras. 228–41.
31. *Prosecutor v. Vasiljević*, Judgement, ICTY Trial Chamber, at paras. 196, 201, Case no. IT-98-32-T (29 Nov. 2002).
32. *Id.* at para. 201.
33. *Id.* at para. 203.
34. *Id.* at para. 204.
35. *See, e.g.*, *Prosecutor v. Milutinović*, Reasons for Decision Dismissing Interlocutory Appeal Concerning Jurisdiction over the Territory of Kosovo, ICTY Appeals Chamber, Case no. IT-99-37-AR-72.2 (8 June 2004).

and judicial decisions."[36] It then reviewed evidence of State practice and *opinio juris* concerning the application of customary humanitarian law to internal conflicts. This sweeping review included, but was not limited to, statements of the Spanish and British governments with regard to the status of combatants in the Spanish Civil War, written instructions given by Mao Tse Tung to the Chinese "people's liberation army," a 1964 statement by the Prime Minister of the Democratic Republic of the Congo with regard to its civil war, the agreement of parties to the 1967 conflict in Yemen, Nigerian, German, New Zealand and U.S. military manuals and prosecutions, a statement of the rebel army in El Salvador, ICRC principles concerning internal conflicts and the record of State compliance with them, statements on behalf of the then 12 members of the European Union with regard to the Liberian conflict and Iraqi human rights abuses, U.S. diplomatic and Defense Department statements, British government publications, a consensus view expressed by various representatives of the international community on the illegality of the domestic use of chemical weapons, the criminal codes of the former Yugoslavia and Belgium and the adoption of various General Assembly and Security Council resolutions.[37] Holding that these various sources provided strong evidence of international custom, the Appeals Chamber found it appropriate to exercise jurisdiction over crimes committed in internal conflicts.[38]

More broadly, the Tribunal's case law discerned and discussed a number of substantive principles of customary law on the basis of careful analysis consistent with the legality principle. For instance, in the context of crimes against humanity, the Tribunal's jurisprudence broached the nexus of such crimes to armed conflict;[39] the distinction between the concepts of "attack" and "armed conflict";[40] the requirement of discriminatory

36. *Prosecutor v. Tadić*, Decision on the Defence Motion for Interlocutory Appeal on Jurisdiction, ICTY Appeals Chamber, at para. 99, Case no. IT-94-1-AR72 (2 Oct. 1995).

37. *Id.* at paras. 96–125. 38. *Id.* at para. 137.

39. *See Prosecutor v. Šešelj*, Decision on the Interlocutory Appeal Concerning Jurisdiction, ICTY Appeals Chamber, at para. 5, Case no. IT-03-67-AR72.1 (31 Aug. 2004) (noting, citing previous decisions, that customary international law does not require that crimes against humanity be committed in an armed conflict, but that this requirement was instead imposed by the ICTY Statute).

40. *See Prosecutor v. Kunarac*, Judgement, ICTY Appeals Chamber, at para. 86, Case no. IT-96-23&23/1-A (12 June 2002) (finding that "under customary international law, the attack could precede, outlast, or continue during the armed conflict, but it need not be part of it").

intent;[41] the elements of crimes against humanity, such as the existence of a plan or policy;[42] the relevance of personal motives;[43] and the *actus reus* of the crime of persecution.[44] Additionally, the Tribunal clarified the customary law of genocide and the question of genocidal intent,[45] in particular in relation to such forms of criminal responsibility as aiding and abetting and complicity.[46] It elaborated on various aspects of the Hague law, including for instance the rule of distinction.[47] The Tribunal elaborated on the definition and the customary law nature of the crimes of torture and rape.[48] It clarified customary aspects of general principles of criminal law, such as the defence of duress.[49] It clarified the immunity of the ICRC from disclosure as a matter of customary law,[50] and addressed customary rules regarding

41. *See*, e.g., *Prosecutor v. Tadić*, Judgement, ICTY Appeals Chamber, at paras. 287–92, Case no. IT-94-1-A (15 July 1999) (finding that customary international law does not require that discriminatory or persecutory intent be established for all crimes against humanity); *Prosecutor v. Kupreškić*, Judgement, ICTY Trial Chamber, at para. 558, Case no. IT-95-16 (14 Jan. 2000) (following *Tadić* and holding that discriminatory intent is only required with regard to the category of "persecutions" under Art. 5(h)).
42. *See*, e.g., *Kunarac* (n. 40), at para. 98 & fn. 114 (holding, based on the consensus of relevant State practice—including judicial precedents in Canada, Australia, Israel, Kosovo and the Nuremberg Tribunal as well as reports of the Secretary-General and the International Law Commission—that crimes against humanity need not be undertaken pursuant to a policy or plan).
43. *See Prosecutor v. Tadić* (n. 41), at paras. 255–70 (holding, based principally on an evaluation of case law from various countries pertaining to the Holocaust, that under customary law, "purely personal motives do not acquire any relevance for establishing whether or not a crime against humanity has been perpetrated").
44. *Prosecutor v. Blaskić*, Judgement, ICTY Appeals Chamber, at paras. 143, 147–9, 152, 156–9, Case no. IT-95-14-A (29 July 2004) (finding, inter alia, that an inherent right to life as well as prohibitions against pillage, deportation and forcible transfer have customary international law status).
45. *Prosecutor v. Krstić*, Judgement, ICTY Appeals Chamber, at para. 25, Case no. IT-98-33-A (19 Apr. 2004) (finding that, according to customary international law, the Trial Chamber was correct to limit the definition of genocide to those acts seeking the physical or biological destruction of all or part of the group). *See also Prosecutor v. Tolimir*, ICTY Appeal Judgement, Case no. IT-05-88/2 A (8 Apr. 2015).
46. *Prosecutor v. Krstić* (n. 45), at paras. 135–44.
47. *Prosecutor v. Blaskić* (n. 44), at paras. 109–16.
48. *See Prosecutor v. Kunarac* (n. 40), at paras. 145–8 (addressing the extent to which the Torture Convention reflects customary international law).
49. *See*, e.g., *Prosecutor v. Erdemović*, Judgement, Joint Separate Opinion of Judge McDonald and Judge Vohrah, ICTY Appeals Chamber, at para. 55, Case no. IT-96-22-A (7 Oct. 1997) (finding that customary international law does not establish whether duress is a defence to a charge of killing innocent human beings).
50. *Prosecutor v. Simić, Ex Parte* Confidential Decision on the Prosecution Motion Under Rule 73 for a Ruling Concerning the Testimony of a Witness, ICTY Trial Chamber, at para. 74, Case no. IT-95-9-PT (27 July 1999) (holding that, under customary law, no question of a balance of interests arises between a confidentiality interest and a claim to non-disclosure of the information).

State sovereignty, such as the issuance of subpoenas to State officials,[51] the examination of documents raising national security concerns[52] and arrest, abduction and international transfer.[53] And in addition to command responsibility, the ICTY addressed the scope of individual liability under customary humanitarian law for participation in joint criminal enterprise[54] and for the crimes of accomplices.[55] And, in a series of seminal cases, the ICTY fleshed out the rather skeletal norms describing crimes against humanity and the crime of genocide.

In some cases, of course, the Tribunal's assessments of the evidence supporting the relevant customary international law principles were comparatively brief; in most of these, it relied on its own precedents instead of revisiting the same issues repetitively, an approach that can hardly be faulted. Still, critics may allege that the Tribunal did not uniformly hew to the strictest methodological conservatism, but sometimes relied to some extent on proxies—such as the long-standing recognition of a principle's customary status by the ICJ—in place of the comprehensive detailing of State practice. As noted earlier, I believe its approach was nonetheless generally consistent with the legality principle, for it relied appropriately on authoritative sources and rules that were foreseeable to potential offenders, and thus avoided crossing the line from recognition of existing customary law to the creation of new law. Moreover, a more relaxed approach to the identification of relevant customary norms may be justified where the norm in

51. *Prosecutor v. Blaškić*, Judgement on the Request of the Republic of Croatia for Review of the Decision of the Trial Chamber II of 18 July 1997, ICTY Appeals Chamber, at paras. 38–60, Case no. IT-95-14-108*bis* (29 Oct. 1997) (finding that, under customary law, State officials cannot suffer the consequences of wrongful acts which are not attributable to them personally but to the State on whose behalf they act, and that subpoenas therefore cannot be issued to State officials acting in their official capacity).

52. *Id.* at paras. 61–6 (concluding that the drafters of Art. 29 departed from international customary law in regard to national security concerns because to grant States a blanket ability to withhold documents for national security reasons would undermine the essential purpose of the international tribunal).

53. *Prosecutor v. Nikolić*, Decision on Interlocutory Appeal Concerning Legality of Arrest, ICTY Appeals Chamber, at paras. 20–4, Case no. IT-94-2-AR73 (5 June 2003) (examining domestic case law and concluding that in cases involving universally condemned offences such as genocide and war crimes, jurisdiction should not be set aside even if there were irregularities in the manner in which the accused was brought before the Tribunal).

54. *See generally*, Steven Powles, *Joint Criminal Enterprise: Criminal Liability by Prosecutorial Ingenuity and Judicial Creativity?*, 2 J. INT'L CRIM. JUST. 606 (2004); Allison Marston Danner & Jennifer (Jenny) S. Martinez, *Guilty Associations: Joint Criminal Enterprise, Command Responsibility, and the Development of International Criminal Law*, 93 CAL. L. REV. 77 (2005).

55. *See Prosecutor v. Tadić* (n. 43), at para. 220 (holding that the notion of common design as a form of accomplice liability is firmly established in customary international law).

question does not concern the substantive scope of the criminal prohibition, or of the defendant's liability, and thus does not directly implicate the *nullum crimen* principle.

Still, tribunals are inevitably constrained in their approaches by their resources, the evidence before them and the arguments put to them by the parties, and some will no doubt criticize the assessments of customary law present in some of the Tribunal's cases. And as a general matter, the greater the confidence that the Tribunal could build in the rigor of its methods, the more effective it would be in building respect for the rule of law. In that regard, the publication of the ICRC report of 2005 on Customary International Humanitarian Law was a very positive development, especially taking into account its ongoing updating by the ICRC. The ICRC's continuing collection, discussion and analysis of evidence of State practice in that study and in the new commentaries on the Geneva Conventions is extremely important for the continued development of customary humanitarian law.

The ICTY declined to engage in an overly formalistic assessment of custom in instances where the criminality of conduct was obvious (or, to use the Nuremberg terminology, where it was clearly established under the relevant "general principles" of law). In its seminal *Interlocutory Decision on Jurisdiction* in the *Tadić* case, the ICTY Appeals Chamber stated that to be subject to prosecution by the Tribunal as a violation of laws and customs of war, an offense must violate either customary law or a treaty that was unquestionably binding on the parties at the time of the alleged offense.[56] Nuremberg, of course, provides a precedent for the principle of legality to be satisfied by reference to treaties that were in force at the time of the offense. However, in the case of the ICTY, such reliance on treaties must be reconciled with the statement in the Secretary-General's 1993 report that the Tribunal should apply rules of international humanitarian law which are beyond any doubt part of customary law. The *Tadić* Bench found that the purpose of that statement was merely to avoid a conflict with the *nullum crimen* principle where a party to the conflict was not a party to a treaty; the statement therefore did not exclude reliance on treaties where there was no potential conflict.[57]

56. *Prosecutor v. Tadić*, Decision on the Defence Motion for Interlocutory Appeal on Jurisdiction, ICTY Appeals Chamber, at paras. 94, 143, Case no. IT-94-1-AR72 (2 Oct. 1995).
57. *Id.* at para. 143. *See* Report of the Secretary-General Pursuant to Paragraph 2 of Security Council Resolution 808 (1993), at para. 34, U.N. Doc. S/25704.

The legality principle likewise governed other international criminal tribunals, including the ICTR and the Special Court for Sierra Leone, and continues to govern the International Residual Mechanism for Criminal Tribunals. In the case of the ICTR, however, that principle had a less restrictive effect because of the less significant role of international custom in that Tribunal's law. Since the conflict in Rwanda was non-international in character, and since (as the Secretary-General noted when the ICTR Statute was adopted) Rwanda had been party to the relevant international humanitarian law treaties, which were part of the law of the land in Rwanda, it was not generally necessary to consider whether a violation of the ICTR Statute was also a violation of customary law at the time of the offense; it was enough that the treaties were violated.[58] There was therefore no obvious need for the ICTR, in its treatment of those provisions, to examine their customary law underpinnings. The Tribunal's contribution to the clarification of customary law was accordingly modest, although the Trial Chambers occasionally discussed the customary status of various principles of law.[59]

The Special Court for Sierra Leone in its decisions on preliminary motions frequently invoked customary humanitarian law, and its Appeals Chamber held that the *nullum crimen* principle must be applied by reference to customary law.[60] In finding that Common Article 3 of the Geneva Conventions enjoyed customary status and applied in both internal and international armed conflicts, the Appeals Chamber relied on the decisions of the ICJ and the ICTY.[61] In finding that customary law precluded the granting of immunity from prosecution based on the Lomé Agreement, it relied, inter alia, on a discussion of ICTY precedent and a Security Council resolution.[62] In concluding that international law did not contain

58. Report of the Secretary-General Pursuant to Paragraph 5 of Security Council Resolution 955 (1994), at paras. 11–12, U.N. Doc. S/1995/134 (13 Feb. 1995).

59. *See*, e.g., *Prosecutor v. Akayesu*, Judgement, ICTR Trial Chamber, at paras. 610, 617, Case no. ICTR-96-4-T (2 Sept. 1998) (addressing the customary status of Art. 4(2) of Additional Protocol II to the Geneva Conventions).

60. *See Prosecutor v. Kallon*, Decision on Constitutionality and Lack of Jurisdiction, Special Court for Sierra Leone (SCSL) Appeals Chamber, at para. 41, Case no. SCSL-2004-15-AR72(E) (13 Mar. 2004).

61. *See Prosecutor v. Fofana*, Decision on Preliminary Motion on Lack of Jurisdiction *Materiae*: Nature of the Armed Conflict, SCSL Appeals Chamber, at paras. 21–4, Case no. SCSL-2004-14-AR72(E) (25 May 2004).

62. *See Prosecutor v. Kondewa*, Decision on Lack of Jurisdiction/Abuse of Process: Amnesty Provided by the Lomé Accord, SCSL Appeals Chamber, at paras. 52, 57, Case no. SCSL-2004-14-AR72(E) (25 May 2004); *Prosecutor v. Gbao*, Decision on Preliminary Motion on the Invalidity of the Agreement Between the United Nations and the Government of Sierra

a peremptory norm providing immunity from criminal prosecution to a head of State, it cited a variety of sources, including the statutes of the various international criminal tribunals, General Assembly resolutions, the ICJ decision in the *Yerodia* case and a British domestic court decision.[63] And in finding that customary law supported the criminalization of child recruitment, it relied on the widespread ratification of several treaties as evidence of State practice.[64]

In contrast to the Statutes of the ad hoc Tribunals, the ICC Statute more closely resembles a civil law code and is meant to be applied as such. Its Statute is the ICC's primary source, while customary law is its secondary source. Unlike pleadings in the ICTY, the gravamen of future pleadings in the ICC will be the interpretation of the Statute, not its customary law underpinnings. Nevertheless, Article 21 of the Statute, which concerns applicable law, opens the door wide to such additional sources of international law as "the principles and rules of international law, including the established principles of the law of armed conflict," as well as "general principles of law derived by the Court from national laws of legal systems of the world."[65] If the Court decides to take advantage of this Article in defining the scope of criminal liability, it should be guided by the legality principle and should, in my view, adopt the cautious approach to the interpretation of custom for which I have argued here.

Moreover, in some situations, the ICC may be forced to address and apply customary law. First, in the case of a referral of a situation to the Court by the Security Council acting under Chapter VII and in accordance with Article 13(b) of the Statute—as, for instance, with the Darfur atrocities—a defendant might argue that he is subjected to *ex post facto* legislation, because the provision under which he is accused is not declaratory of customary law. Second, such an argument might be made when the ICC's jurisdiction is based on a special acceptance by the State concerned, thus necessitating an *ex post facto* inquiry. The success of such an argument would turn on

Leone on the Establishment of the Special Court, SCSL Appeals Chamber, at paras. 6–10, Case no. SCSL-2004-15-AR72(E) (25 May 2004).

63. *See Prosecutor v. Taylor*, Decision on Immunity from Jurisdiction, SCSL Appeals Chamber, at paras. 43–53, Case no. SCSL-2003-01-I (31 May 2004).

64. *Prosecutor v. Norman*, Decision on Preliminary Motion Based on Lack of Jurisdiction (Child Recruitment), SCSL Appeals Chamber, at paras. 18–24, Case no. SCSL-2004-14-AR72(E) (31 May 2004).

65. Art. 21, Rome Statute of the International Criminal Court (1 July 2002), 2187 UNTS 3.

whether the accused understood—or reasonably should have understood—that the act of which he is accused constituted an offence at the time of its commission. In such a case, the Court will have a rare opportunity to clarify the customary law status of the particular provisions.

Selective Accountability

The idea that international criminal justice is a valuable tool for the enhancement of the rule of law both globally and locally is, as I hope I have demonstrated thus far, a compelling one, but it inevitably clashes with the phenomenon of selectivity. The simple fact is that, as I write, atrocities are being committed in Syria, Myanmar and in many other places. Yet, there are presently no proceedings before the ICC in response to these situations, nor has there been any concerted effort on the part of the international community to establish specialized international tribunals to address them (although the U.N. General Assembly has established mechanisms for collection and preservation of evidence for crimes with regard to Syria, Iraq and Myanmar). The selectivity reflected in the assertion of international criminal jurisdiction for some situations and not for others poses an enormous challenge not just for efforts to end impunity but for international justice itself, as the rule of law demands equality of enforcement and non-arbitrariness.

Selectivity is, regrettably, in many ways a political and practical reality. Criminal tribunals at the supranational level are necessarily courts of limited jurisdiction—jurisdiction that may be exercised only over situations in States that have acceded to such jurisdiction or by the mandate of the Security Council under Chapter VII of the U.N. Charter. That limitation subjects the administration of international criminal justice to the vagaries and vicissitudes of politics, where some will prioritize alliances and self-interest over the rule of law. The tribunals and those who would wish to see international criminal jurisdiction asserted over new atrocities are often powerless in the absence of some form of national will or international political consensus.

Making matters worse still is the scarcity of resources, which means that international criminal tribunals are unable to take on all or even most of the cases that fall within their jurisdiction, and resource constraints may undermine the will to create new courts or jurisdictions. Practically speaking, it is simply not possible for international courts to try all of those accused of responsibility for atrocity crimes. In sum, hard choices must be made.

But all of that does not mean we should despair. First, we must appreciate international criminal justice for the modest enterprise that it is, at least at this stage in its evolution. Jurisdiction over some cases is still better than jurisdiction over no cases.

Second, even while acknowledging that selectivity may be an intractable problem, the international community and all of those who care about accountability and international criminal justice can and should take actions to curb the corrosive effects of selectivity on the rule of law by encouraging domestic prosecutions of international crimes, by assisting national judicial systems and hopefully of regional courts to develop the expertise and capacity to handle such cases. Commendably, we have already seen a rising tide of national prosecutions in just the past two decades, and encouraging such prosecutions has been one of the key undertakings of the ICC, through so-called "positive complementarity." The idea is that by using carrots and sticks—for example, the offer of assistance in domestic prosecutions on the one hand, and the threat of international prosecution on the other hand—the ICC can incentivize States to carry the burden jointly with the international community.

Finally, we must endeavor to ensure that practical constraints are not permitted to make things worse. In many cases, the selectivity problem is exacerbated by the unavailability or weakness of evidence. As a practical matter, many cases of international crimes are not investigated and prosecuted until months or years after the relevant events took place, and, as a result, valuable evidence and witnesses are lost. The timely collection of evidence must be made a priority, both by State actors and by the international community. The establishment of mechanisms for Syria, Iraq and Myanmar is a step in the right direction.

Due Process

In his report to the U.N. Security Council pursuant to the Council's Resolution 808 (1993), the Secretary-General wrote that the Trial Chambers of the ICTY should ensure that a trial is fair and expeditious and that proceedings are conducted in accordance with the Rules of Procedure and Evidence and with full respect for the rights of the accused. Fairness of proceedings and due process rights are thus the very foundation of the Tribunals' proceedings and the basis of their legitimacy and credibility.

The ad hoc Tribunals did their best to comply with these standards.

There is of course a major intersection between international and domestic criminal proceedings: fairness and due process of law.

Since World War II, and particularly in the last few decades, there has been a growing recognition, both in the international arena and within individual States, of certain fundamental legal norms protecting individuals during criminal trials. These norms—such as the right to an impartial tribunal, the right to be assisted by a counsel of one's choice, the right to a speedy trial and a number of other norms—are crucial to safeguard individuals from vindictive or abusive prosecutions or abuse of judicial power. These rights can be collectively termed rights to a fair trial, or, particularly in the common law legal system, to due process of law.

These due process rights are important, first and foremost, to the individual, because they provide him or her with important protections when they are confronted with the force of the apparatus of the criminal justice system. But due process also fulfils an important function with respect to the judicial system itself. By ensuring that all participants in the criminal justice process—including the Prosecutors and the Judges—abide by the norms of due process, the trial is made fair and impartial, and the public, as a result, gains a greater respect for the judicial process. Alexander Bickel, a noted scholar of American constitutional law, has remarked that the courts are "the least powerful branch" of the government. The courts have no army, nor do they control the public purse. What the courts have, however, is the authority to determine disputed facts, to explain the law and to apply it to individual violators, and to do so impartially. To carry out this task effectively, and to ensure that their decisions are respected and implemented, the courts must have impeccable moral authority. This moral authority comes from the public perception of courts as both knowledgeable in the law and impartial in its application. Consequently, it is essential for Judges to ensure that norms that govern the fair conduct of criminal trials are respected, recognized and explained in their decisions.

There is, of course, a great deal of similarity between the norms of due process reflected in international law and the norms of due process in the law of individual nations. In fact, the two are interdependent and mutually influence each other. The norms of due process derive from national legal systems. Once formulated in an international instrument—whether that document has the binding force of a treaty or is only a nonbinding reflection of their aspirations—these instruments serve as models or examples to States, and are often incorporated by them into their domestic law. As more States accept a due process norm, the more accepted it becomes as a norm of international law, which is universally binding as customary law, general principle of law or even as a peremptory norm.

One of the most prominent, and most comprehensive, documents codifying due process rights in criminal trials is the International Covenant on Civil and Political Rights (ICCPR), concluded in 1966.

Other instruments, including regional human rights instruments, also contain norms of criminal due process often similar to those in the ICCPR. Particularly authoritative is the European Convention for the Protection of Human Rights and Fundamental Freedoms. The other major instruments are the American Convention on Human Rights and the African Charter on Human and Peoples' Rights. The requirements of due process contained in many of these conventions are further elucidated in the decisions of the regional courts set up to ensure compliance with their requirements. Of particular note in that regard is the extensive jurisprudence of the European Court of Human Rights. That Court has issued many decisions which dealt with, among others, the meaning of the right to representation, the right to a speedy trial and the right to fair and impartial proceedings.

The Statutes of U.N. ad hoc Tribunals contain lists of specific guarantees which seek to ensure that individuals tried in international criminal courtrooms are afforded full protection of due process. These Articles often reflect customary international law. They are similar to and often track the provisions of international human rights documents and especially the ICCPR.

The case law pertaining to fairness and due process is discussed in Chapter X. I would like briefly to introduce here some of the fairness and due process rights particularly important in the work of the ad hoc Tribunals.

The first right I would like to mention is the right to be represented by counsel. This right has been recognized by Article 14(3) of the ICCPR and by Articles 18(3) and 21 of the Statute of the ICTY. I begin with this right because the presence of effective counsel, who is familiar with the law, ensures that norms of due process are respected in criminal proceedings. The right to counsel has several components. Both the ICCPR and the Statute of the ICTY provide that the defendant has a right to select a counsel of his own choosing. This allows an effective defence, because the representation is based on a voluntary relationship of trust between the defendant and counsel. Obviously, this choice is not unconstrained. Counsel engaged by the accused must possess certain mandatory qualifications. Thus, counsel must demonstrate that he or she is admitted to the practice of law in a State, or is a professor of law in a university. Counsel must also speak one of the two working languages of the Tribunals, which are English and French. In certain circumstances, the Tribunals permit a counsel to represent a defendant when he does not speak those languages but speaks the language of the defendant. The defendant must make such a request, and the Tribunal determines whether it would be in the interests of justice to permit that departure from the rules. This procedure allows a counsel with whom the defendant is familiar and has a common linguistic bond to represent him. In a situation where the principal counsel does not speak either of the Tribunals' working languages, there will normally be a co-counsel who speaks either English or French to ensure an effective defence. Of course, the accuracy of the interpretation provided by the Tribunal is of utmost importance. Finally, the counsel must be a member of the association of counsel practicing at the Tribunal. This association is similar to a national criminal defence bar. The members of the association share general information in terms of representation techniques, and, most importantly, are able to bring to the attention of the Tribunal any problems affecting the defence bar which might require action by court officials. The principal administrative official of the Tribunal, the Registrar, has certain powers of oversight over the defence bar, including determination of competency and compensation. The Registrar's decisions in this matter can be appealed to the President of the Tribunal. The trial Judges also have some powers of oversight, especially where a counsel is alleged to be in contempt of court.

For the right to counsel to have meaning, there must be a mechanism to pay his or her fees where the defendant lacks the financial resources to do so themselves. The Statutes provide the defendant with the right to have a free counsel assigned in any case where the defendant lacks sufficient means to pay for legal representation. In the vast majority of cases, counsel is paid by the Tribunal. Where counsel's costs are covered by the Tribunals, international norms of due process do not require that counsel be one of the defendant's own choosing. Where the Tribunals provide free legal aid, the choice of a lawyer rests with the Registry, and the defendant cannot insist that the Registry pays a lawyer he or she selects. I think it is wise, however, to adhere as closely as possible to the principle that the defendant has a right to counsel of his or her choice. As I have already mentioned, where the defendant and counsel have a relationship of mutual trust, representation is more effective and solidifies public confidence in the fairness of the trial. The Tribunals thus try to allow an indigent defendant to select his or her own counsel, typically from a list kept by the Registry of defence lawyers who have been found to meet the necessary professional qualifications. In particular circumstances, the Tribunals allow assignment of counsel whose name is not on the approved list.

Another aspect of the right to counsel, is the right of the defendant to refuse counsel and to conduct his or her own defence. This right is recognized both by the ICCPR and by the Statutes of the Tribunals. This right is controversial and often criticized because, obviously, a defendant who is not trained in the law and not familiar with the complex rules of criminal procedure will often not be able to present as well prepared a defence as a professional lawyer. It is important to remember, however, that it is the guilt or innocence of the defendant himself that is at issue; and the defendant must have the right to present the kind of defence he wishes, even if that defence is less legal and professional than personal. The defendant may decide that he or she would prefer to address the court themselves, rather than to have a lawyer mediate between them and the Judges.

Of course, self-representation itself may give rise to concerns about the fairness of the trial. International law generally, and the Statutes in particular, explicitly recognize the right of the accused to a fair trial. The Tribunals recognize that trial Judges have an obligation to ensure that the defendant's trial is fair. This obligation applies even where the defendant chooses to represent himself. This does not mean that the Judges must act as counsel for the accused; but it does mean that they must make a special effort to ensure that the accused understands the proceedings, and knows with what formalities he or she must comply, for example in filing documents or making motions. The Judges must also ensure that the defendant understands the benefits of professional legal representation he or she is giving up.

In particular situations, additional fairness safeguards might be necessary. For instance, in the case of former President Slobodan Milošević, the Judges decided to appoint a group of three lawyers as "friends of the court." These lawyers were instructed to do everything they deemed necessary to help to ensure that Milošević had a fair trial. They made motions to the court, were present during the hearings, addressed the court on a variety of issues and even appealed the court's rulings to the Tribunal's Appeals Chamber. The friends of the court, however, were not counsel for Milošević. While they took steps for his benefit, they did so pursuant to the Order of the Chamber to help to ensure that the trial was fair and not as agents of the defendant.

In another case, that of the Serbian politician Vojislav Šešelj, who also chose to represent himself, the trial Judges took a different approach. They appointed a "stand-by counsel." This was a lawyer who was present in court during the hearings and with whom Šešelj could consult. He was not, however, acting as his counsel, and could not intervene in the proceedings independently. The Judges indicated that if, at some point during the trial, they concluded that a fair trial was impossible with the defendant continuing to represent himself, they could order the stand-by counsel, who was already familiar with the proceedings, to take over the defence. Of course, such an Order could be appealed, and the Appeals Chamber would consider whether it was consistent with the defendant's right to self-representation.

There are thus various ways of dealing with a defendant's right to represent him or herself, and of addressing the tension between that right and the defendant's right to a fair trial. The choice of method may depend, in part, on a Judge's legal tradition. Common law countries, which view criminal proceedings as adversarial contests between the prosecution and the defence, are more permissive with respect to the right to self-representation. They believe that provided the defendant knows the consequences of his or her choice to proceed without counsel, they should be allowed to do so. Civil law countries, by contrast, view judicial proceedings as a Judge-managed search for the truth. An unassisted defendant is often less able than a defendant assisted by counsel to contribute to that task. Consequently, the civil law tradition is more inclined to impose counsel on the defendant in order to ensure an equitable trial.

Another important norm of due process is the requirement of a speedy trial. This norm has several components. First, there is the right to be released from detention, or at least the right to request to be so released, if the accused is not brought to trial within a reasonable time. This is recognized by Article 9(3) of the ICCPR and in somewhat different terms in Article 21(4)(c) of the ICTY Statute. The prosecutorial and law enforcement organs are required to bring a suspect within a reasonable time before the judiciary for a review of the charges levied against him. Second, there is the right to be tried without undue delay (ICCPR, Art. 14(3)(c)). This right is crucial to the guarantee of a fair trial because undue delays may cause the loss of evidence and the fading of memories of the witnesses. In addition, this right seeks to minimize the emotional strain on the accused caused by lengthy criminal proceedings.

Of course, the requirements that both the detention and the trial last only a reasonable time must be analyzed in the context of a particular case. In the Tribunals, both pre-trial stages and the trials themselves are quite lengthy. This is due to the complexity of the cases, the difficulty in investigating events which took place years earlier, the challenge of bringing in witnesses who reside in other countries, the sheer number of those witnesses and the need to rely on governments for enforcing investigative orders and arrest warrants.

The Tribunals took steps to promote expeditiousness, both during the pre-trial proceedings and during the trials. At the pre-trial stage, borrowing from the civil law, the Tribunals instituted the position of a pre-trial Judge. This position is taken up by one of the three Judges assigned to try a case. The pre-trial Judge is designated by the presiding Judge of the Bench. He or she ensures that the case is ready for trial and can proceed smoothly and efficiently. The pre-trial Judge requests the parties to submit briefs addressing the factual and legal issues in the case and lists of witnesses and exhibits. The pre-trial Judge thus clarifies and narrows the issues between the parties and enables the entire Trial Bench to make a subsequent determination of whether it is necessary to hear all of the listed witnesses. The trial Judges have the authority to require the prosecution to shorten the estimated length of the examination-in-chief; to set the number of prosecution witnesses; and to determine the time available for presenting evidence. The Judges have similar powers vis-à-vis the defence.

The Tribunals also introduced a series of procedures to utilize written statements in lieu of oral testimony. One rule allowed the prosecution to introduce evidence in written form where it did not deal with the acts or conduct of the defendant himself, but rather with accompanying events or circumstances, or with actions taken by individuals under the defendant's command. To admit this evidence, the prosecution had to present stringent guarantees of its veracity and authenticity, and the trial Judges would decide whether the evidence should be admitted. This procedure was often used when the proposed evidence was cumulative of oral evidence already admitted, as when other witnesses had given oral testimony on similar facts. The trial Judges also determined whether the witness whose evidence was presented in a written statement should appear in court for cross-examination. Generally, such cross-examination was allowed when the statement sought to be introduced raised an issue in dispute between the parties. This ensured compliance with yet another norm of international due process—the right of the accused to cross-examine prosecution witnesses. This right is stated in Article 14(3)(e) of the ICCPR and in Article 21(4)(e) of the ICTY Statute. In conformity with that right, Judges insist on oral testimony where the statement sought to be introduced directly implicates the acts or conduct of the defendant.

Another rule allows either party—whether the prosecution or the defence—to introduce in written form oral testimony given by a witness in a different trial. Again, a number of safeguards must be present to ensure that the right of cross-examination is not violated. The witness must be present in court; must publicly attest that his or her earlier testimony is accurate and would be the same today; and must be available for cross-examination and for questioning by the Judges. These procedures are designed to balance the right to a speedy trial with the right to cross-examine the witnesses. Judges impose some limitations on the right of cross-examination to make the trials more expeditious, but balance this with setting up a number of safeguards to ensure that the accused has the right to question witnesses who give evidence against them.

In contrast to Nuremberg, modern international criminal tribunals recognize the right of appeal by both the accused and the prosecution to an Appeals Chamber both on the final conviction and sentence and on certain interlocutory matters. As regards the latter, on matters pertaining to jurisdiction, interlocutory appeals may be filed as a matter of right; on most other matters, interlocutory appeals require a certification of the Trial Chamber.

I now turn to what is perhaps the most fundamental criminal due process right, the presumption of innocence. This guarantee is essential to protect the human dignity of the arrested individual and to preserve the basic concept of justice and fairness. All the major human rights instruments, including the ICCPR, guarantee this right. The ICTY, for example, did likewise in Article 21(3) of the Statute. The presumption of innocence, though obviously crucial at trial, also comes into play in other instances. For example, the Tribunal often faced requests by the individuals arrested to be released provisionally pending trial. In the ICTY's early years, such requests were granted only in exceptional circumstances. In part, this was due to the fact that the ICTY's host country, the Netherlands, was strongly opposed to having arrested individuals released pending trial on its territory, and the Judges did not have adequate assurances that, if the accused were released in their home countries (Serbia, Montenegro, Croatia or Bosnia and Herzegovina), they would return when requested. Judges made it clear that the presumption of innocence was not a bar to denying a defendant's application for provisional release. Over time, however, they began granting such requests with greater frequency, as the guarantees provided by the States of the Balkan region were considered adequate. In fact, all the individuals who were released provisionally returned to face trial.

The presumption of innocence also relates to the issue of guilty pleas.

These are instances in which the prosecution does not need to prove the guilt of the accused because he or she agrees to admit the charges in court. In exchange, the prosecution recommends a sentence lower than the one normally imposed in similar circumstances at the end of the trial, should the guilt be proven.

Guilty pleas accomplish several tasks. First, they free up important prosecutorial and judicial resources by sparing the expense of a lengthy trial. Second, by having the accused openly and voluntarily acknowledge his or her responsibility, he or she may provide victims with greater comfort and satisfaction than a contested judicial determination. The guilty pleas in the Tribunal have been criticized, however, because of the lower sentences imposed. Critics argued that the sentences did not reflect the gravity of the crimes committed by individuals who pled guilty, and therefore did not serve either justice or the interests of victims. These are valid concerns, and any court which accepts a guilty plea should be sensitive to them. One way of assuaging these concerns, and one which has always been present in the Judges' minds, is that the trial Judges who impose the sentence would not be bound by the sentence recommended by the prosecution. They can impose, and in several instances have imposed, sentences which were harsher than the ones recommended. The accused as well as the Prosecutor, can appeal a sentence imposed which departs from that agreed as a condition of the guilty plea. Moreover, Judges usually insist on a statement from the accused acknowledging in some detail the crimes and creating a historical record.

Lastly, I would like to mention two interrelated rights: the right to be tried in one's own presence and the right to a public hearing. I list them together because, while they offer the accused different protections, both are instrumental in ensuring that the judicial proceedings are effective and credible to the public. The first right, which prohibits trials *in absentia*, assumes that the ability of the accused to face his Judge and accusers adds a dimension of credibility to the proceedings, enhances the ascertainment of truth and protects the rights of the accused. The presence of the defendant during his or her trial also allows them to participate effectively in the trial and to present an adequate defence. The international law on this issue is not fully crystallized, however. The ICCPR prohibits trials *in absentia*, guaranteeing the right to be present at one's trial. The Statutes of International Criminal Tribunals grant the right to be present, subject to some limitations, such as for cases where the accused flees the jurisdiction during trial or after having been given notice of the charges, or where the obstructive conduct of the accused renders the continuance of the proceedings in his or her presence impossible. The Statutes of the ad hoc Tribunals specify that the accused has the right "to be tried in his presence." This right both protects the accused and ensures the effectiveness of the proceedings. However, this is not a universally accepted rule. The prohibition of trials *in absentia* is guaranteed in some but not all national jurisdictions. Civil law jurisdictions generally allow *in absentia* trials subject to various safeguards.

The second guarantee, that of a public trial, is designed to protect the accused from secret trials. It also fosters public trust in the administration of criminal justice by opening the courts to public scrutiny. This right is guaranteed by Article 14(1) of the ICCPR, by a number of other human rights instruments and by Article 21(2) of the ICTY Statute. This right, of course, is not unconstrained. The ICCPR, for example, explicitly provides for a number of exceptions. Thus, "the press and public may be excluded from all or part of the trial in the interests of morals, public order or national security in a democratic society, where the interests of juveniles or the protection of the private life of the parties so require, or to the extent strictly necessary in the opinion of the court in special circumstances where publicity would prejudice the interests of justice." The ICTY Statute, similarly, imposes a number of limitations. Judges are particularly concerned with the safety of witnesses. Therefore, Article 22 of the Statute allows Judges to impose such measures as to conduct *in camera* proceedings or to protect the identities of witnesses with voice distortion or pseudonyms where there are reasons to suppose that their safety or the integrity of the proceedings might be at risk.

I have attempted to present not an exhaustive catalog of protections that international due process offers to a criminal defendant, but rather to list those which proved to be particularly important in the work of the Tribunals.

The meaning of any due process guarantee is not always immediately clear from the text of the instrument which contains it. Instead, this meaning has to be clarified by Judges, as they apply these norms to the different circumstances of the cases before them, taking into account their legal traditions and experiences. The application of fairness norms to cases before the Tribunals was not always straightforward. It was necessary to clarify the meaning of those norms and to balance them against each other also bearing in mind the overall reputation, integrity and efficiency of the judicial proceedings.

V

Trying Violations of Human Rights in International Criminal Tribunals

The law of war—today known as international humanitarian law—long predates the modern human rights movement. In keeping with traditional Westphalian precepts, the classic law of war primarily regulated States' behavior toward one another and was based on the principle of reciprocity. When a soldier violated the rules, the State for which he fought was typically liable for the violation not to the victim, but to the victim's State. The remedies available to the injured State were largely methods of self-help: reprisals and, after the war, reparations for war damage.

While international humanitarian law governed relations between States in times of war and protected individuals from enemy powers, international human rights law has historically applied principally in times of peace and has protected individuals from their own governments. Violations of human rights law resulted principally in State responsibility, while violations of international humanitarian law could lead to State responsibility and armed reprisals, and in some cases, to individual criminal liability for the perpetrator. International human rights law has been limited in its application to the territory of the State concerned, while international humanitarian law has also applied extraterritorially, especially to situations of occupation or whenever an army found itself outside its national territory. Even today, most violations of international human rights law are perceived as triggering civil liability of States and not individual criminal liability of the perpetrators.

In recent years, there has been a growing recognition of the extraterritorial application of human rights under Article 2 of the International

Standing Up For Justice. Theodor Meron, Oxford University Press (2021). © Theodor Meron.
DOI: 10.1093/oso/9780198863434.003.0005

Covenant on Civil and Political Rights[1] and Advisory Opinions of the International Court of Justice. And there has been real progress in recognizing that some human rights continue to apply in times of war, international and non-international.

Some prosecutions have been pursued by third party States under the Convention against Torture (1984), a human rights treaty with a penal component establishing universal jurisdiction obligations *inter partes*, which requires domestic prosecution of individuals even in cases where crimes were not committed in a country's territory or against its citizens. But such prosecutions have been rare. So have prosecutions by third party States to the Geneva Conventions, under the grave breaches provisions of the Conventions. Torture is listed as a crime under the statutes of international criminal tribunals.

The Nuremberg Charter conferred jurisdiction over crimes against humanity, but the International Military Tribunal considered that it lacked competence to try such crimes against humanity that were committed before World War II. As regional human rights courts had, and still have, only civil jurisdiction, no individual penal responsibility attached even for gross violations of human rights on the international plane.

Post-World War II Changes

It is no exaggeration, I think, to suggest that the devastating horrors committed during World War II led to a seismic shift in the foundations of international law. This shift fundamentally altered not just how international law governs relations among States but also how it governs the relations of States with individuals—and the responsibilities of both States and individuals for breaches of international law.

Indeed, in the years that followed the end of the war, we saw the birth of a new generation of international instruments of human rights. Underlying these instruments, as well as the more specialized conventions that would

1. Thomas Buergenthal, *To Respect and to Ensure: State Obligations and Permissible Derogations*, in THE INTERNATIONAL BILL OF RIGHTS: THE COVENANT ON CIVIL AND POLITICAL RIGHTS 72, 74 (Louis Henkin ed., 1981); Theodor Meron, *Extraterritoriality of Human Rights Treaties*, 89 AM. J. INT'L L. 78 (1995); Theodor Meron, HUMAN RIGHTS LAW-MAKING IN THE UNITED NATIONS 106–9 (1986)

follow in the decades to come, was the belief that certain rights vest not in the State, but in individuals; that States must not simply refrain from taking certain actions against individuals but also have affirmative duties to provide for individuals' basic needs; and that what a State does to its own citizens and to those within its jurisdiction is not just the concern of that State but of the whole world.

It is small wonder that this tidal change in international law gave rise to extraordinary changes in the law of war as well.

These changes are most evident in the Geneva Conventions for the Protection of Victims of War (1949). The Geneva Conventions marked a movement away from reactively protecting civilians—as in the earlier Hague Conventions on the Laws and Customs of War—to proactively safeguarding their welfare. The Geneva Conventions also helped to transform the law of war from a system based on State-to-State reciprocity to a framework of individual, inalienable rights. Common Article 1 of the Geneva Conventions epitomizes this denial of reciprocity with its analog to the prerogative of all States to invoke obligations *erga omnes* against States that violate fundamental human rights. Several Common Clauses in the Conventions are a prime example of inalienable rights, rights which may not be waived by either States or individuals.

The two Additional Protocols to the Geneva Conventions (1977), especially Protocol II on non-international armed conflicts, constitute important statements of human rights in humanitarian law instruments in the context of international and non-international armed conflicts. This is particularly true of the "fundamental guarantees" clauses of the two Protocols, Article 75 of Additional Protocol I and Article 4, as well as Articles 5 and 6, of Additional Protocol II. Both state a wide-range and enlightened catalog of human rights and due process protections. Article 75 applies its provisions as a minimum for persons who are in the power of a party to the conflict and who do not benefit from more favorable treatment under the Conventions or under Protocol I. Article 4 protects persons who do not take a direct part or who have ceased to take a part in hostilities.

All of this marked a profound humanization of the law of war.[2]

2. Theodor Meron, *The Humanization of the Humanitarian Law*, 94 Am. J. Int'l L. 239 (2000); Theodor Meron, The Humanization of International Law 1 (2006).

The Establishment of International Criminal Tribunals

The creation of the ICTY in 1993 and the ICTR in 1994 was followed by the establishment of other international criminal courts and tribunals, as well as hybrid tribunals—including the world's first permanent international criminal court—representing another tidal shift. This transformative moment comes not from an emphasis on the rights of individuals so much as from a growing focus on individual accountability, and not from promulgation of new rules of State responsibility but from the increased recognition of the criminal responsibility of individual actors based upon norms of behavior first developed principally for States.

This development led to the tendency to fill an important *lacuna* in the law through international criminal tribunals increasingly judging and punishing violations which constitute in effect, even if not in the nomenclature, violations of human rights or, in many cases, violations of both human rights and humanitarian law.

What truly sets modern international criminal courts apart from Nuremberg and from early efforts aimed at ensuring accountability is the degree to which these modern courts—while formally mandated to apply international humanitarian law—have tried gross violations of human rights. This is of great importance because regional human rights courts have exclusively civil competence.

While human rights law has provided a major due process dimension and an interpretative tool in areas of international humanitarian law inadequately addressed by treaty law, through trials of violations of human rights in international criminal courts and tribunals, human rights law has acquired a growing component of individual criminal liability. This led to an increasing impact of international criminal courts and tribunals on human rights protections not only as a matter of principles of fairness, but also as a matter of substantive law.

While human rights treaties have traditionally protected individuals from abuse in times of peace, many of these protections may, alas, be derogated on the ground of national emergency. What is more, these treaties often offer little protection against the acts of non-governmental actors, such as rebel groups during internal armed conflicts. At the same time, instruments governing international humanitarian law, such as the Geneva Conventions, while non-derogable, have generally focused on international armed conflicts. Indeed, Common Article 3 of the Geneva Conventions—a quintessential statement of human rights, albeit in the international humanitarian law context—is the sole Article of the Conventions to expressly apply to internal armed conflicts, and its provisions are far more limited than those applicable to international armed conflicts. There were, thus, gaps both in the conventional protections applicable in internal armed conflicts and in the criminal enforcement of gross violations of human rights.

This situation has undergone a major change thanks in great part to the 1995 *Tadić Interlocutory Decision on Jurisdiction* of the ICTY,[3] where Judge Cassese and his Bench made plain that customary international law rules governing internal armed conflicts have emerged over time and that many of the rules and principles governing international armed conflicts apply to internal armed conflicts as well. This decision stated, also, that those rules established individual criminal responsibility of the perpetrators and not only the civil responsibility of the parties concerned. This decision gained further support from the ICRC Customary International Humanitarian Law Study of 2005. I had the honor of serving on the steering committee of that study and being one of its rapporteurs. In the years that followed, the ICTY was at the forefront of articulating and applying those protections under humanitarian law, thus helping to redress through customary law and case law, gaps between treaty-based human rights law and international humanitarian law.

This is not the only way in which international criminal tribunals such as the ICTY contributed to human rights law and protections. In construing the material elements of crimes under international humanitarian law, international criminal tribunals also had recourse to human rights law and jurisprudence, thereby strengthening human rights law and opening new avenues for its penal enforcement.

Common Article 3 and Crimes Against Humanity

The beginnings of these developments can be traced, first, to the drafting of crimes against humanity clauses in the Nuremberg Charter and,

3. *Prosecutor v. Duško Tadić*, Decision on the Defence Motion for Interlocutory Appeal on Jurisdiction, ICTY Appeals Chamber, at paras. 96–137, Case no. IT-94-1-AR72 (2 Oct. 1995).

second, to the drafting of Common Article 3 of the Geneva Conventions. For the first time in an international treaty, humanitarian law projected into internal conflicts and articulated provisions containing human rights law. As Joyce A. C. Gutteridge, the British delegate to the Fourth Committee of the 1949 Geneva Conference commented, Common Article 3 guaranteed "the observance of certain fundamental human rights."[4] Common Article 3 proved critical for enabling international criminal tribunals to try and punish gross violations of international human rights law.

This prescient comment was certainly true of such proscriptions stated in Common Article 3 as resort to mutilation, cruel treatment and torture, outrages upon personal dignity, humiliating and degrading treatment and passing of sentences except by a regularly constituted court ensuring all the judicial guarantees. At the very least such provisions could be regarded as having a dual character of both human rights and humanitarian norms.

Not only has Common Article 3 become part of the *jus scripta*, it has been applied as a hard norm of law in scores of cases to punish violators of its proscriptions. Thus, in the *Semanza* case, charges were pursued and entered on appeal based on such violations of Common Article 3 as violence to life, health and physical and mental well-being of persons, in particular murder, cruel treatment such as torture, mutilation and any form of corporal punishment.[5]

With the growing criminalization of essentially human rights norms, the question arises, in the context of the ad hoc Tribunals, how to distinguish war crimes from purely domestic offences. The *Kunarac* Appeal Judgement helpfully clarified that "[w]hat ultimately distinguishes a war crime from a purely domestic offence is that a war crime is shaped by or dependent upon the environment—the armed conflict—in which it is committed ... the existence of an armed conflict must, at a minimum, have played a substantial part in the perpetrator's ability to commit it, his decision to commit it, the manner in which it was committed or the purpose for which it was committed."[6]

4. Joyce A. C. Gutteridge, *The Geneva Conventions of 1949*, 26 Brit.Y.B. Int'l L. 294, 300 (1949).
5. *Prosecutor v. Semanza*, Judgement, ICTR Trial Chamber, at para. 522, Case no. ICTR-97-20-T (15 May 2003).
6. *Prosecutor v. Kunarac, Kovač and Vuković*, Judgement, ICTY Appeals Chamber, at para. 58, Case nos IT-96-23 & IT-96-23/1-A (12 June 2002).

And, of course, as the ICRC Commentary on the Geneva Conventions points out, alleged perpetrators of serious violations of Common Article 3 can also be tried by the competent national courts, typically the courts of the State on whose territory the offences were committed.[7]

The commission of the acts prohibited by Common Article 3 has been prosecuted multiple times in U.N. war crimes tribunals. Acts charged have included murder, mutilation, cruel and inhuman treatment, torture, hostage taking and outrages upon personal dignity. The proscription of such acts has been included in the statutes of the ICTY, ICTR, ICC and SCSL. Additional crimes applicable in non-international armed conflicts are listed in Article 8(2)(e) of the ICC Statute.

Of course, the case law of the Tribunals confirms that Common Article 3 protects only those taking no active part in the hostilities, who have laid down their arms, and those placed *hors de combat.*

Importantly, the Tribunals have confirmed the customary law status of Common Article 3, and that the Article states the minimum common yardstick applicable to both non-international and international armed conflicts. The case law has also confirmed that Common Article 3 fulfills the four conditions stated in the *Tadić Interlocutory Decision on Jurisdiction*:[8] the violations must constitute a violation of international humanitarian law; the rule must be customary in nature; the violation must be serious; the violation must entail the individual criminal responsibility of the perpetrator.[9]

In 1998, the Rome Conference made the text of Common Article 3 part of the Rome Statute of the ICC (Art. 8(2)(c)). And, of course, the ICJ, in the *Nicaragua* case (1986), defined Common Article 3 as a "reflection of elementary considerations of humanity," that is customary law.

The humanization of the law of war continued with the definition of crimes against humanity in the Statutes of the ICTY and the ICTR and subsequently in the Statutes of the ICC, the Mechanism and the hybrid courts. Article 5 of the ICTY Statute listed as crimes against humanity the following crimes directed against any civilian population when committed in armed conflict, whether international or internal in character: enslavement, deportation, imprisonment, torture, rape, persecutions on political, racial and religious grounds and other inhumane acts when committed in

7. ICRC, Commentary on the First Geneva Convention, para. 877 (2016).
8. *Prosecutor v. Duško Tadić* (n. 3).
9. *Prosecutor v. Kunarac, Kovač and Vuković* (n. 6), at para. 68.

international and internal armed conflicts. Article 3 of the ICTR Statute listed similar crimes but omitted the requirement of armed conflict. The dual (humanitarian law/human rights) character of these crimes does not detract from the significance of such gross violations of human rights being subjected to the jurisdiction of international criminal tribunals. The Appeals Chamber of the ICTY made it clear that the armed conflict requirement in Article 5 was statutory and jurisdictional only and not customary law.

Article 7(1) of the ICC Statute further developed and fleshed out definitions of crimes against humanity, emphasizing their human rights dimension by eliminating the requirement that they be committed in armed conflict. The requirement that such acts be committed as part of a widespread or systematic attack directed against any civilian population, with the knowledge of the attack means, in effect, that they can be committed not only in situations of armed conflict, whether international or national, but even in situations of peace. Among the crimes listed are enslavement, deportation or forcible transfer of populations, imprisonment or other severe deprivation of physical liberty in violation of fundamental rules of international law, torture, rape (and other gender crimes) and persecution of an identifiable group on political, racial, national, ethnic, cultural, religious, gender or other grounds that are universally recognized as impermissible under international law in connection with any crime within the jurisdiction of the ICC. Persecution is further defined in Article 7(2)(g) as an intentional and severe deprivation of fundamental rights contrary to international law by reason of the identity of the group, that is on discriminatory grounds.

Additional crimes listed in Article 7 are enforced disappearance of persons, apartheid and other inhumane acts of a similar character intentionally causing great suffering or serious injury to body or to mental and physical health. Usefully, Article 7(2) contains interpretations of the crimes listed in Article 7(1). Taken together, this list constitutes an important catalog of mostly human rights norms.

The new relationship between human rights and humanitarian law was recognized by the ICJ. In the *Nuclear Weapons* and the *Construction of a Wall* Advisory Opinions, the ICJ made it clear that human rights continued to apply in times of war, even outside the national territory—subject to the possibility of lawful derogations and to the *lex specialis* status of international humanitarian law with regard to the right to life.

When the ICTY was established, the Secretary-General of the U.N. Boutros Boutros-Ghali stated that the ICTY must take international human rights into account: "It is axiomatic that the International Tribunal must fully respect internationally recognized standards regarding the rights of the accused at all stages of its proceedings."[10]

The Secretary-General's focus was on fair trial rights attaching to the accused. Undoubtedly, international human rights law has been a vital source of procedural protections recognized by the Tribunals. However, the Tribunals have gone further. They have invoked human rights to define, elaborate and interpret substantive humanitarian law. And they have also tried and punished gross violations of human rights.

Crimes against humanity (especially persecution and inhumane treatment) are somewhat indeterminate, of course. They have been an important vehicle through which the Tribunals have imported human rights law into their jurisdiction. But the very flexibility of the appellation "crimes against humanity" has forced the Tribunals to analyze particular charges in some detail so as to guard against overbroad categorizations.

Similar difficulties arise with regard to Common Article 3 which was drafted at a high level of generality. Note, for instance, the proscription of violence to life and person. With regard to both crimes against humanity and Common Article 3, the Tribunals had to be careful not to transgress on the principle of legality.

Thus, in the *Kunarac* Judgement[11] the Trial Chamber, noting the similarity between the two bodies of law—humanitarian law and human rights law—in terms of goals, values and terminology, underscored that such reliance must be undertaken cautiously, given the crucial differences between them.[12] The Trial Chamber noted, in particular, that the law applied by the Tribunals constituted a penal regime, concerned with individual criminal responsibility, whereas the international human rights regime was focused on the State, as both the guarantor and abuser of human rights protections.

An example of how this different focus is pertinent is provided by the Tribunal's consideration of torture in the *Kunarac* case.[13]

10. Report of the Secretary-General Pursuant to Paragraph 2 of Security Council Resolution 808 (1993), U.N. Doc. S/25704, para. 106.
11. *Prosecutor v. Dragoljub Kunarac et al.*, Judgement, ICTY Trial Chamber, at para. 467, Case nos IT-96-23-T & IT-96-23/1-T (22 Feb. 2001).
12. *Id.*, paras. 467–70.
13. *Id.*, paras. 465–97, *upheld and expanded upon at Prosecutor v. Dragoljub Kunarac et al.* (n. 6), at paras. 143–8. Regarding rape as torture, see *id.*, paras. 184–5.

The Torture Convention requires that torture comprises four main elements: namely, the severity of treatment, the deliberate nature of the act, the specific purpose of the act and the requirement that the act be committed by or at the instigation of a public official.

The Trial Chamber reasoned that the public official requirement was a result of the context in which the Torture Convention operates—at the interstate level with States as respondents—and was therefore directed only to States' obligations. For the purposes of the ICTY in that case, however, the involvement of the State did not modify or limit the guilt or responsibility of the individual who carried out the crimes in question.[14]

On that basis, the Trial Chamber held that the presence of a State official or other authority was not necessary for the act to be regarded as torture as a matter of personal culpability of the perpetrator, rather than as a matter of State responsibility. This development strengthened the scope and value of the prohibition of torture.

The Tribunals have also made immense contributions to strengthening the proscriptions of rape as war crimes, crimes against humanity and genocidal acts (Chapter III).

Persecution

Persecution and other inhumane acts are often referred to as "residual" or "umbrella crimes" because they encompass a broad range of conduct. By turning to international human rights law, the Tribunals have been able to provide further precision to crimes against humanity. With respect to persecution, the ICTY Trial Chamber in *Kupreškić*[15] held that persecution is the gross or blatant denial, on discriminatory grounds, of a fundamental right, laid down in international customary or treaty law, reaching the same level of gravity as the other acts prohibited as crimes against humanity. Of course, this definition necessarily implicated international human rights, in order to determine which rights are "fundamental."

An act which does not constitute a crime in itself can constitute persecution due to the presence of a discriminatory element and the severity of the

14. *Prosecutor v. Kunarac et al.* (n. 11), at para. 493.
15. *Prosecutor v. Zoran Kupreškić et al.*, Judgement, ICTY Trial Chamber, at paras. 618–22, Case no. IT-95-16-T (14 Jan. 2000).

deprivation of fundamental rights. As the *Tadić* Appeal Judgement[16] made clear, only the crime of persecution requires a discriminatory intent. Other crimes against humanity listed in Article 5 of the ICTY Statute do not have a discriminatory intent requirement.

In *Blaškić*, the Trial Chamber held that there was no doubt that causing serious bodily and mental harm may be characterized as persecution when members of a group are targeted because they belong to a specific community.[17]

Other cases have also opened the door to using human rights law jurisprudence to address the scope of "persecution." In *Brđanin*, the Appeals Chamber dismissed the argument that the denial of the rights to employment, freedom of movement, proper judicial process and proper medical care did not rise to the level of serious violations of international humanitarian law and therefore did not fall within the jurisdiction of the Tribunal.[18] The Chamber noted that it was settled jurisprudence that the crime of persecution includes not only the acts enumerated in Article 5 of the Statute, or other Articles of the Statute, but also acts which are not listed in the Statute. Furthermore, acts underlying persecution need not even constitute crimes in international law. Rather, the act must be of equal gravity to the crimes listed under Article 5, when considered in isolation or conjunction. Determining whether the acts *actually constitute* persecution is a fact-specific exercise.

In *Simić*, an ICTY Trial Chamber reviewed a number of acts alleged to amount to persecution. It reasoned that persecution can involve a number of discriminatory acts, involving violations of political, social or economic rights. For example, the Trial Chamber noted that the Nuremberg Tribunal found that the requirement that the members of the group marked themselves out by wearing a yellow star amounted to persecution.[19]

Indeed, as the Trial Chamber in *Kupreškić* noted, although every crime against humanity can be described as a gross violation of human rights, "not every denial of a human right may constitute a crime against humanity."

16. *Prosecutor v. Duško Tadić*, Judgement, ICTY Appeals Chamber, at paras. 283–5, Case no. IT-94-1-A (15 July 1999).
17. *Prosecutor v. Tihomir Blaškić*, Judgement, ICTY Trial Chamber, at paras. 220–33, Case no. IT-95-14-T (3 Mar. 2000).
18. *Prosecutor v. Radoslav Brđanin*, Judgement, ICTY Appeals Chamber, at paras. 295–6, Case no. IT-99-36-A (3 Apr. 2007).
19. *Prosecutor v. Blagoje Simić et al.*, Judgement, ICTY Trial Chamber, at paras. 57–63, Case no. IT-95-9-T (17 Oct. 2003).

As such, the Tribunals needed to ensure not only that a right whose violation was the subject of criminal prosecution was truly fundamental and universally recognized, but also that any transgression constituted a violation of the law at the time of its commission.[20]

The principle of legality (Chapter IV) is particularly important when the Tribunals draw on human rights to inform the substantive crimes of international humanitarian law. The issue was discussed extensively in the *Čelebići* case with respect to Common Article 3 of the Geneva Conventions. The defence argued that to punish breaches of Common Article 3 would violate the principle of legality in that it would amount to the creation of law, and would thus be clearly contrary to basic human rights (ICCPR, Art. 15).[21] The Tribunal first considered whether Common Article 3 was customary law applicable to international armed conflicts, and not just non-international armed conflicts.[22] The Appeals Chamber noted that Common Article 3 reflects fundamental humanitarian principles which underlie international humanitarian law as a whole. Indeed, the norms in Common Article 3 were customary even before being codified in the Geneva Conventions, as the most universally recognized humanitarian principles. This conclusion is confirmed by a consideration of human rights law which shares, with the Geneva Conventions, a common core of fundamental standards which are applicable at all times, in all circumstances and to all parties.[23] The Appeals Chamber concluded that it would be legally and morally untenable to hold that Common Article 3, which constitutes mandatory minimum rules, would not be applicable to international armed conflicts.[24] Indeed, the ICJ's holding in the *Nicaragua* Judgment that Common Article 3 is a "minimum yardstick" makes this conclusion compelling.

Turning to the question whether violations of Common Article 3 are criminal, the defence further argued that by excluding the provisions of Common Article 3 from the grave breaches system of the Geneva Conventions, the State Parties intended that individual violators would not face criminal sanction. According to the defence, Common Article 3

20. *Prosecutor v. Zoran Kupreškić* (n. 15), at paras. 507, 618.
21. *Prosecutor v. Zejnil Delalić et al.*, Judgement, ICTY Trial Chamber, at para. 311, Case no. IT-96-21-T (16 Nov. 1998).
22. *Id.*, para. 314.
23. *Prosecutor v. Zejnil Delalić et al.*, Judgement, ICTY Appeals Chamber, at para. 143, Case no. IT-96-21-A (20 Feb. 2001)
24. *Id.*, paras. 149–50.

imposed duties on States, not individuals.[25] The Appeals Chamber rejected that argument, holding that although not expressly provided in the Geneva Conventions, violations of Common Article 3 undoubtedly entailed individual criminal liability.[26] The purpose of the principle of legality is to prevent the prosecution and punishment of individuals for acts which they reasonably believed to be lawful at the time of their commission. Notice is, thus, of the essence. As codified in Article 15 of the ICCPR, which protects individuals from being convicted for acts that did not constitute a criminal offence at the time they were committed, the principle of legality does not prevent the criminalization of acts which are criminal according to the general principles of law recognized by the community of nations. As the Chamber noted, it is undeniable that acts such as murder, torture, rape and inhuman treatment are criminal according to that standard. It would strain credulity to contend that the accused would not understand the criminal nature of those acts.

The entirety of Common Article 3 is not regarded as suitable for criminal enforcement, however. The Trial Chamber thus held in *Vasiljević* that although Common Article 3 of the Geneva Conventions mentions the term "violence to life and person" as a prohibited act, and although the Appeals Chamber had earlier held that customary international law imposed criminal liability for all serious violations of Common Article 3, the Trial Chamber could not convict the accused of "violence to life and person" because that crime was not recognized or defined with sufficient clarity by customary international law.[27] The Trial Chamber therefore acquitted the accused on that charge.

25. *Id.*, para. 157. 26. *Id.*, para. 167.

27. *Prosecutor v. Mitar Vasiljević*, Judgement, ICTY Trial Chamber, at paras. 203–4, Case no. IT-98-32-T (29 Nov. 2002).

VI

Judicial Independence and Impartiality

Since there are major similarities between national and international concepts of judicial independence and impartiality, some of my discussion will be of relevance to both.

As the Bologna and Milan Global Code of Judicial Ethics (2015) makes clear, judicial independence requires that Judges be independent of the legislative and executive branches of the government.[1] Clearly, international Judges must be entirely independent of both governments and international organizations in the performance of their judicial duties. They must be immune from legal actions, at least in the exercise of their judicial functions and they must be impartial and avoid any conduct which might give an appearance of partiality. They must not sit on any case where there is a reasonable suspicion or appearance of partiality and must treat the parties equally, with no partiality or prejudice, with no fear or favor. In international criminal tribunals, this requires treating equally the prosecution and the accused.

With regard to international Judges, the Code provides that Judges should not serve in any case in which they have previously served as agent, counsel or as a member of a court which has considered the subject matter in the dispute, or in a case where they have expressed an opinion in a manner that is likely to affect or may reasonably appear to affect their independence or impartiality.

In the Advisory Opinion on the *Legal Consequences of the Construction of a Wall in the Occupied Palestinian Territory* before the International Court of

1 *See* Bologna and Milan Global Code of Judicial Ethics, 2. Judicial Independence.

Standing Up For Justice. Theodor Meron, Oxford University Press (2021). © Theodor Meron.
DOI: 10.1093/oso/9780198863434.003.0006

Justice (2004), Judge Nabil El-Araby, was criticized by some of his colleagues on the Bench for not recusing himself despite opinions about Palestine he had expressed in the past in a nonjudicial capacity and which were relevant to the question submitted to the Court.[2]

Another difficulty arises where a Judge previously and in a different case has expressed an opinion which may appear to show bias or partiality in a case in which he is sitting and where his recusal or disqualification has been requested. I will return to this matter in Chapter X in discussion of the Tribunals' case law.

Of course, persons typically elected or appointed to judicial positions will come to the court with formed views on many issues, with their own values, traditions, preferences and, yes, even biases. And the critical professional challenge they will face is the will and the ability to overcome their preconceived preferences and consider the case at issue dispassionately, objectively and fairly.

The Global Code is just one of many codes establishing national and international codes of judicial ethics. One of the better known ones is the Basic Principles on the Independence of the Judiciary adopted by the U.N. General Assembly (1985).[3] The Basic Principles deal, however, only with national judiciaries. They articulate provisions on the independence of the judiciary and its impartiality, on qualifications, selection and training, on conditions on service and tenure, professional secrecy and immunity, removal and discipline.

Of particular importance because of their operational and compulsory character are codes adopted by various tribunals respectively. They demonstrate that Judges should be held accountable, but that their accountability should be a matter of decision by Judges, not politicians, or governments. It is the judiciary that should control disciplinary procedures against Judges and not, at least in general, the appointing authority. Such procedures should include enlightened due process safeguards. One of the most recent codes is the Code of Professional Conduct for the Judges of the Mechanism,[4]

2. *See* ICJ Advisory Opinion on the Legal Consequences of the Construction of a Wall in the Occupied Palestinian Territory, para. 8 (9 July 2004).
3. *See* Basic Principles on the Independence of the Judiciary, adopted by the Seventh United Nations Congress on the Prevention of Crimes and the Treatment of Offenders held at Milan from 26 August to 6 September 1985. The Principles were endorsed by U.N. General Assembly Resolutions 40/32 of 29 November 1985 and 40/146 of 13 December 1985.
4. http://www.irmct.org/sites/default/files/documents/180409-judges-code-of-conduct-mict-14.pdf.

adopted by the International Residual Mechanism for Criminal Tribunals (9 April 2018). In its present, revised form, it contains both ethical rules of conduct and disciplinary provisions in the case of serious violations. If two-thirds of the Judges are of the opinion that a complaint against a Judge is well founded and is of sufficient severity to suggest that the removal of a Judge is warranted, the matter would be reported to the U.N. Secretary-General to request the removal of the Judge concerned.[5]

The Code provides that Judges shall not engage in any activity which may affect confidence in their independence and that they must be independent of all external authority or influence. Judges must respect secrecy of deliberations and perform their functions efficiently, fairly and with reasonable promptness. They may not comment on pending cases, be disrespectful of the views of other Judges or express views which might undermine the standing and integrity of the Mechanism.

Why Judicial Independence Matters

Judicial independence[6] is crucial for the rule of law. Most obviously, when Judges are independent from political or other pressures, they will resolve the disputes brought to them fairly, with an eye to the guiding legal principles and without any undue influence. This will solidify public respect for the courts, and lead people to turn to the courts more often for the settlement of their disputes.

The ability to resolve disputes fairly has a wider social consequence: it is essential for a stable economy and polity. The community needs to know that there is an impartial arbiter who will administer the rules of the game and that their expectations based on existing laws and regulations will be honored. Independent Judges play a critical role in this regard. Judges, when they resolve disputes, explain and clarify the existing laws and regulations. When Judges are independent and behave in a rule-based way, their explanations have a certain predictability, because they are based on existing laws, on the prior judicial precedent and on logic. This predictability allows political, military and economic actors to plan their behavior

5. *See* IRMCT Code of Professional Conduct for the Judges of the Mechanism, Art. 14, para. 3.
6. *See* Theodor Meron, Editorial Comment *Judicial Independence and Impartiality in International Criminal Tribunals* 99 AM. J. INT'L L. 359 (2005).

accordingly. This contributes to the political stability and economic prosperity of a society.

Judicial independence is also necessary to effectively protect individual rights, which is the bedrock of any free society. These rights may be enshrined in the country's constitution or laws, but there must exist an authority, such as the courts, which can review—independently and impartially—a citizen's complaint and, if necessary, order that his or her improperly infringed rights be vindicated. To do so effectively, Judges must be assured that, irrespective of their ruling, there will be no unpleasant repercussions on them in terms of salary diminution or threats of dismissal, or adverse effects on career prospects.

Finally, the government is often a party to a lawsuit. One of the most fundamental principles of the rule of law is that no one should be the Judge of his or her own case. There must therefore exist an independent entity, such as the courts, which has the power to determine when the government has violated the legal constraints upon it.

This conclusion has implications not only for the protection of individual rights, but also for the maintenance of the separation of powers. In a system with competing authorities—be they the Executive and the legislature, or the national government and the regional governments—there are bound to be frictions and even outright conflicts. Some of these frictions can, and often will, resolve themselves through political mechanisms. It is unrealistic, however, to expect that all of these conflicts will resolve themselves in this manner. Reliance on political mechanisms alone is potentially dangerous. While some conflicts may be easily resolved through the legislative process, through elections or through other political means, some conflicts may polarize society and produce either an intractable stalemate or a bitterly divisive polity. The existence of a neutral, respected and independent arbiter, such as the courts, provides an alternative way of resolving political and social disputes.

Ensuring an Independent Judiciary

What, then, is necessary to ensure an independent judiciary? There are several relevant indicators. In a well-known U.K. case, *Kearney v. Her Majesty's Advocate*, the complaint alleged that a temporary Judge was not independent, having regard to the manner of his appointment, the term of office, the existence of guarantees against outside pressure and consideration of the question whether the Judge presented the appearance of independence.[7] The Human Rights Committee established under the ICCPR, similarly, but in more detail, stated in General Comment No. 32[8] that the requirement of independence refers to the procedure and qualifications for the appointment of Judges, guarantees relating to their security of tenure until a mandatory retirement age or expiry of their term of office, the conditions governing promotion, transfer, suspension and cessation of their functions and the actual independence of the judiciary from political interference by the Executive branch or the legislature.

A short term of office is not, per se, inconsistent with judicial independence, but may be problematic when it is renewable at the discretion of the executive.

The European Charter on the Statute for Judges (Strasbourg 1998)[9] provides that decisions pertaining to the selection, recruitment, appointment, career or termination of Judges can only be made by an authority independent of the Executive and the legislature and of which at least one-half are Judges elected by their peers.[10] Opinion No. 1 of the Consultative Council of European Judges (2001) states that when a full-time judicial appointment is for a limited period, a decision on reappointment must be made objectively on merit and without taking into account political considerations.[11] The Opinion emphasizes that the guarantee of tenure until a mandatory retirement age or the expiry of a fixed term of office is a fundamental tenet of judicial independence. Sanctions against a Judge for dereliction of duties may only be decided by an authority composed of at least one-half of elected Judges.

The European Court of Human Rights has a rich jurisprudence supporting the principle of judicial independence.

While there are many necessary elements of judicial independence, as indicated earlier, I would suggest that among the most crucial are the

7. [2006] UKPC D1.

8. *See* General Comment no. 32, Art. 14: Right to equality before courts and tribunals and to a fair trial, III. Fair and public hearing by a competent, independent and impartial tribunal, Human Rights Committee, Ninetieth Session (9–27 July 2007).

9. https://rm.coe.int/16807473ef.

10. *See* European Charter on the Statute for Judges, I. General Principles, para. 1.3.

11. *See* Opinion 1 of the Consultative Council of European Judges, Tenure—period of appointment, para. 52, ii.

public's respect for the courts, the Judge's own self perception as an independent and impartial arbiter, the judicial process's transparent nature and the provision of reasoned judicial decisions.

These factors are closely related, for if the courts are viewed as impartial they will be respected; and a court which enjoys public respect will find it easier to display independent judgement and confront, if necessary, powerful institutions and interests.

Judicial Selection

Taking the example of the United States, does the involvement of the U.S. President and the Senate in the selection and appointment of Judges endanger the principle of the separation of powers, and thereby the independence of the judiciary? A somewhat analogous question is often asked with respect to Judges who are selected to sit on international courts. In the case of ad hoc Tribunals, the Judges are nominated by Member States of the U.N. and are then elected by the U.N. General Assembly; in the case of the ICJ, Judges must be elected by both the General Assembly and the Security Council; for the ICC and the European Court of Human Rights, Judges are elected by the Assembly of State Parties for nine-year terms which are not renewable.

Unlike federal Judges in the United States, Judges in the ad hoc Tribunals do not hold tenure for life or, unlike in England, until a mandatory retirement age. Instead, they are elected for a specified term, in ad hoc Tribunals four years which are renewable (in the Mechanism they are now typically extended by the U.N. Security Council for two-year periods), in the case of the ICJ Judges, nine years with the possibility of reelection, for the ICC nine years without the possibility of reelection.

It is possible that overt campaigning by Judges may create a perception of inappropriate politicization, not to mention distraction from the work at hand. I have thought at times that a ban on direct electioneering by Judges might well be attractive. It would certainly raise some practical problems—as campaigning by Judges might simply be replaced by proxy campaigns, for example—but, in principle at least, keeping Judges at one remove from the political process might be beneficial both for the perceived impartiality of the international court, and for the efficiency and effectiveness of individual Judges.

There is often a concern expressed that a Judge on an international court who focuses on the prospects of renomination by his or her government, or reelection, may decide cases in such a way as not to antagonize powerful Member States of the U.N. and, especially, their own State. Let me first underscore that I believe that any conscientious Judge sitting on an international court will decide cases before them only in accordance with the law and their judicial conscience. But the possibility of public perception that a Judge may be biased because of extrajudicial considerations—particularly if those considerations appear self-serving—counsels strongly for international Judges to be scrupulously impartial in their decision-making. This is especially so when a Judge on an international court makes a ruling or writes an opinion favorable to his or her own Member State or a Member State that strongly supports that Judge's candidacy. I am not suggesting, of course, that a Judge should alter his or her view as to the legal outcome in such a case, I only suggest the importance of being sensitive to the possibility of the public perception of bias.

To address the potential conflict of interests posed by government selection of Judges, I would suggest exploring policy solutions that make Judges more independent from the electors. I am on record as preferring longer, single, nonrenewable terms for Judges at international tribunals. Even with regard to the first selection, I would prefer that a nonpolitical committee of experts vets Judges—perhaps in conjunction with subsequent legislative, General Assembly, Security Council or Executive approval—for international courts. Such an approach removes direct threats to judicial independence while still allowing Judges and potential Judges to be held accountable for their performance. The ICC took some steps in this direction.[12]

Governments have a critical responsibility to nominate for international judgeships the most highly qualified candidates. A good practice is for a government to submit two or even more candidates, as is already the practice with regard to World Trade Organization (WTO) panels and the European Court of Human Rights. It is unfortunate that during the political process in the institution electing the Judges, governments often resort to bargaining or the trading of votes, which is not commensurate with the high standards of behavior that should instruct such voting.

12. *See* International Criminal Court, Assembly of States Parties, Advisory Committee on nomination of Judges, Part III National nomination and selection procedures.

Should Judges Respond to Outside Criticism?

The Judges of international courts, as a rule, do not explain their rulings in press interviews, and do not respond directly to public criticism or to allegations of partiality in the media. Instead, international Judges put their efforts into producing reasoned and persuasive opinions, which explain, in language understandable both to lawyers and to the general public, the reasons why the court reached a particular outcome. If an opinion is persuasive and clearly explains why the decision was a correct one in terms of law and evidence, it will resonate as such with the public, and go a long way to counter possible allegations of bias.

Whether Judges should reply to criticism of their judicial work continues to be controversial. There is a strong temptation to reply to extreme, hostile criticism, particularly when it is uninformed and politically inspired. I have myself, as President of the Tribunal or as a Presiding Judge of the Appeal Chamber, been subjected to severe criticism, especially in cases of reversal of convictions on appeal. My policy has always been reticence and stoic silence, thus adhering to the convention that Judges do not extrajudicially discuss individual cases. There is always the risk that responding to criticism would trigger public conflicts between Judges, which, as the Global Code warned, may bring the judiciary into disrepute and diminish the authority of a court. In a public discussion between a Judge and the media, the latter will always have control and the last word. Thus, both for principle and pragmatic reasons, I would not advise Judges to engage in public responses to criticism, however unjustified.

Codes of judicial conduct advocate such restraint. The American Bar Association's Code of Judicial Conduct, Rule 2.10 (A) (2020)[13] provides that a Judge shall not make any public statement that might reasonably be expected to affect the outcome or impair the fairness of a matter pending or impending in any court, or make any public statement that might substantially interfere with a fair trial or hearing.

The Code of Conduct for United States Judges (2019), Canon 3(A)(6)[14] provides that a Judge shall not make any public comment on the merits

13. https://www.americanbar.org/groups/professional_responsibility/publications/model_code_of_judicial_conduct/model_code_of_judicial_conduct_canon_2/rule2_10judicial-statementsonpendingandimpendingcases/.
14. https://www.uscourts.gov/judges-judgeships/code-conduct-united-states-judges#d.

of a matter pending or impending in any court. These prohibitions on public comment on the merits do not extend to public statements made in the course of the Judge's official duties, to explanations of court procedures or to scholarly presentations made for purposes of legal education.

The French *Recueil des obligations déontologiques des magistrats*, Chapter VIII(6) (2019)[15] provides that magistrates may not comment upon or add to their own decisions, which by their reasoning should be self-explanatory.

The U.K. Guide to Judicial Conduct (2019)[16] is particularly detailed. It proclaims that all Judges should be aware that by long convention they should not comment publicly on the merits of individual cases: "All Judges should exercise their freedom to talk to the media with caution. Judges should refrain from answering public criticism of a judgement or a decision, whether from the bench or otherwise."

Judges should be aware that participation in public debate on any topic may entail the risk of undermining public perception in the impartiality of the judiciary whether or not a Judge's comments would lead to recusal from a particular case. This risk arises in part because the Judge will not have control over the terms of the debate or the interpretation given to his or her comments. The risk of expressing views that might be considered as bias or prejudgement in future cases before the Judge is a particular factor to be considered.

Finally, the ICC Code of Judicial Ethics (2005), Article 9(2) and the Code of Professional Conduct for the Judges of the Mechanism provide that Judges shall not comment on pending cases, shall not disrespect the views of other Judges and shall avoid expressing views which may undermine the standing and integrity of their institutions.

Judicial Assignments and Court Presidents

As the Consultative Council of European Judges stated in its Opinion (2016)[17] on the Role of Court Presidents, the principal roles of Court Presidents are to ensure the effective functioning of the courts, to represent

15. https://www.cours-appel.justice.fr.
16. https://www.judiciary.uk/publications/guide-to-judicial-conduct/.
17. https://rm.coe.int/opinion-no-19-on-the-role-of-court-presidents/16806dc2c4, at 1.

the courts and to preside over their judicial work. And they must protect the independence and the impartiality of courts and individual Judges.

The Presidents of the courts must thus protect the courts and their Judges from both external and internal attempts to encroach on their judicial independence. As the 2016 Opinion No. 19 of the Consultative Council of European Judges states, judicial independence requires not only freedom from external encroachment but also internal judicial independence.[18] Thus Presidents must refrain from any directives or pressure on Judges in the context of adjudicating cases.

A subtler concern about influence presents itself in the power of Presidents of ad hoc Tribunals over the make-up of judicial panels. In these Tribunals, the Presidents assign the full panel of Judges for both trials and appeal proceedings. So when a defendant is brought before the Tribunal, it is up to the President to determine which three Judges will decide the defendant's fate at the trial level. Similarly, when a verdict has been entered at the trial level and the defendant or Prosecutor files an appeal or appeals, the President is responsible for naming the Bench of five Appeals Judges who will decide the appeal. It is worth noting that the ICC has a similar but not identical system of panel appointments, in which the ICC presidency selects the Judges that make up both the Pre-Trial Chambers and the Trial Chambers themselves.

How much discretion does this add up to in practice? In terms of raw numbers, the structure of the ad hoc Tribunals leaves much less leeway at the appeals level. But at the trial level, the leeway is much broader: the President appoints trial panels of three Judges from among a larger pool of Judges.

The self-regulating culture of the ad hoc Tribunals, constrains the President's discretion to some extent, since transparent workload surveys show how the work is allocated among Judges. The existence of preexisting criteria is of importance.

Cases should also not be withdrawn from a Judge without compelling reasons, or without the Judge's consent. There is also an essentially political check on the President's activities since, although elected for a fixed term, in many ways he or she serves as President only at the sufferance of the other Judges of the Tribunal. Under this system, the Tribunal must rely on

18. *See* Consultative Council of European Judges Opinion (2016) (n. 17), B. Relations within the court: independence of judges, para. 13.

the conscientious goodwill of the President, as monitored by his or her colleagues, to avoid inappropriate ideological control over panel memberships. But ultimately the integrity of the system rests on the integrity of all Judges, such that the composition of the Bench should have no predictable effect on the judicial result. In some ways, this last reflection holds true for judicial impartiality more generally: the best defense of that principle lies in the culture of judicial independence and integrity that must be fostered at the Tribunals and in the international judiciary throughout the world.

As another example of judicial selection, the Presidents of the ICTY and the ICTR actually controlled the permanent make-up of the Appeals Chamber itself—the body that had the final say on the law that governed both Tribunals. The mechanics of this require some explanation. The two Tribunals actually shared a single seven-Judge Appeals Chamber, of which only one member was determined by the Statute: the ICTY President. So there were six Judges left. Four of them were named by the ICTY President, and two of them by the ICTR President after both Presidents have consulted with the other Judges of their Tribunal. In theory, then, the ICTY President could have stacked the decks in the Appeals Chamber to lock in ideological uniformity. As evidenced by the dissents and vigorous debates in the Appeals Chamber, this did not seem to have happened because of the prevailing culture of judicial integrity, but it is nonetheless a structural element that, in theory, could be seen to have undercut judicial independence.

In my own practice, to avoid appearance of any bias or favoritism, I would assign cases to the Judges on the taxi-stand principle, i.e. next in line. Moreover, I would expect the staff to advise me which Judge was next in line and would routinely follow their recommendations.

The ICTR President's power in that regard was even more striking, since the Rwanda Tribunal's Statute was interpreted to allow midterm transfers. So, for example, part-way through a judicial term, the ICTR President could remove one of his or her appointees from the Appeals Chamber and replace that Judge with a Judge from the ICTR Trial Chamber. Would that implicate judicial independence? It depends. Periodic replacements shifting Judges between the Trial Chamber and the Appeals Chamber on a preset schedule strike me as acceptable from the perspective of judicial independence. Random replacements, on the other hand, could be problematic. The appropriateness of an exercise of that power also depends on the motives of the President. It would clearly be inappropriate if the President shifted Judges from one Chamber to another in order to stifle dissent. I am confident that shifting for such reasons never occurred. But if the President shifted Judges with an eye to balancing the make-up of the Appeals Chamber (in terms of the geographical distribution, for example, or in terms of the different experience or the legal system of the Judges), then it would have presented less of a problem.

Judicial Bias and Recusal

There is another form of possible bias that may also endanger the public perception of impartiality of the judiciary. It is the danger of a preconceived notion in favor of a particular outcome. Judges are expected to approach any case brought before them with an open mind, with the willingness to listen to the parties' arguments and with the intention to decide the case only after they have heard from all the parties and have reviewed the facts of the case and the applicable law. This open-mindedness is crucial to solidifying public respect for the courts. It indicates to every litigant that he or she will have a fair day in court because the Judges are willing to listen to a litigant's arguments and should they have merit, hold for him or her.

Judges are not empty vessels that the litigants fill with content. Judges are appointed, at least in the international courts and in many countries, such as the United States and the United Kingdom, from among prominent members of the legal profession. At some point in their judicial career, they could be called upon to decide cases raising issues with which they have dealt as practicing lawyers or civil servants, or on which they have written as academics. These situations raise the question of whether a Judge should recuse themself, on the basis either that the Judge cannot be impartial or that their impartiality can be questioned by a reasonable observer.

These are two related, but separate, considerations. In the first scenario, if a Judge concludes that he or she cannot be impartial because they have already formed an irreversible opinion on the issue, they must, of course, recuse themselves. In this situation, they are unable to act as a Judge: weighing competing legal positions and assessing the merits of each party's case.

The second scenario is more complicated. There, a Judge actually concludes that he or she can act impartially in the case, but that others may reasonably perceive them as partial. In such a situation, a Judge recuses themself not because they are unable to exercise the judicial function, but in order to preserve the integrity of the court and the rule of law. Lord Hewart, famously remarked in *Ex parte McCarthy*, that: "Justice must not only be done, but should manifestly and undoubtedly be seen to be done."[19] There are situations where the reputation of the judiciary may be compromised if there is even an appearance of bias, and in these situations caution and concern for the reputation of the court often counsel that a Judge recuses themself from deciding that particular case.

What are such situations? The easiest one is where a Judge may have a financial or material stake in the outcome of the decision. Even though that personal interest may be unimportant to the Judge, the public may justly question the impartiality of a Judge who might profit from their decision.

Another situation is where a Judge has a strong personal connection to one of the parties. If this connection is such that it may indicate to an outside observer that a Judge is likely to be swayed by the personal bond, the Judge should recuse themself. Care must be taken, however, that Judges do not feel forced to step aside from deciding cases only because they are either acquainted with some of the litigants or connected to them in some way, but the connection is not so strong as to call into question their ability to render an impartial judgement.

A third, and perhaps the most difficult, question is whether a Judge should recuse themself if the Judge has previously publicly expressed an opinion that can be viewed as prejudging the case now before them. The ICTY faced this issue in *Furundžija*, where the defendant on appeal sought the disqualification of the Presiding Trial Judge (and the *vacatur* of the judgement in which that Judge participated) because the Judge was previously a member of the U.N. Commission on the Status of Women, which investigated allegations of mass and systematic rape in the former Yugoslavia and called for their prosecution by the ICTY.[20] The defendant, who had been convicted of committing rape as a war crime, argued that having that Judge preside over his trial created an appearance of partiality because a reasonable observer could have concluded that the Judge used the trial and the judgement to promote the legal and political agenda of the Commission on the Status of Women that she had helped to create.

The ICTY Appeals Chamber rejected the defendant's claim, and elaborated what I believe is a workable rule for deciding when a Judge should

19. *R v. Sussex Justices, ex parte McCarthy* [1924] 1 KB 256, 259.
20. *Prosecutor v. Anto Furundžija,* Judgement, ICTY Appeals Chamber, Case no. IT-95-17/1-A (21 July 2000).

disqualify themself. The Chamber explained that a Judge is not impartial and should recuse themself if there is a showing of actual bias. It stated that a Judge should recuse themself also if there is an unacceptable appearance of bias. This appearance can be manifested in two ways. First, a Judge should recuse themself if the Judge "is a party to the case, or has a financial or proprietary interest in the outcome of a case, or if the Judge's decision will lead to the promotion of a cause in which he or she is involved, together with one of the parties." Second, a Judge should disqualify themself if the circumstances would lead a reasonable observer, properly informed, to reasonably apprehend bias.

This rule was followed by another international court, the Special Court for Sierra Leone, which was faced with a request from the defense to disqualify the Court's President because, in a book he had previously published he had written that the armed organization to which the defendants belonged was guilty of crimes against humanity. The President of the Sierra Leone Court refused to disqualify himself, but his colleagues disagreed and ordered his recusal.[21] They concluded that a reasonable bystander could, reading the passages in question, have a legitimate reason to fear that the Judge who wrote them lacked impartiality. Notably, the recused Judge accepted the decision and its rationale. He stated that while he held no preconceived views on the guilt or innocence of the defendants, his earlier criticisms of the organization to which they belonged could have given rise to a perception that he could not judge them with an open mind.

Also worth mentioning in the recusal context is one interesting and, generally speaking, rare issue that presented itself in the ICTY *Čelebići* case (so named because of the location where the crimes at issue were committed). Judge Odio Benito, who was on the trial panel in *Čelebići*, was elected as the Second Vice-President of Costa Rica partway through the trial, but continued to serve on the trial panel. On appeal in *Čelebići*, the defendants argued that she should not have continued to sit on the trial panel after her election as Second Vice-President.[22] Most relevantly for present purposes,

21. *Prosecutor v. Issa Hassan Sesay*, Decision on Defence Motion Seeking the Disqualification of Justice Robertson from the Appeals Chamber, SCSL Appeals Chamber, Case no. SCSL-2004-15-AR15 (13 Mar. 2004).

22. *Prosecutor v. Zejnil Delalić et al.*, Judgement, ICTY Appeals Chamber, Case no. IT-96-21-A (20 Feb. 2001). Another case in point is that of ICC Judge Kuniko Ozaki, of Japan, who was appointed as Japan's Ambassador to Estonia. She then requested to transfer to part-time status in the ICC and continued to hear cases. See Kevin John Heller, *Judge Ozaki must Resign or*

they contended that her position in domestic government meant that she no longer possessed the necessary judicial independence required by international law.

In its ruling, the Appeals Chamber appeared to acknowledge that active service as a member of a national executive branch might be incompatible with service in the ICTY. In the circumstances of Judge Odio Benito's case, however, the Appeals Chamber noted that she had declined to assume any vice-presidential functions until completing her duties as a member of the trial panel in *Čelebići*. Had she been serving in an active capacity as Second Vice-President while still actively serving on the *Čelebići* Bench, presumably the Appeals Chamber would have been much more likely to find an appearance of impropriety. In such a case, her dual loyalties—as a political representative of her nation and a member of its political hierarchy, on the one hand, and as an impartial Judge whose positions on the case before her had nothing to do with her nationality, on the other—might well have appeared to be a conflict of interests to a reasonable observer.

A lesson that can be derived from these cases is that while the Judge whose impartiality is challenged should be the first one to assess whether to recuse themself, there may also be situations where, should the Judge refuse to stand aside, the other members of the court may revisit the question and rule on whether it would be proper for that Judge to continue sitting on that case. Care must be taken to ensure that such a decision is taken in the proper spirit of collegiality and that there should not be an abuse of claims of disqualification and requests for recusal.

The case law on disqualifications will be further discussed in Chapter X but I would like to give here an example of a claim which the ICTY Bureau (the Bureau which no longer exists, comprised the President, the Vice-President and the Presiding Judges of the several Chambers), which was then competent to deal with such issues, considered "frivolous and abuse of process." This was the decision of 10 June 2003, on application submitted by Šešelj requesting the disqualification of Judges Schomburg, Mumba and Agius (Case no. IT-03-67-PT). The bases for the claims were Judge Schomburg's German nationality and Germany's membership in NATO, the Catholic religion of Judges Mumba and Agius, the long history of conflict between Serbia and Germany and the long history of conflict

be Removed, Opinio Juris, 29 March 2019. Following criticism of violating the ICC Code of Ethics, she resigned from the ambassadorship and continued as an ICC Judge.

between the Serbian Orthodox Church and the Catholic Church. The Bureau ruled that nationalities and religions of Judges are irrelevant to their ability to hear the cases before them impartially.

Requests for disqualification based on perceived appearance of bias are likely to recur in international tribunals. The Judges on these tribunals come from academic backgrounds or from careers in other sectors of public life, legal practice, the judiciary or the government, and they have usually been chosen precisely because of their expertise in international or criminal law, sometimes evidenced by a lengthy publication trail. The fact that Judges will have spoken or written on some of the issues that come before them in their role as Judges is, thus, to be expected. Usually, when previous writings have not been with reference to specific individuals or specific defendants, I would think that a Judge's prior analysis of a legal problem in an academic context should not be an issue worthy of recusal—certainly not where the Judge has the openness of mind to be willing to reconsider his or her prior position. But drawing lines may be somewhat difficult: when does an expression of a purely academic view about a legal issue in international law raise an appearance of partiality?

The Tribunals strove to determine the best way to resolve such questions where they arose after a Judge whose recusal or disqualification had been requested, declined to step down of their own accord. Following the disqualification of three Judges in the *Mladić* appeal by a single Judge whose controversial decision was not subject to appeal, the Mechanism adopted these revised rules:

Rule 18. Disqualification of Judges (Amended 18 December 2019)

(A) A Judge may not sit in any case in which the Judge has a personal interest or concerning which the Judge has or has had any association which might affect his impartiality. The Judge shall in such circumstance withdraw, and the President shall assign another Judge to the case.

(B) (i) Any Party may apply to the President for the disqualification and withdrawal of a Judge from a proceeding upon the above grounds. The President shall confer with the Judge in question.

(ii) The President shall appoint a three-Judge panel to decide the application. If the decision is to uphold the application, the President shall assign another Judge to sit in the place of the Judge in question.

(iii) The decision of the panel of three Judges shall not be subject to interlocutory appeal.

(iv) If the Judge in question is the President, the responsibility of the President in accordance with this paragraph shall be assumed by the Judge most senior who is able to act and who is not the object of the application, or a related application for disqualification or withdrawal.

(C) The ICTY or the ICTR Judge who has reviewed an indictment against an accused, or the Single Judge who reviews an indictment, shall not be disqualified from sitting as a member of the Trial Chamber or as a Single Judge for the trial of the accused.

(D) No Judge shall sit on any appeal in a case in which that Judge sat in first instance.

Institutional Design and Management

This brings me to another point I would like to make. To maintain the judiciary's reputation for impartiality, it must have a variety of internal mechanisms to either filter out potential bias or to correct it before the result becomes final. One such mechanism is multi-Judge panels. In the ad hoc Tribunals, all trials are conducted by a Bench of three Judges and all appeals by a Bench of five. A majority of those Judges must agree on the outcome and the rationale. This prevents a single member who may be biased from influencing the result. The Judges, moreover, discuss the case among themselves prior to agreeing on a decision, and that discussion helps to correct any latent biases, because a Judge is confronted with, and has to respond to, the arguments of his or her colleagues. I discuss deliberations of Judges in Chapter VII.

Another mechanism is appellate review. In the international criminal tribunals, the governing instruments allow appeals, although with some limitations. Appellate review ensures that decisions of lower courts are accurate and uniform, and that injustice is not committed. Allegations of bias by Trial Judges can be raised earlier or at this stage. Appellate review also enhances judicial independence in another way: by correcting the judicial error internally, it reduces the need for other institutions to step in and deal with abuses or mistakes within the court system. The rules also allow, on certain conditions, interlocutory appeals (further discussed in Chapter VII). Interlocutory appeals challenging jurisdiction can be made as a matter of right. Most interlocutory appeals require, however, certification by the Trial Chamber. Such certifications should be granted if they involve an issue which would significantly affect the fair and expeditious conduct of the proceedings or the outcome of the trial, and on which an immediate resolution by the Appeals Chamber may materially advance the proceedings.

The Presidency and the Prosecution

I have already said that in international criminal tribunals prosecution and defense must be treated equally, applying, as far as possible, the principle of equality of arms. Of course, in these tribunals the prosecution is entirely independent. Under Article 14(2) of the Statute of the Mechanism adopted by the Security Council on 22 December 2010 (Resolution 1966), the Prosecutor, responsible for investigation and prosecution, "shall act independently as a separate organ of the Mechanism. He or she shall not seek or receive instructions from any government or from any other source." In my view, the Prosecutor is an officer of the court and must behave accordingly and be guided by the law, not by politics. In civil law jurisdictions, Judges and Prosecutors are often interchangeable; typically they both belong and are in many ways officials of the ministry of justice and are not subject to the strict common law conventions establishing where it is inappropriate for a Judge to have any *ex parte* contacts or dealings with the Prosecutor. *Inter partes* contacts in which the defence participates are allowed in the courtroom or in a Judge's chambers. In international criminal tribunals the Judges or the chambers are one of three principal organs, the Prosecution and the Registry being the other two organs, with the President being the head of the institution. The organs share a common interest in ensuring the implementation of the mandate of the court, in the efficient disposal of cases and adequate supply of resources from the international community. To ensure the necessary coordination, some contacts between the President and the Prosecutor are necessary as in the Coordination Council, especially for discussion of administrative matters (the Registrar is also a member of the Coordination Council). However, it is clearly inappropriate for the President and the Prosecutor to discuss any judicial matters or any cases before the Tribunal without the presence of the defence, as this could give rise to apprehension or the appearance of bias on the President's part.

The President's role as head of the institution presents other problems. The President is an Appeals Judge and the Presiding Judge of the Appeals Chambers. He or she has overseeing authority of the Registry. But as the head of the institution he or she also has a public, non-judicial role representing the Tribunal/Mechanism in the Security Council, the General Assembly, before the U.N. Secretary-General and more generally before the international community. This inevitably involves them in some political and diplomatic functions, but these must not clash with their judicial functions. In their representative role, the President must explain the role of the Tribunal, and try to ensure maximum political and financial support for the institution. The President must also protect the institution, as a whole, from inappropriate intervention by political organs. An example would be useful here. Following my statement to the Security Council on 9 October 2003, I was asked by the representative of the United Kingdom to describe the appropriate guidance which the Council could give the Prosecutor for the preparation of additional indictments. Here is what I answered:

> It is entirely appropriate for the Security Council to define such broad goals and directives. I must say that it would not be appropriate for the Council to go into great detail in such directives, because such directives should not encroach upon on the prosecutorial independence of the Prosecutor. In other words, broad guidelines, yes; specific guidelines that encroach on her prosecutorial independence, no.[23]

The President has additional roles, such as supervising the Registry and management, but they are not relevant to the present discussion.

Communicating with the Public

Let me speak briefly about the courts' relationship with the public. As the courts decide an increasing number of important issues in public life, they become more visible in the eyes of the public and the media. When the courts render a decision of which certain sections of the government or society disapprove, these latter often express their criticism publicly. Of course, the right to publicly express disagreement with a judicial decision is an integral element of a free society and a free press. Courts are public institutions and should not be immune from criticism. Indeed, there are occasions when such criticism is beneficial. Constructive criticism facilitates self-examination and self-improvement of the judiciary.

23. U.N. Doc. S/PV.4838, at 30 (2003).

In addition, in the instances where a judicial decision interpreting a particular law or statute is being criticized, that criticism may motivate the competent authority to amend it as necessary. There are occasions, however, when criticism goes too far. This happens, for example, when criticism is motivated solely by the dislike of a particular result reached by a court, without adequate regard to the underlying reasoning or the supporting law, or when particular Judges are targeted for criticism for reasons unrelated to their professional performance. The Judges cannot give in to pressure, as this would be a violation of their judicial independence. The Judges are also, as I have already mentioned, limited in their means of responding to criticism.

There are certain things, however, that Judges can do to promote a better understanding on the part of the public of the work they do and, if necessary, defend the independence of the judiciary. One possibility is to recruit media and public affairs officers to the service of the courts. As Judges have to exercise restraint and discretion. it is preferable that in cases where a reaction from the judiciary is really necessary, it should come from the President of the Court (where the President is not the target of the criticism), or collectively from a Court, or from councils of judiciary or bar associations.

The ad hoc Tribunals have a special public affairs office which provides the media with briefings about the work of the Tribunal and its Judges, answers questions from journalists and disseminates a variety of information both to the press and to any interested researcher and also deals with outreach activities. The Tribunals' public affairs officers do not interpret judicial decisions to the media. But what they do is to help journalists—who often work under strict deadlines—to report important court decisions accurately. The public, thus, becomes better informed and hopefully more appreciative about courts.

Rules and Obstructive Behavior of Defendants

I have mentioned official judicial rules codes. While important and helpful, I feel that they may be inadequate in certain extraordinary situations, such as the trial of uncooperative defendants—especially those who are self-represented. This latter issue was particularly difficult in the context of international criminal tribunals such as the ICTY, where certain defendants refused to recognize the legitimacy of the Tribunals and felt they had nothing to gain from cooperating with the Tribunals' procedures. In the trial of former President Slobodan Milošević, for example, ICTY Judges were forced to engage with a self-represented defendant who explicitly embraced obstructive behavior, ignoring courtroom rules and deadlines while harassing witnesses, Judges, and others in the courtroom.

In cases like that of Slobodan Milošević, where rules fail, the Judges' demeanor and intelligence become essential to guaranteeing that a trial resembles neither a circus nor a kangaroo court. The Judges must ensure that they remain in control of the courtroom while avoiding offering any impression that they are giving in to anger at personal insults or frustration at disruptive behavior. Achieving that balanced approach is challenging, but necessary to preserve the sense that a trial is proceeding in an impartial and appropriate manner.

In all courts, Judges are sometimes accused of favoritism or prejudice toward one party or another. In international criminal tribunals, where the crimes at issue are typically committed in an inter-ethnic context, such accusations are routine. Judges must exercise special caution to remain fair but, at the end of the day, they must understand that being subjected to even the harshest criticism is part of their job description.

The Saga of the Turkish Judge Akay

There is nothing new with States trying to exert pressure on international courts and tribunals. I was often a target, for example, of harsh *ad hominem* attacks by the Government of Rwanda, Rwandan NGOs and media because, following the normal and time-honored practice of the Presidents who preceded me, I considered for early release persons who had served two-thirds or three-quarters of their sentences. The case of Judge Akay was different in that it involved the arrest, detention, and criminal conviction of a Judge of the Mechanism whose full diplomatic immunity was formally asserted by the Legal Counsel of the U.N. Given its importance, I will now discuss this case in some detail.

By letter dated 5 October 2016 I informed the U.N. Secretary-General that on or about 21 September 2016, Judge Aydin Sefa Akay, a Judge of the Mechanism and a member of the Appeals Bench in the case of *Prosecutor v. Augustin Ngirabatware* was detained by law enforcement officials of the Government of Turkey for allegations of conduct connected to the events of 15 July 2016 and directed against the constitutional order of Turkey.[24] His arrest and continued detention resulted in his being unable to perform his functions as a Judge of the Mechanism. Thus, he could neither attend the first in-person plenary of Judges at The Hague on 26–7 September 2016, nor continue his work on the *Ngirabatware* case. I requested the Security Council's prompt consideration of the matter so as to enable the Mechanism to complete its work in those proceedings. In discussions with members of the Council, and the Office of Legal Affairs, I explained that under Security Council Resolution 1966, which established the Mechanism, the concept of judicial independence envisaged not only Judges serving at The Hague and in Arusha, but also, and for the most part, Judges working remotely in their States of nationality. Indeed, the Mechanism Statute used the very same language pertaining to the Judges' diplomatic immunities that was used in the Statutes of the ICTR and the ICTY for Judges who worked at the seats of those institutions. It would be incongruous and against the intent of the Statute to grant functional immunity only to most of the Mechanism Judges who, in compliance with the wish of the Council, work remotely from their countries of nationality, in contrast to the few Judges who work at The Hague or in Arusha, and enjoy diplomatic privileges and immunities. I strongly urged that diplomatic immunity be asserted by the U.N. Secretariat for Judge Akay. Such immunity was asserted by the Legal Counsel in October 2016.

On 17 October, I addressed a formal note to the Ambassador of Turkey to the Netherlands noting that under Rule 23 of the Rules of Procedure and Evidence of the Mechanism, I, as President of the Mechanism, coordinated the work of the chambers and that the ongoing detention of Judge Akay had a deleterious effect upon the work of the Mechanism in the *Ngirabatware* case. I requested an authorization to visit Judge Akay for the purpose of discussing with him confidentially the situation and ascertaining his conditions of detention. The Ambassador did not respond. None of the subsequent communications to the embassy received answers or even acknowledgments.

A few days later, in the absence of a response from Turkey, I went public with a press conference in The Hague. I pointed out that the use of a judicial roster and the reliance on Judges working remotely—typically in

24. U.N. Doc. S/2016/841.

their countries of origin—represented innovations adopted by the Security Council enhancing the efficiency and cost-saving of international justice and thus making international justice more viable. When the U.N. Security Council established the Mechanism it decided that the Convention on the Privileges and Immunities of the U.N. should apply to the Mechanism's Judges. Under Article 29 of that Convention, the President and the Judges shall enjoy immunities when engaged in the business of the Mechanism, including immunity from arrest. From the moment that a Judge is assigned to a case or otherwise assigned to carry out functions for the Mechanism, he or she is engaged in the work of the Mechanism and must enjoy the immunities to which they are entitled. Without the assurance of those immunities, the Mechanism's integrity as a court and its feasibility as a new model of international criminal tribunal, as it was at that time, would be in question. Once more, I called upon the Government of Turkey to end Judge Akay's detention.

Given unofficial suggestions that replacing Judge Akay would be an appropriate means to reconstitute the Bench and resume the work on the *Ngirabatware* case, I wrote on 19 October to Ambassador Roselli of Uruguay, Chair of the Security Council Informal Working Group on International Tribunals, invoking Article 14(1) of the ICCPR, Article 2 of the Basic Principles on the Independence of the Judiciary (1985), and Article 2(1) of the Code of Professional Conduct for the Judges of the Mechanism (2015), and rejecting such a possibility:

> ... It has long been a foundational principle of systems of law in all parts of the world that protection of the ability of a Judge to fairly and impartially adjudicate a case according to law, independent of external pressure, is integral to the proper discharge of the judicial function.
>
> ... Through the principle of normative continuity recognized by the Appeals Chamber of the Mechanism, the principle likewise applies fully to the Mechanism and its own discharge of judicial functions. Indeed, the very structure of the Statute of the Mechanism, prescribing qualifications for Judges of the highest order and processes of election and appointment following closest scrutiny, further reinforces the conception of a strong, independent and effective judiciary of the Mechanism, wherever its judicial functions might be discharged.
>
> Given the fundamental importance of judicial independence, I do not, as President of the Mechanism, see it possible to reconcile full respect for that principle with any concession that the consequence of coercive action of domestic authorities taken against a Judge while engaged on the business of

> the Mechanism, with the effect of fully frustrating the performance of lawfully assigned judicial functions, could be the formal removal of a Judge from his duly assigned functions ... to seek to discharge a Judge in such circumstances from a case ... would be to pay lip service to the notion of judicial independence, run tantamount to giving credence within the legal system of the Mechanism to the acts of coercive restraint by the national authorities in question, and would render nugatory the protection afforded by Article 29 of the Statute ... such an outcome cannot have been the intent of the Members of the Security Council in adopting the Statute of the Mechanism in 2010.

I raised the Akay prosecution again in my address to the U.N. General Assembly on 9 November 1916. In that address I was able to inform the Assembly that the U.N. Office of the Legal Counsel had formally asserted the diplomatic immunity of Judge Akay and requested his immediate release from detention and the cessation of all legal proceedings against him. I emphasized that judicial independence was a cornerstone of the rule of law, and that it was long-standing and consistent practice to accord international Judges privileges and immunities in order to protect the independent discharge of their judicial functions.

On 8 November, I met with U.N. Secretary-General Ban Ki-moon and raised the problem of the continuing detention by Turkey of Judge Akay. And I did it again in the U.N. Security Council on 8 December. I repeated that even though some may have believed that the situation could have been resolved by replacing Judge Akay on the *Ngirabatware* case, that option was not open to me as a matter of law and justice. It was not possible to reconcile full respect for the fundamental principle of judicial independence with the removal of Judge Akay from the Bench to which he had been assigned.

On 17 January 2018, I convened a hearing with the representatives of the Prosecutor and Ngirabatware to consider a motion from the latter that an order be issued to Turkey, pursuant to Article 28 of the Statute, to cease its prosecution of Judge Akay so that he could resume his judicial functions as a member of the Bench on that case. The Prosecution expressed doubts whether such an order would be implemented and proposed, instead, principally, that I should proceed through invoking my administrative power, under Article 12 of the Statute and Rule 23(A) of the Rules of Procedure and Evidence to determine the composition of the Review Bench, remove Judge Akay from the *Ngirabatware* Bench and assign him instead to another judicial assignment in the Mechanism. I questioned whether a removal of a Judge from a Bench had ever been carried out without the consent of the Judge concerned. The Prosecutor could not recall any cases in which a Judge had been removed from a Bench without his consent. I asked the counsel for Ngirabatware to state his position on the Prosecutor's proposal. He answered that manipulating the assignment system to give Judge Akay a fictitious assignment would not be a solution, as he, being in jail, could not sit on any case. The proposal would not be fair to him. He added that replacing a Judge on a particular case and shifting him to some meaningless work struck at the very heart of judicial independence.

Following this hearing, I issued, on 31 January 2017, in response to the motion of *Ngirabatware* of 10 November 2016, an Order to Turkey to cease all legal proceedings against Judge Akay, and to release him from detention no later than 14 February 2017 so that he could resume his judicial functions in that case. I pointed out that it was self-evident that justice and the rule of law begin with an independent judiciary and that a guarantee of that independence is stated in Article 29 of the Statute which provides for full diplomatic immunity for Judges during the course of their assignments. Reassignment of Judge Akay to another case would similarly halt proceedings in that case and would impinge on judicial independence in allowing interference by a national authority in the conduct of a case. I made it clear that *Ngirabatware* supported this fundamental principle and opposed the replacement of Judge Akay.

By letter dated 9 March 2017 to the President of the Security Council, I informed the Council that on 6 March 2017 I had issued a decision on non-compliance by Turkey with the judicial Order of 31 January 2017, and with its obligations under Article 28 of the Statute. In my address to the Council of 7 June 2017, I reported on the continued detention of Judge Akay and called upon the Council to take such measures as were necessary to achieve a resolution of the situation, consistent with the Mechanism Statute and with the obligations incumbent on all States under Chapter VII of the U.N. Charter.

On 14 June 2017, Judge Akay was convicted by a Turkish criminal court of first instance on a single charge of being a member of a terrorist group, FETO, to imprisonment of seven years and six months and was provisionally released pending appeal. As elaborated in the Statement of the Mechanism of 15 June, his passport was confiscated and he was prohibited from departing Turkey. Upon his release from detention, I consulted Judge Akay as to whether he would be willing and able to continue on the *Ngirabatware* case and was assured by him that he was. Accordingly, in my fifth annual report to the Security Council of 1 August 2017, I reported that the review proceedings in the case of *Ngirabatware* had resumed in June 2017. In my report to the Council of 17 May 2018, I discussed the continuation of proceedings in the case.

In June 2018, all Mechanism Judges were up for reappointment. Invoking his conviction, Turkey objected to Judge Akay's reappointment by the U.N. Secretary-General on the ground that he no longer possessed the qualifications for appointment to the highest judicial office in Turkey. Qualifications for appointment to the highest judicial office of the Judge's country are required under Article 9(1) of the Statute of the Mechanism. The Legal Counsel consequently informed Judge Akay, by letter dated 8 June 2018, that it was not possible to consider him for reappointment as a Judge of the Mechanism. Following my letter to the Legal Counsel dated 15 June 2018 and his response dated 21 June 2018, I issued, on 3 July 2018, a "Statement of the President on the Non-Reappointment of Judge Akay" which read, in part, as follows:

> [T]he situation has raised serious questions as to whether the immunities to which Judges are entitled and the judicial independence that these immunities serve to protect can be effectively guaranteed for institutions such as the Mechanism where Judges typically work in the countries of their nationality. It is understood that the decision not to reappoint Judge Akay was based on information provided by the Government of Turkey to the UN Secretariat that Judge Akay no longer satisfies the qualifications for Judges identified in Article 9 of the Mechanism's Statute by virtue of his conviction. The President expressed his strong disappointment in this regard stating that "the acquiescence to the position advanced by the Government of Turkey represents a de facto acceptance of a State's action in contravention of the diplomatic immunity asserted by the United Nations, a dangerous precedent to set."

I further underscored that the potential for political or other inappropriate pressure by a government in these circumstances is unlimited, explaining that "there is a great difference between the statutory right of States to nominate their nationals for election and the far more indeterminate and potentially political and arbitrary possibilities of an extra-statutory and still vague procedure that allows States to advocate the removal or non-renewal of their national Judges or even, potentially, Judges of any nationality." I added: "If States are permitted to take action against a Judge in violation of the applicable international legal framework, judicial independence—a cornerstone principle of the rule of law—and the integrity of our court as such are fundamentally at risk, as is the overall project of international criminal justice."

Although I understand the pressure exerted by Turkey on the Office of Legal Affairs, had I been the Legal Counsel, I would have established a committee of respected jurists, national and international, to advise me on the course of action to follow, rather than deciding the matter *intra muros*, especially given the situation then prevailing with regard to the rule of law in Turkey. Thus, in my final address to the Security Council, on 11 December 2018,[25] I stated:

> At a time when the world is facing deeply troubling trends related to the undermining of independent judiciaries and the weakening of the rule of law, we, at the United Nations, simply cannot afford to be anything less than exemplary when it comes to our own handling of interference with judicial independence and actions undertaken in contravention of UN immunities. At the very least, it is imperative that, going forward, fair and transparent processes are developed to determine whether any proposed non-reappointment of a Judge accords with the fundamental principles of the rule of law.

25. https://news.un.org/en/story/2018/12/1028291 or for full address *see* https://www.irmct.org/sites/default/files/statements-and-speeches/181211-address-president-meron-uncs.pdf.

VII

Judicial Decision-Making and Deliberations

Decision-Making

The success of international criminal courts depends in no small part on the transparency of proceedings and reasoning of the Judgements. Transparency is essential to building public confidence in the fair administration of justice—and public confidence is, in turn, essential to building a broad understanding of and support for the Tribunals' work.

Transparency in court proceedings also serves as an important safeguard against judicial arbitrariness and helps to ensure not only the fairness of the proceedings but the independence and impartiality of the Bench. And transparency is perhaps particularly important in criminal courts like the Tribunals, where the issues at stake—including horrific alleged crimes and determinations of the guilt or innocence of an accused and consequently their liberty—make it all the more important to have clear and visible adherence to internationally recognized standards of due process.

This commitment to transparency in court proceedings is not absolute, however. It is limited by other factors, such as the importance of protecting witnesses and victims and the requirement that certain information be kept confidential, such as that provided conditionally by a State. And the courts' commitment to maximum transparency is also limited by the sacrosanct principle of the secrecy of judicial deliberations. The tension between transparency and secrecy is not unique to international tribunals. It also exists in national courts. The difference, however, is that in an international tribunal this tension between the transparency of process and the secrecy of

Standing Up For Justice. Theodor Meron, Oxford University Press (2021). © Theodor Meron.
DOI: 10.1093/oso/9780198863434.003.0007

judicial decision-making is negotiated through a powerful dialectic of differing legal cultures and systems of law, diverse nationalities and languages and a highly political context. This dialectic, in turn, plays an important role in shaping the Tribunals' decisions and procedures.

I will focus my remarks on the process of decision-making in the ICTY, ICTR and the Mechanism.[1]

In identifying questions of particular import to decision-making at the Tribunals, I would draw attention to four specific matters:

a) The uniqueness of the Tribunals and the impact of their special status on decision-making.
b) The diversity of decision-makers at the Tribunals—including Judges, the President and the Registrar.
c) The diverse backgrounds of the Tribunals' Judges and staff.
d) The process of decision-making.

I will be discussing decision-making at the Tribunals largely in terms of process.

The uniqueness of the Tribunals

The Tribunals were created in the early 1990s, half a century after the Nuremberg trials during which the enforcement of international criminal law did not take place at the international level.

The end of the Cold War and the televised atrocities of the Yugoslavia conflict, along with the increasing power of NGOs, the media and public opinion, were key factors in facilitating the adoption by the Security Council of resolutions setting up the ICTY in 1993 and later, in 1994, the ICTR. Their Statutes were adopted after the beginning of the conflicts and after some of the crimes had been committed.

In some ways the Tribunals may appear to have operated like domestic criminal courts—trying individual defendants charged with killing, rape and other offences.

However, many aspects of the Tribunals' work were, and in the case of the Mechanism are, unique. In particular, rather than relying primarily on a Statute, as does the ICC, the Tribunals had to ensure, in accordance with

1. *See generally,* Theodor Meron, THE MAKING OF INTERNATIONAL CRIMINAL JUSTICE: THE VIEW FROM THE BENCH 278 (2001).

the principle of legality, that convictions involved violations of customary international law at the time the offences took place and even before the Statutes' adoption.

The Tribunals had little procedural precedent on which to rely, and had to create many of their procedural rules based on diverse national precedents.

The cases tried before the Tribunals were unprecedented in character and scale, and involved crimes almost never prosecuted on a national level, such as genocide, crimes against humanity and war crimes.

The Tribunals operated in the context of time periods and locations for which they were given jurisdiction—and while defendants were tried as individuals, their fates were often seen as emblematic of broader geopolitical concerns.

Finally, the expectations of the international community made it particularly important to render Judgements that were both carefully reasoned and scrupulously solicitous of the rights of the accused.

Decision-makers

In considering decision-making at the Tribunals, it is important to remember that important decisions emanate not just from the Trial and Appeal Chamber panels, but also from Plenaries of the Judges; the President and the Registrar.

Substantive legal decisions, Judgements and sentences are obviously delivered by the Trial and Appeal Chambers, as are many decisions concerning procedural issues. However, many of the procedural decisions of the Tribunals, which can significantly impact the lives of accused and convicted individuals, are made by other actors, such as the President and the Registrar. I am not mentioning the Prosecutor here, as with regard to judicial decision-making he is a party, not a decider.

Most fundamentally, the Tribunals' Rules of Procedure and Evidence, which govern core aspects of the conduct of trials and appeals, are adopted and subject to change based on decisions by Judges at their Plenaries, including in the Mechanism's remote Plenaries.

The President also plays a significant role in deciding particular issues, such as responding to requests for early release from individuals serving their sentences; addressing requests for the disqualification of Judges; monitoring the enforcement of sentences; appointing Trial and Appeal Benches; adjudicating complaints from detainees at the U.N. Detention Unit in The Hague and the U.N. Detention Facility in Arusha and, at times, also from detainees serving sentences in enforcement-of-sentences States, and reviewing certain decisions by the Registrar.

The Registrar also makes significant decisions. These include decisions on the remuneration of defence counsel and on the conditions under which detainees are held in detention facilities at The Hague and in Arusha, including their access to media, protective measures and other issues.

I also note that certain procedural decisions, such as routine pre-trial and pre-appeal management questions and urgent matters arising during judicial recess, are often decided by a single duty Judge. In the Mechanism, the matters over which a single Judge is competent has been enlarged, including over contempt cases.

Of course, the most fundamental questions, and especially the guilt and innocence of the accused, are decided by panels of Judges.

Judges and staff—background

The diversity of the Tribunals' Judges and staff is one of the Tribunals' sources of strength—but it can also present challenges in reaching decisions.

Election of Judges and recruitment of staff emphasize diverse representation, complying with the general aim of reflecting the world's legal systems and geographic spread. The diversity in Judges' and staff members' cultural, national and linguistic backgrounds helps to bring different perspectives to assessing the status of customary international law, the importance of precedents and the types of procedural rules that should be adopted. This diversity increases both the Tribunals' public legitimacy and operational challenges. For instance, as not all Judges speak the same language, interpretation and translation are needed, and easy, informal communication is difficult to achieve. Diversity in backgrounds also means that judicial decisions must be reached in the context of a dialectic between different legal cultures and legal systems. For example, in the Appeals Chamber, both the Tribunals' Statutes and their Rules of Procedure and Evidence are—despite the enhanced influence of civil law—still primarily a product of the common law. However, while rules of procedure still continue to reflect primarily common law approaches, rules governing evidence have been modified over time and now reflect civil law flexibility such as with regard to the admission of hearsay evidence and far greater openness to admitting written evidence. Under the influence of the civil law, the role of Judges as managers of courtroom proceedings has been strengthened, such as by the introduction of pre-trial and pre-appeal Judges.

Borrowing elements from the two major legal systems of the world, the common law and the civil law, has been part of a trial-and-error process that aimed at increasing the efficiency of international criminal proceedings. While not renouncing their common law sources, the Tribunals enriched their adversarial system by incorporating components of the civil law inquisitorial model. Allowing appeals by the prosecution, reinforcing the role of the pre-trial Judge and pre-appeal Judge, removing barriers to the efficient administration of a trial by permitting the admission of written statements in lieu of *viva voce* testimonies, lowering the threshold of evidence admissibility or facilitating interlocutory appeals—all these and other features of a civil law-leaning adjudicatory model have been injected into the ad hoc Tribunals' rules and jurisprudence, mostly by the Judges themselves, to enhance both the speed of proceedings and the quality of the work product. Addressing challenges inherent in the conduct of criminal trials of such exceptional magnitude and historical importance, the ad hoc Tribunals have built upon their common law foundations a quite unique model of adjudication that combines elements of both the prosecutorial and the adversarial systems.

More broadly, discussions of legal and procedural issues often began from first principles, because in some cases basic understandings—typically shared by individuals operating within one national legal system—were not common to the Tribunals' Judges and staff.

Basic approaches to judicial precedents also may not be shared by all Judges and staff. Common law-trained Judges and staff are typically interested in situating proposed decisions in the context of precedents, and they would make efforts to distinguish any case that did not follow such precedent. Civil law-trained Judges and staff, on the other hand, may refer to past decisions, but they may be less systematic in canvassing existing precedents. They will, instead, take steps to situate their decision in a general theory of law, whether international or not.

Even among Judges from similar legal systems there may be a variation in how they approach decision-making, including the degree to which they are inclined to express their views in separate or dissenting opinions.

In the United States, for instance, panels of Judges generally issue a decision in the form of a single text that may reflect compromises among the Judges, and this in addition to sometimes concurring or dissenting opinions.

In the United Kingdom, it is not uncommon for each Judge on a panel to issue an opinion explaining how he or she reached a particular legal conclusion, even if there is general agreement among the Judges as to the outcome of the case.

Judges—processes

I now turn to the technical decision-making process at the Tribunals, with special emphasis on the Appeals Chamber.

Generally, a team of staff members considers the issues that arise with respect to particular motions or appeals and provides Judges with helpful briefing papers and notes to assist in their decision-making. This assistance is essentially the same as that provided by judicial clerks in the United States, but involves a larger number of staff members, reflecting the complexity and the large scale of the cases before the Tribunals, which often involve dozens of crime sites, thousands of victims and enormous volumes of written material.

With regard to many decisions before the Appeals Chamber, official communication about a case is conducted by Judges by means of exchange of memoranda, usually on the basis of a draft decision prepared by a presiding Judge.

For Judgements and some decisions, Judges on the Appeals Chamber meet for formal deliberations, assisted in most cases by legal staff, though sentencing deliberations are conducted largely by Judges alone.

These formal exchanges are supplemented by extensive discussions between Judges and the staff who assist them in preparing decisions.

Unlike many national jurisdictions, Trial Chambers typically consist of three-Judge panels, a situation which yields its own dynamics, as it requires the panel to deliberate, unlike in those countries where a single Judge may hear and decide a case. I discuss here the technical aspects of the decision-making process at the Tribunals but not the specifics of decision-making discussions in particular cases. Of course, I am aware of Judge Posner's perhaps somewhat cynical view that secrecy in judicial deliberations is "an example of professional mystification" which helps to promulgate what for him is a fiction that judicial deliberations are "unmarred by willfulness, politics, or ignorance."[2] In my view, however, Judges sitting as part of a panel must be free to discuss, develop and sometimes even change their views without fear of repercussions or embarrassment, either personal or for the institution of which they are a part. In other words, secrecy in judicial decision-making plays a crucial role in ensuring the independence and impartiality of the Bench during the decision-making process. It also lends greater authority to the ultimate decision that the Judges pronounce. As commentators have suggested, "[t]he decisions of an appellate court are more authoritative when we know the legal reasoning behind a decision; but not the personal or institutional dynamics."[3]

I have said already that the Tribunals' success depends in no small part on the transparency of their proceedings. The Tribunals' success depends also on effective decision-making at all levels.

To be sure, the diverse expectations of and roles played by the Tribunals—as well as the institutional and logistical challenges they face—tend to make their decision-making processes slower than those in national jurisdictions. However, the diversity of Judges and staff members, and the careful scrutiny to which the Tribunals' decisions are subjected before being issued, are necessary for the Tribunals' historic mission of ending impunity for international crimes. And these decisions—both procedural and substantive—have laid the groundwork for broader enforcement of international criminal law, as exemplified by institutions such as the ICC and other international and hybrid tribunals and more frequent domestic prosecutions of international crimes.

The Deliberation Process at International Criminal Tribunals

To date, very little is known about how Judges at international criminal courts and tribunals deliberate and decide the cases before them. The deliberation process is the very essence of the Judges' mission at both the international and the domestic level. Yet, as far as international courts are concerned, that process is mostly shrouded in secrecy. One notable

2. Richard A. Posner, How Judges Think 3 (2008).
3. Paul R. Bernard, *Transparency and Authority in Appellate Decision-Making*, Mich. Bar J. 44, 46 (Feb. 2008).

exception is the ICJ, which has adopted specific guidelines as to the procedure that culminates in the issuance of a Judgement.[4] International criminal tribunals, however, follow internal procedures that are not entirely transparent.[5] The secrecy of deliberations is, without doubt, a time-honored principle that allows Judges at every court to deliberate free of external influences and reach a decision firmly based in the law and the facts before them. The veil of secrecy, however, only covers the content of the Judges' deliberations—in other words, Judges' views and ultimate votes on the specific judicial matters before them. Each Judge's educational and professional background cannot but influence his or her positions on a broad array of legal matters, such as the weight of jurisprudential precedent or the probative value of hearsay evidence. The secrecy of deliberations prevents public scrutiny of individual Judges' views expressed behind the closed doors of the deliberations chamber and in other exchanges of views between the Judges.

What the principle of secrecy does not protect is the decision-making process itself, i.e. the distinct procedural steps Judges follow to decide the controversies before them. Judges at international criminal tribunals have adopted, over the years, specific working methods and decision-making procedures. The focus of my analysis in this chapter will be the deliberation process at the ad hoc Tribunals—the ICTY, the ICTR and more specifically their common Appeals Chambers—and their successor, the Residual Mechanism for International Criminal Tribunals.

However antithetical they may appear, secrecy in judicial deliberations and transparency in court proceedings actually foster the same goals: independent and impartial decision-making and, as a result, greater public confidence in the Tribunals and in the administration of justice.

While the complexities of judicial decision-making discussions must remain secret and are often not apparent in the Tribunals' Judgements and

4. ICJ: Resolution concerning the Internal Judicial Practice of the Court (Rules of Court, Art. 19) adopted 12 April 1976. *See also* Rules of Court, Art. 21, adopted 14 Apr. 1978.

5. A partial exception may be the Extraordinary Chambers of the Courts of Cambodia (ECCC), the internal rules of which describe with more clarity the procedure for appeals from Judgement before the Supreme Court Chamber—even though those rules still do not speak about the deliberation process itself. In any event, the ECCC is a so-called hybrid institution, i.e. a semi-internationalized annex to the Cambodian court system, which applies Cambodian law and hence is subject to a different regime from purely international tribunals.

decisions, by reading concurring and dissenting opinions one may glean some perspectives on Judges' different views.

Civil Law and Common Law Courts

I start from a very brief overview of the models of judicial deliberations at civil law and common law courts of second and last instance.

In continental systems, Judges of second and last instance deliberate and all but decide the cases assigned to them before the oral presentation of the parties' arguments at a hearing. Typically, once the parties have submitted their written submissions, a *Juge rapporteur* or "reporting Judge" is appointed from the panel of Judges designated to decide a case. That Judge is usually a junior member of the court and, unlike common law Judges, is unaided by "judicial clerks." The reporting Judge does most of the heavy lifting in a case—he or she is charged with reviewing the parties' arguments, conducting the necessary legal research and presenting to his or her colleagues a draft proposal for the resolution of the case. The proposal is, essentially, a draft decision, both in form and substance. Importantly, the role of the reporting Judge is to prepare a draft that reflects not only his or her individual views on the case, but as broad a consensus among their colleagues on the resolution of the case and as solid a legal analysis of the issues involved as possible.

When, and if, a hearing takes place, the Judges arrive at the Bench with very concrete ideas as to the resolution of the appellate case before them. Hearings in continental courts of appeal and last resort are rather perfunctory and not compulsory.

Appellate and supreme courts in common law systems follow a different model of deliberations. Contrary to the practice of continental courts, Anglo-American courts deliberate on and decide cases after oral arguments are heard. Before the hearings, each Judge of the panel reviews the parties' submissions and conducts the necessary legal research individually or with the assistance of their law clerks. The law clerks will typically summarize and analyze the parties' arguments in a memorandum to the Judge, the so-called "Bench memorandum," upon which the Judge relies to prepare for the hearing and to form a first view of the case. There is no reporting Judge. The Bench memorandum is drafted for the benefit of an individual Judge and sometimes, but not always, is circulated to the entire Bench.

Deliberations at the ICTY/ICTR Appeals Chambers

As already suggested, international criminal tribunals are composed of Judges hailing from different legal systems, with diverse education, experience and languages. The model of deliberations at international tribunals reflects this diversity. International criminal courts decide cases through a process that constitutes an amalgam of both civil law and common law practices.

Appeals from Judgements

At the ICTY,[6] an appeal from a Judgement lay as of right for both the prosecution and the defence—a feature borrowed from the continental criminal justice system. Once an appeal was filed, the ICTY President—who was also presiding Judge of the ICTY and the ICTR Appeals Chamber—would appoint a five-member panel to decide the appeal. If the President was a member of the panel, he or she would also preside over the appeal *ex officio*; otherwise, the Judges of the panel would elect one among them as the presiding Judge in the case. The function of the presiding Judge is critical, because, as explained later, they oversee, direct and lead the decision-making process, while also exercising the duties and functions of both the *Juge rapporteur* in civil law appellate courts and the Judge designated in common law courts, to write the court's opinion.

Customarily, but not always, the presiding Judge would also be designated as the 'pre-appeal' Judge in the case. This Judge, as part of his or her administrative duties, decided, *solo*, motions relating to the briefing of the case—such as extensions of time and word limits, lifting the confidentiality of an exhibit or a transcript or issuing public redacted versions of a trial decision—and other housekeeping matters—that did not require the involvement of the entire Bench. More complex pre-appeal matters, however, were submitted to the consideration of the whole panel.

6. All references to the decision-making process at the ICTY henceforth should also be construed as including the ICTR, which officially closed its doors in Dec. 2015. The ICTY closed its doors on 31 Dec. 2017.

Before the hearing

The appellant's brief set in motion the decision-making process at the ICTY and the ICTR Appeals Chambers. That brief presented in detail the arguments of the party that challenged the Trial Judgement in a given case.

The lengthiest—and arguably, most important—phase of the appeal process involved the drafting of a document called in ICTY/ICTR parlance the "preparatory document" or "prepdoc." This was the primary material used by the Judges of the panel to prepare for the appeal hearing and for the ultimate resolution of the case. The "prepdoc" summarized in a comprehensive fashion the findings of the Trial Chamber, the challenges against those findings and the appellees' corresponding responses, somewhat like the "Bench memorandum" in a common law appellate court. The "prepdoc" also analyzed the parties' submissions, discussed their legal arguments and suggested how those arguments should be disposed of. The "prepdoc" did not simply explore different legal avenues for the resolution of the issues arising out of the appeal, but also provided an overview of the applicable principles and the relevant jurisprudence and proposed very concrete conclusions for each specific legal question. If an issue could be resolved in more than one way, the "prepdoc" offered alternative options and analyses. The "prepdoc" thus attempted to be inclusive, detailed and exhaustive. In that sense, it resembled the draft Judgement prepared by the *Juge rapporteur* in the continental deliberative model before the oral hearing. Indeed, the "prepdoc" adopted the form of a draft "Judgement" of the Appeals Chamber, which suggested to the Bench specific dispositions of the issues on appeal. Each proposition in the "prepdoc" was supported by references contained in voluminous footnotes.

The drafting of the "prepdoc" took place under the general direction and oversight of the presiding Judge in the case. The latter and his or her legal officers or law clerks collaborated with the leader of the drafting team (legal staff assigned to drafting in a particular case), to ensure the smooth completion of the "prepdoc." The presiding Judge had the last word as to when a specific section was ready for inclusion in the "prepdoc." The presiding Judge and his or her team also reviewed the legal analysis proposed by the drafting team and would offer their comments as to the suggested legal reasoning and as to how each issue on appeal should be resolved. In fulfilling this role, the presiding Judge engaged in extensive exchanges with the drafting team, but did not usually reach out to other Judges, either formally or informally, to seek their views on specific issues. Unlike the *Juge rapporteur* in a continental appellate court, the Judge presiding over an ICTY appeal would not aim at producing a complete draft Judgement likely to sail through the post-hearing deliberations without objections. On the other hand, the "prepdoc" was not supposed to merely reflect the personal views of the presiding Judge either. The goal was to create a document that (i) presented, in condensed fashion, the findings of the Trial Chamber and all the assertions in the parties' briefs in favor of and against the soundness of the Trial Judgement; and (ii) examined those arguments under the applicable law as objectively and thoroughly as possible, proposing specific conclusions and reasoning in support of the conclusions. The drafting team and the presiding Judge would strive to make the "prepdoc" inclusive and self-contained, so that the Bench was presented with the entire spectrum of possible solutions of the issues involved. Those efforts would result in a document of considerable volume, amounting to hundreds of pages.

The "prepdoc" would be circulated at least a month before the scheduled oral hearing. In more complicated cases, especially those concerning multiple defendants, the "prepdoc" would be finalized and distributed earlier, even three months in advance, so as to allow Judges sufficient time to review it carefully. Upon receipt of the "prepdoc," the Judges would prepare for the hearing. Each Judge prepared mostly individually, in his or her own Chamber, with the assistance of their assigned legal officer who might offer a fresh perspective on the questions arising out of the case, which could deviate substantially from the analysis of the drafting team. Having the benefit of a document as thorough as the "prepdoc," the Judges arrived at the hearing with at least partially formed views as to what the main issues on appeal were and how those issues should be framed, analyzed and disposed of.

The hearing

The hearings allowed the parties one last chance to clarify their positions on key issues, fill in any gaps in their submissions and distill their arguments. Each party was expected to present orally a condensed version of their written submissions, focusing on what constituted, for each party, the heart of the case as well as to answer the questions that the Appeals Chamber wished to see addressed.

It was not unusual for the Appeals Chamber, in the order scheduling the hearing, to draw the parties' attention to specific issues and invite the parties to discuss those issues during their presentations. Such issues ranged from the discussion of an exhibit to very concrete legal questions, such as the correctness of specific trial conclusions. In the case against General Tolimir, for example, the Appeals Chamber invited the parties to discuss during the hearing, inter alia, whether certain incidents constituted genocide and whether the defendant could be found guilty of charged crimes under modes of liability other than commission of the crimes (e.g. aiding and abetting). Such specific questions might offer a glimpse into the panel's thinking about the case (despite the usual disclaimers included in the scheduling order). Yet confining the scope of the appeal hearing to particular issues was often necessary given the limited time at the parties' disposal and the large scope of the appeals heard by the Appeals Chamber, especially those involving multiple defendants and charges. The Appeals Chamber preferred to notify the parties in advance of the issues it considered crucial to the resolution of the appeal so that the parties could make the most efficient use of the time allotted for the hearing.

However, issuing such an invitation to the parties did not preclude the Judges from questioning the parties about other aspects of the appeal during the hearing, even if such questions were not listed in the scheduling order. Questions asked by Judges during the hearing were an attempt to seek clarifications from the parties on legal and factual issues that remained unanswered, or unclear in their briefs. The parties' responses, thus, did matter in the sense that they elucidated their positions and might help the panel to see a critical question through the parties' own prisms.

Because of its important function, the appeal hearing for a single case might last several days, depending on the size of the case and the number of accused individuals. At the end of the hearing it became customary to allow the convicted appellant to make a brief personal address to the Chamber.

After the hearing

The deliberations entered their main stage after the hearing, consistent with the Anglo-American deliberative model. Shortly after the hearing, the presiding Judge would circulate to the other members of the panel a detailed agenda for the post-hearing deliberations. The agenda contained a list of all the issues that the Judges had to consider and decide by vote at the post-hearing conference. In complex cases like those heard by the Tribunal, such a list was indispensable to streamline the Judges' deliberations and ensure that no issue raised by the parties remained unaddressed. For efficiency purposes, the agenda largely followed the structure of the "prepdoc"—not the parties' submissions. The presiding Judge's agenda-setting power added to the significance of their role, since they were in charge of the preparation and circulation of both the "prepdoc" and the deliberations agenda.

Like in common law courts, the presiding Judge also opened and presided over the panel's post-hearing conference. He or she went through the items in the pre-circulated agenda and requested the members of the panel to vote on each of the issues on appeal. The presiding Judge might preface the voting on an issue with a brief statement, but in general, they expressed their views and cast their vote at the end of each voting round, so as not to influence the other Judges' votes. The only issue on which Judges did not deliberate at this stage was sentencing—which was the subject of a separate round of deliberations usually exclusively among Judges, which took place once the main text of the Appeal Judgement was finalized by the majority of the panel.

The post-hearing conference at the ICTY Appeals Chamber was intended more as a preliminary voting session than a forum for detailed discussion of the merits of the case. Given the size of each appeal and the myriad of issues to be decided, the panel could not engage in overly long debates about the substance of the appeal. The primary objective of the post-hearing conference was to canvass the Judges' positions on the various issues and on the analysis proposed in the "prepdoc," so that specific guidance could be provided to the drafting team for the preparation of the first draft Judgement. This was the reason why the senior legal officer leading the drafting team, as well as each Judge's assigned legal officer, were allowed to attend the conference and note each Judge's position and initial vote on the questions in the agenda.

Judges voted on the basis of the very detailed draft analysis contained in the "prepdoc," which was the starting point of the post-hearing deliberations. Having reviewed the "prepdoc," the Judges had to indicate whether they agreed or disagreed with the proposed analysis of each issue in the "prepdoc" and, where applicable, which one of the various options offered they favored. Votes were, in essence, cast in favor or against the "prepdoc."

Disagreements could be expressed not only at the post-hearing conference but at later stages as well. The votes cast at the conference were not definite; Judges reserved the right to revisit their earlier positions and change their votes once they received the first draft of the Appeal Judgement, at which point the deliberations would resume.

An important difference from common law courts was that the preparation of the draft Appeal Judgement at the ICTY was not assigned to a single Judge identified in the Judgement as its author. This task was undertaken by the drafting team, which acted in accordance with the views of the majority of the Judges and under the guidance and oversight of the presiding Judge. The latter had a supervisory role over the drafting process and did not relinquish this function even when he or she was not in agreement with the majority of the panel as to the resolution of a specific issue or even the entire appeal. The presiding Judge did not aspire to prepare a draft reflecting primarily his or her own views, but a draft reflecting the views of the panel's majority, as expressed during the post-hearing conference and perhaps in informal exchanges after the conference. The presiding Judge acted not as the author of the court's opinion, but as the guardian of the integrity, fairness and managerial efficiency of the drafting process, aiming to produce a fine first draft Judgement that was likely to be approved by the other Judges without extensive modifications.

The deliberations entered their most intense phase when the first draft Judgement was delivered to the entire Bench. Depending on the degree of the Judges' approval of the "prepdoc," the preparation of the first draft Judgement could last from a few days or weeks to a few months. The Judges were given ample time—a minimum of four weeks—to examine the first draft Judgement and decide to what extent they agreed with the draft.

Corridor discussions in a search for compromise solutions are a natural part of the decision-making process at all courts, domestic and international. This is, in fact, the quintessence of judicial deliberations: honest, in-depth discussion between the Judges about the issues pending before them.

Informal exchanges notwithstanding, Judges' reactions were formally communicated by means of highly confidential memoranda, stating a Judge's position on the draft Judgement and agreement or disagreement with the analysis of each issue. These memoranda were usually detailed and contained Judges' substantive comments and editorial suggestions, which the drafting team reviewed, in consultation with the presiding Judge, and decided whether to incorporate in the draft. If a proposal gained the support of the majority of the panel, it would be implemented. Otherwise, the drafting team had to weigh carefully whether the reasoning could be revised in accordance with a Judge's request without undermining the overall analysis of an issue. In the end, a refined draft Judgement was recirculated to the Judges who were members of the Bench and who would, again, review it and comment upon it. The same process of revision, circulation and commenting would be repeated until a solid majority expressed its formal support for a final version of the Judgement. Each new draft Judgement inched closer to the final resolution of the appeal, but it must be noted that technically, throughout this stage, Judges were free to revisit and change the preliminary votes cast during the deliberations conference or expressed in any of the previous discussions. They might also announce whether they intend to file a separate opinion—either concurring with or dissenting from the draft Judgement as a whole or in part.

Sentencing deliberations

Once majority support for each conclusion in the draft Judgement consolidated, the drafting team prepared the final section of the Judgement which contained the disposition, i.e. a list of the Appeals Chamber's conclusions on each charge. Using that list, the Judges would confer a second time in person to deliberate on the sentence to be imposed, provided that the defendant was not to be acquitted *in toto*—i.e. assuming that some convictions survived the appellate review or that new convictions were entered on appeal. Sentencing deliberations have a very limited scope: Judges conferred only to discuss the length of the sentence to be imposed. This second in-person conference took place in absolute secrecy. Judges alone participated, unaccompanied by their legal officers or any member of the drafting team, so as to freely discuss the sentence that fitted the surviving convictions. In particularly complex cases, the senior legal officer might be invited to attend the sentencing deliberations to ensure a proper follow-up in drafting. The presiding Judge directed the discussion this time as well, but deliberations were strictly oral and votes cast were final.

In general, Judges have absolute discretion as to the length of the sentence to be imposed; they may shorten, lengthen or affirm the sentence imposed by the Trial Chamber or they may reverse acquittals and impose a sentence on appeal. Typically, an expansion of the scope of criminal liability on appeal (for instance, the entry of fresh convictions or of a conviction for commission of a crime in lieu of a conviction for aiding and abetting) are likely to result in an increase in the length of the sentence. On the other hand, reversals of some convictions could lead to a shorter sentence, but this would necessarily depend on the gravity of the surviving convictions. For the same reasons, the panel's decision on the sentence was only shared with the senior legal officer leading the drafting team who was to insert it in the final version of the Appeal Judgement. After a further review by the Bench, the Judgement was ready for signature and a date for its public delivery was scheduled and announced.

Separate/dissenting opinions

Although the Appeal Judgement itself was not authored by any single Judge, ICTY Judges might, if they wished, attach to the Court's Judgement a dissenting opinion or separate opinion concurring in the draft Judgement but pursuant to a line of reasoning different from that favored by the majority. Such individual opinions were issued as opinions of a particular Judge, consistent with the common law model, and did not bind the parties. Their authoritative value depended on the clarity and strength of the majority opinion. In cases decided by a narrow majority (3 out of 5 votes), separate opinions written by concurring Judges might shed more light on the Tribunal's reasoning, while dissenting opinions might be relied upon by the parties in subsequent cases seeking to attack the earlier Judgement.

Judges could announce at any point during the post-hearing deliberations their intention to dissent or author a concurring opinion. A Judge could indicate as early as at the post-hearing conference their tentative intention to file a separate opinion or dissent if their firmly held views about certain or all the issues on appeal did not gain the support of the majority.

In most cases, and depending on the timeline of each case, drafts of separate and dissenting opinions were circulated well in advance of the scheduled delivery of the Judgement so as to afford the Judges joining the majority the opportunity to reconsider their positions. Separate or dissenting opinions were finalized simultaneously, or earlier, with the Judgement to which they were to be attached. It was very exceptional—but not unprecedented—that a separate or dissenting opinion was not ready for publication on the day of delivery of a Judgement. In any event, because the Appeal Judgement must accurately reflect the views of all Judges, the final text of the Judgement explicitly noted the dissents in its relevant paragraphs, as per the instructions of dissenting and concurring Judges.

Interlocutory appeals, pre-appeal decisions and petitions for review

Appeals from final Judgements were not the only item on the Appeals Chamber's docket. While deliberating on the main appeal, the Judges assigned to a case also had to consider, in the first instance, and dispose of numerous pre-appeal motions by the parties on matters as diverse as the provisional release of the defendants, the admission of newly discovered evidence or the variation of protective measures granted to witnesses who testified at the trial. Simpler matters such as the extension of word and time limits for the parties' submissions were handled by a single member of the panel, the pre-appeal Judge, typically the presiding Judge who was designated for that purpose. More complicated, substantive matters, were decided by the entire Bench.

The Appeals Chamber was also regularly seized of interlocutory appeals, i.e. appeals from non-final rulings of the Trial Chambers on a wide variety of issues, such as the violation of the prosecution's obligation to disclose exculpatory evidence to the defence, the admission of evidence, the judicial notice of factual propositions adjudicated in earlier cases, the prima facie sufficiency of the evidence to support a conviction, challenges to the fairness of the proceeding or simple scheduling matters. Not all of such rulings were automatically appealable to the Appeals Chamber. Appeals as of right lay only from decisions on: (i) the provisional release of the accused individuals; (ii) motions challenging jurisdiction; (iii) the referral of indictments to domestic courts; and (iv) motions by the parties for orders to States for the production of documents, as well as from (v) directions to the prosecution to proceed on only some counts in the indictment.[7] Appeals from all other interlocutory decisions needed to be certified to the Appeals Chamber by the Trial Chamber that issued the decision. Such permission to appeal was granted when the trial ruling involved an issue that would significantly affect the fair and expeditious conduct or the outcome of the trial and thus warranted the immediate

7. *See* Rules 65, 72(B)(i), 11*bis*, 54*bis*(C) and 73*bis*(E), respectively. References to the Rules are to the Rules of Procedure and Evidence of the ICTY.

intervention of the Appeals Chamber so as to materially advance the proceedings.[8] Strict though this threshold was, Trial Chambers tend to grant certification quite often, because the resolution of an issue by the Appeals Chamber before the issuance of the Trial Judgement allows the Trial Chamber to issue its Judgement on firmer grounds and diminishes the scope for a subsequent appeal.

Another part of the Appeals Chamber's workload was the post-appeal review of final Judgements.[9] A party could petition the Appeals Chamber to revisit an earlier final Judgement, in the extraordinary event that new facts of decisive importance for the outcome of the case were discovered after the completion of all proceedings.[10] This standard was applied strictly by the Appeals Chamber, which agreed to a review only once, leading to a partial overturning of its own Judgement in the *Mrkšić and Šljivančanin* case. In the *Ngirabatware* review case (2019), the Appeals Chamber held hearings on the "new fact," rejecting the review, having determined, on the basis of the evidence, that the new fact had not been established. Although the review of a final Judgement is an exceptional remedy, not meant as a second appeal, parties do not hesitate to take advantage of this last resort opportunity to try to relitigate issues decided on appeal, disguising their second appeals as petitions for review. Hearings on review requests are only held if the majority of the Judges on the Bench determine that the new fact, if proved, could have been "decisive" as to the outcome of the case.

Rule 116*bis* explicitly precluded hearings on interlocutory appeals, whether as of right or certified, while hearings on pre-appeal motions were not normally held as a matter of customary practice, unless there was a request from the parties and the Appeals Chamber affirmed the need for a hearing, which was rarely the case.

8. *See* Rules 72(B)(ii) (Preliminary Motions) and 73(B) (Other Motions). Earlier versions provided that permission to file an interlocutory appeal was to be sought and granted by a three-Judge Bench of the Appeals Chamber, not the Trial Chamber that issued the impugned decision. This practice was eventually abandoned, however, because it put considerable strain on the Appeals Chamber's docket and resources, as Appeal Judges had to decide a constant stream of requests for leave to file an interlocutory appeal, in addition to the merits of the limited number of appeals that met the filing threshold.

9. In addition to Judgements rendered on appeal by the Appeals Chamber, Trial Judgements not challenged on appeal also became final upon the expiration of the deadline for the filing of an appeal.

10. *See* Rule 119. Petitions for review could be filed before a Trial Chamber as well, in which case its decision on review would be subject to further appeal pursuant to Rule 121.

Deliberations at the Trial Chambers

Trial Chambers followed different working methods than the Appeals Chamber. A Trial Chamber must decide a myriad of legal, factual and administrative/logistical issues on a day-to-day basis while the trial is ongoing and after it ends. Unlike some domestic courts, trials at the ICTY were conducted by panels of three Judges, not a single Judge. During the trial, Judges would meet almost on a daily basis and decide several issues relating to the conduct of the trial either orally or on the basis of drafts prepared by legal staff members assisting the Chamber, with little time for extensive deliberations. At the same time, Judges deliberated on the resolution of issues that would form part of the Trial Judgement itself. Due to the scope of international criminal trials and the number of evidentiary, procedural, factual and legal issues that must be addressed in a Judgement, trial Judges cannot afford to postpone deliberations until the trial itself concludes, but deliberate on and decide issues once each question is ripe for determination. Questions relating to the credibility of witnesses, for example, were usually determined by the conclusion of each party's case, or earlier. Deliberations enter their most decisive phase after the parties' closing arguments are heard; after that point, Judges devote themselves to the determination of matters still left pending and to the preparation of the Trial Judgement, which would decide whether the accused person's guilt beyond reasonable doubt has been established.

In all those instances, both before and after the conclusion of the trial, trial Judges deliberated on the basis of written drafts prepared by the legal officers who assisted the Chamber. The Judges individually reviewed each of those drafts and convened a confidential meeting at which, in the presence of the legal team leader, they expressed their views and agreement or disagreement with the draft and provided specific directions to the legal support team as to how the draft should be revised. These drafts, once finalized, would then be merged into the voluminous Trial Judgement, which was then reviewed holistically by the Chamber, before its issuance, along with concurring and dissenting opinions. In other words, Trial Chambers did not defer deliberations until a complete draft of the Judgement was prepared by the drafting team; the Trial Judgement was assembled gradually after several rounds of deliberations on various aspects of the case. The model of piecemeal deliberations was devised by ICTY Trial Chambers as a means of coping with the massive scope of ICTY trials and the workload they generated.

Challenges for the Mechanism

The main feature of this new model is its lean structure—the only full-time Judge of the Mechanism is its President, who is appointed by the U.N. Secretary-General after consultations with the Security Council and the other Mechanism Judges. All other Judges of the Mechanism may keep their previous, or find new, professional occupations and work on Mechanism matters, as assigned by the President, on a part-time basis and without being physically present at the seats of the Mechanism in The Hague or in Arusha, unless their physical presence is deemed necessary for the conduct of a hearing, in-person deliberations or in-person plenary. Judges are remunerated per day of work and are not on annual salaries.

As a result of such innovations, judicial deliberations at the Mechanism do not follow the usual pattern followed at the ICTY or ICTR. In most matters handled so far by the Mechanism, Appeals and Trial Chambers deliberations are mostly conducted remotely, through written memoranda transmitted via electronic mail by Judges. This mode of deliberating from a distance, by the members of the panel, had never been implemented before at the international level as the prevalent judicial decision-making process. It certainly poses challenges and raises questions not only about the secure nature of Judges' communications (and thus the secrecy of deliberations) but also about the quality of the deliberative process.

VIII

Keeping POWs Safe

The Ovčara Massacre

Perhaps the most important development concerning the Geneva Conventions during the last two and a half decades has been their reiteration and application in the statutes and in the jurisprudence of international criminal tribunals. Following, but far surpassing, Nuremberg jurisprudence, these developments demonstrate that the Geneva Conventions constitute hard law par excellence, relevant not only to State behavior in capitals and on the battlefield but central also in the courtroom. These developments have enabled the revival of customary humanitarian law and the enhancement of the norms of the Conventions through the interpretative gloss, some would say development, provided by court decisions.

The Fourth Geneva Convention was discussed and applied tens of times in the ICTY. The Third Geneva Convention and the Additional Protocols to the Conventions were also applied. And despite the nature of the ICC Statute as a self-standing civil law-type Statute, the Conventions have been central to the ICC jurisprudence as well. There is no question that the constant citation and application of the Conventions by the international tribunals and the Tribunals have greatly contributed to their standing and centrality.

The Conventions have, of course, benefited from the fact that to ensure the principle of legality and to avoid criticism of *ex post facto* voiced against Nuremberg and Tokyo, the Judges of the Tribunals superimposed on their Statutes the test whether each of the crimes within a Tribunal's jurisdiction reflected customary law at the time of the commission of the crimes. This was clarified by the *Galić* Appeal Judgement.[1] That Judgement also

1. *Prosecutor v. Galić*, Judgement, ICTY Appeals Chamber, at para. 83, Case no. IT-98-29-A (30 Nov. 2006).

Standing Up For Justice. Theodor Meron, Oxford University Press (2021). © Theodor Meron.
DOI: 10.1093/oso/9780198863434.003.0008

confirmed that the prohibition of attacks against civilians may not be derogated from on the ground of military necessity.

Significantly, it was not necessary for the Tribunals to apply the customary law test to the application of the provisions of the Geneva Conventions because of the broad agreement that those provisions are already recognized as customary law or general principles of law.

The Geneva Conventions and especially Common Article 3 have been cited and applied in a multitude of cases by international criminal tribunals. I will mention briefly some examples before focusing on the case of the largest murder of prisoners of war (POWs) in the Yugoslav wars, a case where the Third Geneva Convention formed the gravamen of the Judgement.

Most of the cases on the application of the Geneva Conventions by the international criminal tribunals concerned the Fourth Geneva Convention, Common Article 3 of the Conventions as well as the Additional Protocols to the Geneva Conventions (1977). There were also some cases involving the application of the Third Geneva Convention. In *Naletilić and Martinović* (2001), for example, the ICTY Trial Chamber considered Article 50 of the Third Geneva Convention concerning authorized work by POWs and Article 52 concerning dangerous or humiliating labor.[2] In *Blaškić* (2000), the ICTY Trial Chamber interpreted Article 4 of the Third Geneva Convention with reference to situations in which militias and paramilitary groups could be regarded as persons protected by the Third Geneva Convention. It stated that Bosnian Muslim combatants had been granted protection in line with the Third Convention and that those who did not enjoy protection under that Convention were civilians.[3] In *Simić* (2003), the Trial Chamber explained that POWs may be subjected to involuntary labor but are entitled to suitable working conditions and may not be assigned to dangerous or unhealthy work or humiliating labor.[4] In *Blaškić* (2004) the ICTY Appeals Chamber ruled that requiring protected persons to dig military trenches was a violation of both the Third and Fourth Geneva

2. *Prosecutor v. Naletilić and Martinović*, Decision on Vinko Martinović's Objection to the Amended Indictment and Mladen Naletilić Preliminary Motion to the Amended Indictment, ICTY Trial Chamber, Case no. IT-98-34 (14 Feb. 2001).
3. *Prosecutor v. Blaškić*, Judgement, ICTY Trial Chamber, at para. 147, Case no. IT-95-14-T (3 Mar. 2000).
4. *Prosecutor v. Simić, Tadić and Zarić*, Judgement, ICTY Trial Chamber, at paras. 89–92, Case no. IT-95-9-T (17 Oct. 2003).

Conventions, as permitted labor may not be connected with military operations or have a military character.[5] Such labor constitutes cruel treatment and a violation of Common Article 3(1)(a). In *Delalić* (1998), the Trial Chamber discussed Article 5 of the Third Geneva Convention which provides for the application of the Convention from the time the POWs fall into the power of the enemy until either their final release or repatriation, and Article 4 of the Convention which defines those who are subject to the Convention's protection. The Chamber also discussed Article 13 of the Convention which states that POWs must be treated humanely, may not be subjected to mutilation or medical experiments and must be protected against acts of violence, intimidation, insults and public curiosity.[6] In *Prlić et al.* (2013), the Trial Chamber clarified the language of Article 4(A) of the Third Geneva Convention, stating that the expression "fall into the power" covers not only the case of being captured during combat but also when soldiers become prisoners without fighting, as in the case of surrender.[7]

Few groups of individuals are more vulnerable and more in need of protection than POWs who have been captured by their enemy or by other hostile actors. All too often they are mistreated, tortured or even killed by those who have taken them captive or to whom they have surrendered.

But for all of the risks of mistreatment that arise when POWs are taken into custody by an opposing force or other hostile group, a host of additional dangers emerges when the custody of POWs is transferred from that first (capturing) entity to another. Often the individuals or groups that assume custody of POWs through such transfers are harder to locate, less accountable and less likely to provide POWs with the protections to which they are entitled. And sometimes such transfers lead even to the death of the POWs.

I turn to one case where the Third Geneva Convention was at the center of the issues raised and the decisions made. As it involved perhaps the largest massacre of POWs in the Yugoslav wars, I will discuss it in some detail.

This was the situation in *Prosecutor v. Mile Mrkšić and Veselin Šljivančanin*. The ICTY's 2009 Appeal Judgement in this case, and, in particular, the

5. *Prosecutor v. Blaškić*, Judgement, ICTY Appeals Chamber, at para. 597, Case no. IT-95-14-A (29 July 2004).
6. *Prosecutor v. Delalić*, Judgement, ICTY Trial Chamber, at paras. 210, 238, 526, Case no. IT-96-21-T (16 Nov. 1998).
7. *Prosecutor v. Prlić et al.*, Judgement, ICTY Trial Chamber, at para. 105, Case no. IT-04-74-T (29 May 2013).

Appeals Chamber's discussion of the Third Geneva Convention, is the focus of this chapter.[8]

The problems posed by the transfer of custody of POWs are not new. During World War II, for example, the Wehrmacht authorities would, from time to time, transfer POWs into the custody of the S.S. or the Gestapo, from whom the prisoners received much worse treatment, including murder. Commandos would typically be executed under orders of Hitler ("Kommandobefehl" 1942) in clear violation of the Geneva POW Convention (1929) and international humanitarian law. The Soviet army transferred custody of Polish officer POWs to the NKVD (the Soviet secret police), which executed thousands of them in Katyn.

Such transfers of custody continue to occur even today. For the ICRC and others in the humanitarian sector, transfers of POWs can create difficult, if not insurmountable, challenges in tracing and protecting individual prisoners. These humanitarian tasks are rendered all the more difficult when—as is increasingly the case in modern conflicts—POWs are transferred to the custody of non-State actors. Grave humanitarian difficulties are also caused by the so-called extraordinary renditions of detainees from one State to another State where mistreatment is expected.

The escalating involvement of non-State actors in armed conflicts around the world poses a number of challenges for those who wish to ensure that POWs are protected, because non-State actors typically do not consider themselves bound by—and often operate without regard to—the requirements of international humanitarian law, including the protections enshrined in the 1949 Geneva Conventions. Even when the Geneva Conventions are supposedly applied, violations still occur.

The Third Geneva Convention—the quintessential international treaty for the protection of POWs—states that POWs "must at all times be humanely treated"[9] and enumerates various ways in which POWs shall be protected. Yet, the provisions of the Third Geneva Convention—Common Article 3 excepted—apply in a clear and uncontroversial way only when the conflict at issue is international in character, or when the parties to the conflict have agreed that the Convention or equivalent protective provisions

8. *Prosecutor v. Mile Mrkšić and Veselin Šljivančanin*, Judgement, ICTY Appeals Chamber, Case no. IT-95-13/J-A (5 May 2009).

9. Geneva Convention Relative to the Treatment of Prisoners of War (Third Geneva Convention) (1949) 75 UNTS 136, Art. 13.

will apply. Where a conflict is not international in character, it must therefore be determined whether the warring parties have explicitly or implicitly agreed that POWs should be afforded the protections guaranteed by the Third Geneva Convention.

The events giving rise to the *Mrkšić and Šljivančanin* case took place in the fall of 1991 in and around the municipality of Vukovar, in present-day Croatia. Serb forces had laid siege to Vukovar from August until November 1991, during which time the city was largely destroyed by shelling and hundreds of people were killed. In the final days of the siege, several hundred people sought refuge at the Vukovar hospital in the hope that it would be evacuated in the presence of international observers. Those who took shelter in the hospital were ultimately captured by advancing Serb forces.

One hundred and ninety-four such people—the majority of whom were Croatian POWs—were taken from the Vukovar hospital to Ovčara, where they were mistreated and, after the withdrawal of the last troops of the Yugoslav People's Army (JNA), killed by members of the Territorial Defense (TO) and Serb paramilitaries. The ICTY's Appeals Chamber observed that the Trial Chamber had made no finding as to whether the armed conflict in the municipality of Vukovar was international in nature. The Appeals Chamber did not make any such finding itself. It concluded, however, that certain orders and instructions of Serb military leaders, as well as the provisions of the Zagreb Agreement of 18 November 1991 (reached between representatives of the Republic of Croatia and the JNA concerning the evacuation of the sick and wounded from the Vukovar hospital), extended the protections of the Third Geneva Convention to POWs captured at the hospital. As the Appeals Chamber explained, "these documents provide sufficient evidence to conclude that the JNA had agreed that the Croat forces were to be considered POWs and that the Third Geneva Convention was to apply.[10]

The Appeals Chamber did not anchor its rulings only in the Zagreb Agreement but also in Common Article 3 and customary law.

It was well established—including by the ICTY's own jurisprudence—that Common Article 3 of the Geneva Conventions, which is applicable to both international and non-international armed conflicts, is part of customary international law and binds all parties to the conflict. Common Article 3,

10. *Prosecutor v. Mrkšić and Šljivančanin* (n. 8), at para. 69.

as the *Mrkšić and Šljivančanin* Appeal Judgement explains, "enshrines the prohibition against any violence against the life and person of those taking no active part in the hostilities, including members of armed forces who have laid down their arms and those placed *hors de combat* by sickness, wounds, detention, or any other cause."[11] The Appeals Chamber accordingly reasoned that Common Article 3 "reflects the same spirit of the duty to protect members of armed forces who have laid down their arms and are detained" as the specific protections provided for POWs in the Third Geneva Convention, viewed as a whole.[12]

This conclusion, which turns on customary law, was not unprecedented. During World War II, well before the adoption of Common Article 3 in the 1949 Geneva Conventions, the 1929 Geneva POW Convention, the predecessor of the Third Geneva Convention—was not applicable on the Eastern Front not having been ratified by the Soviet Union. Yet, both the International Military Tribunal established in the wake of the war and the follow-on Nuremberg tribunals did not hesitate to regard the 1929 Geneva Convention as a reflection of long-established principles of customary humanitarian law concerning the treatment of POWs—and to convict Nazi war criminals on that basis.[13] Of course, the customary law character of the Third Geneva Convention, and of its third Article, are no longer questioned. But the Nuremberg jurisprudence was seminal in establishing the customary law character of the main provisions of its predecessor—the 1929 Geneva Convention.

Even if there is a growing jurisprudence concerning the universality of certain duties to protect POWs, there is—or, at least, there was, before the *Mrkšić and Šljivančanin* Appeal Judgement—considerably less guidance concerning if and when those duties may cease to apply. This question was squarely presented by the facts in the *Mrkšić and Šljivančanin* case because the Trial Chamber acquitted Veselin Šljivančanin of the murder of the POWs at Ovčara on the basis that his responsibility for the welfare and security of the POWs ended with the withdrawal of the last JNA troops at Ovčara. The prosecution appealed this aspect of the Trial Chamber's Judgement,

11. *Id.* at para. 70. 12. *Id.*

13. International Military Tribunal (Nuremberg), *Judgment and Sentences* (1947) 41 AM. J. INT'L L. 172; *United States v. Wilhelm von Leeb et al.* (*The High Command* Case), *reprinted in* 11 TRIALS OF WAR CRIMINALS BEFORE THE NUREMBERG MILITARY TRIBUNALS UNDER CONTROL COUNCIL LAW NO. 10, at 533 Vols X–XI (1997).

arguing, in essence, that Šljivančanin—who had command authority over the JNA troops involved in evacuating POWs from the Vukovar hospital—had a continuing legal duty under international humanitarian law to protect the POWs, even after Šljivančanin's co-accused, Mile Mrkšić, ordered the JNA troops' withdrawal from Ovčara. The Appeals Chamber agreed with the prosecution, and I would like to explain why.

First, let us recall that the fundamental principle enshrined in the Third Geneva Convention is that POWs shall be treated humanely and protected from physical and mental harm. The Appeals Chamber concluded that this basic principle mirrored the protective principle found in the Common Articles of the Geneva Conventions and was non-derogable. Under the Third Geneva Convention, this fundamental principle applies from the time POWs fall into the power of the enemy until their final release and repatriation or transfer to another entity capable of ensuring their protection and welfare.

This means that it is the obligation of each agent in charge of the protection or custody of POWs to ensure that their transfer to another agent will not diminish the protection to which the prisoners are entitled. That obligation is so well established that it appears in both Articles 12 and 46 of the Third Geneva Convention, concerning the transfer of POWs to another State Party to the Convention and the transfer of POWs to other locations by a detaining power, respectively. The Appeals Chamber, therefore, made plain in its Appeal Judgement that, before transferring custody of the POWs at Ovčara, the JNA troops should have satisfied themselves of the willingness and ability of the members of the TO—like the JNA, a constituent element of the armed forces of the former Yugoslavia and subordinated to the Supreme Defense Council—to apply the principles enshrined in the Third Geneva Convention.

The Appeals Chamber also made clear that, although the Third Geneva Convention places the responsibility for POWs squarely on the detaining power, this is not to the exclusion of individual responsibility. Drawing upon the text of the Third Geneva Convention, ICRC commentaries and the regulations of the JNA itself, the Appeals Chamber concluded that individuals are personally accountable when they breach the law governing the treatment of POWs. It follows from this that agents of the detaining powers need not be specifically invested with authority over POWs to be subject to international obligations concerning the protection of POWs. Thus, in the view of the Appeals Chamber, all State agents who find themselves with custody of POWs owe the duty of protection regardless of whether the investment of responsibility was made through explicit delegation, such as through legislative enactment or a superior order, or as a result of the State agent finding himself with de facto custody over POWs such as when a POW surrenders to that agent.[14]

Based upon those considerations, the Appeals Chamber concluded that the Trial Chamber had erred in finding that Šljivančanin's duty to protect the POWs held at Ovčara pursuant to the laws and customs of war ended upon Mrkšić's order to withdraw. Šljivančanin was under a duty to protect the POWs evacuated from the Vukovar hospital and taken to Ovčara, and that duty included an obligation not to allow the transfer of custody of the POWs to anyone without first assuring himself that they would not be harmed. Put differently, Mrkšić's order to withdraw the JNA troops did not relieve Šljivančanin of his position as an officer of the JNA. As such, Šljivančanin remained an agent of the detaining power—and, thus, continued to be bound by the Third Geneva Convention not to transfer the POWs to another agent who would not guarantee their safety.

The *Mrkšić and Šljivančanin* Appeal Judgement thus has seminal importance for the proposition that the captor retains responsibility for the protection and welfare of POWs in his or her custody until their transfer to another entity with the will and the capability of ensuring such protection and welfare.

Although certain aspects of the Appeals Chamber's Judgement have been vacated following review proceedings conducted in 2010, nothing in the Appeals Chamber's Review Judgement[15] undermines the logic of the Chamber's earlier delineation of "the legal responsibilities that Šljivančanin bore, and agents of Detaining Powers continued to bear, with respect to the POWs in their custody,"[16] including the obligation to ensure that the transfer of POWs to another agent will not diminish or detract from their protection. "No matter what other procedures might be bypassed in times of stress and conflict, these responsibilities are neither vague nor elective,

14. *Prosecutor v. Mile Mrkšić and Veselin Šljivančanin* (n. 8), para. 73.
15. *Prosecutor v. Veselin Šljivančanin*, Review Judgement, ICTY Appeals Chamber, Case no. IT-95-13/1-R.1 (8 Dec. 2010).
16. *Id.*, Separate Opinion of Judge Meron, para. 3.

and the *Mrkšić and Šljivančanin* Appeal Judgement's careful guidance on this subject remains valid."[17]

The case also throws light on another principle of international humanitarian law and international criminal law, the duty to disobey illegal orders. Assuming that Šljivančanin knew that the order by his superior (Mrkšić) to withdraw the military police guarding the prisoners was illegal, he should have tried to compel the military police to remain in place.[18] Had they remained in place, the murder of the POWs would have become substantially less likely. At the very least, he should have reported to more senior commanders that murder was likely to occur if the regular troops were to withdraw and the POWs were left to the sole custody of the territorial troops.[19] He thus failed to act pursuant to his duty under the laws and customs of war, which substantially contributed to the murder. This justified his conviction for aiding and abetting the murder of the POWs.[20]

17. *Id.*, Separate Opinion of Judge Meron, para. 4.
18. *Prosecutor v. Mile Mrkšić and Veselin Šljivančanin* (n. 8), at para. 96.Ib.
19. *Id.* at paras. 98, 100.
20. *Id.* at para. 103.

IX

General Gotovina

A Controversial Acquittal

The Background

The events giving rise to the present case occurred between July and September 1995. During that time, Croatia initiated a military action called "Operation Storm" for the purpose of taking control of territory in the Krajina region of Croatia. Gotovina was a colonel-general in the HV (Croatian Army) during the Indictment period and was the operational commander of Operation Storm in the southern part of the Krajina region. The Trial Chamber found that Gotovina contributed to the joint criminal enterprise (JCE) the common purpose of which was to permanently remove the Serb civilian population from the Krajina region. The Trial Chamber consequently found Gotovina guilty under the first form of JCE of both persecution and deportation as crimes against humanity. It also found him guilty under the third form of JCE of murder and inhuman acts as crimes against humanity, plunder of public and private property and violations of the laws or customs of war. He was sentenced to a single term of 24 years' imprisonment.

As the documents make plain, the Trial Chamber found that the gravamen of the crimes was the unlawful shelling by Croatian forces of Serbian towns. Illegal shelling was considered to be shelling involving artillery impacts more than 200 meters from a military objective. The Trial Chamber applied this yardstick to all the shellings, whatever the range and weather and the artillery used. The Appeals Chamber unanimously considered that the 200-meter standard was erroneous. The majority and minority differed

Standing Up For Justice. Theodor Meron, Oxford University Press (2021). © Theodor Meron.
DOI: 10.1093/oso/9780198863434.003.0009

on whether other alternative modes of liability should have been resorted to on the appeal level. This is further discussed in my separate opinion which follows.

During my four terms as President of the ICTY and three terms as President of the Mechanism, I chaired many appeals. Most of them resulted in convictions and sentences, sometimes very heavy, some involved acquittals. None of them triggered as harsh and often *ad hominem* criticism as the Gotovina acquittal. Rather than respond to criticisms which, following judicial conventions, I do not do, I have decided to bring here the principal judicial texts on the subject. They should speak for themselves.

I. Excerpts from the Appeals Chamber Majority Judgement of Acquittal of Gotovina

Prosecutor v. Ante Gotovina and Mladen Markač, Appeal Judgement, Case no. IT-06-90-A (16 Nov. 2012)

57. The Trial Chamber's Impact Analysis never deviated from the 200 Metre Standard. With respect to all Four Towns, it found that all impact sites within 200 metres of a target it deemed legitimate could have been justified as part of an attack offering military advantage to HV forces. By contrast, the Trial Chamber found that all impact sites more than 200 metres from a target it deemed legitimate served as indicators of an indiscriminate artillery attack.[1]

[...]

83. In these circumstances, the Appeals Chamber, Judge Agius and Judge Pocar dissenting, finds that the reversal of the Impact Analysis undermines the Trial Chamber's conclusion that artillery attacks on the Four Towns were unlawful. The Trial Chamber's reliance on the Impact Analysis was so significant that even considered in its totality, the remaining evidence does not definitively demonstrate that artillery attacks against the Four Towns were unlawful. In view of the foregoing, the Appeals Chamber, Judge Agius and Judge Pocar dissenting, considers that no reasonable trier of fact could conclude beyond reasonable doubt that the Four Towns were subject to unlawful artillery attacks. The Appeals Chamber thus need not consider the Appellants'

1. *See* Trial Judgement, paras. 1899-1-906, 1917-19-21, 1927-19-33, 1939-41.

remaining arguments challenging the Trial Chamber's findings on the unlawful nature of artillery attacks against the Four Towns.

[...]

91. The Appeals Chamber observes that the Trial Chamber's conclusion that a JCE existed was based on its overall assessment of several mutually-reinforcing findings, but that its findings on the JCE's core common purpose of forcibly removing Serb civilians from the Krajina rested primarily on the existence of unlawful artillery attacks against civilians and civilian objects in the Four Towns.[2] Having reversed the Trial Chamber's findings related to unlawful artillery attacks,[3] the Appeals Chamber, Judge Agius and Judge Pocar dissenting, cannot affirm the Trial Chamber's conclusion that the only reasonable interpretation of the circumstantial evidence on the record was that a JCE aiming to permanently remove the Serb civilian population from the Krajina by force or threat of force existed.

92. More specifically, the Appeals Chamber, Judge Pocar dissenting, recalls that, in the context of Operation Storm, unlawful artillery attacks were identified by the Trial Chamber as the primary means by which the forced departure of Serb civilians from the Krajina region was effected. The Trial Chamber stated that the JCE involved treating "whole towns as targets for the initial artillery attack" in Operation Storm, that removal "of the Krajina Serb population was to a large extent achieved through the unlawful attacks against civilians and civilian objects in Knin, Benkovac, Obrovac, and Gračac,"[4] and that these attacks promoted the JCE's goal of forcing "the Krajina Serbs from their homes."[5] By contrast, the Appeals Chamber, Judge Pocar dissenting, observes that where artillery attacks on settlements were not deemed unlawful, the Trial Chamber was unwilling to characterise Serb civilians' concurrent departures as deportation.[6] The Trial Chamber explained that "The failure by members of the Croatian political and military leadership to make the distinction between the civilian population and the military goes to the very core of the case."[7]

[...]

96. The Appeals Chamber, Judge Agius and Judge Pocar dissenting, underscores again the centrality of unlawful artillery attacks on the Four Towns to the Trial Chamber's findings. The unlawfulness of these attacks constituted the core basis for finding that Serb civilians were *forcibly* displaced. Absent the finding of unlawful artillery attacks and resulting displacement, the Trial Chamber's conclusion that the common purpose

2. *See* Trial Judgement, paras. 2310–2315.
3. *See* Appeals Judgement, 16 November 2012, para. 84.
4. Trial Judgement, para. 2311.
5. Trial Judgement, para. 2310. *See also* Trial Judgement, para. 2314.
6. *See* Trial Judgement, para. 1755.
7. Trial Judgement, para. 2309.

crimes of deportation, forcible transfer, and related persecution took place cannot be sustained.[8] In this context, no reasonable trial chamber could conclude that the only reasonable interpretation of the circumstantial evidence on the record was the existence of a JCE with the common purpose of permanently removing the Serb civilian population from the Krajina by force or threat of force.

97. In view of the Appeals Chamber's reversal of the Trial Chamber's finding that a JCE existed, the Appellants' convictions for the common purpose crimes of deportation, forcible transfer, and persecution fall. The Appellants' remaining convictions for the crimes of plunder, wanton destruction, murder, inhumane acts, and cruel treatment, and associated convictions for persecution were entered via the third form of JCE.[9] The Trial Chamber, in convicting the Appellants for these deviatory crimes, found that the crimes "were a natural and foreseeable consequence of the JCE's implementation."[10] The Appeals Chamber recalls that liability for deviatory crimes attributed via the third category of JCE involves responsibility for crimes committed "beyond the common purpose, but which are nevertheless a natural and foreseeable consequence" of it.[11] Reversal of the Trial Chamber's finding that a JCE existed means that other crimes could not be a natural and foreseeable consequence of that JCE's common purpose. Accordingly, the Appellants' convictions for deviatory crimes entered via the third form of that JCE must also fall.[12]

[...]

108. Having dismissed the Appellants' challenge to its general power to enter convictions on the basis of alternate modes of liability, the Appeals Chamber recalls that its exercise of this power is subject to the Statute's fundamental protections of the rights of the accused.[13] The Appeals Chamber further recalls that, as set out in the Statute, its jurisdiction is focused on reviewing the findings of trial chambers for errors of law which invalidate a decision and errors of fact which occasion a miscarriage of justice.[14] The Appeals Chamber will not enter convictions under alternate modes of liability where this would substantially compromise the fair trial rights of appellants or exceed its jurisdiction as delineated in the Statute.[15]

8. *Cf. Stakić* Appeal Judgement, paras. 278, 317.
9. Trial Judgement, paras. 2372–2374, 2584–2586.
10. Trial Judgement, paras. 2374, 2586.
11. *Kvočka et al.* Appeal Judgement, para. 83.
12. *See* Appeals Judgement, 16 November 2012, paras. 89–90. Judge Agius and Judge Pocar dissent on this paragraph.
13. *See* Art. 21 of the Statute. *See also* Art 20, 23, 25 of the Statute.
14. Art. 25 of the Statute. *Cf.* Art 20, 23 of the Statute; *Orić* Appeal Judgement, para. 11.
15. *Cf.* Art 21, 25 of the Statute.

II. A Separate Opinion on Alternate Modes of Liability

Separate Opinion of Judge Theodor Meron

1. While I join the Majority's analysis as set out in the Appeal Judgement, I write separately primarily to explain my views on the Appeals Chamber's jurisprudence with respect to convictions pursuant to alternate modes of liability.

2. As an initial matter, I observe that the Bench is unanimous in holding that the Trial Chamber erred in deriving the 200 Metre Standard. While not all my Colleagues join the Majority view on the consequences of this error, there is no dispute over its existence.[16]

3. I further observe that the Appeal Judgement makes two clear advances to the criminal procedure precedent of the Tribunal. For the first time, a panel considering entering convictions pursuant to an alternate mode of liability requested explicit briefing from parties on this issue. The Appeal Judgement also helps clarify our jurisprudence by setting out in more detail the judicial rationale underlying the Appeals Chamber's power to enter convictions pursuant to alternate modes of liability.

4. I join the Majority in holding that the Appeals Chamber possesses the power to enter convictions pursuant to alternate modes of liability. However, I would underscore that this authority does not constitute a panacea to address any and all errors by the Prosecution or a trial chamber. Instead, I believe that this power should only be exercised selectively, where: i) any additional, inferences from findings set forth in a relevant trial judgement are restricted; and ii) any differences between the convictions that appellants initially appealed and convictions entered on appeal are limited. Otherwise, the Appeals Chamber risks undermining appellants' fair trial rights, or conducting a second trial rather than reviewing the trial chamber's alleged errors.[17]

5. Whether it is warranted to enter convictions pursuant to alternate modes of liability in a given appeal constitutes a fact-specific question best left to individual Benches. But as a general matter, I do not believe that the Appeals Chamber's authority serves as a licence for wholesale reconstruction or revision of approaches adopted or decisions taken by a trial chamber. In this context, I recall that our jurisprudence has consistently indicated that sudden, significant alterations in the scope of a case may deny individuals their fair

16. See Appeal Judgement, 16 November 2012, para. 61.

17. I would underscore that this discussion refers to convictions pursuant to alternate means of liability which are not requested in an appeal by the Prosecution.

trial rights. Thus, for example, in the Kupreskic et al. Appeal Judgement, the Appeals Chamber found that two appellants had been unacceptably prejudiced by the "drastic change" in the Prosecution's case of which they had no effective notice.[18] Similarly, I note that in past cases where the Appeals Chamber entered convictions pursuant to alternate modes of liability, changes to the structure of the case faced by appellants were limited in nature. For example, the Appeals Chamber entered such convictions to address technical but effectively non-substantive errors in indictments,[19] or after finding that appellants aided a JCE but were not proved to share its common purpose.[20]

6. In the present Appeal Judgement, I am satisfied that the Majority acts prudently and fairly in not entering additional convictions. I also agree with the Majority's logic in addressing those findings with respect to each Appellant which were not reversed. However, were I solely responsible for the Appeal Judgement, I would not have undertaken this latter analysis. In this regard, I first recall that in the Appeal Judgement, the Majority reverses the fundamental conclusions of the Trial Chamber, including the finding that a JCE existed.[21] I also note that discussion of modes of liability other than JCE was almost entirely absent from core trial and appeal briefing.[22]

18. *Kupreškić et al.* Appeal Judgement, para. 121. See also *Kupreškić et al.* Appeal Judgement, para. 122; *Ntagerura et al.* Appeal Judgement, paras. 146–150, 164.

19. *See*, e.g., *Rukundo* Appeal Judgement, paras. 37, 115 (In which the Appeals Chamber replaced Rukundo's conviction for committing certain crimes with convictions for aiding and abetting these same crimes based on its finding that commission as a mode of liability was not pled in the indictment).

20. *See*, e.g., *Krstić* Appeal Judgement, paras. 135-144 (In which the Appeals Chamber found that Krstić did not possess the intent to commit genocide, but instead possessed knowledge of the exact same set of crimes, and did not reverse the finding that a JCE existed); D. *Milošević* Appeal Judgement, paras. 275–282 (In which the Appeals Chamber found that the evidence did not establish that Dragomir Milošević ordered numerous shelling incidents but was responsible as a superior for those crimes). I note that in the *Simić* Appeal Judgement, in which the Appeal Chamber entered an alternate conviction for aiding and abetting after reversing a finding that a JCE existed, the Appeals Chamber underscored that aiding and abetting liability had been extensively discussed both at trial and on appeal. See *Simić* Appeal Judgement paras. 74–191, 301.

21. Appeal Judgement, paras. 84, 98.

22. The Prosecution's arguments at trial and on appeal focused on the existence of a JCE involving unlawful artillery attacks. While the Indictment charged the Appellants with, inter alia, aiding and abetting and superior responsibility, Indictment, paras. 36–37, 45–46, post-Indictment proceedings provided only limited indications that the Prosecution was pursuing these alternate forms of liability. The Prosecution's Pre-Trial Brief and Final Trial Brief consistently focus on the existence of unlawful attacks and a JCE. *Compare* Prosecution Final Trial Brief, paras. 1–123, 383–386, 477–660 (outlining the existence of a JCE and the centrality of the unlawful attacks), *with* Prosecution Final Trial Brief, paras. 124–132, 387–399 (addressing alternate modes of liability). See also Prosecution Pre-Trial Brief, paras. 127–132. Even the Prosecution's brief discussions of other modes of liability often include references to unlawful attacks. See Prosecution Final Trial Brief, paras. 124–133, 387–400. On appeal, the Prosecution devoted only a single footnote to alternate modes of liability in each of its appeal response briefs, see Prosecution Response (Gotovina), para. 333, n. 1112; Prosecution Response (Markač) para. 273,

In circumstances like these, while fully supporting the Appeal Judgement, I do not believe the Appeals Chamber should enter convictions pursuant to alternate modes of liability. Such convictions would, in my view, necessarily involve unfairness to the Appellants, who would be found guilty of crimes very different from those they defended against at trial or on appeal.[23] Accordingly, I consider that analysis of the Trial Chamber's "remaining findings",[24] like that undertaken by the Appeal Judgement,[25] is unnecessary, as the Tribunal's commitment to fair trial rights should, in this case, foreclose the possibility of convictions pursuant to alternate modes of liability.

7. I reiterate that, in appropriate circumstances, the Appeals Chamber's power to enter convictions pursuant to alternate forms of liability can be deployed to serve the interests of justice. This authority must, however, be wielded sparingly, in appropriate circumstances, and only where its exercise does not impinge on the rights of appellants. The Appeal Judgement's holding respects this principle, and this is the basis on which I join the Majority.

Done in English and French, the English text being authoritative.

Judge Theodor Meron

Dated this 16th day of November 2012,
At The Hague,
The Netherlands.

[Seal of the Tribunal]

III. Judgement of the ICJ Supporting the *Gotovina* Majority Decision

The International Court of Justice gave detailed consideration to the criticism voiced by the counsel for Serbia in this case of the *Gotovina* acquittal. The ICJ concluded that the majority Judgement was correct.

n. 958, and referred to the matter only in passing during the Appeal Hearing, see AT. 14 May 2012 p. 102. See also Trial Judgement, paras. 2375, 2587.

23. In this regard I note that I join the Majority in finding that in the circumstances of this case, supplementary briefing would not cure such unfairness. *See* Appeal Judgement, para. 154.
24. Appeal Judgement, para. 150.
25. *See* Appeal Judgement, paras. 111–155.

International Court of Justice Reports of Judgments, Advisory Opinions and Orders

APPLICATION OF THE CONVENTION ON THE PREVENTION AND PUNISHMENT OF THE CRIME OF GENOCIDE (CROATIA *v.* SERBIA) JUDGMENT OF 3 FEBRUARY 2015

468. In its Judgment of 16 November 2012 in the *Gotovina* case, the Appeals Chamber disagreed with the Trial Chamber's analysis and reversed the latter's decision.

The Appeals Chamber held that the "200 Metre Standard" had no basis in law and lacked any convincing justification. The Chamber accordingly concluded that the Trial Chamber could not reasonably find, simply by applying that standard, that the four towns in question had been shelled indiscriminately. It further held that the Trial Chamber's reasoning was essentially based on the application of the standard in question, and that none of the evidence before the Court—particularly the Brioni Transcript—showed convincingly that the Croatian armed forces had deliberately targeted the civilian population (*Gotovina* Appeals Judgment, paras. 61, 64-65, 77-83, 93). The Appeals Chamber accordingly found that the prosecution had failed to prove a "joint criminal enterprise", and acquitted the two accused on all of the counts in the indictment (including murder and deportation) (*ibid.*, para. 158).

469. The Court recalls, as it stated in 2007, that it "should in principle accept as highly persuasive relevant findings of facts made by the Tribunal at trial, unless of course they have been upset on appeal" (see paragraph 182 above).

That should lead the Court, in the present case, to give the greatest weight to factual findings by the Trial Chamber which were not reversed by the Appeals Chamber, and to give due weight to the findings and determinations of the Appeals Chamber on the issue of whether or not the shelling of the Krajina towns during Operation Storm was indiscriminate.

470. Against this approach, Serbia argued that the findings of an ICTY Appeals Chamber should not necessarily be accorded more weight than those of a Trial Chamber. Indeed, according to Serbia, the members of the Appeals Chamber are appointed at random and vary from one case to another, so that they have no greater experience or authority than those of the Trial Chamber having ruled on the same case. Serbia argues that the main difference between the two Benches appears to be that the former consists of five judges, whilst the latter is composed of three judges. Moreover, the decision of the Trial Chamber was unanimous when it convicted Gotovina and Markač, whereas the Appeals Chamber reached its decision to acquit them by a majority of three against two. Serbia points out that, overall, the majority of the judges having sat in the Gotovina case were of the view that

the Croatian forces did engage in indiscriminate shelling of the four above-mentioned Krajina towns.

It would follow, according to Serbia, that in the particular circumstances of the present case the Court should not attach any greater importance to the findings of the Appeals Chamber than to those of the Trial Chamber, and should form its own view of the persuasiveness of the arguments accepted by each of the two Benches.

471. Irrespective of the manner in which the members of the Appeals Chamber are chosen—a matter on which it is not for the Court to pronounce—the latter's decisions represent the last word of the ICTY on the cases before it when one of the parties has chosen to appeal from the Trial Chamber's Judgment. Accordingly, the Court cannot treat the findings and determinations of the Trial Chamber as being on an equal footing with those of the Appeals Chamber. In cases of disagreement, it is bound to accord greater weight to what the Appeals Chamber Judgment says, while ultimately retaining the power to decide the issues before it on the facts and the law.

472. The Court concludes from the foregoing that it is unable to find that there was any indiscriminate shelling of the Krajina towns deliberately intended to cause civilian casualties. It would only be in exceptional circumstances that it would depart from the findings reached by the ICTY on an issue of this kind. Serbia has indeed drawn the Court's attention to the controversy aroused by the Appeals Chamber's Judgment. However, no evidence, whether prior or subsequent to that Judgment, has been put before the Court which would incontrovertibly show that the Croatian authorities deliberately intended to shell the civilian areas of towns inhabited by Serbs. In particular, no such intent is apparent from the Brioni Transcript, which will be subjected to a more detailed analysis below in relation to the existence of the *dolus specialis*. Nor can such intent be regarded as incontrovertibly established on the basis of the statements by persons having testified before the ICTY Trial Chamber in the *Gotovina* case, and cited as witnesses by Serbia in the present case.

[...]

PART III

Selected Decisions

X

Fleshing Out Principles of Fairness

The Tribunals made a major contribution to fleshing out principles of fairness, on which their legitimacy and credibility rests, in matters such as fair trials, recusals, disqualification of Judges, proportionality and sentencing. In this Chapter, I will discuss some of these developments by referring to specific decisions, mostly of the Appeals Chamber.

Prosecutor v. Ngirabatware

Order to the Government of the Republic of Turkey for the Release of Judge Aydin Sefa Akay

Date of Order: 31 January 2017

Judge Meron as a Pre-Review Judge

Order to Turkey to release a Mechanism Judge arrested in violation of his immunity

I start from the Order to Turkey in the case of *Prosecutor v. Ngirabatware* for the release of Judge Aydin Sefa Akay of 31 January 2017 which I issued as a Pre-Review Judge.

The story of the Turkish Judge Akay is fully discussed in Chapter VI.

On 18 December 2014, the Appeals Chamber affirmed Ngirabatware's convictions for committing direct and public incitement to commit genocide and instigating and aiding and abetting genocide.[1] On 8 July 2016,

1. *Prosecutor v. Augustin Ngirabatware*, Order to the Government of the Republic of Turkey for the Release of Judge Aydin Sefa Akay, at para. 2, IRMCT President, Case no. MICT-12-29-R (31 Jan. 2017). *See also Augustin Ngirabatware v. The Prosecutor*, Judgement, IRMCT Appeal Chamber, Case no. MICT-12-29A (18 Dec. 2014).

Standing Up For Justice. Theodor Meron, Oxford University Press (2021). © Theodor Meron.
DOI: 10.1093/oso/9780198863434.003.0010

Ngirabatware filed a request for review of his convictions and on 25 July 2016 a Bench of the Appeals Chamber was assigned to consider the request.[2] On or around 21 September 2016, Judge Akay was detained in Turkey while engaged in business of the Mechanism. The Secretary-General consequently asserted diplomatic immunity with respect to Judge Akay and requested his immediate release pursuant to Article 29 of the Statute and the Convention on the Privileges and Immunities of the United Nations of 13 February 1946.[3] On 28 November 2016, Turkey was invited to file a written response related to the issuance of an Order to cease the prosecution of Judge Akay but failed to do so.[4] On 21 December 2016, a public hearing was ordered to allow Turkey another opportunity to respond to Judge Akay's arrest and detention; however, Turkey failed to attend the hearing, which was held on 17 January 2017.[5] The hearing was to assess how to proceed with Ngirabatware's case without further delays due to Judge Akay's detention—should Judge Akay be replaced on the Bench on this case, should he be reassigned to another matter or should the review proceedings continue in his absence?

An independent judiciary is fundamental for the interests of justice. This Order makes clear that the right to a fair trial stated in Article 19 of the Statute must include the right to be tried before an independent and impartial tribunal: "it is self-evident that justice and the rule of law begin with an independent judiciary."[6] The right to an independent and impartial tribunal is an absolute right and requires the Judges of the Mechanism to be independent from all external factors. This includes independence "from their own States of nationality or residence."[7] Article 29 of the Statute—providing full diplomatic immunity—allows Judges of the Mechanism to properly exercise their judicial functions from their home countries.

In the present case, replacing Judge Akay would violate the principle of an independent judiciary. Reassigning him to another case would not only be unfair but would similarly infringe upon judicial independence. Reassigning Judge Akay would improperly "allow interference by a national authority in the conduct of a case and the exercise of judicial functions."[8]

2. *Id.* at para. 3.
3. *Id.* at para. 6.
4. *Id.* at para. 7.
5. *Id.* at para. 8.
6. *Id.* at para. 11.
7. *Id.* at para. 11.
8. *Id.* at para. 13.

Absent "extraordinary circumstances, Ngirabatware's continued presence on the Bench is essential to the preservation of judicial independence."[9]

Nahimana, Barayagwiza and Ngeze v. The Prosecutor

Appeals Judgement

DATE OF JUDGEMENT: 28 NOVEMBER 2007

INDEPENDENCE, IMPARTIALITY, ALLEGATIONS OF BIAS

Independence is a "functional attribute" where an individual is not subject to the influence of external authorities and retains complete freedom in making a decision. On the other hand, impartiality is a "personal attribute" which implies a lack of bias and prejudice.[10]

The Appeals Chamber emphasized that the independence of the Judges of the Tribunal was "guaranteed by the [high] standards for their selection, the method of their appointment, their conditions of service and the immunity they enjoy." There is a strong presumption of independence and the burden falls on the appellant to rebut this presumption.[11]

The Appeals Chamber recalled that the Prosecutor is a party to the proceedings and his duty "to act independently is distinct from that of the Judges"[12] of the Tribunal, and is found in Article 15(2) of the Statute. The Appeals Chamber held that the appellant had failed to show that the principle of judicial independence was violated.

The requirement of impartiality is a fundamental component of the right of an accused to a fair trial. There is a presumption of impartiality which attaches to Judges of the Tribunal and this presumption cannot be easily rebutted. The burden falls on the appellant to submit sufficient evidence to the Appeals Chamber to rebut this presumption. The Appeals Chamber will resort to the "reasonable observer" test to determine if a properly informed reasonable observer would find actual bias or the appearance of bias.[13]

9. *Id.* at para. 15.

10. *Ferdinand Nahimana, Jean-Bosco Barayagwiza, Hassan Ngeze v. The Prosecutor*, Judgement, ICTR Appeals Chambers, at para. 19, Case no. ICTR-99-52-A (28 Nov. 2007).

11. *Id.* at para. 28.

12. *Id.* at para. 40.

13. *Id.* at paras. 47–8.

None of the allegations made by the appellants met the threshold of proving that the Trial Chamber Judges either relied on certain evidence or past judgements to improperly influence their decisions.

Prosecutor v. Galić

Appeals Judgement

Date of Judgement: 30 November 2006

Fair Trial, Impartiality, Disqualification

I discuss here Ground 2 of the Appeal, the disqualification of a Judge.

Neither the Statute nor the Rules of the Tribunal provide for the suspension of a trial while a motion for disqualification is pending.[14] This does not mean that an accused cannot request a suspension of the proceedings on his or her own accord. However, this request does not have to be granted as the Trial Chamber has discretion whether or not to suspend a trial while a disqualification motion is pending.

The right of an accused to be tried by an independent and impartial tribunal is an integral component of the right to a fair trial found in Article 21 of the Statute.[15] This impartiality requirement covers both subjective and objective bias. It thus protects the accused against both actual bias and the appearance of bias. Regarding the appearance of bias, the "reasonable observer" test is used. This allows for a finding of the appearance of bias when the circumstances of a case would lead a reasonable observer who has been properly informed of all the relevant circumstances of a case to reasonably apprehend bias.[16] However, the Judges of the Tribunal enjoy a presumption of impartiality, and there is a high threshold for rebutting this presumption of impartiality.[17]

The Appeals Chamber held that Judge Orie's confirmation of the *Mladić* Indictment did not establish actual bias or show that the Judge had in any way predetermined Galić's guilt. The Appeals Chamber noted that Galić had failed to understand the "fundamental difference between the

14. *Prosecutor v. Stanislav Galić*, Judgement, ICTY Appeals Chamber, at para. 33, Case no. IT-98-29-A (30 Nov. 2006).

15. *Id.* at para. 37.

16. *Id.* at paras. 39–40.

17. *Id.* at para. 41.

functions of a Judge who confirms an indictment and a Judge who sits at a trial."[18]

To assess whether there was an appearance of bias, the Appeals Chamber had to apply the "reasonable observer" test.[19] The Appeals Chamber held that a properly informed, reasonable observer would not find that Judge Orie's confirmation of the *Mladić* Indictment represented a predetermination of Galić's guilt. That same reasonable observer would recognize that Judge Orie would still be able to properly assess the evidence presented at Galić's trial with an open mind due to his training and professional experience.

Renzaho v. The Prosecutor

Appeals Judgement

DATE OF JUDGEMENT: 1 APRIL 2011

PRESUMPTION OF INNOCENCE

The guarantee of the presumption of innocence of an accused is found in Article 20(3) of the Statute (para. 24). Rule 87(A) of the Rules of Procedure and Evidence of the Tribunal further provides that a majority of the Trial Chamber must be satisfied beyond a reasonable doubt that the accused is guilty before entering a verdict. The Prosecution has the burden of proving the charges beyond a reasonable doubt. However, on appeal the burden shifts to the appellant who must now show that the Trial Chamber violated his or her presumption of innocence.[20]

The Appeals Chamber recalled that the right to a fair trial did not create a right of an accused to participate in any proceeding in which his name may be mentioned. The right to a fair trial and the right to have knowledge of and the opportunity to comment on the evidence given by the other party concerns the specific proceedings of the accused. Additionally, the Appeals Chamber noted that Judges are not disqualified from hearing two or more cases arising out of the same events and involving similar evidence. The

18. *Id.* at para. 42. 19. *Id.* at para. 44.

20. *Tharcisse Renzaho v. The Prosecutor*, Judgement, ICTR Appeals Chamber, at para. 24, Case no. ICTR-97-31-A (1 Apr. 2011).

training and professional nature of the Judges as well as the presumption of impartiality act as safeguards and ensure that Judges will only consider and rely on the evidence presented in the particular case before them.[21]

Prosecutor v. Hadžihasanović and Kubura

Appeals Judgement

Date of Judgement: 22 April 2008

Actual Bias and Appearance of Bias

The Appeals Chamber explained that the duty of impartiality is found in Article 13 of the Statute and is an important component of the right to a fair trial found in Article 21 of the Statute.[22] The Appeals Chamber also recalled that improper bias can take the form of actual bias or the appearance of bias. In this case, the Appeals Chamber considered whether the Trial Judges showed an appearance of bias and decided that it did not.

Prosecutor v. Šešelj

Decision on Defence Motion for Disqualification of Judge Frederik Harhoff and Report to the Vice-President

Date of Decision: 28 August 2013

Before a Chamber of three Judges convened by Order of Vice-President

Finding by a panel of three Judges (one dissenting) that Ad Litem Judge Harhoff demonstrated a bias in favour of convictions and that the presumption of impartiality had been rebutted

By an emailed letter to 56 contacts which was leaked to the press, Judge Harhoff alleged, inter alia, that I exerted pressure on my colleagues in the *Gotovina* and *Perišić* cases to acquit Gotovina and Perišić, that I acted following alleged pressure by the United States and Israel, and that the ICTY took a significant step back from making military leaders responsible for their

21. *Id.* at paras. 25, 43.

22. *Prosecutor v. Enver Hadžihasanović, Amir Kubura*, Judgement, ICTY Appeals Chamber, at para. 78, Case no. IT-01-47-A (22 Apr. 2008).

subordinates' crimes. At that time, Judge Harhoff was serving on the *Šešelj* Trial Bench. On 2 July 2013, Šešelj filed a motion for the disqualification of Judge Harhoff from all further proceedings in his case, on the ground that the letter/email showed a strong inclination to convict accused persons of Serbian ethnicity. By decision of 28 August, the Chamber of Judges Moloto, Hall and Liu (appointed by Vice-President Agius, as I had recused myself) with Judge Liu dissenting, found that Judge Harhoff demonstrated a bias in favour of convictions, that a reasonable observer properly informed would reasonably apprehend bias, that the presumption of impartiality has been rebutted and that the application requesting the disqualification of Judge Harhoff was upheld.[23]

Since Judge Harhoff was an *Ad Litem* Judge assigned only to the *Šešelj* case, he had to leave the ICTY following the disqualification decision.

In its Judgement of 3 February 2015 in the case of the Application of the Convention on the Prevention and Punishment of the Crime of Genocide,[24] the ICJ agreed with the ICTY Appeals Chamber Judgement on Gotovina (which reversed Gotovina's convictions and which was criticized in the Harhoff letter).

Prosecutor v. Mladić

Decision on Interlocutory Appeal Against Decision on Defence Motion for a Fair Trial and the Presumption of Innocence

Date of Decision: 27 February 2017

Allegations by Mladić that his rights to a fair trial and to his presumption of innocence had been compromised because of the engagement of staff members who had previously worked on and participated in the drafting of the *Karadžić* Trial Judgement rejected. Judges' impartiality confirmed.

23. *Prosecutor v. Vojislav Šešelj*, Decision on Defence Motion for Disqualification of Judge Frederik Harhoff and Report to the Vice-President, ICTY Chamber convened by Order of the Vice-President, at paras. 13–14, Case no. IT-03-67-T (28 Aug. 2013).
24. *Application of the Convention on the Prevention and Punishment of the Crime of Genocide (Croatia v. Serbia)*, Judgment, ICJ, at paras. 469–72 and 501–7 (3 Feb. 2015).

On 19 May 2016, Mladić filed a motion before the Trial Chamber alleging that his rights to a fair trial and the presumption of innocence had been compromised because of the engagement of staff members who had previously worked on and participated in the drafting of the *Karadžić* Trial Judgement (referred to as the "Impugned Staff").[25] On 4 July 2016, the Trial Chamber issued a Decision rejecting Mladić's allegation that his rights had been violated by the engagement of the staff.[26] The Trial Chamber noted that the role of the Impugned Staff in the *Karadžić* case did not influence the independent decision-making of the Judges or their impartiality. The Trial Chamber also concluded that the presumption of impartiality of the Judges had not been rebutted by the role of the Impugned Staff in the *Karadžić* case.[27]

Mladić filed the present Appeal on 4 October 2016 and, on 10 October 2016, he filed motions seeking the disqualification of Judge Agius, Judge Pocar and Judge Meron with regards to two interlocutory appeals, including this Appeal.[28]

Though legal officers assisting Judges are not held to the same standards of impartiality as Judges of the Tribunal, this decision acknowledges the possibility of cases where a staff member's participation "may be so problematic as to either impugn the perceived impartiality of the Judges or the appearance thereof."[29] The presumption of impartiality which attaches to Judges cannot be easily rebutted.[30] The Appeals Chamber held that the role of the Impugned Staff did not influence the decision-making ability of the Judges. The role of the impugned staff was limited to providing assistance to the Judges (such as legal research and preparing draft decisions) based on the Judges' instructions.[31] Further, the Appeals Chamber held that the staff's previous work on the *Karadžić* case would not lead a reasonable observer to rebut the presumption of impartiality of the Judges.[32]

25. *Prosecutor v. Ratko Mladić*, Decision on Interlocutory Appeal against Decision on Defence Motion for a Fair Trial and the Presumption of Innocence, ICTY Appeals Chamber, at para. 3, Case no. IT-09-92-AR73.6 (27 Feb. 2017).
26. *Id.* at para. 4.
27. *Id.* at para. 5.
28. *Id.* at para. 7.
29. *Id.* at para. 10.
30. *Id.*
31. *Id.* at para. 30.
32. *Id.* at para. 39.

Prosecutor v. Mladić

Decision on Defence Motions for Disqualification of Judges Theodor Meron, Carmel Agius and Liu Daqun

Date of Decision: 3 September 2018

Judge Antonetti as the Senior Judge

Case Law on Judge Antonetti's decision to disqualify Judges Meron, Agius and Liu from Mladić Appeal

On 18 June 2018, the accused, Ratko Mladić, filed motions seeking the disqualification of Judges Meron, Agius and Liu for actual or apparent bias.[33] As required by Rules 18(B)(iv) and 22(B), the President of the Mechanism withdrew and assigned the next most senior judge, in this case Judge Antonetti, to consider the consolidated motions.[34] As reiterated in this decision, the right to be tried by an impartial court is a fundamental right that is required in order to guarantee a fair trial. Correspondingly, the right to a fair trial is recognized as an "absolute right not subject to exception."[35] To safeguard the right to be tried by an impartial court, a Judge cannot hear a case in which "he has or has had any sort of connection that might compromise or appear to compromise his impartiality."[36]

According to Judge Antonetti, who himself was a member of the Bench in the *Tolimir* appeal, the Judges involved in either the trial or appeal proceedings of the *Krstić*, *Tolimir*, *Popović et al.* and *Blagojević and Jokić* cases had knowledge of incriminating evidence against the accused regarding his criminal responsibility, though Mladić contested his responsibility in his appeal.[37] The findings of the ICTY Trial Chamber concerning Mladić's participation in JCEs, his contribution to the crimes committed in Srebrenica and his knowledge of the crimes committed, could lead a reasonable observer to apprehend bias.[38]

33. *Prosecutor v. Ratko Mladić*, Decision on Defence Motions for Disqualification of Judges Theodor Meron, Carmel Agius and Liu Daqun, IRMCT Judge Antonetti as Senior Judge, at para. 1, Case no. MICT-13-56-A (3 Sept. 2018).

34. *Id.* at para. 2. 35. *Id.* at para. 3. 36. *Id.*

37. *Id.* at para. 32. 38. *Id.*

However, regarding the example included in paragraph 16(iv) of the Motion, pointing to footnote 250 of the *Krstić* Appeal Judgement, this was indeed an example of unacceptable bias according to Judge Antonetti.[39] According to Judge Antonetti, the content of that footnote could no longer be said to simply be referring to preexisting findings of the Trial Chamber, instead implying the criminal responsibility of Mladić.[40] Further findings of the Appeals Chamber that appeared to fall outside the scope of the Trial Chamber's findings included paragraph 32 of the Appeal Judgement, pointing to the genocidal intent of the VRS Main Staff of which Mladić was the Commander, as no explicit reference to the Trial Chamber was made in support of that allegation.[41] In the view of Judge Antonetti, it was difficult for a reasonable observer informed of the particular circumstances of the case to not hold that the findings relating to a "direct subordinate" of Mladić had no influence on Mladić.[42]

Judge Antonetti noted that the references to Mladić in both *Krstić* and *Tolimir* did not directly qualify as "findings" of the Appeals Chamber, however, their "accumulation in two separate appeal judgements presents a problem."[43] Numerous findings of the Trial Chamber pointed to Mladić's genocidal intent, his role in a JCE and his role in planning and committing the crime that he was now contesting on appeal.[44] As a result, Judge Antonetti believed that it would be difficult for Judge Meron to not be influenced by the incriminating evidence that he himself analyzed against Mladić and based his previous findings on.[45] Judge Antonetti further noted that Judge Meron sat in the Appeals Chamber in the *Blagojević and Jović* as well as *Nikolić* cases, all also subordinates of Mladić.[46] Judge Antonetti believed that there was the risk of the appearance of bias if a Judge who found the subordinates of a superior officer guilty was later tasked with deciding the appeal of that same superior officer.[47] The cumulative incriminating references against Mladić demonstrated that there was a reasonable apprehension of bias on the part of Judge Meron.[48] The disqualification motion was therefore granted.

39. *Id.* at paras. 42–3. 40. *Id.* at para. 43. 41. *Id.* at para. 44.
42. *Id.* at para. 48. 43. *Id.* at para. 49. 44. *Id.*
45. *Id.* 46. *Id.* at para. 51. 47. *Id.* 48. *Id.* at para. 52.

Following Judge Antonetti's invitation to the impugned Judges, I wrote to Judge Antonetti on 16 July 2018, explaining why, in my view, the motion failed to meet the requirements of firmly establishing a reasonable apprehension of bias and affirming that I would bring an independent mind to the adjudication of the appeals in the Mladić case.

Following the decision of Judge Antonetti to disqualify the three impugned Judges in the *Mladić* appeal, Karadžić filed on 25 September 2018 a motion before Judge Antonetti seeking my disqualification in his appeal. In response, I issued on 27 September 2018 an Order stating that I was withdrawing from the *Karadžić* appeal, although I would bring to it an impartial mind, because the *Mladić* Disqualification Decision clearly contradicted established jurisprudence and, in my view, harmed the interests of the Mechanism by wrongly suggesting that "there is a risk in terms of appearance where the superior officer [...] is being tried, even on appeal, by the Judge who found his subordinates guilty," and because allowing Judge Antonetti to adjudicate yet another disqualification motion would further harm the interests of the Mechanism. By that Order, I also appointed a replacement Judge. The Order observed that the *Mladić* Disqualification Decision clearly contradicted established jurisprudence and, in my view, harmed the interests of the Mechanism by wrongly suggesting that "there is a risk in terms of appearance where the superior officer [...] is being tried, even on appeal, by the judge who found his subordinates guilty."

See also the Decision of the Appeals Chamber to 1 November 2018 to Strike Karadzic's Second Motion to Disqualify Judge Theodor Meron.

Prosecutor v. Šešelj

Appeal Judgement

Date of Judgement: 11 April 2018

Allegations of denial of fair trial rights of Šešelj, including undue delay and modalities of self-representation, rejected

This case concerned procedural fairness of the proceedings and the fair trial rights of Šešelj. Specifically, the procedural challenges raised by Šešelj in relation to: 1) the Indictment and alleged political bias; 2) self-representation; 3) Šešelj's detention conditions and the preparation of his defence; 4) the admission of witness statements and allegedly false evidence; and 5) undue delay. The Appeals Chamber dismissed all of Šešelj's submissions in their entirety, I comment on the question of undue delay.

Šešelj alleged that the "trial proceedings in his case were the longest in the history of the ICTY and amounted to undue delay."[49]

The Appeals Chamber took considerable time to elaborate on the right to be tried without undue delay. The right can be found in Article 19(4)(c) of the Statute and protects an accused against undue delay, as determined on a case-by-case basis.[50] Numerous factors are considered when assessing whether a delay was "undue", including: "the length of the delay, the complexity of the proceedings, the conduct of the parties, the conduct of the relevant authorities, and any prejudice to the accused."[51] Trial chambers must be "proactive" in protecting this right, independent of whether it is raised by an accused.[52] Though the Appeals Chamber acknowledged that the trial proceedings had been lengthy, the arguments being raised by Šešelj on appeal had already been addressed at trial. In fact, when the ICTY Appeals Chamber upheld the relevant portion of the Decision of 13 December 2013, it recalled that according to the ICTY "jurisprudence, a 12-year incarceration prior to the issuance of a trial judgement does not amount to prejudice *per se*."[53]

Prosecutor v. Galić

Judgement

DATE OF JUDGEMENT: 30 NOVEMBER 2006

RULES GOVERNING TESTIMONY OF WITNESSES DO NOT AUTOMATICALLY APPLY TO THE ACCUSED, AS THE LATTER ENJOYS SPECIFIC PROTECTIONS FOR THE DEFENCE. CLAIMS OF VIOLATION OF FAIRNESS OF TRIAL RIGHTS REJECTED.

The Appeals Chamber explained that there was in fact a fundamental difference between an accused who chooses to testify as a witness, and a

49. *Prosecutor v. Vojislav Šešelj*, Judgement, IRMCT Appeals Chamber, at para. 40, Case no. MICT-16-99-A (11 Apr. 2018).

50. *Id.* at para. 41. 51. *Id.* 52. *Id.* 53. *Id.* at para. 42.

regular witness. Certain Rules are indeed incompatible with the rights of an accused though they would apply to the testimony of a regular witness (e.g., Rule 77(A)(i) or Rule 90(E)). An accused enjoys special protections of his fundamental rights ensuring a fair trial. Consequently, Rule 85(C) should not be interpreted to mean that an accused is subject to the same Rules as a regular witness.[54]

Rule 85(C) of the Rules does not include any explicit parameters restricting the right of the accused to appear as a witness at his trial. Though some guidance can be found in Rules 85(A) and 86 which require that the accused's testimony must take place during the presentation of defence evidence, the only true parameter is to ensure that the fundamental right of the accused to testify at his own trial is preserved.[55] However, the lack of explicit parameters in Rule 85(C) should not be thought to restrict the power of the Trial Chamber regarding the proper administration of a trial. The Trial Chamber acted within its discretion when setting parameters on when Galić could testify at his trial pursuant to Rule 90(F).

Slobodan Milošević v. Prosecutor

Appeals Chamber Decision on Interlocutory Appeal of the Trial Chamber's Decision on the Assignment of Defense Counsel

DATE OF DECISION: 1 NOVEMBER 2004

MODALITIES OF SELF-REPRESENTATION: THE TRIAL CHAMBER FAILED TO RECOGNIZE THAT ANY RESTRICTIONS ON S. MILOŠEVIĆ'S RIGHT TO REPRESENT HIMSELF MUST BE LIMITED TO THE MINIMUM EXTENT NECESSARY TO PROTECT THE TRIBUNAL'S INTEREST IN ASSURING A REASONABLY EXPEDITIOUS TRIAL. WHEN REVIEWING RESTRICTIONS ON FUNDAMENTAL RIGHTS, THE BASIC PROPORTIONALITY PRINCIPLE MUST BE TAKEN INTO ACCOUNT.

54. *Prosecutor v. Stanislav Galić*, Judgement, ICTY Appeals Chamber, at para. 17, Case no. IT-98-29-A (30 Nov. 2006).
55. *Id.* at para. 19.

The right to self-representation is one of the fundamental protections granted to defendants in the interest of justice. The right to self-representation can be found in Article 21 of the ICTY Statute, which the Appeals Chamber interpreted as guaranteeing that right, regardless of a Trial Chamber's judgement that a defendant's case would benefit from the assignment of counsel. However, the right to self-representation is not absolute and can be restricted to better protect the fairness of proceedings.[56] In the present case, the Appeals Chamber had to decide whether the right to self-representation should be limited when allowing a defendant to exercise that very right would significantly interfere with the "proper and expeditious" conduct of the trial.[57] The Appeals Chamber believed that the Trial Chamber did not exceed its discretion in assigning counsel to represent Milošević.

Though the Appeals Chamber agreed with the assignment of counsel, it did not agree with the Trial Chamber's Order on Modalities. That Order greatly undermined Milošević's ability to meaningfully participate in his own case, granting him a "visibly second-tier role" subject to the discretion of the Trial Chamber. Further, though the Order included the possibility of Milošević examining witnesses, that examination would take place only after the assigned counsel had already completed their examination. The Order clearly failed to limit the restrictions on Milošević's right to self-representation to the minimum extent possible to ensure a reasonably expeditious trial. The Appeals Chamber ruled that:

> [t]he Trial Chamber failed to recognize that any restrictions on Milošević's right to represent himself must be limited to the minimum extent necessary to protect the Tribunal's interest in assuring a reasonably expeditious trial. When reviewing restrictions on fundamental rights such as this one, many jurisdictions are guided by some variant of a basic proportionality principle: any restriction of a fundamental right must be in service of "a sufficiently important objective," and must "impair the right … no more than is necessary to accomplish the objective." Similarly, while the International Covenant on Civil and Political Rights allows some restriction of certain civil rights where "necessary to protect national security, public order (*ordre public*), public health or morals, or the rights and freedoms of others," the United

56. *Slobodan Milošević v. The Prosecutor*, Decision on Interlocutory Appeal of the Trial Chamber's Decision on the Assignment of Defense Counsel, at para. 12, Case no. IT-02-54-AR73.7 (1 Nov. 2004).
57. *Id.* at para. 13.

> Nations Human Rights Committee has observed that any such restrictions "must conform to the principle of proportionality; ... they must be the least intrusive instrument amongst those which might achieve the desired result; and they must be proportionate to the interest to be protected." And the ICTY itself has been guided by a "general principle of proportionality" in assessing defendants' suitability for provisional release, noting that a restriction on the fundamental right to liberty is acceptable only when it is "(1) suitable, (2) necessary and when (3) its degree and scope remain in a reasonable relationship to the envisaged target."[58]

The Trial Chamber thus exceeded its discretion with that Order.

Prosecutor v. Slobodan Milošević

Decision on the Interlocutory Appeal by the *Amici Curiae* against the Trial Chamber Order Concerning the Presentation and Preparation of the Defence Case

Date of Decision: 20 January 2004

The Trial Chamber properly balanced the right to a fair trial with the right to an expeditious trial. The Trial Chamber took into account the special concerns that arise from self-representation and explained that it would provide the accused with resources to aid with the preparation of his defence.

This Appeal concerns the Trial Chamber's Order granting the accused three months to prepare his defence and requiring him to file a list of the witnesses and exhibits he intended to present within six weeks of the adjournment.[59]

The Appeals Chamber ruled that the Trial Chamber was in the best position to determine the amount of time needed for the accused to finish preparing his defence because the Trial Chamber had been in charge of conducting the trial for the past two years.[60] The Trial Chamber properly utilized that position to make an informed decision based on the case's factual information and the appropriate legal principles.

58. *Id.* at para. 17.
59. *Prosecutor v. Slobodan Milošević*, Decision on the Interlocutory Appeal by the *Amici Curiae* against the Trial Chamber Order concerning the Presentation and Preparation of the Defence Case, ICTY Appeals Chamber, at para. 1, Case no. IT-02-54-AR73.6 (20 Jan. 2004).
60. *Id.* at para. 18.

The Trial Chamber properly balanced the principle of the right to a fair trial with the right to an expeditious trial. The Trial Chamber took into account the special concerns that arise from self-representation and explained that it would provide the accused with resources to aid with the preparation of his defence.

The Appeals Chamber noted that by choosing to conduct his own defence, the accused deprived himself of the resources a well-equipped legal defence team could have provided. A defendant who decides to represent himself relinquishes many of the benefits associated with representation by counsel. Where an accused elects self-representation, the concerns about self-representation are heightened and a Trial Chamber must be particularly attentive to its duty of ensuring that the trial is fair.[61]

The Appeal was dismissed.

Zigiranyirazo v. The Prosecutor

Decision on Interlocutory Appeal

Date of Decision: 30 October 2006

Right of the accused to be present in court for the testimony of a key witness is not satisfied by a video-link. The restrictions imposed violated the principle of proportionality.

The Appeals Chamber considered that the physical presence of an accused before the court, as a general rule, is one of the most basic and common precepts of a fair criminal trial.[62]

The parties acknowledged that an accused's right to be tried in his or her presence is not absolute. The ICTR Appeals Chamber observed as much, and this Appeals Chamber agreed. An accused/person can waive or forfeit the right to be present at trial. For example, Rule 80(B) of the Rules allows a Trial Chamber to remove a persistently disruptive accused. Referring to the equivalent provision in the ICTY Rules, the ICTY Appeals Chamber observed that an accused's right to be present for his or her trial can be restricted "on the basis of substantial trial disruptions." In assessing a particular limitation on a statutory guarantee, the Appeals Chamber will bear in

61. *Id.* at paras. 19–20.

62. *Protais Zigiranyirazo v. The Prosecutor*, Decision on Interlocutory Appeal, ICTR Appeals Chamber, at para. 11, Case no. ICTR-01-73-AR73 (30 Oct. 2006).

mind the proportionality principle, pursuant to which any restriction on a fundamental right must be in service of a sufficiently important objective and must impair the right no more than is necessary to accomplish the objective. The explicit exception provided by Rule 80(B) and the ICTY Appeals Chamber's reference to "substantial trial disruptions" provided a useful measure by which to assess other restrictions on the right to be present at trial.[63]

The primary question for the Appeals Chamber was whether the Trial Chamber properly exercised its discretion in its restriction of the appellant's right to be present at his trial.[64]

The Trial Chamber's attempts to give full respect to both the right to counsel and the principle of equality of arms did not compensate for the failure to accord the accused what is a separate and distinct minimum guarantee: the right to be present at his own trial. Although one of the appellant's counsel was in the courtroom with the Judges and the witness, the appellant himself was thousands of kilometers away, connected to the proceedings only by means of audio-visual equipment. The appellant's sense of being wronged in such circumstances was well understandable. As the Prosecution and Trial Chamber noted, Mr. Bagaragaza's testimony did not cover simply background information or a matter other than the acts and conduct of the accused. According to the Prosecution's own statement and the Trial Chamber's consideration, Mr. Bagaragaza was a key Prosecution witness against the appellant.[65]

The Trial Chamber's restrictions on the appellant's fair trial rights were unwarranted and excessive in the circumstances and thus failed the test of proportionality. Accordingly, the Trial Chamber committed a discernible error.[66]

The Appeals Chamber considered that:

> It cannot be held that the violation of the Appellant's right to be present constitutes harmless error given the length and purported significance of the testimony to the charges against him. Prejudice therefore can only be presumed, as any attempt to prove or disprove actual prejudice from the record in an ongoing trial before any factual findings have been made would be purely speculative. In the view of the Appeals Chamber, allowing the testimony of Mr. Bagaragaza to remain on the record would seriously damage

63. *Id.* at para. 14.
64. *Id.* at para. 15.
65. *Id.* at para. 21.
66. *Id.* at para. 22.

the integrity of the proceedings. In such circumstances, Rule 95 of the Rules plainly requires the exclusion of such testimony.[67]

Prosecutor v. Prlić, Stojić, Praljak, Petković, Ćorić and Pušić

Decision on Praljak's Request for Stay of Proceedings

DATE OF DECISION: 27 JUNE 2014

LIMITATIONS ON SELF-REPRESENTATION. GIVEN THE INABILITY OF AN APPELLANT TO UNDERSTAND EITHER ENGLISH OR FRENCH, THE LEGAL AND FACTUAL COMPLEXITY OF THE CASE, THE FACT THAT HE HAS NO LEGAL EDUCATION AND THE INEVITABLE LONG DELAYS, HE SHOULD NOT BE ALLOWED TO REPRESENT HIMSELF AND IS ASSIGNED A COUNSEL IN THE INTEREST OF JUSTICE.

Article 21(4)(d) of the Statute states an accused's fundamental right to self-representation during both the trial and appeal phases of a case. However, the right to self-representation is not absolute. Rule 45*ter* allows for the assignment of counsel to an accused, even one who chooses to be self-represented, if it is in the interests of justice.[68]

The Appeals Chamber agreed that Praljak was unable to sufficiently understand English or French to effectively represent himself and would require not only the already agreed upon B/C/S translations but also translations of all future filings. The Appeals Chamber further noted that Praljak did not have any legal education and would not be able to adequately address the complex issues of the appeal. Contrary to other self-represented accused, Praljak did not have any form of legal assistance available to him.[69] This, combined with the required translation efforts, would likely cause significant delays in the proceedings.

The Appeals Chamber held that these delays would negatively affect the right of Praljak and his co-appellants to fair and expeditious appellate proceedings, especially in light of the fact that all of Praljak's co-appellants

67. *Id.* at para. 24.

68. *Prosecutor v. Jadrako Prlić, Bruno Stojić, Slobodan Praljak, Milivoj Petković, Valentin Ćorić, Berislav Pušić*, Decision on Praljak's Request for Stay of Proceedings, ICTY Appeals Chamber, at para. 12, Case no. IT-04-74-A (27 June 2014).

69. *Id.* at paras. 14–15.

were represented by counsel.[70] The Appeals Chamber therefore held that Praljak should not be allowed to represent himself and that the assignment of counsel would be in the interests of justice, in accordance with Rule 45*ter*.[71] As it was previously established that Praljak had sufficient funds to remunerate counsel, Praljak still had to reimburse the Tribunal for the costs already incurred for his defence and future costs stemming from this appeal. However, the Appeals Chamber noted that it could not stay the appeal proceedings until those past costs were reimbursed. Halting the proceedings as opposed to expending further funds would negatively impact Praljak's co-appellants and be contrary to the interests of justice.[72]

Prosecutor v. Karadžić

Decision on Radovan Karadžić's Appeal From Decision on Motion to Vacate Appointment of Richard Harvey

Date of Decision: 12 February 2010

Fairness and the principle of proportionality as they apply to the right of self-representation. Does the Trial Chamber's appointment of stand-by Counsel violate the principle of proportionality and result in prejudice?

The right to self-representation is not absolute and limitations can be proper depending on the specific circumstances of a case. Article 21(4)(d) of the Statute does not provide an accused with the guarantee of both the right to self-representation and the right to counsel of his own choosing.[73] An accused has the right to one or the other, and in the case at hand Karadžić had chosen to exercise his right to self-representation thereby forfeiting his right to be represented by legal counsel. The Appeals Chamber was not persuaded by Karadžić's argument that he should now be granted the same rights as those who chose to be represented by legal counsel due to the Trial

70. *Id.* at para. 16. 71. *Id.* 72. *Id.* at para. 17.

73. *Prosecutor v. Radovan Karadžić*, Decision on Radovan Karadžić's Appeal from Decision on Motion to Vacate Appointment of Richard Harvey, ICTY Appeals Chamber, at para. 26, Case no. IT-95-5/18-AR73.6 (12 Feb. 2010).

Chamber's decision to override his right to self-representation with Harvey's appointment as stand-by counsel.[74] If the Trial Chamber decided to assign counsel to represent Karadžić's interests at trial, it would be because the Trial Chamber had found, within its discretion, that Karadžić's "persistent obstructive behaviour has made it necessary, in the interests of justice, to limit his right to self-representation."[75]

In this case, the Appeals Chamber held that the limitation on the right to self-representation of Karadžić with the appointment of stand-by counsel was justified.

Prosecutor v. Nyiramasuhuko, Ntahobali, Nsabimana, Nteziryayo, Kanyabashi and Ndayambaje

Decision in the Matter of Proceedings under Rule 15*bis*(D)

Date of Decision: 24 September 2003

Continuation of proceedings with a substitute Judge allowed when the substitute Judge certifies that he or she has familiarized himself or herself with the record of the proceedings

This Decision (also known as *Butare* case) concerned a partially heard trial where one of the three Judges of the Trial Chamber was not reelected. The issue at hand was whether the case should continue or start over with a substitute Judge being assigned.

The appellants alleged that the amended Rule 15*bis* was not applicable to the *Butare* trial because it concerned substantive rights and therefore could not apply retrospectively. Though this was a pending trial, the Appeals Chamber agreed to consider the matter retrospectivity as the appellants had a legitimate expectation to be tried in a certain way throughout the entire duration of the trial. The Appeals Chamber therefore had to decide whether the application of the amendment to the rest of the trial was in accordance with the appellants' right to a fair trial.[76] Statutes that amend procedure concern secondary, not primary, conduct

74. *Id.* at para. 27. 75. *Id.*
76. *Prosecutor v. Pauline Nyiramasuhuko & Arsène Shalom Ntahobali, Sylvain Nsabimana & Alphonse Nteziryayo, Joseph Kanyabashi, Elie Ndayambaje*, ICTR Appeals Chamber, at para. 12, Case no. ICTR-98-42-A15*bis* (24 Sept. 2003).

and are applicable to existing proceedings that began before said Statutes were in effect (retrospective application). On the other hand, amendments that affect substantive rights are presumed to have a prospective application. This presumption is rebuttable and, if rebutted, the amendment can apply retrospectively to existing proceedings. Pursuant to Rule 6(C), an amendment enters into force immediately but cannot operate to the prejudice of the accused in a pending case.[77] The Appeals Chamber therefore had to determine whether the new Rule 15*bis* would operate to the prejudice of the appellants.

The Appeals Chamber held that the value of the old safeguard was indeed equivalent to the value of the new one, as provided for in the various procedural requirements of new Rule 15*bis*.[78] Under both the old and new Rule 15, an accused could withhold his consent and be equivalently protected against arbitrariness. The right to consent to continuation of the trial under the old Rule 15*bis* and the application of the new Rule 15*bis* therefore did not prejudice the rights of the appellant in the pending trial.

The Appeals Chamber noted that even in the case of a Judge who has not been reelected and the ensuing right of the appellants to withhold consent under the old Rule 15*bis*, that right could be qualified by the substitution of a safeguard of equivalent value.[79] That safeguard could be found in the new Rule 15*bis*, and the second argument on prejudice was accordingly rejected.

Any inadequacies of the record because of lack of video-recordings, do not invalidate the decision of the Trial Chamber to continue the trial with a substitute Judge. This is because after a substitute Judge joins the Bench, he certifies that he has familiarized himself with the record of the proceedings. If he cannot certify to this, he will not be able to join the Bench. However, the substitute Judge in this case may have decided that the record was complete enough even without the video-recordings to allow him to be familiar with the case. He could decide to join the Bench and the recomposed Trial Chamber could recall witnesses so as to allow the substitute Judge to assess their demeanor.[80] The Appeals Chamber concluded that if the substitute Judge assigned by the President certified that he or she had familiarized themselves with the record of the proceedings (and accompanying lack of video-recordings) and joined the Bench, the recomposed Trial Chamber

77. *Id.* at para. 14. 78. *Id.* at para. 19. 79. *Id.* at para. 21. 80. *Id.* at para. 34.

could recall witnesses to assess matters of credibility based on a witness's demeanor.[81]

Mugenzi and Mugiraneza v. The Prosecutor

Judgement

DATE OF JUDGEMENT: 4 FEBRUARY 2013

THE BREACH OF DISCLOSURE OBLIGATIONS BY THE PROSECUTION DID NOT PREJUDICE THE APPELLANTS

The Trial Chamber acknowledged that the more than 12-year period from arrest to the Trial Judgement was lengthy.[82] In that respect, the Appeals Chamber recalled that the judicial process undertaken by the Tribunal would not always be as expeditious as that undertaken before domestic courts.[83] In the present case, the length of the delay could adequately be attributed to the sheer size and complexity of the proceedings, which also was similar to that of other multi-accused trials where no undue delay had been found. The Appeals Chamber did not consider that the Trial Chamber failed to properly consider the delay in the pre-trial phase of the case, the three-year time period between final trial submissions and the issuance of the Trial Judgement or the impact of the trial Judges' work on other judicial matters.[84]

Under Rule 68(A), the Prosecution must disclose to the Defence any material which in the actual knowledge of the prosecution may suggest the innocence of or mitigate the guilt of the accused.[85] To prove that the Prosecution has breached its disclosure obligation, the applicant bears the burden of: 1) identifying specifically the material sought; 2) presenting a prima facie showing of its probably exculpatory nature; and 3) proving that the material requested is in the custody or control of the Prosecution. If the Defence meets its burden, the Appeals Chamber must then decide whether the Defence has been prejudiced by the failure to disclose.

81. *Id.* at para. 35.
82. *Justin Mugenzi, Prosper Mugiraneza v. The Prosecutor*, Judgement, ICTR Appeals Chamber, at para. 31, Case no. ICTR-99-50-A (4 Feb. 2013).
83. *Id.* at para. 32.
84. *Id.* at para. 35.
85. *Id.* at para. 39.

Regarding Mugenzi's alleged Rule 68 violations, the Appeals Chamber was satisfied that i) Mugenzi had met the required burden of sufficiently identifying the material in question; ii) that the Prosecution did not dispute that the material was in its custody and should have been disclosed; and iii) that Mugenzi had made a prima facie showing of the probably exculpatory nature of the material. The Appeals Chamber therefore found that the Prosecution had breached its disclosure obligations under Rule 68. Turning to the question of prejudice, the Appeals Chamber found that Witness CHC's testimony was consistent with the Trial Chamber's conclusions that there were instances of violence and was cumulative of other evidence on the record.[86]

Regarding Mugiraneza's alleged Rule 68 violations, the Appeals Chamber was also satisfied that Mugiraneza had met the burden of showing that the Prosecution violated its disclosure obligations. However, the Appeals Chamber was similarly not convinced that this disclosure breach prejudiced Mugiraneza. At most, the resulting prejudice was minimal.

As the prejudice was at most minimal, no relief was warranted. However, as both the Appeals Chamber and Trial Chamber found the Prosecution in breach of its Rule 68 obligations on previous occasions, the Appeals Chamber utilized the discussion as an opportunity to remind the Prosecution of the "fundamental importance of its positive and continuous obligation to disclose exculpatory material under Rule 68 of the Rules." The breaches identified by both the Appeals Chamber and Trial Chamber negatively impacted the conduct of the proceedings and clearly prejudiced the interests of justice and a fair trial.[87]

Prosecutor v. Dragan Nikolić

Judgement on Sentencing Appeal

DATE OF JUDGEMENT: 4 FEBRUARY 2005

SENTENCING. THE PRINCIPLE OF PROPORTIONALITY REFERS TO PROPORTIONALITY BETWEEN THE GRAVITY OF THE OFFENCE AND THE DEGREE OF THE

86. *Id.* at para. 44. 87. *Id.* at para. 63.

RESPONSIBILITY OF THE OFFENDER RATHER THAN PROPORTIONALITY BETWEEN SENTENCES OF THE DIFFERENT ACCUSED IN THIS CASE.

The Trial Chamber convicted Dragan Nikolić on the basis of a Confidential Joint Plea Agreement Submission filed by the parties on 2 September 2003.[88] The Trial Chamber found Nikolić guilty of Counts 1 to 4 of the Indictment and entered a single conviction of 23 years' imprisonment for Count 1 incorporating Counts 2 to 4.[89] In this Judgement, the Appeals Chamber dismissed all seven grounds of appeal. This annotation focuses on the first ground of appeal, where the Appeals Chamber discussed the principle of proportionality.

As emphasized by the Appeals Chamber, the inherent gravity of a crime must be determined on a case-by-case basis with reference to the particular circumstances of a case and the form/degree of the accused's participation in the alleged crime.[90] The gravity of the offence can be thought of as "the litmus test" when deciding on an appropriate sentence.[91] As a result of this case-by-case basis, previous sentences rendered by the ICTY and the ICTR could only provide so much guidance and may not have been a "proper avenue" for challenging a Trial Chamber's discretion in imposing a particular sentence.[92] The Appeals Chamber advanced two reasons to justify the limited reach of previous sentences: 1) previous sentences may only be helpful when the offences are not only the same, but were also committed in substantially similar circumstances, meaning in circumstances that included similar mitigating and aggravating factors; and 2) Trial Chambers have an "overriding obligation to tailor a penalty to fit the individual circumstances of the accused and the gravity of the crime, with due regard to the entirety of the case, as the triers of fact."[93] In the present case, the Trial Chamber did review previous sentencing practices, but found that the scale of the sentences had been very broad and individualized. Since the Trial Chamber was not bound by previous sentences, or by the sentencing practice in the former Yugoslavia or other States for that matter, the Trial Chamber did not exceed its discretion in the present case.

88. *Prosecutor v. Dragan Nikolić*, Judgement on Sentencing Appeal, ICTY Appeals Chamber, at para. 3, Case no. IT-94-2-A (4 Feb. 2005).
89. *Id.* at para. 4.
90. *Id.* at para. 18.
91. *Id.*
92. *Id.* at para. 19.
93. *Id.*

The appellant alleged that the Trial Chamber violated the principle of proportionality by equating his offences and his participation to that of the likes of the ICTR defendants.[94] However, it was clear that the appellant misunderstood the principle of proportionality and that the Trial Chamber did indeed apply that principle correctly. The Appeals Chamber agreed with the Trial Chamber, that the principle of proportionality requires that a punishment be "proportionate to the moral blameworthiness of the offender."[95] In order to correctly reflect the "moral blameworthiness" of an accused, a Trial Chamber must take into consideration factors such as deterrence and the social condemnation of the acts. The principle of proportionality focuses on a particular accused, his particular offence, his particular circumstances and his particular form/degree of participation. It does not focus on comparing or achieving proportionality between an accused's sentence and the sentence of the other accused in a trial.

Prosecutor v. Bralo

Judgement on Sentencing Appeal

Date of Judgement: 2 April 2007

Principles governing sentences. In light of the seriousness of the crimes committed and with specific regard to the aggravating circumstances not challenged by the appellant, the Appeals Chamber considers that the appellant failed to demonstrate that the sentence imposed upon him was so unreasonable as to amount to an abuse of discretion by the Trial Chamber. The appellant failed to show that the imposed sentence contradicted the principles governing sentencing at the Tribunal

Though the appellant did not dispute the appropriateness of a sentencing range beginning at 25 years, he disputed the reduction of the sentence by only five years after the Trial Chamber allegedly considered the mitigating evidence and agreed that this evidence merited "substantial modification"

94. *Id.* at para. 21. 95. *Id.*

of the sentence.[96] He argued that by only reducing the sentence by five years, the Trial Chamber abused its sentencing discretion and adopted an overly restrictive view of the powers of the international tribunal.

The Appeals Chamber noted that while securing justice, peace and reconciliation are important goals of sentencing, they are not the only goals. In fact, the purposes of punishment are clearly explained in the jurisprudence of the international tribunal. Examples of such purposes or goals include the principles of retribution and deterrence. According to the Appeals Chamber, these principles and other principles governing sentencing when determining an appropriate sentence were all properly applied by the Trial Chamber.[97]

The weight to be accorded to the mitigating circumstances will differ from case to case and is part of the Trial Chamber's sentencing discretion. The burden falls on the appellant to demonstrate how the Trial Chamber exceeded its discretion when considering the mitigating circumstances and imposing the sentence, a burden which the appellant failed to meet in the case at hand.

The Appeals Chamber found that the Trial Chamber did properly take the mitigating (and aggravating) circumstances into account when determining the sentence and found that a single sentence of 20 years was both the *proportionate* and appropriate punishment.[98] As explained by the Appeals Chamber, mitigating circumstances should not be considered in isolation, any resulting modification of a sentence must be assessed in light of all of the circumstances of the case.[99]

Ntabakuze v. The Prosecutor

Judgement

Date of Judgement: 8 May 2012
The Appeals Chamber set aside the sentence of life imprisonment and replaced it with a sentence of 35 years' imprisonment.

96. *Prosecutor v. Miroslav Bralo*, Judgement on Sentencing Appeal, ICTY Appeals Chamber, at para. 78, Case no. IT-95-17-A (2 Apr. 2007).
97. *Id.* at para. 82.
98. *Id.* at para. 83.
99. *Id.* at para. 85.

Ntabakuze claimed that the Trial Chamber failed to consider certain mitigating circumstances and therefore violated Article 22(2) of the Statute. The Appeals Chamber reiterated that a Trial Chamber is under an obligation to consider mitigating circumstances in a particular case, however, it enjoys a considerable degree of discretion in determining what qualifies as mitigating circumstances and what weight to accord to each circumstance. The Appeals Chamber emphasized that the mere existence of mitigating factors did not automatically imply a certain reduction of a sentence nor did it automatically preclude the imposition of a life sentence. After considering the various mitigating circumstances alleged by Ntabakuze, the Appeals Chamber found that the Trial Chamber did not exceed its discretion, did properly consider mitigating circumstances and did properly accord each circumstance the appropriate weight, except in one circumstance. The Appeals Chamber found that the Trial Chamber did err in not considering Ntabakuze's statement of regret and in therefore not considering whether public and genuine regret constituted a mitigating circumstance. In assessing this error, the Appeals Chamber did not find that the error invalidated the sentence imposed by the Trial Chamber and held that the gravity of the offences and the aggravating factors greatly outweighed that single mitigating factor.

The Appeals Chamber further held that Ntabakuze failed to demonstrate how the sentence imposed on him by the Trial Chamber was out of proportion with the respective sentences imposed on Bagosora and Nsengiyumva. The sentence imposed by the Trial Chamber was proportionate to the form and degree of Ntabakuze's participation. The gravity of the crimes committed by Ntabakuze did warrant similar treatment to those who planned or ordered the atrocities, including the most senior authorities.[100]

Prosecutor v. Mrkšić, Šljivančanin

Judgement

Date of Judgement: 5 May 2009

Principles governing sentencing. for having aided and abetted torture of POWs, discernible error in the exercise of discretion by the Trial Chamber

100. *Aloys Ntabakuze v. The Prosecutor*, Judgement, ICTR Appeals Chamber, at paras. 300–5, Case no. ICTR-98-41A-A (8 May 2012).

The Appeals Chamber held that there was a discernible error in the Trial Chamber's sentencing discretion when it imposed the single sentence of five years on Šljivančanin for having aided and abetted the torture of prisoners of war at the hangar at Ovčara on 20 November 1991 (Count 7 of the Indictment). The Appeals Chamber explained that it was unable to determine how the Trial Chamber chose to weigh the consequences of the torture upon the victims and their families and to what extent it considered the particular vulnerability of the prisoners when determining Šljivančanin's sentence. The particular vulnerability of the prisoners of war included the fact that some of them were already injured because they had been taken from the Vukovar hospital. Those prisoners were nevertheless subjected to extreme cruelty and brutality. Though the Appeals Chamber noted that the Trial Chamber did not commit any errors in its factual findings, it held that the Trial Chamber erred in its consideration of the factual findings when it imposed such an unreasonable sentence of five years' imprisonment. A sentence of five years did not adequately reflect the level of gravity of the crimes committed by Šljivančanin nor did it adequately reflect the totality of his criminal conduct pursuant to Rule 87(C) of the Rules. Accordingly, the Appeals Chamber raised Šljivančanin's sentence to a term of 17 years' imprisonment. However, the sentence for having aided and abetted torture of POWs was reviewed and reduced in a subsequent review Judgement, which is discussed in Chapter VIII on the Massacre in Ovčara.

Prosecutor v. Karadžić

Decision on a Motion to Admit Additional Evidence on Appeal

Date of Decision: 2 March 2018

This Decision focused on Ground 40 of Karadžić's appeal, which alleged that the Trial Chamber erred in finding that he knew of and shared the Srebrenica JCE's expanded common criminal purpose of killing the Bosnian Muslim males of Srebrenica.[101] In making this conclusion, the Trial Chamber

101. *Prosecutor v. Radovan Karadžić*, Decision on a Motion to Admit Additional Evidence on Appeal, IRMCT Appeals Chamber, at para. 5, Case no. MICT-13-55-A (2 Mar. 2018).

relied on an intercepted conversation between Karadžić and Deronjić that took place on 13 July 1995.[102] The Trial Chamber found that during that conversation, Karadžić used coded language to direct Deronjić to transfer the Bosnian male detainees to Zvornik. That interpretation of the coded language was based substantially on evidence provided by Nikolić and his allegation that he overheard a conversation between Deronjić and Beara on 14 July 1995, which the Trial Chamber relied on to emphasize that a decision to kill the Bosnian Muslim men detainees had already been made.

Karadžić sought to admit additional evidence on appeal which undermined the Trial Chamber's conclusion that he shared the expanded common criminal purpose of killing the Bosnian men detainees.[103] Specifically, he sought to admit excerpts of transcripts of Vasić's testimony from the *Perišić* Trial, or alternatively he sought to have Vasić testify before the Appeals Chamber. According to Karadžić, that testimony showed that Deronjić never told Beara that Karadžić had ordered him to transfer the prisoners to Zvornik and that Nikolić did not overhear the conversation between Deronjić and Beara. Though Karadžić did concede that this evidence was available at trial, he alleged that not admitting it on appeal would constitute a miscarriage of justice.

The admission of additional evidence on appeal is governed by Rule 142 of the Rules of Procedure and Evidence of the Mechanism.[104] For additional evidence to be admissible, the applicant must demonstrate that the additional evidence was *not* available at trial (or discoverable). The applicant must also bear the burden of demonstrating that the additional evidence is relevant to a material issue at trial and is credible. Of relevance to the present case, evidence that was available at trial may still have been admissible under Rule 142(C). The applicant would bear the burden of demonstrating that excluding the additional evidence would lead to a miscarriage of justice because had the evidence been admitted at trial, it would have had an impact on the verdict.

Here, Karadžić alleged that Vasić's testimony from the *Perišić* Trial met the requirements of Rule 142(C) as it was relevant to the case at hand, credible and would result in a miscarriage of justice if not admitted on appeal.[105] Turning to those requirements, the Appeals Chamber found that

102. *Id.* at para. 3.
103. *Id.* at para. 6.
104. *Id.* at para. 7.
105. *Id.* at para. 9.

the proposed additional evidence was relevant to material issues at trial and was credible as it was in the form of sworn testimony in a proceeding before the ICTY.[106]

As the evidence was available at trial, the Appeals Chamber had to determine whether excluding it would result in a miscarriage of justice.[107] According to the Appeals Chamber, Vasić's testimony did not contradict the nature of the conversation between Deronjić and Beara from 14 July 1995, which the Trial Chamber relied on to find that Karadžić agreed to the expanded common criminal purpose of killing the Bosnian Muslim male detainees.[108] Furthermore, the Appeals Chamber noted that Vasić's testimony did not undermine Nikolić's ability to overhear the conversation, even if Vasić's evidence suggested that Nikolić was not present during the conversation between Deronjić and Beara. This was due to the fact that Vasić also testified that many people were present when he arrived and failed to remember if there was a path leading to Deronjić's office.[109] It is important to note that the Appeals Chamber did explain that the Trial Chamber did not solely rely on Karadžić's order to move prisoners to Zvornik to then conclude that he had indeed agreed to the alleged expanded common criminal purpose. Rather, the Trial Chamber also relied on Karadžić's subsequent acts following the conversation between Deronjić and Beara from 14 July 1995. Karadžić's proposed additional evidence was mainly based on disputing the content of that conversation and Nikolić's presence, it did not dispute or cast doubt on the Trial Chamber's findings and reliance on those subsequent acts.[110] The Appeals Chamber therefore held that Karadžić had failed to meet his burden under Rule 142(C): Karadžić had failed to demonstrate that Vasić's testimony would have impacted the Trial Chamber's verdict and that excluding it on appeal would result in a miscarriage of justice.[111]

106. *Id.* at para. 11.
107. *Id.* at para. 12.
108. *Id.* at para. 14.
109. *Id.* at para. 15.
110. *Id.* at para. 16.
111. *Id.* at para. 17.

XI

Writing Separately

My Dissenting and Concurring Opinions

Throughout my nearly two decades on the Bench, I exercised restraint in writing dissenting or separate opinions. I wrote such opinions when I felt it worthwhile explaining my own positions on important judicial questions, particularly on aspects of fairness. To share with the readers my own perspectives, I cite and explain some of these opinions in this chapter.

Nahimana, Barayagwiza and Ngeze v. The Prosecutor

Judgement—Partly Dissenting Opinion of Judge Meron

Date of Judgement: 28 November 2007

Hate speech, persecution, principle of legality, due process

A. The Case Should Have Been Remanded

1. The sheer number of errors in the Trial Judgement indicates that remanding the case, rather than undertaking piecemeal remedies, would have been the best course. Although any one legal or factual error may not be enough to invalidate the Judgement, a series of such errors, viewed in the aggregate, may no longer be harmless, thus favoring a remand. Such is the case here. Throughout the Appeals Judgement the Appeals Chamber has identified several errors in the Trial Chamber decision, some of which it deems insufficient to invalidate the Judgement. At other times, the Appeals Chamber has acted as a fact-finder in the first instance and substituted its own findings in order to cure the errors when, in fact, the Trial Chamber is the body best suited to this task.

2. The volume of errors by the Trial Chamber is obvious as demonstrated by the numerous convictions that the Appeals Chamber reverses as well as the

Standing Up For Justice. Theodor Meron, Oxford University Press (2021). © Theodor Meron.
DOI: 10.1093/oso/9780198863434.003.0011

issue that I discuss below. Based on the quashed convictions and the cumulative effect of other errors, I believe that a remand was clearly warranted.

B. Nahimana's Conviction for Persecution (RTLM Broadcasts)

3. The Trial Chamber convicted Appellant Nahimana for persecution pursuant to Articles 3(h), 6(1), and 6(3) of the Statute, and the Appeals Chamber has affirmed the conviction based on Articles 3(h) and 6(3). The conviction rests on Appellant Nahimana's superior responsibility for the post-6 April RTLM broadcasts. My objections to the conviction for persecution are two-fold: first, from a strictly legal perspective, the Appeals Chamber has improperly allowed hate speech to serve as the basis for a criminal conviction; second, the Appeals Chamber has misapplied the standard that it articulates by failing to link Appellant Nahimana directly to the widespread and systematic attack.

4. By way of clarification, when I refer to "mere hate speech," I mean speech that, however objectionable, does not rise to the level of constituting a direct threat of violence or an incitement to commit imminent lawless action. Hate speech, by definition, is vituperative and abhorrent, and I personally find it repugnant. But because free expression is one of the most fundamental personal liberties, any restrictions on speech—and especially any criminalization of speech—must be carefully circumscribed.

1. Mere Hate Speech is Not Criminal

5. Under customary international law and the Statute of the Tribunal, mere hate speech is not a criminal offense. Citing the obligation to ban hate speech under the International Covenant on Civil and Political Rights (ICCPR) and the Convention on the Elimination of all Forms of Racial Discrimination (CERD), the Trial Chamber held that "hate speech that expresses ethnic and other forms of discrimination violates the norm of customary international law prohibiting discrimination." Although the Appeals Chamber does not address the accuracy of this statement, the Trial Chamber incorrectly stated the law. It is true that Article 4 of the CERD and Article 20 of the ICCPR require signatory states to prohibit certain forms of hate speech in their domestic laws, but do not criminalize hate speech in international law. However, various states have entered reservations with respect to these provisions. Several parties to the CERD objected to any obligation under Article 4 that would encroach on the freedom of expression embodied in Article 5 of the CERD and in their own respective laws. For example, France stated: "With regard to article 4, France wishes to make it clear that it interprets the reference made therein to the principles of the Universal Declaration of Human Rights and to the rights set forth in article 5 of the Convention as releasing the States Parties from the obligation to enact anti-discrimination legislation which is incompatible with the freedoms

of opinion and expression and of peaceful assembly and association guaranteed by those texts." With respect to Article 20 of the ICCPR, several states reserved the right not to introduce implementing legislation precisely because such laws might conflict with those states' protections of political liberty. The United States has entered arguably the strongest reservations in light of the fact that the American Constitution protects even "vituperative" and "abusive" language that does not qualify as a "true threat" to commit violence. Critically, no state party has objected to such reservations. The number and extent of the reservations reveal that profound disagreement persists in the international community as to whether mere hate speech is or should be prohibited, indicating that Article 4 of the CERD and Article 20 of the ICCPR do not reflect a settled principle. Since a consensus among states has not crystallized, there is clearly no norm under customary international law criminalizing mere hate speech.

6. The drafting history of the Genocide Convention bolsters this conclusion. An initial provision, draft Article III, stated: "All forms of public propaganda tending by their systematic and hateful character to provoke genocide, or tending to make it appear as a necessary, legitimate or excusable act shall be punished." As the commentary to draft Article III made clear, the provision was not concerned with direct and public incitement to commit genocide, which fell under the purview of draft Article II; rather, draft Article III was aimed unequivocally at mere hate speech. Importantly, the final text of the Convention did not include draft Article III or subsequent proposals by the Soviet delegation that also would have codified a ban on mere hate speech. As a result, the Genocide Convention bans only speech that constitutes direct incitement to commit genocide; it says nothing about hate speech falling short of that threshold.

7. Furthermore, the only precedent of either International Tribunal to address this precise question notes that hate speech is not prohibited under the relevant statute or customary international law. The language of the *Kordić* Trial Judgement of the International Criminal Tribunal for the former Yugoslavia (ICTY) is instructive:

> The Trial Chamber notes that the Indictment against Dario Kordić is the first indictment in the history of the International Tribunal to allege [hate speech] as a crime against humanity. The Trial Chamber, however, finds that this act, as alleged in the Indictment, does not by itself constitute persecution as a crime against humanity. It is not enumerated as a crime elsewhere in the International Tribunal Statute, but most importantly, it does not rise to the same level of gravity as the other acts enumerated in Article 5. Furthermore, the criminal prohibition of this act has not attained the status of customary international law. Thus to convict the accused for such an act as is alleged as persecution would violate the principle of legality.

The Prosecution did not appeal this important determination, and the Appeals Chamber did not intervene to correct a perceived error, lending credence to the notion that the *Kordić* Trial Judgement accurately reflects the law on hate speech. Notably, Article 5 of the Statute of the ICTY, including the prohibition against persecution, is virtually identical in scope to Article 3 of the Statute of the ICTR under which Nahimana was convicted.

8. In light of the reservations to the relevant provisions of the CERD and the ICCPR, the drafting history of the Genocide Convention, and the *Kordić* Trial Judgement, it is abundantly clear that there is no settled norm of customary international law that criminalizes hate speech. Similarly, a close textual analysis demonstrates that the Statute of the ICTR does not ban mere hate speech. This is as it should be because the Statute codifies established principles of international law, including those reflected in the Genocide Convention. Were it otherwise, the Tribunal would violate basic principles of fair notice and legality. The Appeals Chamber asserts that finding that hate speech can constitute an act of persecution does not violate the principle of legality as the crime of persecution itself "is sufficiently precise in international law." I find this statement puzzling. In international criminal law, a notion must be precise, not just "sufficiently precise." The Brief of *Amicus Curiae* correctly observes that "[i]n contrast to most other crimes against humanity … 'persecution' by its nature is open to broad interpretation." Citing *Kordić*, which is given short shrift by the Appeals Chamber, the Brief of *Amicus Curiae* continues: "Mindful of the attendant risks to defendants' rights, international courts have sought to ensure the 'careful and sensitive development' of the crime of persecution 'in light of the principle of *nullem crimen sine lege*'." The Tribunal must proceed with utmost caution when applying new forms of persecution because, of the various crimes against humanity, persecution is one of the most indeterminate. There are difficulties with the rubric or definition of persecution itself, and even more so with the vagueness of its constituent elements. The combined effect of this indeterminacy and the Tribunal's desire to address effectively such an egregious crime as persecution is to gravitate towards expansion through judicial decisions. Understandable as such tendency is, it may clash, as in the present case, with the fundamental principle of legality.

2. Why Hate Speech is Protected

9. The debate over the wisdom of protecting hate speech has raged for decades, and I do not purport to summarize the debate here. While some scholars have defended the protection of hate speech on the ground that tolerant societies must themselves exemplify tolerance or that the best antidote to malevolent speech is rational counterargument (rather than suppression), my objective here is more practical. Because of the extent to which hate

speech and political discourse are often intertwined, the Tribunal should be especially reluctant to justify criminal sanctions for unpopular speech.

10. From an *ex post* perspective, courts and commentators may often be tempted to claim that no harm, and in fact much good, could come from the suppression of particularly odious ideas. In many instances, hate speech seems to have no capacity to contribute to rational political discourse. What, then, is its value? The reason for protecting hate speech lies in the *ex ante* benefits. The protection of speech, even speech that is unsettling and uncomfortable, is important in enabling political opposition, especially in emerging democracies. As *amicus curiae* in the instant case, the Open Society Justice Initiative has brought to the Tribunal's attention numerous examples of regimes' suppressing criticism by claiming that their opponents were engaged in criminal incitement. Such efforts at suppression are particularly acute where political parties correspond to ethnic cleavages. As a result, regimes often charge critical journalists and political opponents with "incitement to rebellion" or "incitement to hatred." The threat of criminal prosecution for legitimate dissent is disturbingly common, and officials in some countries have explicitly cited the example of RTLM in order to quell criticism of the governing regimes. "[S]weepingly overbroad definitions of what constitutes actionable incitement enabled governments to threaten and often punish the very sort of probing, often critical, commentary about government that is of vital importance to a free society." In short, overly permissive interpretations of incitement can and do lead to the criminalization of political dissent.

11. The *ex ante* benefit of protecting political dissent, especially in nascent democracies, is the reason that speakers enjoy a wide berth to air their viewpoints, however crassly presented. Even when hate speech appears to be of little or no value (the so-called "easy cases"), criminalizing speech that falls short of true threats or incitement chills legitimate political discourse, as various countries have recognized. In South Africa, one of the few countries that has removed certain hate speech from constitutional protection, speech may be criminalized only when it "constitutes incitement to cause harm." Similarly, the American Constitution does not protect "true threats" or incitement designed and likely to provoke imminent lawless action. However, "the government may not prohibit the expression of an idea simply because society finds the idea itself offensive or disagreeable."

12. The Statute of the ICTR explicitly prohibits genocide and incitement to commit genocide. When hate speech rises to the level of inciting violence or other imminent lawless action, such expression does not enjoy protection. But for the reasons explained above, an attempt, under the rubric of persecution, to criminalize unsavory speech that does not constitute actual imminent incitement might have grave and unforeseen consequences. Thus, courts must remain vigilant in preserving the often precarious balance between competing freedoms.

3. Mere Hate Speech May Not Be the Basis of a Criminal Conviction

13. In upholding Appellant Nahimana's conviction, the Appeals Chamber has impermissibly predicated the conviction on mere hate speech. As noted above, my colleagues do not decide whether hate speech, without more, can be the *actus reus* of persecution under the Statute, but hate speech nonetheless is an important and decisive factor in the conviction for persecution. In effect, the Appeals Chamber conflates hate speech and speech inciting to violence and states that both kinds of speech constitute persecution. This, to my mind, is a distinction without a meaningful difference.

14. I agree with the Appeals Chamber that under the Tribunal's jurisprudence, cumulative convictions under different statutory provisions are permissible as long as each provision has at least one distinct element that the Prosecution must prove separately. The same act—here, Nahimana's responsibility for the post-6 April RTLM broadcasts—may form the basis for convictions of direct and public incitement to commit genocide as well as persecution; however, the unique element of persecution is that the acts must be part of a widespread and systematic attack on a civilian population. Because of Nahimana's responsibility for the post-6 April broadcasts, the only remaining question concerns whether the unique element of persecution existed.

15. One might argue that the post-6 April broadcasts in themselves are enough to establish the existence of a widespread and systematic attack on a civilian population. The Appeals Chamber recognizes the weakness of such a conclusion; otherwise, the analysis would have been much more straightforward and would not have required a finessing of the hate speech question. Clearly, then, the existence of mere hate speech contributed to the Appeals Chamber's finding of a widespread and systematic attack. My distinguished colleagues defend this approach by noting (1) that "underlying acts of persecution can be considered jointly" and (2) that "it is not necessary that … underlying acts of persecution amount to crimes in international law." According to this view, hate speech, though not criminal, may be considered along with other acts in order to establish that the Appellant committed persecution.

16. The fundamental problem with this approach is that it fails to appreciate that speech is unique—expression which is not criminalized is protected. As Justice Oliver Wendell Holmes has observed: "Every idea is an incitement." But in the case of conflicting liberties, a balance must be struck, and speech that falls on the non-criminal side of that balance enjoys special protection. This stands in stark contrast to other non-criminal acts that have no such unique status and indeed may contribute to the aggregate circumstances a court can consider. The Appeals Chamber, even without deciding whether hate speech alone can justify a conviction, nevertheless permits protected

speech to serve as a basis for a conviction for persecution. Such a tack abrogates the unique status accorded to non-criminal expression and, in essence, criminalizes non-criminal speech.

4. Nexus Between Nahimana and the Widespread and Systematic Attack

17. Having discussed my objections to the legal question of what role, if any, mere hate speech may play in justifying a conviction for persecution, I turn now to a factual problem. In describing the widespread and systematic attack on a civilian population that must underpin the conviction, the Appeals Chamber takes cognizance of a campaign "characterised by acts of violence (killings, ill-treatments, rapes, ...) and of destruction of property." Nowhere in the Judgement, however, does the Appeals Chamber establish a nexus between these vile acts and Appellant Nahimana. Unless there is a causal nexus between the underlying acts committed by an accused and the systematic attack to which they contributed, a conviction for persecution would be based on guilt by association.

18. The Appeals Chamber notes that mere hate speech "contributed" to the other acts of violence and thus constituted an instigation to persecution. It also observes that the hate speech occurred in the midst of a "broad campaign of persecution against the Tutsi population." While the Appeals Chamber has thus correctly recognized the necessity of establishing a causal nexus between Nahimana's actions and the widespread and systematic attack, it has marshaled no evidence to this effect. The supposed nexus rests on nothing more than *ipse dixit* declarations that Nahimana's hate speech "contributed" to a larger attack.

19. It is true that Nahimana's responsibility for the post-6 April broadcasts occurred within the same temporal and geographic context as the wider Rwandan genocide. Generalizations about the atrocities that took place, though, cannot convert Nahimana's conviction for direct and public incitement to commit genocide into a conviction for persecution as well. It is quite possible that a direct link exists between Nahimana's actions and the wider attack, but a vague appeal to various killings, rapes, and other atrocities does not pass muster under norms of legality and due process.

20. The conclusion, then, is that the evidence of Nahimana's connection to a widespread attack rests on only two sources: first, certain post-6 April broadcasts, which the Appeals Chamber itself deemed insufficient when considered alone, to establish that such an attack took place; and, second, non-criminal hate speech, which I have argued should not form the basis, in whole or in part, of any conviction. Nahimana's conviction for persecution is thus left on extremely weak footing and cannot stand.

21. For the foregoing reasons, I believe that the Appeals Chamber should have reversed Nahimana's conviction for persecution.

5. Nahimana's Sentence

22. Because I would reverse the conviction of Appellant Nahimana for persecution, I believe that the only conviction against him that can stand is for direct and public incitement to commit genocide under Article 6(3) and based on certain post-6 April broadcasts. Despite the severity of this crime, Nahimana did not personally kill anyone and did not personally make statements that constituted incitement. In light of these facts, I believe that the sentence imposed is too harsh, both in relation to Nahimana's own culpability and to the sentences meted out by the Appeals Chamber to Barayagwiza and Ngeze, who committed graver crimes. Therefore, I dissent from Nahimana's sentence.

Judgement—Partly Dissenting Opinion of Judge Meron: Annotations

The Partly Dissenting Opinion primarily focuses on Nahimana's conviction and sentencing and asserts that the case should have been remanded. The Trial Chamber committed numerous errors while rendering its Judgement, as demonstrated by the multitude of convictions that the Appeals Chamber reversed in this Judgement. Due to these errors, the Appeals Chamber on several occasions acted as a "fact-finder in the first instance and substituted its own findings in order to cure the errors."[1] The Trial Chamber, not the Appeals Chamber, should be acting as the fact-finder in the first instance as it is in the best position to do so. The Opinion then focuses on Nahimana's conviction for persecution based on his responsibility for the post-6 April RTLM broadcasts. Though the Appeals Chamber decided that Nahimana could not be convicted of persecution under Article 6(1) of the Statute for the post-6 April RTLM broadcasts, it upheld the conviction under Articles 6(3) and 3(h). The Opinion disagrees with Nahimana's conviction for persecution on two grounds: 1) the Appeals Chamber improperly allowed hate speech to be the basis of the conviction; and 2) the Appeals Chamber improperly applied its own standard by failing to link Nahimana directly to the widespread and systematic attack.[2]

1. *See Ferdinand Nahimana, Jean-Bosco Barayagwiza, Hassan Ngeze v. The Prosecutor*, Judgement, ICTR Appeals Chamber, Part XXII. Partly Dissenting Opinion of Judge Meron, at para. 1, Case no. ICTR-99-52-A (28 Nov. 2007).
2. *Id.* at para. 3.

At the center of this Opinion is a fundamental principle: freedom of expression. Given the importance of freedom of expression and opinion, criminalization of speech must be carefully defined according to strict criteria. Hate speech should be protected due to its *ex ante* benefits, primarily its role in promoting the growth of democratic societies by enabling, and protecting, political opposition. Individuals should be free to express their dissenting opinions to a political regime without fear of repercussion in the form of criminal prosecution. Naturally, a distinction must be made between mere hate speech and hate speech that rises to the level of actual imminent incitement such as inciting violence or other lawless action. Such speech will not be protected and will be prosecuted accordingly. The difficulty lies in determining when hate speech rises to the appropriate level of incitement.

Under customary international law and the Statute of the Tribunal, mere hate speech, by itself, is not a criminal offense.[3] Neither Article 4 of the Convention on the Elimination of all Forms of Racial Discrimination (CERD) nor Article 20 of the International Covenant on Civil and Political Rights (ICCPR) reflect a settled principle. Numerous reservations have been entered with respect to both Articles, objecting to any obligation to enact domestic legislation that would infringe on the right to freedom of expression and opinion or the protection of political liberty.

The United States entered a powerful reservation with respect to Article 20 of the ICCPR, holding that the U.S. Constitution "protects even 'vituperative' and 'abusive' language that does not qualify as a 'true threat' to commit violence."[4] This lack of consensus among the States, and the absence of objections to the reservations, clearly illustrates that there is presently "no norm under customary international law criminalizing mere hate speech."[5] This is reinforced by the drafting history of the Genocide Convention and the decision to not include the text of draft Article III in the final iteration. The final text of the Genocide Convention bans only speech that constitutes direct incitement to commit genocide, *not* mere hate speech. Similar reinforcement can be found in the *Kordić* Trial Judgement of the ICTY holding that hate speech alone does not constitute persecution as a crime

3. *Id.* at para. 5. 4. *Id.* 5. *Id.*

against humanity. Importantly, the Trial Chamber emphasized that mere hate speech did not fall within the scope of Article 5 of the Statute of the ICTY, which is "virtually identical in scope to Article 3 of the Statute of the ICTR under which Nahimana was convicted."[6]

This Opinion addresses another significant principle: the principle of legality as it relates to the crime of persecution. It is important to note that the Statute of the ICTR codifies established principles of international law, including those established in the Genocide Convention. This ensures that the principles of fair notice and legality of an accused are protected. In the present Judgement, the Appeals Chamber asserted that holding hate speech as an act of persecution does not violate the principle of legality because the "crime of persecution itself 'is sufficiently precise in international law'."[7] The Opinion draws attention to the use of the word "sufficiently" as flawed: in international criminal law, the relevant standard is for the crime to be precise, not *sufficiently* precise. Given that the crime of persecution is already considered one of the most indeterminate of the various crimes against humanity, the Tribunal should not lightly elaborate on new forms of persecution through its decisions.

Regarding Nahimana's conviction for persecution, the Appeals Chamber failed to establish the requisite nexus between the violent acts of the campaign and Nahimana. A conviction for persecution must include a causal link between the underlying acts and the systematic attack to which they contributed. Instead, the Appeals Chamber explained that mere hate speech contributed to other violent acts and therefore qualified as an instigation to persecution.[8] Stating that Nahimana's hate speech contributed to a larger campaign of persecution against the Tutsi population without providing any evidence to support this causal nexus was wholly insufficient and violated due process. Without such evidence, Nahimana's conviction for direct and public incitement to commit genocide could not be converted into a conviction for persecution.[9] Nahimana's conviction for persecution should therefore have been reversed by the Appeals Chamber.

Reversing Nahimana's conviction for persecution would leave the conviction for direct and public incitement to commit genocide under

6. *Id.* at para. 7. 7. *Id.* at para. 8. 8. *Id.* at para. 18. 9. *Id.* at para. 19.

Article 6(3). As Nahimana did not personally kill anyone or personally made statements that constituted incitement and given the graver crimes committed by Barayagwiza and Ngeze, the Opinion holds that the sentence of 30 years' imprisonment imposed by the Appeals Chamber was too harsh.[10]

Prosecutor v. Galić

Judgement—Separate and Partially Dissenting Opinion of Judge Meron

Date of Judgement: 30 November 2006

Acts or threats of violence the purpose of which is to spread terror as violation of customary international law; the increase of Galić's sentence from 20 years' imprisonment to life sentence incompatible with the standard of review and violates due process

1. I agree with the reasoning of the Appeals Chamber with regard to Galić's Appeal. I write separately for two reasons: first, to add a brief thought on why acts or threats of violence the primary purpose of which is to spread terror among the civilian population are criminal violations of customary international law; and second, to dissent from the decision to grant the Prosecution's Appeal as to the sentence.

I

2. The Appeals Chamber explains why criminal responsibility attaches to acts or threats of violence the primary purpose of which is to spread terror among the civilian population. I believe this conclusion also follows logically from the ban, present at least since the Fourth Hague Convention on the Laws and Customs of War, on "declar[ing] that no quarter will be given." It is a crime to violate principles of customary international law identified in the Fourth Hague Convention. And if threats that no quarter will be given are crimes, then surely threats that a party will not respect other foundational principles of international law—such as the prohibition against targeting civilians—are also crimes. The terrorization at issue here is exactly such a threat.

10 *Id.* at para. 22.

II

3. I respectfully dissent from the Appeals Chamber's decision to increase Galić's sentence from 20 years to life imprisonment. In my view, this increase is incompatible with the standard of review that we have applied in the past.

4. "Sentencing is essentially a discretionary process on the part of a Trial Chamber." Our jurisprudence makes this very clear. We have recognized in numerous cases that "Trial Chambers are vested with broad discretion in determining an appropriate sentence". We have similarly emphasized that "[a]ppeals against sentence, as appeals from a trial judgement, are appeals stricto sensu; they are of a corrective nature and are not trials de novo." Our obligation to give broad deference to the Trial Chamber stems from the standard set forth in Article 25 of the Statute. As the court most familiar with the particulars related to the defendant and his crime, the Trial Chamber is best positioned to identify the proper sentence. Accordingly, our precedents make clear that we can reverse a sentence imposed by the Trial Chamber only where we identify a "discernible error".

5. As the Prosecution concedes, there is no discernible error in the Trial Chamber's factual findings. The Trial Chamber fully acknowledged the gravity of Galić's crimes in its discussion of the sentence. It also noted his "very senior position" in aggravation, and his "exemplary behaviour ... throughout the proceedings before the International Tribunal" in mitigation. Taking into account all these factors, the Trial Chamber imposed a single sentence of 20 years imprisonment. The Appeals Chamber now overturns this sentence and imposes a life sentence on the grounds that a "sentence of only 20 years was so unreasonable and plainly unjust, in that it underestimated the gravity of Galić's criminal conduct."

6. I must dissent from the Appeals Chamber's decision to treat the Trial Chamber's chosen sentence as outside its broad discretion. For where a Trial Chamber properly identifies the relevant factors that should govern its decision and where no new convictions are entered on appeal, I would increase its chosen sentence only if one of two conditions is met: either the sentence is clearly out of proportion with sentences we have given in similar situations, or the sentence is otherwise so low that it demonstrably shocks the conscience. Any more stringent review denies the Trial Chamber the broad discretion vested in it.

7. Neither of these two conditions is satisfied here. As to the first condition, our case law indicates that "in principle, [a sentence] may be thought to be capricious or excessive if it is out of reasonable proportion with a line of sentences passed in similar circumstances for the same offences." This principle is of limited use, given the "multitude of variables, ranging from the number and type of crimes committed to the personal circumstances of the individual," and "[o]ften too many variables exist to be able to transpose the sentence in one case mutatis mutandis to another." Nonetheless, an "overview of the

International Tribunal's cases" can be helpful in assessing whether the sentence was disproportionate.

8. The ICTR Appeals Chamber has applied a comparative analysis in one case: in *Gacumbitsi* it increased a sentence from thirty years to life in keeping with a line of life sentences given in ICTR genocide cases in which there were "no especially mitigating circumstances." The ICTY, however, lacks a comparable line of genocide cases and so *Gacumbitsi* is not applicable here. Indeed, the ICTY Appeals Chamber has been reluctant to apply a comparative analysis.

9. Perhaps partly in consequence of the ICTY's emphasis on individualized sentencing, the final sentences imposed upon convicted individuals have ranged widely. Of the convictions which have become final, 15 individuals have received sentences of less than 10 years; 19 have received sentences of 10–19 years; and only 12 have received sentences of 20 years or more. In no case has an ICTY defendant ended up with a life sentence. This is not to say such a sentence cannot be given. To the contrary, the Appeals Chamber in *Stakić* acknowledged that a life sentence for a "co-perpetrator of extremely serious crimes, including an extermination campaign that the Trial Chamber estimated killed approximately 1,500 people in the Prijedor municipality" fell "within the Trial Chamber's discretion," though the Appeals Chamber did not suggest that such a life sentence was compelled. But in the absence of any ICTY case where a defendant has ended up with a life sentence after appeal, a comparative analysis gives us no basis for finding that the Trial Chamber was obligated to impose a life sentence on Galić. This is true even if, as the Prosecution claims, Galić's "crimes are among the worst that come before the Tribunal."

10. Turning to the second condition I identified, I cannot conclude that a 20-year sentence is so low that it demonstrably shocks the conscience. The war crimes and crimes against humanity committed by Galić are grave indeed. He commanded a lengthy campaign that led to deaths and serious injuries of civilians of all ages and that sought to terrorize countless more. Yet his sentence is hardly insubstantial. It is not a two-and-a-half-year slap-on-the-wrist, but rather a term of 20 years—a sentence that is as long as or longer than the vast majority of sentences imposed by the ICTY to date. And as noted by the Trial Chamber, this sentence is as long as was the longest prison sentence that could be imposed in the former Yugoslavia. The Trial Chamber fully considered the awful nature of Galić's crimes and the individual considerations pertinent to him in meting it out.

11. Reasonable minds can disagree about this sentence, just as they can disagree about whether there was enough evidence to support all the convictions in the first place. Just as we review the convictions on the merits to see whether any reasonable trier of fact could have found the defendant guilty beyond a reasonable doubt rather than considering whether we ourselves would have entered such a conviction, so we review the sentence to see

whether a Trial Chamber could reasonably impose it—rather than whether we ourselves would have done so. Had I sat as a Trial Judge, I might not have found Galić guilty beyond a reasonable doubt of the shelling of Markale market, but I cannot say that all reasonable triers of fact had to reach this conclusion. Similarly, had I sat as a Trial Judge, I might have called for a sentence of a longer term than 20 years, but I cannot say that all reasonable triers of fact were obligated to do the same. The need for a consistent standard of review is particularly high in cases like this one, where the scope of the defendant's guilt presents a closed question. Judge Nieto-Navia, for example, would have found Galić responsible for fewer incidents than did the majority of the Trial Chamber; would have found him guilty only of failing to restrain his subordinates from unlawful conduct that he had reason to know was occurring; and would have sentenced him to ten years. It is most unfair to affirm Galić's convictions by genuinely deferring to the findings of the Trial Chamber majority, and yet to increase Galić's sentence by not deferring (or only nominally deferring) to the Trial Chamber's choice of sentence.

12. Finally, I see no meaningful difference between the Prosecution's appeal in this case and its appeal in Kordić and Čerkez. There, the Prosecution called for us to increase the 25-year sentence imposed by the Trial Chamber on Dario Kordić, who was held responsible for, among other crimes, the persecution of Bosnian Muslims, the murder or wilful killing of hundreds of civilians, inhumane acts, wanton destruction, and plunder committed in and around at least 17 towns and villages in three municipalities of Bosnia-Herzegovina. As in this case, the Prosecutor did "not argue that the Trial Chamber erred in failing to take into account factors that would have called for a longer sentence." Rather, and again parallel to this case, the Prosecution claimed that "the sentence of 25 years' imprisonment is manifestly inadequate in relation to (i) the magnitude, scope—geographic and temporal—and extremely grave nature of the offences, the attacks being committed against defenceless civilians; [and] (ii) Kordić's position, powers, responsibilities as the highest Bosnian Croat political leader in Central Bosnia at the time." We readily held that "The Prosecution has not shown that the Trial Chamber handed down a sentence which did not reflect the gravity of Kordić's conduct." For the same reasons, we should reach the same conclusion in this case.

13. The majority's decision to increase Galić's sentence to life imprisonment may satisfy your sense of condemnation. But this increase disserves the principles of procedural fairness on which our legitimacy rests. As the highest body in our court system, we are not readily accountable to any other authority and thus have a particular obligation to use our power sparingly. We should not substitute our own preferences for the reasoned judgement of a Trial Chamber. A sound method for assuring that we have not fallen prey to such preferences is to measure our choices fully and comprehensively against those made in prior cases. Although precise comparisons may be of limited value, the radically different approach adopted by the majority in this case

requires at least some explanation. Rather than undertaking such an analysis, however, the majority simply offers conclusory statements. I cannot accept the majority's approach. No matter what he has done, Galić is entitled to due process of law—including a fair application of our standard of review. I respectfully dissent.

Judgement—Separate and Partially Dissenting Opinion by Judge Meron: Annotations

Pursuant to an indictment filed on 26 February 1999, Galić was charged with 7 Counts:

- Count 1: "conducting a campaign of shelling and sniping against civilian areas of Sarajevo between 10 September 1992 and 10 August 1994, thereby inflicting terror upon its civilian population"
- Counts 2 to 4: "a protracted campaign of sniper attacks upon the civilian population of Sarajevo, killing and wounding a large number of persons of all ages and both sexes"
- Counts 5 to 7: "a coordinated and protracted campaign of artillery and mortar shelling onto civilian areas of Sarajevo, resulting in thousands of civilians being killed or injured."

On 5 December 2003, the Trial Chamber by a majority found Galić guilty of Counts 1–3 and 5–6 and dismissed Counts 4 and 7 because of the finding of guilt entered on Count 1. Galić was sentenced to a single sentence of 20 years' imprisonment. Both Galić and the Prosecution appealed the Trial Chamber's decision.[11]

This annotation focuses on parts of the Judgement relevant to the Dissenting Opinion—the appeal against the sentence.[12]

Galić argues that the international tribunal is bound by the sentencing laws/practices of the former Yugoslavia where the maximum prison sentence that could be given was 20 years and excluded a sentence of life imprisonment. Regarding that argument, the Appeals Chamber recalled that the international tribunal while "bound to take the sentencing law and

11. *See Prosecutor v. Stanislav Galić*, Judgement, ICTY Appeals Chamber, Part XXI. Separate and Partially Dissenting Opinion of Judge Meron, at para. 4, Case no. IT-98-29-A (30 Nov. 2006).
12. *See Prosecutor v. Stanislav Galić*, Judgement, ICTY Appeals Chamber, Part XII. Appeal Against Sentence, at paras. 391–456, Case no. IT-98-29-A (30 Nov. 2006).

practice of the former Yugoslavia into account, does not have to follow it."[13] The Appeals Chamber accordingly rejected Galić's argument that the maximum sentence that could be imposed was 20 years. The Appeals Chamber similarly rejected Galić's reference to the principle of *lex mitior.*

Galić argued that the Trial Chamber treated certain factors which constituted elements of the alleged crimes as aggravating factors, specifically: "the suffering of the victims, the frequency of the illegal actions of the SRK, the anguishing environment, and his position as a commander."[14] The Appeals Chamber agreed that "an element of the crime cannot constitute an aggravating circumstance"[15] but noted that the first three factors listed by Galić were used to assess the *gravity* of the offence, not aggravating circumstances. Concerning the fourth factor, Galić's position as a commander, the Appeals Chamber noted that "the level of authority may still play a role in sentencing as it is not an element of the mode of liability of 'ordering' that an accused is high in the chain of command and thus wields a high level of authority."[16] The Trial Chamber did not treat Galić's authority to give orders as an aggravating circumstance but rather considered other factors that "emanate from his position of authority as commander and found that he repeatedly breached his public duty from this very senior position, thereby abusing his position of authority."[17]

Galić argued that the Trial Chamber failed to consider several mitigating circumstances when deciding his sentence, specifically the conditions under which Galić commanded the troops, the conditions of urban warfare and his personal and family situation. The Appeals Chamber recalled that a Trial Chamber is granted *considerable discretion* in deciding which mitigating factors to take into account and noted that an appeal is not the "appropriate forum" to raise mitigating circumstances that were available at trial for the first time. Regardless, the Appeals Chamber found that the Trial Chamber did not abuse its discretion by not considering the conditions under which Galić commanded the troops. The Appeals Chamber further found that the Trial Chamber did consider (and decided to not accept) the conditions of urban warfare and that Galić failed to bring that argument at trial as a mitigating circumstance.

13. *Id.* at para. 398.
14. *Id.* at para. 406.
15. *Id.* at para. 408.
16. *Id.* at para. 412.
17. *Id.*

The Appeals Chamber by majority (with Judge Pocar partially dissenting and Judge Meron dissenting) found that the Trial Chamber did indeed commit a "discernible error in assessing the factors in relation to the gravity of the crime, the role and participation of Galić, the aggravating circumstance of abuse of Galić's position of authority, and the single mitigating circumstance regarding his behaviour [his exemplary behavior throughout the proceedings[18]]."[19] The Appeals Chamber explained that the Trial Chamber did not err in its factual findings but instead committed an error in finding that a sentence of 20 years' imprisonment adequately reflected the gravity of the crimes and Galić's participation as a high-ranking officer. The Appeals Chamber held that a sentence of only 20 years was "so unreasonable and plainly unjust"[20] that it could be said that the Trial Chamber abused its sentencing discretion. The Appeals Chamber therefore allowed the Prosecution's appeal.

This Opinion first briefly elaborates on why acts or threats of violence, the primary purpose of which is to spread terror among civilians, constitute criminal violations of customary international law. Another explanation for why criminal responsibility attaches to these acts or threats can be found in the Fourth Hague Convention on the Laws and Customs of War and the ban on declaring that no quarter will be given. If threats that no quarter will be given are crimes, then by extension of the same logic, threats that a party will not respect the prohibition against targeting civilians are also crimes.

The rest of this Opinion focuses on Galić's sentence and dissents from the Appeals Chamber's decision to increase the sentence from 20 years to life imprisonment. The increase was said to be "incompatible"[21] with the standard of review applied in past cases. Instead, it stated that the Trial Chamber's sentence was within its discretionary powers given that there was no error in the factual findings and no new convictions were entered on appeal.

Of particular interest, the Opinion identifies the only two conditions where an increase in sentence would be permissible even with a lack of error in the factual findings: either 1) the sentence given is "clearly out of proportion with sentences" given in similar situations; or 2) the sentence is "otherwise so

18. *Id.* at para. 453. 19. *Id.* at para. 455. 20. *Id.*

21. *See Prosecutor v. Stanislav Galić*, Judgement, ICTY Appeals Chamber, Part XXI. Separate and Partially Dissenting Opinion of Judge Meron, para. 3, Case no. IT-98-29-A (30 Nov. 2006).

low that it demonstrably shocks the conscience."[22] Reasoning falling outside these two conditions would deny the Trial Chamber its broad discretion to identify the proper sentence. Neither of those conditions was satisfied in the present case.

Turning to the first condition, though past cases can be helpful in determining whether a sentence is disproportionate, those cases are not determinative due to their varying factors. A helpful reference is the ICTR Appeals Chamber's Judgement in *Gacumbitsi* where a sentence of 30 years was increased to a life sentence in line with similar ICTR genocide cases. Unfortunately, a comparable analysis cannot be found within the ICTY genocide cases, partially due to the case-by-case sentencing analysis undertaken by the ICTY. Of significance, no ICTY defendant had ever been given a life sentence [prior to *Galić*], though that should by no means have been taken to mean that a life sentence was impermissible and outside the Trial Chamber's discretion. Regardless, the lack of ICTY cases where a sentence was increased to a life sentence after appeal meant that there was no comparative basis for holding that the Trial Chamber was "obligated" to require a life sentence.[23] The Appeals Chamber not only disregarded this lack of similar cases, but also failed to provide an explanation for its approach.

The second condition is also not satisfied—a 20-year sentence is not low enough to shock the conscience. Though the gravity of the crimes committed by Galić is not denied, his sentence was "as long as or longer than the vast majority of sentences imposed by the ICTY to date."[24] The Opinion takes this opportunity to remind us that reasonable minds can differ as to what they would have chosen as the appropriate sentence if they were in the Trial Chamber's position. However, the standard calls for reviewing the sentence imposed by the Trial Chamber to see whether it could reasonably be imposed, not whether it is the "best" possible sentence, or the preferred judgement of the Appeals Chamber. Undermining this standard would be problematic, especially in cases such as this where the scope of the defendant's guilt presented such a close and difficult call.

Similarly to the Judgement in *Kordić and Čerkez*, the Appeals Chamber in *Galić* should have held that the Prosecution had failed to show that the sentence of the Trial Chamber did not reflect the gravity of Galić's conduct. Holding otherwise "disserves the principles of procedural fairness on which

22. *Id.* at para. 6. 23. *Id.* at para. 9. 24. *Id.* at para. 10.

[the Appeals Chamber's] legitimacy rests" and denies Galić not only due process of the law, but a fair application of the well-established standard of review of the Appeals Chamber.[25]

Bagosora and Nsengiyumva v. The Prosecutor

Judgement—Joint Dissenting Opinion of Judges Meron and Robinson

Date of Judgement: 14 December 2011

The conviction entered by the Trial Chamber must be the only possible interpretation of the evidence, not just one reasonable interpretation of the evidence

1. In this Judgement, the Appeals Chamber enters convictions against Nsengiyumva, as a superior under Article 6(3) of the Statute, for the actions of three soldiers linked to killings in Gisenyi town on 7 April 1994. The Majority's approach is based on, inter alia, its conclusion that the Trial Chamber did not err in finding that Nsengiyumva had knowledge of the soldiers' actions. In our view however, no reasonable Trial Chamber could find that this was the only reasonable inference to be drawn from the circumstantial evidence on the record. Accordingly, we respectfully disagree with the Majority's reasoning and with its decision to affirm Nsengiyumva's convictions as a superior with respect to the killings in Gisenyi town.

2. The Trial Chamber found that Nsengiyumva had knowledge of the killings in Gisenyi town based on: (i) its finding that he ordered the attacks; (ii) its general characterisation of the crimes for which he was convicted as "organised military operations requiring authorisation, planning and orders from the highest levels"; (iii) its view that military authorities would be particularly vigilant on 7 April 1994 given the death of President Habyarimana and resumption of hostilities with the RPF; and (iv) the proximity of the crime scene to Gisenyi military camp. The Majority upholds the Trial Chamber's findings that Nsengiyumva possessed the relevant knowledge, noting the Trial Chamber's conclusions regarding "organised military operations" at a time when military authorities would be vigilant, and the proximity of the attacks to Gisenyi military camp.

3. We first observe that with respect to the Gisenyi town attacks, the Appeals Chamber has concluded that the Trial Chamber erred in finding

25. *Id.* at para. 13.

Nsengiyumva responsible for ordering under Article 6(1), and instead enters convictions as a superior under Article 6(3). We also note that the Appeals Chamber has reversed all of Nsengiyumva's convictions related to other crime sites. The gravamen of the Majority's opinion is thus limited to Nsengiyumva's responsibility for the actions of three soldiers who, disguised in civilian clothes, joined a large group of civilians in perpetrating killings in the immediate aftermath of President Habyarimana's death.

4. The Trial Chamber's general conclusion regarding "organised military operations" was based on the pattern of crimes for which it convicted Nsengiyumva, some involving a much larger number of subordinates than those at issue in Gisenyi town. It may well be reasonable to infer that a commander at a time of heightened vigilance would have to know about significant numbers of his subordinates participating in multiple crimes. However, all of Nsengiyumva's other convictions establishing a pattern of "organised military operations" have been reversed, and thus are no longer relevant to his knowledge of the Gisenyi town crimes. In this context, we consider it implausible that the only reasonable inference to be drawn from the limited remaining circumstantial evidence is that Nsengiyumva would have reason to know that three lower-level soldiers from one of the camps in his zone of command would disguise themselves in civilian clothes and commit crimes near their base. It is entirely reasonable to interpret the remaining evidence on the record as demonstrating that the three soldiers took action without Nsengiyumva's knowledge. Finding otherwise comes dangerously close to imposing strict liability on military commanders for any and all crimes committed by subordinates, simply by virtue of the superior-subordinate relationship.

5. In our view the geographical proximity of the killings to Gisenyi military camp is insufficient to justify the Majority's findings as to Nsengiyumva's knowledge. The evidence considered by the Trial Chamber was that the Gisenyi town killings were carried out primarily by a group of civilians, and that the three soldiers who joined this group were disguised as civilians. Absent additional evidence, we cannot see how the only reasonable inference to be drawn from evidence regarding a group of individuals dressed as civilians committing crimes near Gisenyi military camp is that Nsengiyumva knew that three soldiers from one of the bases under his command would join these civilians.

6. We acknowledge that if Witness DO's testimony that the soldiers involved in the Gisenyi town killings met with Nsengiyumva is considered, the Majority's conclusion as to Nsengiyumva's knowledge would be reasonable. Such reliance on Witness DO's testimony, however, is not possible. The Trial Chamber explicitly declined to accept Witness DO's "account of Nsengiyumva's participation in meetings in the absence of corroboration." It

noted, inter alia, Witness DO's status as an accomplice witness serving a life sentence in Rwanda, that Witness DO provided accounts that were at times definitively incorrect and contradictory, and that he may have had an "interest in distancing himself from the crimes." Just as the Appeals Chamber must give deference to the Trial Chamber's acceptance of certain parts of Witness DO's very problematic testimony, so must it defer to the Trial Chamber's conclusion that other parts of Witness DO's testimony are not credible. We also note that although the three soldiers may have interacted with an officer from the Gisenyi military camp while committing crimes, this does not demonstrate that the only reasonable inference available was that Nsengiyumva knew of their actions. The mere fact that the officer was within Nsengiyumva's chain of command does not establish knowledge.

7. We underscore that we would support finding that one reasonable interpretation of the evidence is that Nsengiyumva knew that the three soldiers would participate in the Gisenyi town killings. We cannot agree, however, with the Majority's finding that the Trial Chamber was reasonable in concluding that this was the only reasonable inference to be drawn from the circumstantial evidence. Accordingly, we respectfully dissent.

Judgement—Joint Dissenting Opinion of Judges Meron and Robinson: Annotations

The Dissenting Opinion focuses on the convictions entered by the majority against Nsengiyumva. Nsengiyumva was held to qualify as a superior pursuant to Article 6(3) of the Statute and was held responsible for the actions of three soldiers and their participation in the killings of Gisenyi town on 7 April 1994.[26] The majority based its decision on its conclusion that the Trial Chamber did not err in its finding that Nsengiyumva had knowledge of the soldiers' actions.[27] In the view of the Dissenting Opinion, no reasonable Trial Chamber could have found this to be the "*only* reasonable inference to be drawn from the circumstantial evidence on the record."[28] The Opinion therefore disagrees with the majority's decision to affirm Nsengiyumva's conviction as a superior with respect to the killings in Gisenyi town.

26. *See Théoneste Bagosora, Anatole Nsengiyumva v. The Prosecutor*, Judgement, ICTR Appeals Chamber, Part VI. Joint Dissenting Opinion of Judges Meron and Robinson, at para. 1, pp. 262–4, Case no. ICTR-98-41-A (14 Dec. 2011)

27. *Id.* 28. *Id.* emphasis added.

The Appeals Chamber held that the Trial Chamber erred in finding Nsengiyumva responsible for ordering the attacks under Article 6(1), instead entering its convictions based on his status as a superior under Article 6(3).[29] As all convictions related to other crime sites were also dismissed, the Appeals Chamber based its entire opinion solely on Nsengiyumva's responsibility concerning the actions of the three soldiers.[30]

This Opinion considers it implausible that the only reasonable inference to be drawn from the remaining circumstantial evidence was that Nsengiyumva would have known that three low-level soldiers from one of the camps under his command would choose to disguise themselves in civilian clothing and commit said crimes.[31] The remaining evidence that was left on the record after the dismissal of convictions relating to other crimes was too limited to allow only one reasonable inference to stand. In fact, it would be entirely reasonable to interpret the opposite: that the three soldiers acted without Nsengiyumva's knowledge.[32] Stating that only one reasonable inference can be drawn from the limited record "comes dangerously close to imposing strict liability" on a military commander for all crimes committed by their subordinates.[33]

Likewise, the geographical proximity of the killings to Gisenyi camp was insufficient to justify what the majority held to be the only possible reasonable inference.[34] The finding of the Trial Chamber was simply that the killings were carried out primarily by a group of civilians, and that three soldiers dressed as civilians joined that group. It is not reasonable to infer that Nsengiyumva knew that three soldiers from one of his bases would subsequently join those civilians.

The above reasoning of the Trial Chamber supports the finding that one reasonable interpretation of the evidence is that Nsengiyumva knew that the three soldiers were planning to participate in the Gisenyi town killings. However, as the Opinion makes clear, this is not the only possible interpretation. The majority erred when it agreed with the Trial Chamber's conclusion that this was indeed the only possible inference to be deduced from the available circumstantial evidence.[35]

29. *Id.* at para. 3 30. *Id.* 31. *Id.* at para. 4. 32. *Id.*
33. *Id.* 34. *Id.* at para. 5. 35. *Id.* at para. 7.

Prosecutor v. Strugar

Judgement—Joint Dissenting Opinion of Judge Meron and Judge Kwon

DATE OF JUDGEMENT: 17 JULY 2008

REVERSAL OF BURDEN OF PROOF, NO COMPLICITY IN A SHAM INVESTIGATION

1. We respectfully dissent from the majority regarding its finding as to Strugar's responsibility for the events of 6 December 1991 under Article 7(3) of the Statute. We cannot agree with the majority's decision to uphold the Trial Chamber's finding that Strugar did not fulfil his duty to take measures to punish those responsible for the unlawful shelling of the Old Town on 6 December 1991.

2. The Trial Chamber found that Jokić proposed that he carry out an investigation of the shelling of the Old Town and that Kadijević implicitly accepted this suggestion, and that the former reported back to the latter on the results of the investigation and the disciplinary measures to follow. We note that the Trial Chamber also found that Strugar, "as Admiral Jokić's immediate superior, remained undisturbed and unrestrained in his power and authority to require more to be done by the Admiral, or to act directly himself, had he so chosen."

A. Singleness of Command

3. We are of the opinion that Kadijević's order, albeit an implicit one, that Jokić should investigate the events of 6 December 1991 prevented Strugar in both a de jure and de facto sense from conducting his own parallel investigation. We note in this regard that the oral submissions made by the Prosecution on Appeal that an officer retains his obligation to investigate even where that officer's superior has ordered that officer's subordinate to conduct a legitimate investigation is unacceptable.

4. The principle of singleness of command, adopted as one of the basic principles of command and control within the JNA creates a single, direct channel through which orders will be formulated, received and carried out. It follows that where an officer's competent superior orders an investigation, any attempt by that officer to interfere with or undermine the order by carrying out a parallel investigation would not be tolerated. The fact that Strugar might have become the subject of an investigation actually strengthens the notion that he should not have interfered with any investigation ordered by his superior. Under such circumstances, it would have been especially inappropriate for Strugar to have become involved. Given the singleness of

command doctrine, we do not consider it necessary and reasonable in this case to say that Strugar was obliged to conduct an investigation parallel to the one ordered by the JNA Supreme Command, i.e., Kadijević.

5. In order to find Strugar guilty under Article 7(3) for failure to punish his subordinates for the unlawful shelling of Old Town, despite Kadijević's order, it must be established that the following situation exists, which the Prosecution must prove beyond a reasonable doubt:

(i) the investigation ordered by Kadijević was a sham;
(ii) Strugar knew that the investigation was a sham; and
(iii) Strugar was complicit, with Kadijević and Jokić, in conducting a sham investigation.

B. The Burden of Proof

6. The Trial Chamber states:

> In the Chamber's finding, the facts do not provide a foundation for these submissions. What is submitted is not the legal effect of what occurred, nor, in the Chamber's finding, is there the factual basis in the evidence for any suggestion that the Accused believed this to be the case in 1991. The Chamber is not persuaded in these circumstances that it is revealed that the Accused was, or thought himself to be, excluded from acting, or that he was ordered not to take action in respect of the events of 6 December 1991. Rather, the evidence persuades the Chamber that the Accused was, at the very least by acquiescence, a participant in the arrangement by which Admiral Jokić undertook his sham investigation and sham disciplinary action, and reported to the First Secretariat in a way which deflected responsibility for the damage to the Old Town from the JNA.
>
> The Accused was present throughout the meeting in Belgrade with General Kadijević. It is the evidence that the General was equally critical of both the Accused and Admiral Jokić. It is not suggested by the evidence that the Accused objected or resisted in any way at the meeting, or later, to the proposal of Admiral Jokić that he should investigate, or to General Kadijević's apparent acceptance of that. There is no suggestion in the evidence that at any time he proposed or tried to investigate or to take any action against any subordinate for the shelling of the Old Town, or that he was prevented from doing so by General Kadijević or any other authority.

7. The Trial Chamber has chosen to focus on the absence of proof that Kadijević's order for Jokić to investigate effectively prevented Strugar from conducting a parallel investigation. We consider this to be an inappropriate reversal of the burden of proof. The burden of proof rests squarely with the Prosecution to prove Strugar's guilt beyond a reasonable doubt. As noted above, in order to prove Strugar's guilt, the Prosecution must show that

Strugar was both aware of the sham nature of the investigation ordered by Kadijević and part of the conspiracy with Kadijević and Jokić to conduct the sham investigation. We consider that the Trial Chamber erred by focusing on the absence of evidence that Strugar was prevented from conducting a parallel investigation, as this constitutes a reversal of the burden of proof.

C. The Finding of the Trial Chamber Is Insufficient to Prove That Strugar Knew That the Investigation Was a Sham

8. Assuming that the investigation conducted by Jokić was a sham, the Prosecution still had the burden of proving both Strugar's knowledge of the sham and his complicity in it. We turn first to the question of knowledge.

9. We note the Trial Chamber's finding that Strugar was:

> prepared to accept a situation in which he would not become directly involved, leaving all effective investigation, action and decisions concerning disciplinary or other adverse action to his immediate subordinate, Admiral Jokić, whose task effectively was known to Strugar to be to smooth over the events of 6 December 1991 as best he could with both the Croatian and ECMM interests, while providing a basis on which it could be maintained by the JNA that it had taken appropriate measures.

10. This finding does not go far enough to prove Strugar's guilt, as it makes no mention of Strugar's knowledge that Kadijević ordered Jokić to conduct a sham investigation.

11. The finding of the Trial Chamber that Strugar "effectively" knew that Jokić's investigation was meant "to smooth over the events of 6 December 1991 as best he could" and to "provide a basis on which it could be maintained by the JNA that it had taken appropriate measures" does not, in our opinion, equate to knowledge that the investigation was intended to be a public relations exercise through which no disciplinary action would be taken. Indeed, a totally legitimate investigation could just as easily smooth things over for the JNA in the eyes of the international community.

D. There Is No Evidence to Prove That Strugar Knew That the Investigation Was a Sham

12. The majority notes a number of the Trial Chamber's findings which, in their opinion, support the conclusion of the Trial Chamber. What we consider to be missing from the Trial Chamber's judgement is a finding that Strugar was aware that the investigation, which Kadijević ordered Jokić to undertake, was a sham. Indeed, we are of the opinion that there was no evidence before the Trial Chamber to support such a finding beyond reasonable doubt.

13. We note that the majority, when reaching its conclusion, cites directly from a portion of Jokić's testimony in which Jokić states, inter alia, that he and Strugar discussed the "official version of events" regarding 6 December 1991. However, we note that the Trial Chamber was very careful to select the parts of Jokić's testimony on which it relied, and cast serious doubt on the credibility of a number of other aspects of Jokić's testimony. The Trial Chamber did not use the above portion of Jokić's testimony. Furthermore, the Trial Chamber went on to describe this part of Jokić's testimony as "surprising indeed". For this reason, we do not consider this portion of Jokić's testimony to be appropriate evidence for the Appeals Chamber to rely upon.

E. Strugar's Complicity in the Sham Investigation

14. Furthermore, we also note that there is a paucity of evidence indicating that Strugar was complicit in the sham investigation.

15. The most that the Trial Chamber said about this issue is:

> The Accused was present throughout the meeting in Belgrade with General Kadijević. It is the evidence that the General was equally critical of both the Accused and Admiral Jokić. It is not suggested by the evidence that the Accused objected or resisted in any way at the meeting, or later, to the proposal of Admiral Jokić that he should investigate, or to General Kadijević's apparent acceptance of that.

16. Strugar's mere presence at the meeting in Belgrade does not establish any complicity on his part because there is no evidence that Strugar believed the meeting to be other than in good faith. To the extent that Strugar believed that Kadijević (a) had insisted on a thorough investigation and (b) designated Jokić to undertake the investigation, the fact that the three individuals met together in Belgrade bears no indicia of a conspiracy.

17. Furthermore, any information that Strugar might have acquired after the meeting regarding the sham nature of the investigation likewise would be incapable of establishing Strugar's complicity. As elucidated above, the principle of singleness of command means that once Strugar reasonably believed that Kadijević had designated Jokić to conduct the investigation, Strugar lacked the material ability to intervene.

18. We note the majority's reliance on the Trial Chamber's finding that Strugar "invited Captain Kovačević to nominate outstanding participants in the events of 6 December 1991". We do not consider this to be evidence of Strugar's complicity in the sham investigation. Strugar's interest in recognising exemplary conduct on 6 December 1991 does not equate to evidence that he was also intent on allowing impunity for illegal conduct.

19. For the foregoing reasons, the Trial Chamber failed to establish that Strugar's actions or inactions constituted "acquiescence" (i.e., complicity) in the sham investigation.

F. Conclusion

20. In our opinion, the evidence marshalled by the Trial Chamber fails to establish that Strugar had knowledge of the sham nature of the investigation ordered by Kadijević or, in the alternative, that Strugar was complicit in the sham investigation. Consequently, we maintain that no reasonable trier of fact could have concluded beyond reasonable doubt that Strugar had failed in his duty to punish his subordinates for the crimes committed by them.

21. Accordingly, we would grant Strugar's sub-ground of appeal and reverse his conviction for failure to punish the perpetrators of the unlawful shelling of the Old Town.

Judgement—Joint Dissenting Opinion of Judge Meron and Judge Kwon: Annotations

This Opinion focuses on Strugar's responsibility under Article 7(3) of the Statute, specifically for the events of 6 December 1991. The Opinion disagrees with the majority's decision to uphold the Trial Chamber's finding that Strugar did not fulfill his duty to punish those responsible for the unlawful shelling of the Old Town. The evidence brought forth by the Trial Chamber failed to establish beyond a reasonable doubt that Strugar had knowledge that the investigation ordered by Kadijević was a sham. Alternatively, the Trial Chamber failed to establish beyond a reasonable doubt that Strugar was complicit in the sham investigation. As a result, it could not be concluded that Strugar failed in his duty to punish his subordinates for the crimes they committed.

The Opinion discusses the principle of singleness of command, which was adopted within the JNA and creates a "single, direct channel" for formulating, receiving and carrying out orders.[36] This principle prevented Strugar from conducting his own parallel investigation from both a de jure and de facto perspective. Strugar could not interfere or undermine an investigation ordered by his superior, especially given the likelihood that Strugar himself might become a subject of an investigation. The Trial Chamber's focus on the absence of evidence showing that Kadijević's order for Jokić to investigate prevented Strugar from conducting his parallel investigation creates an "inappropriate reversal of the burden of proof."[37]

36. *See Prosecutor v. Pavle Strugar*, Judgement, ICTY Appeals Chamber, Part XI. Joint Dissenting Opinion of Judge Meron and Judge Kwon, at para. 4, Case no. IT-01-42-A (17 July 2008).

37. *Id.* at para. 7.

The Trial Chamber should instead have focused on whether or not the Prosecution had met its burden of proving that Strugar knew of the sham investigation and was part of the conspiracy to conduct that sham investigation.

Prosecutor v. Halilović

Judgement—Separate Opinion of Judge Meron

Date of Judgement: 16 October 2007

Only statements memorialized on a video or audio tape are sufficiently reliable to be admitted into evidence against an accused thus ensuring voluntariness and reliability

1. I write separately on the issue of Sub-Ground 6. Although I agree with the majority that the Trial Chamber correctly excluded Halilović's 1996 Statement, I believe that such a conclusion necessarily derives from Rule 43 and is not, as the majority holds, a discretionary decision pursuant to Rule 89(D).

2. The majority holds that "[w]hether [Halilović's] statement would also be inadmissible due to a retroactive reading of Rule 43 of the Rules was not a decisive consideration in the Trial Chamber's reasoning." I disagree. In reproducing the Trial Chamber's holding regarding the Statement, the majority omits a critical paragraph from the Trial Judgement:

> Rule 43 provides for audio and video-recording of the interview of suspects and aims at ensuring the integrity of the proceedings, *inter alia*, by providing for an instrument to ascertain the voluntariness of a statement and the adherence to other relevant safeguards as provided for in Rule 42 and Rule 95. The Trial Chamber finds that Rule 43 is a fundamental provision to protect the rights of a suspect and an accused. Moreover, it is a safeguard for a full and accurate reflection of the questions and answers during the interview and thus enables the parties and the Trial Chamber to verify the exact wording of what was said during the interview.

The centrality of Rule 43 in the Trial Chamber's logic could hardly be more clear. Thus, the correct interpretation of Rule 43 is an issue that the Appeals Chamber should address.

3. Rule 43 provides:

> Whenever the Prosecutor questions a suspect, the questioning shall be audio-recorded or video-recorded …

4. The Trial Chamber correctly recognized that two fundamental legal questions arise with respect to Rule 43 and Halilović's Statement: (1) What procedural safeguards applied to the Statement?; and (2) What is the remedy for violations of those safeguards?

5. The first legal question involves the scope of Rule 43, specifically whether it applies only when someone is already a suspect or whether it applies also to questioning that occurred before the person became a suspect. As the Trial Chamber correctly recognized, Rule 43 has a two-fold purpose—ensuring *voluntariness* and *reliability*. Precisely because of concerns about reliability, Rule 43 must apply to all statements by an accused to the Prosecutor. Notwithstanding that a Prosecutor might have acted in good faith by not applying Rule 43 when questioning someone who, at the time, was not a suspect, Rule 43 embodies a substantive policy judgement that only statements memorialized on a video or audio tape are sufficiently reliable to be admitted into evidence against an accused. Therefore, the Trial Chamber correctly determined that Rule 43 was among the procedural safeguards that applied to the Statement.

6. Since Rule 43 applied to the Statement, and given that there is no question that the Statement was not recorded in compliance with the rule, the second question concerns the appropriate remedy. Rule 43 reflects a substantive judgement that unrecorded statements by the accused are, by definition, insufficiently reliable. A Trial Chamber normally assesses reliability on a case-by-case basis under Rule 95 and excludes evidence when there is "substantial doubt" about its reliability. Similarly, it determines probativeness under Rule 89(D). The discretion that a Trial Chamber normally exercises pursuant to these rules is inapposite, though, because an unrecorded statement by an accused is per se unreliable under Rule 43. As an unrecorded statement by an accused is never sufficiently reliable, the only appropriate remedy is exclusion of that statement.

7. My conclusion about the appropriateness of exclusion for violations of Rule 43 is bolstered by the precedents of the Tribunal. The *Čelebići* Appeal Judgement noted that the Appeals Chamber must seek to ensure (1) that procedural safeguards are respected and (2) that the evidence is reliable. (3) The Appeals Chamber there clearly contemplated that, despite scrupulous adherence to all procedural safeguards, some evidence might still be unreliable. It did not indulge the converse (*i.e.*, that despite procedural violations, some evidence might still be sufficiently reliable). A violation of Rule 43 thus incurably taints the evidence.

8. In light of the foregoing analysis, the majority's holding fails to appreciate that a Trial Chamber exercises discretion in assessing probativeness under Rule 89(D), and in determining reliability under Rule 95, only *after* the Trial Chamber has established that the Prosecution respected certain procedural safeguards, including Rule 43. Once it is established that Rule 43 applied, and that it was violated, there is no room for discretion—the statement must be excluded.

9. Finally, I note that Judge Schomburg and I are largely in agreement on this issue. Although we disagree slightly as to the precise scope of Rule 43, we both agree that it applied here, that it was violated, and that exclusion is the only appropriate remedy.

10. Except for these observations, I am in full agreement with the majority opinion.

Judgement—Separate Opinion of Judge Meron: Annotations

On 8 July 2005, the Trial Chamber issued a decision denying admission of the 1996 Statement, a statement that had been given voluntarily by Halilović to the Prosecution during various interviews about five years prior to the Indictment. Both parties agreed that the procedure for questioning suspects found in Rules 42 and 43 was not followed during those interviews because the Prosecution did not consider him a suspect at the time. The Prosecution did inform Halilović of his rights to counsel and to remain silent. After the Prosecution indicated its intent to tender the 1996 Statement from the bar table, Halilović requested details on the interviews, including any existing records. As no such records existed, the Trial Chamber decided that the 1996 Statement was inadmissible as there was no possibility of ensuring that the Statement was indeed a full and complete record of what Halilović had said.

In its decision denying admission of the Statement, the Trial Chamber looked at Rules 42, 43, 63, 89 and 95. The Trial Chamber explained that the focus should be on deciding what safeguards should have been applied by the Prosecution to allow the former statement of a later accused individual into evidence. The Trial Chamber held that the content of the Statement was more of a general reflection with no audio or video record to verify its accuracy. Consequently, the content of the Statement could only be challenged by Halilović waiving his right to remain silent.

The Trial Chamber then notes that Rule 43 was not applied when the Statement was taken and that Halilović had not chosen to waive his right to remain silent. The Trial Chamber did not take into consideration whether the Statement would also be inadmissible based on a retroactive reading of Rule 43. Instead, the Trial Chamber focused on Rule 89(D) in pointing to the unreliability of the Statement and the impact it would have on the right to a fair trial. The Appeals Chamber in turn deferred to the Trial Chamber's discretion regarding the inadmissibility and dismisses sub-ground 6 based on the Prosecution failing to meet its burden of showing that the Trial Chamber had abused that discretion.

Though the Separate Opinion agrees with the majority's decision to dismiss sub-ground 6, it states that the decision to exclude the Statement was not done pursuant to Rule 89(D) but rather was done pursuant to Rule 43. Of interest, the Opinion emphasizes a flaw in the Appeals Chamber's holding that the Trial Chamber did not take into consideration whether or not the Statement would have been inadmissible based on a retroactive reading of Rule 43: the omission of a paragraph from the Trial Judgement pointing to the contrary. This paragraph not only demonstrates the importance of Rule 43 in the Trial Chamber's reasoning, but also proves that the Appeals Chamber should not have limited itself to the interpretation of Rule 89(D). Applying Rule 43 to the present case shows that the Statement was indeed properly excluded as "an unrecorded statement by an accused is per se unreliable."[38] This is in line with the *Čelebići* Appeal Judgement where the Appeals Chamber contemplated that "despite scrupulous adherence to all procedural safeguards, some evidence might still be unreliable."[39]

Once Rule 43 applies, a statement must be excluded, leaving no room or use for the Trial Chamber's discretion under Rules 89(D) and 95.

Gacumbitsi v. The Prosecutor

Judgement—Joint Separate Opinion of Judges Liu and Meron

Date of Judgement: 7 July 2006

A DEFECTIVE INDICTMENT CAN ONLY BE CURED IF THE PROSECUTION PROVIDES THE ACCUSED WITH TIMELY, CLEAR AND CONSISTENT INFORMATION DETAILING THE FACTUAL BASIS UNDERPINNING THE CHARGES AGAINST HIM OR HER

1. We write separately to explain our disagreement with the Majority's conclusion that, though the killing of Mr. Murefu "was not specifically alleged in the indictment", the Trial Chamber could nonetheless have convicted

38. *See Prosecutor v. Sefer Halilović*, Judgement, ICTY Appeals Chamber, Part VI. Separate Opinion of Judge Meron, at para. 6, Case no. IT-01-48-A (16 Oct. 2007).
39. *Id.* at para. 7.

Gacumbitsi of committing genocide solely on the basis of its finding that Gacumbitsi killed this individual.

2. The Appeals Chamber's Judgement does not dispute that, if the Prosecution intended this killing to be the basis of a finding that Gacumbitsi committed offences, the killing should have been mentioned in the indictment. Indeed, this proposition is beyond dispute. "[C]riminal acts that were physically committed by the accused personally must be set forth in the indictment specifically, including where feasible 'the identity of the victim, the time and place of the events and the means by which the acts were committed.'" The Majority, however, is willing to excuse the Prosecution's failure to comply with our pleading requirements because a vague chart-entry summarizing the anticipated testimony of one witness mentions, *inter alia*, the killing of Mr. Murefu and the fact that the witness's testimony "relate[s] to the charge of genocide." In our view, serious flaws in the indictment are not so easily remedied.

3. We fully agree with the ICTY Appeals Chamber's holding in *Kupreškić* that "in some instances, a defective indictment can be cured if the Prosecution provides the accused with timely, clear and consistent information detailing the factual basis underpinning the charges against him or her." This holding, however, had an important caveat: "in light of the factual and legal complexities normally associated with the crimes within the jurisdiction of this Tribunal, there can only be a limited number of cases that fall within that category." Indeed, in order to protect the accused's right to be fully aware of the charges he or she faces, and to ensure that each accused can defend against the Prosecution's charges, it is imperative to apply strictly the rule that only "timely, clear and consistent information" can remedy defects in an indictment. Recognizing this fact—even as it held that a particular defect in the indictment was cured by a witness statement taken together with "unambiguous information" contained in the Pre-Trial Brief and its annexes—the Appeals Chamber made clear in *Ntakirutimana* that the Prosecution cannot be deemed to have charged an accused for every incident described in a document that it makes available to him.

4. Here, in concluding that Gacumbitsi had "clear and consistent" notice that he was alleged to have committed genocide by killing Mr. Murefu, the Majority points to only one document, and indeed, just one small section of a document—namely, the entry on Witness TAQ's anticipated testimony in the Prosecution's Summary of Anticipated Witness evidence. Indeed, in this case, unlike in *Ntakirutimana*, the Prosecution never mentioned the killing of Mr. Murefu in the body of its Pre-Trial Brief. Nor did the Prosecution allege in its Opening Statement that Gacumbitsi killed Mr. Murefu. Hence, as the Majority implicitly acknowledges, the key question is whether the chart-entry, taken alone, provided "clear and consistent" notice that Gacumbitsi was alleged to have committed genocide by killing Mr. Murefu. It did not.

5. First, we question whether notice provided only once can ever be "consistent" notice. Not only does the term "consistent" suggest that there must not be deviation in the material terms of the notice, but "consistent" also could reasonably be read to suggest that there must be some repetition—arguably, a document or statement providing notice is only "consistent" if there is another relevant document or statement that it is consistent with. Such a reading of the term "consistent" would be in accordance with the purposes of the "clear and consistent" notice requirement: safeguarding the accused's right to be clearly and unequivocally informed of the charges against him in a situation where material facts were omitted from the indictment, the place where the accused would expect to find them.

6. Regardless of whether notice provided only once can ever satisfy the "clear and consistent" standard, the notice provided in the chart-entry on Witness TAQ fails to meet this standard, as it was far from clear. The chart shows that Witness TAQ's testimony would relate to the charges of genocide, extermination, and rape. Yet the chart-entry never mentions any mode of liability, let alone explains which aspects of Witness TAQ's testimony would support a conviction for any of the charges pursuant to a particular mode of liability. This omission is all the more serious given how much ground the chart said that witness TAQ's testimony would cover. According to the chart, Witness TAQ was to testify about a lengthy series of events in which Gacumbitsi took part over the course of several days. The killing of Mr. Murefu was just one small part of this series of events. Given that—in relation to the genocide charge—the Prosecution pursued theories of responsibility based on Gacumbitsi's entire course of conduct during this period, Gacumbitsi could reasonably have believed that the killing of Mr. Murefu was mentioned only as part of this course of conduct. Alternatively, as the Prosecution charged Gacumbitsi with instigating genocide, and as the chart-entry says that the killing of Mr. Murefu was immediately followed by a grenade attack on refugees gathered in the church that Mr. Murefu was killed in front of, Gacumbitsi could reasonably have believed that this killing would be used to argue that he instigated genocide. He might also have reasonably believed that the Prosecution viewed this incident only as evidence of his *mens rea* for genocide—evidence that could be rebutted with *mens rea* evidence unrelated to this particular killing. Any of the abovementioned inferences would have been logical ones for Gacumbitsi to have made—indeed, they were likely more logical than the inference that he was charged with committing genocide on the basis of this killing—given that "criminal acts that were physically committed by the accused personally must be set forth in the indictment specifically", and given that the Murefu killing was never mentioned in the indictment.

7. Not surprisingly, the chart does not appear to have led Gacumbitsi to deduce that the Murefu killing was alleged as a basis for the charge that he committed genocide. Discussion of this killing in the Rule 98*bis* filings makes

clear that, even after the completion of the Prosecution's case at trial, the Appellant was still under the impression that the incident had been alleged with respect to the murder charge. Yet not even at this point in the proceedings did the Prosecution clarify that it felt Gacumbitsi should be convicted of committing genocide on the basis of this killing. In fact, the Prosecution waited until the close of the trial to finally make clear that it intended to rely upon the evidence of the killing to support a conviction for genocide. This is not timely notice. We cannot agree to the entry of a conviction on the basis of allegations that were only made clear at the end of trial.

8. According to the Majority, these circumstances "are materially indistinguishable from" circumstances under which the ICTY Appeals Chamber recently found that the Prosecution had cured an indictment defect. We disagree. The Majority refers to the *Naletilić and Martinović* case, and in particular, the ICTY Appeals Chamber's finding that the Prosecution had cured the indictment's failure to provide information about the beating of an individual known as "the Professor". This finding rested in part on an entry in a similar chart of witnesses—although the chart-entry suggested that the witness at issue would be testifying to a few discrete incidents, and the chart-entry was far less lengthy than the one at issue in the present case. Yet the Appeals Chamber also rested its finding on the fact that the relevant "details were specifically reiterated by the Prosecution in its Opening Statement." Indeed, the Prosecution's Opening Statement in *Naletilić and Martinović* not only mentions the beating of "the Professor", it clearly states the counts in the indictment that the allegation relates to. Hence, at the start of his trial, Martinović knew what the Prosecution was trying to prove with its allegations about "the Professor". The value of this second piece of clear, detailed information about the Prosecution's allegation with regard to "the Professor"—like the value of the information in the Pre-Trial Brief that together with the chart of witnesses cured the indictment defect in *Ntakirutimana*—should not be underestimated.

In the present case, where the indictment makes absolutely no mention of the killing of Mr. Murefu—it does not just omit some material facts related to the killing—it is particularly problematic that neither the Prosecution's Pre-Trial Brief nor its Opening Statement reiterated and clarified the information on the killing provided in the chart-entry on Witness TAQ.

9. In conclusion, because the provision of "timely, clear and consistent information" is necessary to cure defects in an indictment, we cannot agree that the Prosecution cured its failure to mention the killing of Mr. Murefu in the indictment, and we therefore cannot agree that Gacumbitsi could be convicted of committing genocide on the basis of this killing alone. Nonetheless, because we agree with the Judgement's conclusion that "[t]he Trial Chamber convicted the Appellant of 'ordering' and 'instigating' genocide on the basis of findings of fact detailing certain conduct that ... should be characterized not just as 'ordering' and 'instigating' genocide, but also as 'committing'

genocide", we support the decision not to vacate the finding that Gacumbitsi committed genocide.

Judgement—Joint Separate Opinion of Judges Liu and Meron: Annotations

Gacumbitsi was convicted based on an Indictment charging him with individual criminal responsibility for certain crimes committed against the Tutsi population of Kibungo Prefecture between 6 and 30 April 1994. The Trial Chamber found Gacumbitsi guilty of genocide and crimes against humanity (extermination and rape) and handed down a single sentence of 30 years' imprisonment.

The Separate Opinion focuses on the scope of the Indictment and if/when a *defective* indictment can be remedied. The majority concluded that even though the killing of Murefu was not mentioned in the Indictment, the Trial Chamber could still convict Gacumbitsi of committing genocide solely on the basis of its finding that Gacumbitsi killed him. The majority did not seek to dispute that if the Prosecution intended this killing to be the basis of a finding that Gacumbitsi committed the alleged offences, the killing should have been stated in the Indictment. However, the majority erroneously chose to excuse the Prosecution's failure to comply with this pleading requirement based on a single piece of evidence: a vague chart-entry that mentioned the killing of Mr. Murefu and that the killing related to the charge of genocide.

The Separate Opinion does not purport to deny the ICTY Appeals Chamber's holding in *Kupreškić* that defective indictments can sometimes be cured, but only when the accused is provided with timely, clear and consistent information of the charges. This standard of clear and consistent notice was plainly not met in the present case because the notice given to Gacumbitsi took the form of a small section of a single, vague document consisting of a chart-entry.

"Consistent" notice most likely entails repeated notice, not notice in the form of a single document. Alternatively, the chart-entry failed to meet the "clear" part of the standard and included serious omissions. Gacumbitsi could reasonably have been led to believe that the killing was mentioned only as part of his entire course of conduct during the relevant period or as part of the murder charge. Gacumbitsi would have been and indeed was unable to deduce that the killing was in fact the basis for the genocide charge, yet the prosecution chose to wait until the end of trial to clarify its intent to rely upon the killing to support the charge of genocide. Neither the Prosecution's Pre-Trial Brief nor the Opening Statement relied on the killing or the chart-entry, a clear distinction from the *Naletilić and Martinović* case where the Prosecution clearly stated the incident at issue in its Opening Statement, thereby curing an indictment defect.

The Separate Opinion concludes by noting that though the defective indictment was not cured in the present case, it still agrees with the Judgement's conclusion that Gacumbitsi did commit genocide.

Prosecutor v. Gotovina and Markač

Judgement—Separate Opinion of Judge Meron

DATE OF JUDGEMENT: 16 NOVEMBER 2012

THE APPEALS CHAMBER'S POWER TO ENTER CONVICTIONS PURSUANT TO ALTERNATE FORMS OF LIABILITY MUST BE WIELDED SPARINGLY AND ONLY WHERE ITS EXERCISE DOES NOT IMPINGE ON THE FAIR TRIAL RIGHTS OF APPELLANTS, I.E. WHERE: I) ANY ADDITIONAL INTERFERENCES FROM FINDINGS SET FORTH IN A RELEVANT TRIAL JUDGEMENT ARE RESTRICTED; AND II) ANY DIFFERENCES BETWEEN THE CONVICTIONS THAT APPELLANTS INITIALLY APPEALED AND CONVICTIONS ENTERED ON APPEAL ARE LIMITED

1. While I join the Majority's analysis as set out in the Appeal Judgement, I write separately primarily to explain my views on the Appeals Chamber's jurisprudence with respect to convictions pursuant to alternate modes of liability.

2. As an initial matter, I observe that the Bench is unanimous in holding that the Trial Chamber erred in deriving the 200 Metre Standard. While not all my Colleagues join the Majority view on the consequences of this error, there is no dispute over its existence.

3. I further observe that the Appeal Judgement makes two clear advances to the criminal procedure precedent of the Tribunal. For the first time, a panel considering entering convictions pursuant to an alternate mode of liability requested explicit briefing from parties on this issue. The Appeal Judgement also helps clarify our jurisprudence by setting out in more detail the judicial rationale underlying the Appeals Chamber's power to enter convictions pursuant to alternate modes of liability.

4. I join the Majority in holding that the Appeals Chamber possesses the power to enter convictions pursuant to alternate modes of liability. However, I would underscore that this authority does not constitute a panacea to address any and all errors by the Prosecution or a trial chamber. Instead, I believe that this power should only be exercised selectively, where: i) any additional inferences from findings set forth in a relevant trial judgement are restricted; and ii) any differences between the convictions that appellants initially appealed and convictions entered on appeal are limited. Otherwise, the Appeals Chamber risks undermining appellants' fair trial rights, or conducting a second trial rather than reviewing the trial chamber's alleged errors.

5. Whether it is warranted to enter convictions pursuant to alternate modes of liability in a given appeal constitutes a fact-specific question best left to individual Benches. But as a general matter, I do not believe that the Appeals Chamber's authority serves as a licence for wholesale reconstruction or revision of approaches adopted or decisions taken by a trial chamber. In this context, I recall that our jurisprudence has consistently indicated that sudden, significant alterations in the scope of a case may deny individuals their fair trial rights. Thus, for example, in the *Kupreškić et al.* Appeal Judgement, the Appeals Chamber found that two appellants had been unacceptably prejudiced by the "drastic change" in the Prosecution's case of which they had no effective notice. Similarly, I note that in past cases where the Appeals Chamber entered convictions pursuant to alternate modes of liability, changes to the structure of the case faced by appellants were limited in nature. For example, the Appeals Chamber entered such convictions to address technical but effectively non-substantive errors in indictments, or after finding that appellants aided a JCE but were not proved to share its common purpose.

6. In the present Appeal Judgement, I am satisfied that the Majority acts prudently and fairly in not entering additional convictions. I also agree with the Majority's logic in addressing those findings with respect to each Appellant which were not reversed. However, were I solely responsible for the Appeal Judgement, I would not have undertaken this latter analysis. In this regard, I first recall that in the Appeal Judgement, the Majority reverses the fundamental conclusions of the Trial Chamber, including the finding that a JCE existed. I also note that discussion of modes of liability other than JCE was almost entirely absent from core trial and appeal briefing. In circumstances like these, while fully supporting the Appeal Judgement, I do not believe the Appeals Chamber should enter convictions pursuant to alternate modes of liability. Such convictions would, in my view, necessarily involve unfairness to the Appellants, who would be found guilty of crimes very different from those they defended against at trial or on appeal. Accordingly, I consider that analysis of the Trial Chamber's "remaining findings", like that

undertaken by the Appeal Judgement, is unnecessary, as the Tribunal's commitment to fair trial rights should, in this case, foreclose the possibility of convictions pursuant to alternate modes of liability.

7. I reiterate that, in appropriate circumstances, the Appeals Chamber's power to enter convictions pursuant to alternate forms of liability can be deployed to serve the interests of justice. This authority must, however, be wielded sparingly, in appropriate circumstances, and only where its exercise does not impinge on the rights of appellants. The Appeal Judgement's holding respects this principle, and this is the basis on which I join the Majority.

Judgement—Separate Opinion of Judge Meron: Annotations

The events giving rise to the present case occurred between July and 30 September 1995. During that time period, Croatian leaders and officials initiated a military action called "Operation Storm" for the purpose of taking control of territory in the Krajina region of Croatia. Gotovina was a colonel-general in the HV (Croatian Army) during the Indictment period and was the operational commander of Operation Storm in the southern part of the Krajina region. The Trial Chamber found that Gotovina contributed to the JCE whose common purpose was to permanently remove the Serb civilian population from the Krajina region. The Trial Chamber consequently found Gotovina guilty under the first form of JCE of both persecution and deportation as crimes against humanity. It also found him guilty under the third form of JCE of murder and inhuman acts as crimes against humanity, plunder of public and private property and violations of the laws or customs of war. He was sentenced to a single term of 24 years' imprisonment.

Markač was the Assistant Minister of the Interior and Operation Commander of the Special Police in Croatia during the Indictment period. The Trial Chamber held that Markač shared the objective of and significantly contributed to the JCE and found him guilty under the first form of JCE of both persecution and deportations as crimes against humanity. It found him guilty under the third form of JCE of murder and inhumane acts as crimes against humanity, acts of plunder of public and private property and violations of the laws or customs of war. He was sentenced to a single term of 18 years' imprisonment.

The convictions of both Gotovina and Markač were reversed and they were thus acquitted.

This Separate Opinion joins the majority and elaborates on the Appeals Chamber's jurisprudence concerning convictions made pursuant to alternate modes of liability.

The Opinion notes that the Appeal Judgement makes two significant contributions regarding modes of liability: 1) "For the first time, a panel considering entering convictions pursuant to an alternate mode of liability requested explicit briefing from the parties on this issue"; and 2) details the rationale behind the Appeals Chamber's power to enter convictions made pursuant to these alternate modes of liability.[40]

It is important to note that the Appeals Chamber's power to enter these convictions should be limited and "exercised selectively."[41] If that power is not exercised with the proper amount of discretion, the Appeals Chamber risks undermining the fair trial rights of the appellant or exceeding its scope to review any alleged errors of the Trial Chamber by conducting a second trial.[42] Clear and consistent notice of the crimes charged must always be accorded to an appellant. This could at times foreclose the possibility of entering a conviction pursuant to an alternate mode of liability.

Prosecutor v. Brđanin

Judgement—Separate Opinion of Judge Meron

DATE OF JUDGEMENT: 3 APRIL 2007

LIABILITY VIA JCE SHOULD ATTACH WHERE A MEMBER OF A JCE USES A NON-MEMBER TO CARRY OUT THE CRIMINAL PURPOSE AT THE ROOT OF THE JCE

1. Today's judgement decides several important issues related to the doctrine of joint criminal enterprise ("JCE"). Given the existing contours of JCE, I agree entirely with the reasoning in the judgement. I write separately to discuss what I view as the appropriate mode of liability for a conviction via JCE where the principal perpetrator is not a JCE member.

40. *See Prosecutor v. Ante Gotovina, Mladen Markač*, Judgement, ICTY Appeals Chamber, Part VII. Separate Opinion of Judge Theodor Meron, at para. 3, Case no. IT-06-90-A (16 Nov. 2012).

41. *Id.* at para. 4.

42. *Id.*

2. Whatever the merits of the overall doctrine of JCE, it is now firmly embedded in our jurisprudence. The question before us is not whether Tadić was correctly decided, but rather how to apply the principles Tadić identified to situations where the principal perpetrators are not proven to belong to the JCE. We have never before directly confronted this question.

3. As today's judgement explains, liability via JCE should attach where a member of a JCE uses a non-member to carry out the criminal purpose at the root of the JCE. Under our existing jurisprudence, if A and B belong to a JCE aimed at unlawfully deporting victims and A personally deports a victim, then B is liable for this deportation via the JCE. The question before us today is whether this result should change where A uses non-member X to commit this same deportation—for example, by ordering X to commit this deportation—rather than personally committing the deportation himself. It would be strange indeed were we to hold that no liability can attach to B via the JCE in this situation simply because A ordered another to commit the criminal act rather than doing it himself. In both cases, A is acting in a criminal way to further the common criminal purpose of the JCE. As his fellow JCE member, B should bear criminal responsibility in both situations.

4. A conviction via JCE can thus occur even when the principal perpetrators are not shown to belong to the JCE. This begs a further question, however: how should we characterize such convictions under the modes of liability identified in Article 7(1) in the Statute? Today's judgement does not address this question. But since we have taken up Ground 1 of the Prosecution's Appeal for the sole purpose of clarifying the law, I think it appropriate to discuss my own views on this subject.

5. In the past, we have generally equated a conviction via JCE with the mode of liability of "committing" in Article 7(1). This is a fiction, of course, but one with some sense to it. Where A and B belong to a JCE and A commits a crime that furthers the common criminal purpose, it seems reasonable to view B as also "committing" this crime due to his identification with A via the JCE.

6. Since we have never before directly considered whether a conviction via JCE can attach where the principal perpetrator is not a member of the JCE, we have also never considered whether "committing" is the proper mode of liability for such convictions. In my view, where a JCE member uses a non-JCE member to carry out a crime in furtherance of the common purpose, then all other JCE members should be liable via the JCE under the same mode of liability that attaches to this JCE member. Thus, where A and B belong to a JCE and A orders non-member X to commit a crime in furtherance of the JCE, then B's conviction for this crime via the JCE should be treated as a form of "ordering" for purposes of Article 7(1) rather than as a form of "committing". Since B's liability for this crime is essentially

derivative of A's, he should not be convicted of a higher mode of liability than that which attaches to A's conduct.

7. This approach has several advantages. First and most importantly, it fits the mode of liability to the behavior at issue. Where a crime in furtherance of the common purpose has not been directly "committed" by a JCE member, then the "committing" of this crime cannot fairly be imputed to the other JCE members via the JCE. Instead, these other JCE members can only be held responsible for a crime that furthers the common purpose to the same extent that another JCE member is responsible for this crime. Second, by requiring the Prosecution to prove and the Trial Chamber to find the proper mode of responsibility, this approach will compel a clear identification of the "link" required under today's judgement between the JCE and the crimes on the ground. Finally, the precision required by this approach will prove valuable to the historical record.

8. I have read with great respect the partially dissenting opinion of my learned colleague Judge Shahabuddeen. He suggests that where a JCE member uses a non-member to commit a crime within the common criminal purpose, other members can only share in this member's liability where "the JCE itself gave authority" to this member to use non-members rather than to commit crimes directly himself. He further suggests that such authority must be specifically shown. I do not subscribe to this view. It seems to me enough that the JCE members all share in the goal of advancing the common criminal purpose and act criminally to further this goal. In no case do we require a showing that JCE member B specifically authorizes JCE member A to commit a crime in a particular manner; and nor should we require a showing that B specifically authorizes A to use nonmembers to commit the crimes rather than to commit them personally. Accordingly, I consider that where a JCE member uses a non-member to carry out a crime within the common criminal purpose, the other members of the JCE have responsibility for this crime that is derivative of their relationship to this JCE member. I thus would equate their convictions for JCE with regard to that crime with whatever mode of liability reflects the responsibility of the JCE member who used the non-member. In my view, this approach will properly match the convictions to the crimes.

Judgement—Separate Opinion of Judge Meron: Annotations

The Prosecution submitted that the Trial Chamber erred when it "(1) dismissed joint criminal enterprise ('JCE') as an appropriate mode of liability for this case and held that the physical perpetrator of a crime must be a member of the joint criminal enterprise concerned; and (2) held that the first category ('basic form') of joint criminal enterprise requires an understanding or agreement between an accused and the physical perpetrator of the crime".[43]

The Tribunal's jurisprudence recognizes three categories of joint criminal enterprise. Regardless of the category, a conviction requires a finding that the accused participated in a joint criminal enterprise.[44] In its Judgement, the Appeals Chamber explained that there are three requirements that need to be satisfied for this finding: 1) a plurality of persons; 2) the existence of a common purpose (or plan) which involved the commission of said crime; and 3) the participation of the accused in that common purpose.[45] After analyzing the relevant jurisprudence, the Appeals Chamber concluded that "what matters in a first category JCE is not whether the person who carried out the *actus reus* of a particular crime is a member of the JCE, but whether the crime in question forms part of the common purpose."[46] Liability through JCE attaches when a member of a JCE uses a non-member to carry out a criminal purpose which forms the basis of the JCE.

The Separate Opinion focuses on the appropriate mode of liability for a conviction via JCE where the principal perpetrator is not a JCE member.[47] This situation is particularly interesting as it had not yet been directly addressed by the Tribunal. From a liability standpoint, what happens when a non-member is ordered to commit a crime? Logically, both members of the JCE should be liable, not just the individual who ordered the non-member (the principal perpetrator) to commit said crime.

This raises another question: what then should be the proper mode of liability under Article 7(1) of the Statute for such convictions? This Opinion suggests that these convictions should be treated as a form of "ordering" as opposed to a form of "committing."[48] This logically follows from the fact that in the non-member scenario, the crime in furtherance of the common purpose is not directly committed by a JCE member. It therefore cannot derivatively be imputed to the other JCE members.

43. *See Prosecutor v. Radoslav Brđanin*, Judgement, ICTY Appeals Chamber, Part XII. Separate Opinion of Judge Meron, at para. 6, Case no. IT-99-36-A (3 Apr. 2007).

44. *See Prosecutor v. Radoslav Brđanin*, Judgement, ICTY Appeals Chamber, at para. 364, Case no. IT-99-36-A (3 Apr. 2007).

45. *Id.* 46. *Id.* at para. 410.

47. *See Prosecutor v. Radoslav Brđanin*, Judgement, ICTY Appeals Chamber, Part XII. Separate Opinion of Judge Meron, at para. 1, Case no. IT-99-36-A (3 Apr. 2007).

48. *Id.* at para. 6.

Muvunyi v. The Prosecutor

Judgement—Dissenting Opinion of Judges Liu and Meron

DATE OF JUDGEMENT: 1 APRIL 2011

THE MAJORITY IGNORES CLEAR GAPS IN THE TRIAL CHAMBER'S ANALYSIS OF THE EVIDENCE BEFORE IT. MUVUNYI'S ACT OF INCITEMENT TOOK PLACE NOT IN EARLY MAY, AS CHARGED IN THE INDICTMENT, BUT IN THE LATTER HALF OF JUNE 1994, WHICH WAS WELL OUTSIDE THE TEMPORAL SCOPE OF INDICTMENT. HE WAS THUS CONVICTED OF A CRIME WITH WHICH HE WAS NOT CHARGED.

1. In this Judgement, the Appeals Chamber affirms Muvunyi's conviction for direct and public incitement to commit genocide based on statements he purportedly made in mid to late May 1994 at a public meeting at the Gikore Trade Center in Nyaruhengeri Commune, Butare Prefecture. In our view, the consistent evidence of all Prosecution witnesses and the Trial Chamber's own findings strongly suggest that Muvunyi's act of incitement took place not in early May, as charged in the Indictment, but in the latter half of June 1994, which is well outside the temporal scope of the Indictment. In these circumstances, no reasonable trier of fact could have found that the crime charged in the Indictment had been proved beyond reasonable doubt. Accordingly, we respectfully disagree with the Majority's reasoning and conclusions on this question, and with its decision to affirm Muvunyi's conviction.

2. At trial, both Prosecution and Defence witnesses gave evidence concerning a public meeting at the Gikore Trade Center attended by Muvunyi. Prosecution witnesses consistently agreed with each other on two issues with respect to the meeting: (1) the identity of the prefect addressing the meeting; and (2) whether Muvunyi made statements inciting genocide. In particular, all four Prosecution witnesses who testified regarding the identity of the prefect at the meeting stated that Alphonse Nteziryayo addressed the meeting in his capacity as prefect of Butare, and that the meeting included statements by Muvunyi inciting genocide. However, all the Defence witnesses who testified regarding the meeting consistently stated that it was Sylvain Nsabimana who addressed them there in his capacity as prefect of Butare, and that the meeting included no statements by Muvunyi inciting genocide. Notably, the Trial Chamber found that Nsabimana was prefect of Butare until 17 June 1994, and that Nteziryayo was prefect of Butare after 17 June 1994.

3. In context, the stark contrast between the evidence of relevant Prosecution and Defence witnesses and the consistency of their respective descriptions readily point to the existence of not one, but two meetings: the first, held before 17 June 1994, while Nsabimana was prefect, and in which Muvunyi did not incite genocide; and the second, held after 17 June 1994,

when Nteziryayo was prefect, and in which Muvunyi directly and publicly incited genocide. This deduction is reinforced by the Trial Chamber's conclusion that the Prosecution witnesses' testimony on these points was credible. Specifically, in assessing Prosecution witnesses' testimony as to the identity of the prefect addressing the meeting, the Trial Chamber confirmed that their "demeanour [...] suggest[ed] that they actually believed that Nteziryayo was [prefect] of Butare during the meeting at Gikore". In addition, we note that three of the four relevant Prosecution witnesses not only stated a belief that Nteziryayo was prefect at the relevant time, but had detailed recollections about the specific manner in which Nteziryayo was introduced as prefect or referred to himself as such during the meeting.

4. Despite the clear and consistent evidence that two meetings occurred, and the equally clear and consistent evidence that Muvunyi's statements inciting genocide were made at the latter of these two meetings, the Trial Chamber dismissed Defence counsel's attempts to show that two meetings took place. Notably, the Trial Judgement fails to consider the possibility of a June 1994 meeting; instead, it analyses and rejects the possibility that multiple meetings occurred in May 1994. This, in our view, is a serious failing.

5. Although the Trial Chamber found Prosecution witnesses to be honest, it dismissed them as being "collectively mistaken" in their testimony about the prefect due to the passage of time. Underlying this conclusion is the Trial Chamber's identification of certain similarities between some of the Prosecution and Defence witnesses' accounts of the meetings and its analysis reconciling the testimony of Prosecution witnesses with respect to the date of the meeting. With respect to the first point, the similarities identified by the Trial Chamber are too generic to undermine the plain evidence that two meetings took place. Indeed, it would be surprising if public meetings in the same locale in the same year differed significantly in terms of location, the number of people attending, the manner in which dignitaries arrived (by car), or the order in which authorities spoke. Divergences that a fact-finder could reasonably expect to be reflected in descriptions of different meetings include the issues addressed, and any changes with respect to which individuals occupied specific official posts within local and national authorities. These are precisely the differences that consistently distinguish the testimony of the relevant Prosecution witnesses from that of the Defence witnesses.

6. With respect to the second point, we acknowledge that three Prosecution witnesses who were asked about the date of the meeting placed it sometime in May. However, we note that a fourth Prosecution witness stated that the meeting could have taken place in June. In light of the Prosecution witnesses' expressed certitude regarding the identity of the prefect who addressed them, we do not find that the Prosecution witnesses' varying testimony regarding the date of the meeting could convince a reasonable trier of fact that the Prosecution had proved beyond a reasonable doubt that Muvunyi's statements inciting genocide were made in May 1994.

7. The Majority claims to defer to the Trial Chamber's discretion over facts, observing that Nteziryayo became prefect soon after the May time-period identified by the Trial Judgement; noting the Trial Chamber's analysis of witness demeanour; and concluding that the Trial Chamber permissibly accepted some but rejected other parts of witnesses' testimony in reaching its conclusion. We do not dispute the Trial Chamber's credibility determinations regarding the relevant Prosecution witnesses or the date on which Nteziryayo became prefect. We find, however, that the Majority ignores clear gaps in the Trial Chamber's analysis of the evidence before it. Most tellingly, the Trial Judgement devotes several paragraphs to explaining how all relevant Prosecution witnesses could be both truthful and wrong regarding the identity of the prefect, without even considering the obvious possibility that they were both truthful and right. This is not a case where the Trial Chamber chose to believe one witness over another. Instead, it chose to discount without convincing explanation the clear implications of the evidence of every single relevant Prosecution witness regarding the critical issue of the identity of the prefect at the meeting.

8. Trial Chambers enjoy considerable and appropriate discretion in their assessment of evidence and their findings of fact may not be lightly overturned on appeal. But a Trial Chamber must be satisfied beyond reasonable doubt that the accused is guilty before a verdict can be entered against him or her, and can only convict if the Prosecution has proved the crime charged. In this case, the Prosecution witnesses' testimony, when viewed in light of the Trial Chamber's own findings, raises reasonable doubt that no trier of fact could ignore. It also raises the distinct possibility that Muvunyi was convicted for statements seemingly made well outside the temporal scope of the Indictment, and thus was convicted for a crime with which he was not charged. Accordingly, we respectfully dissent.

Judgement—Dissenting Opinion of Judges Liu and Meron: Annotations

This case concerned the retrial of Muvunyi for his responsibility for direct and public incitement to commit genocide based on a speech allegedly made at a public meeting at the Butare Prefecture. The Trial Chamber convicted him of this allegation based on his statements made in mid to late May 1994 and sentenced him to 15 years' imprisonment. Muvunyi sought to overturn his conviction while the Prosecution sought to dismiss the appeal and increase the sentence to 25 years' imprisonment.

The Dissenting Opinion focuses on the dismissal of Muvunyi's first group of appeal: the alleged defect in the indictment. Muvunyi argued that the Trial Chamber erroneously convicted him of participating in a meeting which was not pleaded in the Indictment. He argued that the Indictment refers to a meeting that took place at the beginning of May 1994, while the evidence presented at trial focused on a different meeting that took place around mid-June 1994. For an accused to have a right to a fair trial, charges against the accused as well as the material facts supporting those charges must be sufficiently precise so as to provide notice. A Trial Chamber can only convict an accused of crimes that are charged in the Indictment. This leads to the question of whether or not Muvunyi was convicted of the specific crime that was charged in the Indictment. The Appeals Chamber majority held that it was not unreasonable for the Trial Chamber to conclude that the meeting described by the Prosecution witnesses did indeed occur in May 1994 and that the evidence did not undermine the reasonableness of the Trial Chamber's conclusion that only one meeting took place in May 1994. The majority accordingly dismissed Muvunyi's First Ground of Appeal.

The Dissenting Opinion disagrees with the majority's finding that the relevant act of incitement found in the Indictment took place in early May 1994, instead holding that the events took place in the latter half of June 1994, placing them outside the temporal scope of the Indictment.

All of the Defence witnesses who testified about this meeting consistently stated that it was Nsabimana, not Muvunyi, who spoke at the meeting in his capacity as prefect of Butare. This points to not one, but two distinct meetings—one taking place before 17 June 1994 where Muvunyi did not incite genocide, and one taking place after 17 June 1994 where Muvunyi did directly and publicly incite genocide. The Dissenting Opinion emphasizes that there was indeed "clear and consistent evidence that two meetings occurred"[49] and that the Trial Chamber improperly failed to consider the possibility of a June 1994 meeting and improperly failed to take into consideration the identity of the prefect at the meetings. The Prosecution witnesses' varying testimony about the date of the meeting cannot be said to meet the required burden of convincing a reasonable trier of fact that the Prosecution has proved beyond a reasonable doubt that the statements inciting genocide were made in

49. *See Tharcisse Muvunyi v. The Prosecutor*, Judgement, ICTR Appeals Chamber, Part VI. Dissenting Opinion of Judges Liu and Meron, at para. 4, Case no. ICTR-2000-55A-A (1 Apr. 2011).

May 1994. As a result, Muvunyi was "convicted for a crime with which he was not charged."[50]

Prosecutor v. Stakić

Judgement—Joint Separate Opinion of Judges Vaz and Meron

DATE OF JUDGEMENT: 22 MARCH 2006

THE POWER TO ENTER NEW CONVICTIONS ON APPEAL

> We agree with the outcome of today's Judgement but append this separate opinion in order to explain our understanding of the Judgement's disposition section—an understanding in accordance with that of Judge Shahabuddeen. The disposition section, which "resolves" that the Trial Chamber erred in failing to convict the Appellant on certain charges but which does not formally enter new convictions thereon, should not be read to suggest that the Appeals Chamber lacks the power to enter a new conviction. The Appeals Chamber has merely declined, in the exercise of its discretion, to enter new convictions in this case.

Judgement—Joint Separate Opinion of Judges Vaz and Meron: Annotations

The Indictment charged the appellant with genocide, complicity in genocide, extermination, murder as a crime against humanity, murder as a violation of the laws and customs of war, persecutions, deportation and other inhumane acts, all committed while he was President of the Municipality of Prijedor Crisis Staff.[51] The Trial Chamber found the appellant guilty of extermination as a crime against humanity, murder as a violation of the laws and customs of war and persecutions as a crime against humanity. The appellant was consequently sentenced to life imprisonment.[52] Both the appellant and Prosecution appealed the decision.

50. *Id.* at para. 8.
51. *See Prosecutor v. Milomir Stakić*, Judgement, ICTY Appeals Chamber, at para. 4, Case no. IT-97-24-A (22 Mar. 2006).
52. *Id.* at para. 5.

This Opinion agrees with the Appeals Chamber Judgement but clarifies its understanding of the Judgement's disposition section. The disposition section "resolves" that the Trial Chamber erred in entering certain acquittals but does not enter new convictions for these acquittals. This should by no means be thought to imply that the Appeals Chamber did not have the requisite power to enter such convictions. In fact, that power had been exercised by this Tribunal's Appeal Chamber in the *Tadić* Appeal Judgement, the *Kupreškić* Appeal Judgement and the *Krnojelac* Appeal Judgement, in accordance with Article 25 of the Statute. Similarly, the ICTR Appeals Chamber had also exercised that power to enter new convictions in the *Semanza* and *Rutaganda* Appeal Judgements. In the present case, the Appeals Chamber "has merely declined, in the exercise of its discretion, to enter new convictions."

XII

Early Release of Prisoners Decisions

Background

In this chapter I will describe my own practice, as President, on early release of prisoners serving sentences imposed by the ICTY, ICTR or the Mechanism, one which followed the practice of my predecessors. All previous Presidents but one had granted early releases. My successor, who assumed the presidency of the Mechanism on 19 January 2019, has adopted a distinctly different approach. No early releases have been granted on his watch so far.

Early releases or pardons of prisoners are often delicate and controversial in nation-States. In international criminal tribunals, the political, national, ethnic and religious context makes early releases even more difficult and contentious. Interested States, victims' organizations, NGOs and media, often vent their anger at some releases by harsh attacks against the Presidents that rendered them. In Rwanda, early releases of persons convicted by the ICTR or the Mechanism have not been welcome.

In the former Yugoslavia, convicted persons who have been released have often been celebrated upon their return to their own local and national communities. These releases have, however, been criticized by other communities in the former Yugoslavia.

The fact that I followed prior practice by other Presidents, including consultations with Judges of the sentencing chambers, did not save me from such criticism, often *ad hominem*. Yielding to such criticism would violate fundamental principles of judicial independence and human rights of prisoners and, thus, for me, has never been an option. Faithful to the judicial convention that Judges should not respond to criticism of specific decisions,

Standing Up For Justice. Theodor Meron, Oxford University Press (2021). © Theodor Meron.
DOI: 10.1093/oso/9780198863434.003.0012

and that judicial decisions should speak for themselves, I have not answered criticism of my early release decisions.

The Statute of the Mechanism adopted by the Security Council—like the Statutes of the ICTY and the ICTR—provides explicitly for pardon or commutation of sentence, commonly referred to at the Tribunals and the Mechanism as "early release." Providing for the possibility of early release is in accordance with basic human rights principles, according to which prisoners have the prospect of release prior to the completion of their sentences. Early releases also serve an important pragmatic purpose: in view of their human rights obligations, some of the States that enforce sentences of those convicted by the ICTY would not agree to accept prisoners into their prisons in the absence of a possibility of early release. This is particularly true of countries subject to the jurisdiction of the European Court of Human Rights.

The Mechanism's early release practice largely followed the practices of the ICTY and the ICTR and of Presidents of both Tribunals. At all the three institutions, certain fellow Judges are consulted by the President prior to the determination of a request of early release. At all the three institutions, the President weighs a number of specified factors and is guided by the interests of justice and general principles of law. These include treatment of similarly situated prisoners, gravity of crimes, demonstration of rehabilitation, substantial cooperation with the prosecution, views of Judges and, where relevant, humanitarian considerations.

I resisted requests to consult the Prosecutors and the victims, not only because such consultation was not mentioned in the relevant Rules, and would diverge from previous practice of other Presidents, but also because it would have changed the balance of considerations to the disadvantage of the prisoners as the Prosecutors and the victims would typically oppose all early releases.

There are certain exceptions to the similarities between the Mechanism's practices and its two predecessors. The Mechanism considers a convicted person eligible for early release after having served two-thirds of his or her sentence, in line with the ICTY practice. The ICTR practice had been to consider eligibility only after a prisoner had served three-quarters of his or her sentence. In contrast to the ICTR's Rules of Procedure and Evidence, the Mechanism's Rules of Procedure and Evidence do not require that the Government of Rwanda be notified prior to early release.

Since their adoption by the Security Council in 1993 and 1994, respectively, the Statutes of the ICTY and the ICTR have contained provisions allowing for those convicted by the Tribunals to be considered for pardon or commutation of sentence.[1] In view of these statutory provisions, the Judges of the two Tribunals in Plenaries, adopted Rules of Procedure and Evidence that set forth the process by which pardon or commutation of sentence would be considered. Practice Directions were likewise issued to ensure the process's transparency.[2] Since the Mechanism is the successor of both the ICTY and the ICTR, its legal provisions are modeled on that of its precursors. Its Statute, Rules of Procedure and Evidence and relevant Practice Directions, all provide for the possibility of pardon or commutation of sentence.

Article 26 of the Mechanism Statute provides: "If, pursuant to the applicable law of the State in which the person convicted by the ICTY, the ICTR, or the Mechanism is imprisoned, he or she is eligible for pardon or commutation of sentence, the State concerned shall notify the Mechanism accordingly. There shall only be pardon or commutation of sentence if the President of the Mechanism so decides on the basis of the interests of justice and the general principles of law."

The Mechanism's Statute—as adopted by the Security Council—is somewhat different than the relevant provisions of the ICTY and ICTR Statutes, in that it: (a) underscores that the President is the sole decision-maker when it comes to pardon or commutation of sentence; and (b) omits reference to consultations with other Judges.

The Rules of Procedure and Evidence adopted by the Judges, however, provide for such consultations.

1. ICTY: Art. 28 of the Statute: "If, pursuant to the applicable law of the State in which the convicted person is imprisoned, he or she is eligible for pardon or commutation of sentence, the State concerned shall notify the International Tribunal accordingly. The President of the International Tribunal, in consultation with the judges, shall decide the matter on the basis of the interests of justice and the general principles of law."

   ICTR: Art. 27 of the Statute: "If, pursuant to the applicable law of the State in which the convicted person is imprisoned, he or she is eligible for pardon or commutation of sentence, the State concerned shall notify the International Tribunal for Rwanda accordingly. There shall only be pardon or commutation of sentence if the President of the International Tribunal for Rwanda, in consultation with the judges, so decides on the basis of the interests of justice and the general principles of law."
2. ICTY: Rules 123–125 of the ICTY Rules of Procedure and Evidence, IT/32/Rev.50 (8 July 2015); Practice Direction on the Procedure for the Determination of Applications for Pardon, Commutation of Sentence, and Early Release of Persons Convicted by the International Tribunal, IT/146/Rev.3 (16 Sept. 2010). New Practice Direction on the Procedure for the Determination of Applications for Pardon, Commutation of Sentence, or Early Release of Persons Convicted by the ICTR, the ICTY, or the Mechanism, MICT/2/Rev.3 (15 May 2020).

Historically at the ICTY and the ICTR, issues of "pardon or commutation of sentence" have been treated as "early release" and the Mechanism follows this same approach.

The 2015 *Galić* Decision on early release explains the principles involved:

> These general legal principles concerning rehabilitation with an aim of reintegration into society would be rendered meaningless if a prisoner is not afforded the possibility of having his or her sentence reviewed. Indeed, as recently recognized by the European Court of Human Rights ("ECHR"), the rehabilitative principle and respect for human dignity, *inter alia*, require that all prisoners, including those serving life sentences, be afforded both a possibility of review of their sentences and a prospect of release. As the ECHR has explained in this regard, "[i]t is axiomatic that a prisoner cannot be detained unless there are legitimate penological grounds for that detention". It has noted the four classic grounds invoked by justice systems around the world as a justification for detention as criminal punishment: punishment, deterrence, public protection and rehabilitation. For the Grand Chamber, "the emphasis in Europe penal policy is now on the rehabilitative aim of imprisonment. Explaining that the balance between the justifications is not static and may shift during the sentence, especially the lengthy one, [i]t is only by carrying out a review of the justification for continued detention at an appropriate point in the sentence that these factors or shifts can be properly evaluated."[3]

Consistent with these principles, the imprisonment of persons convicted by the ICTR, the ICTY or the Mechanism is focused on the rehabilitation of these convicted persons with the goal of their eventual return to and integration in the society.

At the Mechanism, the practice concerning pardon, commutation of sentence or early release applies uniformly to all convicted persons, regardless of the core crimes for which they were convicted (genocide, crimes against humanity, war crimes), the country where they are serving their sentences or the Tribunal that convicted them.[4] To proceed otherwise would lead to an unacceptable distinction between different categories of prisoners and would run contrary to basic human rights principles and norms of fairness.

3. *Prosecutor v. Stanislav Galić*, Reasons for the President's Decision to Deny the Early Release of Stanislav Galić and Decision on Prosecution Motion (public redacted version), at para. 22, Case no. MICT-14-83-ES (23 June 2015).

4. E.g., *Prosecutor v. Mile Mrkšić & Veselin Šljivančanin*, Judgement, ICTY Appeals Chamber, at para. 375, Case no. IT-95-13I1-A (5 May 2009); *Prosecutor v. Stakić*, Judgement, ICTY Appeals Chambers, at para. 375, Case no. IT-97-24-A (22 Mar. 2006) ("The Appeals Chamber stresses that there is no hierarchy of the crimes within the jurisdiction of the Tribunal and that, contrary to what the Appellant alleges, the sentence of life imprisonment can be imposed in cases other than genocide.").

All convicted persons whose sentence enforcement is supervised by the Mechanism are thus considered eligible for early release upon completion of two-thirds of their sentences. While they are eligible for early release as of two-thirds of their sentence, they are not entitled to release at that time. When the relevant factors weigh against early release, release may well be denied.

Although the two-thirds practice differs from that of the ICTR (which followed a three-quarters practice), I adopted it at the time I served as President of the Mechanism for fundamental fairness and justice and the need to apply a uniform eligibility threshold to all convicted persons within the jurisdiction of the Mechanism.[5] Following the long-standing practice and jurisprudence of the ICTY and the ICTR, at the Mechanism the President may entertain petitions directly from the convicted person as well as, in accordance with the statutory provisions, notifications of eligibility received from enforcement States.

At the Mechanism, it is only in exceptional circumstances, such as cases involving extraordinary cooperation with the prosecution or humanitarian emergencies, such as terminal illness or grave illness that cannot be treated in prison, that early release prior to two-thirds of the sentence having been served may be granted.

In one case, I was asked by the enforcement State (Germany) to consider the release of prisoner Ljubiša Beara prior to him having served two-thirds of his sentence, I determined that, in view of Germany's inability to continue to enforce Beara's sentence and his dire medical prognosis, clear and compelling humanitarian circumstances existed that warranted the conditional release of Beara. I decided, however, that if Beara's condition were to evolve in a non-terminal fashion, I would have the competence to issue such corrective orders as may be necessary, including, inter alia, ordering the enforcement of the remainder of Beara's sentence and his return to the U.N. Detention Unit at The Hague. To this end, I requested the State to which Beara was released to report on a weekly basis about the status of Beara's health. This was the first case where I granted a conditional release. Beara passed away prior to his return to Serbia.

5. *Prosecutor v. Paul Bisengimana*, Decision of the President on Early Release of Paul Bisengimana and on Motion to File a Public Redacted Application (public redacted version), Case no. MICT-12-07 (11 Dec. 2012). *See also Prosecutor v. Kayishema and Ruzindana*, Judgement (Reasons), ICTR Appeals Chamber, at para. 367, Case no. ICTR-95-1-A (1 June 2001).

Key Early Release Decisions

The following are public redacted versions of key early release Decisions.

Prosecutor v. Bisengimana

Date of Decision: 11 December 2012

Before President Meron

For purposes of early release, prisoners convicted by the ICTR must be considered "similarly situated" not only to persons convicted and sentenced by the ICTR, but also to those convicted and sentenced by the ICTY or the Mechanism. All prisoners under the supervision of the Mechanism must be treated equally. Thus, and in accordance with the *lex mitior* principle (requiring the application of a more lenient criminal law to crimes committed before and sentences imposed before the law's enactment), Bisengimana is eligible for early release upon completion of two-thirds of his sentence—like ICTY prisoners—and not upon the completion of three-quarters of his sentence, as was the practice for the ICTR prisoners

[…]

15. In deciding early release applications, I am required, under Rule 151 of the Rules, to consider the treatment of similarly-situated prisoners as a factor. In his Application, Bisengimana submits that this factor should include consideration of the treatment of, *inter alios*, prisoners convicted by both the ICTR and the ICTY.[6] He claims that this interpretation best serves the equal treatment criterion set forth in Rule 151 of the Rules.[7] Accordingly, based on the practice of the ICTY, Bisengimana submits that, having served two-thirds of his sentence, he should be considered eligible for early release. He contends that service of the two-thirds of the sentence is an appropriate eligibility threshold for the Mechanism to apply, in light of established national and international practice.[8]

16. … The question before me is whether, for purposes of early release determinations under Rule 151 of the Rules, persons convicted and sentenced by the ICTR, like Bisengimana, should be considered "similarly-situated" not only to

6. Application, para. 17.
7. *See* Application, paras. 16–18, 23.
8. *See* Application, paras. 24–26.

persons convicted and sentenced by the ICTR, but also to those convicted and sentenced by the ICTY or the Mechanism.

17. For the reasons explained below, I have formed the view that all prisoner populations to be ultimately supervised by the Mechanism should be treated equally. There is no compelling reason why convicted persons whose sentences are, or will ultimately be, supervised by the Mechanism should be treated differently for early release purposes depending on which tribunal convicted or sentenced them. The Mechanism is a single institution that will ultimately succeed both the ICTY and the ICTR (with one branch for each of those tribunals).[9] I therefore consider it fair and just to deem early release applicants "similarly-situated" to all prisoners whose sentences will be supervised by the Mechanism, irrespective of whether they were convicted or sentenced by the ICTR, the ICTY, or the Mechanism itself.

18. The determination that all prisoners applying to the Mechanism for early release should be treated equally is particularly relevant as the ICTR and the ICTY have developed divergent practices on early release eligibility. Before the Mechanism assumed the responsibility for the supervision of prisoners convicted and sentenced by the ICTR,[10] the ICTR's practice was to consider convicted persons eligible to apply for early release only when they had served at least three-quarters of their sentences.[11] That practice was introduced in 2011, in connection with the first grant of early release to a person convicted by the ICTR in the *Bagaragaza* Decision.[12] That decision made it clear that the three-quarters mark was "not intended to create a precedent" at the ICTR and that "future decisions on early release will continue to be determined on a case-by-case basis."[13] The three-quarters threshold established in the *Bagaragaza* Decision has been applied by the ICTR in two other decisions as a factor relevant to the consideration of similarly-situated ICTR prisoners.[14]

19. By contrast, ICTY convicted persons are considered eligible for early release upon completion of two-thirds of their sentences.[15] The two-thirds practice at the ICTY was first introduced in 2003, based on a consideration of the eligibility thresholds for early release that were in effect in the ICTY

9. *See* Resolution 1966, paras. 1, 4.
10. *See* Resolution 1966, para. 1; Article 25(2) of the Statute.
11. *See*, e.g., *The Prosecutor v. Tharcisse Muvunyi*, Case no. ICTR-00-59A-T, Decision on Tharcisse Muvuyni's Application for Early Release, 6 March 2012 ("*Muvunyi* Decision"), para. 12, and cases cited therein.
12. *See The Prosecutor v. Michel Bagaragaza*, Case no. ICTR-05-86-S, Decision on the Early Release of Michel Bagaragaza, 24 October 2011 ("*Bagaragaza* Decision"), paras. 8–10.
13. *Bagaragaza* Decision, para. 17.
14. *See Muvuyni* Decision, para. 12; *The Prosecutor v. Juvénal Rugambarara,* Case no. ICTR-00-59, Decision on the Early Release Request of Juvénal Rugambarara, 8 February 2012 ("*Rugambarara* Decision"), para. 12.
15. *See*, e.g., *Prosecutor v. Dragan Zelenović*, Case no. IT-96-23/2-ES, Decision of President on Early Release of Dragan Zelenović, 30 November 2012 ("*Zelenović* Decision"), para. 14, and cases

enforcing States,[16] and has since been applied consistently by the ICTY.[17] This practice does not mean that every person convicted by the ICTY is automatically granted early release upon completion of two-thirds of his or her sentence, but that these prisoners are eligible to apply for early release once that threshold has been met.[18] The two-thirds mark is, in essence, an admissibility threshold.

20. Given that the early release practice of the ICTR was derived by reference to the long established relevant jurisprudence and practice of the ICTY,[19] and taking into account the *lex mitior* principle—*i.e.*, the retroactive applicability of a more lenient criminal law to crimes committed and sentences imposed before the law's enactment—which is a fundamental principle of criminal law,[20] I am of the opinion that all convicts supervised by the Mechanism should be considered eligible for early release upon the completion of two-thirds of their sentences, irrespective of the tribunal that convicted them.[21] Although the two-thirds practice originates from the ICTY, I believe that fundamental fairness and justice are best served[22] if the ICTY practice applies uniformly to the entire prisoner population to be ultimately supervised by the Mechanism.

21. While I acknowledge that adoption of the two-thirds eligibility threshold might constitute a benefit not previously recognised for persons convicted by the ICTR, I do not consider that this can justify discriminating between the different groups of convicted persons falling under the jurisdiction of the Mechanism. I further emphasise that consideration of an application for early release at the two-thirds mark does not guarantee that release will be granted, nor does it preclude considering every application on its merits in a manner

cited therein; *Prosecutor v. Momčilo Krajišnik*, Case no. IT-00-39-ES, Decision of President on Early Release of Momčilo Krajišnik, 11 July 2011 ("*Krajišnik* Decision"), para. 21, and cases cited therein.

16. *See Prosecutor v. Zdravko Mucić et al.*, Order of the President in Response to Zdravko Mucić's Request for Early Release, Case no. IT-96-21-A *bis*, 9 July 2003, p. 3.
17. *See*, e.g., *Zelenović* Decision, para. 14, n. 26; *Krajišnik* Decision, para. 21, n. 46.
18. *See Zelenović* Decision, para. 14; *Krajišnik* Decision, para. 21.
19. *See Bagaragaza* Decision, paras. 8–10; *Rugambarara* Decision, para. 11; *Muvuyni* Decision, para. 11.
20. *See Prosecutor v. Dragan Nikolić*, Case no. IT-94-2-A, Judgement on Sentencing Appeal, 4 February 2005, paras. 79–86. *See also Scoppola v. Italy*, Application No. 10249/03, Judgment, 17 September 2009 (European Court of Human Rights) ("*Scoppola* Judgement"), para. 106 (describing the international instruments that reflect the *lex mitior* principle and concluding that it has become a "fundamental principle of criminal law.").
21. *Cf. Munyarugarama* Decision, paras. 5–6 (stating that, because of the "normative continuity" between the Statute and the Rules of the Mechanism with the Statutes and the Rules of the ICTR and the ICTY, the Mechanism's Statute and Rules should be interpreted in such a manner as to be consistent with the jurisprudence and practice of both the ICTY and the ICTR, as a matter of "due process and fundamental fairness").
22. *See* Article 26 of the Statute ("There shall only be pardon or commutation of sentence if the President of the Mechanism so decides on the basis of the interests of justice and the general principles of law.").

consistent with the practice of both the ICTY and the ICTR. A convicted person having served two-thirds of his sentence shall merely be eligible for early release and not entitled to such release, which may only be granted by the President of the Mechanism as a matter of discretion.[23]

[...]

26. Moreover, I observe that, in his 9 August Letter, the director of the Koulikoro prison advises that Bisengimana "has demonstrated exemplary behaviour on a daily basis" and "is a calm person who respects the rules of the prison and its authorities, and even his co-detainees."[24] The director of the Koulikoro prison further notes that Bisengimana "shuns laziness in the sense that he is very involved in various commissions managing the community of Rwandan prisoners in Koulikoro" prison, and also that Bisengimana "regrets everything that has happened to his country and wishes to make amends."[25] This information from the prison authorities appears to corroborate Bisengimana's rehabilitation claims. I note that Bisengimana has not been evaluated by a psychiatrist or psychologist during his incarceration in Mali.[26] However, as the availability of these types of services to prisoners held in Mali is unclear, I do not consider this a factor to be accorded any negative weight.

27. Based on the foregoing, I am of the view that there is evidence of Bisengimana's rehabilitation, and that this factor militates in favour of his early release.

[...]

35. Having carefully considered the factors identified in Rule 151 of the Rules, as well as the particular circumstances of Bisengimana's case, I am of the view that Bisengimana should be granted early release, effective immediately. Bisengimana has already completed two-thirds of his sentence and there is evidence of rehabilitation, cooperation with the ICTR Prosecution, [REDACTED] all of which I find counsel in favour of his early release.

36. I note that my colleagues unanimously share my view that Bisengimana should be granted early release.

Done in English and French, the English version being authoritative.

Done this 11th day of December 2012,
At The Hague,
The Netherlands.

____

Judge Theodor Meron
President

23. *See* Article 26 of the Statute; Rule 150 of the Rules.
24. 23 August Memorandum, 9 August Letter.
25. 23 August Memorandum, 9 August Letter.
26. *See* October Memorandum.

Prosecutor v. Ntakirutimana

Date of Decision: 24 April 2014

Before President Meron

Ntakirutimana, convicted by the ICTR, was granted early release after reaching the two-Thirds Mechanism benchmark

[...]

14. I recall that ICTR convicts, like Ntakirutimana, are considered "similarly-situated" to all other prisoners under the Mechanism's supervision and that all convicts supervised by the Mechanism are to be considered eligible for early release upon the completion of two-thirds of their sentences, irrespective of the tribunal that convicted them.[27] Although the two-thirds practice originates from the International Criminal Tribunal for the former Yugoslavia, it applies to all prisoners within the jurisdiction of the Mechanism, given the need for equal treatment of all convicted persons supervised by the Mechanism and the need for a uniform eligibility threshold applicable to both of the Mechanism's branches.[28] However, a convicted person having served two-thirds of his or her sentence shall be merely eligible to apply for early release and not entitled to such release, which may only be granted by the President of the Mechanism as a matter of discretion, after considering the totality of the circumstances in each case.[29]

15. Based on my own calculation, Ntakirutimana had completed more than two-thirds of his twenty five year sentence as of 29 June 2013.[30]

[...]

18. The Akpro-Missérété Warden's description of Ntakirutimana's behaviour while in prison suggests that Ntakirutimana is capable of reintegrating into society if he is released. In this context, I am of the view that there is some evidence from Ntakirutimana's "exemplary" behaviour in prison that he is able to live peacefully with others and to be of use to society. Accordingly, I consider Ntakiturimana's demonstration of rehabilitation to weigh in favour of his early release.

19. The Prosecution asserts that "at no time has Ntakirutimana provided any cooperation to the [Office of the Prosecutor] of the ICTR or the

27. *See Prosecutor v. Obed Ruzindana*, Case no. MICT-12-10-ES, Decision of the President on the Early Release of Obed Ruzindana, 13 March 2014 (public redacted version) ("*Ruzindana* Decision"), para. 14. *See also Prosecutor v. Omar Serushago*, Case no. MICT-12-28, Public Redacted Version of Decision of the President on the Early Release of Omar Serushago, 13 December 2012 ("*Serushago* Decision"), paras. 16–17.

28. *See Ruzindana* Decision, para. 14; *Serushago* Decision, para. 17.

29. *See Ruzindana* Decision, para. 14; *Serushago* Decision, paras. 18, 34.

30. *See* Obagou Report, p. 2.

[Mechanism]".[31] The Prosecution also notes that, unlike the other convicted persons granted early release by the Mechanism thus far, Ntakirutimana did not plead guilty.[32] In his Reply, Ntakirutimana submits that neither the Rules nor the Practice Direction restrict a grant of early release to those convicted persons who have cooperated with the Prosecution.[33]

20. I note at the outset that entering a guilty plea promotes the efficient administration of justice and constitutes cooperation with the Prosecution.[34] However, an accused person is under no obligation to plead guilty or, in the absence of a plea agreement, to cooperate with the Prosecution.[35] I also note that the Prosecution does not indicate whether it or the Office of the Prosecutor of the ICTR sought Ntakirutimana's cooperation at any point during his trial or after he was convicted. I therefore consider that Ntakirutimana's lack of cooperation with the Prosecution or the Office of the Prosecutor of the ICTR is a neutral factor in my determination of whether to grant him early release.

[...]

23. Having carefully considered the factors identified in Rule 151 of the Rules, as well as the particular circumstances of Ntakirutimana's case, I conclude that Ntakirutimana should be granted early release. Specifically, Ntakirutimana has already completed more than two-thirds of his sentence and has demonstrated signs of rehabilitation. I believe that in context, the particular factors and circumstances of Ntakirutimana's case are sufficient to justify his early release.

24. For the foregoing reasons and pursuant to Article 26 of the Statute, Rules 150 and 151 of the Rules, paragraph 9 of the Practice Direction, and Article 8 of the Enforcement Agreement, I hereby **GRANT** the Application.

Done in English and French, the English version being authoritative.

Done this 24th day of April 2014,
At The Hague,
The Netherlands.

____
Judge Theodor Meron
President

31. Prosecution Memorandum, para. 10 (emphasis omitted).
32. Prosecution Memorandum, paras. 12–14. *See also* Prosecution Memorandum, paras. 15–19.
33. Reply, para. I(d).
34. *See Ruzindana* Decision, para. 21.
35. *See Ruzindana* Decision, para. 21, and references cited therein.

Prosecutor v. Lazarević

DATE OF DECISION: 3 DECEMBER 2015

Before President Meron

PERIODS SPENT ON PROVISIONAL RELEASE MAY NOT BE COUNTED AS PERIODS SPENT IN DETENTION FOR PURPOSES OF ELIGIBILITY FOR EARLY RELEASE

[…]

16. Lazarević contends that all of the time he spent on provisional release should be included as part of his sentence served.[36] Alternatively, Lazarević submits that the 94 days he spent in the hospital under police surveillance should be credited towards his sentence served.[37]

17. The Trial Judgement and the Appeal Judgement do not address the manner in which Lazarević's time spent on provisional release should be calculated. I have previously held that in such circumstances, time spent on provisional release is not counted as time in detention for purposes of sentence calculation.[38] Accordingly, as of the date of this decision, Lazarević will have served two-thirds of his sentence as of 3 December 2015.[39]

[…]

20. The Commanding Officer's description of Lazarević's good behaviour while detained at the UNDU suggests that Lazarević is capable of reintegrating into society if he is released. Having carefully reviewed the information before me, I am of the opinion that Lazarević has demonstrated signs of rehabilitation, and I am therefore inclined to count this factor as weighing in favour of his early release.

[…]

22. According to the Prosecution, Lazarević "cooperated with the [ICTY Prosecution] and has been given credit in mitigation of his sentence for this factor."[40] The Prosecution refers specifically to the Trial Chamber's acknowledgement of Lazarević's participation in "an extensive

36. Application, para. 17.
37. Application, para. 22.
38. *Prosecutor v. Nikola Šainović*, Case no. MICT-14-67-ES.1, Decision on Defence Request Regarding Service of Sentence, 28 March 2014 (confidential), p. 2. *See also Prosecutor v. Miroslav Tadić*, Case no. IT-95-9, Decision of the President on the Application for Pardon or Commutation of Sentence of Miroslav Tadić, 24 June 2004, fn. 8.
39. The Prosecution responded to Lazarević's Application arguing that none of Lazarević's time spent on provisional release should be counted towards his time served. *See Prosecutor v. Vladimir Lazarević*, Case no. MICT-14-67-ES.3, Prosecution's Response to Vladimir Lazarević's Supplement or Amendment to His Early Release Request, 19 June 2015 (confidential), para. 5.
40. Prosecution Memorandum, para. 2, *citing* Trial Judgement, Vol. III, para. 1198 and Appeal Judgement, paras. 1819–1821.

interview over the course of several days and providing new documents."[41] According to the Prosecution, "no additional cooperation has been given".[42] I am satisfied that when an accused person participates in interviews with and provides documents to the Prosecution, this constitutes cooperation.

23. While accepting that Lazarević's participation in interviews and his provision of documents was a factor taken into account by the Trial Chamber in relation to sentencing, I place some weight upon it in favour of Lazarević's early release, due to the impact such cooperation has on the efficient administration of justice.

24. Paragraph 9 of the Practice Direction provides that the President may consider "any other information" that the President believes to be "relevant" to supplement the criteria specified in Rule 151 of the Rules. Previous decisions on early release have determined that the condition of a convicted person's health may be taken into account in the context of an application for early release, especially when the seriousness of the condition makes it inappropriate for the person to remain in prison any longer.[43]

[...]

27. The record before me suggests that Lazarević suffers from health issues. However, I am not convinced that his health issues [are] so serious as to be a factor supporting early release. Accordingly, I consider these to be neutral factors in determining whether or not to grant Lazarević early release.

28. In light of the above, and having considered the factors identified in Rule 151 of the Rules, as well as all the relevant information on the record, I hereby grant Lazarević early release, effective 3 December 2015. Although the crimes for which Lazarević was convicted are grave, Lazarević's demonstrated signs of rehabilitation and his cooperation with the Prosecution, counsel in favour of his early release upon completion of two-thirds of his sentence. The view that Lazarević should be granted early release is shared by the Judge of the sentencing Chamber who is a Judge of the Mechanism.

29. For the foregoing reasons and pursuant to Article 26 of the Statute, Rules 150 and 151 of the Rules and paragraph 9 of the Practice Direction,

41. Trial Judgement, Vol. III, para. 1198.
42. Prosecution Memorandum, para. 2.
43. *See*, e.g., *Munyakazi* Decision, para. 22; *Prosecutor v. Gérard Ntakirutimana,* Case no. MICT-12-17-ES, Public Redacted Version of the 26 March 2014 Decision of the President on the Early Release of Gérard Ntakirutimana, 24 April 2014, para. 21; *Prosecutor v. Obed Ruzindana,* Case no. MICT-12-10-ES, Decision of the President on the Early Release of Obed Ruzindana, 13 March 2014 (public redacted version), para. 22. *See also Bisengimana* Decision, para. 32.

I hereby **GRANT** the Application effective 3 December 2015, or as soon as practicable thereafter.

Done in English and French, the English version being authoritative.

Done this 7th day of September 2015,
At The Hague,
The Netherlands.

Judge Theodor Meron
President

Prosecutor v. Galić

Date of Decision: 18 January 2017
Before President Meron

This decision accepts 45 years as the standard of eligibility for early release of persons sentenced for life imprisonment

[...]

3. On 5 December 2003, Trial Chamber, by a majority, found Galić guilty pursuant to Article 7(1) of the ICTY Statute of five counts of the indictment, including charges of murder as a crime against humanity through sniping and shelling, inhumane acts other than murder as crimes against humanity through sniping and shelling, and acts of violence the primary purpose of which was to spread terror among the civilian population as violations of the laws and customs of war.[44] He was sentenced to a single term of 20 years' imprisonment.[45] On 30 November 2006, the Appeals Chamber of the ICTY ("ICTY Appeals Chamber") dismissed all 19 of Galić's grounds of appeal and increased his sentence to life imprisonment.[46]

4. Galić was transferred to Germany to serve the remainder of his sentence on 15 January 2009.[47]

[...]

7. In coming to my decision on whether it is appropriate to grant early release for Galić, I have consulted the Judge of the sentencing Chamber who is a Judge of the Mechanism, pursuant to Rule 150 of the Rules.

44. Trial Judgement, paras. 751, 769. The two other counts charged in the Indictment were dismissed, because the Trial Chamber concluded that they were "subsumed under count 1 [of the Indictment]". *See* Trial Judgement, para. 752.
45. Trial Judgement, para. 769.
46. *Prosecutor v. Stanislav Galić*, Case no. IT-98-29-A, Judgement, 30 November 2006 ("Appeal Judgement"), p. 185, Annex A, para. 4.
47. *See* Press Release, Stanislav Galić Transferred to Germany to Serve Sentence, dated 15 January 2009, *available at* http://www.icty.org/sid/10037.

[...]

19. Rule 151 of the Rules requires the President to consider, as a separate factor, the need for equal treatment of similarly-situated prisoners when deciding early release applications.

20. In this respect, I recall that ICTY convicts, like Galić, are considered "similarly-situated" to all other prisoners under the Mechanism's supervision and that, following previous practice at the ICTY, all convicted persons supervised by the Mechanism are to be considered eligible for early release upon the completion of two-thirds of their sentences, irrespective of the tribunal that convicted them.[48]

21. I further recall that, in accordance with the principle of treating similarly-situated prisoners equally, a person sentenced to life imprisonment shall be considered eligible for early release by the Mechanism upon having served more than two-thirds of the highest fixed terms sentence imposed by the ICTR, the ICTY, or the Mechanism.[49] I note that for purposes of applying the two-thirds practice of the Mechanism to those sentenced to life imprisonment and serving their sentences under the supervision of the Mechanism, a sentence of life imprisonment is to be treated as equivalent to more than a sentence of 45 years.[50]

48. *See Prosecutor v. Emmanuel Rukundo*, Case no. MICT-13-35-ES, Public Redacted Version of the 19 July 2016 Decision of the President on the Early Release of Emmanuel Rukundo, 5 December 2016 ("*Rukundo* Decision"), para. 19. *See also Prosecutor v. Paul Bisengimana*, Case no. MICT-12-07, Decision of the President on Early Release of Paul Bisengimana and on Motion to File a Public Redacted Application, 11 December 2012 (public redacted version) ("*Bisengimana* Decision"), paras. 17, 20.

49. *See Prosecutor v. Stanislav Galić*, Case no. MICT-14-83-ES, Reasons for the President's Decision to Deny the Early Release of Stanislav Galić and Decision on Prosecution Motion, 23 June 2015 (public redacted version) ("*Galić* Decision"), para. 36.

50. *Galić* Decision, para. 35. I note in this regard that, following the issuance of the *Galić* Decision, a fixed-term sentence higher than 45 years was handed down by the ICTR. Specifically, the Appeals Chamber of the ICTR in the case of *Prosecutor v. Pauline Nyiramasuhuko et al.*, Case no. ICTR-98-42-A, reduced the life sentences of Messrs. Arsène Shalom Ntahobali and Élie Ndayambaje to respective sentences of 47 years of imprisonment. *See Prosecutor v. Pauline Nyiramasuhuko et al*, Case no. ICTR-98-42-A, Judgement, 14 December 2015, pp. 1210, 1213. I recall in this regard that the interests of justice and the principle of legal certainty require that no change in the calculation of the eligibility threshold for those sentenced to life imprisonment take place, notwithstanding the fact that a sentence higher than 45 years was handed down. *See Galić* Decision, para. 38. I further note, for clarification purposes, that the two-thirds threshold does not prohibit enforcement States from notifying the Mechanism whenever convicted persons become eligible for pardon, commutation of sentence, or early release under national law, even before the completion of two-thirds of their sentence. *See generally*, Practice Direction, para. 2. Paragraph 3 of the Practice Direction also allows a convicted person to directly petition the President for pardon, commutation of sentence, or early release, if the convicted person believes that he or she is eligible, even before the completion of the two-thirds of his or her sentence. According to the Practice Direction, in such circumstances, the President will still consider a convicted person's application or eligibility for pardon, commutation of sentence, or early release. *See* Practice Direction, para. 3. However, it is only in exceptional circumstances, such as cases involving extraordinary cooperation with

22. However, I note that a convicted person having served two-thirds of his or her sentence shall be merely eligible to apply for early release and not entitled to such release, which may only be granted by the President as a matter of discretion, after considering the totality of the circumstances in each case.[51]

23. Based on the foregoing, Galić shall be considered eligible for early release by the Mechanism upon having served more than two-thirds of 45 years, which amounts to more than 30 years of his sentence. As of the date of this decision, and based on my own calculation, Galić has thus far served approximately 17 years of his sentence.

[...]

29. The description of Galić's behaviour while detained at Freiburg Prison suggests that Galić is capable of reintegrating into society if he is released. Having carefully reviewed the information before me, I am of the opinion that Galić has demonstrated signs of rehabilitation, and I am therefore inclined to count this factor as weighing in favour of his early release.

[...]

34. I note that an accused person is under no obligation to plead guilty or, in the absence of a plea agreement, to cooperate with the Prosecution.[52] In view of the above, I therefore consider that Galić's lack of cooperation with the Prosecution is a neutral factor in determining whether or not to grant him early release.

[...]

39. While I am concerned about Galić's health condition, the reports provided suggest that Galić has been receiving treatment, that his medical condition is stable, and that he is capable of serving his sentence. Accordingly, I am not convinced that Galić's health condition is so serious as to constitute exceptional circumstances that warrant his early release. Nor do I believe that his age plays such a role.

the Prosecution or humanitarian emergencies, that early release prior to the serving of two-thirds of the sentence may be granted, provided that other factors also weigh in favour of early release. *See*, e.g., *Prosecutor v. Dragan Obrenović*, Case no. IT-02-60/2-ES, Decision of President on Early Release of Dragan Obrenović, 29 February 2012 (public redacted version), paras. 15, 25–28, 30 (granting early release in a case involving exceptional cooperation with the ICTY Prosecution); *Prosecutor v. Vladimir Šantić*, Case no. IT-95-16-ES, Decision of the President on the Application for Pardon or Commutation of Sentence of Vladimir Šantić, 16 February 2009 (public redacted version), paras. 8, 1315 (granting early release because of substantial cooperation with the Office of the Prosecutor of the ICTY and because the convicted person had effectively completed two-thirds of his sentence once sentence remissions under national law were recognized).

51. *See Rukundo* Decision, para. 19; *Bisengimana* Decision, paras. 21, 35.

52. *See Prosecutor v. Dominique Ntawukulilyayo*, Case no. MICT-13-34-ES, Decision of the President on the Early Release of Dominique Ntawukulilyayo, 8 July 2016 (public redacted version), para. 31; *Prosecutor v. Gérard Ntakirutimana*, Case no. MICT-12-17-ES, Public Redacted Version of the 26 March 2014 Decision of the President on the Early Release of Gérard Ntakirutimana, 24 April 2014 ("*Ntakirutimana* Decision"), para. 20.

40. In light of the above, and having considered the factors identified in Rule 151 of the Rules, as well as all the relevant information on the record, I am inclined to deny Galić early release. Although Galić has demonstrated some signs of rehabilitation, the crimes for which he has been convicted are very grave, and Galić has failed to demonstrate that there exist exceptional circumstances warranting his early release prior to having served more than two-thirds of his sentence. The view that Galić should be denied early release is shared by the Judge of the sentencing Chamber who is still a Judge of the Mechanism.

41. For the foregoing reasons and pursuant to Article 26 of the Statute, Rules 150 and 151 of the Rules, paragraph 9 of the Practice Direction, and Article 7(2) of the Enforcement Agreement, I hereby **DENY** Galić early release.

Done in English and French, the English version being authoritative.

Done this 18th day of January 2017,
At The Hague,
The Netherlands.

Judge Theodor Meron
President

Prosecutor v. Beara

Date of Decision: 16 June 2017
Before President Theodor Meron

This decision introduces conditional release for a terminally ill person convicted of some of the Srebrenica crimes

[...]

3. On 10 June 2010, Trial Chamber II of the ICTY ("Trial Chamber") found Beara guilty pursuant to Article 7(1) of the ICTY Statute for committing genocide, extermination and persecution as crimes against humanity, and murder as a violation of the laws or customs of war.[53] He was sentenced to life imprisonment.[54]

4. On 30 January 2015, the Appeals Chamber of the ICTY ("Appeals Chamber") reversed, in part, Beara's "convictions for genocide (Count 1 in part), extermination as a crime against humanity (Count 3 in part), murder as a violation of the laws or customs of war (Count 5 in part), and persecutions

53. *See* Trial Judgement, vol. II, p. 833.
54. Trial Judgement, vol. II, p. 833.

as a crime against humanity (Count 6 in part) to the extent they concern[ed] the killing of six Bosnian Muslim men near Trnovo".[55] All other convictions were upheld and a new conviction against Beara for conspiracy to commit genocide was entered.[56] Beara's life sentence was affirmed by the Appeals Chamber.[57]

[...]

19. Rule 151 of the Rules provides that, in making a determination on early release, the President shall take into account the gravity of the crime or crimes for which the prisoner was convicted.

20. The crimes for which Beara was convicted are of very high gravity. In this regard, the Trial Chamber found that Beara was "a driving force behind the murder enterprise",[58] and "a central figure in the organisation and execution of the genocide".[59] It further found that Beara "had the clearest overall picture of the massive scale and scope of the killing operation", and that "he had a very personal view of the staggering number of victims destined for execution".[60] The Trial Chamber found "that Beara's involvement in the murder operation was not characterised by a particular 'zeal', but his actions were cold and calculated. Even in the early stages of the murder operation, Beara's approach is demonstrated by the conversation he had with Deronjić on the night of 13 July, when he announces his intent to 'kill all' the detained men, and without pause to consider or comment upon the horrific nature of his 'orders'".[61]

21. In these circumstances, I am of the view that the high gravity of Beara's offences weighs strongly against his early release.

[...]

23. In this respect, I recall that ICTY convicts, like Beara, are considered "similarly-situated" to all other prisoners under the Mechanism's supervision and that all convicts supervised by the Mechanism are to be considered eligible for early release upon the completion of two-thirds of their sentences, irrespective of the tribunal that convicted them.[62]

24. I further recall that, in accordance with the principle of treating similarly-situated prisoners equally, a person sentenced to life imprisonment

55. *Prosecutor v. Vujadin Popović et al.*, Case no. IT-05-88-A, Judgement, 30 January 2015 ("Appeal Judgement"), Appeal Judgement, p. 713.
56. Appeal Judgement, p. 713.
57. Appeal Judgement, p. 714.
58. Trial Judgement, vol. 2, para. 1314. *See* Appeal Judgement, paras. 1967, 1972.
59. Trial Judgement, vol. 2, para. 2164. *See* Appeal Judgement, paras. 1967, 1972.
60. Trial Judgement, vol. 2, para. 2164. *See* Appeal Judgement, para. 1265.
61. Trial Judgement, vol. 2, para. 2166.
62. *See Prosecutor v. Stanislav Galić*, Case no. MICT-14-83-ES, Decision of the President on the Early Release of Stanislav Galić, 18 January 2017 (public redacted version) ("*Galić* Decision 2017"), para. 20; *Prosecutor v. Paul Bisengimana*, Case no. MICT-12-07, Decision of the President on Early Release of Paul Bisengimana and on Motion to File a Public Redacted Application, 11 December 2012 (public redacted version) ("*Bisengimana* Decision"), paras. 17, 20.

shall be considered eligible for early release by the Mechanism upon having served more than two-thirds of the highest fixed terms sentence imposed by the ICTR, the ICTY, or the Mechanism.[63] I note that for purposes of applying the two-thirds practice of the Mechanism to those sentenced to life imprisonment and serving their sentences under the supervision of the Mechanism, a sentence of life imprisonment is to be treated as equivalent to more than a sentence of 45 years.[64]

[...]

26. Based on the foregoing, Beara shall be considered eligible for early release by the Mechanism upon having served more than two-thirds of 45 years, which amounts to more than 30 years of his sentence. As of the date of this decision, and based on my own calculation, Beara has thus far served approximately 13 years of his sentence.

63. *Galić* Decision 2017, para. 21; *See Prosecutor v. Stanislav Galić*, Case no. MICT-14-83-ES, Reasons for the President's Decision to Deny the Early Release of Stanislav Galić and Decision on Prosecution Motion, 23 June 2015 (public redacted version) ("*Galić* Decision 2015"), para. 36.

64. *Galić* Decision 2017, para. 21. I note in this regard that, following the issuance of the *Galić* Decision 2015, a fixed-term sentence higher than 45 years was handed down by the International Criminal Tribunal for Rwanda ("ICTR"). Specifically, the Appeals Chamber of the ICTR in the case of *Prosecutor v. Pauline Nyiramasuhuko et al.*, Case no. ICTR-98-42-A, reduced the life sentences of Messrs. Arsène Shalom Ntahobali and Élie Ndayambaje to respective sentences of 47 years of imprisonment. *See Prosecutor v. Pauline Nyiramasuhuko et al.*, Case no. ICTR-98-42-A, Judgement, 14 December 2015, pp. 1210, 1213. I recall in this regard that the interests of justice and the principle of legal certainty require that no change in the calculation of the eligibility threshold for those sentenced to life imprisonment take place, notwithstanding the fact that a sentence higher than 45 years was handed down. *See Galić* Decision 2015, para. 38. I further note, for clarification purposes, that the two-thirds threshold does not prohibit enforcement States from notifying the Mechanism whenever convicted persons become eligible for pardon, commutation of sentence, or early release under national law, even before the completion of two-thirds of their sentence. *See generally*, Practice Direction, para. 2. Paragraph 3 of the Practice Direction also allows a convicted person to directly petition the President for pardon, commutation of sentence, or early release, if the convicted person believes that he or she is eligible, even before the completion of the two-thirds of his or her sentence. According to the Practice Direction, in such circumstances, the President will still consider a convicted person's application or eligibility for pardon, commutation of sentence, or early release. *See* Practice Direction, para. 3. However, it is only in exceptional circumstances, such as cases involving extraordinary cooperation with the Prosecution or humanitarian emergencies, that early release prior to the serving of two-thirds of the sentence may be granted, provided that other factors also weigh in favour of early release. *See*, e.g., *Prosecutor v. Dragan Obrenović*, Case no. IT-02-60/2-ES, Decision of President on Early Release of Dragan Obrenović, 29 February 2012 (public redacted version), paras. 15, 25–28, 30 (granting early release in a case involving exceptional cooperation with the ICTY Prosecution); *Prosecutor v. Vladimir Šantić*, Case no. IT-95-16-ES, Decision of the President on the Application for Pardon or Commutation of Sentence of Vladimir Šantić, 16 February 2009 (public redacted version), paras. 8, 1315 (granting early release because of substantial cooperation with the ICTY Prosecution and because the convicted person had effectively completed two-thirds of his sentence once sentence remissions under national law were recognized).

27. I recognize that this is a particularly early point in a lengthy sentence and consider the fact that Beara has only served 13 years of his life sentence to be a factor that weighs strongly against his early release.

[...]

29. As of the date of this decision, I have not received information regarding Beara's rehabilitation, nor do the German authorities intend to submit further information.[65] Nevertheless, I am of the view that the absence of this information, in the present circumstances of this case, should not weigh either way in my consideration of his early release.[66]

[...]

32. I note that an accused person is under no obligation to plead guilty or, in the absence of a plea agreement, to cooperate with the Prosecution.[67] I therefore consider that Beara's lack of cooperation with the Prosecution is a neutral factor in determining whether or not to grant him early release.

[...]

45. I am of the opinion that the ongoing enforcement of Beara's sentence, in such present conditions that (i) [REDACTED]; (ii) [REDACTED]; (iii) curative medical care is no longer medically-indicated and [REDACTED]; (iv) Beara is socially isolated; and (v) his life expectancy is estimated at a few weeks at the most, would be tantamount to violation of Beara's internationally-guaranteed human right not to be subjected to inhuman or degrading treatment or punishment.[68] I adopt the view of the German authorities, consistent with all medical reports received to date, that the severity of Beara's health condition, and the rapid deterioration of his health, have presently become irreconcilable with having his prison sentence executed at a correctional facility.[69]

46. Accordingly, I am satisfied that the clear and compelling humanitarian considerations discussed above weigh strongly in favour of a grant of release from imprisonment.

65. 23 January 2017 Registry Memorandum, para. 2. According to this memorandum, the German authorities confirmed via e-mail to the Registry that they are not intending to submit any additional documentation, unless so requested.
66. *Cf. Prosecutor v. Gérard Ntakirutimana*, Case no. MICT-12-17-ES, Public Redacted Version of the 26 March 2014 Decision of the President on the Early Release of Gérard Ntakirutimana, 24 April 2014 ("*Ntakirutimana* Decision"), para. 17.
67. *See Galić* Decision 2015, para. 34; *Prosecutor v. Dominique Ntawukulilyayo*, Case no. MICT-13-34-ES, Decision of the President on the Early Release of Dominique Ntawukulilyayo, 8 July 2016 (public redacted version), para. 31; *Ntakirutimana* Decision, para. 20.
68. Article 7 of International Covenant on Civil and Political Rights; Article 3 of European Convention on Human Rights. *See also Paposhvili v. Belgium*, no. 41738/10, European Court of Human Rights ("ECHR") Judgement of 13 December 2016, para. 175; *Rozhkov v. Russia*, no. 64140/00, ECHR Judgement of 19 July 2007, para. 104; *Hüseyin Yıldırım v. Turkey*, no. 2778/02, ECHR Judgement of 3 May 2007, paras. 73–74; *Farbtuhs v. Latvia*, no. 4672/02, ECHR Judgement of 2 December 2004, paras. 51–53, 61; *Papon v. France* (no. 1), no. 64666/01, Decision on Admissibility of 7 June 2001, pp. 7–8.
69. Prison Report, p. 3 (emphasis in original). *See also Rozhkov v Russia*, ECHR Judgement of 19 July 2007, para. 104.

47. While I have given due consideration to the particular gravity of the crimes for which Beara was convicted, as well as the early stage of Beara's sentence, it is apparent, given the severe and rapid deterioration of Beara's health condition successively advised by the German authorities and confirmed by United Nations medical personnel, that his present life expectancy has now become highly abbreviated. I further recall that, as confirmed by the German authorities, neither Tegel Correctional Facility, in which Beara has been serving his sentence, nor any other detention facility in Germany, is equipped with the means necessary to address the health needs of seriously-ill patients.[70] Nor does it appear a viable option for him to be returned to The Netherlands. Accordingly, on the basis of the above-mentioned specific medical circumstances, I am of the view on humanitarian grounds, and in accordance with human rights principles, that clear and compelling reasons exist that make it no longer appropriate, at this time, for Beara to remain in prison, notwithstanding the significant factors which weigh against release.

48. My fellow Judges of the Mechanism, who were also Judges of the sentencing Chamber, have agreed that sufficient humanitarian considerations exist to warrant release but have expressed concerns with respect to granting Beara early release. [REDACTED]. Accordingly, it was recommended by the Judges of the sentencing Chamber, who are also Judges of the Mechanism, that Beara be granted a conditional release and that reporting obligations be placed on the State of release to keep the Mechanism informed of Beara's health condition in the event that revocation should become necessary.[71]

70. Notification, p. 2.

71. I note that in the past provisional release was granted to a convicted person who was still in the custody of the UNDU, awaiting transfer to an enforcement state. *See Prosecutor v. Drago Nikolić*, Case no. MICT-15-85-ES.4, Public Redacted Version of the 20 July 2015 Decision of the President on the Application for Early Release or Other Relief of Drago Nikolić, 13 October 2015 ("*Nikolić* Decision"). In the current matter, there are legal as well as practical issues that constrain my ability to consider provisional release. Beara is currently in the custody of Germany, and the regime of provisional release that applies to persons in the custody of the Mechanism is not applicable to individuals serving their sentences in an enforcement State. I also note that the Prosecution appealed the *Nikolić* Decision, arguing, inter alia, that, according to Rule 68 of the Rules, the power to grant provisional release lay explicitly with Trial and Appeals Chambers and that, in considering provisional release, the Prosecution should be heard prior to a convicted person's provisional release. *See Prosecutor v. Drago Nikolić*, Case no. MICT-15-85-ES.4, Prosecution Appeal of the Decision Granting Provisional Release to Drago Nikolić, 27 July 2015 (confidential). While an Appeals Chamber was constituted to deal with this appeal, Drago Nikolić died and therefore the Chamber held that it lacked the jurisdiction to continue the proceedings. *See Prosecutor v. Drago Nikolić*, Case no. MICT-15-85-ES.4, Decision on Prosecution Appeal of the Decision Granting Provisional Release, 22 October 2015. As such, whether as President I have the competence to issue a decision on provisional release, even should the individual remain in the custody of the UNDU, has yet to be resolved by the Appeals Chamber. *See also Prosecutor v. Zdravko Tolimir*, Case no. MICT-15-95-ES, Order Assigning Judges of the Appeals Chamber to Decide a Motion for Provisional Release, 18 November 2015.

While such an approach constitutes a novelty in terms of approaches that have been taken to applications for early release, I am satisfied that the clear and compelling circumstances in this case warrant Beara's discharge from detention but that the gravity of the crimes for which Beara was convicted, coupled with the limited amount of time he has served of his life sentence, warrant the taking of such an approach.

49. Accordingly, having considered the factors identified in Rule 151 of the Rules as well as all the relevant information on the record, given the specific, clear, and compelling humanitarian circumstances that exist at this time, I hereby grant Beara's conditional release effective on this specific humanitarian basis immediately, or as soon as practicable thereafter. I note in that regard that, should Beara's condition evolve in a non-terminal fashion, notwithstanding the consistent views of the German authorities which underlie this decision, I have competence, and reserve the possibility, to issue such corrective orders as may be necessary, including, *inter alia*, ordering the enforcement of the remainder of Beara's sentence and his return to the UNDU.[72] In that respect, I require the State to which Beara is released to report to me within one week of the rendering of this decision on the status of Beara's health and every week thereafter.

50. For the foregoing reasons and pursuant to Article 26 of the Statute, Rules 150 and 151 of the Rules, paragraph 9 of the Practice Direction, and Article 8 of the Enforcement Agreement, I hereby **GRANT** the Notification, effective immediately, or as soon as practicable thereafter.

51. The Registrar is hereby **DIRECTED** to inform the German authorities of this decision as soon as practicable, as prescribed in paragraph 13 of the Practice Direction, and to inform the Serbian authorities of this decision as soon as practicable.

52. I further, **REQUEST** the German authorities to report to the Mechanism on the status of Beara's health, on a weekly basis, pending the implementation of his conditional release to the Republic of Serbia; and

ORDER as follows:

i. During the period of his conditional release, Beara shall abide by the following conditions:

  a. Beara shall remain within the confines of his place of residence in the Republic of Serbia, and—if strictly necessary for the purpose of

72. The Mechanism, in this regard, received guarantees from the Government of the Republic of Serbia, stating that "it will comply with all orders by the Mechanism so that the convicted person will be accessible to the Mechanism at any time". *See* Internal Memorandum from Ms. Åsa Rydberg van der Sluis, Legal Officer, Office of the Registrar, Hague Branch, to Judge Theodor Meron, President, Mr. Ljubiša Beara—Guarantees from the Government of Serbia, dated 6 February 2017, *transmitting* guarantees issued by the Government of the Republic of Serbia in the event Beara is released by the Mechanism, dated 24 January 2017 (transmitted to the Registry on 4 February 2017, translation received 6 February 2017).

medical treatment—the local hospital in Belgrade, Republic of Serbia, apart from his travel to and from these locations and as specifically authorized by me;

b. Beara shall remain under 24-hour armed surveillance by authorized officials of the Ministry of Interior of the Republic of Serbia throughout his presence in the Republic of Serbia;
c. Beara shall surrender all his travel documents to the Public Security Station in the Republic of Serbia for the entire duration of his conditional release;
d. Beara shall have no contact whatsoever or in any way interfere with victims or (potential) witnesses, or otherwise interfere in any way with the proceedings of the Mechanism, the ICTY, or the administration of justice;
e. Beara shall strictly comply with any requirements of the authorities of Republic of Serbia necessary to enable them to comply with their obligations under the present decision; and
f. Beara shall comply with any order I issue varying the terms of or terminating his conditional release, including any order that he return to the custody of the Mechanism; and

REQUIRE the Government of the Republic of Serbia to inform me and the Registrar as soon as practicable, that it will assume responsibility for:

i. Designating the authorized official(s) of the Ministry of Interior of the Republic of Serbia into whose custody Beara shall be delivered and who shall accompany Beara from Germany to the Republic of Serbia, and, if needed, from the Republic of Serbia back to the custody of the Mechanism;
ii. Notifying, as soon as practicable, myself and the Registrar of the name(s) of these designated official(s);
iii. Ensuring Beara's personal security and safety while on conditional release in the Republic of Serbia;
iv. Providing 24-hour armed surveillance of Beara throughout his stay in the Republic of Serbia;
v. Covering all expenses in connection with Beara's conditional release including, but not limited to, the transport from Germany to the Republic of Serbia;
vi. Facilitating, at the Mechanism's request, all means of co-operation and communication and ensuring the confidentiality of any such communications;
vii. Reporting immediately to the Registrar as to the substance of any threats to Beara's security, including full reports of investigations related to such threats;
viii. Detaining Beara immediately should he attempt to escape from the territory of the Republic of Serbia or the custody of the authorized official(s) of the Ministry of Interior of the Republic of Serbia, or should

he in any other way breach the terms and conditions of his conditional release as set out in the present decision, and reporting immediately any such breach to the Registry and myself;

ix. Respecting the primacy of the Mechanism in relation to any existing or future proceedings in the Republic of Serbia concerning Beara;

x. Submitting a weekly written report to the Mechanism confirming the presence of Beara in the Republic of Serbia and his adherence to the conditions of his conditional release and containing information about any change in his health, whether a deterioration or an improvement;

xi. Complying strictly with any other or further requirements concerning this conditional release; and

xii. Complying with any order issued by the President, including any order to return Beara to the custody of the Mechanism.

Done in English and French, the English version being authoritative.

Done this 16th day of June 2017,
At The Hague,
The Netherlands.

Judge Theodor Meron
President

Prosecutor v. Kunarac

Date of Decision: 2 February 2017

Before President Theodor Meron

Unsatisfactory behaviour in prison and thus poor prospects for rehabilitation justify denial of early release

[...]

2. Kunarac surrendered to the International Criminal Tribunal for the former Yugoslavia ("ICTY") on 4 March 1998 and was transferred to the United Nations Detention Unit ("UNDU") in the Hague on that same day.[73] On 22 February 2001, Trial Chamber II of the ICTY ("Trial Chamber") found Kunarac guilty of torture, rape, and enslavement as crimes against humanity, and torture and rape as violations of the laws or customs of war, and sentenced him to 28 years of imprisonment.[74] On 12 June

73. *Prosecutor v. Dragoljub Kunarac et al.*, Case no. IT-96-23-T & IT-96-23/1-T, Judgement, 22 February 2001 ("Trial Judgement"), p. 283. *See also* Press Release, "Dragoljub Kunarac Is the First Accused of Rape and Torture of Bosnian Muslim Women to Turn Himself In", 4 March 1998, *available at* http://www.icty.org/en/sid/7687.

74. Trial Judgement, paras. 883, 885.

2002, the Appeals Chamber of the ICTY affirmed the convictions entered against Kunarac by the Trial Chamber, as well as the 28 year sentence it had imposed.[75]

22. In this respect, I recall that ICTY convicts, like Kunarac, are considered "similarly-situated" to all other prisoners under the Mechanism's supervision and that all convicts supervised by the Mechanism are to be considered eligible for early release upon the completion of two-thirds of their sentences, irrespective of the tribunal that convicted them.[76] However, I note that a convicted person having served two-thirds of his or her sentence shall be merely eligible to apply for early release and not entitled to such release, which may only be granted by the President as a matter of discretion, after considering the totality of the circumstances in each case.[77]

[...]

23. Based on my own calculation, Kunarac served two-thirds of his sentence of 28 years on 1 November 2016.

[...]

26. The Prison Report informs that Kunarac behaves properly towards the prison attendants, but that conflicts with other inmates are "not a rare occurrence".[78] The Prison Report reflects that Kunarac, who has been at Bochum prison since 2002, has a "very rudimentary" knowledge of German.[79] The Prison Report notes in this regard that any attempt at providing Kunarac with German refresher courses "is dropped after a short while" and the Prison Report further observes that Kunarac "obviously seems to show no real interest in learning the language properly".[80]

27. According to the Prison Report, Bochum prison's Social Work Unit states that Kunarac has a "striking history in detention of a variety of breaches and offences", that he has in the past "always proven to be demanding, occasionally insolent, brash and intransigent in his behaviour", and that Kunarac projects his difficulties "onto the nearest prison attendants and his bad mood is acted out on them accordingly".[81] According to the Social Work Unit, Kunarac calmed down to a certain extent since mid-2014, at least insofar as it relates to his interactions with this Unit.[82]

75. *Prosecutor v. Dragoljub Kunarac et al.*, Case no. IT-96-23 & IT-96-23/1-A, Judgement, 12 June 2002, p. 125.

76. *See Prosecutor v. Stanislav Galić*, Case no. MICT-14-83-ES, Decision of the President on the Early Release of Stanislav Galić, 18 January 2017 ("*Galić* Decision"), para. 20. *See also Prosecutor v. Paul Bisengimana*, Case no. MICT-12-07, Decision of the President on Early Release of Paul Bisengimana and on Motion to File a Public Redacted Application, 11 December 2012 (public redacted version) ("*Bisengimana* Decision"), paras. 17, 20.

77. *See Galić* Decision, para. 22; *Bisengimana* Decision, paras. 21, 35.

78. Prison Report, p. 2.

79. Prison Report, p. 2.

80. Prison Report, p. 2.

81. Prison Report, p. 3.

82. Prison Report, p. 3.

28. The Prison Report concludes by stating that Kunarac "has not used his time in prison in a fully positive way" and reflects that even "under the corseted conditions of a closed prison Mr. Kunarac finds compliance with rules and application of behavioural values and standards difficult, however over the years a certain calming down is noticeable".[83]

[…]

37. In an interview that took place at Bochum prison on 21 August 2015, Kunarac stated that he did not commit the crimes of which he was convicted and that he was "shocked" at the allegations of rape that were made against him, "since that was not true".[84] During this interview, Kunarac is to have stated that a "woman climbed on top of [him], overpowered him and had vaginal intercourse with him. He just lay there and didn't move […] Actually, he was the one who was raped".[85]

[…]

53. I note that factors such as, for example, the prisoner's behaviour whilst in detention, his or her willingness to assume responsibility for the crimes of which he or she was convicted, his or her mental state, as well as his/her maintenance of meaningful ties with the outside world are taken into account in determining whether a prisoner has shown sufficient signs of rehabilitation.[86]

[…]

55. Based on the above, I am of the view that while Kunarac's behaviour may have shown some improvement, he has not demonstrated sufficient signs of rehabilitation at this stage. Accordingly, I am of the view that this factor weighs against his early release.

[…]

59. I note that an accused person is under no obligation to plead guilty or, in the absence of a plea agreement, to cooperate with the Prosecution.[87] While accepting that Kunarac's cooperation with the Prosecution was a factor taken into account by the Trial Chamber, I place some weight upon it in

83. Prison Report, p. 14.
84. Prison Report, p. 10. *See also* Prison Report, p. 13.
85. Prison Report, p. 11. *See also* Prison Report, p. 13; Psychiatric Report, p. 28.
86. *See*, e.g., *Galić* Decision, para. 108; *Prosecutor v. Emmanuel Rukundo*, Case no. MICT-13-35-ES, Public Redacted Version of the 19 July 2016 Decision of the President on the Early Release of Emmanuel Rukundo, 5 December 2016, paras. 24, 27; *Prosecutor v. Ferdinand Nahimana*, Case no. MICT-13-37-ES.1, Public Redacted Version of the 22 September 2016 Decision of the President on the Early Release of Ferdinand Nahimana, 5 December 2016, paras. 24–26; *Prosecutor v. Ljubomir Borovčanin*, Case no. MICT-15-85-ES.6, Public Redacted Version of the 14 July 2016 Decision of the President on the Early Release of Ljubomir Borovčanin, 2 August 2016 ("*Borovčanin* Decision"), paras. 21–25; *Prosecutor v. Aloys Simba*, Case no. MICT-14-62-ES.1, Decision of the President on the Early Release of Aloys Simba, 2 February 2016 (public redacted version), paras. 21–23.
87. *Galić* Decision, para. 34; *Prosecutor v. Gérard Ntakirutimana*, Case no. MICT-12-17-ES, Public Redacted Version of the 26 March 2014 Decision of the President on the Early Release of Gérard Ntakirutimana, 24 April 2014 ("*Ntakirutimana*"), para. 20.

favour of Kunarac's release, due to the impact that such cooperation has on the efficient administration of justice.[88]

[...]

68. In light of the above, and having carefully considered the factors identified in Rule 151 of the Rules, as well as all the relevant information on record, I am not in favour of granting Kunarac early release at this time. Although Kunarac has served two-thirds of his sentence as of 1 November 2016, the particular circumstances of this case, including the high gravity of the crimes, and the fact that Kunarac has not demonstrated sufficient signs of rehabilitation, weigh against his early release at this stage.

[...]

70. Lastly, the fact that I am not granting Kunarac early release at this time does not preclude him from applying for early release in the future in accordance with paragraph 3 of the Practice Direction, in particular should Kunarac consider that changed circumstances suggest that he has demonstrated sufficient signs of rehabilitation.

71. For the foregoing reasons and pursuant to Article 26 of the Statute, Rules 150 and 151 of the Rules, paragraph 9 of the Practice Direction, and Article 8 of the Enforcement Agreement, I hereby **DENY** Kunarac early release at the present time, and respectfully **REQUEST** [REDACTED].

72. The Registrar is hereby **DIRECTED** to inform the authorities of Germany of this decision as soon as practicable, as prescribed in paragraph 13 of the Practice Direction.

Done in English and French, the English version being authoritative.

Done this 2nd day of February 2017,
At The Hague,
The Netherlands.

Judge Theodor Meron
President

Prosecutor v. Simba

DATE OF DECISION: 7 JANUARY 2019

Before President Meron

EARLY CONDITIONAL RELEASE—AGREED BY SIMBA—ON HUMANITARIAN GROUNDS CAUSED BY THE SEVERE ILLNESS OF SIMBA. INFORMATION ON THE HEALTH CONDITION OF SIMBA HAS BEEN REDACTED TO PROTECT HIS PRIVACY

88. *See Borovčanin* Decision, para. 29; *Bisengimana* Decision, para. 30.

1. I, Theodor Meron, President of the International Residual Mechanism for Criminal Tribunals ("President" and "Mechanism", respectively), am seised of an application for the early release of Mr. Aloys Simba ("Simba"), dated 25 October 2016 and received on 27 October 2016.[89] I note that the Application has been pending for over two years, which is largely due to expert monitoring of Simba's health condition during this period, including the level of access to medical care he is currently receiving, and partially due, *inter alia*, to the delay in receiving the necessary materials from the relevant Beninese authorities and litigation with the Republic of Rwanda ("Rwanda") in relation to the Application.[90] [...]

[...]

3. On 13 December 2005, Trial Chamber I of the International Criminal Tribunal for Rwanda ("Trial Chamber" and "ICTR", respectively) convicted Simba of committing genocide and extermination as a crime against humanity pursuant to Article 6(1) of the Statute of the ICTR, based on his participation in a joint criminal enterprise to kill Tutsi civilians at Murambi Technical School and Kaduha Parish.[91] The Trial Chamber sentenced Simba to a single sentence of 25 years of imprisonment.[92] On 27 November 2007, the Appeals Chamber of the ICTR ("Appeals Chamber") dismissed the appeals of both Simba and the ICTR Office of the Prosecutor ("ICTR Prosecution") in

89. Letter from Mr. Sadikou Ayo Alao, Counsel for Simba, to Judge Theodor Meron, President, dated 25 October 2016 (with annexes) ("Application"), received on 27 October 2016. The English translation was received on 7 November 2016. All references herein are to the English translation of the Application.

90. *See*, e.g., Internal Memorandum from Judge Theodor Meron, President, to Mr. Olufemi Elias, Registrar, dated 24 March 2017; Internal Memorandum from Judge Theodor Meron, President, to Mr. Olufemi Elias, Registrar, dated 15 May 2017; Internal Memorandum from Judge Theodor Meron, President, to Mr. Olufemi Elias, Registrar, dated 2 June 2017; Internal Memorandum from Judge Theodor Meron, President, to Mr. Olufemi Elias, Registrar, dated 28 July 2017; Internal Memorandum from Judge Theodor Meron, President, to Mr. Olufemi Elias, Registrar, dated 20 September 2017; Internal Memorandum from Mr. Olufemi Elias, Registrar, to Judge Theodor Meron, President, dated 27 October 2017; Internal Memorandum from Judge Theodor Meron, President, to Mr. Olufemi Elias, Registrar, dated 29 January 2018; Internal Memorandum from Mr. Olufemi Elias, Registrar, to Judge Theodor Meron, President, dated 28 February 2018 ("28 February Memorandum"); *Prosecutor v. Aloys Simba*, Case no. MICT-14-62-ES.1, Request to the Republic of Rwanda Related to the Application for Early Release from Mr. Aloys Simba, 26 April 2018 ("Request to Rwanda"); *Prosecutor v. Aloys Simba*, Case no. MICT-14-62-ES.1, Omnibus Response of the Republic of Rwanda on the Requests for Early Release from Aloys Simba, Dominique Ntawukulilyayo and Hassan Ngeze and Request for Extension of Time, 11 May 2018 ("Omnibus Response"); *Prosecutor v. Aloys Simba*, Case no. MICT-14-62-ES.1, Supplementary Request for Documents by the Republic of Rwanda in Respect of the Requests for Early Release from Aloys Simba, Dominique Ntawukulilyayo and Hassan Ngeze, 21 May 2018 ("Supplementary Request"); *Prosecutor v. Aloys Simba*, Case no. MICT-14-62-ES.1, Decision on Supplementary Request for Documents by the Republic of Rwanda, 12 July 2018 ("12 July Decision").

91. Trial Judgement, paras. 419, 426–427.

92. Trial Judgement, para. 445.

their entirety, and affirmed Simba's 25-year sentence.[93] Simba was transferred to the Republic of Benin ("Benin") to serve the remainder of his sentence on 27 June 2009.[94]

[...]

18. In coming to my decision on whether it is appropriate to grant Simba early release, I have consulted with the Judge of the sentencing Chamber who is a Judge of the Mechanism, pursuant to paragraph 7 of the Practice Direction and Rule 150 of the Rules. In addition, as I will be leaving the office of President as from 19 January 2019, I proceeded to seek views on the Application from the incoming President, Judge Carmel Agius, who declined to take part in the decision-making process or convey his position on the merits of the Application.

19. I note that in the 23 October Interim Order, I requested Simba to file confirmation as to whether he would be willing to abide by the conditions, as set forth therein, and in line with the recommendations of the Resolution.[95] In this context, I did not solicit submissions from Rwanda or the Prosecution and accordingly I am of the view that only Simba has *prima facie* standing to make submissions in regard to the 23 October Interim Order.

[...]

21. I consider that while the President has broad discretion to consider information he deems relevant pursuant to the Practice Direction,[96] neither the existence of such discretion alone nor its exercise in the particular circumstances of the present case in which submissions were sought from State authorities, provides a sufficiently compelling reason to change settled practice by allowing Rwanda or the Prosecution to make submissions on broader issues related to the Application. Furthermore, neither the Prosecution nor Rwanda has demonstrated the existence of either compelling reasons or special circumstances that would give them standing to make submissions on the 23 October Interim Order. Paragraph 3 of the Practice Direction provides that a convicted person may directly petition the President for pardon, commutation of sentence, or early release, if he or she believes that he or she is eligible.

[...]

32. Moreover, I note that a convicted person having served two-thirds of his or her sentence shall be merely eligible to apply for early release and not entitled to such release, which may only be granted by the President as a matter of discretion, after considering the totality of the circumstances in

93. *Aloys Simba v. The Prosecutor*, Case no. ICTR-01-76-A, Judgement, 27 November 2007 ("Appeal Judgement"), p. 103 (Disposition).
94. *See* Press Release, Nine ICTR Convicts Transferred to Benin, dated 30 June 2009, *available at* http://unictr.irmct.org/en/news/nine-ictr-convicts-transferred-benin.
95. 23 October 2018 Interim Order, pp. 2-3.
96. *See* Paragraph 4(d) of the Practice Direction.

each case.[97] In this regard, I note that persons convicted by the ICTR with equal or higher sentences and with convictions for crimes of graver than or of equal magnitude to those of Simba, including convictions of genocide, have been granted early release upon reaching the two-thirds benchmark.[98]

[…]

34. In this context, as of the date of this Decision, and based on my own calculation, Simba has served two-thirds of his 25-year sentence on 27 July 2018. Accordingly, as of that date, Simba became eligible to apply for early release. I note, however, that the Application was filed prior to that date. Given the foregoing, and taking into account the established jurisprudence of the Mechanism in this regard, I consider that the fact that Simba has already served almost five months more than the two-thirds benchmark of his sentence weighs in favour of his early release.

[…]

40. […] notwithstanding the mitigating circumstances considered by the Trial Chamber in determination of Simba's sentence, I am of the view that the high gravity of Simba's offences weighs against his early release, notwithstanding the fact that he has served two-thirds of his sentence as of 27 July 2018, and has thus served almost five months more than the two-thirds benchmark of his sentence.

[…]

44. Although Simba does not accept responsibility for his crimes, I note that while there is limited case law of the ICTY which provides for remorse as a primary requirement for commutation of sentence specifically,[99] remorse

97. Second *Miletić* Decision, para. 23; Second *Lukić* Decision, para. 17; *Pušić* Decision, para. 35; *Miletić* Decision, para. 21; *Beara* Decision, para. 25; *Prosecutor v. Mladen Naletilić*, Case no. IT-98-34-ES, Public Redacted Version of the 29 November 2012 Decision of the President on Early Release of Mladen Naletilić, 26 March 2013, para. 20; *Bisengimana* Decision, paras. 21, 35.

98. *See*, e.g., *Prosecutor v. Obed Ruzindana*, Case no. MICT-12-10-ES, Decision of the President on the Early Release of Obed Ruzindana, 13 March 2014 (public redacted version) ("*Ruzindana* Decision"); *Prosecutor v. Gérard Ntakirutimana*, Case no. MICT-12-17-ES, Public Redacted Version of the 26 March 2014 Decision of the President on the Early Release of Gérard Ntakirutimana, 24 April 2014 ("*Ntakirutimana* Decision"); *Prosecutor v. Alphonse Nteziryayo*, Case no. MICT-15-90, Decision of the President on the Early Release of Alphonse Nteziryayo, 9 March 2016 (I note that Nteziryayo had completed two-thirds of his sentence before the conclusion of his appeal); *Prosecutor v. Ferdinand Nahimana*, Case no. MICT-13-37-ES.1, Public Redacted Version of the 22 September 2016 Decision of the President on the Early Release of Ferdinand Nahimana, 5 December 2016 ("*Nahimana* Decision").

99. *See*, e.g., *Prosecutor v. Milomir Stakić*, Case no. IT-97-24-ES, Decision of President on Early Release of Milomir Stakić, 18 July 2011 (public), paras. 30–31, 34, 38 (denying sentence remission); *Prosecutor v. Mlado Radić*, Case no. IT-98-30/1-ES, Decision of the President on Commutation of Sentence, 22 June 2007, para. 15. The then-ICTY President denied Mr. Mlado Radić's request for commutation of sentence, based on the fact that he did not consider Radić to have demonstrated clear signs of rehabilitation, stating that "[w]hile his behaviour in detention has generally been good, this is outweighed by his denial of having committed rape and sexual assault".

is not generally considered as such. It is mainly considered as just one of a number of factors that may be taken into account.[100] Indeed numerous requests for early release have been granted where there was no clear indication of remorse[101] and in some instances where the convicted person expressly denied the crimes for which they were convicted.[102] I do not consider that remorse should be treated as a determining factor in this case or in determining early release applications more generally. Rule 151 of the Rules provides that I must take into account "a prisoner's demonstration of rehabilitation"

100. *See*, e.g., *Pušić* Decision, paras. 37, 66 (early release was granted based on signs of rehabilitation and that Pušić had already served two-thirds of his sentence); *Prosecutor v. Dominique Ntawukulilyayo*, Case no. MICT-13-34-ES, Decision of the President on the Early Release of Dominique Ntawukulilyayo, 8 July 2016 (public redacted version) ("*Ntawukulilyayo* Decision"), paras. 25, 37 (early release was denied on the basis that he had not as yet completed two-thirds of his sentence, although he expressed remorse); *Prosecutor v. Drago Nikolić*, Case no. MICT-15-85-ES.4, Public Redacted Version of the 20 July 2015 Decision of the President on the Application for Early Release or Other Relief of Drago Nikolić, 13 October 2015, paras. 24, 44 (early release was denied based on gravity of crimes and that he had not as yet completed two-thirds of his sentence, but he was granted provisional release for a fixed-term period); *Prosecutor v. Vinko Pandurević*, Case no. MICT-15-85-ES.1, Public Redacted Version of the 9 April 2015 Decision of the President on the Early Release of Vinko Pandurević, 10 April 2015, paras. 26, 30 (early release was granted based on signs of rehabilitation, noting his statements of remorse, and that he had completed two-thirds of his sentence); *Prosecutor v. Ranko Češić*, Case no. MICT-14-66-ES, Public Redacted Version of the 30 April 2014 Decision of the President on the Early Release of Ranko Češić, 28 May 2014, paras. 20, 25 (early release was granted based on signs of rehabilitation, including his expressions of remorse, and that he had completed more than two-thirds of his sentence); *Prosecutor v. Momir Nikolić*, Case no. MICT-14-65-ES, Public Redacted Version of the 14 March 2014 Decision on Early Release of Momir Nikolić, 12 October 2015, paras. 22–24, 35 (early release was granted prior to completion of two-thirds of his sentence based on his signs of rehabilitation and his guilty plea at trial, as well as humanitarian reasons); *Prosecutor v. Dragan Zelenović*, Case no. MICT-15-89-ES, Public Redacted Version of the 28 August 2015 Decision of the President on the Early Release of Dragan Zelenović, 15 September 2015 ("*Zelenović* Decision"), paras. 18, 21, 23 (early release was granted taking into account his guilty plea at trial).
101. *See*, e.g., *Prosecutor v. Emmanuel Rukundo*, Case no. MICT-13-35-ES, Public Redacted Version of the 19 July 2016 Decision of the President on the Early Release of Emmanuel Rukundo, 5 December 2016; *Prosecutor v. Nikola Šainović*, Case no. MICT-14-67-ES.1, Public Redacted Version of the 10 July 2015 Decision of the President on the Early Release of Nikola Šainović, 27 August 2015; *Prosecutor v. Innocent Sagahutu*, Case no. MICT-13-43-ES, Public Redacted Version of the 9 May 2014 Decision of the President on the Early Release of Innocent Sagahutu, 13 May 2014; *Ntakirutimana* Decision.
102. *See*, e.g., *Prosecutor v. Ljube Boškoski and Johan Tarčulovski*, Case no. IT-04-82-ES, Decision of President on Early Release of Johan Tarčulovski, 8 April 2013 (public), paras. 20, 23; *Prosecutor v. Haradin Bala*, Case no. IT-03-66-ES, Decision of the President on Early Release of Haradin Bala, 28 June 2012 (confidential), paras. 25–27, 31 (early release was granted despite his attitude towards the deeds for which he was convicted, which were noted to weigh against his application for early release, however, this was ultimately considered as neutral given that Bala had issues adjusting to the conditions of detention in France); *Prosecutor v. Vinko Martinović*, Case no. IT-98-34-ES, Decision of the President on Early Release of Vinko Martinović, 9 January 2012 (public), paras. 21, 26 (maintaining that he was not responsible for acts committed).

in determining whether early release is appropriate, but the applicable legal framework of the Mechanism (following that of its predecessor institutions, the ICTY and the ICTR) does not stipulate that remorse must be present.

45. The prison warden's description of Simba's behaviour while detained in Benin, as well as the Psychiatric Report's portrayal that Simba is social, cooperative, and has family to support him upon release, suggest that Simba is capable of reintegrating into society and is not at risk of reoffending, if he is released. Accordingly, I believe that in context, and having carefully reviewed the information before me, including that Simba does not deny the existence of genocide in Rwanda and condemned the massive slaughter that occurred,[103] I am of the opinion that Simba has demonstrated some signs of rehabilitation, and I am therefore inclined to count this factor as weighing in favour of his early release.[104]

[...]

49. I do not consider that Simba's decision not to join in the strike with other ICTR detainees in 2004, or his compliance with the Trial Chamber during his proceedings, amount to cooperation with the Prosecution. However, I note that an accused person is under no obligation to plead guilty or, in the absence of a plea agreement, to cooperate with the Prosecution.[105] I therefore consider that Simba's lack of cooperation with the Prosecution and ICTR Prosecution is a neutral factor in determining whether or not to grant him early release.

66. Paragraph 4(d) of the Practice Direction provides that the President may obtain any further information considered relevant for his judicial determination of a request for pardon, commutation of sentence, or early release, through the Registry. In this regard, I issued the Request to Rwanda, in which I requested the authorities of Rwanda to file their views on the Application, if any, and I granted Simba the right to reply to Rwanda's submissions, if any.[106]

[...]

67. Rwanda opposes the Application "in the strongest terms" and states that it "must" be rejected,[107] arguing that (i) early release is "unwarranted" because of the gravity of Simba's crimes, and that accordingly Simba should serve his full sentence;[108] (ii) Simba's early release would cause "untold psychological harm" to the survivors and victims;[109] (iii) the rationale for the

103. Trial Judgement, para. 441.
104. *See also* Decision on First Application, paras. 23–34. *Cf. Zelenović* Decision, paras. 18–20.
105. *See Pušić* Decision, para. 42; *Lukić* Decision, para. 49; *Miletić* Decision, para. 34; *Beara* Decision, para. 32; *Ntawukulilyayo* Decision, para. 20.
106. Request to Rwanda, p. 3.
107. *See* Omnibus Response, pp. 2, 17, 19; Rwanda Statement, pp. 308-307 (Registry pagination).
108. *See* Omnibus Response, pp. 2-7; Rwanda Statement, pp. 308, 306, 304 (Registry pagination); Supplemental Brief, pp. 2-4, 12, 17.
109. *See* Omnibus Response, pp. 2, 4-14; Rwanda Statement, pp. 306, 304 (Registry pagination); Supplemental Brief, p. 2. In support of this argument, Rwanda attaches and references

Application is "unsubstantiated", as Simba has not referenced medical reports or opinions that would demonstrate his severe health condition, and that Simba has shown no remorse or taken responsibility for the crimes of which he was convicted;[110] (iv) the Mechanism's legal provisions do not provide for unconditional early release after completion of two-thirds of a convicted-person's sentence,[111] and that the ICTR considered ICTR-convicted persons eligible to apply for early release upon completion of three-fourths of their sentences, which was a "more appropriate" standard to apply;[112] and (v) according to Rule 149 of the Rules, eligibility for early release depends on the law of the enforcement State, that Benin does not provide for unconditional early release, and that the Mechanism therefore does not have the "apparent authority to authorize it".[113] In addition, Rwanda requests a hearing during which the victims' views could be solicited and considered in my determination of the Application.[114]

[...]

70. I have taken note of the information provided by Rwanda, including the statements of, *inter alia*, victims, academic scholars, purported experts, and ICTR Prosecution Counsel. As a preliminary matter, allow me to reiterate that regardless of whether Simba is eligible for early release under the domestic law of Benin, the early release of persons convicted by the ICTR falls exclusively within the discretion of the President, pursuant to Article 26 of the Statute, Rules 150 and 151 of the Rules, and paragraphs 9 and 12 of the Practice Direction.[115] Furthermore, I note Rwanda's submissions related to the gravity of crimes for which Simba was convicted. In this regard, I recall that I have taken into account the very high gravity of the crimes of which

affidavits of victims voicing their opposition to Simba's potential early release, as well as a statement from an alleged mental health expert detailing the "ongoing damage and trauma" that the victims endure to this day, and statements from former counsel from the ICTR Office of the Prosecutor ("ICTR Prosecution Counsel") working on Simba's case. *See* Rwanda Statement, pp. 306-305 (Registry pagination), Annexes A-D, F; Supplemental Brief, pp. 4-9, Annexes F-Q, R. I note that Annexes S-T of the Supplemental Brief relate only to Mr. Hassan Ngeze and not Simba. Accordingly they will not be considered herein.

110. *See* Omnibus Response, pp. 3, 14-16; Rwanda Statement, p. 307 (Registry pagination); Supplemental Brief, pp. 12.

111. *See* Omnibus Response, pp. 3, 16; Rwanda Statement, p. 304 (Registry pagination); Supplemental Brief, p. 2, 12.

112. *See* Rwanda Statement, p. 304 (Registry pagination); Supplemental Brief, pp. 2, 12.

113. *See* Omnibus Response, p. 17; Rwanda Statement, p. 304 (Registry pagination); Supplemental Brief, pp. 10-12; Additional Submissions, pp. 3-4, 474-468 (Registry pagination). In this regard, it further argues that the enforcement State has not notified the Mechanism of Simba's eligibility for early release in accordance with its laws, pursuant to Article 26 of the Statute, and accordingly, Simba cannot be granted early release. *See* Supplemental Brief, pp. 10, 13.

114. *See* Rwanda Statement, p. 306 (Registry pagination); Supplemental Brief, p. 4.

115. *See also* paragraph 11 of the Practice Direction.

Simba was convicted and that I determined that this factor weighs against granting his early release.[116]

[...]

72. [...] I recall that the Statute, the Rules, and the Practice Direction do not provide for the victims' views on an application for early release, commutation of sentence, or pardon by persons convicted by the ICTR, the ICTY, or the Mechanism. I recall, in this regard that the fact that the President has broad discretion to consider information he deems relevant pursuant to paragraph 4(d) of the Practice Direction, does not provide a sufficiently compelling reason to allow victims to make submissions on issues related to the Application, or to compel me to consider them in my judicial determination thereof.[117] In addition, I note that it has been long standing practice at the ICTR, the ICTY and the Mechanism, not to consult with the victims in making a judicial determination of an application for pardon, commutation of sentence, or early release of convicted persons. Nevertheless, I take note of the various statements made by the victims, and other individuals as attached to the Rwanda Statement and Supplemental Brief, and referenced in both documents.[118]

[...]

74. Allow me to reiterate, at this juncture, that it is long-standing practice of the Mechanism that each application for early release is considered on a case-by-case basis and is ultimately a matter of discretion for the President. Following careful consideration of the totality of submissions filed by Rwanda in this regard, and based on the foregoing, I am of the opinion that, notwithstanding the submissions concerning conditional release, in line with the Resolution, Rwanda has otherwise not provided any compelling reasons warranting a departure from the long-standing practice of the Mechanism. I therefore consider the submissions filed by Rwanda to be a neutral factor in determining whether or not to grant Simba early release.

75. In response to the 10 October Interim Order, I note that Simba has provided proof that his family members [REDACTED] are willing and able to accept full responsibility for him should his Application be granted, and that they are financially able to provide Simba with adequate medical care.[119] Although Simba is currently unable to provide proof that [REDACTED] is willing to accept him in its territory should he be granted early release, I note that Simba has initiated the procedure [REDACTED] in this regard and that his family members had an appointment with the relevant authorities

116. *See supra*, para. 40.
117. *See*, e.g., 12 July Decision, para. 17.
118. *See* Rwanda Statement, pp. 306-305 (Registry pagination), Annexes A-D, F; Supplemental Brief, pp. 4-8, Annexes F-Q.
119. Additional Proof, para. 3; Annex 1, Additional Proof, pp. 560-559 (Registry pagination); Annex 3, Additional Proof, p. 546 (Registry pagination); Attestation.

regarding the status of this process, in November 2018.[120] In this regard, Simba indicates that his family members [REDACTED] have made arrangements to accommodate him, and have committed to cater for his daily needs, [REDACTED].[121]

[...]

79. Notwithstanding the high gravity of Simba's crimes, which are somewhat mitigated by the Trial Chamber's reasoning in determining the ultimate sentence imposed on Simba, as upheld by the Appeals Chamber, I note that Simba has completed two-thirds of his sentence on 27 July 2018, having presently served almost five months more than the two-thirds benchmark of his sentence, and just over 16 years of his 25-year sentence. [REDACTED].[122]

80. Furthermore, I note the additional proof that Simba's family [REDACTED] are willing and able to accept full responsibility for him and that they are able to provide him with adequate medical care, should the Application be granted.[123] I also take into account Simba's indicated willingness to sign an undertaking to abide by conditions as set forth in the 23 October Interim Order.[124]

81. In light of the above, and having considered the factors identified in Rule 151 of the Rules, as well as all the relevant information on the record, I am inclined to grant the Application, on the condition that Simba signs and files on the record the document contained in Annex 1 by the date set forth herein. The view that Simba should be granted early release at this time is shared by Judge Liu Daqun, the Judge of the sentencing Chamber who is a Judge of the Mechanism, who was consulted pursuant to Rule 150 of the Rules. Judge Liu has informed me that having considered all the relevant documentation provided in accordance with the Practice Direction, he believes that Simba qualifies for early release. As a member of the Appeals Chamber in Simba's case, Judge Liu states that he understands that although the crimes for which Simba was convicted are very serious, compared with other convicted persons they are not the "most serious".[125] Judge Liu also noted that Simba has already served two-thirds of his sentence and he stated that Simba's health constitutes "an extraordinary circumstance" in this regard.[126]

82. For the foregoing reasons and pursuant to Article 26 of the Statute, Rules 150 and 151 of the Rules, and paragraph 9 of the Practice Direction, I hereby

120. Additional Proof, para. 4; Annex 2, Additional Proof. *See also* Additional Proof, paras. 5–8.

121. Additional Proof, para. 5; Annex 4, Additional Proof. *See also* Attestation.

122. [REDACTED].

123. Psychiatric Report, pp. 5-6 (Registry pagination); Statement; Additional Proof, paras. 3, 5; Annex 1, Additional Proof, pp. 560-559 (Registry pagination); Annex 3, Additional Proof, p. 546 (Registry pagination); Annex 4, Additional Proof; Attestation.

124. Additional Proof, para. 9.

125. *See* Electronic Mail from Judge Liu Daqun, to Mr. Thomas Lay for the attention of Judge Theodor Meron, President, 3 December 2018 ("Judge Liu Email").

126. Judge Liu Email, *supra* note 125.

GRANT Simba early release as soon as practicable, following his filing on the record of the signed document contained in Annex 1 by 14 January 2019.

[...]

Done in English and French, the English version being authoritative.

Done this 7th day of January 2019,
At The Hague,
The Netherlands.

Judge Theodor Meron
President

Prosecutor v. Ćorić

DATE OF DECISION: 15 JANUARY 2019

Before President Meron

EARLY CONDITIONAL RELEASE GRANTED FOLLOWING THE PRESIDENT'S CONSULTATIONS WHICH WERE LIMITED TO JUDGES AND EXCLUDED THE PROSECUTOR AND THE VICTIMS. AT THE MECHANISM, AS AT THE ICTY AND THE ICTR, IT HAS BEEN THE GENERAL PRACTICE THAT THE PRESIDENT WOULD GRANT EARLY RELEASE WHERE, INTER ALIA, TAKING INTO ACCOUNT THE PRESIDENT'S OWN VIEWS AND THOSE OF THE JUDGES CONSULTED PURSUANT TO RULE 150 OF THE RULES, A MAJORITY WAS IN FAVOR OF GRANTING EARLY RELEASE, AND, CONVERSELY, THAT THE PRESIDENT WOULD DENY EARLY RELEASE WHERE, INTER ALIA, TAKING INTO ACCOUNT THE PRESIDENT'S OWN VIEWS AND THOSE OF THE JUDGES CONSULTED PURSUANT TO RULE 150 OF THE RULES, A MAJORITY WAS OPPOSED.

[...]

13. On 4 September 2018, Ćorić, *inter alia*, reiterated his contention that neither the Prosecution nor the victims have standing to make submissions other than as provided for in the Statute, the Rules, or the Practice Direction, in relation to Ćorić's request for early release.[127]

[...]

14. I recall that pursuant to Rule 151 of the Rules and paragraph 4(c) of the Practice Direction, the Prosecution is consulted in relation to an application for early release with respect to the substantial cooperation, if any, provided by the convicted person to the Prosecution during the pre-trial,

127. Response ofValentin Ćorić in Opposition to Prosecution Request to Re-Classify Non-Party "Letters" and Ćorić's "Submissions to Same", 4 September 2018 (confidential) ("Reply"), paras. 6–8.

trial, or appeal phase of his or her case and the significance thereof. I further recall that it has been repeatedly held that, in principle, the Prosecution has no standing to make submissions on sentence enforcement matters under the Statute and the Rules other than when consulted in the context of early release applications.[128]

15. I note that, notwithstanding the long-standing practice at the ICTY and the established jurisprudence of the Mechanism, the Prosecution has failed to explicitly address the question of its standing to make submissions in relation to the Application beyond the consultations contemplated by Rule 151 of the Rules and paragraph 4(c) of the Practice Direction.[129]

16. In addition, I consider that the Prosecution has failed to demonstrate the existence of either compelling reasons or special circumstances that would give the Prosecution standing to make submissions in this case or cogent reasons to depart from the principles set forth in earlier judicial rulings more generally.[130]

[…]

128. *See*, e.g., *Prosecutor v. Radivoje Miletić*, Case no. MICT-15-85-ES.5, Decision of the President on the Early Release of Radivoje Miletić, 23 October 2018 (public redacted version) ("2018 *Miletić* Decision"), para. 18; *Prosecutor v. Berislav Pušić*, Case no. MICT-17-112-ES.1, Public Redacted Version of the 20 April 2018 Decision of the President on the Early Release of Berislav Pušić, 24 April 2018 ("*Pušić* Decision"), para. 24 ("Neither the Rules nor the Practice Direction provides the Prosecution, a party to the proceedings, standing to make submissions on whether an application for early release should be granted, beyond with respect to whether the convicted person has provided substantial cooperation to the Prosecution."); *Prosecutor v. Sreten Lukić*, Case no. MICT-14-67-ES.4, Public Redacted Version of 30 May 2017 Decision of the President on the Early Release of Sreten Lukić, 11 August 2017 ("*Lukić* Decision"), para. 17; *Prosecutor v. Stanislav Galić*, Case no. MICT-14-83-ES, Reasons for the President's Decision to Deny the Early Release of Stanislav Galić and Decision on Prosecution Motion, 23 June 2015, para. 8; *Prosecutor v. Sreten Lukić*, Case no. MICT-14-67-ES.4, Decision on Sreten Lukić's Request for Determination by the President of Time Served, 29 May 2015, p. 2. *See also Prosecutor v. Hazim Delić*, Case no. IT-96-21-ES, Decision on Hazim Delić's Motion for Commutation of Sentence, 24 June 2008 (public redacted), para. 10 ("While I appreciate the information provided, I do not consider it appropriate at this stage of the International Tribunal's history to change its long standing practice by allowing the Prosecution to make submissions on a convicted accused's application for early release. Accordingly, I do not consider that the material placed before me by the Prosecution, which goes beyond that identified in the Practice Direction, should be considered in rendering a determination on the Request of Mr. Delić."), *annexed to Prosecutor v. Hazim Delić*, Case no. IT-96-21-ES, Order Issuing a Public Redacted Version of Decision on Hazim Delić's Motion for Commutation of Sentence, 16 July 2008.

129. *See generally*, Prosecution Submissions.

130. In this context, I am of the view that the mere invocation by the Prosecution of the interests of justice and general principles of law is inadequate to demonstrate that the Prosecution Submission should be taken into account in the context of my judicial determination of the Application. While the Prosecution contends that the Prosecution Submission is well-founded because it relates, inter alia, to the "need to consider the views of affected parties", *see* Response to Motion to Strike, para. 2, the Prosecution does not, and does not purport to, represent such affected parties. *See generally*, Article 14 of the Statute. *Cf.* 2018 *Miletić* Decision, para. 20.

18. Finally, in Judge Agius's communications, respectively dated 26 October 2018 and 13 January 2019, Judge Agius, *inter alia*, is "strongly against" granting the Motion to Strike[131] referencing paragraph 9 of the Practice Direction and Rule 151 of the Rules where the President is "entrusted to take into consideration" the interests of justice, the general principles of law and any other information that he considers relevant, which the President invoked when seeking the opinion of the Government of Rwanda in other early release cases of persons convicted by the ICTR.[132] Judge Agius considers that it is not in the interest of justice to accept information from various entities, including the medical officer at the UNDU, and the Commanding Officer of the UNDU, but not to consider information from the Prosecution, who may have "important information relevant to rehabilitation issues as a matter of principle".[133]

19. I am grateful for Judge Agius's remarks. However, in regard to those remarks concerning consultation with stakeholders, particularly his remarks concerning my decision to consult with the Government of Rwanda in other early release cases of ICTR-convicted persons but not accepting the Prosecution Submissions in this instance, I note that my consultation with Rwanda in that regard derived from Rule 125 of the ICTR Rules of Procedure and Evidence which required "notification" of such matters to the Government of Rwanda. With regard to the consultation or acceptance of the views of the Prosecution, or the victims, in this context, no such antecedent exists. Accordingly, in my view, such consultation with the Prosecution should only be undertaken if approved by formal amendment of the Rules. Consequently, I respectfully disagree with Judge Agius's views in this context. Moreover, I note that Judge Antonetti states that in relation to the Prosecution Submissions, the Prosecution's position is "open to criticism", and that the Prosecution "relentlessly hounds" the convicted persons who are "entitled to be reintegrated into society and not to be permanently excluded".[134] In this regard, I note that neither Judge Antonetti nor Judge Liu has expressed their support for Judge Agius's arguments and as such Judge Agius's views reflect the views of the minority in this context.

20. Based on the foregoing, I hereby grant the Motion to Strike.

131. Internal Memorandum from Judge Carmel Agius, to Judge Theodor Meron, President, dated 26 October 2018 ("Judge Agius's 26 October Memorandum"), p. 3; Electronic Mail from Judge Carmel Agius, to Ms. Daniella Rudy, dated 13 January 2019, for the attention of President Theodor Meron ("Judge Agius's Email").

132. Judge Agius's 26 October Memorandum, p. 3. Judge Agius also states that in the section entitled "Humanitarian Considerations" in the Early Release Memorandum, the President references paragraph 9 of the Practice Direction. *See* Judge Agius's 26 October Memorandum, pp. 3-4.

133. Judge Agius's 26 October Memorandum, p. 3.

134. Judge Antonetti's 19 October Memorandum, paras. 13, 20.

21. On 10 August 2018 and 17 August 2018, respectively, I received two letters from victims in Bosnia and Herzegovina opposing the Application.[135] On 24 August 2018, Ćorić filed a submission, requesting that the President disregard the Victims' Submissions, given that they have no standing to make such submissions in relation to the Application.[136]

22. I recall that the Statute, the Rules, and the Practice Direction do not provide for the victims' views on an application for early release, commutation of sentence, or pardon by persons convicted by the ICTR, the ICTY, or the Mechanism.

23. I recall, in this regard that the fact that the President has broad discretion to consider information he deems relevant pursuant to paragraph 4(d) of the Practice Direction, does not provide a sufficiently compelling reason to allow victims to make submissions on issues related to the Application, or to compel me to consider them in my judicial determination thereof.[137] In addition, I note that it has been long standing practice at the ICTR, the ICTY and the Mechanism, not to consult with the victims in making a judicial determination of an application for pardon, commutation of sentence, or early release of convicted persons. I do not consider that there exist cogent reasons to depart from this long standing practice by granting the victims standing to make submissions or by considering the Victims' Submissions in the present case.

24. In addition, I take note of Judge Agius's comments that he is, *inter alia*, "strongly against" granting the Submission on Non-Party Letters.[138] Specifically, Judge Agius states that I "very unwisely" propose to grant Ćorić's motion to dismiss the Victims' Submissions,[139] explaining that the Practice Direction provides the President with a broad discretion to consider information he deems relevant, which the President invoked when seeking the opinion of the Government of Rwanda in other early release cases of persons convicted by the ICTR.[140] Judge Agius requests that I "seriously reconsider" this proposed course of action.[141]

135. The Request of Victims from Bosnia and Herzegovina to Prevent Preterm Release of Valentin Ćorić from Custody, 17 August 2018; Letter from Armin Kmetaš re Valentin Ćorić possible release, 23 August 2018. The above-mentioned filings will collectively be referred to herein as "Victims' Submissions".

136. Submission of Valentin Ćorić as to Non-Party "Letters", 24 August 2018 ("Submission on Non-Party Letters").

137. *See*, e.g., *Prosecutor v. Dominique Ntawukulilyayo*, Case no. MICT-13-34-ES, *Prosecutor v. Hassan Ngeze*, Case no. MICT-13-37-ES.2; *Prosecutor v. Aloys Simba*, Case no. MICT-14-62-ES.1, Decision on Supplementary Request for Documents by the Republic of Rwanda, 12 July 2018, para. 17.

138. Judge Agius's 26 October Memorandum, p. 3; Judge Agius's Email.

139. Judge Agius's 26 October Memorandum, p. 4. *See also* Submission of Valentin Ćorić as to Non-Party "Letters", 24 August 2018 ("Submission on Non-Party Letters").

140. Judge Agius's 26 October Memorandum, p. 4.

141. Judge Agius's 26 October Memorandum, p. 4.

25. I am grateful for Judge Agius's remarks and at this juncture, I reiterate that my consultation with Rwanda in regard to other early release cases of ICTR-convicted persons derived from Rule 125 of the ICTR Rules of Procedure and Evidence which required "notification" of such matters to the Government of Rwanda. With regard to the consultation or acceptance of the views of the victims, in this context, no such antecedent exists. Accordingly, and as set forth above, in my view, such consultation should only be undertaken if approved by formal amendment of the Rules. Consequently, I respectfully disagree with Judge Agius's views in this context.

26. In addition, I note that although Judge Antonetti recognises that the situation regarding the victims is more "sensitive" as their "misery is never-ending", he states that "our mission goes beyond their trauma and involves bringing back into society those who have transgressed while ensuring that they do not reoffend".[142] In this regard, I note that neither Judge Antonetti nor Judge Liu has expressed their support for Judge Agius's arguments and as such Judge Agius's views reflect the views of the minority in this context.

[…]

47. In these circumstances, and notwithstanding the relatively low sentence imposed on Ćorić by the Trial Chamber based on, *inter alia*, the mitigating circumstances, I am of the view that the high gravity of Ćorić's offences weighs against his early release, notwithstanding the fact that he has served two-thirds of his sentence as of 24 September 2018, and has thus served over three months more than the two-thirds benchmark of his sentence.

52. The overall description of Ćorić's conduct while detained at the UNDU, as well as Dr. Falke's analysis of Ćorić's current mental health, suggest that Ćorić is capable of reintegrating into society should he be released. In this regard, I note the progress made by Ćorić since he was sanctioned for the offences he committed while in detention prior to 2015 and that no further offences have been recorded since then. In addition, I recall that Ćorić voluntarily surrendered to the ICTY very shortly after the indictment filed against him was made public.[143] Having carefully reviewed the information before me, I am of the opinion that Ćorić has demonstrated some signs of rehabilitation, particularly from 2015 onward, and I am therefore inclined to count this factor as weighing in favour of his early release.

54. The Prosecution Memorandum states that Ćorić has never cooperated with the Prosecution during the proceedings against him or others, nor at any point while serving his sentence.[144]

55. I note that the Prosecution does not indicate whether they sought Ćorić's cooperation at any point during his trial or after he was convicted.[145]

142. Judge Antonetti's 19 October Memorandum, para. 15.
143. Trial Judgement, Vol. IV, para. 1371.
144. Prosecution Memorandum, para. 2.
145. *See generally*, Prosecution Memorandum.

I further note that an accused person is under no obligation to plead guilty or, in the absence of a plea agreement, to cooperate with the Prosecution.[146] I therefore consider that Ćorić's lack of cooperation with the Prosecution or the ICTY Prosecution is a neutral factor in determining whether or not to grant him early release.

[...]

59. I recall that while it is within my discretion as President to determine whether to grant early release, this discretion is exercised "in consultation with" certain other Judges, as specified in Rule 150 of the Rules. Such consultations form a meaningful part of the President's assessment of applications for pardon, commutation of sentence, or early release at the Mechanism, as they did for the Presidents at the ICTY and the ICTR. Indeed, at the Mechanism, as at the ICTY and the ICTR, it has been the general practice that the President will grant early release where, *inter alia*, taking into account the President's own views and those of the Judges consulted pursuant to Rule 150 of the Rules, a majority are in favour of granting early release, and, conversely, that the President will deny early release where, *inter alia*, taking into account the President's own views and those of the Judges consulted pursuant to Rule 150 of the Rules, a majority are opposed, absent compelling circumstances requiring otherwise.[147]

60. In this regard, I note that of the remaining Judges of the sentencing Chamber who are also Judges of the Mechanism, Judge Jean-Claude

146. *See* 2018 *Miletić* Decision, para. 40; *Pušić* Decision, para. 42; *Lukić* Decision, para. 49; *Miletić* Decision, para. 34; *Beara* Decision, para. 32; *Prosecutor v. Dominique Ntawukulilyayo*, Case no. MICT-13-34-ES, Decision of the President on the Early Release of Dominique Ntawukulilyayo, 8 July 2016 (public redacted version) ("*Ntawukulilyayo* Decision"), para. 31; *Ntakirutimana* Decision, para. 20.

147. *See*, e.g., 2018 *Miletić* Decision, para. 44; *Miletić* Decision, para. 35; *Pušić* Decision, para. 67; *Beara* Decision, para. 48; *Ntawukulilyayo* Decision, para. 36; *In the case against Florence Hartmann*, Case no. MICT-15-87-ES, Decision of the President on the Early Release of Florence Hartmann, 29 March 2016, para. 29; *Prosecutor v. Drago Nikolić*, Case no. MICT-15-85-ES.4, Public Redacted Version of the 20 July 2015 Decision of the President on the Application for Early Release or Other Relief of Drago Nikolić, 13 October 2015 ("*Nikolić* Decision"), para. 43; Prosecutor v. Dragan *Zelenović*, Case no. MICT-15-89-ES, Public Redacted Version of the 28 August 2015 Decision of the President on the Early Release of Dragan Zelenović, 15 September 2015, para. 22; *Prosecutor v. Youssouf Munyakazi*, Case no. MICT-12-18-ES.1, Public Redacted Version of the 22 July 2015 Decision of the President on the Early Release of Youssouf Munyakazi, 22 July 215, para. 25; *Prosecutor v. Vinko Pandurević*, Case no. MICT-15-85-ES.1, Public Redacted Version of the 9 April 2015 Decision of the President on the Early Release of Vinko Pandurević, 10 April 2015, para. 29; *Prosecutor v. Ranko Češić*, Case no. MICT-14-66-ES, Public Redacted Version of the 30 April 2014 Decision of the President on the Early Release of Ranko Cešić, 28 May 2014, para. 25; *Sagahutu* Decision, para. 23; *Prosecutor v. Darko Mrđa*, Case no. IT-02-59-ES, Decision of President on Early Release of Darko Mrđa, 18 December 2013, para. 31; *Prosecutor v. Mile Mrkšić*, Case no. IT-95-13/1-ES.2, Decision of the President on the Early Release of Mile Mrkšić, 13 December 2013 (public redacted version), paras. 29–30.

Antonetti is of the overall view that the Application should be granted,[148] as it is "fair" to do so, stating that Ćorić was a "pawn like many others" and it is important to show "fairness" when considering his role in the events compared to the greater role of others.[149] Judge Antonetti further states that the convicted persons are "entitled to be reintegrated into society and not to be permanently excluded".[150] Judge Liu is of the view that the Application should be granted based on the analysis provided herein.[151]

[...]

62. Furthermore, Judge Agius states that the information provided in the Behavioural Report, in this regard could be considered as a "measure of rehabilitation" in some countries "with some able persuading", but that for the purposes of "the crimes [...] for which our prisoners have been convicted [...] and always keeping in mind the context of peace and security, this understanding of rehabilitation is bad and [...] a disservice to international criminal [law] and the legacy of the two ad hoc tribunals".[152] In Judge Agius's Email, Judge Agius further states that, "[t]his decision once more continues to understand and apply rehabilitation in a way that I've criticized over the years. It's an understanding of rehabilitation which makes sense at the domestic level and in a context of normal crimes and normal criminals, but it does not make sense in a context of the gravest crimes against humanity, war crimes and genocide. My view is that I'm not satisfied that based on what is contained in part E of the [...] decision there is enough evidence of rehabilitation on the part of Ćorić."[153]

63. Based on the information before me and discussed in further detail above,[154] I respectfully disagree with my Colleague's view that Ćorić has not shown any signs of rehabilitation. The record before me reflects that Ćorić's behaviour following his conviction generally appears to have been positive and focused on rehabilitation.[155] I therefore remain of the view that Ćorić has shown some signs of rehabilitation.

148. Internal Memorandum from Judge Jean-Claude Antonetti, to Judge Theodor Meron, President, dated 19 October 2018 ("Judge Antonetti's 19 October Memorandum"), paras. 12–20. *See also* Electronic Mail from Judge Jean-Claude Antonetti, to Ms. Isabelle Lambert, for the attention of Judge Theodor Meron, President, dated 28 December 2018.

149. Judge Antonetti's 19 October Memorandum, paras. 18–20. *See also* Internal Memorandum from Judge Jean-Claude Antonetti, to Judge Theodor Meron, dated 29 October 2018 ("Judge Antonetti's 29 October Memorandum"), paras. 5, 8–9.

150. Judge Antonetti's 19 October Memorandum, paras. 13, 20.

151. Electronic Mail from Judge Liu Daqun, to Ms. Isabelle Lambert, for the attention of Judge Theodor Meron, President, dated 4 January 2019 ("Judge Liu's Email"); Electronic Mail from Judge Liu Daqun, to Mr. Thomas Lay, for the attention of Judge Theodor Meron, President, dated 29 October 2018

152. Judge Agius's 26 October Memorandum, pp. 2-3.

153. Judge Agius's Email.

154. *See supra*, paras. 49–52.

155. *See supra*, paras. 49–52.

64. Nevertheless, I also supported Judge Agius's views and considered it necessary and appropriate, in the interest of justice, and in accordance with the relevant provisions of the Practice Direction, to obtain additional information from Ćorić in line with Judge Agius's 26 October Memorandum. Accordingly, in the Interim Order, I requested, *inter alia*, that Ćorić file an explanation justifying the statement he made in the Application, that he "has demonstrated by his behavior to date that he has always respected the proceedings of the tribunal" in light of the statement that he made during the Appeal Hearing, as quoted herein.[156]

65. In response, Ćorić submits that he is "surprised and distraught" that his words have been "understood" in a manner which was "neither intended by him nor reflect his intended expression of feelings during the Appeals Hearing".[157] He "regrets" this and "genuinely" "apologizes to the Chamber for his perhaps inartful [*sic*] expression of his words", attributing this to the insufficient time he had to "elaborate with clarity", and his "elevated medical condition" which was exacerbated by the effects of medication he took before the Appeal Hearing, and his emotional and stressed state at that time.[158] Ćorić further clarifies that he "neither intended to accuse nor attack the Court or the Prosecution", that he "very strongly does not share [the] sentiment" of the statement made by Judge Agius,[159] and is "perplexed as to how those words have been cited and attributed" to him.[160] In addition, Ćorić contends that there were errors made in the initial interpretation of his statements that were later rectified and highlights that the corrected transcripts reflected the most important aspects of his remarks.[161] He states that during the Appeal Hearing, he said: "I most sincerely regret each victim, especially civilian victims and their suffering caused by this unfortunate war. If I have done anyone any injustice or caused them misfortune during the war, I sincerely beg their forgiveness".[162] He hopes that these words of "regret, repentance and atonement to victims" are now understood.[163]

66. Based on the foregoing, as well as the record before me, I remain of the view that Ćorić has shown some signs of rehabilitation. While I respect my Colleague's concerns in this respect, I believe that in context, and having carefully reviewed the information before me, including the information contained in Ćorić's Additional Submissions, that Ćorić has demonstrated some signs of rehabilitation. Accordingly, I am inclined to count this factor as weighing in favour of his early release.

156. Interim Order, p. 4. *See also supra*, para. 61.
157. Additional Submissions, p. 3.
158. Additional Submissions, pp. 3–5.
159. Additional Submissions, pp. 3, 5.
160. Additional Submissions, p. 4.
161. Additional Submissions, p. 5.
162. Additional Submissions, p. 5. Ćorić submits that these words were not translated in the courtroom and were omitted from the initial transcripts.
163. Additional Submissions, p. 6.

[...]

73. In Security Council resolution 2422 of 27 June 2018 ("Resolution"),[164] the Security Council of the United Nations noted the views and concerns expressed by some Member States during the Security Council debate on 6 June 2018 about the current approach of the Mechanism to early release of persons convicted by the ICTR, and encouraged the Mechanism to consider an appropriate solution, including by considering putting in place conditions on early release in appropriate cases.[165] In this regard, I have already considered imposing conditions on an early release case concerning an ICTR-convicted person.[166] Accordingly, and while noting my Colleague, Judge Liu's, concerns regarding the imposition of conditions on convicted persons following their release following the long-standing practice at the ICTY and the Mechanism not to do so,[167] I consider that it would be appropriate to also impose conditions on the early release of ICTY-convicted persons, in line with the Resolution, certain past practice of the Mechanism in regard to ICTY-convicted persons,[168] and in this case, in particular, in line with the recommendations of the WISP Report, as well as to harmonise the approach to early release across both branches of the Mechanism, as it falls within my discretion to do.

74. In light of the above, and having considered the factors identified in Rule 151 of the Rules, as well as all the relevant information on the record, I am inclined to grant Ćorić's early release subject to the conditions outlined herein. In reaching this conclusion, I have given due consideration to the long standing practice of granting requests for early release upon completion of two-thirds of a given sentence absent particular circumstances that warrant against it. I consider that Rule 151 of the Rules mandates consistency in terms of treatment of similarly-situated prisoners by the ICTR, the ICTY and the Mechanism and that the proper exercise of my discretion mandates that I follow past practice and jurisprudence. Accordingly, I consider that despite the gravity of the crimes for which he was convicted, the fact that Ćorić has already completed two-thirds of his sentence as of 24 September 2018, and has therefore already served over three months past that date, and the fact that he has demonstrated some signs of rehabilitation, weigh in favour of his early release subject to the conditions outlined herein, as soon as practicable.

75. The view that Ćorić should be granted early release at this time is shared by Judge Antonetti and Judge Liu, a majority of the remaining Judges of the sentencing Chamber who are Judges of the Mechanism, whom I consulted pursuant to

164. United Nations Security Council Resolution 2422, U.N. Doc. S/RES/2422 (2018), 27 June 2018.

165. *See* Resolution, para. 10.

166. *See Prosecutor v. Aloys Simba*, Case no. MICT-14-62-ES.1, Interim Order for Further Submissions, 23 October 2018.

167. *See* Judge Liu's Email.

168. *See*, e.g., *Nikolić* Decision (although this case relates to conditions imposed on provisional release, I consider it relevant in this regard); *Beara* Decision.

Rule 150 of the Rules. In this regard, I also take note of Judge Agius's comments that "he is not prepared to grant early release to Ćorić until the [Prosecution Submissions and Victims' Submissions] have been duly given adequate consideration by the President".[169] As stated above, I stand by my decision to grant the Motion to Strike and the Submission on Non-Party Letters.

76. For the foregoing reasons and pursuant to Article 26 of the Statute, Rules 150 and 151 of the Rules, and paragraph 9 of the Practice Direction, I hereby **GRANT** Ćorić early release based on the conditions outlined herein, effective immediately, or as soon as practicable thereafter.

I further **ORDER** that Ćorić shall abide by the following conditions:

a. Ćorić shall have no contact whatsoever, directly or indirectly try to harm, intimidate or otherwise interfere, with victims or witnesses who testified at his trial or the trial of other ICTY-convicted persons, or otherwise interfere in any way with the proceedings of the Mechanism, or the administration of justice;
b. Ćorić shall conduct himself honourably and peacefully in the community to which he is released, and shall not engage in secret meetings intended to plan civil unrest or engage in any political activities;
c. Ćorić shall not discuss his case, including any aspect of the events in the former Yugoslavia that were the subject of his trial, with anyone, including the media, other than *pro bono* counsel, if any;
d. Ćorić shall not purchase, possess, use or handle any weapons;
e. Ćorić shall not commit any offence;
f. Ćorić shall be held in contempt of court, pursuant to Rule 90 of the Rules, if he violates any of the conditions as stated herein;
g. The decision granting Ćorić conditional release shall be revoked if he violates any of the conditions as stated herein, and his conditional release will be terminated;
h. Ćorić shall be subject to the terms of the conditions as stated herein, unless these conditions are revoked or modified, until the expiration of his sentence; and
i. Any change in the foregoing conditions can only be authorised by the President.

Done in English and French, the English version being authoritative.

Done this 15th day of January 2019,
At The Hague,
The Netherlands.

Judge Theodor Meron
President

169. Judge Agius's Email.

Epilogue

XIII

The Road Ahead

Does International Justice Work?

Invigorate the New Era of Accountability

When the ICTY was established by the U.N. Security Council in 1993, followed by the establishment of the ICTR in 1994, to try individuals accused of war crimes, crimes against humanity and genocide (atrocity crimes),[1] it marked in many ways a turning point in international law and relations. The creation of the ICTY grounded in cries not simply to bring an end to the horrible violence then ongoing in the Balkans but also to answer a groundswell of demands to end impunity for violations of international law more generally.

In the years that followed, the ICTY and the ICTR demonstrated in concrete terms that accountability for international crimes was possible, in full compliance with norms of fairness and due process, and it showed practically how this could be done. During the past 30 years since the ICTY's creation, a number of other international or internationalized courts have been established, including the ICTY's sister court, the ICTR, as well as the ICC. Each one has been proof of an emerging consensus at the international level that—with sufficient political will and resources—principled accountability for violations of international law can be achieved.

During this same period, and after decades of virtual inaction since Nuremberg, an increasing number of authorities in national jurisdictions have undertaken domestic criminal trials of individuals alleged to have committed atrocity crimes. We saw this in the Balkans (thanks in part to the

1. *See* Security Council Resolution 827, U.N. Doc. S/RES/827 (25 May 1993).

Standing Up For Justice. Theodor Meron, Oxford University Press (2021). © Theodor Meron.
DOI: 10.1093/oso/9780198863434.003.0013

completion strategy of the ICTY, which called for that Tribunal to support national judicial systems) as well as in a great many other jurisdictions from Guatemala to Canada and from Sweden and Germany to Rwanda.

Taking stock of all the developments since the establishment of the ICTY, there is much to be heartened by. Indeed, I have referred to these developments as the dawning of a new era of accountability, an era in which accountability is increasingly the expectation, rather than the exception.[2] Notwithstanding the evident positive momentum toward ending impunity for violations of international law, the fact remains that there is a huge gap between the actual accountability efforts undertaken, and the far larger number of individuals who are believed to be responsible for atrocity crimes.

Close the Accountability Gap

Why is this? First, and most simply, we must recall that international justice—by which I refer in this context to the pursuit of accountability for international crimes or atrocities—is still a relatively new field in its current incarnation, and one that, for all that it is built upon well-accepted humanitarian norms and principles of criminal responsibility, reflects fundamental changes in our understanding of international law. It takes time and, perhaps, targeted and sustained advocacy at many levels for any new paradigm to be fully accepted and for international norms to be internalized and implemented effectively.

A second reason for the accountability gap is the matter of basic resources and infrastructure. At present, the great majority of those who are alleged to have perpetrated violations of international law will never be brought to justice at the international level because doing so is simply not practically or financially possible. For accountability to truly take hold, it will necessarily fall to officials in national jurisdictions to take on the lion's share of this work. Yet, even where national jurisdictions may have the will to act, they may, nonetheless, lack the resources and infrastructure to do so. That leaves better resourced third States as well as regional bodies to step in to fill the void—something they have, for the most part, failed to do to date.

2. *See* Theodor Meron, *A New Era of Accountability*, Autumn/Winter INTERSECTIONS MAG. 7 (2016). *See also* Theodor Meron, *Reflections on the Prosecution of War Crimes by International Tribunals*, 100 AM. J. INT'L L. 551, 577–9 (2006).

The third reason for the continuing accountability gap stems from a variety of legal hurdles. Courts—whether international, regional or national—must have jurisdiction over the alleged crimes and over the alleged perpetrator for any investigation or trial to take place. Yet, in many countries, the penal laws do not enable the prosecution of international crimes, or do not do so in a manner in keeping with international law. Traditional jurisdictional limits often circumscribe the degree to which extraterritorial crimes may be considered in national courts. What is more, for there to be true accountability, the accused must be afforded a fair trial, requiring States to ensure the observation of the full panoply of due process rights guaranteed under international law. And even if all of these factors are adequately addressed, prosecutors and courts may be faced with evidentiary deficits or other challenges as they seek to meet the legal standards applicable to atrocity crimes.

The fourth reason for the gap is undoubtedly political. Whether at the national, regional or international level, political decisions often dictate when accountability efforts are undertaken—and when they are not. States may prioritize the self-interest of senior officials and alliances among governments over adherence to other principles; we see this in the Security Council, which has thus far been unwilling or unable to refer the situations in Syria or Myanmar to the ICC, and arguably in the failure of States to execute the ICC arrest warrant for Omar Al-Bashir. We also see this in the absence of referral of situations to the ICC since the referral of Libya in early 2011.

A final reason for the accountability gap may come down to paralysis, or at least, inertia. In effect, international organizations, regional bodies and States can do more to strengthen and support accountability efforts, and simply do not. Importantly, this is not necessarily because they reject the principle of accountability for atrocity crimes. Rather, it would seem to result from competing priorities, a lack of perceived political benefit and perhaps even, when it comes to an individual State, a desire not to overreach or otherwise interfere with events outside that State's borders.

The challenges I have just outlined are not insignificant—but they are also not insurmountable. And surmount them we must. The reason why we insist on accountability for violations of international law is because that is how we defend the law and demonstrate our insistence on respect for the law going forward. If we fail to ensure accountability across the board, we risk undermining the very beneficial effects that the nascent accountability drive that has built since the establishment of the ICTY. We risk telling

States and individuals that the requirements set forth in international law—whether customary or conventional in nature—are not actually binding. That is the last message we should wish to send.

What is more, a failure to close the accountability gap reflects, in essence, acceptance of selectivity in the enforcement of the law. Such selectivity or uneven enforcement of the law is anathema to the rule of law. Those of us who wish to see international law and the rule of law strengthened, and those of us who wish to make every effort to ensure accountability, should not accept such a state of affairs.

After a period of expansion of international and internationalized tribunals and of optimism about the future of international justice, sadly, we have reached a period of retraction and concern. The ICTY, the ICTR and the Special Court for Sierra Leone have completed their work and spawned residual mechanisms. The Kosovo Specialist Chambers began their operations in 2016. The ICC is subject to criticism for both the quantity and the quality of its judicial output as well as leadership and management issues. The political climate in the U.N. Security Council is not conducive to referral of cases to the ICC or to the creation of additional tribunals. Advocates of criminal justice hope that the expert review triggered by the ICC Assembly of State Parties will result in meaningful reforms. But for the moment there is significant disappointment with the performance of the ICC with doubts shared even by strong supporters of the Court.

Criticisms include lacunae in the Rome Statute. The Rome Conference on the establishment of the ICC (1998) was a remarkable success in all that it achieved, and the Rome Statute is groundbreaking. Yet as the experience since then has demonstrated, the legal framework to which the Rome Conference gave rise suffers from various lacunae, some textual and jurisprudential, some in the area of procedure and inadequate implementation, some in policy and management. These difficulties require sensitivity to the ICC's broader context, both political and legal.

Beginning with the Court's docket, criticism has been voiced about lack of consistency and coherence of judicial decisions and the long and indeterminate duration of preliminary examinations. There is an absence of guidance in the Rome Statute regarding the duration of the preliminary examinations.[3] The indeterminacy of preliminary examinations can feed

3. Gabrielle McIntyre, The impact of a lack of consistency and coherence: how key decisions of the International Criminal Court have undermined the Court's legitimacy, *QIL* Zoom-in 67,

perceptions that international politics affect prosecutorial decisions, though there has been a trend toward increasing transparency. There is some dissatisfaction with the selection process for Judges.[4] Of course, States necessarily control the selection of Judges. The creation of an Advisory Committee on Nominations has helped to provide some guidance, but it still falls on States to take the Committee's recommendations seriously. The replacement of one-third of the Court's 18 Judges in each periodic election poses a real challenge to the efficiency and judicial cohesion of the Court.[5]

The critical issue of States' failure to enforce arrest warrants, has been acute.[6] The real political and economic pressure applied by the European Union and the United States that produced the delivery of accused to the ICTY was far more effective than the lack of concerted pressure to enforce ICC arrest warrants.

Finally, there are problems concerning the role of customary international law in filling lacunae in the Rome Statute itself.[7] The Rome Statute departs from the ad hoc Tribunals insofar as it treats statutory provisions as primary authority and customary law as secondary authority. Because the Rome Statute thus gives priority to the Statute over customary law, it has led to limited application of customary law by the Court. There is a danger that the ICC's application of customary law may lead to differences in the application of customary law between the ad hoc Tribunals and the ICC, and, thus, increasing fragmentation of international law. There are problems with head-of-State immunity, particularly those involving non-parties to the Rome Treaty.[8] And there has been criticism of the jurisprudence of the ICC on gender violence.[9]

More positively, apocalyptic visions of unmanageable crises and a mass exodus of African members from the ICC have not transpired, which is in

25 (2020), http://www.qil-qdi.org/. *See also* David Bosco, *Putting the Prosecutor on the Clock? Responding to Variance in the Length of Preliminary Examinations*, 112 AM. J. INT'L L. UNBOUND 158 (2018).

4. Silvia Fernández de Gurmendi, *Judges: Selection, Competence, Collegiality*, 112 AM. J. INT'L L. UNBOUND 163 (2018).
5. *Id.*
6. Adrian Fulford, *Who Arrests Those Accused by the ICC?*, 112 AM. J. INT'L L. UNBOUND 168 (2018).
7. Fausto Pocar, *Transformation of Customary Law Through ICC Practice*, 112 AM. J. INT'L L. UNBOUND 182 (2018).
8. Dapo Akande, *The Immunity of Heads of States of Non-Parties in the Early Years of the ICC*, 112 AM. J. INT'L L. UNBOUND 172 (2018).
9. Gabrielle Louise McIntyre, *The Pace of Progress: Addressing Crimes of Sexual and Gender-Based Violence in the Generation After Rome*, 112 AM. J. INT'L L. UNBOUND 177 (2018).

itself a cause for celebration for all those who hold dear the project of international criminal justice. But it is also undeniable that the Rome project still falls short of the expectations of the participants at the groundbreaking Rome Conference, with their visions of creating the best international criminal court possible: one that is efficient, economic and fair, and one that applies a full panoply of human and due process rights.

Let me set forth a number of concrete steps that can and should be taken to close, or at least reduce, the accountability gap when it comes to atrocity crimes.[10] The suggestions here are far from novel.

Comply with Existing Obligations

The first and simplest step toward closing the accountability gap is for States to meet their existing treaty obligations—and to take steps to encourage other States to do likewise.

This means, as an initial matter, that States must fully transform into domestic law the relevant provisions of the principal conventions setting forth norms of humanitarian and criminal law. Thus, for example, the Genocide Convention of 1948, the Geneva Conventions of 1949 and the U.N. Convention against Torture of 1984, all include obligations on States to enact implementing legislation[11]—obligations that have been satisfied to varying degrees. Of the States that have signed on to the Rome Statute of the International Criminal Court, many have not enacted the complementarity and cooperation legislation necessary to ensure that the Rome Statute takes full effect.[12] Of those States that have enacted such legislation, many have enacted legislation that has been deemed incomplete or flawed.[13] For

10. There are, of course, a great many other prohibitions arising in international law that could be the subject of criminal proceedings, including most notably violations of international human rights guarantees. I will limit my focus to those violations of international law to which I have referred as atrocity crimes. However, I note that many egregious violations of fundamental human rights guarantees may be addressed under the rubric of atrocity crimes. *See* Chapter V.
11. *See* Convention on the Prevention and Punishment of the Crime of Genocide, Art. V, 9 Dec. 1948, 78 UNTS 277; Geneva Convention [No. IV] Relative to the Protection of Civilian Persons in Time of War, Art. 146, 12 Aug. 1949, 6 UST 3516, 75 UNTS 287; Convention against Torture and Other Cruel, Inhuman or Degrading Treatment or Punishment, Arts 2 and 4, 10 Dec. 1984, S. Treaty Doc. No. 100-20 (1988), 1465 UNTS 85.
12. Parliamentarians for Global Action, *Implementing Legislation on the Rome Statute*, http://www.pgaction.org/campaigns/icc/implementing-legislation.html. *See also* Parliamentarians for Global Action, *Parliamentary Kit on the International Criminal Court* (6 Dec. 2016), at 6.
13. *See* Parliamentarians for Global Action, *Implementing Legislation on the Rome Statute* (n. 12).

the complementarity system envisaged by the Rome Statute to work—and for the ICC itself to be able to better conduct its cases—it is essential that those States that have ratified the Rome Statute enact all necessary legislation.[14]

The benefits of enacting legislation addressing atrocity crimes include enabling a State to pursue cases itself and to accept cases transferred from other jurisdictions or entities. But even where States have incorporated the provisions of international law related to atrocity crimes into their domestic legal frameworks, however, there is more to be done. Very few State Parties to the Geneva Conventions have taken steps to abide by their obligations under the provisions of the Conventions that require them to extradite or punish those accused of perpetrating grave breaches of the Conventions. Even in countries that have complied with these provisions, it has simply been a matter of only a handful of cases per jurisdiction.[15] Robust public, political and diplomatic pressure can and should be brought to ensure that States take action to implement their obligations under the principle of *aut dedere, aut judicare*.[16]

The 1948 Genocide Convention likewise envisages that States shall enact legislation to give effect to the Convention and provides that States shall undertake prosecutions in national courts in the territory where the crime took place.[17] In recent years, Bosnia and Herzegovina, Croatia, Kosovo and Rwanda have all tried cases arising under the Convention, as have the Extraordinary Chambers in the Courts of Cambodia. With rare exceptions, other countries where genocide has been alleged to have occurred have been conspicuously inactive, reflecting perhaps the challenge inherent in the Convention's requirement that the crime of genocide must be tried in the courts of the territory where it took place (or in an international court).

When it comes to the Rome Statute, adopting adequate implementing legislation is, of course, essential—but actually giving effect to that legislation and abiding by obligations arising under the Statute, such as by

14. *See generally*, Rome Statute of the International Criminal Court, Preamble, Art. 88, *opened for signature* 17 July 1998, 2187 UNTS 90.
15. *See* Ward Ferdinandusse, *The Prosecution of Grave Breaches in National Courts*, 7 *J.* INT'L CRIM. JUST. 723, 725–9 (2009) (noting that prosecutions for grave breaches of the Geneva Conventions before national courts are scarce).
16. *But see*, e.g., Adam Roberts, *The Laws of War: Problems of Implementation in Contemporary Conflicts*, 6 DUKE J. COMP. & INT'L L. 11 (1995) (discussing vulnerabilities in the *aut dedere, aut judicare* requirements).
17. *See* text accompanying n. 11.

executing arrest warrants and orders to produce evidence, are steps that are no less important. Regrettably, State cooperation with the ICC remains imperfect[18] and is, perhaps, one of the biggest obstacles to that Court's effective conduct of its mandate.

Even for those States that are in full compliance with their treaty obligations, there are steps that they can take when it comes to encouraging other States to meet their own treaty obligations, such as by sharing model legislation, urging States that have adopted legislation that only partially reflects international norms to revise their approach and, whenever appropriate, conditioning aid and other actions on compliance with international obligations.

Encourage and Invigorate Prosecutions under the Principle of Universal Jurisdiction

We need a more robust resort to prosecutions under the principle of universality of jurisdiction.

Typically, States do not prosecute persons alleged to have committed crimes abroad, even if the persons are present in their territories, in the absence of a strong nexus with the accused, the victim or the place in which the crime was committed. There is, however, a compelling case to be made—and, indeed, that has already been made—for making an exception to this traditional practice when it comes to the treatment of atrocity crimes. States may thus adopt and implement legislation enabling them to prosecute individuals alleged to have committed atrocity crimes regardless of the nationality of the accused, the nationality of the victim or the locus where the crime is alleged to have been committed. The exercise of such

18. *See generally*, e.g., ICC, *Report of the Court on Cooperation*, delivered to the Assembly of States Parties, ICC-ASP/16/16 (26 Oct. 2017) (in particular, para. 40, providing that, "[a]t this time, 15 individuals against whom arrest warrants have been issued are still at large"). *See also Prosecutor v. Al Bashir*, Decision on the Non-Compliance by the Republic of Uganda with the Request to Arrest and Surrender Omar Al-Bashir to the Court and Referring the Matter to the United Nations Security Council and the Assembly of State Parties to the Rome Statute, Case no. ICC-02/05-01/09-267 (11 July 2016); *Prosecutor v. Al Bashir*, Decision on the Non-Compliance by the Republic of Djibouti with the Request to Arrest and Surrender Omar Al-Bashir to the Court and Referring the Matter to the United Nations Security Council and the Assembly of State Parties to the Rome Statute, Case no. ICC-02/05-01/09-266 (11 July 2016).

jurisdiction in the absence of the more traditional jurisdictional requirements is referred to as universal jurisdiction.

The rationales underlying the adoption and deployment of universal jurisdiction vary. By some accounts, universal jurisdiction reflects the egregiousness of the violations of international law and the idea that such crimes affect the interests of all States (crimes *erga omnes*).[19] By other accounts, universal jurisdiction is based on the principle that atrocity crimes harm the international order itself and that individual States have a right to act as a result of this harm.[20] Whatever the reasoning, it is clear that by adopting and implementing universal jurisdiction, States could greatly contribute to reducing the accountability gap.

Estimates vary as to how many States have adopted universal jurisdiction over atrocity crimes depending on the interpretation of existing legislation and variations between the definitions used in certain national legislation and the definitions found in international law.[21] By some accounts, universal jurisdiction has been increasingly and effectively deployed in recent years—including by States such as France, Germany, the United Kingdom and Argentina—that may set a salutary example for other States.[22] Nevertheless, the use of universal jurisdiction continues to raise questions and concerns.

For example, is the invocation of universal jurisdiction permissible where genocidal acts are alleged to have taken place in a State other than where the alleged offender is present? If, as the text of the Genocide Convention suggests, genocide may only be prosecuted in the territory in which it occurred or by an international tribunal,[23] the accountability gap when it comes to that crime might never close. Importantly, however, the prohibition of genocide has become a norm of *jus cogens*, allowing—and perhaps

19. *See*, e.g., Christopher Keith Hall, *Universal Jurisdiction: New Uses for an Old Tool*, *in* JUSTICE FOR CRIMES AGAINST HUMANITY 47, 55–6 (Mark Lattimer & Philippe Sands eds, 2003).
20. *See*, e.g., International Justice Resource Center, *Universal Jurisdiction*, *at* http://www.ijrcenter.org/cases-before-national-courts/domestic-exercise-of-universal-jurisdiction/#gsc.tab=0.
21. *Compare*, e.g., Amnesty International, *Universal Jurisdiction: Strengthening this Essential Tool of International Justice*, IOR 53/020/2012 (Oct. 2012), at 23 *with* Ryan Goodman, *Counting Universal Jurisdiction States: What's Wrong with Amnesty International's Numbers [Updated]*, *at* https://www.justsecurity.org/4581/amnesty-international-universal-jurisdiction-preliminary-survey-legislation-world/.
22. In the course of 2017, 126 suspects were investigated or prosecuted for atrocity crimes under the principle of universal jurisdiction. *See* Trial International, *Universal Jurisdiction Annual Review 2018*, at 5, Federation for Human Rights *at* https://www.fidh.org/en/issues/international-justice/make-way-for-justice-4-international-momentum-towards-accountability.
23. Convention on the Prevention and Punishment of the Crime of Genocide, Art. VI, 9 Dec. 1948, 78 UNTS 277.

requiring—every State to take steps to prosecute accused persons present in their territory.[24]

A strong argument can also be made to the effect that customary law recognizes a norm giving a third State a right—and perhaps an obligation—to prosecute the crime of genocide even when the accused is not present in the prosecuting (third) State's territory. The counter-argument is that by prosecuting persons not in the territory of the prosecuting State, and thus resorting to trials *in absentia*, the door is open to politically motivated prosecutions as well as to prosecutions lacking in guarantees of fairness or adequate evidence. While *in absentia* trials are anathema to principles of criminal justice in common law countries, they are generally recognized in civil law jurisdictions.[25] Should they be a priori excluded in genocide cases where a nexus between the crime and the prosecuting State is lacking but guarantees against abusive prosecutions and due process are guaranteed?

These obstacles and concerns are not insignificant. Notwithstanding these challenges, I remain somewhat encouraged by the growing number as well as the geographic spread of countries prosecuting atrocity crimes under the principle of universality of jurisdiction, as the use of this tool is essential if the accountability gap is to be closed. States should also review existing extradition treaties as well as immigration laws and procedures, with a view to ensuring that these States do not become—or do not remain—a safe haven for those alleged to have committed atrocities elsewhere.

Review and Revise Laws and Practices to Ensure Due Process, Fair Trials and Judicial Independence

Conducting a trial of an individual accused of committing war crimes, crimes against humanity or genocide in a domestic court may appear to be an important step forward in the fight to end impunity. However, such a step is meaningless—if not outright problematic—if the trial and all related activities (from investigation through final appeal and sentence enforcement, where applicable) are not conducted in accordance with fundamental

24. *See*, e.g., *Case Concerning Armed Activities on the Territory of the Congo (New Application: 2002) (Democratic Republic of the Congo v. Rwanda)*, Jurisdiction and Admissibility, 2006 ICJ Rep. 32, at para. 64.
25. Ryan Rabinovitch, *Universal Jurisdiction in Absentia*, 28 FORDHAM INT'L L.J. 500, 526 (2004).

principles of fairness and internationally recognized human rights guarantees. Indeed, atrocity crime trials conducted with manifest disregard for—or simply inadequate attention to—fair trial requirements and trials conducted in violation of basic and commonly recognized principles of criminal law (such as in *dubio pro reo*) may do far more damage than good when it comes to broader accountability aims.

So what is needed when it comes to ensuring what I refer to as *principled* accountability? International and regional human rights instruments and the authoritative interpretations of these instruments—such as by the competent treaty bodies—on matters of due process and conditions of detention offer vital guidance, as does the large corpus of jurisprudence addressing fair trial guarantees at international tribunals such as the ICTY and ICTR. Complementarity analyses under the Rome Statute and the jurisprudence of the ad hoc Tribunals in their consideration of what cases may be transferred for trial to national jurisdictions can also be informative,[26] as can assessments conducted by national courts themselves when considering matters such as extradition to a foreign jurisdiction.[27]

Whatever the reference point, it is important to recognize that some variation will be inevitable across jurisdictions. For example, countries following the civil law tradition will, in many instances, address the investigative process differently than their common law counterparts. Such differences, however, are not problematic so long as basic defense rights are respected and protected, including when it comes to the ability of the defense to prepare effectively for trial.

In other national systems, witness protection and support offices will need to be put in place or, if in place, provided with sufficient resources

26. *See*, e.g., *Prosecutor v. Stanković*, Decision on Referral of Case under Rule 11*bis*, Case no. IT-96-23/2-PT (17 May 2005); *Prosecutor v. Mejakić et al.*, Decision on Joint Defence Appeal against Decision on Referral under Rule 11*bis*, Case no. IT-02-65AR11*bis*.1 (7 Apr. 2006); *Prosecutor v. Munyakazi*, Decision on the Prosecution's Appeal against Decision on Referral under Rule 11*bis*, Case no. ICTR-97-36-R11*bis* (8 Oct. 2008).

27. *See*, e.g., Proposals for extradition of Sylvère Ahorugeze to the Republic of Rwanda, Sahögsta Domstolen [Supreme Court of Sweden] (26 May 2009) (Swed.) (ruling in favor of extraditing Ahorugeze to Rwanda); *R v. Bow St. Metropolitan Stipendiary Magistrate, ex parte Pinochet Ugarte (No. 1)* [1998] UKHL 41, [2000] 1 AC 61 (holding that Pinochet was not entitled to immunity from criminal proceedings and could be extradited in a decision subsequently set aside on the basis of an undisclosed conflict of interest); *Government of Rwanda v. Nteziryayo et al.* [2017] EWHC 1912 (Admin) (rejecting extradition based on considerations of fair trials). *See also Questions relating to the Obligation to Prosecute or Extradite (Belgium v. Senegal)*, Judgment, 2012 ICJ Rep. 422 (20 July).

to enable meaningful services. In still other national systems, it may prove necessary to revisit basic provisions related to judicial selection and, as applicable, reappointment or reelection criteria and processes so as to ensure judicial independence. Without the protection of Judges from political or other interference and without adherence by Judges to the highest judicial ethics and judicial independence, principled accountability is not possible, in either national or international jurisdictions,[28] just as it is not possible without robust adherence to other fundamental fairness guarantees.

Invest in Justice Infrastructure

It is undeniable that, for many States, taking steps to ensure accountability for atrocity crimes such as those outlined earlier may remain difficult, if not impossible, in the absence of significant investments in judicial, prosecutorial and investigative infrastructures. This is particularly true for developing countries and countries that have recently emerged from armed conflict, these latter being the very countries where atrocity crimes are most likely to have been committed.

While closing the accountability gap depends on the involvement of individual States—as I believe that it does—this does not mean that each State can or must act in a vacuum. Rather, it is incumbent upon all States and key actors and influencers to do all that we can to facilitate that engagement in each State. This may include more developed and wealthier nations participating directly in strengthening the national justice infrastructure in less fortunate States through investment, aid, capacity-building training and other means. Such other means may include the creation of specialized judicial chambers and prosecutorial offices composed of national as well as international Judges and staff,[29] practices by which capacity building and

28. *See generally*, Theodor Meron, *Judicial Independence and Judicial Impartiality*, *in* THE MAKING OF INTERNATIONAL CRIMINAL JUSTICE: A VIEW FROM THE BENCH. SELECTED SPEECHES 255 (Theodor Meron, 2011); Theodor Meron, *Decision Making in International Criminal Tribunals*, *in* THE MAKING OF INTERNATIONAL CRIMINAL JUSTICE: A VIEW FROM THE BENCH. SELECTED SPEECHES 278 (Theodor Meron, 2011); Theodor Meron, *Justice and Leadership Dilemmas in Shakespeare*, *in* THE MAKING OF INTERNATIONAL CRIMINAL JUSTICE: A VIEW FROM THE BENCH. SELECTED SPEECHES 286 (Theodor Meron, 2011).

29. *See*, e.g., Regulation 64 Panels in the Courts of Kosovo, UN Interim Admin. Mission in Kosovo, Reg. no. 2000/64 on Assignment of International Judges/Prosecutors and/or Change of Venue, UNMIK/REG/2000/64 (15 Dec. 2000); Special Panels for Serious Crimes in East Timor, U.N. Transitional Admin. in East Timor, Reg. no. 2000/11 on the Organization

norm accretion may be accelerated through practical engagements and collaboration. Reinforcing national capacity in these ways will go a long way toward helping States to improve their capability to try atrocity crime cases while, at the same time, paying dividends for the judicial, prosecutorial and investigative infrastructures—and society and the rule of law—more generally.

Consider and Support Regional Accountability Initiatives

When the African Union adopted the Malabo Protocol some commentators expressed concern that this effort to provide for a regional court to address, inter alia, atrocity crimes undermined the aims of the ICC.[30] I disagree. The establishment of regional bodies with jurisdiction to try cases related to atrocity crimes is, in my view, a welcome innovation that complements rather than detracts from the aims underlying the Rome system, provided that such regional bodies ensure due process and adhere to the tenets of international law.[31]

Regional courts endowed with jurisdiction over atrocity crimes do not simply multiply the number of fora in which accountability can function. They also, and importantly, allow for judicial processes to be more tailored to those applicable in the region itself (so long as such tailoring conforms to international norms), to be conducted in languages more

of Courts in East Timor, UNTAET/REG/2000/11 (6 Mar. 2000); War Crimes Chamber for Bosnia and Herzegovina, Agreement between the High Representative for Bosnia and Herzegovina and Bosnia and Herzegovina on the Establishment of the Registry for Section I for War Crimes and Section II for Organised Crime, Economic Crime and Corruption of the Criminal and Appellate Divisions of the Court of Bosnia and Herzegovina and the Special Department for War Crimes and the Special Department for Organised Crime, Economic Crime and Corruption of the Prosecutor's Office of Bosnia and Herzegovina, Official Gazette of BiH, No. 12/04, 1 Dec. 2004.

30. *See*, e.g., Chacha Bhoke Murungu, *Towards a Criminal Chamber in the African Court of Justice and Human Rights*, 9 J. INT'L CRIM. JUST. 1067 (2011); Max du Plessis, *Implications of the AU Decision to Give the African Court Jurisdiction Over International Crimes*, 235 INST. FOR SEC. STUD. 1 (2012); Ademola Abass, *The Proposed International Criminal Jurisdiction of the African Court: Some Problematical Aspects*, 60 NETH. INT'L L. REV. 27 (2013); Amnesty International, MALABO PROTOCOL. LEGAL AND INSTITUTIONAL IMPLICATIONS OF THE MERGED AND EXPANDED AFRICAN COURT (2016), at 35.

31. While supporting regional accountability initiatives in general, I do not support those that, like the Malabo Protocol, recognize head of State immunity.

relevant to the region and to take place in locations closer to the communities affected by the alleged crimes.[32] At the same time, regional courts offer the beneficial possibility of justice at some remove from the affected communities—allowing greater perceived impartiality in the adjudication of the often highly politicized cases concerned—and they permit the pooling of resources among wealthy and less wealthy States to ensure a consistent approach is applied in all such cases. All in all, I believe that initiatives aimed at enhancing accountability at the regional level are to be welcomed, and actively encouraged.

To date, the unratified Malabo Protocol represents a unique example of measures taken to endow an existing regional human rights court with jurisdiction over atrocity crimes. However, there is no reason that, following Malabo, consideration cannot be given to establishing regional criminal courts elsewhere in the world or adding criminal chambers to existing regional human rights courts. To be sure, the resources necessary to adequately support criminal trials are considerable, and for human rights courts designed to hear cases after the exhaustion of national remedies, serving as a venue for first instance (and subsequent) proceedings may represent a dramatic and perhaps even difficult shift. On the other hand, as the examples of the ad hoc Tribunals and other courts established at the international level suggest, creating new courts from the ground up can be an expensive and time-consuming proposition in its own right, and there is something to be said for simply expanding the mandate of an existing, proven and respected judicial institution.

Develop Innovative Solutions to Foster Greater Accountability—and Revisit or Recycle Past Approaches Where Appropriate

As the preceding discussion suggests, if the accountability gap is to be closed, we must not shy away from exploring and, indeed, pioneering new approaches.

32. *See*, e.g., Miles Jackson, *Regional Complementarity: The Rome Statute and Public International Law*, 14 J. Int'l Crim. Just. 1061 (2016).

The U.N. General Assembly did just this when it established the International, Impartial and Independent Mechanism (IIIM) for Syria, the U.N. Investigative Team for Accountability of Islamic State (UNITAD) in Iraq and the Independent Investigative Mechanism for Myanmar (IIMM), in the face of political gridlock in the U.N. Security Council. Notably, the IIIM is not a court but an agency mandated to collect, preserve and analyze evidence of violations of international law with the aim of ultimately sharing that information with jurisdictions carrying out prosecutions for international crimes committed in Syria. This work is intended to ease the investigative burden on national prosecutors when it comes to case preparation and to preserve evidence for cases that may not be tried for years, if not decades.[33] Unlike the Commission of Inquiry established by the Human Rights Council to investigate violations of human rights in Syria, the IIIM is expected to collect evidence pertaining not simply to violations of international law but also to individual criminal responsibility and is not required to report publicly on all aspects of its work, both significant distinctions in view of the IIIM's mandate.[34]

Importantly, steps to gather, preserve and present evidence for further action need not be taken only by States or intergovernmental organizations. To the contrary, examples abound of civil society organizations operating either nationally or internationally to collect, preserve and present for prosecution case files pertaining to violations of international law.[35] These organizations are actively seeking to collect, preserve and present evidence in a manner that will ensure its usability in future court proceedings. Indeed, active engagement by civil society organizations operating within a State

33. *See generally*, G.A. Res. 71/248, U.N. Doc. A/71/248 (11 Jan. 2017), at para. 4.

34. *See* Report of the International, Impartial and Independent Mechanism to Assist in the Investigation and Prosecution of Persons Responsible for the Most Serious Crimes under International Law Committed in the Syrian Arab Republic since March 2011, U.N. Doc. A/72/764 (28 Feb. 2018), at paras. 4–12.

35. For instance, in relation to the Rohingya crisis, the ICC Prosecutor relied on evidence collected by Fortify Rights and Human Rights Watch. *See* Prosecution's Request for a Ruling on Jurisdiction under Article 19(3) of the Statute, Case no. ICC-RoC46(3)-01/18-1 (9 Apr. 2018), at para. 7. The use of evidence collected by NGOs, however, may pose certain difficulties. *See*, e.g., Human Rights First, The Role of Human Rights NGOs in Relation to ICC Investigations (Sept. 2004), at 3 ("[m]ost NGOs do not employ trained criminal investigators. There may be differences in the mandates and policies of NGOs and the ICC. NGOs also may have particular concerns regarding the protection of confidential relationships or sources. Human rights NGOs also need to be aware that their actions could actually harm an ICC investigation. By gathering multiple Statements from a witness, NGOs may create difficulties for that witness when testifying in ICC proceedings. In addition, untrained collection of physical or forensic evidence could limit its value before the Court").

where crimes are alleged to have occurred may be the key to enabling prosecutions well beyond that State's borders by means of coalitions formed with other civil society actors, as the *Hissène Habré* case demonstrates. Over time, such efforts can even yield important accountability dividends in the State where the underlying crimes occurred, as that case likewise demonstrates.[36]

The *Habré* case was tried before an internationalized chamber in the courts of Senegal, part of a growing trend to establish special chambers within national courts mandated to try specific types of cases, either with or without international personnel and Judges. From Cambodia to Kosovo and from Senegal to Guatemala and, most recently, Colombia, this practice of establishing special chambers to adjudicate politically sensitive and international crimes can serve as an important new model for how to address atrocity crimes within national courts provided such work is undertaken with appropriate safeguards and the creation of special chambers is intended to facilitate principled accountability (rather than to limit the procedural guarantees or transparency of the proceedings),

Those committed to pursuing every avenue to ensure greater accountability for atrocity crimes would do well to consider whether and in what circumstances national military courts may also play an important role in that regard. Although their trials often receive less attention, military courts in a number of States already can try, and have tried, cases involving atrocity crimes, whether they are characterized as such or under more ordinary rubrics.[37] While questions as to who should come within the jurisdiction of such courts and how to enhance their due process still need to be considered,[38] we should not a priori rule out the potential of these fora when it comes to expanding accountability efforts at the national level. Finally,

36. *See generally*, Reed Brody, *Bringing a Dictator to Justice: The Case of Hissène Habré*, 13 J. Int'l Crim. Just. 209 (2015). A key element in the prosecution against Habré was the collection of evidence by civil society actors, such as Human Right Watch and the Fédération Internationale des Ligues des Droits de l'Homme. *See* Reed Brody, *Victims Bring a Dictator to Justice: Updated Edition After the Final April 2017 Verdict*, 14 (2d ed. 2017).

37. *See*, e.g., Niyonteze, *Tribunal Militaire de Cassation [Military Court of Cassation]*, 27 April 2001 (Switz.), *at* https://casebook.icrc.org/case-study/switzerland-niyonteze-case; *R v. Payne*, General Court Martial, 30 April 2007 (U.K.); Joshua Kelly, *Re Civilian Casualty Court Martial: Prosecuting Breaches of International Humanitarian Law Using the Australian Military Justice System*, 37 Melb. U.L. Rev. 342 (2013).

38. The Military Commissions of Guantánamo have been much-criticized for their adherence to fair trial standards. Despite some improvements to their legal framework, objections still remain as to whether these Commissions comply with standards of due process and international law. *See generally*, e.g., David J. R. Frakt, *Applying International Fair Trial Standards to the Military Commissions of Guantanamo*, 37 S. Ill. U. L.J. 551 (2013).

we cannot preclude the possibility that, in the future, the creation of a new, ad hoc international criminal tribunal will be deemed necessary to address crimes alleged to have occurred in a given armed conflict. I must underscore that such a move does not detract in any way from the role or importance of the ICC. As should be clear by now, achieving accountability on a global scale necessarily entails a multifaceted, multidimensional approach, and where such an ad hoc Tribunal is needed, it should receive all due support and cooperation.

Likewise, we should not ignore the potential of more traditional approaches under international law, such as the preparation and promulgation of new treaties or other such legal instruments. In this regard, I note in particular the significant work of the International Law Commission preparing a Convention on the Prevention and Punishment of Crimes Against Humanity, an endeavor that advances accountability efforts as a general matter but also reflects a welcome focus on issues such as enhancing interstate cooperation.[39]

Foreswear Amnesties and Targeted Immunities

Speaking of past practice, it bears noting that it has not been uncommon for peace accords concluded over the course of the last decades to include provisions providing for amnesties for those engaged in the conflict.[40] Such

39. *See generally*, Sean D. Murphy, *Crimes against Humanity and other Topics: The Sixty-Ninth Session of the International Law Commission*, 111 AM. J. INT'L L. 970 (2018). The International Law Commission has decided to transmit the draft Articles to governments and international organizations, inter alia, for comments. *See id.* at 978.

40. *See*, e.g., Peace Agreement between the Government of Sierra Leone and the Revolutionary United Front of Sierra Leone, Art. IX, 7 July 1999, U.N. Doc. S/1999/777 (Lomé Agreement) (signed with a caveat by the U.N. Special Representative in Sierra Leone that the U.N. would not recognize amnesty for atrocity crimes, *see* Secretary-General, *Seventh Report of the Secretary-General on the United Nations Observer Mission in Sierra Leone*, U.N. Doc. S/1999/836 (30 July 1999), at para. 7). I note that amnesties are called for under Art. 6(5) of Additional Protocol II to the Geneva Conventions, which recommends granting the broadest possible amnesty to persons who have participated in the armed conflict or were deprived of liberty for reasons related to the armed conflict. However, that provision, as interpreted by the ICRC, is understood not to apply to amnesties for atrocity crimes. *See* Letter from Toni Pfanner, Chief of the Legal Division of the International Committee of the Red Cross, Central Office in Geneva, to Douglass Cassel, Executive Director of the International Institute of Human Rights and the Jeanne and Joseph Sullivan Program for Human Rights in the Americas, University of DePaul, School of Law (15 Apr. 1997) (filed with the addressee), *quoted in* Douglass Cassel, *Lessons from the Americas: Guidelines for International Response to Amnesties for Atrocities*, 59 LAW & CONTEMP. PROBS 197, 218 (1996).

amnesties, and, in particular, their validity when it comes to violations of international law (especially with regard to *jus cogens* norms), remain the subject of considerable debate.[41] While I will not seek to dwell on that debate here, I nonetheless underscore my view that any peace accord that provides for broad amnesties for those who may have committed atrocity crimes undercuts overall accountability efforts. All those involved in peace negotiations should do their utmost to find a way to attain peaceful resolution through means other than amnesties.

Efforts to insulate senior political or military leaders from accountability efforts are equally, if not more, problematic. While recognizing a number of promising ideas stated in the Malabo Protocol, I am, thus, concerned about the Protocol's Article 46A(*bis*), which states that no charges may be brought before the criminal jurisdiction of the African Court of Justice and Human Rights against any serving AU head of State or government, or anybody acting or entitled to act in such capacity, or other senior State officials based on their functions, during their tenure. This provision would take international criminal law all the way back to before Nuremberg.[42] I recognize, of course, that the Protocol has not entered into force, that it is still far from obtaining the required number of ratifications and that it limits the immunities to the period in which the officials concerned are still serving in their official functions.[43] Nonetheless, it sets a troubling precedent, as does the saga of Omar Al-Bashir.[44]

The rule of law demands equality of all individuals before the law. The more that this principle is made subject to exceptions—and the more that

41. *See*, e.g., Office of the U.N. High Commissioner for Human Rights, *Rule of Law Tools for Post-Conflict States*, HR/PUB/09/1 (2009), at 16. *See also* Murphy (n. 39), at 977.
42. *See* Agreement for the Prosecution and Punishment of the Major War Criminals of the European Axis, Art. 1, 8 Aug. 1945, 59 Stat. 1544, 82 UNTS 279, 282. *See also* Geoffrey Robertson, *Ending Impunity: Criminal Law Can Put Tyrants on Trial*, 38 CORNELL INT'L L.J. 649 (2005).
43. *See* Protocol on Amendments to the Protocol on the Statute of the African Court of Justice and Human Rights, Arts 11(1), 46A(*bis*), 27 June 2014; List of Countries which Have Signed, Ratified/Acceded to the Protocol on Amendments to the Protocol on the Statute of the African Court of Justice and Human Rights (8 Feb. 2018), *at* https://au.int/en/treaties/protocol-amendments-protocol-statute-african-court-justice-and-human-rights. *See also* Gerhard Werle & Moritz Vormbaum, *Creating an African Criminal Court*, *in* THE AFRICAN CRIMINAL COURT. A COMMENTARY ON THE MALABO PROTOCOL 3, 13 (Gerhard Werle & Moritz Vormbaum eds, 2017).
44. *See*, e.g., the decisions on non-compliance in *Prosecutor v. Al Bashir* (n. 18).

such exceptions benefit those in positions of privilege or power—the weaker the rule of law and the overall imperative to end impunity become.[45]

Sustain Support for and Cooperation with Existing Accountability Mechanisms

As I have made clear earlier, the success of efforts to close the accountability gap turns, in a very large part, on the active engagement by States in accountability efforts and by actions to be taken at the national and at times regional levels. But that should not be read to suggest that international courts are now, or will become in the future, irrelevant to broader accountability goals. It would be an extraordinary and welcome day were we to reach a moment in time when the ICC is no longer needed. But until that day comes, it will remain essential that States continue to lend their support to those international and internationalized courts that are often the most visible representatives of the fight to end impunity for atrocity crimes and to the ICC in particular.

This must amount to more than simple diplomatic verbiage. Support entails practical and tangible cooperation (such as by executing arrest warrants, facilitating access to witnesses and evidence and enforcing sentences in national prisons) and active engagement (such as by encouraging cooperation by fellow States and serving as prominent advocates and allies for the courts in diplomatic and political fora). It is also necessary to ensure adequate financial backing (without which courts will struggle to carry out their basic mandates), and, in the context of the ICC, to adopt and fully

45. I note with satisfaction that Draft Article 7 provisionally adopted by the International Law Commission in 2017 under the topic "Immunity of State Officials from Foreign Criminal Jurisdiction" lists atrocity crimes in respect of which immunity *ratione materiae* shall not apply. ILC, *Report on the Work of its Sixty-Ninth Session*, U.N. Doc. A/72/10 (11 Sept. 2017), at 176. In its commentary on Draft Article 7, the Commission notes that "there has been a discernible trend towards limiting the applicability of immunity from jurisdiction *ratione materiae* in respect of certain behavior that constitute crimes under international law." *Id.* at 178–9, *quoted in* Curtis A. Bradley, *Introduction to the Symposium on the Present and Future of the Foreign Official Immunity*, 112 AM. J. INT'L L. UNBOUND 1, 2 (2018). Draft Article 7 has nonetheless been the subject of some controversy. *See generally*, *Symposium on the Present and Future of Foreign Official Immunity*, 112 AM. J. INT'L L. UNBOUND 1 (2018). I am concerned about the pardons granted by President Trump to U.S. military personnel, *see* Jean Galbraith, *Issuing Several Pardons, President Trump Intervenes in Proceedings of U.S. Troops Charged or Convicted of Acts Amounting to War Crimes*, 114 AM. J. INT'L L. 307 (2020).

implement all legislation required under the Rome Statute or necessary to enable complementarity. Support also entails taking affirmative steps to reinforce respect for these courts and their work, including for their rulings, their officers and the integrity with which the courts and their officers carry out mandated functions. If the ability of these courts to operate as courts of law, responsible for upholding the rule of law, is allowed to be brought into serious question by either politically motivated criticism or even basic misunderstandings—and if the courts' orders are not carried out by States or the independence of their Judges is made subject to State interference—the capability of the courts to fulfill their mandated role risks being compromised. Simply put, State support remains critically important if international and internationalized courts are to carry out their missions.

This is not to suggest that international and internationalized courts are above reproach—far from it. While these courts have served as important models for how to ensure principled accountability for atrocity crimes during the last almost 30 years, setting vital and at times groundbreaking legal, procedural and practical precedents addressing everything from sexual violence to the parameters of fair trial rights, there are also, undeniably, ways in which the work of international courts could have been, and still could be, improved. Indeed, in recent years there has been an ever-increasing focus on how to enhance the efficiency and effectiveness of these courts, a focus evident both within the courts themselves and in the legislative and other bodies that provide oversight.

With the creation of the International Residual Mechanism for Criminal Tribunals in 2010, the U.N. Security Council introduced a number of efficiency-inspired innovations as compared to the Mechanism's predecessor Tribunals (such as the utilization of single Judges rather than full Benches for various judicial tasks and the expectations that Judges will typically work remotely from the physical seats of their courts and will only receive payment per day of work rather than full salaries). Since its establishment, the Mechanism has continued to seek additional ways in which to extend its efficiency and heighten its efficacy, while underscoring its commitment to abiding by the highest principles and reflecting best practices.[46]

46. *See*, e.g., International Residual Mechanism for Criminal Tribunals, *Assessment and Progress Report of the President of the International Residual Mechanism for Criminal Tribunals, Judge Theodor Meron, for the Period from 16 May to 15 November 2017*, U.N. Doc. S/2017/971 (17 Nov. 2017), at para. 6. Recognizing that the independence and impartiality of Judges is fundamental to ensuring public confidence, the Mechanism, for example, adopted a judicial code of conduct

At the ICC, meanwhile, the Court's leadership has announced that enhancing efficiency and effectiveness is a top priority for the Court.[47] Considerable attention has been paid both within the Court and among outside experts to concrete ways to achieve this, such as by taking steps to reduce the time and resources needed to investigate and try each case.[48] Efforts such as these, aimed at helping international judicial mechanisms evolve, are crucial if international courts are to remain a viable option in the long run. The creation of the Mechanism by the Security Council has already arguably influenced the judicial procedures of the Kosovo Specialist Chambers, hopefully resulting in economies.[49]

Leaving aside issues of efficiency and cost-effectiveness, the past 30 years have also provided lessons about how important it is to make the proceedings at international and internationalized courts more accessible to communities around the world. Approaches include formal outreach programs, increased use of internet and social media platforms to share information in real time, targeted information-sharing exercises with State authorities, civil society and community leaders and translations of key rulings and instruments into local languages. This is not simply a matter of increasing awareness of, and ideally support for, the work of international courts in national and local communities. It is also a crucial way in which members of the public, civil society and judicial and prosecutorial officials around the world can be sensitized to accountability efforts more generally, to how principled accountability is ensured and to the availability of a wealth of useful precedents at the international level that can help to support national efforts to advance accountability for atrocity crimes. International and internationalized courts can and should continue to enhance their efforts in these regards

in 2015 and more recently adopted a revision to that code to address alleged violations thereof. *See* International Residual Mechanism for Criminal Tribunals, *Code of Professional Conduct for the Judges of the Mechanism*, MICT/14/Rev.1 (9 Apr. 2018).

47. Silvia Fernández de Gurmendi, President of the ICC, Keynote Remarks at Plenary Session of the 16th Session of the Assembly of States Parties to the Rome Statute on the Topic of the 20th Anniversary of the Rome Statute, New York (13 Dec. 2017).

48. *See generally*, e.g., Panel of Independent Experts, *Expert Initiative on Promoting Effectiveness at the International Criminal Court* (Dec. 2014); ICC, *Enhancing the Court's efficiency and effectiveness—a top priority for ICC Officials, Press Release* (24 Nov. 2015). *See also*, e.g., David Bosco, *Discretion and State Influence at the International Criminal Court: the Prosecutor's Preliminary Examinations*, 111 AM. J. INT'L L. 395 (2017).

49. *Compare*, e.g., SC Res. 1966, Annex 1, Art. 8, U.N. Doc. S/Res/1966 (22 Dec. 2010) *with* Law on Specialist Chambers and Specialist Prosecutor's Office, Arts 2, 29, No. 05/L-053 (3 Aug. 2015) (Kosovo).

going forward, as, by doing so, they serve overall accountability aims at all levels.

Tackle Apathy, Intransigence and the Absence of Political Will

At base, much of the failure or slowness to act to ensure accountability for atrocity crimes comes down not to the inability of States to take such steps—typically, related to resource constraints—but to a lack of political will.

The absence of political will to take action to ensure accountability—whether in the national context or in conjunction with other States, such as in the U.N. Security Council—can reflect a variety of root causes. There may be no desire to act due to the fact that the violations of international law take place far outside the nation's borders or because competing diplomatic, political, domestic or strategic concerns and allegiances are seen as a higher priority. A State may lack political will to act because the violations at issue are perpetrated by that State or that State's allies or because that State holds the view that accountability efforts are not undertaken solely in their own right but instead reflect geopolitical strategic moves that the State does not support. Political will may also be lacking where there are strongly held perceptions that there is no urgency to develop and implement accountability frameworks, that there is no actual obligation to act to ensure accountability for international crimes, that the accuracy of the information suggesting the need to act is in doubt or that existing accountability mechanisms are not reliable. And States or, more accurately, State leaders may not wish to take action where, quite simply, personal self-interest is in play, such as where there is a desire to ensure that national leaders are not subjected to investigation and prosecution, whether now or in the future.

Each of these barriers to action can and must be addressed if the accountability gap is to be closed. Doing so, of course, is no easy task. But simply because something is not easy does not mean it cannot be done. Coordinated campaigns by civil society organizations to capture public attention and outrage, the deployment of targeted incentives and sanctions by individual States or groups of States and vocal support for accountability initiatives by community leaders and other key stakeholders have all proven effective in the past when it comes to overcoming political intransigence or apathy.

These and no doubt many other measures should be deployed in a targeted and nuanced fashion going forward to overcome the continuing obstacle of political inaction.

In short, ensuring accountability for atrocity crimes should not be seen as a mere political option: one choice among many facing national authorities and diplomats. It should be understood as a political, legal and fundamentally human and humanitarian imperative.

None of the examples and suggestions I have set forth here will be sufficient to close the accountability gap on their own. Nevertheless, concerted action on multiple fronts can and will narrow the accountability gap significantly by helping to advance the momentum to end impunity that began in earnest nearly 30 years ago and to transform the current ad hoc and piecemeal approach to accountability for atrocity crimes to a synergistic, multi-leveled and comprehensive (if not wholly coordinated) global system.

All of the steps described earlier, while directed toward ensuring accountability for grave violations of international law, will yield important benefits in other areas as well. For instance, increased investment, aid and capacity-building will help to strengthen national justice systems in ways that can be expected to help all litigants appearing before them, reifying the rule of law locally. Enhanced information-sharing means that standards set in international courts and in the context of their cases (such as with regard to evidentiary issues or witness protection measures) or in national courts and proceedings may serve as models for reforms in national processes and approaches to the adjudication of domestic crimes elsewhere. Efforts to ensure compliance with existing international obligations regarding atrocity crimes will help to reinforce international law more generally. It is difficult to imagine that increased efforts to prosecute atrocity crimes at the national level would not also benefit initiatives aimed at ensuring accountability for human rights violations that do not amount to atrocities, or that both types of efforts would not lead to greater compliance with international law more generally.[50] And efforts to protect judicial independence and to enhance

50. *See*, e.g., Kathryn Sikkink & Hun Joon Kim, *The Justice Cascade: The Origins and Effectiveness of Prosecutions of Human Rights Violations*, 9 ANNU. REV. L. SOC. SCI. 269, 280 (2013) (discussing how analysis shows "that countries that have prosecuted human rights violations have better human rights practices than do countries that have not. In addition, transitional countries that have experienced more prosecutions over time (and thus a greater likelihood of punishment for past human rights violations) have better human rights practices than countries that have not had, or had fewer, prosecutions. Contrary to the arguments made by some scholars, prosecutions of human rights violations have not tended to exacerbate human rights violations").

adherence to due process guarantees in civilian and military courts alike will undoubtedly serve the communities in which these Judges and courts function as well as the individuals coming before them.

In sum, by taking the steps I suggest previously, we will not only be helping to close the accountability gap when it comes to atrocity crimes; we will also be enhancing respect for the rule of law more generally—internationally as well as nationally—with all the many benefits that greater respect for the rule of law entails.

Measure Success

In light of the previous discussion, I now return to the question which appears in the sub-title of this chapter, does international justice work? As a Judge and past President of war crimes tribunals, I have strong incentives to answer that question in the affirmative, or at least with a "Yes, but ...". However, I have tried to put aside my biases and critically evaluate the system to which I belong.

This has not been an entirely comforting enterprise. Much as I would like to think that our system of international criminal justice works, and works well, the answer is much more mixed. While in some ways this system works very well indeed, in other ways it works poorly, or not at all.

Before elaborating on these points, however, I wish to make a more fundamental one. It is noteworthy, and remarkable, that today we are asking questions like "Does International Criminal Justice Work?" Twenty five years ago, we would not have asked that question—we would have asked instead "Will There Ever Be Another International Criminal Tribunal?" or, in pessimistic moments, "Is There Such a Thing as International Criminal Justice?" This is because, twenty five years ago, international criminal justice was largely a memory of Nuremberg, as discussed in Chapter III.

To address the question, Does international criminal justice work? I will set forth and evaluate five criteria. The first of these—the most basic one—is the extent to which we are apprehending and trying the suspected perpetrators of international crimes. On this front, international criminal justice works fitfully.

First, there are whole swathes of the world that remain outside the jurisdiction of any international criminal tribunal; Russia, China, India, Indonesia, Pakistan and most of the rest of Asia, the Middle East and North

Africa and, of course, the United States. In these countries, which account for most of the world population and which are not State Parties to the ICC, no international court has jurisdiction over international crimes committed by citizens of those countries on their soil. This means that to have an international institution with competence over the subject and the party concerned, it may be necessary to establish international or hybrid tribunals to coexist with the ICC. Setting aside the possibility of the exercise of jurisdiction by courts in other States, such as through the principle of universal jurisdiction, or in the territory of a party to the ICC, we can rely only on these countries' own domestic courts for the enforcement of international criminal justice.

Interestingly, one argument often brought in support of the American refusal to ratify the Rome Statute is precisely that U.S. personnel suspected of having committed war crimes are already held accountable and tried before U.S. courts-martial and that there is therefore no deficit of justice compelling the United States to accept the jurisdiction of the ICC.[51] The critiques made by human rights defenders focus on the failure of U.S. military justice to seriously investigate the responsibility of high-ranking military and security personnel for planning and implementing a policy of mistreatment of detainees in the War on Terror. I am not confident on improvements in prosecuting persons beyond those involved in rogue operations. Moreover, the number of pardons by President Trump of military personnel accused or convicted of killings Afghans gives rise to concerns.[52]

There is little domestic prosecution when international crimes are committed by members or affiliates of the government in power. In Russia, for example, there have been virtually no effective prosecutions with regard to crimes committed by Russian forces in Chechnya. With regard to one set of such crimes, the European Court of Human Rights observed in 2007 that "no meaningful result whatsoever has been achieved in the task of identifying and prosecuting the individuals who had committed the crimes" and that "the astonishing ineffectiveness of the prosecuting authorities in this case can only be qualified as acquiescence in the event."[53] Similarly, the

51. See Bureau of Political-Military Affairs, *Frequently Asked Questions About the U.S. Government's Policy Regarding the International Criminal Court, Fact Sheet* 30 July 2003, http://www.State.gov/t/pm/rls/fs/23428.htm; see also J. Bolton, *The United States and the International Criminal Court*, 14 Nov. 2002, *see* http://www.State.gov/t/us/rm/lSlS8.htm.
52. *Trump's Pardons for Servicemen Raise Fears that Laws are History*, NEW YORK TIMES, 16 Nov. 2019.
53. European Court of Human Rights, *Musayev et al. v. Russia*, App. Nos 57941/00, 58699100 and 60403/00, Judgment (26 July 2007), para. 164.

prosecutions in Indonesia with regard to international crimes committed by Indonesian forces in East Timor have been as pro forma as were the German domestic prosecutions that followed World War I.[54]

Even where an international criminal tribunal has jurisdiction, it lacks police powers and it is entirely dependent on the cooperation of sovereign States. We thus have no certainty that indicted individuals will be apprehended and brought to trial. In its early years, the ICTY had enormous difficulties getting Balkan governments to help to apprehend indicted individuals. Eventually all indictees, including such senior figures as Milošević, Mladić, Karadžić and Gotovina, faced international justice at The Hague, sometimes with the help of third States' intelligence services.

The ICTR had fewer initial difficulties in apprehending suspects because of the change of regime in Rwanda. The Tutsi-led government had unsurprisingly been quite willing to do what it could to help the ICTR prosecute prominent Hutu leaders accused of taking part in the genocide against the Tutsis. But the ICTR Prosecutor has not indicted any members of the RPF—which is the army associated with the Tutsis—and it is unclear whether cooperation from Rwanda would prove forthcoming were this to happen.

The ICC has also been experiencing difficulties in apprehending suspects. Al-Bashir is still detained in Sudan and has not been delivered to the ICC. On the positive side, Ali Kushayb, an alleged leader of the *Janjaweed* in the atrocities in Darfur (2003–4), was arrested by the Central African Republic and was delivered up to the ICC on 9 June 2020, following an ICC arrest warrant issued in 2007.[55]

In a 2004 Statement, the Prosecutor of the ICC emphasized that the Office of the Prosecutor would take a "positive approach to complementarity" and "encourage national proceedings whenever possible."[56] In making this Statement, the Prosecutor might simply be making the best of the situation before him. Given that the Rome Statute clearly grants national

54. Report to the Secretary-General of the Commission of Experts to Review the Prosecution of Serious Violations in Timor-Leste (then East Timor) in 1999, U.N. Doc. S/2005/458, Annex II, paras. 169–71. *See also* http://www.etan.org!et2006/marchll8/13i-top.htm. Note that the U.N. Serious Crimes Unit in East Timor during the transitional period issued many indictments against Indonesian leaders, but they have had virtually no success in getting those leaders handed over for trial.

55. New York Times, 11 June 2020.

56. Statement of the Prosecutor to the Diplomatic Corps (12 Feb. 2004), *available at* http://www.icc-cpi.intllibrary/organs/otp/LOM 20040212 En.pdf.

jurisdictions the first shot at trying war crimes suspects, as required by the principle of complementarity, the Prosecutor will be more likely to be effective if he or she works closely with these jurisdictions from the start. Nonetheless, this Statement on the part of the Prosecutor reflects more than simply recognition of the realities at hand. It also reflects the ideal that countries will themselves take direct responsibility for bringing to justice suspected war criminals within their jurisdiction.

The ideal of States taking responsibility for prosecution of war crimes is a valuable one, and was essential in the negotiations of the Statute and in promoting adherence to it. But what does it mean for the ICC as an institution? Here, I think we must ask some rather hard questions. First, will there be enough work left for the ICC? Obviously, the Office of the Prosecutor will always have work, whether investigating possible crimes or supporting domestic jurisdictions in their own investigations or prosecutions. But that work must include at least some prosecutions. For without a critical mass of actual cases, the ICC Judges and chambers will have little to do. This in turn may cause State Parties and other actors to wonder whether the ICC is worth sustaining.

This concern may be overstated. Of course, the ICC will have cases where national jurisdictions are unwilling or genuinely unable to prosecute. National jurisdictions may be unwilling where they resent the intervention of the ICC—something most likely to occur in the context of Security Council resolutions. National jurisdictions may also be unwilling to prosecute due to practical difficulties, such as other priorities for their resources. In such cases, these nations may refer matters to the ICC—as Uganda did. However, referring to the ICC cases of the opponents of a government is not unproblematic. Finally, national jurisdictions may be genuinely unable to prosecute due to internal conflict, the danger of exacerbating domestic strife or other reasons. Given all the ways for the ICC to end up with cases, then perhaps the concern raised earlier about a critical mass of work is overstated. But I am not sure. For one thing, we face another problem of appearances. The national jurisdictions that lack the will, the resources or the ability to prosecute war crimes suspects are likely to be overwhelmingly from developing countries. Of course, some very wealthy and powerful jurisdictions may lack the will to prosecute war crimes suspects, but there might be no ICC jurisdiction in these cases—especially since Security Council resolutions with regard to these jurisdictions are unlikely. Thus, it seems likely that most or all of the ICC's cases will come from poorer States or failed States. In cases of self-referral, there is an easy answer to charges of elitist imposition. But if the ICC's docket consists entirely or almost entirely of cases from Africa, a continuing groundswell of resentment is probable.

The difficulties in apprehension often mean that trials occur years after the atrocities, if at all. The Cambodia Tribunal deals with crimes that stem from the Khmer Rouge. Few of the 1970s witnesses are still around and able to testify and most of the Khmer Rouge genocidaires have died in the meantime having escaped accountability. Thus very few persons have been prosecuted and convicted. With regard to the people of Cambodia, justice delayed is literally justice denied.

Each trial before an international criminal tribunal also takes enormous time and resources. Although the length of these trials has been criticized, I think that, realistically, international criminal trials will usually be long ones. Typically, they involve multiple crimes, committed over long periods of time and in many localities. They involve travel of witnesses and translations of voluminous documents. In this regard, I note that while the mandate of the Special Court for Sierra Leone included a strong emphasis on efficiency, the shortest trial in that court lasted over two years. I realize that judicial output is a function of the size of the docket but it is also a function of efficiency and leadership. A brief comparison of the output of the international criminal tribunals with the ICC is thus useful.

During its first ten years, the ICTY issued 23 Trial Judgements and 10 Appeal Judgements, in the first 15 years, 50 Trial Judgements and 32 Appeal Judgements. Compare the ICC: during the first 10 years of its operation (until 2012), the ICC issued one conviction, later appealed and confirmed (in 2014), one Judgement not confirming charges, and one Judgement terminating a case (by death). In its first 15 years (until 2017), the ICC issued four convictions (two resulted from appeals, one from a conviction by a Trial Chamber, and one from a guilty plea), one acquittal (by a Trial Judgement), one Judgement not confirming charges, and one Judgement terminating a case (by death). Clearly, these ICC results are disappointing. The reach of international criminal justice thus remains limited.

Now, what can be said on the positive side of the ledger?

For one thing, with regard to the first criterion, we have succeeded in bringing a substantial number of high-level suspects from the former Yugoslavia and from Rwanda to justice and a small number of high-level suspects from African countries before the ICC. The experiences of the

ICTY and ICTR have shown that where the international community provides sufficient resources and political support for tribunals, and where States, the European Union, the United States, the U.N. and NGOs encourage or pressure recalcitrant but susceptible States to hand over suspects, then we achieve results. For another thing, we do have some domestic prosecution for international crimes, whether taken *sua sponte* or under pressure from the international community. In particular, the experiences of the ICTR, and particularly the ICTY, show us the importance of international encouragement and support for domestic prosecutions. In the former Yugoslavia, such cases have helped to achieve and demonstrate a measure, still incomplete, of governmental recognition of crimes committed by its own side in the conflict.

Given the limited capacity of international criminal courts, it is reassuring that there is a small but significant trend of individual States, such as Germany, enforcing international law by holding accountable those who serve as accomplices to regimes that commit atrocities.

My second criterion for measuring success is the extent to which we give a fair trial to the suspected perpetrators of international crimes. We do not want to create individual accountability for international humanitarian law at the expense of international human rights law.

Fair trial requires not only the application of advanced due process norms in trials of genocide, crimes against humanity and war crimes, but also the existence, at the time the offenses were committed, of substantive and detailed norms of international criminal law requiring that the principle of legality and the prohibition of retroactive penal legislation be fully satisfied. The Statutes of the ICC and the Tribunals together with customary norms to fill the interstices of the *lex scripta*, establish such a corpus of international criminal law. Additionally, the hundreds of decisions of the Tribunals, on both substantive and procedural/evidentiary issues, demonstrate that war crimes law is finally coming of age. With regard to this criterion, I believe that international criminal tribunals are doing very well indeed. We have certainly improved upon the protections available at Nuremberg. To give one example, I mentioned that there were three acquittals in Nuremberg—but I should add that there was no provision protecting acquitted individuals from being tried again for the same crimes. These acquitted men were seized and tried again by a German court. This cannot happen today. The guarantees now accorded to defendants in the foundational statutes of international criminal tribunals and in the case law are substantial, and the transparency with which international tribunals act provides a further safeguard.

The record is much more mixed in domestic courts trying individuals for international crimes. The proceedings—or lack of proceedings—with regard to the men held at Guantánamo Bay have triggered grave concerns. Concerns also exist with regard to the domestic proceedings undertaken in Rwanda and the former Yugoslavia.

My third criterion relates to the state of international criminal law applied by international criminal tribunals and the ICC. There is no question that tremendous progress has occurred in international criminal law in comparison to Nuremberg and Tokyo. As a result of the Statutes, Rules of Procedure and Evidence, the elements of crimes (for the ICC) and the jurisprudence of the various international courts and tribunals, the skeletal descriptions of the crime of genocide (which did not even exist in the corpus of international criminal law in Nuremberg), the crimes against humanity, gender crimes and war crimes have all been fleshed out and developed by a rich case law.[57] Thus, both as regards due process norms and substantive law, the developments have been positive. These much more mature and nuanced norms will, hopefully, provide a salutary model to national prosecutions of atrocity crimes.

My last two criteria have to do with the broader role of international criminal justice in promoting peace or, at least, in promoting the strictly lawful conduct of hostilities. This broader role is important because international justice is a very expensive proposition.

Unless the productivity of the ICC greatly increases, it is inevitable that questions will arise as to whether those costs are worth it if the only benefit of international criminal justice is retribution in a very limited number of cases. This cost–benefit analysis could be greatly improved if it could be shown that international justice deters international crimes.

My fourth criterion, thus, is the extent to which international criminal justice deters the commission of international crimes. Unfortunately, there is very little hard evidence on this front. We do have a plethora of sweeping and anecdotal statements and guesses. The Preamble to the Rome Statute speaks of State Parties "determining to put an end to impunity for the

57. See Guénaël Mettraux, International Crimes Law and Practice, Vol. I: Genocide (2019), Vol. II: Crimes against Humanity (2020).

perpetrators of [international] crimes and thus to contribute to the prevention of such crimes."

Similar pronouncements exist with regard to the ICTY and ICTR. Nonetheless, I do have doubts about whether specific awareness of the existence of international criminal tribunals with jurisdiction will deter fanatical and genocidal leaders from committing international crimes. In this regard, I note that the genocide in Srebrenica (1995) occurred several years after the establishment of the ICTY.

Perhaps the fear of prosecutions is a bit more real now, but only the future will tell. Then there is the question of generalized deterrence through norm-changing. I will not discuss this at length, but the idea is that the international criminal tribunals contribute to a culture in which humanitarian law and human rights law are better ingrained in the fabric of society and therefore more likely to be adhered to. At Nuremberg, Justice Robert H. Jackson referenced something along these lines in his opening remarks, when he told the International Military Tribunal that "I am too well aware of the weaknesses of juridical action alone to contend that in itself your decision under this Charter can prevent future wars.... But the ultimate step in avoiding periodic wars, which are inevitable in a system of international lawlessness, is to make Statesmen responsible to law ...".[58]

In this regard, high hopes are pinned on the ICC. The universe of the ICC and the Tribunals creates a culture in which governments find it more and more difficult to openly tolerate impunity.

The possibility of international prosecutions should, however, be considered as only one possible tool of deterrence. Additional tools include targeted sanctions, seizure of assets, restrictions on travel, fear of arrest, national prosecutions in third States and exercise of universal jurisdiction which create real dangers for the wrongdoers and are likely to increase the potential of deterrence, provided that States and the organized international community do not give up on the past momentum for ending impunity and establishing more effective accountability processes.

My fifth criterion is the extent to which international criminal justice helps to bring healing to the region at issue. Again, international documents demonstrate expectations on this front. Establishing the ICTY in Resolution 827, the Security Council stated that it was "Convinced that

58. 2 *Trial of the Major War Criminals before the International Military Tribunal, Nuremberg, 14 November 1945*–1 October 1946, at 153–4 (1947) (Opening Statement).

in the particular circumstances of the former Yugoslavia the establishment as an ad hoc measure by the Council of an international tribunal and the prosecution of persons responsible for serious violations of international humanitarian law ... would contribute to the restoration and maintenance of peace."

And once again, it is difficult to measure quantitatively whether and to what extent international criminal tribunals have in fact had a positive influence on the establishment of regional peace. We can, however, try to draw some conclusions on this front from the experiences of the ICTY, the ICTR and the ICC to date. At the most basic level, these tribunals can contribute to regional peace by providing an internationally reputable mechanism for the removal of abusive leaders. Peace and ethnic harmony in the former Yugoslavia became much more of a possibility with the removal from the region of the senior leadership suspected of international crimes against members of other ethnicities. The removal of Karadžić from power and his indictment was essential for the implementation of the Dayton Agreements. The indictment of Charles Taylor had a positive effect in calming the situation in Liberia. But there is a flip side to this point, which is that peace may also become more difficult to achieve if leaders know that they will face international criminal prosecutions once the hostilities are over.[59]

So, while international criminal tribunals may make peace settlements initially more difficult, once a tenuous regional stability has been established then they can further this stability by removing past bad actors from the scene.

What else can they do for regional peace and stability? A common claim is that in the course of holding wrongdoers accountable, international criminal tribunals break the cycle of vengeance and allow people to start moving forward. Moreover, the very existence of international criminal jurisdictions introduces the paradigm of resolving conflicts by resorting to justice, due process and law, rather than to pogroms and vendettas. I support this argument both in the short-term process and in the longer term as part of educational and cultural changes. I admit that it is hard to assess the frequency, time frame and scale of such positive developments.

59. *Report on the Special Court for Sierra Leone*, Submitted by the Independent Expert Antonio Cassese, 12 Dec. 2006, para. 30, *available at* http://www.sc-sl.org/documents/independentexpertreport.pdf.

As I have mentioned before, international criminal tribunals can bring only a small percentage of suspected perpetrators of international crimes to justice and they do so at locations removed from the region. This distance may diminish the value of international criminal tribunals and the resonance of their decisions to residents of the regions in question.

While we have theories and some indications of how international criminal justice can best contribute to peace, I believe we have a long way to go before we can speak with certainty on this issue. Further assessment is also needed with regard to the effectiveness of other mechanisms, such as truth and reconciliation commissions, and how such mechanisms can complement or conflict with the mechanisms of international criminal justice.[60]

In conclusion, I am particularly happy that we have well-developed standards under the statutes of international criminal courts and tribunals and under customary international law for what constitutes an international crime and in what context. I note that international conferences such as those that adopted Additional Protocols I and II to the Geneva Conventions could not reach agreement on a broad application of international humanitarian law to non-international armed conflicts. Yet, through the seminal ICTY 1995 *Tadić* Decision, international criminal tribunals have fostered acceptance of such a broad application of these norms almost overnight by a robust interpretation of its Statute and the customary law. This development was later recognized in the ICC Statute and, surprisingly perhaps, is not even questioned by many of the governments that opposed a more expansive role for the Additional Protocols to the Geneva Conventions.

Despite the current retraction of international criminal tribunals, I recognize the great importance of the increased commitment of the international community to international criminal justice. International criminal tribunals have demonstrated that international prosecution and trial is both feasible and credible. But I am concerned with the fact that large swathes of the world remain outside the reach of effective and timely international criminal justice. I realize that we have a long way to go in demonstrating and strengthening the link between international criminal justice and either peace or, at the very least, the strictly lawful conduct of hostilities and the

60. Sierra Leone had both a Special Court and a Truth and Reconciliation Commission, and a somewhat uneasy relationship existed between the two. There is some literature on this, but I think it is far too early for definitive evaluations.

prevention of atrocities. In this chapter I have suggested some steps that should be taken in these directions.

As we look to the future of international justice and the eventual closure of the last ad hoc Tribunal, the Mechanism, we would do well to ask ourselves how this new era may change over time—how international justice can and should evolve to better meet its goals, including with regard to the rule of law in particular, while also evolving to address the criticisms, concerns and constraints faced by courts operating at the international level.

Already, with the Residual Mechanism for International Criminal Tribunals—we see some evolution that is taking place. The Mechanism was established not simply to assume responsibility for completing the outstanding trials and appeals, but for the so-called residual functions of the ICTY and ICTR and to demonstrate that a new, smaller and more cost-effective model of an international criminal court was possible.

But, of course, the Mechanism is still an ad hoc Tribunal, like its predecessors, and we would do well to ask ourselves whether questions of efficiency demand that such ad hoc international criminal courts be phased out over time in light of the establishment of a permanent court with more comprehensive (if by no means fully comprehensive) jurisdiction: the ICC.

The role of the ICC is, of course, vital, but is it realistic to expect that—even if it has jurisdiction over some current and future atrocities—it will have the resources and the capacity to address, with a fair degree of promptness, the mounting number of cases that call for prosecutions? Even with structural and administrative reforms at the ICC aimed at ensuring more effective and efficient processes, is it wise to exclude the possibility that there may be a need for additional, perhaps ad hoc, international criminal tribunals in the future, particularly in circumstances where the assertion of jurisdiction by the ICC is problematic or uncertain? In the U.N. General Assembly's recent resolutions concerning the absence of action by the U.N. Security Council in relation to Syria, Iraq and Myanmar, and the creation of mechanisms especially to collect evidence of crimes, we already see one response to that question. Whatever the answer may be on the international level, to my mind there is no question that we must do our utmost to find ways to encourage States to prosecute war crimes before national judiciaries in accordance with international legal norms, and to facilitate their efforts in doing so. Indeed, while international criminal tribunals have created the normative model and key practical examples, much of the future work can and should be done on the national and on the regional levels. This is not simply a question of numbers and practicality; this is an imperative if the new era of accountability is to truly take hold both globally and locally.

Reflecting on my Personal Journey

As I am close to ending my judicial journey, I feel that at a time when the multilateral rule system is increasingly called into question, we must redouble our efforts to give renewed vitality to the principle of accountability both internationally and domestically. Our lodestar must always be fairness and justice, principles on which legitimacy of our project rests. These are the principles that have guided me on my life journey. Standing up for them is vital, now more than ever, when principles of international law and accountability are challenged.

Although my career has followed a circuitous path, the constant theme has been an attempt to grapple with the chaos and pain of war. War shuttered my childhood and gave me both a craving for education and the desire to use the law to bring an end to atrocities. War led me to write my legal opinion against settlements on the West Bank. Later, as a law professor, I taught the law of war. And as a Judge of an international criminal tribunal, I heard cases of individuals accused of atrocities in times of armed conflict.

International criminal courts are, in many ways, like criminal courts in national jurisdictions around the world. They weigh evidence, follow due process, ensure the parties are heard and apply and abide by the law and human rights.

At the same time, international criminal courts—and the cases they hear and the challenges they face—are extraordinary. The cases are of tremendous breadth, often involving alleged crimes of massive scale committed over long periods (in the former Yugoslavia) and across many localities. The magnitude of evidence is enormous. This evidence must be obtained without any independent police force—and with the cooperation of sovereign States, which is not always available. The crimes can have complex political dimensions, not least because the individuals charged are frequently a country's top leaders.

Because of their unique role and the nature of the crimes charged, international criminal courts are also often seen as something more than criminal courts. Their Judgements are sometimes expected to be definitive histories of the conflict. Their mission is sometimes said to be to foster reconciliation among parties to a conflict or to bring victims closure through convictions. Indeed, sometimes members of the public, including victims, equate the bringing of heads of State, leaders of political parties and military or paramilitary groups "to justice" with the entering of convictions. Accused who come before international criminal courts thus often come with—in the public mind—an existing narrative of guilt.

But different stakeholders have different expectations or visions of international criminal justice. But for Judges—including myself, of course!—bringing someone to justice means simply that the individual charged shall be tried: fairly, soberly, in accordance with the law and the evidence, having heard from the parties and observing the time-honored principles of fairness and the presumption of innocence. This is what the rule of law requires on a domestic level and it requires no less on the international level.

However, the operation of international criminal courts in this way has often led to criticisms and even the claim that international criminal justice is failing. Several Judgements of acquittal at the war crimes tribunal of which I was the President were decried as evidence of this failing. Nothing is farther from the truth.

Acquittals, and often early releases of prisoners (as discussed in Chapter XII) in any system cause some level of controversy, and they unquestionably bring victims of crimes real pain. This controversy can be magnified at the international level, given the dimensions of the crimes alleged and the political implications of those allegations. Indeed, for victims an acquittal may feel like a denial of what happened to them, and a betrayal of their hopes and expectations. For others, an acquittal may be seen as a rewriting of history or a failure of the international court to serve its purpose as part of a broader transitional justice agenda.

In my view, a true failure of international criminal justice would be if international courts were to convict an individual where there is an inadequate evidentiary or legal basis to do so. When the law or the evidence do not support a finding that a person is guilty beyond a reasonable doubt of the specific crimes for which he or she has been charged, it is the duty of international judges—it is my duty—to rule accordingly. In so doing, Judges are not declaring an individual innocent, they are not redefining history and they are not thinking about the impact on national or transnational reconciliation. They are—or rather we are—carrying out our responsibility to follow the dictates of the law—no more and no less.

Judges cannot be swayed by outside sentiment, by popular perceptions or criticisms or by preexisting narratives of guilt. Justice is and must be blind to all of that. Indeed, although one must be careful not to make sweeping generalizations, acquittals, just as convictions, can be seen as a sign of a mature system of law, an independent system, a system focused on its actual, narrow mandate to try those charged, rather than on trying to satisfy the myriad and sometimes conflicting expectations of victims, observers, civil society groups and others.

Criticisms suggest the importance of strengthening respect for and understanding of the rule of law. Establishing respect for the rule of law is critically important for ensuring protections for human rights and for building and maintaining peaceful and productive societies. And respect for the rule of law requires that we accept not only those judicial decisions with which we agree, but also those decisions with which we disagree. An à la carte approach to accepting court rulings is a denial of the fundamental principles of the rule of law.

So, my life, in many ways, has come full circle: from World War II to trying war criminals, and doing it justly and fairly.

In doing my work as a Judge in a principled way, come what may in terms of criticism, I have helped to ensure the strength and integrity of international criminal justice. And in years to come, I trust that others will see these first decades of international criminal justice for what they are: a time where vital and difficult issues were confronted, and where fledgling courts succeeded in making profoundly important contributions to the larger shared goals of ending impunity and upholding human rights and dignity.[61]

61. See my Tedx Hague Academy, "International Justice on Trials" (9 Sept. 2013), *YouTube link* https://www.youtube.com/watch?v=S3UBZ3MYY5c&t=155s&ab_channel=TEDxTalks.

Index

Note: In order to avoid multiple entries under P and to make the index more reader-friendly, cases are indexed by name of accused only, eg *Bralo* instead of *Prosecutor v. Bralo*. Only authors discussed are included in the index.

200 Metre Standard 173, 174, 177, 180, 250

abduction 87
access to witnesses and evidence, facilitation of 329
accomplices, crimes of 87
accountability 22, 32, 69
  establishment of international criminal tribunals 106
  human rights violations and ICTs 106
  ICTY 40, 43
  judicial independence and impartiality 117
  judicial selection 122
  selective accountability 91–2
  see also accountability and whether international justice works
accountability and whether international justice works 311–47
  amnesties and targeted immunities 327–9
  apathy, intransigence and absence of political will 332–4
  closing accountability gap 312–16
  compliance with existing obligations 316–18
  Courts apprehending and trying suspected perpetrators of international crimes 334–9
  due process, fair trials and judicial independence: review and revision of laws and practices 320–2
  fair trial rights 339
  infrastructures, judicial, prosecutorial and investigative 322–3
  innovative solutions to foster better accountability 324–7
  international criminal justice acting as deterrent to commission of crimes 340–1
  international criminal justice helping bring regional peace and stability 341–2
  international criminal law applied by international criminal tribunals and ICC 340–1
  measuring success 334–45
  new era of accountability 311–12
  principled accountability 321–2, 326, 330–1
  regional accountability initiatives 323–4
  support and cooperation with existing mechanisms 329–32
  universality of jurisdiction principle and encouragement of prosecutions 318–20
acquittals 23, 25, 31, 38, 346
  due process 54, 61
  Gotovina and Markač 253
  legality principle 84
  Nuremberg proceedings 52, 53, 339
  persecution 115
  Šljivančanin 169
  viewed as failure of justice 37
actus reus of crime 86, 220, 256

ad hoc Tribunals 23, 62, 93, 344
Common Article 3 of Geneva Conventions and crimes against humanity 108
institutional design and management 132
judicial assignments and Court Presidents 125
judicial decision-making 147
judicial selection 121
public affairs office 135
Statutes 94
see also in particular Extraordinary Chambers in the Courts of Cambodia (Khmer Rouge Tribunal); ICTR; ICTY; Special Court for Sierra Leone (SCSL)
admission of additional evidence on appeal (*Karadžić*) 212–14
adversarial systems 147
Advisory Committee on Nominations 315
Aerial Incident (1955) 8
Africa 338
African Charter on Human and Peoples' Rights 94
African Court of Justice and Human Rights 328
African Union 323, 328
aggravating circumstances
Bralo 209–10
Galić 230–1
Ntabakuze 211
Agius, Judge 130, 174–5, 176 n.12, 191–5, 291, 300–1, 304–5, 307
Ago, Roberto 9
Ahorugeze, Sylvère 321 n.27
aiding and abetting 86
deliberations at ICTY/ICTR Appeals Chambers 155, 159
Mrkšić, Šljivančanin (torture of POWs) 211–12
murder of prisoners of war 172
Ngirabatware (genocide) 185
Akande, Dapo 29
Akay, Judge Aydin Sefa and diplomatic immunity 136–42, 185–7
Akayesu 49
Al-Bashir 313, 318 n.18, 328, 336
Al-Khasawneh, Judge 78 n.6
Aldrich, George H. 14
Aleksovski 83
Allied Control Council Law No. 10 40
Alstein, Merel xi
Alston, Philip 29
alternate forms of liability (*Gotovina and Markač*) 177–9
Amanpour, Christiane 10
American Bar Association—Code of Judicial Conduct 123
American Convention on Human Rights 94
Amicus Curiae Brief 199–200, 218
Amin, Idi 41
amnesties and targeted immunities 327–9
Anglo-American deliberative model 155
Annan, Kofi 69
Antonetti, Judge 193–5, 300, 302, 303–4, 306
apartheid 110
apathy, tackling 332–4
appeal, right of 51, 99
Appeals Chamber *see* fairness principles and decisions of Appeals Chamber; ICTY/ICTR Appeals Chambers—deliberations
appellate courts 151
appellate review 132
appointment of Judges 120
apprehension of suspects, difficulties of 338
arbitrariness, avoidance of 72
Argentina 319
armed conflict 74, 108
and attack distinction 85
internal 107, 109
national 110
non-international 49–50, 73, 75, 105, 109, 114, 168
non-State 167
see also international armed conflict
armed reprisals 103
arrest, fear of 341
arrest warrants 315, 318, 329
assets, seizure of 341

assignment of counsel
Milošević 198
Prlić et al. 202–3
whose name is not on approved list 96
atrocity crimes
accountability and measures of success 311–13, 316–19, 326, 329, 331, 340
apathy, intransigence and lack of political will 333
due process, fair trials and independence 321
judicial infrastructure investment in 322–3
universal jurisdiction 318–20
Australia 86 n.42
aut dedere, aut judicare principle 317
authority of courts 38

Bagaragaza 201, 269
Bagosora and Nsengiyumva 233–6
Bala 293 n.102
Barayagwiza 222
Basic Principles on the Independence of the Judiciary (1985) 117, 138
Baxter, Richard 7, 14, 15, 21
Beara 267, 279–86
Bench memorandum 151
beyond a reasonable doubt 25, 38, 238, 260, 346
Galić 227–8
Gotovina 174
Muvunyi 257–9
Renzaho 189
Strugar 238–9, 241
bias 117, 124, 127–32
actual 129
Galić 188
Hadžihasanović and Kubura 190
allegations of 123, 132
Nahimana, Barayagwiza and Ngeze 187–8
apparent (*Mladić*) 193
appearance of 126, 131
Galić 188
Hadžihasanović and Kubura 190
Mladić 194
apprehension of 129
Mladić 193–4
improper (*Hadžihasanović and Kubura*) 190
political (*Šešelj*) 196
public perception of 122
Šešelj 190–1
subjective and objective (*Galić*) 188
unacceptable (*Mladić*) 194
Bickel, Alexander 93
Bisengimana 267 n.5, 268–71, 277 n.48, 280 n.62, 287 n.76
Bizimana, death of 56
Blagojević and Jokić 193, 194
Blaškić 113, 165
Bloch, Julie xi
Blum, Yehuda 13
Bologna and Milan Global Code of Judicial Ethics (2015) 32, 116, 123
Bormann, Martin 61
Borovčanin 288 n.86
Bosnia and Herzegovina 44, 317
Boulding, Dame Hilary xi, 29
Boutros-Ghali, Boutros 110
Bradley, Curtis A. 329 n.45
Bralo 209–10
Brđanin 113, 253–6
Brioni Transcript 180–1
Brownlie, Ian 29
Buergenthal, Judge 21, 78 n.6, 104 n.1
burden of proof 51, 61
reversal (*Strugar*) 237–42

Cambodia 326, 338
see also Extraordinary Chambers in the Courts of Cambodia (ECCC) (Khmer Rouge Tribunal)
Canada 86 n.42, 312
capacity-building 322, 333
case law 193, 226, 292, 296, 339–40
due process 58–9, 94
human rights 107, 109
independence and impartiality 117, 130
legality principle 71, 74, 78 n.6, 82, 85, 86 n.43, 87 n.53

Cassese, Judge 107
Čelebići 78, 83, 114, 129, 243, 245
Češić 293 n.100, 303 n.147
Charania, Shehzad 26
child recruitment 90
Chirac, J. 6
circumstantial evidence 48, 175–6
  Bagosora and Nsengiyumva 233–6
citizen-to-citizen criminal liability 55
civil law jurisdictions 34, 35, 151
  accountability 321
  deliberations 151
  deliberations at ICTY/ICTR Appeals Chambers 152
  due process 55, 58, 97–8, 101, 321
  fair trials and independence 321
  judicial decision-making 146–7, 151
  legality principle 90
  Presidency and the Prosecution 133
  universal jurisdiction 320
civil liability of States 103
civil society organizations 325, 332
civilian courts 334
clear and consistent evidence (*Muvunyi*) 260
clear and consistent notice of crimes charged 253
  Gacumbitsi 245–50
  Gotovina 253
co-counsels 95
Code of Conduct for United States Judges (2019) 123
Colombia 326
command and control principles 237
command responsibility theory 50, 79, 81–3, 87
common criminal purpose crimes 176, 212–14, 251, 254–6
common law jurisdictions 34, 35, 151
  accountability 321
  deliberations 151
  deliberations at ICTY/ICTR Appeals Chambers 152, 159
  due process 55, 93, 97, 321
  fair trials and independence 321
  judicial decision-making 146–7, 151
  legality principle 77
  Nuremberg proceedings 51
  Presidency and the Prosecution 133
  universal jurisdiction 320
commutation of sentence *see* early release of prisoners decisions
complementarity principle 92, 336–7
compliance 32, 316–18
complicity 86, 239–40, 261
concurring Opinions 148, 151
  see also dissenting and concurring Opinions
conditional release
  Beara 267, 283–6
  Ćorić 299–307
  Simba 289–98
conduct of trials and appeals 145
confidential information 143
  see also secrecy of judicial deliberation
Confidential Joint Plea Agreement Submission 208
conflicts of interests 122, 130, 321 n.27
conscientious goodwill 126
conspiracy 51, 61
  liability 53
Consultative Council of European Judges Opinions 120, 125
continuation of proceedings with substitute judge (*Nyiramasuhuko et al.* (*Butare* case)) 204–6
Control Council Law No. 10 46, 47, 62, 63
Convention against Torture (1984) 48, 104, 112, 316
Convention on the Elimination of all Forms of Racial Discrimination (CERD) 217–18, 223
Convention on the Non-Applicability of Statutory Limitations to War Crimes and Crimes against Humanity (1968) 59
Convention on the Prevention and Punishment of Crimes against Humanity 327
Convention on the Privileges and Immunities of the U.N. 138

conviction of crime with which person not charged (*Muvunyi*) 257–61
conviction entered by Trial Chamber must be the only possible interpretation of the evidence (*Bagosora and Nsengiyumnva*) 233–6
cooperation with Prosecution and early release of prisoners 264, 267, 281 n.64
  Bisengimana 271
  Ćorić 298
  Galić 278
  Kunarac 288
  lack of cooperation 273, 278, 282, 294, 303
  Lazarević 274–5
  Ntakirutimana 272
Coordination Council 133
Corfu Channel 81
Ćorić 299–307
corporal punishment 108
corridor discussions (informal exchanges) 157
cost-benefit analysis 340
cost-effectiveness and efficiency of Courts 331
counsel representation, defendant's right to 93–5
  Halilović 244
  Zigiranyirazo 201
Courts apprehending and trying suspected perpetrators of international crimes, extent of 334–9
creativity of Judge 34
credibility of courts 3, 35, 38, 42, 162, 185, 206, 240
  due process 93, 100
  legality principle 78
crimes against humanity 21
  accountability 311, 339–40
  Beara 279
  Common Article 3 of Geneva Conventions and crimes against humanity 111–12
  Ćorić 304
  due process 54–9, 320
  early release of prisoners 266
  fair trials and independence 320
  Gacumbitsi 249
  Galić 227, 276
  Gotovina and Markač 173, 252
  human rights violations and ICTs 104
  ICTY 41, 43
  judicial decision-making 145
  Kunarac 22, 286
  legality principle 76, 78, 85–7
  Nahimana et al. 218, 224
  non-international armed conflicts 50
  Nuremberg proceedings 50, 53
  persecution 112–13
  rape and sexual slavery 23, 48
  rule of law 72
  Simba 290
  Stakić 261
  state of the law and the rape example 43, 47, 48–9
crimes against peace 50, 53, 59, 76
crimes *erga omnes* 319
criminal law 58, 86, 316, 321
  see also international criminal law
criminal liability
  citizen-to-citizen 54–5
  individual 103, 106
criminal responsibility principles 82–3, 86, 312
criminality of conduct 88
Croatia 317
cross-examination of witnesses 51, 98–9
cruelty and brutality 108
  Mrkšić, Šljivančanin 212
Crystal, Willow xi
customary humanitarian law 79, 88, 164, 168–9
customary international law 33, 47
  accountability 315, 343
  due process 53, 62, 94
  establishment of international criminal tribunals 107
  Galić 225–33
  judicial decision-making 145–6
  legality principle 73–6, 79, 81, 87
  Nahimana et al. 216–18, 223
  persecution 115

customary law
  accountability 320
  Common Article 3 of Geneva Conventions and crimes against humanity 109
  due process 58, 59, 62, 63
  legality principle 77, 80, 82–6, 88–9, 94
  persecution 114
  prisoners of war protection 164
  universal jurisdiction 320
  see also customary humanitarian law; customary international law

Darfur atrocities 90
Dauchy case 19–20
Dayton Agreements 342
de Sousa Mendes, Aristides 6
decision-making 143–9
  decision-makers 145
  judges—processes 148–9
  judges and staff - background 146–8
  Tribunals, uniqueness of 144–5
Declaration of the High-level Meeting of the U.N. General Assembly (2012) 71
defense preparation (*Šešelj*) 196
degree of responsibility of offender (*Nikolić*) 207–9
Delalić 166
deliberations of Judges 32, 153–6
  civil law and common law 151
  formal 148
  international criminal tribunals 149–51
  Trial Chambers 162–3
  see also ICTY/ICTR Appeals Chambers - deliberations; secrecy of judicial deliberations
Delić 299 n.128
deportation 39, 109–10
  Brđanin 254
  Gotovina and Markač 173, 176, 252
  Stakić 261
dereliction of duty by Judges, sanctions against 120
detention conditions 321
  Šešelj 196
deterrence principle 266
  Bralo 210
  Dragan Nikolić 209
diplomatic immunity and Akay, Judge Aydin Sefa 136–7, 139–42, 186
discernible error
  Galić 226
  Mrkšić and Šljivančanin 211–12
disciplinary provisions for serious violations by Judges 118
disclosure obligations (*Mugenzi and Mugiraneza*) 206–7
discretion 34, 125
  see also sentencing discretion
discriminatory intent 85–6
disqualification of Judges 32, 185
  bias and recusal 130–1
  decision-making 145
  Galić 188–9
  independence and impartiality 117, 130–1
  Mladić 192–5
  Šešelj 190–1
disruptions of trial (*Zigiranyirazo*) 200
dissenting and concurring Opinions 215–62
  Bagosora and Nsengiyumva 233–6
  Brđanin 253–6
  Gacumbitsi 245–50
  Galič 225–33
  Gotivina and Markač 250–3
  Halilović 242–5
  Muvunyi 257–61
  Nahimana, Barayagwiza and Ngeze 215–25
  Stakić 261–2
  Strugar 237–42
dissenting Opinions 147–8, 151, 159–60
  see also dissenting and concurring Opinions
distinction, rule of 86
domestic courts 55, 93–4, 311, 320, 335, 339–40
domestic law 57, 94, 316–17
double jeopardy 61
draft decisions 148, 151, 192
dubio pro reo 321
due process 15, 22, 24, 36, 37, 38, 53–65, 93–102, 345

accountability and measures of success 311, 313, 316, 320–2, 326, 339–40, 342
apathy, intransigence and absence of political will 334
establishment of international criminal tribunals 106
Galić 225–33
human rights violations and ICTs 105
ICTY 41
judicial decision-making 143
judicial independence and impartiality 117
legality principle 74
Nahimana et al. 215–25
regional accountability initiatives 323
review and revision of laws and practices 320–2
rule of law 71
duration of trial 338
see also speedy trial, right to
duress, defence of 86
duty to disobey illegal orders 172

early life and road to judgeship of author 3–30
academia 16–17
Ambassador to Canada 8, 15
American Journal of International Law articles 15
Cambridge University 7, 18
Częstochowa 4
Dauchy case 19–20
departure from Poland 4
diplomatic life 8
Foreign Ministry (Israel) 8
ghettos and work camps 4
Harvard University 7, 9
Hersch Lauterpacht Memorial Lectures on "Human Rights in Internal Strife" 18
high school in Haifa 7
Holocaust 4–7
Human Rights and Humanitarian Norms as Customary Law 16
Human Rights in Internal Strife (Sir Hersch Lauterpacht Memorial Lectures 16
Human Rights Law-Making in the United Nations 16
Human Rights Watch 17
Humanization of International Law 16
ICRC/NYU seminar for U.N. diplomats on international humanitarian law 17
International Committee of the Red Cross (ICRC) 5, 11, 17–19
International Law in the Age of Human Rights 16
Investment Insurance in International Law (1976) (first book) 15
Jerusalem University 7
judgeships 21–6
Kalisz 4
Legal Adviser of the Foreign Ministry (Jerusalem) 8–9
military service 7
NYU School of Law 8, 16–17, 20, 27
Ottawa University 15
Oxford 26, 29
Palestine 7–9
Palestine Opinions 9–15
Permanent Mission of Israel to the U.N. (New York) 8–9
Permanent Mission to the U.N. (Geneva) 8, 16
Rockefeller Foundation Fellowship 19
Shakespeare, interest in 26–9
Six-Day War 9
State Department (USA) 20–1
UNITAR—visiting fellow 15
United Nations Secretariat: The Rules and the Practice, The (1977) 15
United States as home 8
early release of prisoners decisions 38, 136, 145, 263–307, 346
background 263–7
Beara 279–86
Bisengimana 268–71
Ćorić 299–307
Galić 276–9
Kunarac 286–9
Lazarević 274–6
Ntakirutimana 272–3
Simba 289–98

efficiency and judicial cohesion of the Court 315
Eichmann, Adolf 41
El-Araby, Judge 78 n.6, 117
election of Judges 146
electioneering by Judges 121
eligibility threshold 267, 277 n.50, 281 n.64
 Bisengimana 268–9
 Ntakirutimana 272
enforced disappearance of persons 110
enforcement of sentences 145, 329
enslavement 63, 109–10
 Kunarac 286
 sexual 22, 48
equal treatment of similarly situated prisoners 264, 268–71
 Beara 280
 Bisengimana 268
 Galić 277
 Kunarac 287
 Ntakirutimana 272
equality of all individuals before the law 328
equality of arms principle 133
 Zigiranyirazo 201
equality of enforcement 72, 91
ethical rules of conduct 32, 118, 322
ethnic cleansing 43, 44, 47
European Charter on the Statute for Judges 120
European Convention for the Protection of Human Rights and Fundamental Freedoms 62, 94
European Court of Human Rights 62, 94, 120–2, 264, 266, 335
European Union 315, 339
even-handedness of Judges 71
evidence
 adequate 320
 admissibility 147
 circumstantial 48, 175–6, 233–6
 clear and consistent 260
 collection 344
 false 196
 hearsay 147
 mens rea 247
 mitigating 209
 obtained without any independent police force and with cooperation of sovereign States 24, 72, 305, 345
 orders to produce 318
 unavailability or weakness of 92
 written 147
evidentiary issues 34, 72
evidentiary rules 34
ex abundante cautela rules 32
execution 39
exemplary behaviour 226, 271, 272
expanded common criminal purpose (*Karadžić*) 212–14
expeditious trial rights *see* speedy trial, right to
extermination
 Beara 279
 Gacumbitsi 247, 249
 Simba 290
 Stakić 261
 see also ethnic cleansing; genocide and incitement to commit genocide
extradition 320, 321
Extraordinary Chambers in the Courts of Cambodia (ECCC)(Khmer Rouge Tribunal) 57, 150 n.5, 299, 317, 338

fair notice principle (*Nahimana et al.*) 218, 224
fair trial rights 92–3, 185
 accountability and whether international justice works 313, 320–2, 330, 339
 Common Article 3 of Geneva Conventions and crimes against humanity 111
 Galić 188–9, 196–7
 Gotovina and Markač 179, 250–3
 Halilović 244
 Karadžić 203
 Milošević 199
 Mladić 191–2
 Muvunyi 260
 Nahimana, Barayagwiza and Ngeze 187
 Ngirabatware 186

Nyiramasuhuko et al. (*Butare* case) 204
Prlić et al. 202
public comment to outside criticism, prohibitions on 123
Renzaho 189
review and revision of laws and practices 320–2
Šešelj 195–6
Zigiranyirazo 200–1
fairness 22, 24–5, 33, 36, 38, 345–6
accountability 311, 320
Akay, Judge Aydin Sefa 142
Bisengimana 270
Ćorić 304
deliberations at ICTY/ICTR Appeals Chambers 157
due process 61, 63, 92–4, 96, 99, 102
early release of prisoners 266–7
establishment of international criminal tribunals 106
Galić 228, 232
ICTY 41
judicial decision-making 143
Karadžić 203–4
Milošević 198
public comment on outside criticism, prohibitions on 123
rule of law 70, 71
universal jurisdiction 320
see also fair trial rights; fairness principles and decisions of Appeals Chamber
fairness principles and decisions of Appeals Chamber 185–214
Bralo 209–10
Galić 188–9, 196–7
Hadžihasanović and Kubura 190
Karadžić 203–4, 212–14
Milošević 197–200
Mladić 191–5
Mrkšić, Šljivančanin 211–12
Mugenzi and Mugiraneza 206–7
Nahimana, Barayagwiza and Ngeze 187–8
Ngirabatware 185–7
Nikolić 207–9
Ntabakuze 210–11
Nyiramasuhuko et al. 204–6
Prlić et al. 202–3
Renzaho 189–90
Šešelj 190–1, 195–6
Zigiranyirazo 200–2
false evidence (*Šešelj*) 196
favoritism 126
Fédération Internationale des Ligues des Droits de L'Homme 326 n.36
financial backing for courts 329
financial or material stake of Judge in outcome of decision 128
Flood, Zoe xi
former Yugoslavia 23, 44, 46, 57, 82, 345
see also ICTY
Fortify Rights 325 n.35
France 124, 319
Franck, Thomas 8, 15
free legal aid 95
freedom of expression (*Nahimana et al.*) 216–17, 223
"friends of the court" (*amicus curiae*) 96, 219
fundamental guarantees clauses 105
Furundžija 48, 128

Gacumbitsi 227, 232, 245–50
Galbraith, Jean xi, xii
Galić 79, 164, 188–9, 196–7, 225–33, 266, 276–9, 280 n.62, 281 n.63, 287 n.76, 299 n.128
Gaza 9
gender crimes 43, 340
see also rape; sexual slavery; sexual violence
gender violence 315
see also rape
general principles of justice 63, 76
general principles of law 63, 115, 165, 299 n.130, 300
early release of prisoners 264–5 , 270 n.22
legality principle 78, 80, 88, 90
Geneva Conventions for the Protection of Victims of War (1949) 10, 13, 105, 316–17
and Additional Protocols 46, 55, 64, 79, 83, 105, 164–5, 343
and Common Article 3 43, 84, 89, 107–12, 114–15, 165, 168

Geneva Conventions for the Protection of Victims of War (1949) (*cont.*)
Common Articles 170
compliance with existing obligations 316–17
due process 55, 60, 62, 64
establishment of international criminal tribunals 106
Fourth 11, 14, 46, 60, 164–5
human rights violations and ICTs 104
ICTY 41
legality principle 78, 80–2, 88
persecution 114–15
prisoners of war, protection of 62, 164, 167
state of the law and the rape example 47
Third 164–6, 167, 170–1
violations 43
Geneva Prisoner of War (POW) Convention (1929) 76, 167, 169
Genocide Convention (1948) 49, 55, 316–17, 319
Nahimana et al. 217–18, 221–3
genocide and incitement to commit genocide 23, 33
accountability and measures of success 311, 317, 319, 320, 336, 339–41
Beara 279
Cambodia 317
Common Article 3 of Geneva Conventions and crimes against humanity 112
Ćorić 304
due process 56, 57, 320
early release of prisoners 266
fair trials and judicial independence 320
Gacumbitsi 227, 232, 246–7, 249
ICTR Statute 219
ICTY 41, 43
ICTY/ICTR Appeals Chambers deliberations 155
judicial decision-making 145
Krstić 22
legality principle 78, 86–7
Mladić 194
Muvunyi 257–8, 260
Nahimana et al. 219–20, 224
Ngirabatware 185
non-international armed conflicts 50
rule of law 72
Simba 290, 292
Stakić 261
state of the law and the rape example 43, 49
universal jurisdiction 319
see also Genocide Convention (1948)
geographical proximity of killings (*Bagosora and Nsengiyumva*) 234, 236
Germany 45–6, 51, 82, 312, 319, 339
Golan Heights 9, 12
Gorenberg, Gershom 10
Gotovina: controversial acquittal at ICTY 173–81, 190, 191
200 metre standard 173, 174, 177, 180
alternate modes of liability: separate Opinion 177–9
Appeals Chamber majority judgement 174–6
background 173–4
Brioni Transcript 180–1
crimes against humanity 173
cruel treatment 176
deportation 173, 176
deviatory crimes 176
dolus specialis 181
forcible transfer 176
Four Towns 175
HV forces (Croatian Army) 173, 174
Impact Analysis 174
inhumane acts 173, 176
joint criminal enterprise (JCE) 173, 175–6, 180
judgement of ICJ supporting majority decision 179–81
Krajina region 173
murder 173, 176
Operation Storm 173, 175, 180
persecution 173, 176, 178
plunder of public and private property 173, 176
Serb civilian population removal 173

unlawful shelling and artillery attacks against civilians 173, 175
violations of the laws or customs of war 173
wanton destruction 176
Gotovina and Markač 250–3, 336
see also Gotovina: controversial acquittal at ICTY
gravity of crimes 264
Beara 280, 283
Ćorić 302, 306
Galić 230–2
Mrkšić, Šljivančanin 212
Nikolić 207–9
Ntabakuze 211
Simba 292, 294–5, 297
Guantánamo Bay 340
Guatemala 312, 326
Guillaume, Judge 78 n.6
guilty pleas and lower sentences 100, 294 n.100, 338
Gush Etzion settlement 13
Gutteridge, Joyce A.C. 108

Habré 326
Hadžihasanović, Alagic and Kubura 81–2, 190
Hague Conventions on the Laws and Customs of War 14, 105, 225
Fourth 62, 76, 81, 225, 231
Hague Regulations concerning the Laws and Customs of War on Land 12–13, 45
Halilović 242–5
Hall, Judge 191
HaMoked (NGO) 10
Harhoff, Judge 190–1
harm of international order 319
Hartmann 303 n.147
Harvey, Richard 203–4
hate speech (*Nahimana et al.*) 215–25
Hay, Alexandre 19
head-of-State immunity 51, 315
health issues and early release
Beara 279, 282–4
Galić 278
Lazarević 275
Simba 295, 297
hearsay evidence 147
Helsinki Declaration 20–1
Henkin, Louis 18
Hewart, Lord 127–8
Higgins, Judge 78 n.6
Holocaust 4–7
hostage taking 109
Howard, Sir Michael: Holocaust speech to Oxford Chabad Society 7
human dignity, respect for 99, 109, 266, 347
human rights 14, 18, 20, 24–6, 30, 345, 347
accountability and measures of success 316, 321, 335, 339, 341
apathy, intransigence and absence of political will 333
Beara 282–3
due process 58, 62, 94, 101, 321
early release of prisoners 263, 266
fair trials and independence 321
ICTY 40–1
lectures 18
legality principle 74, 83
regional accountability initiatives 324
rule of law 70–2
state of the law and the rape example 44, 48
teaching 10, 16
see also human rights violations and international criminal tribunals
Human Rights Council—Commission of Inquiry 325
human rights violations and international criminal tribunals 103–15
Common Article 3 of the Geneva Conventions and crimes against humanity 107–12
establishment of tribunals 106–7
international instruments 104
persecution 112–15
post-World War II changes 104–5
regional courts 104
Human Rights Watch 17, 325 n.35, 326 n.36

humanitarian considerations and early release of prisoners 264, 267, 278 n.50, 281 n.64
Beara 82, 284
Simba 289–98
humanitarian law 17, 26, 28, 30, 312
accountability and measures of success 312, 316, 341
Common Article 3 of Geneva Conventions and crimes against humanity 110–11
compliance with existing obligations 316
due process 58
human rights violations and ICTs 105, 108
legality principle 73, 84
persecution 114
teaching 10, 16
see also customary humanitarian law; international humanitarian law
humiliating and degrading treatment 108
Humphrys, Matthew xi
Hun Joon Kim 333 n.50
Hussein, Saddam 41, 65 n.87
hybrid Tribunals 55, 69, 106, 109, 149

ICTR 23, 69
accountability and measures of success 311, 314, 321, 336, 339, 341–2, 344
Bisengimana 270
Common Article 3 of Geneva Conventions and crimes against humanity 109
deliberation process at international criminal tribunals 150, 162–3
diplomatic immunities 137
due process 55–6, 64, 321
early release of prisoners 38, 264, 266–72, 277, 281, 290, 294–5, 298–307
establishment 106
fair trials and judicial independence 321
fairness 208
human rights violations and ICTs 106
judicial assignments and Court Presidents 126
judicial bias and recusal 132
judicial decision-making 144
legality principle 75, 89
President (author as) 23, 263
rule of law 72
state of the law and the rape example 49
see also ICTY/ICTR Appeals Chambers—deliberations
ICTR Rules of Procedure and Evidence 264
ICTR Statute 57, 64, 89, 110, 218–19, 224
diplomatic immunity 137
due process 59, 62
early release of prisoners 264–5
legality principle 89
ICTY 39–43
accountability and measures of success 311, 313, 315, 321, 336, 338–9, 341, 344
Common Article 3 of Geneva Conventions and crimes against humanity 109–10, 112
creation 69
deliberation process at international criminal tribunals 150, 152–63
diplomatic immunities 137
due process 55–6, 60, 63, 92, 99, 321
early release of prisoners 38, 264, 266, 268–71, 277, 280, 286, 294, 296, 298–307
establishment 106
fair trials and independence 321
fairness 190
five-member panel 152
human rights violations and ICTs 106
immunity from disclosure 87
Judge (author as) 21, 31
judicial assignments and Court Presidents 126
judicial bias and recusal 130, 132
judicial decision-making 144
legality principle 73–5, 77–80, 87–9

obstructive behavior of defendants 135
President 152
President (author as) 23, 174, 263
prisoners of war, protection of 164, 168
rule of law 70, 72
see also ICTY/ICTR Appeals Chambers—deliberations
ICTY Bureau 130
ICTY Statute 198, 218, 264–5
Beara 279
diplomatic immunity 137
due process 59, 62, 94, 97, 99, 101
early release of prisoners 276, 279
Galić 276
persecution 113
ICTY/ICTR Appeals Chambers —deliberations 152–63
appeals from judgements 152
deliberations at Trial Chambers 162–3
hearing 154–5
interlocutory appeals 160–1
petitions for review 160–1
post-hearing 155–8
pre-appeal decisions 160–1
pre-hearing 153–4
presiding Judge 152–3, 156, 160
sentencing deliberations 158–9
separate/dissenting opinions 159–60
immigration laws and procedures 320
immunity from arrest 138
immunity from disclosure 86
impartiality *see* independence and impartiality
imprisonment or severe deprivation of liberty 109–10
in absentia trials 42, 60, 101, 320
independence and impartiality of the judiciary 32, 33, 35–6, 37–8, 116–42
accountability 320–2
Akay, Judge Aydin Sefa 136–42
deliberation process at international criminal tribunals 150
due process 93–4
early release of prisoners 263
ensuring independent judiciary 119–21
Galić 188–9
importance of independence 118–19
institutional design and management 132–3
judicial assignments and Court Presidency 124–7
judicial bias and recusal 127–32
judicial decision-making 143, 149
judicial selection 121–2
Mladić 191–2, 193
Nahimana, Barayagwiza and Ngeze 187–8
Ngirabatware 186
obstructive behaviour of defendants 135–6
Presidency and the prosecution 133–4
public comment and response to outside criticism by judges, prohibitions of 123–4
public, communication with 134–5
regional accountability initiatives 324
Renzaho 190
rule of law 71
Šešelj 190–1
Independent Investigative Mechanism for Myanmar (IIMM) 325
individual criminal liability 87, 106
individual criminal responsibility 42, 103
individual rights protection 119
Indonesia and East Timor 336
inertia and accountability 313
information-sharing, enhanced 333
infrastructures, judicial, prosecutorial and investigative 312, 322–3
inhabitants, rights of 10
inhumane acts and treatment 48, 78, 108–11, 115
Galić 276
Gotovina and Markač 173, 176, 252
Stakić 261
innocence, presumption of 99, 346
Mladić 191–2
Renzaho 189–90
institutional design and management 132–3

integrity 32, 37, 126–7, 138, 157
interests of justice 34
Beara 281 n.64
Bisengimana 270 n.22
Ćorić 299 n.130, 300, 305
due process 60, 95, 101, 264–5
Galić 278 n.50
Gotovina and Markač 179, 252
Karadžić 204
Milošević 198
Mugenzi and Mugiraneza 207
Ngirabatware 186
Prlić et al. 202–3
interlocutory appeals 99, 131–2, 147, 160–3
internal armed conflict 107, 109
international armed conflict 73, 106, 109–10, 114, 168
International Committee of the Red Cross (ICRC) 11, 17–19, 46–7
Commentary on the Geneva Conventions 81, 109
Customary International Humanitarian Law Study (2005) 60, 88, 107
immunity from disclosure as matter of customary law 86
prisoners of war, protection of 167, 170
Warsaw Summer Course on International Humanitarian Law lecture 5
International Court of Justice (ICJ) 19, 110
Advisory Opinions 104
deliberation process at international criminal tribunals 150
Gotovina 179–81
judicial selection 121
legality principle 80, 87, 89
International Covenant on Civil and Political Rights (ICCPR) 62, 104, 115, 120, 138
due process 62, 94, 96–7, 99, 101
Milošević 198
Nahimana et al. 216–18, 223
International Criminal Court (ICC) 24–5, 35–6, 69, 345
accountability and whether international justice works 311, 313–15, 317–18, 327, 329, 331, 335–7, 341, 344
Assembly of State Parties 314
Code of Judicial Ethics (2005) 124
Common Article 3 of Geneva Conventions and crimes against humanity 109–10
due process 55–6, 62
Elements of Crimes 49
establishment 24, 106
human rights violations and ICTs 106
judicial assignments and Court Presidents 125
judicial decision-making 143–4, 149
judicial selection 121–2
justification for international criminal tribunals 66
legality principle 90
prisoners of war protection 164
regional accountability initiatives 323
role of 344
rule of law 70
Rules of Procedure and Evidence of the Tribunals 49, 340
selective accountability 91–2
Statute 49, 59, 90, 109, 164, 339–40, 343
see also Rome Conference on the establishment of the International Criminal Court (ICC); Rome Statute of the International Criminal Court (ICC)
international criminal judge (author as) 31–8
international criminal justice deterring commission of crimes, extent of 340–1
international criminal justice helps bring regional peace and stability, extent to which 341–2
international criminal law 21, 30, 172
applied by international criminal tribunals and ICC 340–1

due process 55, 59
judicial decision-making 144, 149
non-international armed conflicts 49–50
prisoners of war, protection of
international criminal tribunals
deliberation process 149–51
institutional design and management 132
justification for 65–6
legality principle 74
prisoners of war, protection of 165, 172
rule of law 71
see also human rights violations and international criminal tribunals; specific Tribunals
international customary law 22
international humanitarian law 14, 16, 21
accountability 339, 342–3
Common Article 3 of Geneva Conventions and crimes against humanity 109
due process 59, 64
establishment of international criminal tribunals 106
human rights violations and ICTs 103
ICTY 39, 41, 42
legality principle 75, 77, 88
non-international armed conflicts 49
persecution 114
prisoners of war, protection of 167, 170, 172
state of the law and the rape example 44–5, 48
International, Impartial and Independent Mechanism (IIIM) for Syria 325
international law 9, 26, 69, 110
due process 57, 94
legality principle 80
see also customary international law
International Law Commission 327
International Military Tribunal (IMT) 40
Charter 61
due process 54, 58, 61, 62
human rights violations and ICTs 104
justification for international criminal tribunals 65
legality principle 76
Nuremberg proceedings 51, 52, 53
prisoners of war, protection of 169
International Residual Mechanism for Criminal Tribunals (IRMCT) 69
accountability 330, 344
Akay, Judge Aydin Sefa 136–7, 140, 186
challenges 163
Code of Professional Conduct for the Judges of the Mechanism 32, 117–18, 124, 138
Common Article 3 of Geneva Conventions and crimes against humanity 109
deliberation process at international criminal tribunals 150
due process 64
early release of prisoners 264–6, 268–71, 277, 280–1, 283–5, 287, 291–2, 294–6, 298–307
eventual closure 344
judicial bias and recusal 131
judicial decision-making 144–5
judicial selection 121
legality principle 89
Practice Directions 265
President 163, 265, 271, 272
President (author as) 174, 263, 267
Rules of Procedure and Evidence 264–5
Statute 47, 104, 133, 137, 265
international transfer 87
internet and social media platforms 331
interpretation and translation of cases 146
intransigence 332–4
investment in justice system 333
Iraq 41, 91, 92, 344
U.N. Investigative Team for Accountability of Islamic State (UNITAD) 325
Israel 86 n.42

Jackson, Judge 52, 54, 65, 341
Jackson, Miles xi

Japan 45
Johnson, Karen xi
joint criminal enterprise (JCE) 87
Gotovina 173, 175–6, 180, 251–2
Karadžić 212
Mladić 193–4
Simba 290
Jokić 237–41
judges 116
background 146–8
processes 148–9
judgeships (of author) 21–6
judicial assignments and Court Presidency 124–7
judicial roster 137
jus cogens norms 328
justice 36, 70, 76, 99, 267, 345
Bisengimana 270

Kabuga arrest 56
Kadijević 237–41
Kampelman, Max 20, 21
Karadžić 191–2, 195, 203–4, 212–14, 336, 342
Karski, Jan 6
Kearney 119
Keen, Maurice 27
Ki-moon, Ban 139
Kooijmans, Peter 44 n.2, 78 n.6
Kordić 79, 217–18, 223, 228, 232
Kordić and Čerkez 228, 232
Kosovo 86 n.42, 317, 326
see also Specialist Chambers for Kosovo
Krajišnik 270 n.15
Krnojelac 262
Krstić 6, 22, 178 n.20, 193, 194
Kubura, Amir 82
Kunarac et al. 22, 48, 108, 111, 286–9
Kuntze 83
Kupreškić 112–13, 178, 246, 249, 251, 262
Kushayb, Ali 336
Kwon, Judge 237–41

Lambert, Isabelle xi
Lauterpacht, Sir Hersch 7
Lazarević 274–6
Lebanon *see* Special Tribunal for Lebanon (Hariri Tribunal)
legal certainty 72
Legal Consequences of the Construction of a Wall in the Occupied Palestinian Territory Advisory Opinion 110, 117
legality principle (*nullum crimen sine lege*) 33, 73–91
accountability and measures of success 339
Common Article 3 of Geneva Conventions and crimes against humanity 111
due process 62–3
ICTY 41
judicial decision-making 145
Nahimana et al. 215–25
persecution 114–15
prisoners of war protection 164
rule of law 71
legitimacy of courts 38, 93, 185
Galić 228, 233
lex mitior principle 230
Bisengimana 268–71
liability
alternate forms of (*Gotovina and Markač*) 250–3
civil 103
conspiracy 53
criminal, citizen-to-citizen 54–5
individual 87, 103, 106
via joint criminal enterprise (JCE) where member uses non-member to carry out criminal purpose (*Brđanin*) 253–6
Liberia 342
Libya 313
Lieber Instructions 45
life imprisonment sentence replaced with lesser sentence (*Ntabakuze*) 210–11
life, right to 110
Liu Daqun, Judge 191, 193–5, 245–8, 249–50, 257–61, 297, 297 n.126, 300, 302, 304, 306
Lomé Agreement 89

London Charter *see* Nuremberg Charter
Lukić 299 n.128

McCarthy 128
McDonald, Judge 86 n.49
Macintyre, Donald 10, 13
McIntyre, Gabrielle xi
McNichol, Jack xi
Malabo Protocol 323, 328
managerial efficiency 157
Martinović 248, 250, 293 n.102
mass internment 39
Mazowiecki, Tadeusz 44
Mechanism *see* International Residual Mechanism for Criminal Tribunals (IRMCT)
media, increasing power of 144
media and public affairs officers to service of courts 135
Meir, Golda 9
memoranda 148, 157, 163
merit principle 15
"Meron gap" 18
methodological conservatism 79
Miletić 299 n.128
Military Commission of Guantánamo 326 n.38
military courts 326, 334
Milošević 96, 136, 178 n.20, 197–200, 336
Milutinović and others 84
ministries of justice 71–2
miscarriage of justice (*Karadžić*) 213–14
mitigating circumstances
  Bralo 209–10
  Ćorić 302
  Galić 230
  Ntabakuze 211
  Simba 292
Mladić 131, 188, 191–5, 336
Moloto, Judge 191
moral authority 93
moral blameworthiness of an accused 209
Mothers of Srebenica 25
Mrđa 303 n.147
Mrkšić 170, 303 n.147
Mrkšić and Šljivančanin 161, 166, 168–9, 171, 211–12
Mucić 270 n.16
Mugenzi and Mugiraneza 206–7
multi-Judge panels 132
Mumba, Judge 130
Munyakazi 303 n.147
murder 63, 78, 108, 109, 115
  Beara 279
  Galić 276
  Gotovina and Markač 173, 176, 252
  Nahimana et al. 221
  prisoners of war (POWs), protection of 166–7, 172
  Stakić 261
mutilation 108–9
mutual trust between defendant and counsel 96
Muvunyi 257–61, 269 n.11
  Nsabimana, Sylvain 257, 260
  Ntezirayayo, Alphonse 257–9
Myanmar 91, 92, 313, 344
  Independent Investigative Mechanism for Myanmar (IIMM) 325

Nahimana, Barayagwiza and Ngeze 187–8, 215–25, 288 n.86, 292 n.98
  case should have been remanded 215–16
  persecution conviction (RTLM broadcasts) 216–22
    mere hate speech is not criminal 216–18
    mere hate speech may not be basis of criminal conviction 220–1
    nexus between Nahimana and widespread and systematic attack 221
    why hate speech is protected 218–19
  sentence 222
Naletilić 248, 250, 292 n.97
Naletilić and Martinović 165
national armed conflict
national decrees 40
national emergency and establishment of international criminal tribunals 106
national jurisdictions 312, 321, 337

national prosecutions in third States 341
national security concerns 87
Ndayambaje 277 n.50, 281 n.64
Neier, Aryeh 17
Netherlands 45 n.8
new convictions on appeal, power to enter 261–2
Ngeze 222, 290 n.90, 295 n.109
Ngirabatware 136–7, 139–40, 161, 185–7
Nicaragua 80–1, 109, 114
Nieto-Navia, Judge 228
Nikolić 194, 207–9, 283 n.71, 293 n.100, 303 n.147
no complicity in sham investigation (*Strugar*) 237–42
non-governmental organizations (NGOs) 10, 106, 136, 144, 325 n.35, 339
non-international armed conflicts 49–50, 73, 75, 105, 109, 114, 168
non-State armed conflict 167
norm accretion 323
normative continuity principle 138
notice, clear and consistent, of crimes charged 245–50
Ntabakuze 210–11
Ntahobali 277 n.50, 281 n.64
Ntakirutimana 246, 272–3, 275 n.43, 278 n.52, 282 n.66, 288 n.87, 292 n.98
Ntawukulilyayo 278 n.52, 282 n.67, 290 n.90, 293 n.100, 303 n.146
Nteziryayo 257, 292 n.98
Nuclear Weapons Advisory Opinion 110
Nuremberg Charter (1945) 46, 50–1, 52, 104
  due process 52, 53, 57–8, 60, 62
  human rights violations and ICTs 107
  legality principle 76
Nuremberg principles 60, 82
Nuremberg proceedings and Tribunals 23, 40, 50–3, 86 n.42, 341
  acquittals 339
  criticisms 42, 60
  due process 62, 63
  interrogation 51
  legality principle 76, 83, 88
  persecution 113
  prisoners of war, protection of 169
Nuremberg tenets 40
Nyiramasuhuko et al. 204–6

Obrenović 278 n.50, 281 n.64
obstructive behaviour of defendants 134–6
  Karadžić 204
Odio, Benito 129
Office of Legal Affairs 137, 142
Office of the Prosecutor 337
Officer of the Order of Merit (Poland) 5
Oil Platforms case 21
Open Society Justice Initiative 219
Operation Storm 173, 175, 180, 252
opinio juris 81
Opinions
  reasoned and persuasive 123
  separate 147, 159–60
  see also dissenting and concurring Opinions
Order on Modalities 198
organised military operations (*Bagosora and Nsengiyumva*) 233–4
Orie, Judge 189
outcome conservatism 80
outreach programs 331
Ovčara massacre 164–72
Oxford (author's time at) 29
Ozaki, Judge 129 n.22

Palestine (author living in) 7–9
Palestine Opinions 9–15
Pandurević 293 n.100, 303 n.147
Papon, Maurice 41
pardon *see* early release of prisoners
past decisions (civil law) 147
past precedents 34
payment per day of work as opposed to full salaries for Judges 330
peace accords 328
Pérez, Lucía xi
periodic replacements of Judges on preset schedule 126
Perišić 190, 213
persecution 109–15
  actus reus 86, 220

Beara 279
Gotovina and Markač 173, 176, 178, 252
Nahimana et al. 215–25
Stakić 261
Persian Gulf War 41
personal connection of Judge to one of the parties 128
personal dignity, outrages upon 108–9
personal motives 86
petitions for review 160–1, 267
physical presence of accused in court not satisfied by video-link (*Zigiranyirazo*) 200–2
Pinochet 321 n.27
Plenaries of the Judges 145
plunder of public and private property (*Gotovina and Markač*) 173, 176, 252
plurality of persons 256
Pocar, Judge 174–5, 176 n.12, 192, 231
political decisions and accountability 313
political liberty, protection of 223
political will, absence of 332–4
politically motivated prosecutions 320
Popović et al. 193
position of authority, abuse of 230–1
Posner, Judge 148
post-appeal review of final Judgements 161
post-hearing conference 156–7, 159
post-hearing deliberations 155–8, 159
agenda 156
pre-appeal decisions 160–1
pre-appeal Judge 147, 152, 160
pre-hearing deliberations 153–4
pre-trial Judge 98, 147
pre-trial and pre-appeal management questions 146
precedents 34, 72, 80, 118, 145–7
see also past precedents
predictability in non-criminal areas of law 78
preliminary examinations, duration of 314
preparatory document (prepdoc) 146, 153, 156–7
presentation and preparation of defense case
(*Milošević*) 199–200
(*Šešelj*) 196
Presidency 124–7, 145
and the prosecution 133–4
Presidents as decision-makers 145
prisoners of war (POWs), protection of 164–72
mistreatment 166–8
murder 166–7, 172
torture 166
transfer of custody to another agent 167, 170–1
Prlić et al. 166, 202–3
probativeness (*Halilović*) 243
procedural decisions 149
procedural issues 72
procedural right to fair notice of the law 73
procedural rules 34, 145–6
procedural safeguards (*Halilović*) 243, 245
promotion of cause in which Judge is involved together with one of the parties 129
property destruction or confiscation 39, 173, 176
proportionality 185
Karadžić 203–4
Milošević 197–9
Nikolić 207–9
Zigiranyirazo 200–2
proprietary interest in outcome of case 129
prosecutorial systems 147
prostitution, enforced 45
provisional release not counted as periods spent in detention for purposes of early release eligibility 274–6
proxy campaigns 121
public comment and response to outside criticism by judges, prohibition on 123–4
public, communication with 134–5
public hearing, right to 100
public opinion, increasing power of 144
public protection and early release of prisoners 266

publicly expressed opinion viewed as prejudgement of case 128
Pušić 293 n.100, 299 n.128

Radić 292 n.99
Ranjeva, Vice-President 78 n.6
rape 22, 39, 115
absence of consent 48
Gacumbitsi 247, 249
human rights violations and ICTs 109–10, 112
Kunarac 22, 286
legality principle 78, 86
Nahimana et al. 221
persecution 115
and state of the law 43–9
Ravanides, Christos xii
reappointment or reelection criteria 322
reasonable inference (*Bagosora and Nsengiyumva*) 235–6
reasonable observer test
Galić 188
Mladić 193
Nahimana, Barayagwiza and Ngeze 187
Šešelj 191
reasoned and persuasive opinions 123
reasoning of Judgements 143
reciprocity principle 103, 105
recruitment of Judges and staff 120, 146
Recueil des obligations déontologiques des magistrats (France) 124
recusal of Judges 32, 117, 127–32, 185
Red Cross *see* International Committee of the Red Cross (ICRC)
Redgwell, Catherine 29
refusal of counsel by defendant and conducting own defence *see* self-representation
regional accountability initiatives 323–4
regional courts 94
Registrars 145
rehabilitation, demonstration of and early release 264, 266
Bisengimana 271
Ćorić 300, 302, 304–5, 306
Galić 278
Lazarević 274–5
Ntakirutimana 272–3
Simba 294
release of defendant from detention, right of if not brought to justice within reasonable time 97
see also speedy trial, right to
reliability (Halilović) 242–5
remorse (*Simba*) 292–3
remote working of Judges 137, 163, 330
Renzaho 188–9
reparation 103
reporting Judge (*Juge rapporteur*) 151, 152–3
representation, right to *see* counsel representation, defendant's right to
reprisals 103
resources and infrastructure 91, 312, 324, 338
retribution principle (*Bralo*) 210
retroactive penal legislation, prohibition of 339
reversal of convictions on appeal 123
Review Bench 139
Roberts, Sir Ivor xi, 29
Robertson, Judge 129 n.21
Robinson, Judge 233–6
Rohingya crisis 325 n.35
Rome Conference on the establishment of the International Criminal Court (ICC) 65, 109, 314, 316
Rome Statute of the International Criminal Court (ICC)
accountability and measures of success 314, 330, 335–6, 340
Common Article 3 of Geneva Conventions and crimes against humanity 109
compliance with existing obligations 316–17
due process, fair trials and independence 56, 321
legality principle 83
regional accountability initiatives 323
Roselli, Ambassador 138
Rosenne, Shabtai 7
Rugambarara 269 n.14

Rukundo 178 n.19, 277 n.48, 288 n.86, 293 n.101
Rule 68 violations 207
rule of law 22, 25, 32, 37, 38, 69–71, 346
  accountability and measures of success 314, 344
  amnesties and targeted immunities 328
  apathy, intransigence and absence of political will 334
  judicial bias and recusal 127
  judicial independence 119, 139–40, 142
  legality principle 73, 74, 88
  reification of principles 71–2
  selective accountability 91–2
Rules of Procedure and Evidence 92, 145–6, 265
  Akay, Judge Aydin Sefa 139
  Ćorić 302
  Karadžić 213
  Renzaho 189
Ruskin-Tompkins Joy xi
Russia 217, 335
Rutaganda 262
Ruzindana 272 n.27, 275 n.43, 292 n.98
Rwanda 23, 57, 136, 312, 317
  see also ICTR

Sagahutu 293 n.101
Šainović 293 n.101
Salam, Nawaf 15
sanctions against Judges for dereliction of duty 120
sanctions, targeted 341
Šantić 278 n.50, 281 n.64
Schachter, Oscar 15, 18
Schomburg, Judge 130, 244
secrecy of judicial deliberations 117–18, 143, 148, 150, 158, 163
secret trials 101
Segev, Tom 10
selection of Judges 117, 120, 121–2, 315, 322
self-representation 96, 135
  Karadžić 203–4
  Milošević 197–9
  Prlić et al. 202–3
  Šešelj 97, 195–6
Semanza 108, 262
Senegal 326
sentence of 20 years changed to life imprisonment (*Galić*) 225–33
sentencing 108, 185
sentencing deliberations 148, 158–9
sentencing discretion
  Bralo 210
  Mrkšić, Šljivančanin 211–12
separate Opinions 147, 159–60
separation of powers principle 119, 121
serious bodily and mental harm 49
seriousness of crimes (*Bralo*) 209–10
Serushago 272 n.27
Šešelj 97, 130, 190–1, 195–6
severe pain or suffering (including mental suffering) 22, 48
sexual slavery 22, 48
sexual violence 330
Shahabuddeen, Judge 255, 261
Shakespeare, author's interest in 26–9
Shamgar, Justice Meir 13
Sierra Leone *see* Special Court for Sierra Leone (SCSL)
Sikkink, Kathryn 333 n.50
silent, right to remain (*Halilović*) 244
Simba 289–98
Simić 113, 165
single Judges as opposed to full Benches 330
singleness of command (*Strugar*) 237–8, 240–1
Six-Day War 9
social condemnation of acts 209
Sohn, Louis 7, 21
South Africa 219
Special Court for Sierra Leone (SCSL) 343 n.60
  accountability and measures of success 314, 338
  Common Article 3 of Geneva Conventions and crimes against humanity 109
  due process 56, 64
  judicial bias and recusal 129
  legality principle 89
Special Tribunal for Lebanon (Hariri Tribunal) 57

Specialist Chambers for Kosovo 57, 314, 331
specialized judicial chambers and prosecutorial offices 322
specificity principle 64
speedy trial, right to 93–4, 97–9
  Milošević 197–9
  Prlić et al. 202
  Šešelj 195–6
Stakić 261–2, 292 n.99
stand-by counsel, appointment of 97
  Karadžić 203–4
standard of eligibility as 45 years for early release of persons sentenced to life imprisonment 276–9
standard of review (*Galić*) 225–33
State practice and *opinio juris* 80, 81, 84–5, 87
State sovereignty 87
statement of regret (*Ntabakuze*) 211
statements memorialized on video or audio tape ensuring voluntariness and reliability 242–5
States, rights and obligations of 10
Statute and Convention on the Privileges and Immunities of the United Nations 186
Statute of the International Tribunal 47
Strugar 237–42
  burden of proof 238–9
  complicity in sham investigation 240
  finding of Trial Chamber insufficient to prove Strugar knew investigation was a sham 239
  JNA 237–9, 241
  no evidence to prove Strugar knew investigation was a sham 239–40
  sham investigation 237–42
  singleness of command 237–8, 240–1
subpoenas 87
substantial doubt (*Halilović*) 243
substantial modification of sentence (*Bralo*) 209
substantive law 55, 72, 73, 106, 149, 340
substitution of a safeguard of equivalent value 205
success, measurement of 334–45
supreme courts 81–2, 151
Sweden 312
Syria 91, 92, 313, 325, 344
Tadić 49, 60, 63, 70, 83–4, 88, 107, 109, 113, 254, 262, 274 n.38, 343
Tarčulovski 293 n.102
targeted immunities and amnesties 327–9
targeted incentives and sanctions 332
targeted information-sharing exercises 331
targeting civilians, prohibition against (*Galić*) 225
taxi-stand principle 126
Taylor, Charles 343
tenure guarantee until mandatory retirement age or expiry of fixed term of office 120
terminal illness or grave illness 267, 279–86
termination of appointment of Judges 120
terror, infliction of upon civilian population (*Galić*) 229
three-Judge panels 148
three-quarters of sentence served (ICTR) 38, 136, 264, 267
  Bisengimana 269
  Simba 295
Tolimir 22, 155, 193, 194
torture 39
  Common Article 3 of Geneva Conventions and crimes against humanity 108–10
  due process 63
  Kunarac 111, 286
  legality principle 78, 86
  persecution 115
  prisoners of war 166
  state of the law and the rape example 48, 49
  see also Convention against Torture
Toyoda, Admiral 46 n.9
transfer of populations, forced 110, 176
translations of key rulings and instruments into local languages 331

transparency 33
accountability and measures of success 340
Akay, Judge Aydin Sefa 142
deliberation process at international criminal tribunals 150
early release of prisoners 265
judicial decision-making 143, 149
rule of law 72
travel restrictions 341
tried in one's own presence, right to be 100
Trump, Donald 329 n.45, 335
truth and reconciliation commissions 343
two-thirds of prison sentence served (ICTY) 38, 136, 264, 267
Beara 280–1
Bisengimana 268–71
Ćorić 302, 306
Galić 277, 279
Kunarac 287, 289
Lazarević 274–5
Ntakirutimana 272–3
Simba 291–2, 295, 297

Uganda 41, 337
U.N. Administrative Tribunal (UNAT) 20
U.N. Charter 20, 39, 48, 57, 91, 140
U.N. Coalition 41
U.N. General Assembly 82, 91, 121, 134, 139
Basic Principles on the Independence of the Judiciary (1985) 117, 138
U.N. Holocaust Memorial Ceremony keynote speech 5
U.N. Human Rights Committee 120, 199
U.N. Investigative Team for Accountability of Islamic State (UNITAD) in Iraq 325
U.N. Kalshoven Commission and interim report 42
U.N. Office of Legal Affairs 137
U.N. Office of the Legal Counsel 136, 139
U.N. resolutions 39, 41, 48, 89, 137, 306, 337, 341, 344
U.N. Secretary-General 64, 118, 134, 141
U.N. Secretary-General's 1993 report to the Security Council 64, 88
U.N. Security Council 3, 12, 36
accountability 313–14, 325, 330, 344
Akay, Judge Aydin Sefa 137–40, 142
apathy, intransigence and absence of political will 332
due process 56, 57, 64, 92
ICTY 39, 41
judicial decision-making 144
judicial selection 121
legality principle 77
Poland presidency (2019)(author) 5
Presidency and the Prosecution 133–4
selective accountability 91
state of the law and the rape example 44, 47–8
Statutes 59
U.N. Statutes 62
U.N. War Crimes Tribunals 6, 49, 109
uniqueness of Tribunals 144–5
United Kingdom 37, 77, 82, 121, 127, 148, 319
United Kingdom Guide to Judicial Conduct (2019) 124
United States 37, 315, 335, 339
Code of Conduct for United States Judges (2019) 123
Constitution 217, 219, 223
due process 55
judicial bias and recusal 127
judicial decision-making 148
judicial selection 121
legality principle 77, 82
Nuremberg proceedings 50
State Department 47
State Department (author's time at) 20–1
state of the law: rape example 47
Supreme Court 81–2
Universal Declaration of Human Rights 216
universality of jurisdiction principle and encouragement of prosecutions 318–20, 335, 341

unsatisfactory behaviour in prison justifying denial of early release (*Kunarac*) 286–9
urgent matters arising during judicial recess 146

Vasiljević case 84, 115
Vaz, Judge 261–2
Versailles Treaty 40, 59
victims' justice 36
violations of the laws or customs of war
 Beara 279
 Gotovina and Markač 173, 252
 Kunarac 286
 Stakić 261
violence, acts or threats of, purpose of which is to spread terror (*Galić*) 225–33, 276
violence to life and person 108, 111
Vohrah, Judge 86 n.49
voluntariness (Halilović) 242–5
Vukovar hospital 168, 170

waiving or forfeiting right of accused to be present at trial 200
war crimes 21, 23
 accountability and measures of success 311, 320, 339–40
 Common Article 3 of Geneva Conventions and crimes against humanity 108, 112
 Ćorić 304
 distinguished from purely domestic offence 108
 due process 54–6, 57, 60
 early release of prisoners 266
 fair trials and independence 320
 Galić 227
 judicial decision-making 145
 legality principle 76
 non-international armed conflicts 50
 Nuremberg proceedings 23, 50, 53
 rule of law 72
 state of the law and the rape example 43, 45, 47, 49
Warsaw, University of and honorary doctorate for author 5
Wechsler, Herbert 52
Wendell Holmes, Justice Oliver 220
Weschler, Lawrence 28
West Bank 9, 13, 14, 24
widespread and systematic attack (*Nahimana et al.*) 222, 224
WISP Report 306
witness credibility 162
witness cross-examination 51, 98–9
witness interrogation 51
witness protection, importance of 143
witness protection and support offices 321
witness safety and *in camera* proceedings, voice distortion and pseudonyms 101
witness statement admissions (*Šešelj*) 196
witness testimony
 Bagosora and Nsengiyumva 234–5
 Galić 196–7
working languages of Tribunals 95
World Trade Organization (WTO) 122
written evidence 147
written form oral testimony given by witness in different trial 99
written statements in lieu of oral testimony and veracity and authenticity guarantees 98

Yad Vashem Holocaust remembrance center 6
Yamashita 81–2
Yerodia 90
Yugoslav People's Army (JNA) 168–71, 237–9, 241

Zagreb Agreement 168
Zelenović 269 n.15, 293 n.100, 303 n.147
Zigiranyirazo 200–2

Sea-Level Rise and the Legal Stability of Maritime Zones

FRANCES ANGGADI

Australian National Centre for Ocean Resources and Security, University of Wollongong, Australia

OXFORD
UNIVERSITY PRESS

OXFORD
UNIVERSITY PRESS

Great Clarendon Street, Oxford, OX2 6DP,
United Kingdom

Oxford University Press is a department of the University of Oxford.
It furthers the University's objective of excellence in research, scholarship,
and education by publishing worldwide. Oxford is a registered trade mark of
Oxford University Press in the UK and in certain other countries.

Published in the United States of America by Oxford University Press
198 Madison Avenue, New York, NY 10016, United States of America.

British Library Cataloguing in Publication Data
Data available

Library of Congress Control Number: 2026933417

ISBN 9780198973508

DOI: 10.1093/9780198973515.001.0001

Printed and bound by
CPI Group (UK) Ltd., Croydon, CR0 4YY

The manufacturer's authorised representative in the EU for product safety is
Oxford University Press España S.A. of El Parque Empresarial San Fernando de Henares, Avenida de Castilla, 2 – 28830 Madrid (www.oup.es/en or
product.safety@oup.com). OUP España S.A. also acts as importer into Spain
of products made by the manufacturer.

MIX
Paper | Supporting responsible forestry
FSC® C013604

Preface and Acknowledgements

The initial thinking that led me to write this book can be traced back to a period from 2017 to 2019 when I was the legal advisor for the Pacific Maritime Boundaries Project. This was a role I undertook while serving with the Australian Government Attorney-General's Department, working closely with Pacific countries to support their endeavours to settle their maritime zones. Many Pacific countries were undertaking intense efforts to modernize their domestic maritime zones legislation, and to negotiate and bring into force maritime boundary treaties, with the aim of 'securing their rights and responsibilities over these large areas of ocean space'.[1] This work awakened my curiosity about whether this practice in the Pacific region was unique, or whether coastal States in other regions of the world were also taking similar actions to secure their maritime zones. If the latter, since this practice was done to implement maritime zones, I wondered whether that practice could also have legal significance beyond being mere instances of domestic implementation: could such State practice meet the requirements of scale and consistency to shape the interpretation of the international legal rules themselves?

These questions took on even greater significance as international attention began to focus on the legal implications of sea-level rise for maritime zones. My interest in gathering and assessing State practice began to sharpen, as I wondered whether there might be any connections between the domestic maritime zones legislation I had noticed earlier and the increasing references to the 'legal stability of maritime zones' underpinning an interpretation of the UN Convention on the Law of the Sea. Springing from these lines of curiosity, the book takes part in an ongoing conversation amongst scholars, organizations, and States seeking to make sense of a fast-moving area of the law. In so doing, the book strives also to strengthen the connections between scholarship and practice by drawing attention to the potential legal significance of State practice for a contemporary understanding of the law.

I feel privileged to have followed the remarkable developments on this topic while in a range of roles—first as a government lawyer, then as a PhD researcher, teacher, and author—so I have many to thank who have supported

[1] Cristelle Pratt and Hugh Govan, *Framework for a Pacific Oceanscape: A Catalyst for Implementation of Ocean Policy* (*Pacific Oceanscape*).

me and this project along the way. This book is based on my doctoral research which I commenced at the Australian National University and completed at the University of Sydney (2020–23). I greatly appreciate the support of my main PhD supervisors at the respective universities, Professor Don Rothwell and Professor Tim Stephens, who guided that research and continue to be generous and wise mentors, and my thesis examiners, whose comments helped to sharpen the focus of this book. I also gratefully acknowledge the financial support my doctoral research received from the collaboration between Geoscience Australia and the Marine Studies Institute at the University of Sydney.

I am also extremely appreciative of the support and encouragement I have received from many colleagues at the Australian National Centre for Ocean Resources and Security (ANCORS) at the University of Wollongong, led by Professor Stuart Kaye, which I have found to be a rich and stimulating professional environment in which to prepare this book. I would like to especially thank Camille Goodman for her confidence in me, fierce encouragement of this project, and generous friendship as always. My thanks also go to Dawoon Jung, Farjana Hossain, Derin Yonel, and visiting fellow Kazumi Wakita for their help in following up particular aspects of State practice, with special thanks to Lucky Wuwung for expertly preparing some of the book's illustrations. This book has also benefited greatly from discussions with my former colleagues in the Australian government, in particular, officers from the Office of International Law at the Australian Government Attorney-General's Department, the Sea Law section at the Department of Foreign Affairs and Trade, and Geoscience Australia (of course, all views and any errors in the book are my own). The preparation of this book has also benefited from kind and insightful readers, who reviewed parts of the book: thank you to Lauren Burke, Alex P Dela Cruz, Millicent McCreath, and Gulardi Nurbintoro for lending your expertise. I am grateful for support from Conor McLaughlin who assisted during the final stages of this book's preparation, and Laina Meg Hall for her friendship and wise counsel on art and life.

Finally, my deepest gratitude goes to all of my family, but especially to my first and steadfast reader, Jonathan Pickering, for your patient listening, at times inconveniently on-point questions, and incomparable sense of curiosity and fun; and to Will and Louis, for all the hugs.

Parts of Chapters 3, 4, 6, and 8 have drawn from, adapted, or updated my previous publications (to varying extents and with varying degrees of revision), and I acknowledge that those publications are reproduced with the generous permission of the publishers:

- Frances Anggadi, 'Reconceptualising the "Ambulatory Character" of baselines: The International Law Commission's Work on Sea-Level Rise and International Law' (2021) 22(2) Melbourne Journal of International Law 163;

- Frances Anggadi, 'What States Say and Do about Legal Stability and Maritime Zones, and Why it Matters' (2022) 71(4) International & Comparative Law Quarterly 767;
- Frances Anggadi, 'Establishment, Notification, and Maintenance: The Package of State Practice at the Heart of the Pacific Islands Forum Declaration on Preserving Maritime Zones' (2022) 53 Ocean Development & International Law 19; and
- Frances Anggadi, 'The Relevance of Habitability (and its Loss) for the Status of "Islands"' (*Opinio Juris*, 24 April 2023).

The work takes into account the ICJ's Advisory Opinion in *Obligations of States in Respect of Climate Change*, although the bulk of the research underpinning the project took place in anticipation of it. To the best of my knowledge, the work is current up to 31 July 2025. All website addresses were accurate on this date and have been archived online at http://archive.org/web/ where they will remain accessible in their original form even if the original website is altered or removed.

Inspired by Hilary Charlesworth's discussion of James Crawford's choice of book covers,[2] this book's cover image is *Sea Wave* (1931), by Australian artist Grace Cossington Smith (1892–1984). Taking a post-impressionist approach to depicting the coast near Thirroul and Bulli (on the south coast of New South Wales, Australia), the painting resonates strongly with the book's critique of the naturalist foundations of an ambulatory theory of baselines. Cossington Smith's artwork is a representation of the coast; similarly, the concept of the baseline in the international law of the sea can be understood as the legal representation of the coast. Both the artwork and the baseline have a strong nexus with the coast and, indeed, give an *impression* of that coast. But as representations of the coast they are of course distinct from the physical coast itself. As such, the maker—whether the artist or the State—must make choices as to how the coastline should be represented. *Sea Wave* vividly speaks to the book's focus on the choices States have made in establishing their baselines, and the significance of those choices, particularly for the legal stability of maritime zones.

Frances Anggadi
Ngunnawal country/Canberra, 31 July 2025

[2] Hilary Charlesworth, 'James Crawford and the Art of Law' (2022) 35 Leiden Journal of International Law 417.

Contents

List of Figures xiii
List of Tables xv
List of Appendices xvii
Table of Cases xix
List of Abbreviations xxi

1. Treaty, Practice, and Interpretation: Towards a Contemporary Understanding of the LOSC 1
 1.1 Sea-level rise and maritime zones 1
 1.2 An interpretative claim for the legal stability of maritime zones 3
 1.3 Situating the book 9
 1.4 The approach of the book 13
  1.4.1 Gathering evidence of State practice 14
  1.4.2 The significance of State practice for the law of the sea 17
 1.5 Overview of the chapters 21

2. The Legal Framework and Scholarship on Sea-level Rise, Baselines, and Maritime Zones 26
 2.1 Introduction 26
 2.2 The applicable law relating to baselines and maritime zones in the international law of the sea 26
  2.2.1 The LOSC framework for unilateral maritime zones 26
  2.2.2 The relationship between baselines and maritime boundary delimitation 29
 2.3 Situating legal stability: Responses from scholars and expert bodies to questions of sea-level rise 34
  2.3.1 First phase of scholarship: The 'ambulatory' theory of baselines (and its problem of instability) 35
  2.3.2 Second phase of scholarship: Situating legal stability within the existing LOSC system 39
  2.3.3 Third phase of scholarship: Legal stability and the 'contemporary interpretation' of the LOSC 43

3. Unpacking the Legal Stability of Maritime Zones 47
 3.1 Introduction 47
 3.2 Securing a stable 'order of the seas and oceans' 49
 3.3 The drafting history of Article 5 52
  3.3.1 Opting for a charts-based definition of the normal baseline 53
  3.3.2 A qualified primacy for charts: guarding against abuse 58

3.4 Invoking the legal stability of maritime zones 61
3.4.1 Achieving legal stability for maritime zones: the importance of stabilizing legislation 64
3.4.2 Achieving legal stability for maritime zones: no duty to update 65
3.4.3 Achieving legal stability for maritime zones: the relevance of entitlement 66
3.5 Identifying elements of the legal stability of maritime zones 68

4. Spatial Stability: The Baseline in National Legislation 71
4.1 Introduction 71
4.2 A fresh study of normal baseline legislation 73
4.2.1 Findings on the normal baseline 75
4.2.2 Discussion of overall findings of the legislative study 84
4.3 The significance of the legislative study for the LOSC 87
4.3.1 Legislation implementing the normal baseline as 'subsequent practice' for the purposes of Article 31(3)(b) of the VCLT 88
4.3.2 Article 5's ordinary meaning, context, and the object and purpose of the LOSC 89
4.3.3 'Subsequent practice' and the need for interpretative agreement 93
4.4 Implications for spatial stability under the LOSC 99

5. Temporal Stability: Baseline Change Over Time 110
5.1 Introduction 110
5.2 The baseline change study 111
5.2.1 Findings on baseline change 115
5.2.2 Discussion of overall findings of the case study 121
5.3 The significance of the baseline change study for the LOSC 122
5.3.1 Baseline change in existing scholarship: is there a legal duty to update established baselines? 122
5.3.2 An implied duty to update established baselines: justifications and critiques 124
5.3.3 Treaty silence: applying the general rule of interpretation, with caution 127
5.3.4 Revisiting ordinary meaning, context, and object and purpose 130
5.3.5 Baseline change as 'subsequent practice' for the purposes of Article 31(3)(b) of the VCLT 133
5.4 Implications for temporal stability under the LOSC 138

6. Stability of Legal Status? The Effect of Sea-Level Rise on Maritime Entitlements 151
6.1 Introduction 151
6.2 Interrogating the causes of destabilization: the relevance of habitability and elevation for the legal status of features 153
6.2.1 Habitability and maritime entitlement: competing views on the interpretation of Article 121 154
6.2.2 Elevation and maritime entitlement: submergence of features 170

6.3 What does it mean to destabilize the legal status of features? 172
6.3.1 Transformation and non-transformation of legal status: the distinction between physical and legal processes 173
6.3.2 The legal transformation of features: the role of State practice relating to baseline legislation and baseline change 177
6.4 Sea-level rise and 'archipelagic status' 180
6.5 Stability for the legal status of features under the LOSC 188

7. Achieving Stable Maritime Zones: Options for Domestic and International Actions 190
7.1 Introduction 190
7.2 Domestic action: implementing spatially stable baselines in legislation 190
7.3 International action: solidifying the legal stability of maritime zones among States 191
7.4 Bringing the legal stability of maritime zones before international courts and tribunals 196

8. Advancing a Contemporary Interpretation of the LOSC 205
8.1 Introduction 205
8.2 The legal stability of maritime zones and the interpretation of the LOSC 206
8.2.1 The contemporary interpretation of the LOSC 207
8.2.2 Customary international law 209
8.3 Addressing questions of sea-level rise 213
8.3.1 Applying a contemporary interpretation of the LOSC 213
8.3.2 How much legal stability is available? 215
8.4 The significance of State practice for international law scholarship 219

Selected Bibliography 223
Index 233

Figures

4.1 Types of normal baseline definition used by coastal States (LOSC Parties and non-Parties); percentages relate to the number of instances of each definition type as a proportion of all observed definitions. 76

4.2 Extract from table in Article 3, Decree No 2015-958 of 31 July 2015, showing coordinates on the Mediterranean coast of mainland France; fifth column indicates the type of line to be used from one point to the next in the list 79

4.3 Trend lines for usage of each definition type, showing the number of coastal States implementing that type of normal baseline in each time band (not cumulative) 87

4.4 Diagram showing various tidal datums 89

6.1 Two-part model of the regime of islands under Article 121 159

6.2 Three-part model of the regime of islands under Article 121 165

Tables

4.1 Typology of definitions of the normal baseline 75
4.2 Coastal States which use the normal baseline, grouped by definition type 77
4.3 Usage of normal baseline definition types according to UN Regional Group 86
5.1 Coastal States included in the baseline change study 114
5.2 Findings in relation to legislative actions effecting baseline change 115
6.1 Archipelagic States and their membership of PIF and/or AOSIS 187

Appendices

1.1 Membership of the PIF, AOSIS, and Commonwealth 24

4.1 Legislation referred to in the legislative study (grouped by definition type) 103

5.1 Baseline change study—selection of coastal States 141

5.2 Baseline change study—representativeness of included coastal States 143

5.3 Baseline change study—legislative actions effecting baseline change 145

5.4 Baseline change study—legislation in relation to which there were no legislative actions effecting baseline change 149

Table of Cases

Aegean Sea Continental Shelf Case (Greece v Turkey) (Judgment) [1978] ICJ Rep 3 . . . 32–34, 151n.2
Alleged Violations of Sovereign Rights and Maritime Spaces in the Caribbean Sea (Nicaragua v Colombia) (Judgment) [2022] ICJ Rep 266. . . . 31, 95–96, 97n.141, 197n.25
Bay of Bengal Maritime Boundary Arbitration (Bangladesh v India) (Award) (2014) LOSC Arbitral Tribunal, 7 July 2014 . . . 32–34
Case concerning the Aerial Incident of July 27th, 1955 (Israel v Bulgaria) (Preliminary Objections) ICJ Rep 127 . . . 128–29
Dispute concerning the delimitation of the maritime boundary between Mauritius and Maldives in the Indian Ocean (Mauritius/Maldives) (Preliminary Objections) (2021) (ITLOS Case No. 28, 28 January 2021) . . . 151n.3
Dispute concerning the delimitation of the maritime boundary between Mauritius and Maldives in the Indian Ocean (Mauritius/Maldives) (Merits) (2023) (ITLOS Case No. 28). . . . 31, 42–43
Delimitation of the Maritime Boundary between Bangladesh and Myanmar (Bangladesh/Myanmar) (Judgment) (2012) ITLOS Reports . . . 31n.36
Fisheries (United Kingdom v Norway) [1951] ICJ Rep 116. . . . 15–16, 56, 89, 138, 189, 197n.25, 208–9
Japan – Alcoholic Beverages II, WT/DS8/AB/R, WT/DS10/AB/R and WT/DS11/AB/R (1 November 1996). . . . 94–95, 96, 207
Kasikili/ Sedudu Island (Botswana/ Namibia) (Judgment) [1999] ICJ Rep 1045. . . . 18–19
M/V "Virginia G" (Panama /Guinea-Bissau) (Judgment) (2014) ITLOS Reports . . . 18–19, 97
M/V Saiga (No. 2) (St Vincent and the Grenadines v Guinea) (Judgment) (1999) ITLOS Reports . . . 197n.28
Maritime Delimitation (Eritrea/Yemen) (Second Phase (Award)) (1999) 119 ILR 417. . . . 197n.25
Maritime Delimitation and Territorial Questions between Qatar and Bahrain (Qatar/Bahrain) (Judgment) [2001] ICJ Rep 40. . . . 182n.150, 183–84, 197n.25
Maritime Delimitation in the Black Sea (Romania v Ukraine) (Judgment) [2009] ICJ Rep 61 . . . 29–31
Monte Confurco Case (Seychelles v France) (Judgment) (2000) 125 ILR 203 . . . 162
North Sea Continental Shelf (Federal Republic of Germany v Denmark) (1969) ICJ Rep 3. . . . 26–27, 151n.2
Obligations of States in Respect of Climate Change (Advisory Opinion of 23 July 2025) . . . 5, 6–7, 110, 131–32, 137–38, 203
Philippines v China (Award) (2016) (Permanent Court of Arbitration, PCA Case N° 2013-19) . . . 18–19, 158, 174–75
Request for an Advisory Opinion submitted by the Sub-Regional Fisheries Commission (SRFC) (Advisory Opinion) (2015) ITLOS Case No. 21 . . . 8–9, 131, 219–20n.48
Request for an advisory opinion submitted by the Commission of Small Island States on Climate Change and International Law (2023) (ITLOS Case No. 31) . . . 198
Sovereignty over Pulau Litigan and Pulau Sipadan (Indonesia/Malaysia) (Judgment) ICJ Rep 625 . . . 129, 130–31

Temple of Préah Vihéar (Cambodia v Thailand) (Merits) [1962] ICJ Rep 6 . . . .32–34, 96n.138
Territorial and Maritime Dispute (Nicaragua v Colombia) (Judgment) [2012] ICJ Rep 624. . . . . .171–72, 197n.25
United States – Standards for Reformulated and Conventional Gasoline, WT/DS2/AB/R (20 May 1996) 90
Volga Case (Russian Federation v Australia) (Judgment) (2003) 42 ILM 159. . . . . 162, 163–64, 196–97

Abbreviations

AOSIS	Alliance of Small Island States
ARSIWA	Articles on Responsibility of States for Internationally Wrongful Acts
COSIS	Commission of Small Island States
DAC	Development Assistance Committee
DOALOS	UN Division for Ocean Affairs and the Law of the Sea
EEZ	exclusive economic zone
ENC	electronic navigational chart
GHG	greenhouse gases
Hague Conference	1930 League of Nations Conference for the Codification of International Law
HHEL	human habitation or economic life
ICJ	International Court of Justice
ICJ Statute	Statute of the International Court of Justice
ILA	International Law Association
ILA Baselines Committee	International Law Association Committee on Baselines
ILA SLR Committee	International Law Association Committee on International Law and Sea Level Rise
ILC	International Law Commission
IPCC	Intergovernmental Panel on Climate Change
ITLOS	International Tribunal for the Law of the Sea
LAT	lowest astronomical tide
LECZ	low elevation coastal zone
LLIC	low-lying islands and coasts
LOSC	United Nations Convention on the Law of the Sea (opened for signature 10 December 1982, entered into force 16 November 1994) 1833 UNTS 3
nm	nautical mile
PIF	Pacific Islands Forum
2021 PIF Declaration	2021 Declaration on Preserving Maritime Zones in the Face of Climate Change-Related Sea-Level Rise
SFRC	Sub-Regional Fisheries Commission
UN	United Nations
UN DOALOS	UN Division for Ocean Affairs and the Law of the Sea

UNCLOS II	Second UN Conference on the Law of the Sea
UNCLOS III	Third UN Conference on the Law of the Sea
UNGA	UN General Assembly
VCLT	Vienna Convention on the Law of Treaties (opened for signature 23 May 1969, entered into force 27 January 1980) 1155 UNTS 331

1

Treaty, Practice, and Interpretation

Towards a Contemporary Understanding of the LOSC

1.1 Sea-level rise and maritime zones

In 2021, the Alliance of Small Island States (AOSIS) declared that 'climate change continues to pose the most serious threat to our very existence, territorial integrity, viability and survival'.[1] This recalled another declaration made a month earlier by the Pacific Islands Forum (PIF), that recognized 'the threats of climate change and sea-level rise as the defining issue that imperils the livelihoods and wellbeing of our peoples and undermines the full realisation of a peaceful, secure and sustainable future for our region'.[2] Indeed, climate hazards are projected for every region in the world,[3] and, in particular, climate change is intensifying coastal hazards such as sea-level rise.[4] Rising sea levels are likely to lead to significant coastal erosion and inundation, especially for low-lying areas. A range of social, economic, and environmental impacts are expected as a result: for example, small island developing States are home to around 65 million people, many of whom live in coastal areas. There is growing concern that, in some cases, the severity of climate change impacts such as sea-level rise will challenge island sustainability in terms of the availability of arable land and fresh water on atoll islands, raising the prospect of community relocation.[5] Over 10 million people also live in coastal 'megacities' situated in

[1] Leaders' Declaration of the Alliance of Small Island States (signed 22 September 2021) <www.aosis.org/launch-of-the-alliance-of-small-island-states-leaders-declaration/> (2021 AOSIS Declaration).

[2] Declaration on Preserving Maritime Zones in the Face of Climate Change-Related Sea-Level Rise (signed 6 August 2021) <www.forumsec.org/2021/08/11/declaration-on-preserving-maritime-zones-in-the-face-of-climate-change-related-sea-level-rise/> (2021 PIF Declaration).

[3] IPCC, 2023: Summary for Policymakers, in 'Climate Change 2023: Synthesis Report. Contribution of Working Groups I, II and III to the Sixth Assessment Report of the Intergovernmental Panel on Climate Change' (2023) Statement B.2.1.

[4] This book hyphenates 'sea-level rise' unless the term is otherwise expressed in a name, title or direct quote (eg 'International Law Association Committee on International Law and Sea Level Rise').

[5] AK Magnan and others, 'Cross-Chapter Box 9: Integrative Cross-Chapter Box on Low-Lying Islands and Coasts' in H-O Pörtner and others (eds), *IPCC Special Report on the Ocean and Cryosphere in a Changing Climate* (2019) 663.

Sea-Level Rise and the Legal Stability of Maritime Zones. Frances Anggadi, Oxford University Press.
 DOI: 10.1093/9780198973515.003.0001

low-lying areas (such as Jakarta, Lagos, and Cairo), and such cities are predicted to face increasing costs of coastal protection, and experience disruptions to transport and supply networks that depend on coastal infrastructure such as ports.[6] Furthermore, almost half of terrestrial species at risk of extinction are found in island habitats, since small islands host significant levels of global terrestrial biodiversity.[7]

Against this backdrop, PIF leaders have also pointed to 'the long-standing concern in our Pacific region for preserving maritime zones in the face of climate change-related sea-level rise'.[8] Maritime zones are the means by which the international law of the sea organizes ocean spaces. In each of the main maritime zones of national jurisdiction—archipelagic waters, the territorial sea, contiguous zone, exclusive economic zone (EEZ), continental shelf—States have different rights, responsibilities, and interests. A clear, global system of maritime zones, with agreed maximum breadths for each zone, was one of the key achievements of the United Nations Convention on the Law of the Sea (LOSC), bringing order to the chaos that had been created by conflicting national claims for jurisdiction in ocean space in past decades.[9] The zonal approach was also central to the aim to settle 'all issues relating to the law of the sea',[10] in that the rules applicable to particular issues depend on the maritime zone in which the activity occurs, whether it be navigation, fishing, or seabed mining. Some of these rights can be highly valuable, as is certainly the case in relation to the fishing rights of Pacific States in their EEZs.[11] This makes the global system of maritime zones essential for determining what rights and interests States have in each part of the ocean, critical for upholding a balance of interests between different ocean stakeholders, and a major contributor in 'the maintenance of peace, justice and progress for all peoples of the world'.[12]

[6] ibid.

[7] M Mycoo and others, 'Small Islands' in H-O Pörtner and others (eds), *Climate Change 2022: Impacts, Adaptation and Vulnerability Contribution of Working Group II to the Sixth Assessment Report of the Intergovernmental Panel on Climate Change* (Cambridge University Press 2022) Executive Summary.

[8] 2021 PIF Declaration (n 2).

[9] See Section 3.2.

[10] United Nations Convention on the Law of the Sea (opened for signature 10 December 1982, entered into force 16 November 1994) 1833 UNTS 397 (LOSC) Preamble.

[11] PIF, 'Submission to the International Law Commission on the Sub-topics of Sea-Level Rise in Relation to Statehood and to the Protection of Persons Affected by Sea-Level Rise (72nd Session of the International Law Commission)' (2021) Information Paper. For deeper perspectives on the economic value of the EEZ, particularly for Pacific countries, see Deborah Cass, 'The Quiet Revolution: The Development of the Exclusive Economic Zone and Implications for Foreign Fishing Access in the Pacific' in Kim Rubenstein (ed), *Traversing the Divide: Honouring Deborah Cass's Contributions to Public and International Law* (ANU Press 2021) and Johann D Bell and others, 'Pathways to Sustaining Tuna-Dependent Pacific Island Economies during Climate Change' (2021) 4 Nature Sustainability 900.

[12] LOSC, Preamble.

Under the international law of the sea, a coastal State's entitlement to maritime zones flows from its sovereignty over land territory, creating an important relationship between the land and the sea in the LOSC framework. Characteristics of that land territory exert a strong influence on the establishment of maritime zones. Land is relevant to the question of *maritime entitlement*, that is, which of the maritime zones might be supported by any particular portion of land, because the legal status of a land feature determines whether or not it can support the full suite of maritime zones. Particular characteristics of the coastline also influence the *baseline*, the zero-mark from which the breadths of maritime zones are measured to their *outer limits* (whether that be 12 nautical miles (nm) for the territorial sea, or 200 nm for the EEZ). In this way, maritime zones can be seen as a form of legal architecture for the oceans, a structure of legally significant lines and spaces supporting the 'legal order of the seas and oceans'.[13]

However, the relationship between land and sea underpinning the rules of maritime entitlement and baseline rules prompts the question: if a coastline retreats, might maritime zones shrink or be lost altogether?

1.2 An interpretative claim for the legal stability of maritime zones

For decades, the most widely expressed answer given in scholarship was that in general, baselines and associated maritime zones 'ambulate' with the coastline; this was commonly known as the 'ambulatory theory of baselines'.[14] Under this view of the law, if a coastline recedes as the sea-level rises, the baseline recedes with it, potentially causing a shrinking of the maritime zones drawn from that baseline.

Following this reasoning, sea-level rise would indeed imperil baselines and maritime zones, which would bring potentially dramatic consequences, especially for 'large ocean states'.[15] For instance, the Federated States of Micronesia has established an EEZ of approximately 100,000 km^2 around its southernmost atoll island, Kapingamarangi.[16] But under the ambulatory theory of baselines, Micronesia would stand to lose areas of its maritime zones—and the

[13] ibid.

[14] See discussion in Chapter 2.

[15] Wesley Morgan, 'Large Ocean States: Pacific Regionalism and Climate Security in a New Era of Geostrategic Competition' (2022) 39 East Asia 45.

[16] Rosemary Rayfuse, 'Sea Level Rise and Maritime Zones: Preserving the Maritime Entitlements of "Disappearing" States' in Michael B Gerrard and Gregory E Wannier (eds), *Threatened Island Nations: Legal Implications of Rising Seas and a Changing Climate* (Cambridge University Press 2013) 175.

significant resource rights and economic benefits that they bring—if its islands (such as Kapingamarangi) were to become submerged. And because low-lying coastal areas are distributed globally, and include both developed and developing States,[17] such potential losses are clearly a concern both within and beyond the Pacific region.

However, many States, with increasing frequency and clarity, have in recent years offered a different answer, advancing the position in a number of landmark collective declarations that their maritime zones may be preserved notwithstanding climate-change induced sea-level rise. In August 2021, PIF leaders issued the Declaration on Preserving Maritime Zones in the Face of Climate Change-Related Sea-Level Rise:

> Recognising the principles of legal stability, security, certainty and predictability that underpin the Convention and the relevance of these principles to the interpretation and application of the Convention in the context of sea-level rise and climate change [...]
>
> [We] Record the position of Members of the Pacific Islands Forum that maintaining maritime zones established in accordance with the Convention, and rights and entitlements that flow from them, notwithstanding climate change-related sea-level rise, is supported by both the Convention and the legal principles underpinning it.[18]

One month later, AOSIS made a similar declaration.[19] In October 2024, the Commonwealth Heads of Government adopted the Commonwealth Ocean Declaration, which similarly affirms that 'members can maintain their maritime zones, as established and notified to the Secretary-General of the United Nations in accordance with UNCLOS, and the rights and entitlements that flow from them, shall continue to apply, without reduction, notwithstanding any physical changes connected to climate change-related sea-level rise'.[20] These declarations make clear that in the view of these seventy Parties[21] to the

[17] See global distribution of low-lying islands and coasts particularly at risk from sea level rise in Magnan and others, 'Cross-Chapter Box 9' (n 5) Fig CB9.1. The total area of the world's combined exclusive economic zones is estimated at 37,745,000 square miles, amounting to 36 per cent of the ocean's surface: Huan-Sheng Tseng and Ching-Hsiewn Ou, 'The Evolution and Trend of the Traditional Fishing Rights' (2010) 53 Ocean & Coastal Management 270, 270.

[18] 2021 PIF Declaration (n 2).

[19] 2021 AOSIS Declaration (n 1).

[20] Apia Commonwealth Ocean Declaration (signed 26 October 2024) <https://thecommonwealth.org/news/chogm2024/commonwealth-nations-adopt-ocean-declaration> (Commonwealth Ocean Declaration).

[21] See Appendix 1.1 for the current membership of the PIF, AOSIS, and Commonwealth.

LOSC, sea-level rise does not result in the loss or diminution of their established maritime zones.

Reflecting on these and other interventions from States, the Final Report of the International Law Commission (ILC) Study Group on sea-level rise and international law found in 2025 that '[t]he preservation of legal stability, certainty and predictability is directly linked to an interpretation of the United Nations Convention on the Law of the Sea and other rules of international law that allows for the preservation of baselines, the outer limits of maritime zones and associated entitlements notwithstanding changes to the coastline as a result of climate change-related sea-level rise'.[22] This conclusion clearly resonates with the scholarly recommendations advanced in 2018 by the International Law Association's Committee on International Law and Sea Level Rise (ILA SLR Committee), which proposed an 'interpretation of the 1982 Law of the Sea Convention in relation to the ability of coastal and archipelagic States to maintain their existing lawful maritime entitlements'.[23] This demonstrates a strong alignment between certain States and experts and scholars as to the broad position that international law permits the preservation of maritime zones in circumstances of sea-level rise, and does so as a matter of interpretation of the LOSC.

Furthermore, in its Advisory Opinion on the *Obligations of States in Respect of Climate Change*, the International Court of Justice (ICJ) affirmed on 23 July 2025 that:

> the provisions of UNCLOS do not require States parties, in the context of physical changes resulting from climate-change related sea level rise, to update their charts or lists of geographical co-ordinates that show the baselines and outer limit lines of their maritime zones once they have been duly established in conformity with the Convention. For this reason, States parties to UNCLOS are under no obligation to update such charts or lists of geographical co-ordinates.[24]

The Court also noted that it formed this view in contemplation of the PIF, AOSIS, and other declarations, as 'practice [...] relevant for the purposes of the

[22] Study Group on sea-level rise in relation to international law, 'Final Report of the Study Group on Sea-Level Rise in relation to International Law', UN Doc A/80/10, Annex I [27] (2025 ILC Study Group Final Report).

[23] See eg ILA (Committee on International Law and Sea Level Rise) Res 5/2018 (ILA 2018 Resolution); discussed further in Section 2.3.2.

[24] *Obligations of States in Respect of Climate Change* (Advisory Opinion) [2025] [362] (*Obligations of States in Respect of Climate Change*) <https://www.icj-cij.org/case/187>.

interpretation of UNCLOS'.[25] This is a very significant and welcome development, as the first judicial recognition of the view that the LOSC does not oblige States to update established maritime zones in response to climate-change induced sea-level rise.

It is notable, however, that these interpretative claims have developed rapidly against the backdrop of decades of scholarship which, until around 2018, had tended to favour a rather different view of the relevant law. The disconnection between these two positions—one envisaging a baseline that ambulates with a sea-level rise impacted coastline; the other asserting the possibility of stable baselines and maritime zones notwithstanding sea-level rise—raises several questions that the book seeks to answer.

First, if both positions purport to offer interpretations of the relevant rules in the international law of the sea, which position should be preferred as the best understanding of those rules today? The ILC has affirmed that '[m]embers generally considered that the existing legal framework remained applicable in the context of sea-level rise, and added that the scope of application of such rules could be made clearer'.[26] The ICJ has now made clear that a key factor in coming to its conclusion is the absence of a duty to update in the terms of the LOSC, and this is undoubtedly a significant development. However, such a conclusion leaves unaddressed how we should approach the interpretation of the other provisions of the LOSC that are central to baselines and maritime zone entitlement. Achieving stable maritime zones requires careful and legally sound interpretation of those provisions as well, particularly since the LOSC has been interpreted in previous scholarship to provide for ambulatory baselines and maritime zones. This book will identify such provisions of the LOSC, gather and analyse relevant State practice, and offer a contemporary interpretation of the LOSC.

Secondly, although it is clear that there is growing support for legal stability in connection with maritime zones, how does an interpretation of the LOSC achieve or promote that goal? As explained in Chapter 3, the concept of legal stability has gained increasing prominence, but its contours remain blurry. As noted by Judge Aurescu, the Advisory Opinion does not mention this concept, expressing the view that a 'most notable absence is the principle of legal stability, security, certainty and predictability'.[27] Is legal stability

[25] ibid [360].

[26] ILC, 'Report of the International Law Commission covering the Work of its Seventy-Sixth Session' (28 April–30 May 2025) UN Doc A/80/10 [54] (2025 ILC Report).

[27] *Obligations of States in Respect of Climate Change* (n 24) Separate Opinion of Judge Aurescu [4].

to be assimilated to States' overarching concerns for security, certainty, and predictability threatened by sea-level rise?[28] Or is a more focused meaning useful, as explained by Papua New Guinea, which stated that '[b]y "legal stability", we mean the need to preserve the baselines and outer limits of maritime zones'?[29]

The book proceeds on the latter view, contending that a more robust and substantial understanding of the legal stability of maritime zones is essential for understanding how the LOSC might be interpreted to achieve the preservation of baselines and maritime zones. To this end, the book identifies key elements for achieving the legal stability of maritime zones—*how* to preserve baselines and outer limits—and connects these explicitly with particular aspects of the interpretation of the LOSC:

- the first element pertains to the spatial stability of the baseline (the capacity for a baseline, as a practical matter, to remain in the same location on the Earth's surface), and relates to a coastal State's implementation of the relevant baseline provisions of the LOSC in its legislation;
- the second element pertains to the baseline's temporal stability (the maintenance of its baseline over time notwithstanding coastal changes), and relates to the absence in the LOSC of any express duty to update baselines, as recognized by the ICJ; and
- the third element of legal stability relates to the status of features (the maintenance of a feature's legal status notwithstanding physical changes to that feature), essential to the maintenance of the feature's maritime entitlements pursuant to Article 121 in particular.

Thirdly, how should we make sense of these rapid developments in this area of the law, in relation to the challenge of sea-level rise? Given that the text of the LOSC has of course remained as it was from 1982, is it that there has been a shift in scholarship in how to view that law; that, despite the language of the LOSC itself staying the same, the substance of the law has nevertheless evolved or developed; or that there have been developments outside of the LOSC itself, such as in customary international law; or perhaps some combination of these possibilities?

[28] This is one approach noted by the ILA SLR Committee: ILA (Committee on International Law and Sea Level Rise) 'Report (Athens Conference)' note 47 (2024 ILA SLR Report).

[29] Papua New Guinea, 22nd Meeting of the Sixth Committee, 76th Session (28 October 2021) <www.un.org/en/ga/sixth/76/pdfs/statements/ilc/22mtg_papuanewguinea_2.pdf>.

Resolving the tensions between old and new statements of the law—as well as between the perspectives of States and scholars—is essential given the dramatic difference between the potential legal outcomes and the high stakes for States already facing the practical and social effects of climate change. Before the ICJ's Advisory Opinion was handed down, States demonstrated an interest in further clarification that would build on previous thinking, particularly on that of the ILA and the ILC: for example, the European Union stated that while 'no State has contested the notion of legal stability and the preservation of maritime zones [. . .] the precise way in which the Convention ought to be interpreted and how the objective of legal stability is to be secured legally and in practice may require careful consideration'.[30] The large number of States seeking clarification on the preservation of maritime zones in advisory proceedings before international courts and tribunals is also a clear indication of that desire for greater legal certainty;[31] and while the Advisory Opinion is a significant statement on one important aspect of that discussion—the lack of any obligation to update established baselines—several outstanding matters remain to be resolved. To contribute to such efforts towards clarification, this book takes a fresh look at whether a claim for the legal stability of maritime zones has merit under today's international law of the sea.

The book contends that increasing recognition of the legal stability of maritime zones should be seen as a paradigm example of the evolution of the LOSC, demonstrating its character as a 'living instrument'.[32] This evolution is discernible by a systematic application of the framework for treaty interpretation; namely, by identifying and analysing the potential legal significance of the practice of States in the application of particular provisions of the LOSC. In this way, treaty interpretation offers the analytical means to connect academic scholarship with States' claims, as well as a means to understand the tension between old and new statements of the law as an expression of the law's evolution. By making these connections, the book takes seriously the interpretative claim in the PIF Declaration that 'maintaining maritime zones established in accordance with the Convention, and rights and entitlements that flow from them, notwithstanding climate change-related sea-level rise, is supported by both the Convention and the legal principles underpinning it',[33] testing this

[30] European Union, 23rd Meeting of the Sixth Committee, 78th Session (23 October 2023) <www.un.org/en/ga/sixth/78/pdfs/statements/ilc/23mtg_eu_1.pdf>.

[31] See Section 7.4.

[32] Judge Lucky referred to the LOSC and the Statute of the International Tribunal for the Law of the Sea as 'living instruments': *Request for an Advisory Opinion submitted by the Sub-Regional Fisheries Commission (SRFC)* (Advisory Opinion) (2015) Case no 21 [18] (*Request for an Advisory Opinion submitted by the Sub-Regional Fisheries Commission (SRFC)*).

[33] 2021 PIF Declaration (n 2).

claim against standards for legally significant State practice and interpretative agreement.

In so doing, the book builds a case for the contemporary (re)interpretation of the international law of the sea, arguing that there is strong evidence that today's law has now developed to be capacious enough to permit the preservation of maritime zones. Offering a reasoned account of such a development makes transparent one of the key modalities for change in international law—interpretation by subsequent practice—demonstrating the capacity of the law of the sea to respond to changing circumstances, thereby providing a foundation for the law's continued relevance and legitimacy. As explained by Allot, 'interpretation is an act of power across time and space. We interpret in the present, here and now, something created elsewhere in the past. [. . .] In interpreting a text, we make choices about reconciling the past and the present, the close and the remote, as we launch our interpretation into an unknowable and uncontrollable future.'[34] The book's engagement with treaty interpretation explicitly traces these connections between text and practice, as well as old and new understandings of the law. Furthermore, in aiming to demonstrate how the identification and analysis of State practice can significantly influence a contemporary understanding of international law rules, the approach of the book also endeavours to speak to international law scholars more generally: as an attempt to reflect and apply the international law method for the interpretation of treaties, and in giving a practical answer to the question 'is international law international?',[35] in its efforts to take into account practice from different regions and languages.[36]

1.3 Situating the book

At the outset, it is essential to situate the book's scope and argument within the broader context of debates on the legal implications of sea-level rise for maritime zones among States and within academic scholarship.

First, the book focuses on the situation where maritime zones may be established unilaterally, noting that there are distinct legal issues which arise

[34] Philip Allott, 'Interpretation: An Exact Art' in Andrea Bianchi, Daniel Peat, and Matthew Windsor (eds), *Interpretation in International Law* (Oxford University Press 2015) 374.

[35] Anthea Roberts, *Is International Law International?* (Oxford University Press 2017).

[36] For an earlier account of the method underlying this book, see Frances Anggadi and Camille Goodman, 'Please Mind the Gap: A Venn Diagram Story of Method in International Law' (*Critical Legal Thinking*, 31 January 2023) <https://criticallegalthinking.com/2023/01/31/please-mind-the-gap-a-venn-diagram-story-of-method-in-international-law/>.

where there is a delimited maritime boundary between States.[37] The stability of delimited maritime boundaries may be grounded in sources outside the LOSC itself, such as the continued application of a maritime boundary treaty between its signatories,[38] or the finality of an adjudicated maritime delimitation decided by a court or tribunal.[39] While the law of baselines and maritime boundary delimitation are related to each other,[40] this book focuses on the former. Accordingly, the applicable rules forming the focus of this book are those in the LOSC governing baselines (normal, straight, or archipelagic); the outer limits of maritime zones (such as the maximum breadth of 200 nm for an EEZ); and the rules of maritime zone entitlement (important because not all land features generate entitlement to all maritime zones in the same way). As detailed in Chapter 2, these rules (and their parallels in customary international law) are determinative regarding the location and extent of unilateral maritime zones, and, accordingly, the standard by which the legality of such baselines or maritime zones must be assessed under international law.

Secondly, this book argues for a renewed appraisal of the *lex lata* (the existing law), consistent with the approach suggested by the ILC, and taken by the ICJ in its Advisory Opinion. Even though many writers take the view that baselines and maritime zones ambulate with the coastline, it is also widely recognized by those writers that this is an undesirable result.[41] Diagnosed as a problem with—or a lack within—the existing laws, many have suggested options *de lege ferenda* (in relation to a potential, future law), such as engaging the LOSC amendment provisions under Article 312, adopting a new implementing agreement under the LOSC, or perhaps negotiating a modification agreement under Article 311(3).[42] Noting the difficulty of those pathways as a means to

[37] See discussion in Section 2.2.2. Both unilateral and delimited maritime boundaries are considered within the ILA and ILC's studies on sea-level rise and international law.

[38] Maritime boundaries delimited in a treaty are generally considered to be more stable than unilateral maritime zones: see Bogdan Aurescu and Nilüfer Oral, Co-Chairs of the Study Group on sea-level rise in relation to international law, *Additional paper to the first issues paper* (Seventy-Fourth Session of the International Law Commission) (13 February 2023) UN Doc A/CN.4/761 [120] (*Additional paper to the first issues paper*) and Julia Lisztwan, 'Stability of Maritime Boundary Agreements' (2012) 37 Yale Journal of International Law 153.

[39] LOSC, art 296(1).

[40] See Chapter 2 on the relationship between baselines and maritime boundary delimitation.

[41] See Section 2.3.1.

[42] These and other options oriented towards *lex ferenda* are discussed in eg Jenny Grote Stoutenburg, *Disappearing Island States in International Law* (Brill 2015) ch 3; Moritaka Hayashi, 'Sea-Level Rise and the Law of the Sea: Future Options' in Davor Vidas and Peter Johan Schei (eds), *The World Ocean in Globalisation* (Brill Nijhoff 2011) 187; Clive Schofield and David Freestone, 'Options to Protect Coastlines and Secure Maritime Jurisdictional Claims in the Face of Global Sea Level Rise' in Michael B Gerrard and Gregory E Wannier (eds), *Threatened Island Nations: Legal Implications of Rising Seas and a Changing Climate* (Cambridge University Press 2013); ILA (Committee on International Law and Sea Level Rise), 'Report (Sydney Conference)' (2018); Karen Scott, 'Rising Seas and Pacific Maritime

achieve the successful preservation of maritime zones, interpretation of the existing rules in the LOSC has been identified by States and scholars as the most promising legal foundation for a response to sea-level rise impacts.[43] This is not to say, however, that the substance and application of the law of baselines and maritime zones has remained static since the conclusion of the LOSC in 1982. On the contrary, the book argues that a thoroughgoing interpretation of those rules today (following the approach explained in Section 1.4) reveals the evolution of those rules towards stable maritime zones.

Thirdly, this book is prompted by the phenomenon of sea-level rise, responding to questions raised within the international community about its legal implications for maritime zones. The scientific basis for such concerns is now well accepted. The Sixth Assessment Report of the Intergovernmental Panel on Climate Change (IPCC) states that it is '*virtually certain* that global mean sea level will continue to rise over the 21st century',[44] explaining that '[a]s of 2018, global average sea level was about 15–25 cm higher than in 1900, and 7–15 cm higher than in 1971. Sea level will continue to rise by an additional 10–25 cm by 2050',[45] and, in the longer term, sea level is 'committed to rise for centuries to millennia due to continuing deep-ocean warming and ice-sheet melt and will remain elevated for thousands of years'.[46] One of the main physical impacts of sea-level rise is coastal inundation and erosion: approximately '6000 to 17,000 km^2 of land is expected to be lost during the 21st century due to enhanced coastal erosion associated with [sea-level rise], in combination with other drivers'.[47] There is high confidence that coastal erosion will increase in all geographic regions,[48] with low-lying islands and coasts being at greater risk of impact.[49] Coastal erosion is 'generally accompanied by shoreline retreat, which can occur as a gradual process (eg due to sea-level rise) or as an episodic event due to storm surge and/or extreme waves, especially when combined with high tide',[50] which—in extreme cases—might result in the total inundation

Boundaries' (*Australian Outlook: Australian Institute of International Affairs*, 2018) <www.internationalaffairs.org.au/australianoutlook/rising-seas-and-pacific-maritime-boundaries/>.

[43] See Section 1.2 and further discussed in Section 2.3.3.
[44] IPCC, 'Climate Change 2021: The Physical Science Basis. Working Group I Contribution to the Sixth Assessment Report of the Intergovernmental Panel on Climate Change' (2021) 21 (original emphasis).
[45] ibid 1318.
[46] ibid 21.
[47] H-O Pörtner and others, 'IPCC Special Report on the Ocean and Cryosphere in a Changing Climate' (2019) 378.
[48] IPCC, 'Climate Change 2021: The Physical Science Basis' (n 44) Table TS.5.
[49] See generally Magnan and others, 'Cross-Chapter Box 9' (n 5).
[50] IPCC, 'Climate Change 2021: The Physical Science Basis' (n 44) 1803.

of small, low-lying coastal features. For example, Micronesia has several low-elevation atolls that are vulnerable to sea-level rise,[51] and sea-level rise trends in Micronesia are reported to have recently outpaced the global average, measuring at 6.7 mm/year at Kapingamarangi (over the period 1993 to 2019).[52]

Accordingly, the book answers questions about the implications of sea-level rise for maritime zones; but in framing its inquiry around the legal stability of maritime zones more broadly, the book also makes a wider argument about the legal stability of maritime zones under today's international law of the sea. This broad framing is notable for two reasons. As a practical matter, it is apparent that coastlines may be subject to change as a result of many factors, such as submergence caused by land subsidence, or changes brought about by earthquakes and volcanic eruptions.[53] Climate change conditions intensify or increase particular coastal hazards, affecting the coast in different ways depending on many factors, including the type of coast (eg sandy, rocky, or reef-lined) and its location and elevation in relation to sea level. For example, for low-lying coasts increasing severe storms might cause greater intensity of storm-induced coastal flooding and erosion, saltwater intrusion of freshwater reservoirs, and damage to coastal infrastructure; while increasing sea surface temperature is likely to result in more frequent bleaching and mortality events on coral reef-lined coasts.[54] Sea-level rise is one of these climate-related hazards, with significant impacts alone and in interaction with other hazards. The book's conclusions offer answers regarding the extent of legal stability available in the particular circumstance of sea-level rise, and also address how such conclusions might apply more broadly.

As a legal matter, framing the book as an inquiry about the legal stability of maritime zones expands the group of States that are potentially affected by the book's conclusions. It might be argued that the legal stability of maritime zones claimed by the leaders of the PIF, and by other groupings of States, might be a position of limited relevance, being only applicable to and opposable among members of those groups. This sentiment underlies the view that pronouncements such as the PIF Declaration have a limited effect, for example pointing

[51] Leonardo Bernard and others, 'Securing the Limits of Large Ocean States in the Pacific: Defining Baselines Limits and Boundaries amidst Changing Coastlines and Sea Level Rise' (2021) 11 Geosciences 394.

[52] Meghna Sengupta, Murray R Ford, and Paul S. Kench, 'Shoreline Changes in Coral Reef Islands of the Federated States of Micronesia since the mid-20th Century' (2021) 377 Geomorphology 107584.

[53] ECF Bird, *Coastal Geomorphology: An Introduction* (2nd edn, Wiley 2008) 9–10.

[54] Magnan and others, 'Cross-Chapter Box 9' (n 5) Table CB9.1; on effects for coral reef islands, see Thomas E Fellowes and others, 'Stability of Coral Reef Islands and Associated Legal Maritime Zones in a Changing Ocean' (2022) 17 Environmental Research Letters 17.

to the development of a particular customary rule.[55] However, resting upon such a conclusion ignores the fact that the PIF Declaration is framed as a universal claim: as explained by Samoa, because the PIF Declaration's claim for legal stability is 'grounded on an interpretation of the existing law of the sea as reflected in UNCLOS, States from outside the [PIF] membership are welcome to endorse and apply the approach of the [PIF] Declaration, including those that are not States Parties to UNCLOS'.[56] If the relevant benchmarks for treaty interpretation are satisfied, then such endorsement—where offered—is no longer merely political nor offered only in solidarity.[57] Rather such support must properly be considered as having legal significance, forming the foundation for an interpretation of the LOSC applicable to all Parties, and, as Samoa indicated, potentially also more broadly through custom.

As documented throughout the book, States in all UN Regional Groups are increasingly expressing such support. To what extent do such statements, weighed with other relevant evidence, support an interpretative claim for the legal stability of maritime zones? The following section explains how the book approaches the identification of relevant State practice, and the method of interpretation the book applies to evaluate its legal significance for today's law of the sea.

1.4 The approach of the book

In suggesting possible ways forward, the ILC Study Group on Sea-Level Rise and International Law suggested, among other things, that 'existing instruments and rules of international law may be applied in a manner that addresses the impact of sea-level rise so as to allow for a contemporary interpretation',[58] and, more specifically, a suggestion was also made to do so in accordance with 'more established approaches of interpretation [including] subsequent agreements and subsequent practice, as provided for in the Vienna Convention

[55] See references to 'regional State practice' and 'the emergence of a particular regional customary rule' in Bogdan Aurescu and Nilüfer Oral, Co-Chairs of the Study Group on sea-level rise in relation to international law, *First issues paper by Bogdan Aurescu and Nilüfer Oral* (28 February 2020) UN Doc A/CN.4/740 (*First issues paper*).

[56] Samoa, 28th Meeting of the Sixth Committee (1 November 2022) Seventy-Seventh Session of the United Nations General Assembly (UNGA77) <www.un.org/en/ga/sixth/77/ilc.shtml>. A summary of this statement is recorded in UN Doc A/C.6/77/SR.28.

[57] Some ILC members referred to 'the importance of the concept of solidarity in relation to challenges posed by sea-level rise': 2025 ILC Report (n 26) [75].

[58] 2025 ILC Study Group Final Report (n 22) [58(a)].

on the Law of Treaties, in addition to the original meaning of the terms of the treaty and taking into account its object and purpose'.[59] This book takes up that invitation here, posing this overarching question: to what extent does a contemporary interpretation of the LOSC provide for the legal stability of maritime zones?

To answer this question, the book takes a systematic doctrinal approach to interpret particular international legal rules, namely, the rules in relation to baselines and maritime zones contained within the LOSC, with an emphasis on identifying and evaluating relevant State practice. As elaborated in Chapter 2, the book considers the rules in Articles 5, 7, 47, and 121 of the LOSC, with a particular emphasis on Article 5 on the normal baseline. This emphasis is chosen not only because the normal baseline is the most commonly used baseline but also because it is the baseline type traditionally considered by scholars to be the paradigm 'ambulatory' baseline.[60]

1.4.1 Gathering evidence of State practice

It is widely accepted that State practice can take many forms, including the actions of all branches of the government of the State, other acts attributable to that State, and can include conduct in connection with treaties, legislative and administrative acts, and decisions of national courts.[61] The form of State practice which has received the most attention amongst commentors is the concentration of statements made by States, individually or collectively, on the topic of sea-level rise and maritime zones. For example, the ILA SLR Committee has closely studied this trend,[62] and the Final Report of the ILC Study Group also remarked that:

[59] 2025 ILC Report (n 26) [60].

[60] Relatedly, because straight and archipelagic baselines are commonly (if not always) defined by reference to coordinates, they much more readily demonstrate the spatial stability that appeared to be lacking in relation to the normal baseline. It is not necessary to examine State practice in the implementation of straight and archipelagic baselines (including through a comprehensive interpretation of arts 7 and 47), since their spatial stability is already generally understood. The book does, however, make conclusions that embrace all baseline types.

[61] ILC, Draft Conclusions on Subsequent Agreements and Subsequent Practice in relation to the Interpretation of Treaties, with Commentaries, UN Doc A/73/10) (ILC Draft Conclusions on Subsequent Agreements and Subsequent Practice) 73, Draft Conclusion 6(2).

[62] See 2024 ILA SLR Report (n 28) and ILA (Committee on International Law and Sea Level Rise) 'Report (Lisbon Conference)' (2022 ILA SLR Report); see also Davor Vidas and David Freestone, 'Legal Certainty and Stability in the Face of Sea Level Rise: Trends in the Development of State Practice and International Law Scholarship on Maritime Limits and Boundaries' (2022) 37 The International Journal of Marine and Coastal Law 1.

> General State practice exists, as evidenced by statements expressing widespread and consistent support, with regard to the preservation of baselines and the outer limits of maritime zones notwithstanding sea-level rise, in the interests of maintaining legal stability, certainty and predictability.[63]

Similarly, the ICJ pointed to similar statements as practice relevant to interpretation.[64] However, relatively little attention has been given in recent years to other potentially relevant forms of State practice, such as legislation. Building on earlier studies,[65] this book aims to enlarge the scope of material examined as potentially relevant State practice by focusing on the collection and evaluation of maritime zones legislation, a readily recognizable form of State practice, as the principal form of State practice examined in the book.[66] Legislative acts are, of course, unilateral actions undertaken by a coastal State and, of themselves, cannot answer questions about the substance of international law rules. Indeed, maritime zones legislation (as an example of a unilateral action by a State) offers a clear example of the complex relationship between international law and its implementation. As a starting point, the ICJ has recognized that domestic legislation establishing unilateral maritime zones necessarily touches upon the interests of other States and the international community:[67]

> The delimitation[68] of sea areas has always an international aspect; it cannot be dependent merely upon the will of the coastal State as expressed in its

[63] 2025 ILC Study Group Final Report (n 22) [32].

[64] *Obligations of States in Respect of Climate Change* (n 24) [360].

[65] Legislation as a form of practice did receive some early consideration, such as in the ILA Baselines Committee study on the normal baseline, on which this book builds: see ILA (Committee on Baselines under the International Law of the Sea), 'Baselines under the International Law of the Sea (Sofia Conference)' (2012 ILA Baselines Committee Report) and discussion in Chapter 4.

[66] While unilateral or collective statements made by States on the topic can be considered State practice, as they would amount to 'official statements regarding its interpretation' of the LOSC: ILC Draft Conclusions on Subsequent Agreements and Subsequent Practice (n 61) Commentary to Draft Conclusion 4, in discussing the constitutive elements of custom, the ILC notes that the same evidentiary material may form the basis of either general practice or *opinio juris*: ILC, Draft Conclusions on Identification of Customary International Law, with Commentaries, UN Doc A/73/10) 94 (ILC Draft Conclusions on Identification of Custom) Commentary to Draft Conclusion 10. This book takes the approach of considering the pronouncements of States as evidence relevant to discerning the 'common understanding' of LOSC Parties regarding its interpretation, to be evaluated together with maritime zones legislation (as subsequent practice), discussed below.

[67] Jill Barrett, 'The UN Convention on the Law of the Sea: A "Living" Treaty?' in Jill Barrett and Richard Barnes (eds), *Law of the Sea: UNCLOS as a Living Treaty* (British Institute of International and Comparative Law 2016) 30.

[68] Here, and in the literature, there is some variance in the use of the terms 'delimitation' and 'delineation'. While the ICJ here has referred to 'delimitation', it is clear from the context that it is referring to the unilateral act of the coastal State (Norway), rather than to the delimitation of a maritime boundary between two or more States. The book takes the approach of interpreting the meaning of the terms 'delimitation' and 'delineation' in judgments and literature by reference to the overall context for the term.

> municipal law. Although it is true that the act of delimitation is necessarily a unilateral act because only the coastal State is competent to undertake it, the validity of the delimitation with regard to other States depends upon international law.[69]

It follows that the validity of any such unilateral act vis-à-vis other States falls to be determined by reference to the relevant rules of international law. However, the substance of those very same rules of international law is capable of being influenced by domestic legislation too. A single instance of domestic implementation will not have such an effect. But if evidentiary conditions can be satisfied at the scale of the entire LOSC membership (eg a pattern of practice among States, a 'common understanding'),[70] domestic legislation can have a direct influence on the interpretation of international law rules. Given the important role played by State practice of this type, and its abundance (since almost all coastal States have some kind of domestic legislation establishing their baselines and maritime zones), the book contends that any contemporary understanding of the relevant legal rules must comprehensively account for such State practice.

In so doing, the book aims to expand the evidence base for examining relevant State practice, applying each element of legal stability to identify potentially significant aspects of coastal States' domestic legislation on baselines and maritime zones. Following the account of legal stability presented in Chapter 3, the book systematically identifies and evaluates State practice in relation to each element of legal stability:

- A legislative study of coastal States' implementation of the normal baseline yields evidence relevant to the spatial element of legal stability (Chapter 4);
- A baseline change study answers questions about whether there is any legal obligation to update established baselines over time, illuminating the temporal element of legal stability (Chapter 5); and
- A re-evaluation of State practice relating to the circumstances in which States claim (and maintain) the legal status of an 'island' offers a basis for considering the element of legal stability relating to status (Chapter 6).

However, the book itself consistently uses 'delineation' in a unilateral context, and 'delimitation' where there are two or more States.

[69] *Fisheries (United Kingdom v Norway)* [1951] ICJ Rep 116 [132].
[70] These evidentiary conditions are elaborated and applied in detail in Section 4.3 and Section 5.3.

While these chapters take a global focus to the identification of State practice, the evidence-gathering stage was necessarily constrained within certain parameters. Chapter 4 presents evidence primarily on the normal baseline but also offers conclusions on the legal stability available for baselines more broadly. Straight and archipelagic baselines are typically defined using coordinates, meaning that the location of these baselines does not automatically vary with coastal change. These types of baselines are often contrasted with normal baselines, but if in fact normal baselines frequently use coordinates as well, then the distinction between these baseline types is not as great as is often assumed. Insofar as the same, stable means of baseline implementation can be seen across all baseline types (legislation describing the location of the baseline by geographic coordinates), this means that findings on the stability of the normal baseline have potential relevance for all baseline types.

Another parameter is that legislation establishing the outer limits of maritime zones was not included within the scope of the book. Since maritime zones are usually established by reference to a maximum breadth from the baseline, the baseline serves as a useful proxy for examining the legal stability of maritime zones, but it remains a partial one. For example, a coastal State may use one legislative method to define the location of its baseline, but a different method to define its outer limit. In such circumstances, the combined effect of a coastal State's baseline and outer limits legislation might together influence the overall legal stability of the maritime zone (eg even if a baseline has not been established using coordinates, an EEZ might still have a degree of spatial stability if its outer limit has been established by coordinates). However, such situations have not been examined in this study.

1.4.2 The significance of State practice for the law of the sea

Because of the almost universal membership of the LOSC—which presently has 169 States Parties, 139 of which are coastal States[71]—State practice in the implementation of baselines and maritime zones is principally of significance for the interpretation of the relevant provisions of the LOSC. Such interpretation is governed by Articles 31 and 32 of the Vienna Convention on the Law of Treaties (VCLT),[72] provisions which are also reflective of

[71] See UN Treaty Collection, 'United Nations Convention on the Law of the Sea (status as at 18 March 2024)' <https://treaties.un.org/pages/ViewDetailsIII.aspx?src=TREATY&mtdsg_no=XXI-6&chapter=21&Temp=mtdsg3&clang=_en>.

[72] Vienna Convention on the Law of Treaties (opened for signature 23 May 1969, entered into force 27 January 1980) 1155 UNTS 331.

custom.[73] In this context, the practice of States is principally relevant as a matter of 'subsequent practice in the application of the treaty which establishes the agreement of the parties regarding its interpretation' under Article 31(3)(b) of the VCLT. The effect of the unitary interpretative approach under Article 31 is that subsequent practice is considered together in 'the crucible of interpretation'[74] with other elements of the general rule, these being the ordinary meaning of the terms of the treaty, the context in which those terms occur, and the object and purpose of the treaty.[75] Recognizing that subsequent practice is an 'authentic'[76] means of interpretation also entails an acknowledgement 'that the common will of the parties, which underlies the treaty, possesses a specific authority regarding the identification of the meaning of the treaty, even after the conclusion of the treaty'.[77] Article 31(3)(b) also requires that the subsequent practice demonstrate the interpretative agreement of the Parties (a matter on which other forms of State practice such as individual or collective statements will be especially relevant to include).

Interpretation by subsequent practice is well accepted by international courts and tribunals, as recognized by the ICJ when remarking that 'when called upon to interpret the provisions of a treaty, the Court has itself frequently examined the subsequent practice of the parties in the application of that treaty'.[78] However, the discussion of subsequent practice in such contexts is often brief, including in relation to the interpretation of the LOSC. For example, in interpreting the extent of coastal State jurisdiction to regulate the bunkering of fishing vessels, the International Tribunal for the Law of the Sea (ITLOS) referred to 'the national legislation of several States, not only in the West African region but also in some other regions of the world'.[79] The Arbitral Tribunal in *Philippines v China* also confirmed the relevance of State practice to the interpretation of the LOSC, concluding simply that 'as far as the case before it is concerned, there is no evidence for an agreement based upon State practice on the interpretation of Article 121(3) which differs from

[73] ILC Draft Conclusions on Subsequent Agreements and Subsequent Practice (n 61) Draft Conclusion 2(1). See also Anthony Aust, *Modern Treaty Law and Practice* (3rd edn, Cambridge University Press 2013) 207.

[74] Richard Gardiner, *Treaty Interpretation* (Oxford University Press 2015) 230.

[75] VCLT, art 31(1).

[76] ILC Draft Conclusions on Subsequent Agreements and Subsequent Practice (n 61) Draft Conclusion 3.

[77] ILC, 'Report of the International Law Commission covering the Work of its Seventieth Session' (30 April–1 June and 2 July–10 August 2018) UN Doc A/73/10, 24 (2018 ILC Report).

[78] *Kasikili/Sedudu Island (Botswana/Namibia)* (Judgment) [1999] ICJ Rep 1045 [50].

[79] *M/V 'Virginia G' (Panama/Guinea-Bissau)* (Judgment) (2014) Case no 19 [218].

the interpretation of the Tribunal'.[80] Neither example offers a detailed analysis of the State practice which might have informed such assertions. Against this backdrop, the book aims to make visible an expanded body of State practice relevant to the legal stability of maritime zones, as well as to demonstrate its legal significance for the interpretation of the LOSC.

Climate change was not contemplated when the LOSC was negotiated (1973–1982), largely reflective of the nascent understanding of climate science within the international community at the time. Like many areas of international law (such as that relating to statehood or the general law of jurisdiction),[81] the establishment of the legal order of the oceans by means of a system of maritime zones assumed a high degree of geographic stability,[82] such that the stability of land territory could form the basis for a stable jurisdictional architecture for the oceans. Now, against the backdrop of virtual certainty that there will be significant coastal erosion and inundation resulting from sea-level rise induced by climate-change, what unfolds throughout the book's analysis of State practice is a clear trajectory towards stable maritime zones, demonstrating the capacity for interpretation to be an instrument of change in the international law of the sea. A convergence of States' views and practice on legal stability is what makes such an assertion possible today, compared to the relative lack of such evidence decades ago, when the LOSC was first concluded or when scholars first sought to understand the legal implications of sea-level rise and maritime zones.

Given this shift, is the approach taken in the book rightly understood as one of interpretation, or is it instead pointing to the tacit modification of the LOSC? Crawford observes that '[t]he process of interpretation through subsequent practice is legally distinct from modification, although the distinction is often a fine one',[83] and Goodman explains that the precise legal basis for tacit modification remains controversial.[84] The ILC has taken the view that it is 'presumed that the parties to a treaty, by an agreement or a practice in the application of

[80] *Philippines v China* (Award) (2016) (PCA Case no 2013-19) [553]. This case, and the significance of State practice in the interpretation of art 121, are discussed further in Chapter 6.

[81] Daniel Bethlehem, 'The End of Geography: The Changing Nature of the International System and the Challenge to International Law' (2014) 25 European Journal of International Law 9.

[82] Davor Vidas and others, 'International Law for the Anthropocene? Shifting Perspectives in Regulation of the Oceans, Environment and Genetic Resources' (2015) 9 Anthropocene 1, 4. See also Davor Vidas, 'Sea-Level Rise and International Law: At the Convergence of Two Epochs' (2014) 9 Climate Law 70.

[83] James Crawford, *Brownlie's Principles of Public International Law* (9th edn, Oxford University Press 2019) 372.

[84] Camille Goodman, *Coastal State Jurisdiction over Living Resources in the Exclusive Economic Zone* (Oxford University Press 2021) 17.

the treaty, intend to interpret the treaty, not to amend or to modify it'.[85] Indeed, the wording of the PIF Declaration is a clear illustration of this stance, explicitly framing the position of PIF leaders as one relating to the '*interpretation and application* of the Convention in the context of sea-level rise and climate change'.[86] Noting the difficulty with identifying an instance of tacit modification, the book opts to take the PIF Declaration at face value, and to test its claim as an interpretative claim.

In so doing, it is crucial to address perhaps the key concern behind understanding whether a legal change is brought about by means of tacit treaty modification or some other process: the centrality of the consent of treaty Parties. Whereas 'formal norm-creating processes and treaty-based mechanisms for change are based more directly on state consent, or the consent underlying a formalised procedure',[87] the consent required to substantiate and legitimate change brought about through interpretative practice is translated into the requirement to meet the benchmarks reflected in the VCLT. Interpreting the LOSC to accommodate legal stability in meeting the challenges of sea-level rise shows that treaty interpretation

> is an ultimate art of the possible, and the possible includes a better kind of law for a better kind of international society. [...] But its effectiveness in changing minds and causing social change depends on pragmatic respect for conventionally determined expectations limiting its inherent freedom, expectations that are indeterminate but numerous and powerful.[88]

While some aspects of the VCLT's evidentiary benchmarks may indeed remain somewhat indeterminate,[89] the book nevertheless invokes the 'conventionally determined expectations' of the VCLT to serve as a framework for transparent and 'verifiable anchor points' in legal argumentation,[90] offering a solid foundation to justify and constrain change through interpretation.

Because State practice in respect of baselines and maritime zones is likely to be referrable to the applicable provisions of the LOSC, the book primarily focuses on the legal significance of State practice for the interpretation of the LOSC. However, Chapter 8 also offers conclusions on the relevant customary

[85] ILC Draft Conclusions on Subsequent Agreements and Subsequent Practice (n 61) Draft Conclusion 7(3).
[86] 2021 PIF Declaration (n 2) (emphasis added).
[87] Rozemarijn J Roland Holst, *Change in the Law of the Sea: Context, Mechanisms and Practice* (Brill 2022) 168.
[88] Allott, 'Interpretation: An Exact Art' (n 34) 392.
[89] eg the degree of agreement required to satisfy art 31(3)(b), discussed in Chapter 4, II.C.
[90] Roland Holst, *Change in the Law of the Sea* (n 87) 244.

international law on baselines and maritime zones, to which the State practice of LOSC non-Parties relates.[91] The starting point to ascertain the content of those rules is that used for the identification of custom.[92] As is stated in the Statute of the ICJ, the identification of a rule of customary international law requires the establishment of 'evidence of a general practice accepted as law'.[93] The ILC confirms that this basic approach means that 'one must look at what States actually do and seek to determine whether they recognize an obligation or a right to act in that way'.[94] Accordingly, in this context, State practice relates to the material or objective element of 'general practice';[95] the subjective element relating to 'acceptance as law' is also commonly referred to as *opinio juris*.

1.5 Overview of the chapters

Following this Introduction (Chapter 1), Chapter 2 introduces the applicable rules of international law for baselines and entitlement to maritime zones, and situates this book's study of the legal stability of maritime zones in the context of an already rich body of scholarship engaging with the legal implications of sea-level rise. Chapter 3 establishes the book's conceptual focus on legal stability by examining what States say in relation to legal stability and maritime zones. It synthesizes observations from the three main contexts in connection with the LOSC in which States have ventilated such concerns: first, it outlines the importance of legal stability in the development of the legal order of the LOSC through negotiations at the Third United Nations Conference on the Law of the Sea (UNCLOS III), which led to the adoption of the LOSC currently in force. Secondly, the chapter shows that although the impacts of sea-level rise on baselines were not envisaged at the time, the drafting records relating to Article 5 of the LOSC (normal baseline) indicate that States were

[91] There are fourteen non-Party coastal States, see Section 4.2. Judge Aurescu also expressed concern at the lack of any discussion of customary international law in the Advisory Opinion: see *Obligations of States in Respect of Climate Change* (n 24) Separate Opinion of Judge Aurescu.

[92] While there is no express framework for the interpretation of customary international law per se, there is some debate on the interpretability of custom. See eg Danae Azaria, '"Codification by Interpretation": The International Law Commission as an Interpreter of International Law' (2020) 31 European Journal of International Law 171; Orfeas Chasapis Tassinis, 'Customary International Law: Interpretation from Beginning to End' (2020) 31 European Journal of International Law 235; and Panos Merkouris, *Interpretation of Customary International Law: Of Methods and Limits* (Brill 2024).

[93] Statute of the International Court of Justice, art 38(1)(b).

[94] ILC Draft Conclusions on Identification of Custom (n 66) Commentary to Draft Conclusion 2.

[95] Although the ILC makes clear that general practice need not be exclusively the practice of States: 'the requirement of a general practice ... refers primarily to the practice of States and that in certain cases, the practice of international organizations may be relevant'; ibid Draft Conclusion 4.

cognizant of 'normal' coastal variability, and this was seen as a practical challenge that the newly codified law of the sea should seek to overcome. Thirdly, in collective declarations in in their interventions at the UN General Assembly (UNGA) and in connection with the ILC's processes on sea-level rise, States have given increasing precision and substance to the meaning of legal stability and its significance for the preservation of maritime zones. On the basis of these observations about what States say about legal stability, the chapter unpacks the legal stability of maritime zones into three key elements, pointing to the requirements for spatial stability (the capacity for a baseline to have an absolute location on the Earth's surface), temporal stability (the capacity for a baseline to maintain its location over time), and stability in relation to the legal status of features under the law of the sea.

Chapter 4 presents a global study of coastal States' legislation implementing the normal baseline and proposes a typology of definitions embracing all observed definition types. It finds that there is more diversity in the implementation of the normal baseline than either the ambulatory or fixed theories of baselines suggest, indicating that neither theory is able to offer a complete account of State practice. Chapter 4 concludes that the existing law of the normal baseline should be understood to embrace this diversity, demonstrating that the law can accommodate a spatial dimension of stability in this sense. Furthermore, the chapter argues that because this conclusion is rooted in the widespread use of coordinates to define the normal baseline—and its general acceptance—conclusions about the spatial stability of the normal baseline are also applicable to other baseline types which are also defined by coordinates, such as straight and archipelagic baselines.

Chapter 5 presents a study of selected coastal States' baselines legislation over time, testing the proposition advanced by some scholars that there is an implied duty to update established baselines. It finds that practice is mixed, providing insufficient support to substantiate a duty to update established baselines. Instead, in finding support for the opposite interpretation of the LOSC that there is no such obligation—as seen in the view of the ICJ in *Obligations of States in Respect of Climate Change*—Chapter 5 concludes that the existing law of baselines can accommodate a temporal dimension of legal stability, allowing for the maintenance of established baselines over time, without review.

Chapter 6 examines whether, as suggested by some States, stability might also be relevant to questions of legal status under the law of the sea. Despite concerns that sea-level rise might result in the loss or reduction of a feature's maritime entitlements, the chapter finds that such concerns rely on an unsettled interpretation of the LOSC, and that State practice suggests a different result. Further, the chapter argues that these concerns obscure the process of legal transformation implied by the idea that, for example, an island which is submerged might 'become' a low-tide elevation, and that (as is also the case with the ambulatory theory) it is not necessarily the case that changes to the characteristics of a feature result in changes to its legal classification. Rather, the chapter argues that if a coastal State has implemented its maritime zones by fixed means, it is possible that, under certain conditions, such maritime zones might be maintained notwithstanding the submergence of the island. For these reasons, the chapter concludes that the existing law on the maritime entitlements of features does embrace certain elements of stability, in the sense that sea-level rise impacts will not automatically destabilize the status of features, nor will a feature's maritime entitlements automatically be lost or reduced. The chapter concludes with a consideration of 'archipelagic status' and sea-level rise.

Chapter 7 identifies that despite the growing consensus around a contemporary interpretation of the LOSC that accommodates the preservation of maritime zones, there remain some areas in which action to achieve stable maritime zones might still be needed or desired. The chapter outlines steps that could be taken at the domestic and international level to further promote the legal stability of maritime zones, including matters that could be clarified in an interpretative statement. And noting that sea-level rise has already been explicitly raised in advisory proceedings before both ITLOS[96] and the ICJ,[97] the book offers some observations on how the legal stability of maritime zones—and the State practice underpinning it—might arise in international proceedings.

Chapter 8 completes the book, synthesizing conclusions on the law of baselines and maritime entitlements and whether there is a legal duty to update established baselines (as a matter of both treaty interpretation and custom) and applying the findings of the book to answer key questions arising from the effects of sea-level rise on coastlines and features. Importantly, the chapter also offers comment on how far legal stability might stretch *in extremis*, such as in cases of complete submergence of a feature or of a State's entire land territory, and connects the arguments of the book to contemporary scholarship on the continuity of statehood.

[96] *Request for an Advisory Opinion submitted by the Commission of Small Island States on Climate Change and International Law* (2023) ITLOS Case no 31.
[97] *Obligations of States in Respect of Climate Change* (n 24).

Appendix 1.1

Membership of the PIF, AOSIS, and Commonwealth

	Country	PIF member	AOSIS member	Commonwealth member
	(LOSC non-Parties indicated in italics)			
1.	Antigua & Barbuda		x	x
2.	Australia	x		x
3.	Bahamas		x	x
4.	Bangladesh			x
5.	Barbados		x	x
6.	Belize		x	x
7.	Botswana			x
8.	Brunei			x
9.	Cameroon			x
10.	Canada			x
11.	Cape Verde		x	
12.	Cook Islands	x	x	
13.	Comoros		x	
14.	Cuba		x	
15.	Cyprus			x
16.	Dominica		x	x
17.	Dominican Republic		x	
18.	Eswatini			x
19.	Fiji	x	x	x
20.	*French Polynesia*	x		
21.	Gabon			x
22.	The Gambia			x
23.	Ghana			x
24.	Grenada		x	x
25.	Guinea-Bissau		x	
26.	Guyana		x	x
27.	Haiti		x	
28.	India			x
29.	Jamaica		x	x
30.	Kenya			x
31.	Kiribati	x	x	x
32.	Lesotho			x
33.	Malawi			x
34.	Malaysia			x
35.	Maldives		x	x

	Country	PIF member	AOSIS member	Commonwealth member
	(LOSC non-Parties indicated in italics)			
36.	Malta			x
37.	Marshall Islands	x	x	
38.	Mauritius		x	x
39.	Micronesia	x	x	
40.	Mozambique			x
41.	Namibia			x
42.	Nauru	x	x	x
43.	*New Caledonia*	x		
44.	New Zealand	x	x	x
45.	Nigeria			x
46.	Niue	x	x	
47.	Pakistan			x
48.	Palau	x	x	
49.	Papua New Guinea	x	x	x
50.	Rwanda			x
51.	Saint Kitts and Nevis		x	x
52.	Saint Lucia		x	x
53.	Saint Vincent and the Grenadines		x	x
54.	Samoa	x	x	x
55.	São Tomé and Principe		x	
56.	Seychelles		x	x
57.	Sierra Leone			x
58.	Singapore		x	x
59.	Solomon Islands	x	x	x
60.	South Africa			x
61.	Sri Lanka			x
62.	Suriname		x	
63.	Tanzania			x
64.	Timor-Leste		x	
65.	Togo			x
66.	Tonga	x	x	x
67.	Trinidad and Tobago		x	x
68.	Tuvalu	x	x	x
69.	Uganda			x
70.	United Kingdom			x
71.	Vanuatu	x	x	x
72.	Zambia			x

2
The Legal Framework and Scholarship on Sea-level Rise, Baselines, and Maritime Zones

2.1 Introduction

This chapter lays out the contextual material for the book, outlining first the international law applicable to unilateral maritime zones, also making some observations about how those legal rules relate to the law of maritime delimitation. The chapter then examines the development of a rich body of scholarship considering the implications of sea-level rise for established maritime zones, tracing how their (legal) stability was initially considered to be a goal to be sought outside the law of the sea, before scholars began to gesture at its possibility within it.

2.2 The applicable law relating to baselines and maritime zones in the international law of the sea

2.2.1 The LOSC framework for unilateral maritime zones

The international law of the sea draws a close nexus between the sea and the land in the sense that a coastal State's maritime entitlements flow from its sovereignty over land. This is reflected in the terms of the United Nations Convention on the Law of the Sea (LOSC), since it is 'coastal States' (rather than all States) which have entitlements to maritime zones adjacent to their land territory, and also in the well-known principle that 'the land dominates the sea'.[1] As part of the historical balancing of interests in this body of international law, the law of the sea developed rules for the allocation of maritime

[1] *North Sea Continental Shelf (Federal Republic of Germany/Denmark; Federal Republic of Germany/Netherlands)* (Judgment) [1969] ICJ Rep 3 [96] (*North Sea Continental Shelf*). For a useful modern discussion of this concept, see Irini Papanicolopulu, 'The Land Dominates the Sea (Dominates the Land Dominates the Sea)' (2018) 47 Questions of International Law: Zoom-in 39.

Sea-Level Rise and the Legal Stability of Maritime Zones. Frances Anggadi, Oxford University Press.
 DOI: 10.1093/9780198973515.003.0002

space 'that did not depend on physical use or possession but instead on geographical proximity'.[2] In general, a coastal State enjoys greater rights in the maritime space most proximate to its coasts: a coastal State has sovereignty in the territorial sea, while the broader international community has interests in the high seas and the Area.[3] The spatial organization of jurisdiction of the ocean into maritime zones is complemented by the allocation of substantive subject-matter jurisdiction (such as fisheries, marine environmental protection, pollution) to coastal States, flag States, and port States under the LOSC.[4]

The term 'baseline' refers to a juridical concept that has strong links to a particular part of the land: the coast. A baseline is 'the legal expression of the coast',[5] and certain physical characteristics of that coast will influence the type of baseline available to be used in any particular geographic area. There are three types of baseline, and the dominant type of baseline in use is the *normal baseline*,[6] defined as 'the low-water line along the coast as marked on large-scale charts officially recognized by the coastal State'.[7] Where the relevant coast is located on an island situated on an atoll or having fringing reefs, the seaward low-water line of the reef may be used as the baseline.[8] A coastal State may also employ *straight baselines* 'in localities where the coastline is deeply indented and cut into, or if there is a fringe of islands along the coast in its immediate vicinity' and where a number of other geographic criteria are met.[9] And a coastal State may opt for a system of *archipelagic baselines* in accordance with the requirements in Part IV of the LOSC, including qualification as an archipelagic State[10] and specifications for the land to water ratio and the length of baseline segments.[11]

[2] Lea Brilmayer and Natalie Klein, 'Land and Sea: Two Sovereignty Regimes in Search of a Common Denominator' (2001) 33 New York University Journal of International Law and Politics 703, 710.

[3] The 'Area' is one of the few terms that is expressly defined in the LOSC, meaning 'the seabed and ocean floor and subsoil thereof, beyond the limits of national jurisdiction': art 1(1).

[4] Camille Goodman, *Coastal State Jurisdiction over Living Resources in the Exclusive Economic Zone* (Oxford University Press 2021) 12.

[5] Coalter G Lathrop, 'Baselines' in Donald R Rothwell and others (eds), *The Oxford Handbook of the Law of the Sea* (Oxford University Press 2015) 69.

[6] See Clive Schofield, 'Departures from the Coast: Trends in the Application of Territorial Sea Baselines under the Law of the Sea Convention' (2012) 27 The International Journal of Marine and Coastal Law 723, 724.

[7] LOSC, art 5.

[8] LOSC, art 6. For examples of where such 'reef baselines' are used in State practice, see Frances Anggadi, 'The Meaning and Legal Significance of "Fringing Reefs" in the LOSC, and Importance for Contemporary Challenges in the Law of the Sea' in Pierandrea Leucci and Illaria Vianello (eds), *ASCOMARE Yearbook on the Law of the Sea 2021: Law of the Sea, Interpretation and Definitions*, vol 1 (Luglio Editore 2022).

[9] LOSC, art 7.

[10] LOSC, art 46.

[11] LOSC, art 47.

A coastal State may use a combination of baseline types.[12] In addition, in order to construct a continuous baseline, the LOSC provides for the drawing of straight segments of the baseline across the mouth of a river or a bay.[13] Also, in certain circumstances, permanent harbour works can be regarded as part of the coast for the purposes of determining the baseline,[14] and lighthouses or similar installations may be built on 'low-tide elevations' to allow such elevations to be used in the drawing of straight baselines (which otherwise would not be permitted).[15] This reinforces the general position that a low-tide elevation, being 'a naturally formed area of land which is surrounded by and above water at low tide but submerged at high tide', may only contribute to the baseline in certain geographic circumstances.[16]

The principal significance of the baseline in the law of the sea is that it is the starting point for determining the location and extent of a coastal State's maritime zones. A coastal State has sovereignty over the territorial sea,[17] which may be established with a breadth of up to 12 nm from the baseline.[18] A coastal State may establish a contiguous zone of up to 24 nm from the baseline[19] and an exclusive economic zone (EEZ) of up to 200 nm from the baseline.[20] A coastal State also has sovereign rights in respect of the natural resources of the continental shelf,[21] the seabed adjacent to the coast and beyond the territorial sea. The extent of the zone of the continental shelf is at least 200 nm from the baseline, or may extend further to the edge of the continental margin under certain conditions.[22] Coastal States may establish maritime zones adjacent to

[12] LOSC, art 14. Also, an archipelagic State need not enclose all of its islands within a single archipelagic baseline system. For examples of using multiple archipelagic systems, and where archipelagic States have used a combination of other baseline types, see Kevin Baumert and Brian Melchior, 'The Practice of Archipelagic States: A Study of Studies' (2015) 46 Ocean Development & International Law 60.

[13] There is also evidence supporting the use of straight lines to close gaps in reefs: see Robyn Frost and others, 'Redrawing the Map of the Pacific' (2018) 95 Marine Policy 302, 306, and UN Office for Ocean Affairs and the Law of the Sea, *Baselines: An Examination of the Relevant Provisions of the United Nations Convention on the Law of the Sea* (United Nations 1989) 11.

[14] LOSC, art 11. In addition, State practice supports the view that certain coastal protective works on the natural coast are permitted to contribute to the baseline: see Chris Carleton, 'Problems Relating to Non-Natural and Man-Made Basepoints Under UNCLOS' in Clive R Symmons (ed), *Selected Contemporary Issues in the Law of the Sea* (Brill 2011) 42.

[15] LOSC, art 7(4).

[16] LOSC, art 13.

[17] LOSC, art 1. Note also that a coastal State's sovereignty in the territorial sea is subject to the right of foreign vessels to exercise innocent passage through those waters: LOSC, art 17.

[18] LOSC, art 4.

[19] LOSC, art 33.

[20] LOSC, art 57.

[21] LOSC, art 77.

[22] LOSC, art 76.

continental land, as well as in relation to insular land features.[23] The baseline is also significant in that it delineates the territorial sea from internal waters, a maritime area in which the coastal State has full sovereignty akin to that exercised on land;[24] for archipelagic States, the archipelagic baseline delineates the territorial sea from archipelagic waters.[25] It is also important to note that while there is some debate whether the entirety of the LOSC is either reflective of or has passed into custom,[26] it is generally considered that the LOSC provisions on baselines and maritime zones outlined above are reflective of customary international law.[27] In this way, the applicable law is sourced in both treaty and custom.

2.2.2 The relationship between baselines and maritime boundary delimitation

Because the book focuses on situations where maritime zones may be established unilaterally by the coastal State, the legal framework described above (Section 2.2.1) is applicable and determinative regarding the location and extent of maritime zones.

At the outset, a distinction must be made between that body of law and the law and practice relating to maritime boundary delimitation.[28] Where there are overlapping maritime entitlements, a maritime boundary will need to be delimited between affected States, either through negotiation or third-party

[23] LOSC, art 121(2). Although not all land features generate all maritime zones in the same way: Chapter 6, Section 6.2 outlines the particulars of the rules governing maritime zone entitlements, examining how the international law of the sea allocates particular maritime zones to particular categories of geographic features.

[24] LOSC, art 8.

[25] LOSC, arts 48 and 49.

[26] eg Crawford considers whether the provisions relating to the outer edge of the continental shelf beyond 200 nm in art 76 should be considered part of custom: James Crawford, *Chance, Order, Change: The Course of International Law, General Course on Public International Law* (Brill 2014) 133.

[27] See generally James Crawford, *Brownlie's Principles of Public International Law* (9th edn, Oxford University Press 2019) 724; RR Churchill, AV Lowe, and Amy Sander, *The Law of the Sea* (4th edn, Manchester University Press 2022) 53; and, for an examination of specific Articles and their customary status, see J Ashley Roach, 'Today's Customary International Law of the Sea' (2014) 45 Ocean Development & International Law 239. The United States has publicly expressed the view that it considers LOSC pt II (containing baseline rules) to be binding as a matter of custom: see United States, 'Comments of the United States regarding Sea-Level Rise in Relation to the Law of the Sea' (14 February 2020) (2020 US ILC Submission).

[28] For an extended discussion of sea-level rise and delimited maritime boundaries, see Snjólaug Árnadóttir, *Climate Change and Maritime Boundaries: Legal Consequences of Sea Level Rise* (Cambridge University Press 2022). See also Julia Lisztwan, 'Stability of Maritime Boundary Agreements' (2012) 37 Yale Journal of International Law 153 and Kate Purcell, *Geographical Change and the Law of the Sea* (Oxford University Press 2019) ch 5.

decision. There are benefits for a State in having established baselines ahead of the negotiation of a maritime boundary treaty, and the selection and justification of basepoints generally plays a key role in the early stages of such negotiations.[29] In a judicial context, the well-established methodology is the 'three-stage approach', involving the drawing of a provisional equidistance line, considering adjustments to that equidistance line, and finally conducting a check for disproportionality.[30] In both delimitation contexts, the baseline (and the LOSC rules governing their establishment) plays a nuanced role, and although a 'basepoint' is simply 'any point on the baseline',[31] it does not necessarily follow that a basepoint used by a coastal State for its baseline must be used where a maritime delimitation is required. As explained by the International Court of Justice (ICJ) in *Black Sea*:

> [T]he issue of determining the baseline for the purpose of measuring the breadth of the continental shelf and the EEZ and the issue of identifying base points for drawing an equidistance/median line for the purpose of delimiting the continental shelf and the EEZ between adjacent/opposite States are two different issues.[32]

Following that approach, the ICJ did not accept Romania's proposal to use a basepoint on the seaward end of Sulina Dyke (which Romania had used for part of its territorial sea baseline) for the purposes of the construction of a provisional equidistance line. Observing that the coastal State is entitled to establish its own baseline in conformity with international law, when required to delimit maritime boundary between two Parties, the ICJ 'should not base itself solely on the choice of base points made by one of those Parties' and instead must 'select base points by reference to the physical geography of the relevant coasts'.[33]

[29] See David Anderson, 'Negotiating Maritime Boundary Agreements: A Personal View' in Rainer Lagoni and Daniel Vignes (eds), *Maritime Delimitation* (Brill Nijhoff 2006).

[30] As articulated in *Maritime Delimitation in the Black Sea (Romania v Ukraine)* (Judgment) [2009] ICJ Rep 61 [115] (*Black Sea*). This book does not attempt a comprehensive discussion of the law of maritime delimitation, to which many scholarly works have already devoted much attention, including Stephen Fietta and Robin Cleverly, *A Practitioner's Guide to Maritime Boundary Delimitation* (Oxford University Press 2016); Massimo Lando, *Maritime Delimitation as a Judicial Process* (Cambridge University Press 2019); Yoshifumi Tanaka, *Predictability and Flexibility in the Law of Maritime Delimitation* (2nd edn, Hart 2019); Prosper Weil, *The Law of Maritime Delimitation: Reflections* (Grotius 1989).

[31] UN Division for Ocean Affairs and Law of the Sea, *Handbook on the Delimitation of Maritime Boundaries* (United Nations 2000) 148, Annex V.

[32] *Black Sea* (n 30).

[33] ibid [137].

Subsequent jurisprudence affirms the distinction made in *Black Sea* between the selection of a basepoint for the purposes of a delimitation between States and the validity of the use of a certain basepoint for establishment of the baseline of a particular coastal State. The ICJ considered a similar issue in *Alleged Violations of Sovereign Rights*[34] when examining the appropriateness of Nicaragua's reliance on Edinburgh Cay as a part of its straight baseline system. Although the ICJ had in its earlier delimitation of the EEZ and continental shelves of Nicaragua and Columbia placed a basepoint on that feature for the purposes of constructing the provisional equidistance line, it 'did not at that time consider the appropriateness of this feature for the purpose of drawing straight baselines'.[35] Conversely, in *Mauritius/Maldives*, the Special Chamber of the International Tribunal for the Law of the Sea (ITLOS) considered that even though Mauritius was entitled to place basepoints on Blenheim Reef for the purposes of its archipelagic baseline, 'this does not necessarily mean that Blenheim Reef should be considered a site of base points for the purpose of delimitation'.[36] These examples illustrate that the suitability of a basepoint for the purposes of a baseline is not conclusive of that same basepoint's suitability for delimitation, and vice versa. Separate conclusions may be reached by reference to the separately applicable bodies of law (the law of baselines and the law of maritime delimitation).

Even though 'the baselines are not necessarily always used as basepoints for a maritime boundary delimitation',[37] baselines should be regarded as a 'major ingredient' in maritime delimitation between States.[38] Indeed, baselines are often the 'starting point'[39] for maritime boundary delimitations.[40]

[34] *Alleged Violations of Sovereign Rights and Maritime Spaces in the Caribbean Sea (Nicaragua v Colombia)* (Judgment) [2022] ICJ Rep 266 (*Alleged Violations of Sovereign Rights*).

[35] ibid [250].

[36] *Dispute concerning Delimitation of the Maritime Boundary between Mauritius and Maldives in the Indian Ocean (Mauritius/Maldives)* (Merits) (2023) ITLOS Case no 28 TBC, 146 (*Mauritius/Maldives*). In its consideration, the Special Chamber of ITLOS expressly affirmed *Black Sea*, as well as citing with approval the reasoning in *Delimitation of the Maritime Boundary between Bangladesh and Myanmar (Bangladesh/Myanmar)* (Judgment) ITLOS Reports 2012 (*Bangladesh/Myanmar*): 'while coastal States are entitled to determine their base points for the purpose of delimitation, the Tribunal is not obliged, when called upon to delimit the maritime boundary between the parties to a dispute, to accept base points indicated by either or both of them. The Tribunal may establish its own base points, on the basis of the geographical facts of the case' [264]

[37] UN Division for Ocean Affairs and Law of the Sea (n 31) [12].

[38] Satya N Nandan, Myron H Nordquist, and Shabtai Rosenne, *United Nations Convention on the Law of the Sea 1982: A Commentary* (Brill 2013) 82.

[39] ILA (Committee on Baselines under the International Law of the Sea), 'Baselines under the International Law of the Sea (Sofia Conference)' 5 (2012 ILA Baselines Committee Report).

[40] This is both in a mathematical (or geometrical) sense, in terms of contributing geographic coordinates for the construction of an equidistance line but also as part of the broader threshold question of establishing the overlapping maritime entitlements that necessitate delimitation in the first place, the latter being a relatively under-examined issue in the doctrine: Jean-Pierre Cot, 'The Dual Function of

They are especially important for the delimitation of the territorial sea boundary since the LOSC expressly states that, in principle, the line of delimitation will be 'the median line every point of which is equidistant from the nearest points on the baselines from which the breadth of the territorial seas of each of the two States is measured'.[41] While the equivalent provisions in the LOSC dealing with the delimitation of the EEZ and continental shelf do not mention baselines, referring instead to the need to 'achieve an equitable solution',[42] Anderson emphasizes that 'baselines have played an important role in the construction of equidistance lines that have been accepted, often with some modification, as maritime boundaries'.[43] Accordingly, the role of baselines in delimitation is 'qualified':[44] this could be because an equidistance line constructed by reference to coastal States' baselines (eg in the manner envisaged in Art 15 LOSC) might nevertheless be adjusted (eg because of 'special circumstances' or to 'achieve an equitable solution'). Or it might be because basepoints selected for the construction of the equidistance line do not fully correspond with that coastal State's baseline in the first place (as in the jurisprudence discussed earlier).[45] Accordingly, noting the need to treat the determination of the baseline as a separate issue from the process of inter-state delimitation, the book focuses on the international law applicable to the former.

Scholars have also considered a related question about the durability of a maritime boundary treaty if sea-level rise causes subsequent changes to the coasts by reference to which the treaty was originally negotiated. Debate has largely focused on whether such circumstances give rise to an entitlement of one treaty party to unilaterally withdraw from the treaty, a question which raises questions of treaty law. Under the Vienna Convention on the Law of

Base Points' in Holger Hestermeyer (ed), *Coexistence, Cooperation and Solidarity: Liber Amicorum Rüdiger Wolfrum* (Brill Nijhoff 2012) 820.

[41] LOSC, art 15.

[42] LOSC, arts 74 and 83. For a discussion of how these different approaches developed in the LOSC, see Malcolm Evans, 'Maritime Boundary Delimitation' in Donald Rothwell and others (eds), *The Oxford Handbook of the Law of the Sea* (Oxford University Press 2015) and Gulardi Nurbintoro, 'International Tribunals Approach Toward Maritime Boundaries Delimitation of an Archipelagic State' (2024) 21 Indonesian Journal of International Law 2.

[43] David H Anderson, 'Baselines in the Modern Law of the Sea' in Michael Lodge and Myron H Nordquist (eds), *Peaceful Order in the World's Oceans* (Brill Nijhoff 2014) 61.

[44] ibid 62.

[45] On the selection of basepoints, see the excellent analysis in 'Constructing an Equidistance Line' of Lando, *Maritime Delimitation* (n 30) ch 4, and 'The Creeping Subjectivity of Base Point Selection: A Lurch Toward a 'Four Stage Approach' (or a Return to Equitable Principles?)' in Fietta and Cleverly, *A Practitioner's Guide to Maritime Boundary Delimitation* (n 30) 575.

Treaties (VCLT), in certain circumstances a party to a treaty may invoke a 'fundamental change of circumstances' to terminate or withdraw from the treaty, except 'if the treaty establishes a boundary'.[46] While scholars have expressed varying views,[47] many States have strongly taken the position that sea-level rise should not affect maritime boundaries, and further, 'no State has expressed the view that the principle of fundamental change of circumstances, as codified in Article 62, paragraph 1, of the Vienna Convention on the Law of Treaties, would apply to maritime boundaries as a result of sea-level rise'.[48] This conclusion was affirmed in the Final Report of the ILC Study Group on sea-level rise in international law.[49] While the book seeks to answer some of the outstanding questions about the stability of baselines and maritime zones, it is reasonably clear that delimited maritime boundaries are unlikely to be disturbed as a result of sea-level rise, largely due to the stabilizing effect of treaty law. This outcome is consistent with judicial observations about the importance of stability in relation to a maritime boundary. In *Bangladesh v India*, the Arbitral Tribunal noted that 'maritime delimitations, like land boundaries, must be stable and definitive to ensure a peaceful relationship between the States concerned in the long term'.[50] In a similar way, the ICJ noted (in considering the exclusion of 'boundary agreements' from the rule permitting unilateral treaty termination where there is a fundamental change of circumstance) that 'whether it

[46] Vienna Convention on the Law of Treaties (opened for signature 23 May 1969, entered into force 27 January 1980) 1155 UNTS 331, art 62(2)(a).

[47] Some express concern that sea-level rise might destabilize existing maritime boundaries (eg David D Caron, 'Climate Change, Sea Level Rise and the Coming Uncertainty in Oceanic Boundaries: A Proposal to Avoid Conflict' in Seoung-Yong Hong and Jon M Van Dyke (eds), *Maritime Boundary Disputes, Settlement Processes, and the Law of the Sea* (Brill Nijhoff 2009) 13; Jonathan Lusthaus, 'Shifting Sands: Sea Level Rise, Maritime Boundaries and Inter-State Conflict' (2010) 30 Politics 113, 115; Snjólaug Árnadóttir, 'Termination of Maritime Boundaries Due to a Fundamental Change of Circumstances' (2016) 32 Utrecht Journal of International and European Law 94. Others assert that maritime boundary agreements are 'highly stable despite coastline shift' (eg Lisztwan, 'Stability of Maritime Boundary Agreements' (n 28).

[48] Bogdan Aurescu and Nilüfer Oral, Co-Chairs of the Study Group on Sea-Level Rise in relation to International Law, *Additional paper to the first issues paper* (Seventy-Fourth Session of the International Law Commission [ILC]) (13 February 2023) UN Doc A/CN.4/761 [125] (*Additional paper to the first issues paper*). The ILA SLR Committee affirmed this observation, also noting that among those States supporting the stability of maritime boundary treaties were those who themselves maintained ambulatory baselines within their national systems: ILA (Committee on International Law and Sea Level Rise), 'Report (Athens Conference)' 45 (2024 ILA SLR Report).

[49] 'The principle of fundamental change of circumstances (*rebus sic stantibus*), as codified in article 62, paragraph 1, of the Vienna Convention on the Law of Treaties, does not apply to maritime delimitation agreements, as they are covered by the exclusion for treaties establishing boundaries under article 62, paragraph 2 (a)': Study Group on sea-level rise in relation to international law, 'Final Report of the Study Group on Sea-Level Rise in relation to International Law', UN Doc A/80/10, Annex I, [33] (2025 ILC Study Group Final Report).

[50] *Bay of Bengal Maritime Boundary Arbitration (Bangladesh v India)* (Award of 7 July 2014) (2014) PCA Case no 2004-02, [216].

is a land frontier or a boundary line in the continental shelf that is in question, the process is essentially the same, and inevitably involves the same element of stability and permanence'.[51] As observed in *Bangladesh v India*, the stability of a maritime boundary between two States should be seen as an expression, in a maritime context, of the general principle in international law on the stability of land boundaries. A clear enunciation of that general principle may be found in *Temple of Préah Vihéar*, where the ICJ stated that 'when two countries establish a frontier between them, one of the primary objects is to achieve stability and finality'.[52] If (as the book argues) the law does indeed embrace stability for unilaterally established baselines and maritime zones, then such a conclusion would align well with the importance of stability for delimited maritime boundaries.

2.3 Situating legal stability: Responses from scholars and expert bodies to questions of sea-level rise

From as early as 1989,[53] scholars have identified the need to consider whether sea-level rise impacts on coastlines raise questions for the system of maritime zones established pursuant to the LOSC, and have raised concerns about the prospect of uncertainty, instability, and maritime jurisdictional loss. It is useful to survey this literature in terms of three (roughly chronological) phases. In the first phase (1989 onwards), the scholarship focuses on identifying the most plausible 'theory' of baselines, in which scholars tended to favour what has come to be known as the 'ambulatory' theory of baselines over the 'fixed' theory. In the second phase (approximately 2018 onwards), scholarship began to point to the possibility of legal stability existing within the existing law, thereby offering a basis for achieving the preservation of baselines and maritime zones. In the third phase (approximately 2022 onwards), scholars began to more clearly articulate and apply the frameworks of international law applicable to treaty and customary sources of the legal rules, offering preliminary conclusions about whether required standards (such as those relating to State practice) had been satisfied or not.

[51] *Aegean Sea Continental Shelf Case (Greece v Turkey)* (Judgment) [1978] ICJ Rep 3 [85].

[52] *Temple of Préah Vihéar (Cambodia v Thailand)* (Merits) [1962] ICJ Rep 6 [34].

[53] A comprehensive early treatment of this issue may be found in E Bird and V Prescott, 'Rising Global Sea Levels and National Maritime Claims' (1989) 1 Marine Policy Reports 177.

2.3.1 First phase of scholarship: The 'ambulatory' theory of baselines (and its problem of instability)

Writing in 1990, Caron referred to the 'current system of ambulatory baselines',[54] explaining that:

> If the baseline moves, the boundary moves. If a baseline point such as an exposed rock disappears, the boundary generated by that point also disappears. Although this is obviously an important principle, it often goes unstated.[55]

Under this view, both the baseline and maritime zone outer limit (which Caron refers to as the maritime 'boundary') shift as the coastline shifts. Caron (and most scholars) developed their views in relation to the normal baseline and the terms of Article 5, but the ambulatory theory also has relevance for other types of baselines (such as straight baselines under Article 7) to the extent that they must still connect to the low-water line on the coast to create a unified baseline system.[56]

The ambulatory theory of baselines is reflected in the work of many writers. Some scholars may be seen to take this view without expressly using the lexicon of 'ambulatory' baselines: for example, discussing the general legal rules concerning the normal baseline, Soons writes that, '[a]s a consequence of sea level rise, this line is shifting landward or, in cases of low-lying islands and low-tide elevations, may even disappear completely. [. . .] Because of the landward shift of the baseline, the outer limits of the territorial sea and EEZ will also shift landward accordingly.'[57] Klein,[58] Freestone,[59] Sefrioui,[60] and Grima[61] take a similar

[54] David D Caron, 'When Law Makes Climate Change Worse: Rethinking the Law of Baselines in Light of a Rising Sea Level' (1990) 17 Ecology Law Quarterly 621, 646.

[55] ibid 634.

[56] See discussion of the placement of straight baselines in relation to the normal baseline in UN Office for Ocean Affairs and the Law of the Sea (n 13) 24.

[57] AHA Soons, 'The Effects of a Rising Sea Level on Maritime Limits and Boundaries' (1990) 37 Netherlands International Law Review 207, 216.

[58] Natalie Klein, 'Land and Sea: Resolving Contested Land and Disappearing Land Disputes under the UN Convention on the Law of the Sea' in Chiara Giogetti and Natalie Klein (eds), *Resolving Conflicts in the Law* (Brill Nijhoff 2018) 22.

[59] David Freestone, 'International Law and Sea Level Rise' in Robin Churchill and David Freestone (eds), *International Law and Global Climate Change* (Graham & Trotman 1991) 110.

[60] Sarra Sefrioui, 'Adapting to Sea Level Rise: A Law of the Sea Perspective' in Gemma Andreone (ed), *The Future of the Law of the Sea* (Springer 2017) 10.

[61] Antoine Grima, *Sea Level Change and Maritime Boundaries* (Routledge 2023) s 2.11.

view, and the position may also be seen in earlier general commentary on the normal baseline not directed to the phenomenon of sea-level rise.[62] Scholars who explicitly take up the language of ambulatory baselines include Bernard et al.,[63] Schofield,[64] Rayfuse,[65] Cogliati-Bantz,[66] and Lusthaus.[67] Reed, for example, wrote that 'the coast line, or baseline, is the mean low-water line. As that line moves landward and seaward with accretion and erosion, so does the baseline. As the baseline ambulates, so does each of the maritime zones measured from it.'[68]

The key features of the 'ambulatory theory' of baselines are, first, that a geographic feature (the low-water line along the coast) is identified with the baseline, and second, that changes to the former automatically result in changes to the latter. Some scholars offer a variation of this view, suggesting that baseline changes are not necessarily automatic, but that there is an obligation 'to update [baselines] in the event of significant geographic change'.[69]

This variation gives a nod to the 'fixed' theory of baselines, which posits that baselines may be 'fixed' as a matter of international law. An early statement of this position (not specifically expressed in the context of sea-level rise) was offered by Kapoor and Kerr:

> [O]nce the normal baseline has been established and cartographically depicted on large scale charts, it remains in place until such time as it is

[62] eg DP O'Connell, *The International Law of the Sea*, vol I (IA Shearer, ed, Clarendon Press 1984) 682 and Lewis M Alexander, 'Baseline Delimitations and Maritime Boundaries' (1983) 23 Virginia Journal of International Law 503, 535.

[63] Leonardo Bernard and others, 'Securing the Limits of Large Ocean States in the Pacific: Defining Baselines Limits and Boundaries amidst Changing Coastlines and Sea Level Rise' (2021) 11 Geosciences 394.

[64] Schofield, 'Departures from the Coast' (n 6) 725.

[65] Rosemary Rayfuse, 'Sea Level Rise and Maritime Zones: Preserving the Maritime Entitlements of "Disappearing" States' in Michael B Gerrard and Gregory E Wannier (eds), *Threatened Island Nations: Legal Implications of Rising Seas and a Changing Climate* (Cambridge University Press 2013) 173.

[66] Vincent Cogliati-Bantz, 'Sea-Level Rise and Coastal States' Maritime Entitlements' (2020) 7 Journal of Territorial and Maritime Studies 86 and Vincent Cogliati-Bantz, 'The Way Forward is not Fast-Forward: Sea-Level Rise, Maritime Zones and Back to Basics' in Lan Anh T Nguyen and Hai Dang Vu (eds), *Viability of UNCLOS amid Emerging Global Maritime Challenges* (Springer 2024).

[67] Lusthaus, 'Shifting Sands' (n 47).

[68] Michael W Reed, *Shore and Sea Boundaries: The Development of International Maritime Boundary Principles through United States Practice*, vol 3 (AL Shalowitz ed, US Government Printing Office 2000) 185.

[69] Lathrop, 'Baselines' (n 5) 77. Hayashi adds that the possibility of temporary 'fixing', due to an implied obligation to update if there is significant coastal change, could also extend to the outer limits of maritime zones: Moritaka Hayashi, 'Sea Level Rise and the Law of the Sea: How Can the Affected States Be Better Protected?' in Clive H Schofield, Seokwoo Lee, and Moon-Sang Kwon (eds), *The Limits of Maritime Jurisdiction* (Brill Nijhoff 2014) 612. The existence of an implied duty to update established baselines is the focus of Chapter 5.

redrafted, irrespective of whether or not the actual low-water line has physically moved.[70]

Under this view, 'it is the chart that is the legal document determining the position of the normal baseline and this remains the case even where the coastline's configuration has changed. Thus, if the coastline has altered, but it has not been published, the legal baseline is that on the published chart.'[71] So in circumstances where there has been a physical change to the coastline, 'the normal baseline will only come to reflect the physical change in the coastline if a fresh survey is undertaken and the chart correspondingly updated'.[72] Purcell goes further, making a 'positive case for the conclusion that, while the coastal State is in most cases entitled to redraw established maritime limits, geographical change does not trigger a legal obligation to do so'.[73] However, in this phase of scholarship, the fixed theory of baselines did not attract broad support as a plausible understanding of the existing law.

The International Law Association (ILA) established a Baselines Committee (ILA Baselines Committee) which undertook the first major collaborative research on this topic, examining the breadth of the literature available at the time. In its 2012 report, the ILA Baselines Committee affirmed the dominance of the ambulatory theory of baselines in the context of its work on the identification of the existing law on the normal baseline. The ILA Baselines Committee framed its work in this way: 'the question before the Committee is, in essence, whether the Article 5 normal baseline is a line on a chart (the charted low-water line) or a line on the "ground" (the actual low-water line)'.[74] The ILA Baselines Committee considered that 'the preponderance of the scholarship in this area appears to support the view that charts are not determinative of the naturally ambulatory normal baseline',[75] concluding that 'the legal normal baseline is the actual low-water line along the coast at the vertical datum, also known as the chart datum, indicated on charts officially recognized by the coastal State'.[76] The wide support for the 'ambulatory theory' of baselines in this phase of the scholarship was also recognized by the ILC, which noted: 'the doctrine had interpreted the Convention to the effect that

[70] DC Kapoor and Adam J Kerr, *A Guide to Maritime Boundary Delimitation* (Carswell 1986) 31.

[71] Chris Carleton and Clive H Schofield, *Developments in the Technical Determination of Maritime Space: Charts, Datums, Baselines, Maritime Zones and Limits*, vol 3 (International Boundaries Research Unit 2001) 24.

[72] ibid.

[73] Purcell, *Geographical Change and the Law of the Sea* (n 28).

[74] 2012 ILA Baselines Committee Report (n 39).

[75] ibid 22.

[76] ibid 25.

the baselines and outer limits of the territorial sea, contiguous zone and exclusive economic zone were ambulatory.'[77]

However, many of the same scholars have been quick to identify its unsatisfactory consequences. Schofield writes that the 'direct relationship between the position of normal baselines and the limits of maritime jurisdiction is potentially and increasingly problematic',[78] and Rayfuse refers to the 'baseline dilemma' which she considers is 'immediately apparent in the context of sea level rise'.[79] Caron and other writers recognized the risks of conflict and wasted resources devoted to coastal protection.[80] Klein considers that 'the prospect of the outer limit of maritime zones shifting is problematic for stability in terms of changing the allocation of rights and duties in different maritime space. States risk losing rights to natural resources as a result.'[81] Writers have also identified the impracticality of the ambulatory theory, noting that 'rigid adherence to this view might logically result in a coastal State's obligation to provide real-time notification of changing baselines and limits through continuous detection, depiction, and dissemination of the physical and legal geography'.[82] Purcell remarks that 'established rights and legal limits [are] vulnerable to the vicissitudes of nature'[83] if baselines automatically ambulate. Further, the theory does not adequately account for the inherent dynamism of coasts, since

> off many coasts, the low-water line varies considerably from tide to tide, following the lunar cycle: accordingly, some means has to be found to define this line for legal purposes, both domestic and international. In other words, the line cannot be completely ambulatory and undefined.[84]

To overcome these difficulties, scholars have suggested a range of responses,[85] including to amend the law to provide for fixed baselines,[86] confirming also

[77] ILC, 'Report of the International Law Commission covering the Work of its Seventy-Fourth Session' (24 April–2 June and 3 July–4 August 2023) UN Doc A/78/10 [141] (2023 ILC Report).
[78] Schofield, 'Departures from the Coast' (n 6) 725.
[79] Rayfuse 'Sea Level Rise and Maritime Zones' (n 65) 173.
[80] On risks of waste and conflict, see Caron, 'When Law Makes Climate Change Worse' (n 54); on international security dimensions, see also Lusthaus, 'Shifting Sands' (n 47).
[81] Klein, 'Land and Sea' (n 58) 23.
[82] Lathrop, 'Baselines' (n 5) 77.
[83] Purcell, *Geographical Change and the Law of the Sea* (n 28) 10.
[84] Anderson, 'Baselines in the Modern Law of the Sea' (n 43).
[85] See works cited in Chapter 1, n 33.
[86] eg Caron, 'When Law Makes Climate Change Worse' (n 54) 41. Murphy broadly identifies three kinds of approach to these problems: in addition to fixing baselines, other options include fixing outer limits, or 'according preferential rights of exploitation to the coastal State in areas where it previously enjoyed sovereignty or sovereign rights' despite ambulatory baselines: Sean Murphy, 'Ambulatory Versus Fixed Baselines Under the Law of the Sea' (2023) 38 American University Law Review 721, 726.

their view that fixing baselines was not generally seen as available under existing law.

2.3.2 Second phase of scholarship: Situating legal stability within the existing LOSC system

As suggested by some writers (such as Klein, above),[87] the ambulatory theory raises problems relating to stability. This reasoning gestures simultaneously to the importance of the stability of maritime zones and to its elusiveness. Under this view, legal stability is constructed as something outside the existing LOSC framework which—under the ambulatory theory—should be seen as a shortcoming of the current rules under conditions of sea-level rise, therefore requiring some legal remediation in order to realize it.

This second phase of scholarship on sea-level rise and maritime zones marks the beginnings of a shift in understanding where the notion of legal stability might be situated vis-à-vis the existing LOSC system. A marker of this development can be seen in the work of the ILC's work on sea-level rise and international law, which took the first steps towards a reconceptualization of the meaning of 'ambulatory' and the place of stability, as informed by States' submissions. In 2018, the ILC decided to recommend the inclusion of the topic 'sea-level rise in relation to international law' in its programme of work.[88] This inquiry was understood at the outset to have implications beyond the law of the sea, such as on questions of statehood and the protection of persons. The *First issues paper* from the Co-Chairs of the ILC Study Group on sea-level rise in international law (*First issues paper*), focusing on the law of the sea, was released in the 72nd Session of the ILC (2020–21).[89]

In the *First issues paper*, Aurescu and Oral observed that, 'at the time of the negotiation of the United Nations Convention on the Law of the Sea, sea-level rise and its effects were not perceived as an issue that needed to be addressed. The Convention was thus interpreted as prescribing an ambulatory character for baselines and the outer limits of the maritime zones measured therefrom.'[90] In support of this view, the *First issues paper* noted the submission of the United

[87] See Section 2.2.3.
[88] ILC, 'Report of the International Law Commission covering the Work of its Seventieth Session' (30 April–1 June and 2 July–10 August 2018) UN Doc A/73/10, Annex B (2018 ILC Report).
[89] Bogdan Aurescu and Nilüfer Oral, Co-Chairs of the Study Group on Sea-Level Rise in relation to International Law, *First issues paper by Bogdan Aurescu and Nilüfer Oral* (28 February 2020) UN Doc A/CN.4/740 (*First issues paper*).
[90] ibid.

Kingdom which states that its domestic legislation 'provides for ambulatory baselines',[91] the submission of the Netherlands which reports on 'the practice of the Kingdom of the Netherlands with regard to ambulatory baselines',[92] and the view expressed by the United States in its submission that 'coastal baselines are generally ambulatory'.[93] The *First issues paper* also pointed to examples from State practice that it considered to amount to 'an ambulatory baselines system',[94] even though the coastal State does not expressly describe it as such. An example is the domestic legislation of Romania which, in setting out coordinates for its straight baselines, also envisages that such coordinates may be reviewed and 'the coordinates of the new points are established through Governmental Decision'.[95] It is clear that these examples of State practice expressly contemplate change to the baseline or maritime zone in one way or another, whether this be through substitution of new coordinates or a chart update. This idea that a baseline and maritime zone may change over time is consistent with the central idea of change underpinning the 'ambulatory theory'.

However, a closer examination reveals that the 'ambulatory character' highlighted by the *First issues paper* in its examples did not always envisage that the baseline is *identified* with the coast, in the sense that 'changes in the shoreline, however and how quickly effected, result in changes in the baseline from which the territorial sea is measured'.[96] Rather, information submitted by the Netherlands, the United States, and Romania made clear that there is a process undertaken by those coastal States to make changes to the baseline; in these examples it is not necessarily the case that changes to the baseline are automatic.[97]

The *First issues paper*'s idea of 'ambulatory character', in common with scholars proposing the ambulatory theory of baselines, had at its core the idea that a baseline and/or maritime zone may change over time. But such scholars

[91] 'Submission of the United Kingdom and Great Britain and Northern Ireland', discussed in ibid [88].

[92] Kingdom of the Netherlands, 'Submission of the Netherlands to the International Law Commission' (27 December 2019) 2 (2019 Netherlands ILC Submission).

[93] 2020 US ILC Submission (n 27) 2.

[94] *First issues paper* (n 89) [88].

[95] Law no 17/1990 concerning the Legal Regime of the Internal Waters, the Territorial Sea and the Contiguous Zone of Romania, art 2(3) as included in Romania, 'Submission of Romania to the ILC' (9 January 2020) (2020 Romania ILC Submission).

[96] O'Connell *The International Law of the Sea* (n 62) 682.

[97] The legislation of one coastal State considered by the *First issues paper* does identify the baseline with the coast: the United Kingdom refers to ambulatory baselines expressly, yet does not disclose any particular process to review or change its baselines 'established in accordance with the relevant provisions of the United Nations Convention on the Law of the Sea': The Territorial Sea (Baselines) Order 2014 (United Kingdom) art 2(1). However, the explanatory memorandum makes clear that, 'generally the baseline will follow the low-water line': Explanatory Memorandum to The Territorial Sea (Baselines) Order 2014 (United Kingdom) [7.1].

considered either that the baseline is identified with the coast or, where a chart is used, that 'charts are not determinative of the naturally ambulatory normal baseline'.[98] In contrast, the examples of national legislation considered by the *First issues paper* to be 'an ambulatory baselines system' suggest the possibility that different methods of domestic implementation may reveal such an ambulatory character, including where the baseline is identified with the low-water line with the coast, or defined by reference to an official chart or coordinates.

Informed by its consideration of State practice, the *First issues paper* developed the idea of 'ambulatory character' beyond the notion that baseline is 'naturally' ambulatory; rather, it is more that 'ambulatory character' is revealed by whether the domestic framework[99] of the coastal State shows that a baseline is envisaged to change over time. If the domestic framework does contemplate such change, then the *way* in which the baseline may change is also a product of that domestic framework, such that it may be 'natural', as suggested in the United Kingdom's legislation, or change may follow coastal State action, as in the Netherlands, United States, and Romanian examples.

In this way, the *First issues paper* offered a way to understand how a certain degree of stability is not necessarily incompatible with an ambulatory baselines system. At least to this extent, this marked a shift to recognizing that existing rules on the baseline may have the capacity to embrace elements of stability, rather than legal stability needing to be found wholly outside the LOSC framework. Despite this, at the time, the Co-Chairs, Aurescu and Oral, offered the preliminary observation that:

> [t]he ambulatory theory/method regarding baselines and the limits of maritime zones measured from them does not respond to the concerns expressed by Member States that are prompted by the effects of sea-level rise, especially as regards the rights of the coastal State in the various maritime zones, and the consequent need to preserve legal stability, security, certainty and predictability.[100]

Reinforcing this conclusion, evidence of State practice on fixed baselines that might have been relevant to understanding legal stability under the existing LOSC framework was instead considered as relevant to 'the emergence of a

[98] 2012 ILA Baselines Committee Report (n 39) 22.

[99] eg the *First issues paper* 'noted that the legislation accompanying notifications is a publicly available source of information with respect to baselines, as it may indicate that a State implements ambulatory baselines through its domestic legislation'; *First issues paper* (n 89) [101].

[100] ibid [104(d)].

particular or regional customary rule (or even of a general customary rule) of international law regarding the preservation of baselines and of outer limits of maritime zones',[101] about which Aurescu and Oral considered it too early to draw conclusions at the time.

The second development marking a shift in understanding whether the notion of legal stability might be situated outside or inside the LOSC system comes from the work of the ILA Committee on International Law and Sea Level Rise (ILA SLR Committee). The ILA SLR Committee was mandated to study the possible impacts of sea-level rise under international law and in particular to 'develop proposals for the progressive development of international law in relation to the possible loss of all or parts of State territory and maritime zones due to sea level rise, including the impacts on statehood, nationality, and human rights'.[102] Adopting the recommendations of the ILA SLR Committee, the ILA in 2018 resolved that, 'on the grounds of legal certainty and stability, provided that the baselines and the outer limits of maritime zones of a coastal or an archipelagic State have been properly determined in accordance with the 1982 Law of the Sea Convention, these baselines and limits should not be required to be recalculated should sea level change affect the geographical reality of the coastline',[103] making clear that this should be considered an 'interpretation of the 1982 Law of the Sea Convention in relation to the ability of coastal and archipelagic States to maintain their existing lawful maritime entitlements'.[104]

Like the ILA Baselines Committee, the ILA SLR Committee's outputs represent a collaborative scholarly effort to tackle these issues. The ILA SLR Committee's recommendation shows an increasing awareness of the significance of legal stability (and certainty) for maritime zones and sea-level rise, and, importantly, a connection with the interpretation of the LOSC rather than, for example, its amendment. This represents a shift away from viewing legal stability as a deficit of the existing LOSC baseline rules (under an ambulatory theory of baselines) but also from the limited stability that might be accommodated within an 'ambulatory baseline system' (as reconceptualized by the ILC). Here, the ILA SLR Committee is suggesting that 'legal certainty and stability' might in some way animate an interpretation of the LOSC baseline

[101] ibid [104(i)].
[102] ILA (Committee on International Law and Sea Level Rise) 'Report (Lisbon Conference)' 1 (2022 ILA SLR Report).
[103] ILA (Committee on International Law and Sea Level Rise) Res 5/2018 (ILA 2018 Resolution).
[104] ibid.

rules itself, underpinning the ability of coastal States to maintain established maritime zones.

2.3.3 Third phase of scholarship: Legal stability and the 'contemporary interpretation' of the LOSC

In this phase, from approximately 2022 onwards, scholars increasingly express the view that the international law rules relating to baselines and maritime zones are not only rules that could or should change, but rather, that 'this is an area of the international law of the sea that is in the process of evolution'.[105]

Two main themes can be discerned in this phase. First, there is a clear effort to move beyond the 'ambulatory theory', seeing it as an increasingly outdated understanding of law that can no longer effectively serve contemporary purposes. In 2023, the ILC remarked that:

> [a]lthough, in the past, before the Commission had embarked on the topic of sea-level rise, the doctrine had interpreted the Convention to the effect that the baselines and outer limits of the territorial sea, contiguous zone and exclusive economic zone were ambulatory, Member States had, in ever-increasing numbers, expressed the contrary view, pointing to an interpretation of the Convention in the sense that it did not forbid or exclude the option of fixing baselines.[106]

Secondly, discussions at the ILC also give prominence to the concept of 'legal stability' with the emergence of an updated understanding of the law:

> [L]egal stability (and security, certainty and predictability) is viewed among Member States as having a very concrete meaning, and has been linked to the preservation of maritime zones through the fixing of baselines (and outer limits of maritime zones measured from those baselines): in other words, States affected by sea-level rise are not required to update their notifications of coordinates and charts, resulting in their baselines being fixed even if the physical coast moves landward because of sea-level rise. No States—not even

[105] Clive Schofield, 'Sea Level Rise: Implications for Baselines, Limits and Boundaries' in Lan Anh T Nguyen and Hai Dang Vu (eds), *Viability of UNCLOS amid Emerging Global Maritime Challenges* (Springer 2024) 71.

[106] 2023 ILC Report (n 77) [141].

> those with national legislation providing for ambulatory baselines—have expressed positions contesting the option of fixed baselines.[107]

This begins to illuminate the contours of a 'pragmatic interpretation'[108] underpinned by legal stability.

The ILA SLR Committee also observed that 'there is increasingly wide and strong support among States for [its] 2018 recommendation that as a matter of interpretation of the LOSC there is no legal requirement for a coastal State to update its national charts to reflect changes in their coastlines brought about by sea level rise.'[109] While some scholars point out that there remain other potential options for baseline preservation (such as amending the LOSC),[110] Murphy considers that, given the unfeasibility of successfully mobilizing the LOSC's formal amendment provisions, 'the current approach by States seems to be to address the problem of rising sea levels by *interpreting* the Convention through State practice'.[111] Taking a similar view, Roland Holst points out that 'state practice—as long as it is not expressly and widely objected to—may well prove a perfectly adequate means for immediately affected states to assert their rights and safeguard their interests'.[112] In this phase, an interpretative approach appears to be gaining favour as the most promising modality through which the preservation of maritime zones might be achieved. This was also recognized by the ILC in its suggestion in 2025 that '[a]n approach may be adopted that allows for the interpretation and application of existing instruments and rules of international law to take into account the adverse impact of sea-level rise. For example [. . .] existing instruments and rules of international law may be applied in a manner that addresses the impact of sea-level rise so as to allow for a contemporary interpretation.'[113]

And while this third phase of scholarship is still ongoing, at the time of writing, scholarly assessments are that State practice does not yet meet the

[107] *Additional paper to the first issues paper* (n 48) [98].
[108] ibid [94].
[109] 2022 ILA SLR Report (n 102) 21.
[110] See eg Massimo Lando, 'Baseline Preservation as a Response to Sea-Level Rise' (2025) 56 Ocean Development and International Law 100 (including for an excellent discussion of customary international law).
[111] Murphy (n 86) 728 (original emphasis).
[112] Rozemarijn J Roland Holst, *Change in the Law of the Sea: Context, Mechanisms and Practice* (Brill 2022) 284.
[113] ILC, 'Report of the International Law Commission covering the Work of its Seventy-Sixth Session' (28 April–30 May 2025) UN Doc A/80/10 [58] (2025 ILC Report). See also 2025 ILC Study Group Final Report (n 49) [58] and Patrícia Galvão Teles, Nilüfer Oral, and Juan José Ruda Santolaria, 'Final Consolidated Report of the Co-Chairs of the Study Group on Sea-Level Rise in Relation to International Law' (3 February 2025) UN Doc A/CN.4/783 [502] (Final Consolidated Report of the Co-Chairs).

relevant legal standards that would be required to establish such an interpretation of the LOSC; that is, although the law of baselines might be in the process of evolution, the prevailing sentiment is that such a change has not yet been fully achieved. For example, in 2022, the ILA SLR Committee identified three stages in the development of State practice from 2010 to the present,[114] focusing on regional and national statements from certain Pacific States and groupings, the submissions of UN Member States to the ILC, and statements to the UN General Assembly, collectively demonstrating 'rapidly evolving State practice and a certain level or consolidation or uniformity of practice among some of the States concerned',[115] well developed among Pacific Islands Forum (PIF) members and also observable in other geographic regions. It also noted national legislation in certain countries (Republic of the Marshall Islands, Kiribati, and Tuvalu) which unilaterally declares those countries' baselines and maritime zones using modern geographic coordinates.[116] On balance, however, the ILA SLR Committee considered that it was 'still arguable' as to whether the level of State support for an interpretation of the LOSC that permitted baseline preservation 'amounts to sufficient evidence'[117] to qualify as 'subsequent practice in the application of [the LOSC] which establishes the agreement of the parties regarding its interpretation',[118] nor to amount to a 'subsequent agreement' of LOSC Parties as to its interpretation or application.[119]

Revisiting this question in 2024, the ILA SLR Committee noted the increasing support from UN Member States for the legal stability of maritime zones, including the adoption of 'new policies specifically addressing the legal stability of baselines and the limits of maritime zones in the context of physical changes to coastlines as a result of climate change-related sea level rise'.[120] The ILA SLR Committee recommended that 'an explicit recognition of a solution at a globally agreed level would significantly contribute to facilitating legal certainty concerning the stability of baselines and maritime limits in the context of sea-level rise'.[121] Such a recommendation suggests that the ILA SLR Committee remains unconvinced that without such global recognition, State practice could be considered sufficiently mature. Lando also considers

[114] 2022 ILA SLR Report (n 102) 7.
[115] ibid 19.
[116] ibid 8. This legislation was also noted in the earlier work of this Committee: see ILA (Committee on International Law and Sea Level Rise), 'Report (Sydney Conference)' (2018) 17 (2018 ILA SLR Report).
[117] 2022 ILA SLR Report (n 102) 21.
[118] VCLT, art 31(3)(b).
[119] VCLT, art 31(3)(a).
[120] 2024 ILA SLR Report (n 48) 42.
[121] ibid 44.

that existing State practice 'is not sufficiently consistent to use it to interpret the relevant UNCLOS provisions';[122] similarly, Schofield concludes that 'it remains to be seen whether the international community will accept this potential evolution in the interpretation of the law of the sea such that declared baselines, limits and boundaries will prove to be opposable to other States'.[123] Cogilati-Bantz[124] and Murphy[125] are similarly unconvinced.

There has clearly been significant development in the literature since 1989, signalling both an immense scholarly effort—on the part of individual scholars and in expert groups—and 'an unusual and fruitful interplay between international law scholarship and State practice'.[126] However, several major questions remain. If we appreciate 'legal stability' to have 'a very concrete meaning' that is 'linked to the preservation of maritime zones through the fixing of baselines',[127] how might this insight influence the exercise of treaty interpretation, for example, the identification of relevant State practice? How, in 'concrete' terms, does a State secure the legal stability of the baseline and maritime zone? Is it only coastal States in the Pacific region which have adopted national legislation to fix baselines, or might there be broader practice? At the same time, if some coastal States adopt ambulatory baselines (such as the United Kingdom and the Netherlands), how might such practice be reconciled with an emerging 'contemporary interpretation' that promotes legal stability? And if there is no duty set out in the LOSC to update established baselines, how does this relate to the interpretation of the LOSC as a whole?

To begin to answer those questions, Chapter 3 takes a closer look at the notion of legal stability, unpacking the 'legal stability of maritime zones' as it might relate to an emerging 'contemporary interpretation' of the LOSC.

[122] Lando, 'Baseline Preservation' (n 110) 15.

[123] Schofield, 'Sea Level Rise' (n 105) 71.

[124] Cogliati-Bantz, 'The Way Forward is not Fast-Forward' (n 66) 91–92.

[125] Murphy (n 86) 730.

[126] Davor Vidas and David Freestone, 'Legal Certainty and Stability in the Face of Sea Level Rise: Trends in the Development of State Practice and International Law Scholarship on Maritime Limits And Boundaries' (2022) 37 The International Journal of Marine and Coastal Law 1, 52.

[127] *Additional paper to the first issues paper* (n 48) [98].

3
Unpacking the Legal Stability of Maritime Zones

3.1 Introduction

Despite States' increasing invocation of legal stability in connection with the United Nations Convention on the Law of the Sea (LOSC) and the challenges of sea-level rise, the meaning of the term 'legal stability' in this context is not self-evident. As outlined in Chapter 2, scholars have recognized the increasing emphasis placed on legal stability in discussions about the implications of sea-level rise for maritime zones, pointing to, for example, the importance of preserving maritime zones 'on the grounds of legal certainty and stability'.[1] Until the work of the International Law Association Sea Level Rise Committee (ILA SLR), legal stability was largely considered to be a value situated outside the existing LOSC system, despite being a sought-after goal in the context of addressing the effects of sea-level rise. Discussions at the International Law Commission (ILC) pointed to the existence of legal stability within the law of the sea, 'linked to the preservation of maritime zones through the fixing of baselines (and outer limits of maritime zones measured from those baselines)',[2] as well as a 'contemporary interpretation'[3] of the LOSC. But if this is the case, *how* precisely is legal stability linked to such an interpretative outcome?

This chapter begins with a historical perspective to demonstrate that concerns for stability in the LOSC system of maritime zones are long-standing. But there are also signs that the limited measure of stability originally envisaged for baselines in the development of the LOSC is now in the process of expanding. Three settings have been important for the ventilation of States'

[1] ILA (Committee on International Law and Sea Level Rise) Res 5/2018 (ILA 2018 Resolution).
[2] Bogdan Aurescu and Nilüfer Oral, Co-Chairs of the Study Group on Sea-Level Rise in relation to International Law, *Additional paper to the first issues paper* (Seventy-Fourth Session of the ILC, 13 February 2023) UN Doc A/CN.4/761 [98] (*Additional paper to the first issues paper*).
[3] ILC, 'Report of the International Law Commission covering the Work of its Seventy-Sixth Session' (28 April–30 May 2025) UN Doc A/80/10 [58] (2025 ILC Report).

Sea-Level Rise and the Legal Stability of Maritime Zones. Frances Anggadi, Oxford University Press.
 DOI: 10.1093/9780198973515.003.0003

concerns about legal stability in connection with maritime zones. Moving chronologically, the chapter first demonstrates the importance of stability in the development of the legal order of the oceans, examining how stability featured in debates at UNCLOS III (Section 3.2). The chapter then revisits the drafting records relating to Article 5 of the LOSC, arguing that even in the context of the normal baseline, the type of baseline considered by many scholars to be the paradigm ambulatory baseline,[4] a degree of stability was envisaged (Section 3.3). In this light, States' choice for a charts-based definition in what was to become Article 5 demonstrates an awareness that States could implement a normal baseline that was not necessarily identified with the low-water line along the coast. Significantly, this meant some degree of discrepancy between the normal baseline and the coastline should be expected and, in some circumstances, tolerated. From these two historical contexts, it is evident that legal stability should not be considered a novel concern. It should instead be considered a long-held value that relates generally to the LOSC system of maritime zones, including in relation to the normal baseline. The chapter finally examines the views of States in the period 2017–25 (Section 3.4). Forty years after the conclusion of the LOSC, States accord increasing prominence to legal stability in connection with debates on sea-level rise and maritime zones. In this period, many States have affirmed the relevance of legal stability to the LOSC legal order, and also made calls for the need to 'preserve'[5] and 'maximize'[6] the stability of baselines and maritime zones.

Synthesizing these observations from States, the chapter demonstrates that States' concerns disclose several key elements of the legal stability of maritime zones. These elements illustrate how the legal stability of a baseline or maritime zone can be achieved as a 'concrete' matter, as well as offering clues as to the legal means by which this could be accomplished. Noting that the ICJ in *Obligations of States in Respect of Climate Change* did not take the opportunity to clarify this key concept,[7] the chapter offers a way to unpack 'the legal stability of maritime zones' into its key elements: spatial stability, temporal stability, and the stability of the legal status of land features.

[4] See Section 2.3.
[5] Germany, 'Summary Record of the 21st Meeting' UN GAOR Sixth Committee 76th Session (29 October 2021) UN Doc A/C.6/76/SR.21.
[6] Australia, 'Summary Record of the 23rd Meeting' UN GAOR Sixth Committee 73rd Session (24 October 2018) UN Doc A/C.6/73/SR.23 (Summary Record of the 23rd Meeting).
[7] This omission was criticized by Judge Aurescu in his Separate Opinion [3]–[4].

3.2 Securing a stable 'order of the seas and oceans'

Delegates representing a range of geographic regions and maritime interests expressed the hope and intention that the work of the Third UN Conference on the Law of the Sea (UNCLOS III) would 'promote stability'[8] in the oceans. The first President of UNCLOS III encapsulated this sentiment when observing that:

> a convention or conventions ensuring a generally acceptable, stable and durable law of the sea would be not only a monument to the patience, perseverance, diplomatic skill and spirit of fraternal cooperation of the participants and the States they represented, but would also honour the highest ideals of the Charter and other international legal instruments which sought to express the aspirations and yearnings of all peoples of the world.[9]

Indeed, this need for stability had become pressing by the mid-twentieth century, a period described by the third President of UNCLOS III as one in which 'the old legal order had collapsed and the world was faced with a plethora of conflicting claims for jurisdiction and resources by coastal States. Instead of order, we had chaos.'[10] At this time, the question of the breadth of the territorial sea remained unresolved (not having been agreed in discussions at the Hague Conference in the 1930s, the 1958 Convention on the Territorial Sea and Contiguous Zone,[11] or at the Second UN Conference on the Law of the Sea (UNCLOS II) in 1960). Meanwhile many coastal States had asserted some form of maritime jurisdiction exceeding the traditionally recognized breadth of the territorial sea of 3 nm: these included the United States' 1946 Truman Proclamation claiming jurisdiction over its adjacent continental shelf; the 1952 Declaration by Santiago by Chile, Peru, and Ecuador of their sovereignty and jurisdiction over its ocean not less than 200 nm from its coast;[12] and claims

[8] Sri Lanka, 187th Meeting of the Resumed Eleventh Session of the Plenary, 7 December 1982, Official Records of the Third United Nations Conference on the Law of the Sea, vol XVII (Plenary Meetings, Summary Records and Verbatim Records, as well as Documents of the Conference, Resumed Eleventh Session and Final Part Eleventh Session and Conclusion) UN Doc A/CONF.62/121, 50.

[9] Sri Lanka, 1st Meeting of the General Committee, 20 June 1974, Official Records of the Third United Nations Conference on the Law of the Sea, vol I (Summary Records of Plenary Meetings of the First and Second Sessions, and of Meetings of the General Committee, Second Session) UN Doc A/CONF./BUR/SR.1, 4.

[10] Tommy Koh, *Building a New Legal Order for the Oceans* (NUS Press 2020) 4.

[11] Convention on the Territorial Sea and Contiguous Zone (opened for signature 29 April 1958, entered into force 10 September 1964) 516 UNTS 206 (Geneva Convention on the Territorial Sea and Contiguous Zone).

[12] Discussed in DP O'Connell, *The International Law of the Sea*, vol I (IA Shearer ed, Clarendon Press 1984) 553.

by Indonesia and the Philippines to enclose the interconnecting waters of their outermost islands as internal waters.[13]

Against this backdrop, some States expressed the concern during the negotiations at UNCLOS III that an unfettered ability to determine national maritime zones would 'create permanent instability and a proliferation of legal conflicts among States'.[14] Particularly salient, having regard to the significant participation of newly independent States in UNCLOS III, the path towards avoiding such instability would require balancing the full range of interests:

> resolved in a spirit of accommodation, so that the necessary consensus could be reached. But consensus did not mean the majority bowing to an intransigent minority, or the bullying of a minority by an unthinking majority. All States would benefit if, by yielding a little, they could attain stable legal rights and benefits.[15]

At the conclusion of UNCLOS III, Indonesia remarked that this approach to negotiations also contributed to the political legitimacy and durability of the resulting treaty, because it was:

> the result of long years of negotiation and represented compromises that balanced all the conflicting interests of different States. As such it offered the best guarantee for the stability and orderly development of the world's oceans and there was no viable alternative for promoting law and order in ocean affairs.[16]

[13] See Clive R Symmons, 'Article 47—Archipelagic Baselines' in Alexander Proelss (ed), *United Nations Convention on the Law of the Sea: A Commentary* (1st edn, CH Beck 2017) 356.

[14] Paraguay, 6th Meeting of the Second Committee, 17 July 1974, Official Records of the Third United Nations Conference on the Law of the Sea, vol II (Summary Records of Meetings of the First, Second and Third Committees, Second Session) UN Doc A/CONF.62/C.2/SR.6, 149. Nicaragua also made a similar intervention: 'The contemporary world needed a stable and certain law of the sea. Unilateral declarations, although made by peoples in exercise of their sovereignty, their right of self-determination and in justifiable defence of their interests and needs, were not the best means of establishing that law': 29th Plenary Meeting, 4 July 1974, Official Records of UNCLOS III, vol I (n 9) 186.

[15] Cameroon, 41st Meeting of the First Committee, 14 April 1978, Official Records of the Third United Nations Conference on the Law of the Sea, vol IX (Summary Records, Plenary, General Committee, First, Second and Third Committees, as well as Documents of the Conference, Seventh and Resumed Seventh Session) UN Doc A/CONF.62/BUR/SR.44, 53.

[16] Djalal (Indonesia), 165th Plenary Meeting, 1 April 1982, Official Records of the Third United Nations Conference on the Law of the Sea, vol XVI (Summary Records, Plenary, First and Second Committees, as well as Documents of the Conference, Eleventh Session) UN Doc A/CONF.62/SR.165, 77. On the importance of the participation of developing and developed countries in reaching an agreed outcome, and relevance to the creation of a 'stable international regime for the oceans', see Bernard H Oxman, 'The Rule of Law and the United Nations Convention on the Law of the Sea' (1996) 7 European Journal of International Law 353, 361.

Stevenson and Oxman explain that 'the goal was a stable accommodation of coastal and maritime interests both within and between coastal States that would be respected by each state's *class politique* as a continuing restraint upon its jurisdictional choices'.[17] In this way, the stabilizing purpose underlying the zonal allocation of jurisdiction in the LOSC was not only set against the mischief of a 'plethora of conflicting claims for jurisdiction and resources' but also intended to uphold a new balance of interests in the ocean that reflected the geopolitics of the time. States identified political and practical implications of the new regime, such as 'the importance of navigation and overflight through straits for the global flow of trade and communications and for a stable and peaceful world order',[18] and how common rules to govern exploitation of natural resources may promote equity and avoid conflict.[19] Indeed, States viewed the new legal order of the oceans as vital 'for the promotion of the rule of law in international affairs, and hence the shaping of a peaceful world with a stable and equitable world order'.[20]

The resulting 'package deal'[21] of the LOSC was adopted in 1982 and its preamble sets out the aspirations of States Parties to establish

> 'a new legal order for the seas and oceans which will facilitate international communication, and will promote the peaceful uses of the seas and oceans, the equitable and efficient utilization of their resources, the conservation

[17] John R Stevenson and Bernard H Oxman, 'The Future of the United Nations Convention on the Law of the Sea' (1994) 88 The American Journal of International Law 488, 492.

[18] USA, 12th Meeting of the Second Committee, 22 July 1974, Official Records of the Third United Nations Conference on the Law of the Sea, vol II (Summary Records of Meetings of the First, Second and Third Committees, Second Session) UN Doc A/CONF.62/C.2/SR.6 128.

[19] See eg the intervention of Ghana: 'There was urgent need for a convention to regulate the exploration and exploitation of the sea-bed beyond the limits of national jurisdiction, which had been proclaimed the common heritage of mankind, before a state of anarchy was reached in the area, with consequent potential danger to world peace and stability', 12th Meeting of the First Committee, 7 August 1974, Official Records of UNCLOS III, vol II (n 18) 60; and Bangladesh: 'Bangladesh attached great importance to the procedure of dispute settlement, since, as a developing country, it would be depending more and more on the extensive exploitation and exploration of sea resources, which could be carried out only when the interests of countries like Bangladesh were secure and an atmosphere of peace reigned over the ocean', 62nd Plenary Meeting, 7 April 1976, Official Records of the Third United Nations Conference on the Law of the Sea, vol V (Summary Records, Plenary, General Committee, First, Second and Third Committees, as well as Documents of the Conference, Fourth Session) UN Doc A/CONF.62/SR.62, 41.

[20] Canada, 65th Plenary Meeting, 12 April 1976, Official Records of UNCLOS III, vol V (n 19) 51. See also the intervention of Germany: 'They hoped that the Conference would justify the hopes for the establishment of a universal and equitable law of the sea, which would greatly enhance peace and stability in the world': 1st Plenary Meeting (3 December 1973) Official Records of UNCLOS III, vol I (n 9) 4.

[21] For a useful discussion of this oft-used term to describe the result of UNCLOS III, see Xuexia Liao, 'The LOSC as a Package Deal and Its Implications for Determination of Customary International Law' (2020) 35 The International Journal of Marine and Coastal Law 704.

of their living resources, and the study, protection and preservation of the marine environment'.[22]

This setting demonstrates the concern of States for legal stability in connection with the overall system of maritime zones, at risk in the 'chaos' of unfettered and conflicting maritime claims, and brought to order in the agreement of the LOSC framework.

3.3 The drafting history of Article 5

As many have pointed out,[23] discussions at UNCLOS III did not canvass sea-level rise, climate change more broadly, nor any of their possible legal impacts on the LOSC jurisdictional framework.[24] This is unsurprising, since it was only after the conclusion of the LOSC in 1982 that the international community began seriously to engage with such matters. For example, the Intergovernmental Panel on Climate Change (IPCC) was established in 1988, issuing its First Assessment Report in 1990.[25] From the early twenty-first century, scholars began to articulate the emergence of the Anthropocene,[26] a new geological epoch characterized by pervasive human impacts on the Earth. While the Holocene was characterized by relative stability in the Earth's conditions, the Anthropocene is a period in which 'human influences become decisive in affecting the parameters of the Earth system, accompanied by the potential to generate instability and even catastrophic shifts in the character of the whole system [. . .] of the sort that are common in the planet's deeper history, but unknown in recorded human history'.[27] Vidas, considering the

[22] LOSC, Preamble.

[23] This section updates and develops material which was previously published in Frances Anggadi, 'Reconceptualising the "Ambulatory Character" of Baselines: The International Law Commission's Work on Sea-Level Rise and International Law' (2021) 22 Melbourne Journal of International Law 163.

[24] See eg Alan Boyle, 'Law of the Sea Perspectives on Climate Change' in David Freestone (ed), *The 1982 Law of the Sea Convention At 30: Successes, Challenges and New Agendas* (Brill 2013); David D Caron, 'When Law Makes Climate Change Worse: Rethinking the Law of Baselines in Light of a Rising Sea Level' (1990) 17(4) Ecology Law Quarterly 621, 635–36; Rosemary Rayfuse, 'Sea Level Rise and Maritime Zones: Preserving the Maritime Entitlements of "Disappearing" States' in Michael B Gerrard and Gregory E Wannier (eds), *Threatened Island Nations: Legal Implications of Rising Seas and a Changing Climate* (Cambridge University Press 2013) 180; Clive Schofield, 'Departures from the Coast: Trends in the Application of Territorial Sea Baselines under the Law of the Sea Convention' (2012) 27(4) The International Journal of Marine and Coastal Law 723, 726.

[25] See IPCC, *Climate Change: The 1990 and 1992 IPCC Assessments* (1992).

[26] The precise date at which the Anthropocene commenced is a matter of debate, and to some extent necessarily arbitrary: see Karen N Scott, 'International Law in the Anthropocene: Responding to the Geoengineering Challenge' (2012) 34 Michigan Journal of International Law 309, 315.

[27] John S Dryzek and Jonathan Pickering, *The Politics of the Anthropocene* (Oxford University Press 2019) 2.

significance of this growing understanding of the Earth system to international law, identifies

> the assumption, based on our experience so far, of constantly stable circumstances of the late Holocene. Many aspects of international law are based on such understanding of the stability of the Earth conditions.[28]

However, it would be incorrect to deduce from these (Holocene) assumptions that it was unnecessary for the LOSC to envisage any degree of legal stability at all.

For example, many scholars have pointed to the LOSC provisions on the outer limits of the continental shelf (under Article 76) and for deltaic baselines (under Article 7(2)) as provisions that expressly provide for stability.[29] For such scholars, these express provisions in the LOSC are an exhaustive account of the LOSC's capacity to provide for stable baselines and outer limits, and the normal baseline's 'naturally ambulatory'[30] character should be seen in contrast to such provisions. However, this section revisits the drafting history of Article 5 to demonstrate that drafters did envisage some degree of stability for the normal baseline too, even though the participants of UNCLOS III operated under Holocene assumptions of geographic stability.

As will be explained, this section suggests that two propositions may be drawn from the drafting history: first, difficulties in reaching agreement on a way to refer to the low-water line along the coast led drafters to adopt a charts-based definition of the baseline; and secondly, drafters envisaged that minor discrepancies between the chart and the coast should not attract legal challenge. The drafters recognized the ability for the normal baseline to remain in place in those circumstances.

3.3.1 Opting for a charts-based definition of the normal baseline

The starting point in the development of draft articles on the normal baseline lies in the work of the League of Nations Conference for the Codification of International Law (the Hague Conference), which took place in 1930.

[28] Davor Vidas and others, 'International Law for the Anthropocene? Shifting Perspectives in Regulation of the Oceans, Environment and Genetic Resources' (2015) 9 Anthropocene 1, 4.

[29] See eg Caron, 'When Law Makes Climate Change Worse' (n 24).

[30] ILA (Committee on Baselines under the International Law of the Sea), 'Baselines under the International Law of the Sea (Sofia Conference)' 22 (2012 ILA Baselines Committee Report).

Ultimately, the codification of an overall conventional regime of the territorial sea eluded the Hague Conference, largely owing to a failure to agree on the question of its breadth and the emerging concept of the contiguous zone.[31] Sub-Committee II of the Hague Conference (which had been tasked to consider baselines in detail) developed the first textual formulation on the subject, in the form of a draft article on the 'base line':

> For the purposes of this Convention, the line of low-water mark is that indicated on the charts officially used by the coastal State, provided the latter line does not appreciably depart from the line of mean low-water spring tides.[32]

The accompanying observations, reflecting the replies of governments, noted that the traditional expression 'low-water mark' is capable of being interpreted in different ways and required further definition. Finland noted that the low-water level varies considerably 'in different parts of the world, and is lowest at the new and at the full moon, highest at the second quarter, and at the mean four days before and four days after the new and the full moon', and therefore called on any draft Convention to specify exactly which line of low water should be used for the purposes of the baseline.[33] To address this concern, some countries proposed a particular line of low water (such as South Africa, which suggested mean low-water spring tides)[34] and Germany proposed that a draft article could refer to the 'sea level adopted in the charts',[35] thereby accommodating a range of methods currently used by various countries.

While the replies of governments affirmed the principle of the 'line of low water mark following all the sinuosities of the coast',[36] at no stage was this proposed as potential article text. Instead, Sub-Committee II considered the possibility of defining the 'low-water mark' as either the low-water mark as indicated on the charts officially used by the coastal State, or as the line of mean low-water spring tides. In what appears to follow the approach suggested by Germany, Sub-Committee II opted for the charts-based formulation because

[31] Donald R Rothwell and Tim Stephens, *The International Law of the Sea* (3rd edn, Bloomsbury 2023) 4.

[32] 'Report of the Second Sub-Committee' in League of Nations, *Conference for the Codification of International Law [1930]*, vol 4 (Oceana Publications 1975) 1419.

[33] ibid Reply of Finland.

[34] ibid Reply of South Africa.

[35] ibid Reply of Germany.

[36] Point IV, 'Determination of the Base Line for Measurement of the Breadth of Territorial Waters' in League of Nations, *Conference for the Codification of International Law [1930]*, vol 2 (Oceana Publications 1975) 253.

it was 'more practical'.[37] The result was that the first drafting effort to articulate the law on the baseline did not refer to the coastline itself, but to a visual representation of the coast at the time of charting.

In its work to 'identify the existing law on the normal baseline',[38] the ILA Baselines Committee referred to this drafting history in asking whether the Article 5 normal baseline is a line on a chart (the charted low-water line) or a line on the 'ground' (the actual low-water line).[39] Its conclusion on the drafting history of Article 5 was that:

> to the extent that the wording of Article 5 is vague, the Committee considers that this was deliberate, and was intended to 'paper over' the practical difficulties resulting from the absence of a universally agreed vertical datum for defining low water. The insertion of the reference to charts was intended to address these difficulties, and was not intended to give primacy to the charted line.[40]

This chapter partially agrees with these views: as illustrated above, the inclusion of charts into the draft article was indeed intended to address the difficulties relating to the tidal datum. But the drafting history shows that despite inevitable discrepancies caused by different tidal datums, this difficulty was to be addressed by giving the charted line a degree of 'primacy' over the 'actual' low-water line insofar as the charted line was intended to serve as the default legal baseline. In this way, the charted line could—indeed, was intended to—constitute the normal baseline.

This view is supported by the discussion around a reference to what the book will refer to as the 'shoreline provision' in the drafting history, and its eventual omission from the text. The 'shoreline provision' originally formed part of the Report of the Committee of Experts on technical questions concerning the territorial sea[41] (Experts' Report), and was included verbatim as the final sentence of new provisional Article 4, entitled 'Normal baseline', and adopted in 1954 by the ILC:

[37] 'Report of the Second Sub-Committee' in League of Nations, *Conference for the Codification of International Law [1930]* (n 32) 1419.

[38] ILA (Committee on Baselines under the International Law of the Sea), 'Baselines under the International Law of the Sea (Sofia Conference)' 1.

[39] ibid 3.

[40] ibid 12.

[41] JPA François, Special Rapporteur, 'Second Report on the Regime of the Territorial Sea' Fifth Session UN Doc A/CN.4/61 (Second Report on the Regime of the Territorial Sea) Annex 'Report of the Committee of Experts on Technical Questions concerning the Territorial Sea' 1–2. The Committee of Experts comprised the following members serving in their personal capacity: LE Asplund (Sweden), SW Boggs (USA), PR Couillault (France), RH Kennedy (UK), AS Pinke (Netherlands).

> Subject to the provisions of Article 5 ['Straight base lines'] and to the provisions regarding bays and islands, the breadth of the territorial sea is measured from the low-water line along the coast, as marked on the largest-scale chart available, officially recognized by the coastal State. *If no detailed charts of the area have been drawn which show the low-water line, the shore line (high-water line) shall be used.*[42]

Mentioned by only a handful of scholars who have engaged with the preparatory material for Article 5,[43] the content of the 'shoreline provision' directly bears on the relationship between the legal definition of the baseline, the low-water line along the coast, vertical datum, and charts. During debate at the ILC, the Special Rapporteur explained that the intention behind the 'shoreline provision' had been to provide for a solution where there were no charts of the area showing the low-water line; in that situation, the high-water line of the shoreline should be used. The term 'high-water line' refers to a tangible, visible manifestation of the coast: it is the 'mark left by the tide at high water. The line or level reached, especially the highest line ever reached.'[44]

In contrast to the options considered by the Hague Conference, the high-water line is not a representation of the coast in the way that a chart or a specific vertical datum is. The Proposed language was intended to reflect the practicalities of navigation: 'The official charts of most countries showed the low-water line, but where no such indication was given, ships at sea could only rely on the high-water line which, being identifiable with the shoreline, was always visible.'[45] Ultimately, the 'shoreline provision' was discarded in 1955 because some considered it might imply that a coastal State was obliged to use the high-water line as the baseline. This would be inconsistent not only with State practice but with the finding of the ICJ in the *Fisheries case*[46] that the low-water mark, rather than high-water mark, should be used for measuring the breadth of the territorial sea.[47]

[42] ILC, 'Report of the International Law Commission covering the Work of its Sixth Session' (3 June–28 July 1954) UN Doc A/2693 (Report of the International Law Commission covering the Work of its Sixth Session) 154 (emphasis added).

[43] The 'shoreline provision' is mentioned by Purcell in the context of consideration by drafters of the high- or low-water line: Kate Purcell, *Geographical Change and the Law of the Sea* (Oxford University Press 2019) 172. See also Myres Smith McDougal and William T Burke, *The Public Order of the Oceans: A Contemporary International Law of the Sea* (New Haven Press 1987) 325.

[44] International Hydrographic Organization, *Hydrographic Dictionary: IHO Publication S-32* (5th edn, 1994): 'high-water mark'.

[45] ILC, Summary Record of the 254th Meeting, Sixth Session UN Doc A/CN.4/SR.254 (Summary Record of the 254th Meeting).

[46] *Fisheries (United Kingdom v Norway)* [1951] ICJ Rep 116, 128 [137].

[47] JPA François, Special Rapporteur, 'Third Report on the Regime of the Territorial Sea' Sixth Session UN Doc A/CN.4/77, 7 (Third Report on the Regime of the Territorial Sea).

Although the 'shoreline provision' was omitted to make clear the entitlement of the coastal State to make use of the low-water line as the baseline for measuring the territorial sea, no concerns were raised about the notion that the shoreline could be used to determine the baseline *if* no appropriate chart existed.[48] Two observations can be drawn from this examination of the fate of the 'shoreline provision' in the drafting history. First, a key objective of the drafters was to develop a legal definition of the baseline that was practical, in the sense that it could provide for a readily identifiable spatial reference point for the inner limit of the territorial sea. Concern for mariners seeking to navigate in the absence of charts indicating the low-water line shows that the drafters sought to provide for jurisdictional clarity in a very practical way. Secondly, this debate demonstrates that drafters considered using the shoreline (high-water line) as the baseline where there were no applicable charts. This suggests that the drafters assumed that if there *was* an applicable chart, then that chart would most readily identify the low-water line to be used as the baseline.

Trümpler, reflecting on this drafting history, considered that it is 'at least possible to interpret the history as also indicating that the charted low-water line is to be considered as the baseline'.[49] This chapter argues that if the role of 'the shoreline provision' is taken into account, a stronger case can be made that the drafting history of Article 5 supports the view that the charted low-water line is intended to be the default baseline. Where such a chart was absent, then the shoreline—that is, the actual coastline, rather than a vertical tidal datum—could be used because this presents a practical solution to finding a visible, identifiable reference point for the territorial sea. The records demonstrate that the drafters intended that the charted low-water line would have primacy over use of a specific vertical datum for the purposes of a definition of the baseline, and that in the absence of a charted low-water line, the fallback would be to use the shoreline (whether high-water line or otherwise).

This account of the drafting history demonstrates that the baseline need not be identified with the low-water line along the coast; indeed, preferably it should not be, to avoid the difficulties with directly using the coastline as a legal line. Drafters opted for a charts-based definition of the baseline for the practical advantages of that approach in contrast to other options considered, which were 'actual' lines on the coast (that is, the high-water line, or 'all the sinuosities of the coast') or a specific vertical tidal datum (such as mean low-water

[48] See also McDougal and Burke, 'The Public Order of the Oceans' (n 43) 325–26.

[49] Kai Trümpler, 'Article 5—Normal Baseline' in Alexander Proelss (ed), *United Nations Convention on the Law of the Sea: A Commentary* (1st edn, CH Beck 2017) 54.

spring times, suggested by South Africa). In so doing, the resulting formulation of Article 5 envisages a degree of legal stability for the normal baseline stemming not from any particular language referring to stability or permanence but from the practical reality that a chart is a visual representation of the coast at a particular point in time. Compared to the discarded options, the charts-based approach was ultimately selected because it was a more certain and stable solution to defining the normal baseline. However, as the following section will discuss, the stability offered by means of the 'primacy' of charts was not envisaged to be absolute.

3.3.2 A qualified primacy for charts: guarding against abuse

Key to understanding the limits of the legal stability envisaged for the normal baseline is what is known in the preparatory documents as the 'proviso'. Originally proposed at the Hague Conference 'in order to guard against abuse, [. . .] the proviso has been added that the line indicated on the chart must not depart appreciably from the more scientific criterion: the line of mean low-water spring tides'.[50] This language was included in text considered at the ILC's Fourth Session in 1953:[51]

> Article 5 Base Line
>
> 1. As a general rule and subject to the provisions regarding bays and islands, the breadth of the territorial sea is measured from the line of low-water mark along the entire coast.
> 2. [new text on straight baselines]
> 3. The line of low-water mark is that indicated on the charts officially used by the coastal State, *provided the latter line does not appreciably depart from the line of mean low-water spring tides.*

Debate at the Fourth Session of the ILC on 'the proviso' showed that ILC members certainly envisaged the possibility—however remote—of a dispute about a discrepancy between the charted line and the low-water line along the coast (at a particular vertical datum, such as mean high-water spring tides). Amado

[50] 'Report of the Second Sub-Committee' in League of Nations, *Conference for the Codification of International Law [1930]* (n 32) 1419.

[51] JPA François, Special Rapporteur, 'Report on the Regime of the Territorial Sea', Fourth Session UN Doc A/CN.4/53, 21 (Special Rapporteur's First Report on the Regime of the Territorial Sea) (emphasis added).

considered 'the proviso' could be deleted, because 'if the low-water mark in official charts departed appreciably from the line of mean low-water spring tides, those charts would not be accurate and their validity would be questioned by any legal tribunal'.[52] Yepes also held the view that 'if a dispute arose as to whether a chart did or did not "appreciably" depart from that criterion, it could be referred to an international tribunal', though he concluded that for this reason the proviso should be retained.[53]

When the matter was next debated at the ILC, Spiropolous expressed the similar sentiment that 'if the line drawn on an official chart differed to any great extent from the tide-line a protest could be made and the chart corrected'.[54] Importantly, by this stage the proviso had been discarded from the draft text following the recommendation of the Experts' Report. The ILC considered the proviso to be unnecessary in the sense that the likelihood of any such discrepancy was low.[55] Spiropolous' intervention at this stage suggests that ILC members did not consider that omission of this language affected the underlying view that a charted line which 'departed appreciably' from the low-water line along the coast could be the subject of protest or challenge.

Some have concluded from this aspect of the drafting history of Article 5 that the ability to challenge charts supports the conclusion that it is the actual low-water line, rather than the charted line, that constitutes the normal baseline.[56] This section has argued that there is evidence that drafters did indeed intend charts to be used as the baseline (where applicable charts were available). How can this suggestion be reconciled with the fact that the possibility of challenging or disputing charts was clearly in the mind of the drafters? To wrestle with this issue, it is necessary to focus on the circumstances in which the drafters envisaged a possible challenge to a charted low-water line.

A starting point lies in the wording of the proviso itself. The idea was that any exercise by a coastal State to select any particular line of low water should

[52] ILC, Summary Record of the 169th Meeting, UN Doc A/CN.4/SR.169 (Summary Record of the 169th Meeting) 172.

[53] ILC, Summary Record of the 170th Meeting, UN Doc A/CN.4/SR.170 (Summary Record of the 170th Meeting) 178.

[54] Summary Record of the 254th Meeting (n 45) 65.

[55] This is confirmed by the Special Rapporteur at the beginning of discussion at the 254th Meeting: 'The Committee of Experts which met at The Hague in 1953 had come to the conclusion that the provision referring to that possibility was unnecessary and should be deleted': ibid.

[56] See Michael W Reed, *Shore and Sea Boundaries: The Development of International Maritime Boundary Principles through United States Practice*, vol 3 (AL Shalowitz ed, US Government Printing Office 2000) 179, and 2012 ILA Baselines Committee Report (n 30) 12 and 25.

not 'depart appreciably' from a particular scientific criterion (i.e. mean low-water spring tides). While it appears there was nothing particular about the selection of mean low-water spring tides other than its use by some of the League members at the time,[57] Sub-Committee II dealt expressly with its use of the phrase 'departed appreciably' and the circumstances in which it might apply:

> The term 'appreciably' is admittedly vague. Inasmuch, however, as this proviso would only be of importance in a case which was *clearly fraudulent*, and as, moreover, absolute precision would be extremely difficult to attain, it is thought that it might be accepted.[58]

This recalls the explanation by the Special Rapporteur that the intention of 'the proviso' was to guard against 'cases of *possible bad faith* on the part of States in determining the limits of their territorial waters'.[59] In the view of the ILC, the scenario that 'the proviso' sought to address was one in which 'Governments [. . .] shift the low-water lines on their charts unreasonably';[60] it was precisely because the ILC considered this scenario unlikely that it considered that 'the proviso' could be discarded.

Though some vagueness remains, the drafting history does shed light on the types of discrepancy between the charted low-water line and the actual shoreline that, in the view of the drafters, may fall within the remit of the proviso and thereby be amenable to challenge or protest. These circumstances were those in which there was a physical discrepancy of a certain magnitude ('departed appreciably', or 'differed to any great extent'), or where there was an element of *mala fides* or unreasonableness ('clearly fraudulent' or shifting the charted line 'unreasonably'). Indeed, the Hague Conference drafters expressly contrasted the type of discrepancy engaging the proviso with those discrepancies which it considered to be acceptable and necessary consequences of its proposal for a charts-based definition:

> The divergencies due to the adoption of different criteria on the different charts are *very slight and can be disregarded*. In order to guard against abuse, however, the proviso has been added that the line indicated on the chart must

[57] Purcell, *Geographical Change and the Law of the Sea* (n 43) 167.
[58] 'Report of the Second Sub-Committee' in League of Nations, *Conference for the Codification of International Law [1930]* (n 32) 1419 (emphasis added).
[59] Summary Record of the 254th Meeting (n 45) (emphasis added).
[60] 'Special Rapporteur's First Report on the Regime of the Territorial Sea' (n 51) 21.

> not depart appreciably from the more scientific criterion: the line of mean low-water spring tides.[61]

Following this logic, these comments suggest that the former of these discrepancies—those which are slight, such as those relating to the adoption of different vertical tidal datum—may be disregarded and should not attract challenge to the charted low-water line. For such minor discrepancies, the baseline was envisaged to remain in place, offering a measure of legal stability so long as it remained unchanged, and with a concomitant certainty that it should not be subject to challenge in such circumstances.

This examination of the drafting history demonstrates that the primacy given to charts in Article 5 is the practical means by which the LOSC envisages legal stability for the normal baseline. In this way, this reading of the drafting history seeks to show that even though the term 'legal stability' would not itself emerge for decades, a degree of legal stability was indeed contemplated for the normal baseline, albeit in this limited sense.

3.4 Invoking the legal stability of maritime zones

As explained in Chapter 2, the second phase of scholarship saw a recognition of the possibility of legal stability within the LOSC system rather than outside it,[62] and it was this period that saw the emergence of some of the key phrases that would become part of the lexicon for continued discussions on sea-level rise and maritime zones. In 2018, the ILA pointed to the importance of 'the grounds of legal certainty and stability';[63] in 2020, the *First issues paper* referred to the 'need to preserve legal stability, security, certainty and predictability',[64] language with clear resonances to the ILA's resolution.[65]

[61] 'Report of the Second Sub-Committee' in League of Nations, *Conference for the Codification of International Law [1930]* (n 32) 1419.

[62] See Section 2.3.2.

[63] ILA 2018 Resolution (n 1).

[64] Bogdan Aurescu and Nilüfer Oral, Co-Chairs of the Study Group on Sea-Level Rise in relation to International Law, *First issues paper by Bogdan Aurescu and Nilüfer Oral* (28 February 2020) UN Doc A/CN.4/740 [104(d)] (*First issues paper*).

[65] On the parallel work of the ILA SLR Committee and the SLR on this topic, and their influence on the engagement of States, see Davor Vidas and David Freestone, 'Legal Certainty and Stability in the Face of Sea Level Rise: Trends in the Development of State Practice and International Law Scholarship on Maritime Limits and Boundaries' (2022) 37 The International Journal of Marine and Coastal Law 1.

At that time, it appears that only one State, Romania, explicitly used the term 'legal stability' in connection with the topic of sea-level rise and maritime zones, though many more States referred to the importance of stability in the overall international system.[66] This dramatically changed in 2021, a year which saw the making of the 2021 Pacific Island Forum (PIF) Declaration which recognizes 'the principles of legal stability, security, certainty and predictability that underpin the Convention',[67] and the 2021 Alliance of Small Island States (AOSIS) Declaration which (without explicitly mentioning 'legal stability') similarly affirms:

> that there is no obligation under the United Nations Convention on the Law of the Sea to keep baselines and outer limits of maritime zones under review nor to update charts or lists of geographical coordinates once deposited with the Secretary-General of the United Nations, and that such maritime zones and the rights and entitlements that flow from them shall continue to apply without reduction, notwithstanding any physical changes connected to climate change-related sea-level rise.[68]

From this period onwards, it is evident that States have given increasing attention to the legal stability of maritime zones in connection with sea-level rise. For example, in examining the statements given in the UNGA Sixth Committee in 2021 relating to the ILC's work on sea-level rise and international law, Aurescu and Oral note that 'the meaning of legal stability, security, certainty and predictability' was a key concern in the statements of approximately twenty-five delegations speaking before the UN General Assembly.[69] Similarly, the Final Consolidated Report of the Co-Chairs noted that:

> In the course of the debate in Sixth Committee at the seventy-eighth session of the General Assembly, in 2023, many Member States from different regions affirmed their interpretation of the United Nations Convention on the Law of the Sea as allowing coastal States to preserve baselines and maritime zones

[66] See *First issues paper* (n 64) [17]–[18].

[67] Declaration on Preserving Maritime Zones in the Face of Climate Change-Related Sea-Level Rise (signed 6 August 2021) <www.forumsec.org/2021/08/11/declaration-on-preserving-maritime-zones-in-the-face-of-climate-change-related-sea-level-rise> (2021 PIF Declaration).

[68] Leaders' Declaration of the Alliance of Small Island States (signed 22 September 2021) <www.aosis.org/launch-of-the-alliance-of-small-island-states-leaders-declaration> (2021 AOSIS Declaration).

[69] The *Additional paper to the first issues paper* notes that twenty-five statements referred to legal stability, noting that many other statements made implicit references: *Additional paper to the first issues paper* (n 2) [13] note 17.

> that have been lawfully established under the Convention and international law, regardless of the physical changes to the coastline as a result of sea-level rise. Many States expressly linked such preservation to the need to ensure legal stability, certainty and predictability.[70]

ILA SLR Committee has observed that this trend can usefully be seen as part of a 'consolidation phase' of State practice from about 2021 onwards,[71] showing increased 'common thinking'[72] amongst States on the preservation of maritime zones.

So while there is some variation in the exact language used, it is clear that the idea of legal stability has gained significant traction among States. Put at its simplest, the 'issue of legal stability is closely connected to the preservation of maritime zones as they were before the effects of sea-level rise';[73] or, put another way, that 'preserving baselines and maritime entitlements would give expression to these foundational principles of legal stability and equity'.[74] This sentiment is explained best by Fiji (on behalf of the Pacific Islands Forum), when it stated that 'when we refer to the need for legal stability, security, certainty, and predictability in relation to the [ILC's] subtopic of the law of the sea, we mean that this is achieved through the preservation of maritime zones and the rights and entitlements that flow from them despite climate change-related sea-level rise'.[75]

Looking more closely at States' interventions, it is possible to discern three key elements of the legal stability of maritime zones: the importance of stabilizing legislation, the need to maintain established maritime zones, and the need to maintain the foundation for maritime entitlement in recognizing the stability of a feature's legal status.

[70] Patrícia Galvão Teles, Nilüfer Oral, and Juan José Ruda Santolaria, 'Final Consolidated Report of the Co-Chairs of the Study Group on Sea-Level Rise in relation to International Law' (3 February 2025) UN Doc A/CN.4/783 [60] (Final Consolidated Report of the Co-Chairs). The views of a large number of States are canvassed extensively: [60]–[119].

[71] ILA (Committee on International Law and Sea Level Rise), 'Report (Lisbon Conference)' 7 (2022 ILA SLR Report).

[72] ibid 14.

[73] Italy, full statement at <www.un.org/en/ga/sixth/78/ilc.shtml>; an official summary is recorded in Summary Record of the 23rd Meeting, UN GAOR, Sixth Committee 78th Session (23 October 2023) UN Doc A/C.6/78/SR.23.

[74] New Zealand, full statement at <www.un.org/en/ga/sixth/78/ilc.shtml>; an official summary is recorded in Summary Record of the 25th Meeting, UN GAOR, Sixth Committee, 78th Session (25 October 2023) UN Doc A/C.6/78/SR.25.

[75] Fiji, full statement at <www.un.org/en/ga/sixth/76/ilc.shtml>; an official summary is recorded in Summary Record of the 19th Meeting, UN GAOR, Sixth Committee 76th Session (28 October 2021) UN Doc A/C.6/76.SR.19.

3.4.1 Achieving legal stability for maritime zones: the importance of stabilizing legislation

One element that emerges from some States' comments relates to the significance of how the relevant LOSC provisions have been domestically implemented, that is, in the establishment of baselines and maritime zones by a coastal State, usually by way of legislation. For example, Belize (on behalf of AOSIS) outlines how '[m]any small island and low-lying States had taken political and legislative measures to preserve their baselines and the existing extent of their maritime zones by adopting domestic laws, concluding maritime boundary agreements and depositing charts or coordinates along with declarations'.[76] Micronesia gives an example of this position, explaining how it had in 2019 'deposited with the Secretary-General lists of geographical coordinates of points, accompanied by illustrative maps, for the maritime zones of the Federated States of Micronesia',[77] accompanied by its observations that 'it understood that it was not obliged to keep under review the maritime zones reflected in the deposit; and that it intended to maintain those zones in line with that understanding, notwithstanding climate change-induced sea-level rise'.[78] Solomon Islands explained it had also taken this approach, describing that: '[i]n accordance with international law and regional practice, the Solomon Islands had deposited geographic coordinates for nearly all its maritime zones with the Secretary-General. Those zones were fixed and should not be altered, despite sea-level rise'.[79] Similarly, the Maldives expressed the view that 'once a State deposited the appropriate charts and/or geographic coordinates with the Secretary-General, those entitlements were fixed and would not be altered by any subsequent physical changes to the State's geography as a result of sea-level rise'.[80] Jamaica, too, explained that it

[76] Belize (on behalf of AOSIS), Summary Record of the 13th Meeting, UN GAOR, Sixth Committee 75th Session UN Doc A/C.6/75/SR.13 (Summary Record of the 13th Meeting).

[77] ibid Federated States of Micronesia [54].

[78] ibid Federated States of Micronesia. See Observations made on 24 December 2019, and revised on 15 January 2020, by the Federated States of Micronesia in connection with the official deposit of lists of geographical coordinates of points, accompanied by illustrative maps, for maritime baselines and maritime zones in accordance with the 1982 United Nations Convention on the Law of the Sea, at <www.un.org/depts/los/LEGISLATIONANDTREATIES/STATEFILES/FSM.htm>. The Cook Islands has also made similar observations: see Observations made on 12 August 2021 by the Cook Islands in connection with the official deposit of lists of geographical coordinates of points, accompanied by illustrative maps, for maritime baselines and maritime zones in accordance with the 1982 United Nations Convention on the Law of the Sea, at <www.un.org/depts/los/LEGISLATIONANDTREATIES/STATEFILES/COK.htm>.

[79] ibid Solomon Islands [74].

[80] ibid Maldives [57]; see also Statements of Australia, Tonga, and Micronesia at the 21st Meeting of the United Nations Open-ended Informal Consultative Process on Oceans and the Law of the Sea

> is one of the many states that have adopted legislation to preserve its baselines and maritime zones. Jamaica has promulgated the Maritime Areas Act, which sets out inter alia that Jamaica is an archipelagic state, establishes Jamaica's sovereignty over the archipelagic waters, prescribes its internal waters, territorial waters, exclusive economic zones, contiguous zones and continental shelf.[81]

In these comments, States have drawn attention to the importance of particular domestic actions to establish their baselines and maritime zones in connection with the goal of stability: namely, the use of charts and/or geographic coordinates to define the relevant lines and areas in order to 'fix' their location on the surface of the Earth. This is key to understanding that there is a *spatial* dimension of legal stability: defining a baseline or outer limits by means of a chart and/or coordinates is a key part of what makes those lines *capable* of remaining in the same location, which is what gives the legal artefacts of the baseline and the maritime zone the capacity to occupy the same location and space on the surface of the Earth. As Chapter 4 will demonstrate, this kind of stabilizing legislation is widely found in the practice of many States, not only in relation to straight and archipelagic baselines but also for those coastal States using the normal baseline.

3.4.2 Achieving legal stability for maritime zones: no duty to update

Another element that emerges from States' comments is that achievement of legal stability lies in the importance of maintaining established maritime zones, the corollary of recognizing that there is no express obligation in the LOSC to update established maritime zones. The effect of this view is that validly established maritime zones (when given effect through appropriately stabilizing legislation) may be maintained as established. Many States signalled their agreement with Aurescu and Oral's early observation that the LOSC does not contain any express obligation to update maritime zones information once established and published.[82] Fiji,[83] on behalf of the PIF, drew attention to the 2021

(2021) (noting these are all PIF members), available at <www.un.org/depts/los/consultative_process/consultative_process.htm>.

[81] Jamaica, full statement at <www.un.org/en/ga/sixth/78/ilc.shtml>; an official summary is recorded at Summary Record of the 28th Meeting, UN GAOR Sixth Commission 78th Session (27 October 2023) UN Doc A/C.6/78.SR.28.

[82] Bogdan Aurescu and Nilüfer Oral, *First issues paper* (n 64) [104(e)–(f)].

[83] Fiji (n 75).

PIF Declaration, which relevantly states that 'the Convention imposes no affirmative obligation to keep baselines and outer limits of maritime zones under review nor to update charts or lists of geographical coordinates once deposited.'[84] In very similar terms, Antigua and Barbuda pointed out that the leaders of the members of AOSIS had also in 2021 affirmed 'that there is no obligation under the United Nations Convention on the Law of the Sea to keep baselines and outer limits of maritime zones under review nor to update charts or lists of geographical coordinates once deposited with the Secretary-General of the United Nations.'[85] The position is explained well by The Bahamas, which stated that 'once countries have deposited their maritime baselines in accordance with UNCLOS, they do not update them. This is evidenced by prevailing state practice (including that of The Bahamas in its legislation), and by the absence of any provisions in UNCLOS requiring revision or updates of such baselines, once submitted.'[86] Germany points out the stability that results from the non-update of maritime zones, taking the view that 'while being entitled to update their baselines, [States] are under no obligation to do so, even when the low-water line changes due to sea-level rise. From this it follows that the territory and maritime zones remain stable until the coastal state decides to update them.'[87]

These statements demonstrate that States see a *temporal* dimension to the achievement of legal stability of maritime zones, in the sense that once the baselines or outer limits of maritime zones have been established pursuant to official charts and/or coordinates by the coastal State, then that baseline and maritime zone may remain in place over time without any obligation to revise them. Seen in this way, the spatial and temporal dimensions of legal stability are both necessary elements in the preservation of maritime zones.

3.4.3 Achieving legal stability for maritime zones: the relevance of entitlement

Finally, the third theme that emerges from a handful of States relates to the issue of maritime entitlement and legal status under the LOSC. As outlined

[84] 2021 PIF Declaration (n 67).

[85] Antigua and Barbuda (on behalf of the AOSIS), Summary Record of the 19th Meeting, UN GAOR Sixth Committee 76th Session (28 October 2021) UN Doc A/C.6/76/SR.19 (Summary Record of the 19th Meeting) [78].

[86] The Bahamas, 'Submission to the ILC in regard to Sea-Level Rise in relation to International Law' (18 November 2024) (2024 Bahamas ILC Submission).

[87] Germany, 'Comments and Observations by the Federal Republic of Germany on the Issue of Sea-Level Rise, International Law and its Impact on Statehood' (December 2024) (2024 Germany ILC Submission).

in Chapter 2, certain questions of legal status have a close nexus to the land. For example, an island is 'a naturally formed area of land, surrounded by water, which is above water at high tide';[88] and only States which are constituted by archipelagos—meaning 'a group of islands, including parts of islands, interconnecting waters and other natural features which are so closely interrelated that such islands, waters and other natural features form an intrinsic geographical, economic and political entity, or which historically have been regarded as such'—may have status as an 'archipelagic State'.[89] Questions of status are key for maritime zones since not all maritime zones are available for all types of maritime features: under Article 121 of the LOSC, an 'island' is entitled to the full suite of maritime zones, while '[r]ocks which cannot sustain human habitation or economic life of their own shall have no exclusive economic zone or continental shelf'.[90] Similarly, 'archipelagic waters'[91] are available only to archipelagic States. Considering the possibility that sea-level rise might impact the geographic features relevant to these kinds of legal status—and therefore calling into question the extent of those features' maritime entitlements—Antigua and Barbuda took the view that 'sea-level rise cannot lead to the requalification of islands as rocks'.[92] In a similar vein, Papua New Guinea expressed the concern that 'potential loss, owing to sea-level rise, of small islands and other features that served as basepoints could affect existing maritime zone entitlements and could compromise the ability of an archipelagic State to maintain that status',[93] noting also the relationship between maritime entitlement with statehood: '[a]s only States could generate maritime zones, it was essential for island States to maintain statehood in order to preserve their maritime zones'.[94] Once again, Germany makes the point perhaps most clearly when it explained that:

[88] LOSC, art 121(1).

[89] LOSC, art 46.

[90] LOSC, art 121(3). The differing entitlements of different features within 'regime of islands' were considered by the Arbitral Tribunal in *South China Sea Arbitration (Philippines v China)* (Award) PCA Case no 2013-19 (LOSC Arbitral Tribunal, 2016), where much depended on the Tribunal's assessment of whether a feature was above or below high tide in its natural state in order to assess whether the feature should be considered a 'fully entitled island' or a 'rock' within the meaning of art 121: see discussion in Chapter 6.

[91] LOSC, art 49.

[92] Antigua and Barbuda, 'Antigua and Barbuda's Submission on the Effects of Sea Level Rise on the Law of the Sea, Submission of Antigua and Barbuda to the ILC' 10. <https://legal.un.org/ilc/sessions/72/pdfs/english/slr_antigua_barbuda.pdf> (Antigua and Barbuda Submission).

[93] Papua New Guinea, Summary Record of the 30th Meeting, UN GOAR Sixth Committee 74th Session UN Doc A/C.6/74/SR.30) (Summary Record of the 30th Meeting).

[94] ibid Papua New Guinea. See also comments of Japan, Romania, and Lebanon who raised questions of statehood more generally in connection with sea-level rise: ibid.

> the principle of 'legal stability' should equally apply to baselines and maritime zones derived from islands and rocks pursuant to Art. 121 para. 1 and 3 UNCLOS, when these natural land features are subsequently submerged due to sea level rise. According to Art. 121 para. 2 UNCLOS, the maritime zones of islands and rocks are determined in accordance with the provisions of the Conventions applicable to other land territory. As I said, in our view, Coastal States have no duty to regularly review and update their baselines and maritime zones derived from continental land territory. It seems to follow from a contemporary reading and interpretation of the Convention that they also have no duty to regularly review whether naturally formed land features have subsequently changed their nature or become submerged after the maritime zones around them were duly established, published and deposited in accordance with the Convention.[95]

This can be usefully considered as the third theme from States' discourse that gives substance to the meaning of legal stability for maritime zones, in the sense that some States identify the stability of a maritime feature's legal *status* as an 'island' under Article 121(1) as another essential element of what is entailed in the legal stability of the maritime zones supported by that feature.

3.5 Identifying elements of the legal stability of maritime zones

Taken together, what States say about legal stability and maritime zones shows that stability was an important value in the creation of the LOSC, and continues to be in the context of sea-level rise discussions more than four decades later. For this reason, a claim for the legal stability of maritime zones should be seen as an expression of a long-held value for stability in the context of the LOSC system of maritime zones. Despite this continuity, it is clear that the concept of legal stability is thickening, the discourse of States revealing concerns for the importance of stabilizing legislation, the absence of a duty to update established baselines, and the relevance of stable legal status for stable maritime zones.

[95] Germany, full statement at <www.un.org/en/ga/sixth/78/ilc.shtml>; an official summary is recorded at Summary Record of the 24th Meeting, UN GAOR Sixth Committee 78th Session (23 October 2023) UN Doc A/C.6/78/SR.24.

This chapter has demonstrated that the text of Article 5 of the LOSC reflects the dominant practice at the time of its negotiation: as described in Section 3.3.1, the text opts for a charts-based definition of the normal baseline where the low-water line on an officially recognized chart could be given legal significance as the baseline in order to overcome difficulties with the 'natural' low-water line. In recent years, States point to an increasing reliance on other methods, such as coordinates, which should be treated as a method analogous to charts for the purpose of depicting the baseline.[96] This suggests a broadening of State practice on the implementation of the normal baseline. Considering the importance identified by States of choosing a method capable of 'fixing' the location of a baseline or outer limit, what is the significance of this emerging diversity in methods used by States to define the normal baseline? Are such methods permissible, despite not being expressly contemplated by the language of Article 5? What can be made of the seemingly paradoxical observation by Aurescu and Oral that '[n]o States, even those that have national legislation providing for ambulatory baselines, have contested the option of fixed baselines':[97] making sense of such a view calls not only for a better understanding of States' national legislation but also its significance as State practice with potential legal significance for the interpretation of the international law rules they implement.

The chapter also argued that the drafters of the LOSC contemplated that a charted baseline may be open to challenge where there is a significant departure from the coast (but that the baseline may be maintained where there are only minor discrepancies).[98] No State has expressly recalled this discussion in recent years, such as in their statements to the UN General Assembly. Rather, some States have supported the idea that once the baseline and outer limits have been established, there is no legal duty to update them. This raises the question of whether the degree of tolerance originally envisaged for the normal baseline may have potentially increased, as States' appreciation of geographic instability due to sea-level rise has also increased. Assuming no issues of fraud or bad faith, is it still the case that States would contemplate that a baseline may be maintained only where there are *minor* discrepancies from the coast? Or does States' increasing emphasis on the legal stability of maritime zones—relating to space, time, and status—mean that a baseline and its associated maritime zone may be lawfully maintained where there is a more significant discrepancy from the coast?

[96] Section 3.4.
[97] *Additional paper to the first issues paper* (n 2) [84].
[98] Section 3.3.2.

These questions can only be answered by reference to the relevant rules of international law, to which the book now turns. The book approaches this inquiry by considering each of the three elements of the legal stability of maritime zones in turn, identifying relevant State practice and evaluating it for the purposes of interpreting relevant provisions of the LOSC. States draw attention to the importance of their domestic actions to implement their baselines and maritime zones in connection with the achievement of legal stability, especially as some methods (such as coordinates) are what gives a baseline the capacity to remain 'fixed' in a particular location: Chapter 4 examines this element of *spatial stability*, investigating how all coastal States have implemented the normal baseline and what this means for an interpretation of Article 5 of the LOSC (and other baseline provisions as well). States also assert that they are not obliged to keep established baselines under review, or to update them: Chapter 5 examines this element of *temporal stability*, examining whether (and if so, how often) States have revisited established baselines, and what this means for the existence of a legal duty to update established baselines. And States suggest that the legal status of an island might be maintained notwithstanding changes to geographic characteristics: Chapter 6 examines the potential for *stability in relation to legal status*. Noting that there are a number of questions of legal status that can affect maritime entitlements,[99] Chapter 6 focuses on 'island' status under Article 121 of the LOSC in light of the physical impacts of sea-level rise on islands—especially small and low-lying islands—to consider whether such impacts result in the destabilization of 'island' status.

Taking up Orford's encouragement to 'evaluate, choose among, or create methods based not on whether they are "correct" but on what they help to make visible or possible',[100] this chapter takes these three elements as its framework for inquiry because they make visible the kinds of State practice that should be taken into account in an understanding of international law, but which previous studies have not fully examined. The book now moves to identify that State practice and to assess its legal significance for the interpretation of the LOSC.

[99] eg whether a State is the relevant 'coastal State' for the purposes of the establishment of maritime zones: see discussion in Chapter 5, n 2.

[100] Anne Orford, *International Law and the Politics of History* (Cambridge University Press 2021) 11.

4

Spatial Stability

The Baseline in National Legislation

4.1 Introduction

This book has identified that a key element of the legal stability of baselines and maritime zones relates to spatial stability. Chapter 3 outlined how States have articulated how they have taken practical steps to achieve stable maritime zones, namely through the use of spatially stable means of baseline definition which are capable of remaining in the same location on the Earth's surface.[1] The connection made by such States between the goal of stability and legislative actions to establish the baseline invites a broader inquiry: how common is the use of such spatially stabilizing legislation among coastal States?

While the use of coordinates in baseline definition is standard for straight and archipelagic baselines, less is known about the use and prevalence of such an approach for normal baselines. Article 5 of the United Nations Convention on the Law of the Sea (LOSC) defines the normal baseline as 'the low-water line along the coast as marked on large-scale charts officially recognized by the coastal State'. Schofield explains that the normal baseline should be considered the predominant baseline and the 'default' baseline type 'in that they require no formal declaration or due publicity'.[2] Lathrop recognizes the centrality of

[1] Some writers use the term 'fixed' baseline to describe the implementation of baselines through coordinates (eg Jenny Grote Stoutenburg, *Disappearing Island States in International Law* (Brill 2015); Nilufer Oral, 'UNCLOS and Sea Level Rise' (2023) 149 Marine Policy 1; Rosemary Rayfuse, 'Sea Level Rise and Maritime Zones: Preserving the Maritime Entitlements of "Disappearing" States' in Michael B Gerrard and Gregory E Wannier (eds), *Threatened Island Nations: Legal Implications of Rising Seas and a Changing Climate* (Cambridge University Press 2013), particularly in contrast to the ambulatory baseline considered by most scholars to be the correct understanding of the legal character of the normal baseline. However, this book generally opts to describe such methods as 'spatially-stable' methods of domestic implementation, or stabilizing legislation, because it more neutrally describes the spatial effect of using coordinates to maintain a certain and precise location on the Earth's surface, leaving open the question of its validity as a method under international law as a separate question for consideration.

[2] Clive Schofield, 'Departures from the Coast: Trends in the Application of Territorial Sea Baselines under the Law of the Sea Convention' (2012) 27 The International Journal of Marine and Coastal Law 723, 724.

Sea-Level Rise and the Legal Stability of Maritime Zones. Frances Anggadi, Oxford University Press.
 DOI: 10.1093/9780198973515.003.0004

the normal baseline in comparison to other baseline types, commenting that 'the low-water line will continue to play a central role in baselines law as the primary baseline along much of the world's coastlines and as the anchoring feature for most artificial baselines'.[3]

This chapter focuses on the normal baseline because of these two factors—the wide usage of the normal baseline and the centrality of the 'low-water line' for this type of baseline—and also because the normal baseline is the focus of scholarship examining the legal implications of sea-level rise for maritime zones.[4] As explained in Chapter 2, most scholars have for decades considered that 'the normal baseline is ambulatory',[5] being directly and necessarily tied to the low-water line along the coast, wherever it may be from time to time. However, this chapter agrees with the observation of the International Law Commission (ILC) observation that this should be regarded as a statement of past doctrine,[6] and that a fresh perspective is required to take into account contemporary challenges and, as this chapter will argue, a broad view of contemporary State practice. Section 4.2 presents a comprehensive global study of coastal States' legislation on the normal baseline, offering a typology of definitions to classify the different approaches observed. The findings of this study are important because they show that, as a practical matter, there is more stability for the normal baseline than suggested by an 'ambulatory theory' of baselines, casting doubt on the continued ability of that theory to give a full account of the present state of the law.

Section 4.3 evaluates the findings of the legislative study, arguing that because the legislation examined in the legislative study should be treated as State practice, it bears upon the interpretation of the LOSC. As a legal matter, the chapter proposes that a better view of the law on the normal baseline—taking full account of the body of State practice—recognizes that there is a margin of appreciation[7] in how a State may define the normal

[3] Coalter G Lathrop, 'Baselines' in Donald R Rothwell and others (eds), *The Oxford Handbook of the Law of the Sea* (Oxford University Press 2015) 74.

[4] As previously discussed in Section 2.3.

[5] International Law Association (Committee on Baselines under the International Law of the Sea), 'Baselines under the International Law of the Sea (Sofia Conference)' 31 (2012 ILA Baselines Committee Report).

[6] See ILC, 'Report of the International Law Commission covering the Work of its Seventy-Fourth Session' (24 April–2 June and 3 July–4 August 2023) UN Doc A/78/10 [141] (2023 ILC Report), discussed in Section 2.3.3.

[7] This chapter uses the term 'margin of appreciation' in the general sense of introducing 'a degree of flexibility in the operation of the law': Jean-Pierre Cot, 'Margin of Appreciation', *Max Planck Encyclopedia of International Law* (2007) [1]. While the term has mainly been used in the jurisprudence of the European Court of Human Rights, this chapter takes its cue from O'Connell's reference to a 'margin of appreciation' in relation to the use of straight baselines: see discussion in Section 4.4.

baseline at its establishment, and that such a margin embraces a spectrum of more or less spatially stabilizing methods. Furthermore, the chapter contends that its conclusions on the spatial stability of the normal baseline have broader significance and shape our understanding of baselines more generally.

4.2 A fresh study of normal baseline legislation

This study[8] builds upon two previous studies which have collected information on the normal baseline. The first was conducted by the International Law Association (ILA) Baselines Committee, which undertook to 'identify, categorize, and provide representative examples of a robust sample of relevant state practice through a survey of the practice of Committee members' home States, among other States'.[9] However, the Committee focused on the use or non-use of charts in legislation[10] and did not discuss the prevalence or significance of other approaches to define the normal baseline. The second study is that recently concluded in the ILC, led by the Study Group on Sea-Level Rise. While Aurescu and Oral have noted that 'there is a body of State practice under development regarding the preservation of baselines and of outer limits of maritime zones measured from the baselines [and that] State practice relates to the establishment of fixed baselines and outer limits of maritime zones measured from the baselines',[11] they[12] and the ILC as a whole[13] remarked that further evidence of State practice is needed.

Like these previous efforts, this study was designed to observe how the legislation of coastal States provides for the establishment of the normal baseline. Building on other studies, this study has sought to be as comprehensive

[8] This section updates and elaborates material which was previously published in Frances Anggadi, 'What States Say and Do about Legal Stability and Maritime Zones, and Why it Matters' (2022) 71 International & Comparative Law Quarterly 767.

[9] 2012 ILA Baselines Committee Report (n 5) 16.

[10] The Report identified four categories relating to use and non-use of charts in definitions on the normal baseline: '(1) the normal baseline is described with no reference to a charted line; (2) the normal baseline is described with an explicit reference to a charted line; (3) the normal baseline is described with an implied reference to a charted line; and (4) the State does not have a normal baseline'; ibid.

[11] Bogdan Aurescu and Nilüfer Oral, Co-Chairs of the Study Group on Sea-Level Rise in relation to International Law, *First issues paper by Bogdan Aurescu and Nilüfer Oral* (28 February 2020) UN Doc A/CN.4/740 [104(g)] (*First issues paper*).

[12] ibid [104(i)].

[13] ILC, 'Report of the International Law Commission covering the Work of its Seventy-Second Session' (26 April–4 June and 5 July–6 August 2021) UN Doc A/76/10 [268] (2021 ILC Report).

as possible in examining the legislation of all coastal States. Out of 193 UN Member States,[14] 150 are coastal States (comprising 136 Parties to the LOSC and fourteen non-Parties).[15] In addition to these, and for consistency with the approach taken by the United Nations Division of Ocean and Law of the Sea (UN DOALOS), this study also included LOSC Parties the Cook Islands, Niue,[16] and the State of Palestine,[17] bringing the overall sample size to 153 coastal States.

In terms of the legislation examined, the study identified coastal State baselines legislation based on publicly available material such as that deposited at UN DOALOS, on the country's own official government web pages, or other consolidations such as the FAOLEX database[18] or PacLii.[19] The study took a broad approach in characterizing the relevant 'legislation' for the purposes of the survey, including both primary and secondary legislation, as well as other instruments within the relevant national framework (eg an order, decree, or proclamation).[20] The publicly available sources and titles of legislation examined for the study are listed in Appendix 4.1.

The study examined the legislation of each coastal State to identify whether that coastal State has legislation establishing (or enabling the establishment of) its baseline, and, if so, whether that legislation (or associated practice) discloses the use of the normal baseline. In considering that normal baseline, the study then examined *how* the normal baseline is defined, looking at whether the legislation defines the normal baseline by reference to terms/concepts such as 'low-water line' and 'charts' (reflective of LOSC Article 5), or by reference to other concepts (including those not expressly reflective of LOSC Article 5), such as coordinates. The study then took an inductive approach to develop categories describing States' methods of implementation.

[14] United Nations, 'Member States' <www.un.org/en/about-us/member-states>.

[15] Landlocked States excluded for the purposes of this study are those indicated as such in the following: UN Division for Ocean Affairs and the Law of the Sea, 'Status of the United Nations Convention on the Law of the Sea, the Agreement relating to the Implementation of Part XI of the Convention and the Agreement for the Implementation of the Provisions of the Convention relating to the Conservation and Management of Straddling Fish Stocks and Highly Migratory Fish Stocks, as at 31 July 2024' <www.un.org/depts/los/reference_files/StatusTablesEnglish.pdf>.

[16] The Cook Islands and Niue are independent self-governing countries in free association with New Zealand: New Zealand Ministry of Foreign Affairs and Trade, 'About Cook Islands' <https://www.mfat.govt.nz/en/countries-and-regions/australia-and-pacific/cook-islands>.

[17] Considered a non-member observer State to the UN: United Nations, 'Member States' (n 14).

[18] Food and Agriculture Organization of the United Nations, 'FAOLEX Database' <www.fao.org/faolex/country-profiles/en/>.

[19] Pacific Islands Legal Information Institute, 'PACLII' <www.paclii.org/>.

[20] Where legislation was not in English (or no official English translation was provided), the legislative study relied on Google Translate.

4.2.1 Findings on the normal baseline

4.2.1.1 Summary of overall findings

Out of 153 coastal States surveyed, the study was able to identify legislation establishing (or enabling the establishment of) its baseline in relation to 148 States,[21] and among those, 110 use the normal baseline.[22] Noting that many coastal States use a combination of methods in the context of their overall baseline system (either implementing the normal baseline in different ways for different segments of the coast and/or using a combination of normal, straight, or archipelagic baselines), the survey identified 118 uses of normal baseline definition.[23]

The study classified those 118 definitions of the normal baseline into a typology comprising four types of definitions, as set out in Table 4.1.

Table 4.1 Typology of definitions of the normal baseline

Typology of definitions: the normal baseline is . . .	
. . . the low-water line (along the coast)	Type 1
. . . defined by reference to coordinates	Type 2
. . . defined by reference to (the low-water line) as marked on charts	Type 3
. . . determined/proclaimed in accordance with international law	Type 4

As shown in Figure 4.1, the first of these—legislation which specifies that the normal baseline *is* the low-water line along the coast—is the most commonly used method, comprising approximately 41 per cent of methods observed. The next most prevalent method is legislation which specifies the location of the normal baseline by reference to coordinates (approximately 31

[21] The study was not able to locate maritime zones legislation in relation to Jordan, Montenegro, or Democratic People's Republic of Korea. Also, while the study could identify some maritime zones legislation for Singapore and Brunei, that legislation did not refer to the baseline.

[22] For the remaining coastal States for which baselines legislation was identified, the study confirmed that either it was not possible to confirm that the normal baseline was used or that it exclusively used straight or archipelagic baselines (eg Maldives uses a completely archipelagic baseline system). Some coastal States' legislation referred to the normal baseline, but other information suggested that only other baseline types are used (eg Malaysia, as discussed in Clive Schofield and Robert van de Poll, 'Claims to Straight Baselines in the Asia-Pacific: Contrary to Customary International Law?' (2022) 7 Asia-Pacific Journal of Ocean Law and Policy 313). Such coastal States have accordingly been classified as not using the normal baseline for the purposes of this study.

[23] Note that this number is higher than the 101 coastal States, because a coastal State can use more than one definition type, along different parts of its coast. For example, Australia uses a Type 1 definition for most of its mainland coast and Type 4 for its external territories, so this is one coastal State that is included as using two types of definition.

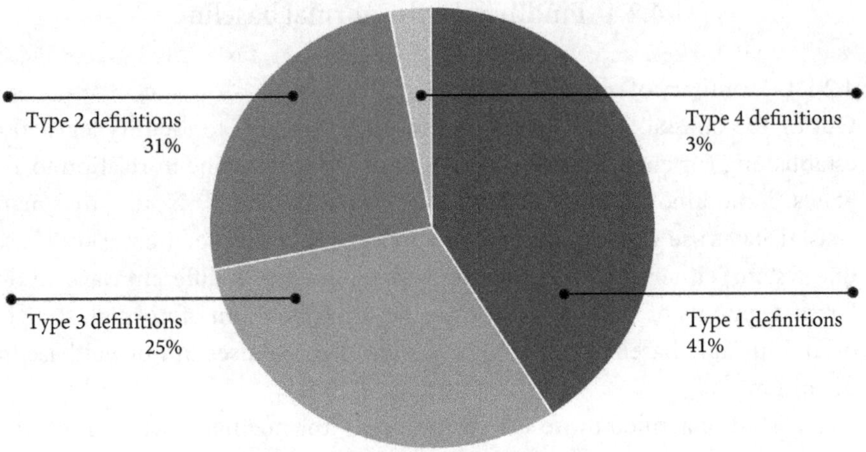

Figure 4.1 Types of normal baseline definition used by coastal States (LOSC Parties and non-Parties); percentages relate to the number of instances of each definition type as a proportion of all observed definitions.

per cent), followed by legislation which specifies that the normal baseline is the low-water line as marked on charts (approximately 25 per cent). A handful of coastal States using the normal baseline (approximately 3 per cent) specify that the baseline is determined in accordance with international law.[24] Table 4.2 lists which coastal States have used each definition type.

The following section discusses each of these methods in decreasing order of prevalence, giving examples to illustrate each type of definition.

4.2.1.2 Type 1: Normal baseline is the low-water line (along the coast)

The survey identifies forty-eight occurrences in which a coastal State defines the normal baseline as the low-water line along its coast; of these, forty-two examples are in the legislation of coastal States Parties to the LOSC, and six in that of non-Parties. The survey classified a definition as Type 1 if it defines the normal baseline *only* by reference to the low-water line along the coast, and not also by reference to other concepts such as charts or coordinates.

A central feature of this type of definition is that the legislation *identifies* the normal baseline with the low-water line along the coast (whether or not the coast is expressly referred to). For example, the legislation of Honduras

[24] For the avoidance of doubt, a Type 4 definition is one whose express terms define the baseline by reference to no other concept or method than 'determined in accordance with international law', or similar. For the purposes of this typology of definition types, it does not mean that Types 1–3 are inconsistent with international law, only that Types 1–3 do not contain express references to international law in the definition of the baseline.

Table 4.2 Coastal States which use the normal baseline, grouped by definition type

	Coastal States which use the normal baseline, grouped according to definition type ***(LOSC non-Parties indicated in italics)***
Type 1 (low-water line)	Australia, Barbados, Belize, Bulgaria, Cameroon, Canada, Côte d'Ivoire, Djibouti, Equatorial Guinea, The Gambia, Georgia, Germany, Greece, Grenada, Guatemala, Guinea, Haiti, Honduras, Ireland, Kenya, Kuwait, Lebanon, Madagascar, Mauritania, Monaco, Namibia, New Zealand, Nicaragua, Nigeria, Poland, Romania, Saint Kitts and Nevis, Saint Lucia, Senegal, Slovenia, Somalia, South Africa, Spain, Sri Lanka, Sweden, Tonga, Tunisia (42)
	Colombia, El Salvador, Eritrea, Iran, Israel, Syria (6)
Type 2 (coordinates)	Angola, Argentina, Bangladesh, Benin, Brazil, Canada, Congo, Cook Islands, Costa Rica, Democratic Republic of Congo, Denmark, Estonia, Fiji, France, Iceland, India, Indonesia, Kiribati, Lithuania, Marshall Islands, Mauritius, Micronesia, Nauru, Niue, Norway, Palau, Papua New Guinea, Samoa, Saudi Arabia, Seychelles, State of Palestine, Togo, Tuvalu, Ukraine, Uruguay, Vanuatu (36)
	Peru (1)
Type 3 (charts)	Angola, Argentina, Bangladesh, Belgium, Brazil, Croatia, Gabon, Ghana, Guyana, India, Italy, Japan, Republic of Korea, Liberia, Mexico, Mozambique, Netherlands, Palau, Portugal, Russian Federation, Sierra Leone, Solomon Islands, Sudan, Suriname, Tanzania, Timor-Leste, Yemen (27)
	Türkiye, Venezuela (2)
Type 4 (international law)	Australia, Qatar, United Kingdom (3)
	United States (1)

provides that the 'normal baseline for measuring the breadth of the Honduran territorial sea and other maritime areas is the low-water line along the coast';[25] similarly, the legislation of Guinea states that 'baselines are comprised of the low-water *mark* and the straight baseline',[26] and that of Slovenia states that 'the baseline shall be the hydrographic zero line running along the coast'.[27]

[25] Act on Honduran Maritime Areas 1999 (Honduras), art 3. Full source details for this and all other legislation considered for this study are included in Appendix 4.1.

[26] Decree no D/2015/122/PRG/SGG (Guinea), art 7. Noting that Guinea uses the term 'low-water mark', this study has used the terms 'low-water line' and 'low-water mark' interchangeably, consistently with the approach taken by UN DOALOS: see entry for 'low-water line/low-water mark' in UN Office for Ocean Affairs and the Law of the Sea, 'Baselines: An Examination of the Relevant Provisions of the United Nations Convention on the Law of the Sea' (United Nations 1989) 58. The drafting history also shows that the term 'low-water mark' was also used in earlier versions of what became art 5 of the LOSC, but no particular reason is apparent for the adoption of one version of the phrase over the other: see Satya N Nandan, Myron H Nordquist, and Shabtai Rosenne, *United Nations Convention on the Law of the Sea 1982: A Commentary* (Brill 2013) para 5.4(b).

[27] Maritime Code (PZ) 2001 (Slovenia) art 13.

The study includes such variations in this category where the apparent meaning is that the normal baseline is in principle defined as a line along the coast, taking from the coast its direction and shape.

In this way, a Type 1 definition locates the normal baseline by pointing to a specific physical feature on the surface of the Earth, which is the low-water line along the coast.[28] And importantly (and in contrast to Type 2 and Type 3 definitions, discussed below), in this type of definition, the legislation refers to the coast as the sole reference point for locating the normal baseline.

4.2.1.3 Type 2: Normal baseline is located by reference to coordinates

The second most prevalent group is the Type 2 definition, where the normal baseline is located by reference to coordinates. The survey identified thirty-seven instances of these: thirty-six are in the legislation of LOSC Parties and one in a non-Party.

The study revealed two ways in which coordinates are used in the context of the normal baseline. First, some coastal States use coordinates to link segments of a mixed baseline system, that is, linking the normal baseline together with other baseline types. A good example is the legislation of France concerning the continental mainland and Corsica, which provides that 'the baselines from which the breadth of the territorial sea adjacent to the Mediterranean continental seaboard is measured, shall be defined by the following basepoints and lines'.[29] As illustrated in the extract at Figure 4.2, the Decree specifies that the baseline is to be located by reference to the listed geographic coordinates, as well as specifying the type of line that links those coordinates, which 'may be a rhumb line (a straight baseline) ["loxodromie"] or the low-water line ["laisse de basse mer"]'.[30]

A similar approach is found in the legislation of Canada,[31] Costa Rica,[32] Denmark,[33] Democratic Republic of the Congo,[34] Estonia,[35] Iceland,[36]

[28] Or seaward low-water line of a fringing reef, as the case may be (eg Maritime Zones Act 2009 (Tonga)).

[29] Decree no 2015-958 of 31 July 2015 defining the baselines from which the breadth of the French territorial sea adjacent to the territory of mainland France and Corsica is measured (France) art 3.

[30] ibid art 1.

[31] ibid art 1.

CRC c 1550 (Canada).

[32] Decree 18581-RE (concerning straight baselines in the Pacific Ocean, 14 October 1988) (Costa Rica), art I(A).

[33] Executive Order no 680 of 18 July 2003, amending Executive Order no 242 of 21 April 1999 concerning the Delimitation of Denmark's Territorial Sea (Denmark).

[34] Law Delimiting the Maritime Areas of the Democratic Republic of the Congo (2009) (Democratic Republic of the Congo).

[35] Law on the Boundaries of the Maritime Tract, 10 March 1993 (Estonia).

[36] Law no 41 of 1 June 1979 concerning the Territorial Sea, the Economic Zone and the Continental Shelf (Iceland).

POINT	DÉSIGNATION	LATITUDE	LONGI-TUDE	NATURE DE LA LIGNE
–	Point terminal de la frontière terrestre France-Espagne	–	–	Laisse de basse mer
MD01	Embouchure du Grau de Palavas-les-Flots	43° 31' 20" N	03° 55' 59" E	Loxodromie
MD02	Pointe de l'Espiguette	43° 28' 58" N	04° 08' 10" E	Laisse de basse mer
MD03	Grau d'Orgon	43° 27' 03" N	04° 23' 29" E	Loxodromie
MD04	Pointe de Beauduc ou du Sablon	43° 22' 21" N	04° 33' 40" E	Laisse de basse mer
MD05	Embouchure du Grand Rhône	43° 19' 46" N	04° 50' 01" E	Loxodromie

Figure 4.2 Extract from table in Article 3, Decree No 2015-958 of 31 July 2015, showing coordinates on the Mediterranean coast of mainland France; fifth column indicates the type of line to be used from one point to the next in the list

Indonesia,[37] Lithuania,[38] Mauritius,[39] Norway,[40] Peru,[41] Ukraine,[42] Uruguay.[43] Common to these examples is that coordinates are specified in the legislation with information that the points are to be linked by the low-water line along the coast, or similar wording (such as 'the coastal line'[44] in Danish legislation).

A variation of this kind of approach can be seen in the legislation of a handful of coastal States which, instead of specifying that the normal baseline is the low-water line between particular coordinates, refer to a charted low-water line

[37] The Government Regulation of the Republic of Indonesia no 38 of 2002 as amended by the Government Regulation of the Republic of Indonesia no 37 of 2008 (Indonesia).

[38] Annex 1 to Res 1597 of 6 December 2004 of the Government of the Republic of Lithuania, 'Coordinates of Turning Points of the Limits of the Territorial Sea of the Republic of Lithuania' (Lithuania).

[39] Maritime Zones (Baselines and Closing Lines) Regulations 2024 (Mauritius). In addition to specifying the normal baseline for the entirety of Agalega and Tromelin islands by coordinates, the Regulation also contains a 'Description of Lines Connecting the Basepoints' which makes clear that the overall baseline system of Mauritius comprises a variety of different lines connecting specified coordinates, including the low-water line along the coast (or reef edge), discussed below.

[40] Royal Decree of 30 August 2002 pursuant to the Constitution of Norway of 17 May 1814 and Royal Decree of 22 February 1812 (§ 2), relating to Jan Mayen.

[41] Law no 30223—adapts Law no 28621, Law of Baselines of the Maritime Domain of Peru, in Accordance with the Ruling of the International Court of Justice of 2014 (Peru).

[42] List of geographical coordinates of points defining the baselines for measuring the breadth of the territorial sea, exclusive economic zone and the continental shelf in the Black Sea [1991] (Ukraine).

[43] Act 17.033 of 20 November 1998 establishing the Boundaries of the Territorial Sea, the Adjacent Zone, the Exclusive Economic Zone, and the Continental Shelf (Uruguay).

[44] Executive Order no 680 of 18 July 2003, amending Executive Order no 242 of 21 April concerning the Delimitation of Denmark's Territorial Sea, s 2.

between specified points. The legislation of Brazil defines the normal baseline as 'the low-water lines as indicated in the large-scale nautical charts published by the Directorate of Hydrography and Navigation of the Brazilian Navy'[45] and also stipulates that the 'coordinates of the starting and final points, as well as those of the points defining the continental and insular SBL [straight baselines] that constitute the Baseline of Brazil are contained in the Annex'.[46] This approach is also taken in Angola,[47] Argentina,[48] Bangladesh,[49] and India.[50]

The second way in which coordinates are used to locate the normal baseline is where coordinates are used for the entirety of the normal baseline around a whole feature or coastal front. For example, Samoa declared that its 'Territorial Seas Baseline shall comprise of a series of successive geographical coordinates located on the outermost reef edge points around and classified as normal baseline',[51] and Palau lists coordinates for the normal baseline along fringing reefs at North Coast and East Coast.[52] Illustrative maps deposited by some States make clear that the prescribed coordinates pertain to the entirety of the feature, following its contours rather than enclosing it in a system of straight baseline segments. For example, 559 points are listed for Pocklington Island, Papua New Guinea,[53] forming a continuous and complete normal baseline that follows the contours of the feature.[54]

The Cook Islands,[55] Federated States of Micronesia,[56] Fiji,[57] Kiribati,[58] Republic of the Marshall Islands,[59] Mauritius,[60] Nauru,[61] Niue,[62]

[45] Decree no 8.400 (4 February 2015) (Brazil) art 2.

[46] ibid art 5.

[47] Law no 17/14 defining the Baselines for the Delimitation and Demarcation of Maritime Zones of Angola (Angola).

[48] Act no 23.968 of 14 August 1991 (Argentina).

[49] Ministry of Foreign Affairs, Notification of 4 November 2015 (Bangladesh).

[50] Notification of the Government of India, 11 May 2009 (India).

[51] Maritime Zones Order 2017 (Samoa).

[52] Maritime Boundary Contention 2008 (Palau).

[53] Maritime Zones Act 2015 (Papua New Guinea), (1c) Schedule of Coordinates—Pocklington Island Territorial Sea Baseline.

[54] Illustrative map 'PNGMBDP 2015/04 Pocklington Island Territorial Sea Baseline', as deposited by Papua New Guinea, available at <www.un.org/depts/los/LEGISLATIONANDTREATIES/STATEFILES/PNG_Deposit_MZN164.htm>.

[55] Maritime Zones Act 2018 and Maritime Zones (Baselines of Territorial Sea) Regulations 2020 of 29 September 2020 (Cook Islands).

[56] Federated States of Micronesia Maritime Boundaries, pt I, Annex I Title 18 of the FSM Code (Annotated), and Permanent Regulation on Maritime Boundaries and Maritime Zones of the Federated States of Micronesia Pursuant to 18 FSMC 101, 102, 104, 105A, and 107, as Amended by Public Law no 19-172 (2017) (Federated States of Micronesia).

[57] Marine Spaces (Rotuma and Its Dependencies) Order 2012 (Fiji), pt 3 in relation to Ceva-I-Ra Island.

[58] Territorial Sea Baselines of Kiribati Regulations 2014 (Kiribati).

[59] Baselines and Outer Limits of Maritime Zones Declaration 2016, Part 2 (Republic of the Marshall Islands), noting that archipelagic baselines are declared in pt 1.

[60] Maritime Zones (Baselines and Closing Lines) Regulations 2024 (Mauritius).

[61] Sea Boundaries Act 1997 and Sea Boundaries Proclamation 1997 (Nauru).

[62] Territorial Sea Baseline Notice 2013 (Niue).

Palestine,[63] Papua New Guinea,[64] Seychelles,[65] Tuvalu,[66] and Vanuatu[67] all take a similar approach in their usage of the normal baseline for particular features.

Coordinates express location by referring to a geographic grid created by 'two sets of imaginary lines around our earth', allowing the statement of 'the absolute location of any point on the earth by calculating the degrees of latitude north or south of the equator and the degrees of longitude east and west of the prime meridian'.[68] Where a Type 2 definition uses coordinates as turning points in a mixed baseline system, normal baseline segments are anchored to an 'absolute location' by the same coordinates that are the endpoints of neighbouring straight or archipelagic baseline segments. Notably, these anchored segments of normal baseline rely on the physical coast or reef, or chart, for the location and shape of the line between the coordinates, a characteristic which a Type 2 definition has in common with Type 1 and Type 3. Where a Type 2 definition uses coordinates for the entirety of a normal baseline around whole features, that whole baseline may be seen to have an 'absolute location' too, in that it may be located solely by reference to coordinates (even if the legislation refers to a coast or reef, or provides an illustrative chart).

4.2.1.4 Type 3: Normal baseline is the low-water line as marked on official charts

The survey identified twenty-nine occurrences in which a coastal State defines the normal baseline as the low-water line marked on officially recognized charts. Of these, twenty-seven examples are in the legislation of coastal States Parties to the LOSC, and two in that of a non-Party.

Many examples of legislation in this category employ language which closely mirrors all the elements of Article 5 of the LOSC on the normal baseline. Some, like that of the Republic of Korea, closely replicate that wording, stating that 'the normal baseline for measuring the breadth of the territorial sea is the low-water line along the coast as marked on large-scale charts officially recognized by the Republic of Korea'.[69] Other legislation refers to charts in the context of

[63] Declaration of the State of Palestine regarding the Maritime Boundaries of the State of Palestine in Accordance with the United Nations Convention of the Law of the Sea, 24 September 2019 (Palestine).
[64] Maritime Zones Act 2015, sch 1 in relation to Pocklington Island, Tauu Islands, and Nukumanu Islands; the illustrative chart makes clear that the baselines around these islands are normal baselines.
[65] Maritime Zones Baselines Order SI of 2008 (Seychelles).
[66] Declaration of Territorial Sea Baselines 2012 (Tuvalu).
[67] Schedule of the Maritime Act [Cap 138] in relation to Mathew Island and Hunter Island (Vanuatu).
[68] Michael N DeMers, *Fundamentals of Geographic Information Systems* (4th edn, Wiley 2009) 42.
[69] Territorial Sea and Contiguous Zone Act promulgated on 31 December 1977 (Republic of Korea) s 2(1).

defining or specifying the term 'low-water line'. For example, after stating that the territorial sea shall be measured from the low-water line along the coast, the legislation of the Netherlands states that 'the low-water line shall be defined as the line indicating the depth of 0 metres on the large-scale Dutch sea charts issued upon the instructions of the Minister of Defence'.[70] Similarly, Timor-Leste legislation states that '"Low-tide line" means the low-tide line of the sea-shores of the territory of Timor-Leste, as shown in official larger-scale maps officially recognized by the Government of Timor-Leste',[71] and that the normal baseline shall be 'the low-tide line along the coast'.[72]

Understanding the purpose of a chart sheds light on how a Type 3 definition works in practice. In the context of the LOSC, which refers to charts in numerous provisions in addition to Article 5 on the normal baseline, a chart is understood to mean a nautical chart,[73] which is a 'map specially designed to meet the needs of marine navigation'.[74] It is apparent that national legislation also uses the term 'chart' in this way. Given the purpose of charts, where terrestrial maps focus on accurately depicting features of the land, a chart will focus only on those land features significant for navigation (whether for positioning, or which present a potential hazard).[75] According to the International Hydrographic Organization (IHO), a 'chart' is:

> specifically designed to meet the requirements of marine navigation, showing among other things depths, nature of the seabed, elevations, configuration and characteristics of the coast, dangers, and aids to navigation. Nautical charts provide a graphical representation of relevant information to mariners for executing safe navigation.[76]

And today, a chart is not confined to an analogue (paper) form (with historical antecedents including the Portolan charts of the Middle Ages, commonly understood to mark the beginning of European cartography).[77] However,

70 Netherlands Territorial Sea (Demarcation) Act of 9 January 1985 (Netherlands) s 1(2).

71 National Parliament Law no 7/2002 on Maritime Borders of the Territory of the Democratic Republic of Timor-Leste (Timor-Leste) art 1(g).

72 ibid art 2.

73 Nandan, Nordquist and Rosenne, *United Nations Convention on the Law of the Sea 1982: A Commentary* (n 26) 90.

74 George K Walker, *Definitions for the Law of the Sea: Terms Not Defined by the 1982 Convention* (Martinus Nijhoff 2012) 126.

75 Joaquim Alves Gaspar and Henrique Leitão, 'Early Modern Nautical Charts and Maps: Working Through Different Cartographic Paradigms' (2019) 23 Journal of Early Modern History 1, 5.

76 IHO, *S-66: Facts about Electronic Charts and Carriage Requirements* 7 (S-66).

77 See discussion of the practical nature of Portolan maps in Mark Denny, *The Science of Navigation: From Dead Reckoning to GPS* (Johns Hopkins University Press 2012).

there are discussions in the international charting community about the future of the paper chart.[78] Rather, coastal States increasingly use electronic charts, which can either be a raster chart (a static image of a paper chart) or a vector chart, which is 'a digital database of all the objects (points, lines, areas, etc.) represented on a chart',[79] also known as an electronic navigational chart (ENC). A low-water line on an ENC will be a line made up of points, each of which corresponds to certain geographic coordinates.[80] In this way, if a coastal State uses an ENC for the purposes of its normal baseline, the charted low-water line very much resembles a line that is specified by reference to coordinates; it is just that the ENC presents a visual representation of the information, in a way that a bare list of coordinates does not. Many countries now use or produce ENCs,[81] including those identified here as using a Type 2 definition of the baseline (eg Canada).[82]

For these reasons, legislation adopting a Type 3 definition of the normal baseline relies on a 'graphical representation' of relevant information about the coast, or, in the case of an ENC, embedded digital information as well.

4.2.1.5 Type 4: Normal baseline is determined in accordance with international law

The survey identified four occurrences in which a coastal State using the normal baseline defines the baseline as determined under, or in accordance with, international law.[83] Of these, three examples are in the legislation of LOSC Parties, and one in that of a non-Party.

The United Kingdom's legislation refers to 'the baselines from which the breadth of the territorial sea adjacent to the United Kingdom, the Channel Islands and the Isle of Man [which] shall be established in accordance with the

[78] See eg IHO (Nautical Cartography Working Group), 'The Future of the Paper Nautical Chart—Final Report' (The Future of the Paper Nautical Chart Final Report).

[79] *S-66* (n 76) 10.

[80] See IHO, *IHO Electronic Navigational Chart Product Specification S-101* (November 2018) (*IHO Electronic Navigational Chart Product Specification S-101*) s 4.8 (Geometry).

[81] See a visual representation of global ENC coverage at IHO, 'ENC Coverage Catalogue' <www.arcgis.com/apps/webappviewer/index.html?id = 06d967702c7f4094bbc5b4f8e485b712>.

[82] See ENCs produced by the Canadian Hydrographic Service at Government of Canada, 'Electronic Navigational Chart (ENC) Maritime Chart Service DFO' <https://open.canada.ca/data/en/dataset/12b769c8-48b8-4562-80fb-4a2e5ee9b45b>.

[83] It should be noted that some coastal States' legislation also referred to baselines determined in relation to international law, but they were not included in this category if it was not possible to confirm the use of the normal baseline, as opposed to other baseline types. For example Decree-Law no 8 of 20 April 1993 (Bahrain) provides that '[t]he breadth of the territorial sea of the State of Bahrain shall be twelve nautical miles, measured from baselines drawn in accordance with the United Nations'; similarly Law no 37-17 (Morocco) provides that '[t]he breadth of the territorial sea of the Kingdom of Morocco extends to a distance not exceeding twelve (12) nautical miles measured from the baselines established in accordance with the provisions of the United Nations Convention on the Law of the Sea.'

relevant provisions of the United Nations Convention on the Law of the Sea'.[84] The Explanatory Memorandum makes clear that this includes the use of the normal baseline insofar as '[g]enerally the baseline will follow the low-water line, except that a straight line can be drawn across bays'.[85] Similarly, 'the territorial sea of the United States henceforth extends to 12 nm from the baselines of the United States determined in accordance with international law'[86] and for the external territories of Australia, maritime zones are measured from 'baselines established under international law'.[87] Although the baseline type is not explicitly mentioned in this legislation, the United States[88] and Australia's external territories do use the normal baseline.[89] Since this definition type does not specify any particular method for locating the normal baseline, the degree of spatial stability relevant to any of these coastal States' segments of normal baseline specified in this way will depend on practical or policy factors outside the legislation itself (eg if the coastal State in practice uses coordinates or an official chart for the purposes of its baseline).

4.2.2 Discussion of overall findings of the legislative study

Four observations about the normal baseline and its stability may be drawn from this chapter's legislative study.

First, the results show that there is a greater diversity in the types of definition of the normal baseline than appreciated in previous scholarship and that these may be usefully considered in terms of the four-part typology of definitions (Types 1–4). Not only is there a distinction between the use and non-use of charts (as identified in the ILA Baseline Committee's 2012 study), but this study has identified a new category (Type 2, relying on coordinates) which is the second most commonly used type of definition of the normal baseline.

[84] Territorial Sea (Baselines) Order 2014 (United Kingdom) art 2(1).

[85] Explanatory Memorandum to The Territorial Sea (Baselines) Order 2014 (United Kingdom) para 7.1.

[86] Territorial Sea of the United States of America by the President of the United States of America; A Proclamation of 27 December 1988 (USA).

[87] Proclamation under Seas and Submerged Lands Act 1973 made under section 10B Seas and Submerged Lands Act 1973 (Cth) (26 July 1994) (Australia).

[88] eg United States, Comments of the United States regarding Sea-Level Rise in Relation to the Law of the Sea (14 February 2020) (2020 US ILC Submission); United States, Comments of the United States regarding Sea-Level Rise in Relation to the Law of the Sea (14 February 2020): 'The United States, as a matter of long standing practice, uses the normal baseline.'

[89] eg the visual representation of the baseline around Cocos (Keeling) Islands in the Australian Marine Spatial Information System indicates the normal baseline: Geoscience Australia, 'Australian Marine Spatial Information System' <www.ga.gov.au/scientific-topics/marine/jurisdiction/amsis>.

Secondly, the definition types differ in the way they locate the normal baseline in relation to the surface of the Earth. These differences are relevant to understanding the spatial stability of the normal baseline, because some types (Types 2 and 3) offer a greater stabilizing effect than others (Type 1): a line defined by reference to coordinates or a chart may be located independently from the physical coastline to which it refers. Accordingly, the spatial stability of a particular coastal State's normal baseline is directly influenced by its choice of definition type. If Types 2 and 3 are grouped together on the basis that both charts and coordinates offer some stabilizing effect, they may collectively be considered spatially stable approaches to defining the normal baseline, representing 66 out of 118 uses of the normal baseline (approximately 56 per cent).

Thirdly, there is no apparent trend or concentration of definition types in terms of their geographical distribution (see Table 4.3). The definition types are used across all UN Regional Groups[90] (though less evident in relation to the Type 4 normal baseline, since only four instances were observed). This distribution challenges the idea that some methods—such as the use of coordinates—are regional phenomena. For example, there has been some reference to the use of 'fixed baseline' in the context of emerging regional State practice in the Pacific region.[91] Yet the use of coordinates for the normal baseline is not confined to the Pacific (even though it is widely used there), showing that its use has significance beyond any one specific region.

Fourthly, it is nonetheless possible to discern some temporal trends in the usage of the four different definition types. As illustrated in Figure 4.3, the Type 2 definition (coordinates) has been increasingly used by coastal States, while the Type 1 definition (normal baseline is the low-water line) has been in decreasing use.

These trends show that a Type 1 definition that identifies the normal baseline with the low-water line was most often used prior to the conclusion of the LOSC in 1982, and since that time, coastal States have used other definition types, increasingly Type 2, in the establishment of normal baselines. A practical reason for the increase in the usage of a coordinates-based definition over

[90] United Nations, 'Regional Groups of Member States' <http://un.org/dgacm/en/content/regional-groups>.

[91] See eg *First issues paper* (n 11) [104] and David Freestone and Clive Schofield, '2016 Maritime Zones Declaration Act: Drawing Lines in the Sea' (2016) 31 International Journal of Marine and Coastal Law 732, 740. See discussion of practice in the Pacific region in Frances Anggadi, 'Establishment, Notification, and Maintenance: The Package of State Practice at the Heart of the Pacific Islands Forum Declaration on Preserving Maritime Zones' (2022) 53 Ocean Development & International Law 19.

Table 4.3 Usage of normal baseline definition types according to UN Regional Group

Usage of normal baseline definition types according to UN Regional Group
(LOSC non-Parties indicated in italics)

	Type 1	Type 2	Type 3	Type 4
African Group	Cameroon, Côte d'Ivoire, Djibouti, Equatorial Guinea, The Gambia, Guinea, Kenya, Madagascar, Mauritania, Namibia, Nigeria, Senegal, Somalia, South Africa, Tunisia; *Eritrea*	Angola, Benin, Congo, Democratic Republic of Congo, Mauritius, Seychelles, Togo	Angola, Gabon, Ghana, Liberia, Mozambique, Sierra Leone, Sudan, Tanzania	-
Asia-Pacific Group	Kuwait, Lebanon, Sri Lanka, Tonga; *Iran, Syria*	Bangladesh, Fiji, India, Indonesia, Kiribati, Marshall Islands, Micronesia, Nauru, Niue, Palau, Papua New Guinea, Samoa, Saudi Arabia, Tuvalu, Vanuatu	Bangladesh, India, Japan, Republic of Korea, Palau, Solomon Islands, Timor-Leste, Yemen; *Türkiye*	Qatar
Eastern Europe Group	Bulgaria, Georgia, Poland, Romania, Slovenia	Estonia, Lithuania, Ukraine	Russian Federation	-
Latin American and Caribbean Group	Barbados, Belize, Grenada, Guatemala, Haiti, Honduras, Nicaragua, Saint Kitts and Nevis, Saint Lucia; *Colombia, El Salvador*	Argentina, Brazil, Costa Rica, Uruguay; *Peru*	Argentina, Brazil, Guyana, Mexico, Suriname; *Venezuela*	-
Western Europe and Others Group	Australia, Canada, Germany, Greece, Ireland, Monaco, New Zealand, Spain, Sweden; *Israel*	Belgium, Canada, Denmark, France, Iceland, Norway	Belgium, Croatia, Italy, Netherlands, Portugal	Australia, United Kingdom; *United States*
Others not formally included in UN Regional Groups	-	Cook Islands, Palestine	-	-

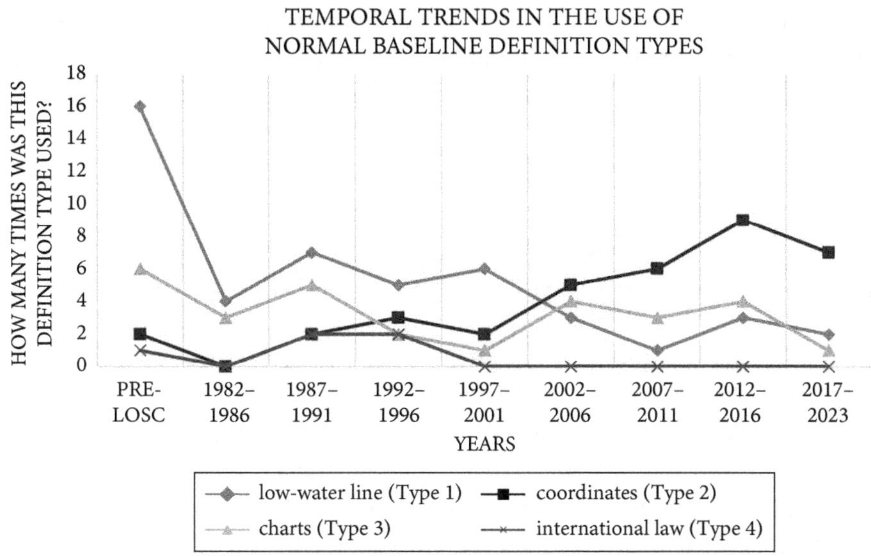

Figure 4.3 Trend lines for usage of each definition type, showing the number of coastal States implementing that type of normal baseline in each time band (not cumulative)

this period may lie in the increasing availability of technological improvements enabling surveys of the coastline at a level of detail not previously possible (or, for many States, economically viable).

4.3 The significance of the legislative study for the LOSC

In addition to the practical significance of the legislative study's findings, the book argues that such findings carry significance for our understanding of existing international law on the normal baseline, namely, Article 5 of the LOSC. Assessing such significance requires the application of the relevant analytical frameworks under public international law relating to the interpretation of the LOSC. Section 4.3 first considers the relevance of evidence of legislation as 'subsequent practice' as a matter of treaty interpretation, guided by the rules of the Vienna Convention on the Law of Treaties (VCLT). Since the LOSC currently has 170 Parties (139 of which are coastal States), State practice in respect of baselines is most likely to be referrable to the applicable provisions of the treaty and accordingly, the following analysis focuses only on the practice of coastal States which are LOSC Parties, which use the normal baseline. However, especially noting there are fourteen non-Parties to the LOSC which are coastal States, there are also implications for customary international law: these are considered for the book as a whole in Chapter 8.

4.3.1 Legislation implementing the normal baseline as 'subsequent practice' for the purposes of Article 31(3)(b) of the VCLT

As outlined in Chapter 1, treaty interpretation is governed by Articles 31 and 32 of the VCLT, provisions which the International Court of Justice (ICJ) has recognized as reflective of custom.[92] In the context of the LOSC baseline provisions, the practice of States is relevant as a matter of 'subsequent practice in the application of the treaty which establishes the agreement of the parties regarding its interpretation' under Article 31(3)(b) of the VCLT. The evidence identified in the legislative study can readily be considered as 'practice' for this purpose, since 'subsequent practice' encompasses legislative acts.[93]

Article 31 sets out the 'general rule of interpretation'. The effect of the unitary interpretative approach under Article 31 is that subsequent practice is considered together in 'the crucible of interpretation'[94] with other elements of the general rule, such as the ordinary meaning of the terms of the treaty, the context in which those terms occur, and the object and purpose of the treaty.[95] Aust emphasizes that these elements do not indicate any hierarchy, but rather should be seen as a 'logical progression, nothing more. One naturally begins

[92] See Section 1.4.

[93] ILC, Draft Conclusions on Subsequent Agreements and Subsequent Practice in relation to the Interpretation of Treaties, with Commentaries, UN Doc A/73/10) (ILC Draft Conclusions on Subsequent Agreements and Subsequent Practice) Draft Conclusion 6(2).

[94] Richard Gardiner, *Treaty Interpretation* (Oxford University Press 2015) 224.

[95] The interpretative approach taken in this book (focusing on subsequent practice under art 31(3)(b)) has some overlap with what is referred to as the 'evolutionary treaty approach' (or evolutionary interpretation) in the sense that both have the purpose of 'allowing treaties to develop over time, ensuring the instrument's survival and adaptation to contemporary priorities': Irina Buga, *Modification of Treaties by Subsequent Practice* (Oxford University Press 2018) 93. However, the two approaches differ in that generally, 'evolutionary interpretation relies on the parties' original intention of codifying treaty terms that are evolutionary in nature, [while] interpretation (or modification) by subsequent practice focuses on the intention of the parties at the time of application, in *addition* to their original intention', 97 (original emphasis). Overall, the book takes a broader view in line with the approach of Roland Holst, who concludes that 'there is arguably no need to label a particular interpretative approach as an 'evolutionary interpretation', or to "house" it specifically under either article 31(3)(c) or (b) VCLT, as is sometimes suggested, considering that one or more of the approaches set out in the general rule may lead to the same result': Rozemarijn J Roland Holst, *Change in the Law of the Sea: Context, Mechanisms and Practice* (Brill 2022) 196.

with the text, followed by the context, and then other matters, in particular, subsequent material.'[96] As a logical preliminary to this section's focus on legislation as subsequent practice, it is necessary to address these other elements of the general rule.

4.3.2 Article 5's ordinary meaning, context, and the object and purpose of the LOSC

We begin with the 'ordinary meaning' to be given to Article 5, which provides that the normal baseline 'is the low-water line along the coast as marked on large-scale charts officially recognized by the coastal State'. While this language makes clear that the normal baseline relies on 'the intersection of *low* water with the shore'[97] (rather than, say, the line of water at high tide),[98] uncertainties remain as to which line of low water should be used for the baseline.[99]

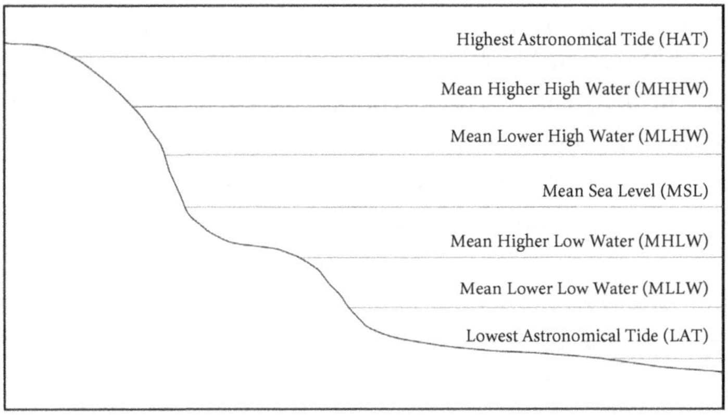

Figure 4.4 Diagram showing various tidal datums

Note: Figure 4.4 is a simplified diagram compiled by the author from a range of sources, including Nuno Sergio Marques Antunes, *The Importance of the Tidal Datum in the Definition of Maritime Limits and Boundaries* (IBRU 2000) and United Nations Office for Ocean Affairs and the Law of the Sea, *Baselines: An Examination of the Relevant Provisions of the United Nations Convention on the Law of the Sea* (United Nations 1989)

[96] Anthony Aust, *Modern Treaty Law and Practice* (3rd edn, Cambridge University Press 2013) 208.
[97] IHO, *Hydrographic Dictionary: IHO Publication S-32* (5th edn, 1994) (emphasis added).
[98] *Fisheries (United Kingdom v Norway)* [1951] ICJ Rep 116, 137.
[99] Questions have also been raised about the ordinary meaning of other aspects of art 5, such as what features might qualify for inclusion within the meaning of 'coast': see RR Churchill, AV Lowe, and Amy Sander, *The Law of the Sea* (4th edn, Manchester University Press 2022) 59.

As outlined in Chapter 3, Hague Conference delegates debated variations in States' choice of low water.[100] The main approaches are illustrated in Figure 4.4. Each of these is a type of vertical tidal datum. A vertical datum can be understood as a level of reference for vertical measurements such as depths, height of tide, and elevations; a tidal datum is a subset of the term vertical datum in that it refers to a level of reference for the measurement of tides. This is relevant to the ordinary meaning of 'low-water line' because the vertical tidal datum determines the conditions under which the intersection of the land with the sea at low tide is determined at any particular moment.[101] Lowest astronomical tide (LAT) is the vertical tidal datum now recommended for navigational purposes by the IHO,[102] meaning 'the lowest tide level which can be predicted to occur under average meteorological conditions and under any combination of astronomical conditions'.[103] LAT is, like any other vertical tidal datum, a statistical representation of the low-water line along the coast under certain physical and temporal conditions (and since it is the lowest of all the vertical tidal datum options, is in practice very seldom visible).[104]

As explained in Chapter 3, a reference to charts was inserted into what would become Article 5 in order to overcome practical difficulties associated with observing the 'low-water line' and variation in the approaches taken by States.[105] As a result, the language of Article 5 does not refer to the 'low-water line along the coast' in isolation; instead it uses the single phrase 'low-water line along the coast as marked on large-scale charts officially recognized by the coastal State'. The principle of effectiveness assists here, as it points to the need to

> give meaning and effect to all the terms of the treaty. An interpreter is not free to adopt a reading that would result in reducing whole clauses or paragraphs of a treaty to redundancy or inutility.[106]

So in the context of Article 5, if the normal baseline was simply 'the low-water line along the coast'—the 'actual' low-water line—then this would not give

[100] See Section 3.3.2.

[101] See 'low water mark': IHO, *Hydrographic Dictionary: IHO Publication S-32* (n 97).

[102] IHO, *A2.5 – Technical Resolution on Datums and Benchmarks* (*A2.5 – Technical Resolution on Datums and Benchmarks*) para 6.

[103] IHO, *Hydrographic Dictionary: IHO Publication S-32* (n 97).

[104] 'The actual low-water line defined using the LAT datum will only be visible once every full metonic cycle of 18.6 years provided the meteorological conditions are normal. This means the low-water line will actually be underwater during all but the very lowest tides': 2012 ILA Baselines Committee Report (n 5) Annex.

[105] Section 3.3.2.

[106] *United States—Standards for Reformulated and Conventional Gasoline* (20 May 1996) WT/DS2/AB/R (Appellate Body Report) (*United States—Gasoline*).

effect to Article 5's reference to charts, and therefore is unlikely to reflect the ordinary meaning of that provision. This is the view put forward by Purcell[107] and by Churchill, Lowe, and Sander.[108] The ILA Baselines Committee was more equivocal about the ordinary meaning:

> [T]he English version of Article 5 could lead to two different meanings of 'the normal baseline for measuring the breadth of the territorial sea': (1) the low-water line along the coast (the actual low-water line), or (2) the low-water line as marked on charts officially recognized by the coastal State (the charted low-water line). Put more simply, the charted line could *be* the legal normal baseline or the charted line could *illustrate* the legal normal baseline. The Committee has reached the view that an analysis of the equally authentic texts in other languages provides no indication regarding which meaning should prevail.[109]

However, even if we consider these two possibilities, it appears that the second meaning identified by the ILA Baselines Committee (which it calls 'the charted low-water line') should be preferred because it is the only meaning that gives effect to the entirety of the text of Article 5. Since there is some ambiguity in the meaning of Article 5, it is relevant to recall that this second meaning is also supported by the conclusions on the drafting history of Article 5.[110] In this way, the 'preparatory work of the treaty'[111] tends to confirm that the ordinary meaning of Article 5 is that the normal baseline is a charted line rather than the 'actual' low-water line. Indeed, such preparatory work suggests that a charted line that does not 'depart appreciably' from the coast, and is not 'clearly fraudulent', might also be considered consistent with the requirement for good faith.[112]

We now turn to context, since the 'the ordinary meaning of a term is not to be determined in the abstract but in the context of the treaty'.[113] 'Context' here refers to the need to consider a provision in light of the treaty as a whole.[114]

[107] Kate Purcell, *Geographical Change and the Law of the Sea* (Oxford University Press 2019) 161.
[108] Churchill, Lowe, and Sander, *The Law of the Sea* (n 99) 58.
[109] 2012 ILA Baselines Committee Report (n 5) 8 (original emphasis).
[110] Section 3.3.2.
[111] VCLT, art 32.
[112] See discussion of 'the proviso' in Section 3.3.2. The VCLT articulates the rule of 'pacta sunt servanda', which provides that '[e]very treaty in force is binding upon the parties to it and must be performed by them in good faith' (art 26).
[113] ILC, Draft Articles on the Law of Treaties, with Commentaries, UN Doc A/CN.4/SER.A/1966/Add.l, 221 (Draft Articles on the Law of Treaties, with Commentaries).
[114] Aust, *Modern Treaty Law and Practice* (n 96) 210 and Mark E Villiger, *Commentary on the 1969 Vienna Convention on the Law of Treaties* (Brill 2008) 421.

Relevant to our inquiry, Gardiner explains that context should also include consideration of provisions that relate to or contrast with the provision being studied.[115] While scholars considering Article 5 have not expressly framed their reasoning as a matter of context, we can clearly see contextual analysis at work where they have looked to other provisions of the LOSC to inform their understanding of the provision. On the basis of a comparison of Article 5 with Article 7(2) and Article 76(8) and (9), Caron and others have reasoned that a negative implication may be drawn from the fact that there is an express provision for retention of the deltaic baseline in certain circumstances, and reference to the permanent establishment of the outer limits of the continental shelf, and, in contrast, no similar language of permanence or retention is present in Article 5.[116]

While this is true as a conclusion about the comparison of different terms of the LOSC, many scholars rely on this reasoning to justify the broader claim that the absence of such terms in Article 5 should be taken to indicate that no such retention or permanence is available for the normal baseline. This is a claim about the interpretation of Article 5 as a whole and overstates the weight to be given to textual context without the potentially tempering influence of the other elements of the general rule. For example, if we take into account the ordinary meaning of the whole phrase 'low-water line along the coast as marked on charts officially recognized by the coastal State', a textual comparison with Article 7(2) and Article 76(8) and (9) might yield a different possible reading. It is open to reason that there was no need to use the language of retention or permanence in Article 5, because the reference to charts already refers to a representation of the coastline; it is the reference to charts that signals the practical stability of the normal baseline, inherent in the stability of a charted line.

Finally, we consider the object and purpose of the LOSC, an exercise that brings a functional dimension to treaty interpretation. One of the key goals of the LOSC is to establish an equitable allocation of ocean space, where sovereignty over land territory functions as the basis for maritime entitlement.[117] In this framework, the principle that the 'land dominates the sea' has relevance and finds expression in the LOSC baseline rules, which make clear that it is '*coastal* States' that may establish baselines. This might tend to support an interpretation of Article 5 that gives emphasis to the dominance of

[115] Gardiner, *Treaty Interpretation* (n 94) 205.

[116] See discussion in Section 2.3.

[117] Lea Brilmayer and Natalie Klein, 'Land and Sea: Two Sovereignty Regimes in Search of a Common Denominator' (2001) 33 New York University Journal of International Law and Politics 703, 726.

the land—including changes to the land—in influencing the character of the normal baseline. However, the LOSC (like many treaties) has several objects and purposes,[118] many of which are listed in its Preamble. It would be misleading to overlook another of the purposes of the LOSC potentially relevant to the interpretation of Article 5: stability. Stability is a long-standing value and goal of the LOSC system, as made clear in the comments of States in the negotiation of the LOSC, and more recently.[119] A constantly mobile baseline—with similarly mobile maritime zones—would challenge the realization of stability. On balance, the objects and purposes of the LOSC give some qualified support to an interpretation preferring the stability of the 'charted low-water line', consistent with its ordinary meaning.

Overall, these first steps in applying the general rule of interpretation tend to support a reading of Article 5 in which the normal baseline is a charted line (rather than the 'actual' low-water line along the coast, whatever its location from time to time); but it remains a mixed picture.

4.3.3 'Subsequent practice' and the need for interpretative agreement

The reach of the general rule of interpretation set out in Article 31 of the VCLT goes further than a consideration of ordinary meaning, context, and object and purpose. Article 31(3) also refers to the potential significance of subsequent agreements and subsequent practice for treaty interpretation, to be taken into account together with context. Subsequent practice is particularly relevant to this chapter's focus on coastal States' legislation implementing the normal baseline and has particular importance for treaty interpretation because it is an 'authentic means of interpretation', being the 'objective evidence of the understanding of the parties as to the meaning of the treaty'.[120] This means that the practice of States—as subsequent practice—is capable of possessing 'a specific authority regarding the identification of the meaning of the treaty, even after the conclusion of the treaty'.[121] Since the legislative study has

[118] Villiger, *Commentary on the 1969 Vienna Convention* (n 114) 427.

[119] See Section 3.3.

[120] ILC Draft Conclusions on Subsequent Agreements and Subsequent Practice (n 93): the Commentary to Draft Conclusion 3 explains that together with subsequent practice, subsequent agreement, and the treaty's ordinary meaning, context and object and purpose are also authentic means of interpretation: 24.

[121] The ILC observes that the VCLT 'thereby accords the parties to a treaty a role that may be uncommon for the interpretation of legal instruments in some domestic systems': ibid.

found that a degree of spatial stability is available for the normal baseline as a practical matter, how does this influence our interpretation of Article 5?

In applying Article 31(3)(b) of the VCLT in relation to the practice of LOSC Parties examined in this legislative study, Gardiner sets out four elements to consider: (1) the meaning of 'subsequent practice'; (2) that it be in the application of the treaty; (3) which Parties need to participate in the practice; and (4) what is it that establishes interpretative agreement.[122] Elements 1 and 2 are straightforward, since the practice under consideration is national legislation implementing the normal baseline.[123]

Elements 3 and 4 require greater consideration. The legislative study presents abundant evidence on the implementation of the normal baseline in national legislation: it examines 108 definitions as employed by 100 coastal States Parties. This represents the practice of approximately 72 per cent of LOSC Parties that are coastal States. Even though it is not necessary for all the Parties to a treaty to engage in the relevant practice,[124] the breadth of the evidence gathered in this legislative study represents a significant proportion of LOSC Parties. Furthermore, even though there is a concentration of certain practice in particular regions (eg a high number of Type 2 definitions in the Pacific), all types are in use across all geographic regions. Responding to Gardiner's third element ('which Parties?'), it may be seen that a significant number of LOSC Parties, representing all geographic regions, have engaged in the practice.

However, in considering Element 4 as to whether the practice establishes interpretative agreement, some issues arise from the diversity of practice observed. The ILC has explained that an important factor in the weight to be given to practice relates to 'whether and how it is repeated'.[125] While it is not strictly necessary to show the existence of 'a "concordant, common and consistent" sequence of acts or pronouncements [. . .] to establish a discern[i]ble pattern implying the agreement of the parties',[126] it remains necessary to show that the practice demonstrates the 'common understanding of the parties'.[127] The difficulty lies in what to make of the diversity of legislative approaches

[122] Gardiner, *Treaty Interpretation* (n 94) 254.

[123] '[S]ubsequent practice under articles 31 and 32 may consist of any conduct of a party in the application of a treaty, whether in the exercise of its executive, legislative, judicial or other functions': ILC Draft Conclusions on Subsequent Agreements and Subsequent Practice (n 93) Draft Conclusion 5.

[124] See ibid Draft Conclusion 10(2): 'The number of parties that must engage in subsequent practice in order to establish agreement under article 31, paragraph 3(b) may vary', and Commentary at 79.

[125] ibid Draft Conclusion 9(2).

[126] *Japan—Alcoholic Beverages II*, WT/DS8/AB/R, WT/DS10/AB/R, and WT/DS11/AB/R (1 November 1996) (Appellate Body Report) (*Japan—Alcoholic Beverages II*).

[127] See discussion on the requirement for 'common understanding' in ILC Draft Conclusions on Subsequent Agreements and Subsequent Practice (n 93) 73.

taken by coastal States in the implementation of the normal baseline. Should such diversity be considered to reflect '[c]onflicting positions regarding interpretation expressed by different parties to a treaty',[128] precluding an interpretative agreement and therefore preventing the 'concretization of the meaning' of Article 5?[129]

This question was considered in relation to the implementation of a different kind of baseline: straight baselines pursuant to Article 7 of the LOSC. Churchill, Lowe, and Sander expressly considered the potential weight to accord diverse State practice as a matter of the interpretation of Article 7:

> Although the amount of State practice in drawing straight baselines that arguably is not in conformity with UNCLOS is quite substantial, it probably represents not much more than about a quarter of coastal States parties to UNCLOS. Furthermore, this practice is quite diverse, in the sense that it does not point to any particular way in which straight baselines should be drawn: in reality, it seems to suggest no more than that a coastal State may draw straight baselines however it likes. Such diversity, coupled with the protests referred to above, indicate that current State practice does not amount to an agreed interpretation of article 7 or a new rule of customary international law.[130]

Even though the ICJ has confirmed that Article 7 is reflective of customary international law, its reasoning does not disclose any evaluation of State practice supporting that conclusion, nor any particular view on the relationship between diversity of State practice and the content of relevant international rules.[131] The Dissenting Opinion of Judge ad hoc McRae criticized this omission, stating that 'there is no doubt that the law relating to straight baselines is in need of clarification'[132] and that 'the imprecision of the terms in Article 7 might well be lessened by considering how States in practice have interpreted and applied those provisions'.[133] So in the interpretation of Article 7, the diversity of practice in the implementation of straight baselines at the very least

[128] ibid 76.

[129] Buga, *Modification of Treaties by Subsequent Practice* (n 95) 29.

[130] Churchill, Lowe, and Sander, *The Law of the Sea* (n 99) 71; see also study of protests in relation to straight baselines in ILA (Committee on Baselines under the International Law of the Sea) 'Baselines under the International Law of the Sea (Sydney Conference)'.

[131] *Alleged Violations of Sovereign Rights and Maritime Spaces in the Caribbean Sea (Nicaragua v Colombia)* (Judgment) [2022] ICJ Rep 266 [243] (*Alleged Violations of Sovereign Rights*).

[132] ibid [81] (Judge ad hoc McRae).

[133] ibid [78] (Judge ad hoc McRae).

raises questions about the existence of any interpretative agreement (if not actually precluding it, as in the view of Churchill, Lowe, and Sander).

In view of the evidence set out in this chapter, the position in relation to State practice in the implementation of the normal baseline is arguably different. Although there is diversity in the practice, it is not the case that the practice points 'to no particular way'[134] in which normal baselines should be drawn. There is instead a 'discernible pattern'[135] in that the 108 definitions of the normal baseline used by LOSC Parties may be readily classified into a typology of four definition types, and that Types 1, 2, and 3 are clearly the most commonly used (42, 36, and 27 uses, respectively).[136] All observed definitions used by coastal States fall into one of these four types, strongly suggesting a concentration of certain types of practice, rather than a random distribution. Indeed, there is a connection between the use of a particular definition type and its resulting stability: defining the normal baseline by reference to coordinates and/or charts (Types 2 and 3) is what gives them a spatial stability by making those lines capable of remaining in the same location on the Earth's surface, independently of the behaviour of the coastline. Seen in this way, the definition types may be seen on a spectrum from those having less of this kind of stabilizing effect, to those which have more. Considering also that this 'pattern' embraces the practice of over 70 per cent of coastal States Parties to the LOSC (and 100 per cent of coastal States Parties known to use the normal baseline), there is a strong case that—unlike the position for straight baselines—State practice on the implementation of the normal baseline is capable of establishing interpretative agreement for the purposes of Article 31(3)(b) of the VCLT.

The ILC has explained that silence or inaction can contribute to agreement if the circumstances call for some reaction in relation to State conduct.[137] If so, this might meet the requirement for 'awareness', and a lack of objection might amount to 'acceptance' of the practice.[138] Does this pattern of practice show the 'common understanding' of the Parties, thereby influencing the interpretation of Article 5? Arguably yes, following the approach of the International

[134] Churchill, Lowe, and Sander, *The Law of the Sea* (n 99) 71.

[135] *Japan—Alcoholic Beverages II* (n 126).

[136] See summary of overall findings in Section 4.2.2—noting that the figures given in this chapter reflect the normal baseline definitions of LOSC Parties only.

[137] See ILC Draft Conclusions on Subsequent Agreements and Subsequent Practice (n 93), especially the discussion of *Temple of Préah Vihéar (Cambodia v Thailand)* (Merits) [1962] ICJ Rep 6 (*Temple of Préah Vihéar*).

[138] On the need for awareness and acceptance, see ILC Draft Conclusions on Subsequent Agreements and Subsequent Practice (n 93) Draft Conclusion 10.

Tribunal for the Law of the Sea (ITLOS) in interpreting Articles 56, 58, and 73 of the LOSC:

> The Tribunal acknowledges that the national legislation of several States, not only in the West African region, but also in some other regions of the world, regulates bunkering of foreign vessels fishing in their exclusive economic zones in a way comparable to that of Guinea-Bissau. The Tribunal further notes that there is no manifest objection to such legislation and that it is, in general complied with.[139]

Similarly, there is 'no manifest objection' to the large sample of legislation on the normal baseline examined here (108 definitions used by 100 coastal States Parties). Following the reasoning of ITLOS in *Virginia G*, this might alone be sufficient, but there are also other factors that support a conclusion that there is both awareness and acceptance of this body of State practice. First, while diplomatic protest is an established means of challenging the validity of baselines,[140] no such practice has developed in relation to normal baselines. In contrast, it is particularly evident in relation to straight baselines, and a number of studies have comprehensively examined such protests.[141] None of these studies has included any examination of protests relating to conformity of a coastal State's normal baseline with the requirements of Article 5.[142]

Secondly, the language used in most definitions departs from that found in Article 5 itself, but this has not emerged as a basis for criticism. This is the case for the two most prevalent groups: Type 1 definitions omit Article 5's reference to official charts, and Type 2 definitions rely on coordinates instead of (or, in some instances, as well as) charts. The lack of objection to these practices departing from the language of Article 5 is suggestive of a common understanding that such legislative choices are within the margin of appreciation available to coastal States when establishing the normal baseline.

Thirdly, there is evidence of an increasing explicit awareness amongst States as to the diversity of legislative approaches to implementation of the baseline.

[139] *M/V 'Virginia G' (Panama/Guinea-Bissau)* (Judgment) (2014) Case no 19 [218].

[140] *Alleged Violations of Sovereign Rights* (n 131) [4] (Judge Bennouna).

[141] See J Ashley Roach, *Excessive Maritime Claims* (4th edn, Brill 2021) 77 and ILA (Committee on Baselines under the International Law of the Sea), 'Baselines under the International Law of the Sea (Sydney Conference)' (2018 ILA Baselines Committee Report).

[142] Although protests have been made on other grounds, such as disputed sovereignty. See eg Communication from the Government of France dated 6 December 2010 relating to Vanuatu's Maritime Zones Act 2010, which established baselines drawn from the low-water line of the Mathew (Umaenupne) and Hunter (Leka) islands: <www.un.org/depts/los/LEGISLATIONANDTREATIES/PDFFILES/DEPOSIT/communicationsredeposit/mzn78_2010_fra_en.pdf>.

For example, in the context of the ILC's work on sea-level rise and maritime zones, the United Kingdom, Netherlands, and United States have referred to their own baselines in 'ambulatory' terms.[143] At the same time, increasing attention has been drawn to coastal States adopting 'fixed' baselines, including by LOSC Parties which implement ambulatory baselines[144] (and by LOSC non-Parties too, as discussed in Chapter 8 in the context of implications for customary international law). This terminology (clearly influenced by the framing of early scholarly debate on this issue) also maps onto the definition types identified by this book: an 'ambulatory' baseline type aligns with a Type 1 definition (where the normal baseline is defined as the low-water line); a 'fixed' baseline type aligns more with Types 2 and 3 (coordinates and charts-based definitions, respectively). While discussions among States on these issues are ongoing, there are signs that States are giving increasing visibility to their legislative choices in implementing their baseline, and that, at least thus far, the emerging picture of diversity has not encouraged criticism.

Overall, these factors tend to support the conclusion that there is general acceptance of a diversity of methods to implement the normal baseline in domestic legislation, and that this acceptance includes methods which define the normal baseline by reference to coordinates.[145] Evaluating the body of State practice on the normal baseline by reference to the general rule of treaty interpretation points us to a more nuanced interpretation of Article 5 than can be accommodated by either an 'ambulatory' or a 'fixed' view of baselines.

Accordingly, this chapter proposes that Article 5 should be interpreted more flexibly than allowed by either of these two theoretical approaches. The provision points to the low-water line (rather than, say, the high-water line) along the coast as the relevant geographic reference point for the establishment of the normal baseline, and the coastal State may choose the precise way of referring to the location of that normal baseline for the purposes of its legislative

[143] Kingdom of the Netherlands, 'Submission of the Netherlands to the International Law Commission' (27 December 2019) (2019 Netherlands ILC Submission); 2020 US ILC Submission (n 88); and United Kingdom of Great Britain and Northern Ireland, 'Submission of the United Kingdom to the International Law Commission' (10 January 2020) (2020 UK ILC Submission).

[144] See United Kingdom of Great Britain and Northern Ireland, Government Response to the United Kingdom House of Lords International Relations and Defence Committee Inquiry on 'UNCLOS: the Law of the Sea in the 21st Century' (UK Government Response to House of Lords Inquiry); although it must also be noted that in 2024, the UK has also expressed its support for the preservation of baselines through the Commonwealth Ocean Declaration.

[145] Indeed, UNGA endorsement of IHO work on *S-121* (a data standard for an international, coordinates-based, representation of maritime boundaries and their associated rights, restrictions, and responsibilities that is authoritative and easy to interpret) also tends to support such general acceptance of this method: see Oceans and the Law of the Sea, GA Res 76/72 (9 December 2021) UN Doc A/RES/76/72 (UNGA Oceans Res 2021) and Michael Sutherland and others, 'S-121: A New Standard for Maritime Limits and Boundaries' (2018) Hydro International 19.

implementation. However, Article 5 does not *require* that the normal baseline be defined in this way. Many coastal States (over half of the coastal States using the normal baseline) define the location of the normal baseline by reference to a chart and/or coordinates. This means that a degree of spatial stability is available for those normal baselines because of the ability of charts and coordinates to express location independently from the physical coast they represent. The broad body of practice examined in the legislative study, and lack of manifest objection to it, strongly indicate the agreement of LOSC Parties that Article 5 embraces a margin of appreciation as to how coastal States define the location of the normal baseline, including means that produce more or less spatial stability.

4.4 Implications for spatial stability under the LOSC

Rayfuse, writing in 2013 in relation to fixed baselines, considered the possibility that 'by accretion of State practice, baselines may become "fixed" at the geographical coordinates expressed in domestic legislation'.[146] A decade later, the 'accretion of State practice' in relation to so-called 'fixed' baselines is indeed substantial. However, it would be a mistake to focus only on 'fixed' baselines, or indeed only on 'ambulatory' baselines, as to do so would be to overlook a larger body of State practice and its legal significance.

This chapter has demonstrated that global practice in relation to the implementation of the normal baseline, unlike that concerning straight baselines, constitutes a body of generally accepted practice. In further contrast to the picture of global straight baselines usage, the legislative study has shown that there is a 'discernible pattern' in the implementation of the normal baseline, evident in classification of all normal baseline definitions into a typology of definition types. Offering a way to classify the normal baseline definitions of 110 coastal States (both Parties and non-Parties to the LOSC), this typology offers the foundation for a strong explanatory narrative for the normal baseline. The two key features of that narrative are its diversity and its spatial differentiation. The diversity of definitions in the typology demonstrates a general acceptance that a coastal State may choose its method among a number of permissible methods: from this perspective, 'ambulatory' and 'fixed' can more usefully be seen as descriptive terms for particular legislative choices. Furthermore, a key practical dimension of these legislative methods is that they differ from each

[146] Rayfuse, 'Sea Level Rise and Maritime Zones' (n 1).

other in how they express location in a more (or less) stable way. Seen in this way, 'ambulatory' and 'fixed' sit at opposite ends of a spectrum of less or more spatial stability.[147]

To be clear, it is not so much that the chapter argues that States' legislative choices in implementing the normal baseline are per se indicative of international law standards; to do so would be to conflate the content of international law with instances of its domestic implementation. However, the scale and convergence of evidence of this particular kind—the legislative implementation of the normal baseline—means that, collectively, domestic actions can take on significance at an international level. The global reach of the legislative study uncovered a discernible pattern of practice amongst coastal States on the use of spatially stable methods, and at a global scale. In addition, a convergence of evidence of such legislation (subsequent practice) and its general acceptance (interpretative agreement) meet the benchmarks for interpretative significance within the framework of treaty interpretation under the VCLT.

For these reasons, it becomes clear that adopting either an 'ambulatory' or a 'fixed' theory of baselines provides only a partial view of the contemporary scope of Article 5. The better view is that in the establishment of the normal baseline, a coastal State has a margin of appreciation in choosing how to define the location of that baseline in its legislation. It may establish the normal baseline by defining it as the low-water line, or use more spatially stable means to express its location, such as coordinates. General acceptance of the diversity of methods across the typology shows that the choice of a particular definition type does not signal legal conformity or non-conformity; rather, it shows that international law accommodates a degree of choice in how a coastal State establishes its baseline, including as to whether it opts for more or less spatially stable types of definition.

Two observations can be drawn from this chapter's conclusions on the normal baseline. Firstly, the apparent acceptance by States of an increasingly common recourse to the stabilizing effect of coordinates points to a similarity between the application of Article 5 and other baseline types using coordinates: straight baselines established under Article 7 and archipelagic baselines under Article 47. Discussing straight baselines, O'Connell wrote that:

[147] Some discussion in the ILC has mentioned a similar approach, that 'there might be a continuum of intermediate possibilities between the two options discussed in the first issues paper—ambulatory versus permanent baselines—that deserved a full and detailed examination': 2021 ILC Report (n 12) [275].

> [t]he concept of the 'general direction' of the coast is a matter of appreciation, not of scientific discovery, and necessarily requires that a considerable margin of appreciation be applied in favour of the coastal State.[148]

Translating this to the context of the normal baseline, this might mean that a coastal State is permitted—within a margin of appreciation—to use a representation of the low-water line as the normal baseline, whether it be through charts or coordinates. That is, the normal baseline need not be a matter of 'scientific discovery' as to where the low-water line is at any particular moment. The influence of State practice on this view of the existing law is crucial for grasping the degree of legal stability available for the normal baseline. It is not necessarily the case that the location of the normal baseline is a fact to be 'discovered'; as a legal artefact, it is also the product of State choices in implementation, including to use more or less stabilizing methods of expressing location.

Indeed, the chapter's findings suggest an even deeper connection between normal baselines and straight and archipelagic baselines (against which normal baselines are usually contrasted). In its finding that thirty-seven coastal States use coordinates to define their normal baseline (Type 2, the second most commonly used type of normal baseline definition),[149] this chapter has identified a strong link between normal baselines and other baseline types.[150] Straight baselines (used by ninety coastal States)[151] and archipelagic baselines (used by twenty-two coastal States)[152] predominantly define turning points for such baselines by means of coordinates.[153] If we conceive of the use of coordinates as a spatially stable method of defining a line on the surface of the Earth, capable of expressing absolute location, then this understanding holds

[148] DP O'Connell, *The International Law of the Sea*, vol I (IA Shearer ed, Clarendon Press 1984) 214. Purcell gestures to a similar idea, in referring to 'latitude in the baselines provisions': Purcell, *Geographical Change and the Law of the Sea* (n 107) 24.

[149] See Section 4.3.2.

[150] Interestingly, some States have also remarked on a similarity between normal and straight baselines, in the sense that the LOSC grants coastal States 'room for manoeuvre when it comes to taking the initiative to modify, or maintain declared data regarding baselines and limits of their maritime zones [. . .] That is the case for normal baselines, under Article 5 of the Convention, but also for straight baselines': France, 'Comments and Observations of the French Republic relating to the Subtopic of Sea-Level Rise in Relation to the Law of the Sea' (29 November 2022) (2022 France ILC Submission). Similarly, Germany stated that 'UNCLOS does not contain any explicit obligations to update neither normal baselines that have been marked (Article 5 UNCLOS) nor straight baselines that have been marked, published and deposited (Article 16 UNCLOS)': Germany, 'Sea-Level Rise in relation to International Law' (30 June 2022) (2022 Germany ILC Submission).

[151] 2018 ILA Baselines Committee Report (n 141).

[152] Donald R Rothwell, *Islands and International Law* (Bloomsbury 2022) Table 5.1.

[153] Though not exclusively, since some coastal States use place names as turning points for straight baselines, see eg Decree of 28 August 1968 delimiting the Mexican Territorial Sea within the Gulf of California.

whether the line so described is a normal, straight, or archipelagic baseline (or, for that matter, a bay closing line, reef closing line, or other line defined by coordinates, contributing to a coastal State's baseline system), although often a greater number of coordinates are required to define the normal baseline in order to account for the contours of the low-water line along the coast. The use of coordinates for straight and archipelagic baselines is uncontroversial and long accepted; the evidence presented in this chapter makes clear however that a sizeable number of coastal States use the same approach for normal baselines too, without 'manifest objection'.

A second, related observation concerns the scope of this chapter's conclusions. The interpretation advanced here pertains to the availability and acceptability of spatially stable methods of establishing the normal baseline in the implementation of Article 5. As such, this is not an interpretation limited to the circumstance of sea-level rise (eg it is not the case that only coastal States concerned to preserve their baselines notwithstanding sea-level rise are permitted to adopt such legislative means). Rather, the chapter makes the more straightforward proposition that there is a generally accepted 'menu' of methods for implementing the normal baseline in domestic legislation, some of which include means such as coordinates which have the practical effect of achieving a spatially stable normal baseline.

While not limited to circumstances of sea-level rise, this conclusion is highly pertinent to it, because if baselines and maritime zones are to be preserved, they must as a practical matter first be capable of remaining in a stable location. If it is assumed that the normal baseline is 'naturally ambulatory',[154] the idea of a spatially stable normal baseline might seem puzzling: this apparent paradox is demonstrated in the sentiment that while the lack of any express duty to update or resurvey straight baselines 'is helpful in developing a pragmatic legal solution for straight baselines and the maritime limits measured from them [...] [t]he question of how to fix baselines formed by the low-water line along the coast is more problematic'.[155] The legislative study offers an answer to this, showing that thirty-seven coastal States have used coordinates to fix their normal baselines (and that many more use coordinates underlying an electronic navigational chart). This chapter argues that implementing a spatially stable baseline is a crucial first step in the pursuit of stable maritime zones that are capable of preservation.

[154] 2012 ILA Baselines Committee Report (n 5) 22.
[155] Ireland, 'International Law Commission's Study Group in relation to International Law' (January 2025) (Ireland 2025 ILC Submission).

Today, it cannot be said that the normal baseline has an inherently ambulatory character in terms of its spatial definition. Instead, the spatial character of the normal baseline must be seen as a product of the way it is established in national legislation, which means that some normal baselines will have an ambulatory character (those using a Type 1 method, such as Australia) and some will have a spatially stable character (eg those using a Type 2 method, such as Mauritius). It follows that straight and archipelagic baselines—because they are almost always defined by coordinates—also have a spatially stable character. However, the ability of a spatially stable baseline—once established—to be maintained over time, and in circumstances of (more or less) coastal change, engages the baseline's temporal stability. This will be the focus of Chapter 5 on the baseline over time.

Appendix 4.1

Legislation referred to in the legislative study (grouped by definition type)[156]

Type 1—Normal baseline is the low-water line (along the coast)

	Coastal State	Legislation and public source
1	Australia	*Seas and Submerged Lands (Territorial Sea Baseline) Proclamation 2016* (section 7)
2	Barbados	*Territorial Waters Act 1977* (section 4)
3	Belize	*Maritime Areas Act 1992* (section 4)
4	Bulgaria	*Maritime Space, Inland Waterways and Ports Act of the Republic of Bulgaria 28 January 2000* (article 16(2))
5	Cameroon	*Loi n° 2000/02 du 17 avril 2000 relative aux espaces maritimes de la République du Cameroun*^ (article 5)
6	Canada	*Oceans Act 1996* (section 5)
7	Colombia*	*Act No 10 of 4 August 1978 establishing rules concerning the Territorial Sea, the Exclusive Economic Zone and the Continental Shelf and regulating other matters* (article 4)
8	Côte d'Ivoire	*Law No 77-926 delimiting the Maritime Zones placed under the National Jurisdiction of the Republic of Ivory Coast of 17 November 1977* (article 1)

[156] In this Appendix, * indicates a LOSC non-Party and ^ indicates that Google Translate was used to review the legislation.

	Coastal State	Legislation and public source
9	Djibouti	*Law No 52/AN/78 concerning the territorial sea, the contiguous zone, the exclusive economic zone, the maritime frontiers and fishing* (article 4)
10	El Salvador*	*Constitution of 13 December 1983* (article 84)
11	Eritrea*	Maritime Proclamation No 137 of 1953 (article 6) <www.un.org/Depts/los/LEGISLATIONANDTREATIES/PDFFILES/ERI_1953_Proclamation.pdf>
12	Equatorial Guinea	*Act No 15/1984 of 12 November 1984 on the Territorial Sea and Exclusive Economic Zone of the Republic of Equatorial Guinea* (article 3)
13	The Gambia	*Territorial Sea and Contiguous Zone Act 1968* (article 2)
14	Georgia	*Law of Georgia on the Maritime Space 1998* (article 6)
15	Germany	*Proclamation of 11 November 1994 by the Government of the Federal Republic of Germany concerning the extension of the breadth of the German territorial sea* (article I)
16	Greece	*Decree of 6/18 September 1931 to define the extent of the territorial waters for the purposes of aviation and the control thereof*
17	Grenada	*Grenada Territorial Sea and Maritime Boundaries Act 1989* (section 4)
18	Guatemala	*Legislative Decree No 20-76 of 9 June 1976 concerning the breadth of the Territorial Sea and the establishment of an Exclusive Economic Zone*
19	Guinea	*Decree No D/2015/122/PRG/SGG* (article 7)
20	Haiti	*Decree No 38 of 8 April 1977* (article 1)
21	Honduras	*Act on Honduran Maritime Areas 1999* (article 3)
22	Iran*	*Act on the Marine Areas of the Islamic Republic of Iran in the Persian Gulf and the Oman Sea 1993* (article 3)
23	Ireland	*Maritime Jurisdiction Act 2021* (section 6)
24	Israel*	Interpretation Law No 5741/1981 (section 3)
25	Kenya	*Maritime Zones Act 1989* (First Schedule)
26	Kuwait	*Decree No 317 of 2014 concerning the delimitation of maritime areas* (article 2)
27	Lebanon	*Legislative Decree No 138 concerning territorial waters and sea area of 7 September 1983* (article 1)
28	Madagascar	*Decree No 2018-1008 establishing the baselines for measuring the breadth of the various maritime zones under the national jurisdiction of the Republic of Madagascar* (article 4)
29	Mauritania	*Ordinance 88-120 of 31 August 1988 establishing the limits and the legal régime of the territorial sea, the contiguous zone, the exclusive economic zone and the continental shelf of the Islamic Republic of Mauritania* (article 1)
30	Monaco	*Sovereign Ordinance No 5094 delimiting the Territorial Waters of Monaco of 14 February 1973*
31	Namibia	*Territorial Sea and Exclusive Economic Zone of Namibia, Act No 3 of 1990* (article 2)

	Coastal State	Legislation and public source
32	New Zealand	*Territorial Sea, Contiguous Zone, and Exclusive Economic Zone Act 1977* (section 5)
33	Nicaragua	*Ley N° 420—Ley de espacios marítimos de Nicaragua^* (article 3)
34	Nigeria	*Territorial Waters Act 1998* (section 1)
35	Poland	*Act on the maritime areas of the Republic of Poland and maritime administration (Journal of Laws of 2022, item 457)* (Article 5)
36	Romania	*Act concerning the Legal Regime of the Internal Waters, the Territorial Sea and the Contiguous Zone of Romania, 7 August 1999* (article 1)
37	Saint Kitts and Nevis	*Maritime Areas Act 1984* (section 4)
38	Saint Lucia	*Maritime Areas Act 1984* (section 4)
39	Senegal	*Decree No 90-670 of 18 June 1990 on the Drawing of Baselines* (article 1)
40	Slovenia	*Maritime Code 2001* (article 13)
41	Somalia	*Law on the Somali Territorial Sea and Ports, Law No 37 of 10 September 1972* (article 2)
42	South Africa	*Maritime Zones Act, No 15 of 1994* (section 2)
43	Spain	*Act No 10/1977 of 4 January 1977* (article 2)
44	Sri Lanka	*Presidential Proclamation of 15 January 1977 in pursuance of Maritime Zones Law No 22 of 1 September 1976* (section 2)
45	Sweden	*Lag (2017:1272) om Sveriges sjöterritorium och maritima zoner^*
46	Syria*	Law No 28 of 2003 on the Territorial Sea, Continental Shelf and Exclusive Economic Zone (article 1)
47	Tonga	*Maritime Zones Act 2009* (section 4)
48	Tunisia	Decree No 73-527 of 3 November 1973 concerning baselines (article 1)

Type 2—Normal baseline is defined by reference to coordinates

	Coastal State	Legislation and public source
1	Angola	Lei n° 14/10 de 14 de Julho^ (article 6) and Lei n° 17/14 de 29 de Setembro^ (Anexo 1)
2	Argentina	Act of 23.968 of 14 August 1991 (article 1 and Annex 1)
3	Bangladesh	SRO No 328-Law/2015/MOFA/UNCLOS/113/2/15 (section 1)
4	Benin	*Decree No 2021-253 of 19 May 2021 establishing the coordinates for the nautical chart of Benin* (article 6 and 7)
5	Brazil	*Decree No 8.400, of 4 February 2015* (articles 1–2 and Schedule)
6	Canada	*Oceans Act 1996* (section 5) and *Territorial Sea Geographical Coordinates Order CRC, c 1550* (subsection 4(2) and Schedule II)
7	Congo	*Ordinance No 049/77 of 20 December amending article 2 of Ordinance 26/71 of 18 October 1971* and deposited coordinates

	Coastal State	Legislation and public source
8	Cook Islands	*Maritime Zones Act 2018* (section 6) and *Maritime Zones (Baselines of Territorial Sea) Regulations 2020 of 29 September 2020*
9	Costa Rica	Decree 18581-RE, 14 October 1988 (article 1(A))
10	Democratic Republic of Congo	*Law No 09/002 of 7 May 2009 delimiting the maritime areas of the Democratic Republic of the Congo* (article 2)
11	Denmark	*Executive Order No 680 of 18 July 2003, amending Executive Order No 242 of 21 April concerning the Delimitation of Denmark's Territorial Sea* (section 2)
12	Estonia	*Law on the boundaries of the maritime tract, 10 March 1993* (article 3 and appendix 1)
13	Fiji	*Marine Spaces (Territorial Seas) (Rotuma and its Dependencies) (Amendment) Order 2012* (order 5)
14	France	*Decree No 2015-958 of 31 July 2015 defining the baselines from which the breadth of the French territorial sea adjacent to the territory of mainland France and Corsica is measured* (articles 1-4)
15	Iceland	*Law No 31 of 1 June 1979 concerning the Territorial Sea, Exclusive Economic Zone and the Continental Shelf* (article I)
16	India	*Notifications of the Government of India dated 11 May 2009 and 20 November 2009*
17	Indonesia	*Act No 6 of 8 August 1996 regarding Indonesian Waters* (article 5) and *the list of geographical coordinates of points of the Indonesian archipelagic baselines based on the government regulation of the Republic of Indonesia number 38 of 2002 as amended by the government regulation of the Republic of Indonesia number 37 of 2008*
18	Kiribati	*Maritime Zones (Declaration) Act 2011* (section 4(1)) and *Territorial Sea Baselines of Kiribati Regulations 2014*
19	Lithuania	*Annex I to Resolution 1597 of 6 December 2004 of the Government of the Republic of Lithuania* (table 1)
20	Marshall Islands	*Maritime Zones Declaration Act 2016* and *Baselines and Maritime Zones Outer Limit Declaration 2016* (Part 2)
21	Mauritius	*Maritime Zones Act 2005* and *Maritime Zones (Baselines and Closing Lines) Regulations 2024*
22	Micronesia	*Permanent Regulation on Maritime Boundaries and Maritime Zones of the Federated States of Micronesia Pursuant to 18 FSMC 101, 102, 104, 105A and 107, As Amended by Public Law No 19-172* (Part I, Annex I Title 18 of the FSM Code (Annotated)) and Permanent Regulation on Maritime Boundaries and Maritime Zones of the Federated States of Micronesia Pursuant to 18 FSMC 101, 102, 104, 105A and 107, as amended by Public Law No 19-172.
23	Nauru	*Sea Boundaries Act 1997* (section 2) and *Sea Boundaries Proclamation 1997* (schedule)
24	Niue	*Maritime Zones Act 2013* (section 4) and *Territorial Sea Baselines Notice* 2013

	Coastal State	Legislation and public source
25	Norway (Jan Mayen)	*Royal Decree of 30 August 2002 pursuant to the Constitution of Norway of 17 May 1814 and Royal Decree of 22 February 1812* (§ 2)
26	Palau	*Maritime Boundary Contention 2008*
27	Papua New Guinea	*Maritime Zones Act 2015* (Section 4 and Schedule 1)
28	Peru*	*Ley No 28621^* (2005) (Anexo 1)
29	Samoa	*Maritime Zones Act 1999* (section 2) and *Maritime Zones Order* 2017
30	Saudi Arabia	*Royal Decree No 33 of 16 February 1958* (article 5) and *Royal Decree No M/4 dated 12 January 2010* (coordinates and illustrative chart)
31	Seychelles	*Maritime Zones Act 1999* (section 3) and *Maritime Zones (Baselines) Order, 2008* (SI 88 of 2008) (Schedule 2)
32	State of Palestine	*Declaration of the State of Palestine regarding the maritime boundaries of the State of Palestine in accordance with the United Nations Convention of the Law of the Sea, 24 September 2019* (article 2)
33	Togo	Ordinance No 24 delimiting the Territorial Waters and creating a protected Economic Maritime Zone of 16 August 1977 (article 1) and deposited coordinates
34	Tuvalu	Maritime Zones Act 2012 (section 7) and Declaration of Territorial Sea Baselines 2012
35	Ukraine	*Statute of Ukraine concerning the State frontier, 4 November 1991* (article 5) and *List of geographical coordinates of points defining the baselines for measuring the breadth of the territorial sea, exclusive economic zone and the continental shelf in the Black Sea*
36	Uruguay	*Act 17.033 of 20 November 1998 establishing the boundaries of the territorial sea, the adjacent zone, the exclusive economic zone, and the continental shelf* (article 14 and Annex I)
37	Vanuatu	*Maritime Zones Act 2010* (section 7(2)(b)) and *Ministerial Order No 81 of 29 July 2009*

Type 3—Normal baseline is the low-water line as marked on charts

	Coastal State	Legislation and public source
1	Angola	Lei nº 14/10 de 14 de Julho^ (article 6)
2	Argentina	Act No 23.968 of 14 August 1991 (article 1 and Annex II) and deposited charts
3	Bangladesh	SRO No 328-Law/2015/MOFA/UNCLOS/113/2/15 (section 1)
4	Belgium	Act establishing the breadth of the territorial sea of Belgium, 6 October 1987
5	Brazil	*Decree No 8.400, of 4 February 2015* (article 2)

	Coastal State	Legislation and public source
6	Croatia	*Pomorski Zakonik^* (2004) (article 18(3))
7	Gabon	*Decree 002066/PR/MHCUCDM of 4 December 1992* (article 3)
8	Ghana	Maritime Zones (Delimitation) Law 1986 (section 1)
9	Guyana	*Maritime Zones Act 2010* (section 2 and 5)
10	India	*Notifications of the Government of India dated 11 May 2009* (paragraph (a))
11	Italy	*Presidential Decree No 816 implementing Act of 8 December 1961, No 1658, concerning the accession and implementation of the Convention on Territorial Sea and Contiguous Zone, adopted in Geneva on 29 April 1958^*
12	Japan	*Enforcement Order of the Law on the Territorial Sea and the Contiguous Zone* (Cabinet Order No 210 of 1977, as amended by Cabinet Order No 383 of 1993, Cabinet Order No 206 of 1996 and Cabinet Order No 434 of 2001) (article 2(6))
13	Republic of Korea	*Territorial Sea and Contiguous Zone Act*, promulgated on 31 December 1977, amended by Law No 14607, which was promulgated on 21 March 2017 (article 2)
14	Liberia	*Executive Order 48* (section 1)
15	Mexico	*Federal Act relating to the Sea, 8 January 1986* (articles 26 and 39)
16	Mozambique	*Mozambique Council of Ministers Decree Law No 31/76 of 19 August 1976* (article 1)
17	Netherlands	Netherlands Territorial Sea (Demarcation) Act of 9 January 1985 (section 1)
18	Palau	Palau National Code (section 141)
19	Portugal	Lei nº 34/2006^ (article 5)
20	Russian Federation	*Federal Act on the internal maritime waters, territorial sea and contiguous zone of the Russian Federation (1998)* (article 4)
21	Sierra Leone	Maritime Zones (Establishment) Decree, 1996 (article 2)
22	Solomon Islands	*Delimitation of Marine Waters Act, 1978* (section 2)
23	Sudan	*Territorial Waters and Continental Shelf Act, 1970* (section 6(1)(a))
24	Suriname	*Act regulating the Maritime Zones of the Republic of Suriname and amending the Offshore Fisheries Act 1980* (article 1(c))
25	Tanzania	*Territorial Sea and Exclusive Economic Zone Act, as amended by the Written Laws (Miscellaneous Amendment) No 2 Act* (section 5)
26	Timor-Leste	*Law No 7/2002 Maritime Borders of the Territory of the Democratic Republic of Timor-Leste* (article 1)
27	Türkiye*	*Act No 2674 of 20 May 1982, on the Territorial Sea of the Republic of Türkiye* (article V)
28	Venezuela*	Aquatic Areas Organic Act Decree No 1,446 of 17 November 2014 (article 9)
29	Yemen	Law No 37/1991 concerning the Territorial Sea, Contiguous Zone, Exclusive Economic Zone and Continental Shelf (article 4)

Type 4—Normal baseline is determined in accordance with international law

	Coastal State	**Legislation and public source**
1	Australia	*Proclamation under Seas and Submerged Lands Act 1973 made under section 10B of the Seas and Submerged Lands Act 1973* (paragraph (a)(2))
2	Qatar	*Decree No 40 of 1992 defining the Breadth of the Territorial Sea and Contiguous Zone of the State of Qatar, 16 April 1992*
3	United Kingdom	*Territorial Sea (Baselines) Order 2014* (article 2(1))
4	USA*	*Territorial Sea of the United States of America By the President of the United States of America A Proclamation of 27 December 1988*

5
Temporal Stability
Baseline Change Over Time

5.1 Introduction

This chapter now examines the *temporal* element of the legal stability of maritime zones, as introduced in Chapter 3: once a baseline is established, do coastal States revisit that baseline over time? If so, how, and under what circumstances?

Among the three elements of the legal stability of maritime zones identified in this book, this was the sole element mentioned in *Obligations of States in Respect of Climate Change*, in which the ICJ stated its view that 'the provisions of UNCLOS do not require States parties, in the context of physical changes resulting from climate-change related sea level rise, to update their charts or lists of geographical co-ordinates that show the baselines and outer limit lines of their maritime zones once they have been duly established in conformity with the Convention. For this reason, States parties to UNCLOS are under no obligation to update such charts or lists of geographical co-ordinates.'[1] However, this view is at odds with the long-dominant ambulatory theory of baselines in scholarship, and the reasoning of the Court leaves unclear how it has arrived at this interpretation of the United Nations Convention on the Law of the Sea (LOSC), and what role was played by the State practice it identified. This chapter tests the robustness of the Court's conclusion (as well as this dimension of the ambulatory theory of baselines) by identifying a broader body of relevant State practice and evaluating that practice through the framework of treaty interpretation reflected in the Vienna Convention on the Law of Treaties (VCLT).

To begin, Section 5.2 presents the first globally representative study examining the baselines of coastal States over time. Its findings (in Section 5.2.2)

[1] *Obligations of States in respect of Climate Change* (Advisory Opinion) [2025] [362] (*Obligations of States in respect of Climate Change*) <https://www.icj-cij.org/case/187>.

Sea-Level Rise and the Legal Stability of Maritime Zones. Frances Anggadi, Oxford University Press.
 DOI: 10.1093/9780198973515.003.0005

include that practice varies as to whether or not coastal States take legislative action amending established baselines; and that there are few if any commonalities among the circumstances where such baseline change does occur. Following the approach taken in Chapter 4, Section 5.3 then moves to consider the legal significance of these findings for the relevant rules of international law. Revisiting the scholarship on the nature of the baseline, Section 5.3.3 focuses on the question of an implied duty to update baselines, arguing that insufficient justification can be found to support the implication of a positive duty to update baselines by application of the general rule of treaty interpretation. While the study's findings should be regarded as State practice relevant to the interpretation of the LOSC, the chapter concludes that variations in the conduct and statements of coastal States mean that there is insufficient basis for the implication of a duty on coastal States to update established baselines. Rather, there is increasing support for the opposite proposition, that the absence of a duty to update established baselines means that they may be preserved over time. For these reasons, the chapter concludes that the existing law of baselines can accommodate a temporal dimension of legal stability, allowing for the maintenance of established baselines over time, without review.

5.2 The baseline change study

The phenomenon of baseline change remains understudied as a concept and in practice. This chapter uses the term 'baseline change' to mean where a coastal State has taken action that has the effect of bringing about a change relating to an established baseline. Little has been written on the practice of States in updating baselines once they have been established. Trümpler observes that publicized coordinates seem to be rarely updated, commenting that:

> [t]his may be an indication that States are willing to accept a less frequent updating of charts and associated basepoints as a 'price' for the legal certainty gained by publication; though a conclusive study of State practice in this particular regard is yet to be undertaken.[2]

Most visible is the practice of the Netherlands and the United States. Through well-publicized national practice and official statements, it is well known that

[2] Kai Trümpler, 'Article 5—Normal Baseline' in Alexander Proelss (ed), *United Nations Convention on the Law of the Sea: A Commentary* (1st edn, CH Beck 2017) 60.

these are coastal States which have a rigorous coastal survey practice as well as internal policy for baseline review. This practice will be considered below in Section 5.2.2. But is this practice typical of coastal States generally? The baseline change study presented in this chapter aims to improve understanding on this issue by presenting a snapshot of State practice on baseline change. This study is designed to observe baseline change effected by legislative action: that is, where a coastal State has taken legislative action that has the effect of bringing about a change in the location of an established baseline.

The case study in Chapter 4 examined the national legislation of 153 coastal States[3] to discover similarities and differences in the approach to defining the normal baseline at a single point in time. However, given the difficulty of tracking the baselines of the same 153 coastal States over a period of time, the baseline change study uses the concept of the 'low elevation coastal zone' (LECZ) as a basis to select a smaller subset of coastal States to examine. McGranahan et al define the LECZ as 'the contiguous area along the coast that is less than 10 metres above sea level. Overall, this zone covers two per cent of the world's land area but contains 10% of the world's population and 13% of the world's urban population.'[4] The IPCC relies on the concept of the LECZ in the context of its findings on 'low lying islands and coasts' (LLIC)—defined as certain islands, megacities, and deltas within the LECZ—which it observes 'are already experiencing the impacts of climate-related changes to the ocean and cryosphere, for both extreme events and slow onset changes, due to their low elevation, narrow ecological zonation, climate sensitive ecosystems and natural resources, as well as increasing anthropogenic pressures'.[5] The IPCC's Special Report on the Oceans and the Cryosphere in a Changing Climate observes that 'LLIC are particularly at risk from climate-related changes to the ocean and the cryosphere, whether they are urban or rural, continental or island, at any latitude and regardless of level of development',[6] and these risks result in multiple and compound effects, including shoreline change.[7] For these reasons, this study also uses the concept of the LECZ to narrow its inquiry on baseline change because these are the coastal States which have experienced

[3] For a discussion of how the figure of 153 coastal States is derived, see Section 4.2.1, which discusses this question in terms of the design of legislative study.

[4] Gordon McGranahan, Deborah Balk, and Bridget Anderson, 'The Rising Tide: Assessing the Risks of Climate Change and Human Settlements in Low Elevation Coastal Zones' (2007) 19 Environment and Urbanization 17.

[5] AK Magnan and others, 'Cross-Chapter Box 9: Integrative Cross-Chapter Box on Low-Lying Islands and Coasts' in H-O Pörtner and others (eds), *IPCC Special Report on the Ocean and Cryosphere in a Changing Climate* (2019) 658.

[6] ibid 667.

[7] ibid (see Table CB9.1 and preceding discussion).

shoreline change at least in part due to their low elevation; for the same reason, they are also likely to be at increased risk of future shoreline changes as well.

This study draws on three existing studies of countries in the LECZ to define its sample. First, Neumann et al identified the 'top 25 countries with the highest LECZ population in the year 2000', representing the countries likely to experience population-level impacts of coastal change, and also most likely to contribute anthropogenic factors to such change.[8] McGranahan et al also undertook a similar study on population, including those countries with the greatest *share* of population in the LECZ, including smaller populations. The third study (also by McGranahan et al) identified the countries with the greatest share of land area in the LECZ. Since population and land area are two key reasons why the LECZ is a useful category,[9] this case study proceeds on the basis of a compilation of those countries identified by Neumann et al and McGranahan et al (some countries having been identified in both). If Cayman Islands, French Polynesia, and Turks and Caicos are set aside on the basis that they are neither UN Member States nor LOSC Parties,[10] this yields a sample size of *thirty-eight coastal States* which rank highly in terms of the proportion of their population or land area in the LECZ, listed in Table 5.1.

Appendix 5.1 shows details of how the thirty-eight coastal States were derived from the Neumann et al and McGranahan et al studies. This sample also includes representation across all UN Regional Groups, developed and developing countries, and usage of all baseline types (normal, straight, and archipelagic), as shown in Appendix 5.2.

For each coastal State, the study asked two key questions. First, it examined whether, after first establishing its baseline, the coastal State had taken legislative action relevant to baseline change in the period 1982–2025.[11] Secondly, if such legislative action had been taken, the study examined the effect of such action (eg replacing coordinates for straight baseline endpoints) and the reasons for taking that action. Similar to the approach taken in Chapter 4, this case study's focus on 'legislative action' is broad, encompassing the enactment or amendment of primary or secondary legislation, and irrespective of whether such legislation may be entitled a decree, order, proclamation, or regulation.

[8] Barbara Neumann and others, 'Future Coastal Population Growth and Exposure to Sea-Level Rise and Coastal Flooding—a Global Assessment' (2015) 10 PloS one e0118571.

[9] McGranahan, Balk, and Anderson, 'The Rising Tide' (n 4) 17.

[10] This approach is consistent with the approach taken in the case study in Chapter 3 to include coastal States which are UN members, with the addition of any LOSC Parties which are not UN members: Section 3.3.1.

[11] This time period was selected as it marks the time between the conclusion of the LOSC (1982) and date of this book (2025).

Table 5.1 Coastal States included in the baseline change study

Coastal States included in the baseline change study *(LOSC non-Parties indicated in italics)*	
Argentina	Republic of Korea
Bahamas	Malaysia
Bangladesh	Maldives
Belize	Marshall Islands
Brazil	Mexico
Cambodia	Myanmar
China	Netherlands
Cuba	Nigeria
Denmark	Pakistan
Djibouti	Philippines
Egypt	Qatar
The Gambia	Russian Federation
Germany	Spain
Guinea-Bissau	Suriname
Guyana	Thailand
India	Tuvalu
Indonesia	UK
Italy	*United States*
Japan	Viet Nam

The rationale for focusing on 'legislative action' is that it is often the most visible manifestation of a coastal State's implementation of the baseline, therefore offering the optimal point of comparison among coastal States. However, 'legislative action' by definition does not encompass other actions of a coastal State which may relate to its baseline, such official statements claiming baselines in a certain area,[12] or actions of a national hydrographic service to update official navigational charts. Since these actions are also important to consider in relation to baseline change, Section 5.2.2 complements the findings of the

[12] eg China has made official statements referring to straight baselines in relation to 'Dongsha Qundao, Xisha Qundao, Zhongsha Qundao, Nansha Qundao and all the other islands belonging to China': People's Republic of China, 'China Adheres to the Position of Settling Through Negotiation the Relevant Disputes Between China and the Philippines in the South China Sea' <www.fmprc.gov.cn/mfa_eng/wjdt_665385/2649_665393/201607/t20160713_679474.html#:~:text=China%20has%20conducted%20consultations%20with,and%20properly%20managing%20relevant%20disputes.&text=74> . These areas are not otherwise specified in China's relevant legislation.

case study with a discussion of selected coastal States' non-legislative actions (particularly as they relate to cases of legislative inaction).

5.2.1 Findings on baseline change

Of the thirty-eight coastal States, the case study identified eighteen coastal States which show evidence of baseline change in the period 1982–2025. The remaining twenty coastal States did not show evidence of such baseline change. These groupings are summarized in Table 5.2.

The following section first discusses these findings of baseline change, followed by a consideration of situations in which there was no evidence of legislative action effecting baseline change.

5.2.1.1 Where there is evidence of legislative action effecting baseline change

It is immediately apparent that there is no single circumstance or characteristic common to the eighteen coastal States which have taken legislative action to revisit their baseline following its establishment. This group of coastal States spans all UN geographic regions, includes developed and developing countries, and usage of all three baseline types. All such legislative actions in this grouping are detailed in Appendix 5.3.[13]

Nevertheless, some smaller clusters of similar practice emerged. Some coastal States undertook actions to review or update their baselines in connection with the implementation of the LOSC. The clearest example of this may

Table 5.2 Findings in relation to legislative actions effecting baseline change

Coastal States which took legislative actions effecting baseline change	**Coastal States which did not take legislative action effecting baseline change**
(LOSC non-Parties indicated in italics)	
Brazil, China, Denmark, Guinea-Bissau, Guyana, Indonesia, Japan, Republic of Korea, Malaysia, Marshall Islands, Mexico, Myanmar, Philippines, Qatar, Suriname, Thailand, Tuvalu, United Kingdom	Argentina, Bahamas, Bangladesh, Belize, *Cambodia*, Cuba, Djibouti, Egypt, The Gambia, Germany, India, Italy, Maldives, Netherlands, Nigeria, Pakistan, Russian Federation, Spain, *United States*, Viet Nam

[13] See Appendix 5.3 for details of all legislative actions undertaken by eighteen coastal States. Full URL references to relevant legislation are included in that Appendix.

be seen in the United Kingdom's Territorial Sea (Baselines) Order 2014, which provides that 'the baselines from which the breadth of the territorial sea adjacent to the United Kingdom, the Channel Islands and the Isle of Man shall be established in accordance with the relevant provisions of the United Nations Convention on the Law of the Sea',[14] amending an earlier provision which had simply referred to the low-water line along the coast.[15] Japan's 1996 amendment introduced the term 'straight baseline' to its baseline system,[16] providing specifically that '(s)traight baselines referred to in the preceding paragraph shall be prescribed by Cabinet Order, in accordance with article 7 of the United Nations Convention on the Law of the Sea'.[17] Indonesia and the Philippines amended particular points in their baseline systems to bring them into conformity with the LOSC, including the technical requirements of Article 47.[18]

Some coastal States have taken legislative action directed to improving the accuracy of their baselines.[19] In 2003, Denmark updated coordinates for its normal and straight baselines (as well as outer limits of the territorial sea), and explained that 'the new coordinates represent a technical improvement reflecting more precisely the positions of the relevant geographical points'.[20]

[14] art 2(1).

[15] Territorial Waters Order in Council 1964 (United Kingdom) art 2(1).

[16] Law on the Territorial Sea and the Contiguous Zone (Law no 30 of 1977, as amended by Law no 73 of 1996) art 2(1).

[17] ibid art 2(2). This amendment was also accompanied by Cabinet Order no 206 of 1996 giving coordinates for straight baseline segments.

[18] See list of geographical coordinates of points of the Indonesian archipelagic baselines based on the Government Regulation of the Republic of Indonesia no 38 of 2002 as amended by the Government Regulation of the Republic of Indonesia no 37 of 2008, discussed in Clive Schofield and I Made Andi Arsana, 'Closing the Loop: Indonesia's Revised Archipelagic Baselines System' (2009) 1 Australian Journal of Maritime & Ocean Affairs 57. In relation to the Philippines' baseline legislation, see Republic Act no 9522: An Act to amend Certain Provisions of Republic Act no 3046, as amended by Republic Act no 5446, to Define the Archipelagic Baselines of the Philippines, and for Other Purposes (Philippines), discussed in Solomon F Lumba, 'The Philippines Archipelagic Baselines Law' (2009) 2 Journal of East Asia and International Law 296 and Jay L Batongbacal, 'The Maritime Territories and Jurisdictions of the Philippines and the United Nations Convention on the Law of the Sea' (2001) 76 Philippines Law Journal 123. See also Republic of the Philippines, 'Inputs on the International Law Commission's Subtopic of "Sea-Level Rise in relation to International Law"' (18 July 2022) (2022 Philippines ILC Submission). It appears there is some difference of views as to whether Republic Act no 3046 established archipelagic baselines or a form of straight baselines. The Philippines' archipelagic baseline was confirmed in the 2024 Republic Act no 120641: An Act Declaring the Maritime Zones under the Jurisdiction of the Philippines (Philippines Maritime Zones Act).

[19] The study has included Malaysia in this group, since the Baselines of Maritime Zones (Declaration of Geographical Coordinates of Base Points) Order 2022 is generally understood to confirm Malaysia's straight baseline system, setting out the coordinates of its turning points for the first time: see Clive Schofield and Robert van de Poll, 'Claims to Straight Baselines in the Asia-Pacific: Contrary to Customary International Law?' (2022) 7 Asia-Pacific Journal of Ocean Law and Policy 313 and Leonardo Bernard, 'The Straits of Malacca and Singapore' (2023) Melbourne Asia Review <https://melbourneasiareview.edu.au/the-straits-of-malacca-and-singapore/?print=pdf>.

[20] Circular Note Addressed to Heads of Mission Accredited to Denmark (12 August 2003), reproduced in Law of the Sea Bulletin no 53, relating to Executive Order no 680 of 18 July 2003, amending Executive Order no 242 of 21 April 1999: p 44.

Similarly, the explanatory memorandum accompanying Suriname's 2018 Maritime Zones Act[21] clarifies that, 'in view of the importance of the baseline for the purposed of defining the extent of Suriname's maritime zones, it is considered appropriate to give a more precise definition of the baseline':[22] repealing the earlier Law, the 2018 Law defined the normal baseline as the low-water line as marked on official charts recognized by the Surinamese government (specifying also the updated chart numbers), and also provided for new straight baselines. Notably, future updates to the baseline are also envisaged in response to changes in the Surinamese coastline, as the explanatory memorandum also states:

> The low-water line along the coast of Suriname is subject to constant changes. Recordings along the coast of Suriname by the Suriname Maritime Authority will point out these changes and subsequently result in a modification of the low-water line along the coast on the relevant nautical charts. The latter modification may result in a modification of the position of the closing lines in the major rivers of Suriname and the outer limit of the territorial sea, the contiguous zone and the exclusive economic zone of Suriname.[23]

A similar process may also be seen in the 1998 updates[24] to certain straight baseline coordinates for the United Kingdom 'which result from the publication of a new larger scale chart of the area'.[25] Notably, some of these actions appear to demonstrate a correlation between the goal of improving accuracy and a change in the type of normal baseline definition used.[26] While not elaborating specific reasons for the legislative action, Mexico also changed from using a Type 1 definition of the normal baseline[27] to Type 3 (by reference to charts),[28] and Tuvalu similarly changed from using a Type 1 normal baseline to using Type 2 (by reference to coordinates).[29]

[21] Act of 7 April 2017 Act regulating the Maritime Zones of the Republic of Suriname and amending the Offshore Fisheries Act 1980 and the Mining Decree (Maritime Zones Act) 2017.

[22] Explanatory Memorandum, under 'Article 4' (baseline).

[23] Explanatory Memorandum, under 'Article 21' (on due publicity).

[24] Territorial Sea (Amendment) Order 1998 (United Kingdom).

[25] ibid Explanatory Note.

[26] Specifically, the United Kingdom changed from using a Type 1 definition to a Type 4 definition, Suriname from Type 1 to Type 3.

[27] Decree of 28 August 1968 delimiting the Mexican Territorial Sea within the Gulf of California (Mexico).

[28] Federal Act relating to the Sea, 8 January 1986 (Mexico) art 39.

[29] Marine Zones (Declaration) Act 1983 (repealed) s 2; Declaration of Territorial Sea Baselines (2012).

Most of these legislative actions have resulted in a change in the location of the baseline. Most clearly, this can be seen where coastal States have added new baseline segments,[30] or replaced the normal baseline with straight baselines[31] or new archipelagic baselines.[32] There are also several examples where original coordinates establishing the baseline have been revised. In addition to the United Kingdom and Denmark mentioned above, Brazil updated coordinates for its baseline system in 2004[33] and again in 2015,[34] affecting both straight and normal baselines. Both were updates of original baseline coordinates from 1994, with a view to supporting Brazil's Submission to the Commission on the Limits of the Continental Shelf.[35]

5.2.1.2 Where there is no evidence of legislative action effecting baseline change

For twenty out of thirty-eight coastal States,[36] the case study did not find evidence of legislative action effecting baseline change in the period 1982–2025. This group includes those coastal States using normal, straight, and archipelagic baselines, as well as all types of normal baseline definition. Appendix 5.4 lists all coastal States which fall into this category.[37]

[30] eg Guyana added river closing lines in Maritime Zones (Internal Waters and River Closing Baselines) Regulations of 22 July 2015. Thailand proclaimed straight baselines in a fourth area: Announcement of the Office of the Prime Minister concerning straight baselines and internal waters of Thailand Area 4, 17 August 1992. Other examples are the 2024 declarations by China of new straight baselines in the Beibu Gulf (also known as the Gulf of Tonkin) and Huangyan Dao (also known as Bajo de Masinloc by the Philippines; or also Scarborough Reef): Statement of the Government of the People's Republic of China on the Baselines of the Territorial Sea Adjacent to the North Part of the Beibu Gulf (1 March 2024) and The Chart of Baselines of Territorial Sea of Huangyan Dao (Minzhu Jiao) of the People's Republic of China (10 November 2024).

[31] eg Myanmar replaced the normal baselines around Preparis Islands and Coco Islands with straight baselines in 2008: Law amending the Territorial Sea and Maritime Zones Law of 5 December 2008, confirmed in Territorial Sea and Maritime Zones Law (Pyidaungsu Hluttaw Law no 14, 2017) of 17 July 2017.

[32] eg, Tuvalu's 1983 legislation referred to archipelagic baselines, but no such baselines were declared under those laws. Its 2012 laws provided for that framework and the establishment of archipelagic baselines in Declaration of Archipelagic Baselines 2012.

[33] Deposit of the list of geographical coordinates of points defining the straight baselines along the coast of Brazil (2004). Although this list refers only to straight baselines, because Brazil's legislation uses coordinates to link both straight and normal baselines, these coordinates also affect the location of its normal baseline segments.

[34] Decree no 8.400, of 4 February 2015, pursuant to Law no 8.617, of 4 January 1993 (Brazil).

[35] Alexandre Pereira da Silva, 'From Rocks to an Archipelago: The Brazilian Interpretation and Application of Article 121 of the United Nations Convention on the Law of the Sea with Respect to the St. Peter and St. Paul Insular Features' (2020) 51(4) Ocean Development and International Law 330, 346

[36] LOSC Parties: Argentina, Bahamas, Bangladesh, Belize, Cuba, Djibouti, Egypt, The Gambia, Germany, India, Italy, Maldives, Netherlands, Nigeria, Pakistan, Russian Federation, Spain, Viet Nam; and non-Parties Cambodia and United States.

[37] Full URL references to relevant legislation are included in Appendix 5.4.

For those coastal States defining the normal baseline simply by reference to the low-water line (Type 1),[38] no particular legislative action need be taken to result in a change in the location of the baseline. This is the type of normal baseline definition that exhibits an 'ambulatory character'[39] most clearly. However, some of the considerations mentioned in the preceding section (such as technical improvements, or legislative update following the release of an updated chart) might conceivably apply to the sixteen coastal States that define some or all of their baselines by reference to charts or coordinates.[40] In that context, the absence of legislative action to revise such charts or coordinates appears to indicate a kind of 'set-and-forget' approach to the establishment of baselines by those coastal States, and their maintenance over time.

It is certainly the case that for baselines defined by reference to coordinates (whether they be normal, straight, or archipelagic), those baselines will remain in that established location unless the coordinates are changed. So for Argentina, Bahamas, Bangladesh, Belize, Cambodia, Cuba, Djibouti, Egypt, Germany, India, Italy, Maldives, Netherlands, Russian Federation, Spain, and Viet Nam, such baselines established by reference to coordinates have remained in place in the period 1982–2025, strongly demonstrating a temporal dimension of stability. The Bahamas has explicitly explained this aspect of its legislative practice, stating that '[o]nce countries have deposited their maritime baselines in accordance with UNCLOS, they do not update them. This is evidenced by prevailing state practice (including that of The Bahamas in its legislation).'[41]

The same conclusion is not readily available in relation to those coastal States which define some or all of their normal baseline by reference to a chart. This group comprises Argentina, Bangladesh, India, Italy, Netherlands and the Russian Federation. The United States might also be considered in this group because even though charts are not referenced in the United States' baseline legislation, charting practice is central to the administration of its baseline and maritime zones in general.[42] The issue is whether, despite an absence of

[38] Belize, Djibouti, The Gambia, Germany, Nigeria, Spain.

[39] Bogdan Aurescu and Nilüfer Oral, Co-Chairs of the Study Group on Sea-Level Rise in relation to International Law, *First issues paper by Bogdan Aurescu and Nilüfer Oral* (28 February 2020) UN Doc A/CN.4/740 (*First issues paper*).

[40] Argentina, Bahamas, Bangladesh, Belize, Cambodia, Cuba, Djibouti, Egypt, India, Italy, Maldives, Netherlands, Pakistan, Russian Federation, Spain, Viet Nam.

[41] The Bahamas, 'Submission to the International Law Commission in regard to "Sea-level Rise in relation to International Law"' (18 November 2024) 2 (2024 Bahamas ILC Submission).

[42] See Meredith A Westington and Matthew J Slagel, 'US Maritime Zones and the Determination of the National Baseline' <www.gc.noaa.gov/pdfs/Westington_Slagel_2007.pdf> and United States, 'Comments of the United States regarding Sea-Level Rise in Relation to the Law of the Sea' (14 February 2020) (2020 US ILC Submission).

legislative action effecting baseline change on the part of these coastal States, changes to the baseline might instead have occurred as a result of changes to the low-water line as marked on charts?

Charting practice is difficult to study. Global efforts to issue and update charts are uneven,[43] and many nautical charts are only available through commercial providers.[44] In this context, it is instructive to examine the Netherlands and the United States, which have explained their approach to baseline change and charts in the context of the International Law Commission's (ILC) study on sea-level rise.

The Netherlands explains that its normal baseline

> is defined by the low-water line along the coast. The Act lays down that the low-water line shall be defined as the line indicating the depth of 0 meters on the large-scale Dutch sea charts issued upon the instructions of the Minister of Defence. [. . .] Due to a high re-survey frequency and a dynamic seabed, the low water line has a dynamic behaviour. Additionally, low tide elevations within the distance of the 12 NM appear and disappear, causing further changes to the determination of the normal baselines. When such a change occurs at a distance exceeding 0.1 NM, the normal baselines are adjusted accordingly.[45]

This approach results in relatively frequent changes to the Dutch baseline,[46] with, for example, the period 2007–19 seeing five changes to the baseline in the Southern North Sea.[47]

The United States describes a similar approach:

> The United States conducts routine surveys of its coasts and evaluates potential resulting changes to its baselines. For shifts other than de minimis ones (i.e., shifts that are greater than 500 meters), an interagency baseline committee reviews and approves any changes to the U.S. baselines. In these

[43] eg the IHO expresses concern about the coverage of large-scale charts in the Western Pacific and Oceania: IHO, 'Analysis of the Status of Charting' <https://iho.int/en/analysis-of-the-status-of-charting>. See also IHO, *C-55: Status of Hydrographic Surveying and Charting Worldwide* (*C-55*).

[44] See eg guidance in relation to Dutch charts: Netherlands Ministry of Defence, 'Nautical Charts' <https://english.defensie.nl/topics/hydrography/nautical-products/nautical-charts>.

[45] Kingdom of the Netherlands, 'Submission of the Netherlands to the International Law Commission' (27 December 2019) (2019 Netherlands ILC Submission).

[46] The Netherlands' Hydrographic Service publishes details of its baseline changes, indicating changes every year in the period 2020–25: Netherlands Ministry of Defence, 'Maritime Limits and Boundaries' <https://english.defensie.nl/topics/hydrography/maritime-limits-and-boundaries>.

[47] 2019 Netherlands ILC Submission (n 45) Annex II.

instances, any associated changes to the outer limits of maritime zones are also made on official charts.[48]

While no similar information was identified in relation to the charting practice of Argentina, Bangladesh, India, Italy, and the Russian Federation, the International Hydrographic Organization (IHO)'s survey[49] indicates that all of these coastal States have a reasonable degree of survey and chart coverage, suggesting that they do undertake at least some level of charting update or review.

This means that for this group of twenty coastal States for which the study found no evidence of legislative action effecting baseline change, the significance of that observation depends on the way in which the coastal State has established the relevant baseline. Where the baseline is defined by reference to coordinates, no legislative action may reasonably indicate the stability of that baseline over time. Where it is a normal baseline defined by reference to the low-water line along the coast, no legislative action is needed to result in any change to the location of the baseline, since the location of the baseline is tied by operation of law to the coastline itself. And where the baseline is defined by reference to an official chart, then the absence of legislative action does not preclude possible (perhaps likely) changes to the baseline, as mediated by the domestic charting practices of the particular coastal State.

5.2.2 Discussion of overall findings of the case study

The purpose of this case study was to seek evidence illuminating the practice of States as to updating established baselines.

The case study has found that such evidence amongst the sampled coastal States is mixed. First, the prevalence of baseline change effected by legislative action is variable (eighteen coastal States show evidence of such change; twenty do not). There is no apparent correlation between whether or not such legislative action was taken, and other variables (such as whether the coastal State is a LOSC Party or not; the baseline type used by the coastal State). Even though coastal survey is a resource-intensive undertaking, it was not only developed countries that undertook legislative action effecting baseline change. For example, Indonesia, Marshall Islands, Philippines, Suriname, and Tuvalu are among those coastal States showing evidence of legislative action to change

48 2020 US ILC Submission (n 42).
49 See entries for each coastal State in *C-55* (n 43).

their established baselines in the period 1982–2025. Accordingly, it is not possible to discern any trends fully accounting for which coastal States have updated their baselines and which have not.

Secondly, if we focus on the eighteen coastal States that have updated their baselines, coastal States have given varying reasons (including implementation of the LOSC, improving the accuracy of baseline information, and making additional or new baseline claims). From these, it is similarly difficult to discern any circumstances or trends common to those coastal States which have updated established baselines.

5.3 The significance of the baseline change study for the LOSC

In addition to their practical significance, the book also argues that such findings have legal significance for our understanding of existing international law. Following the approach taken in Chapter 4, Section 5.3 now considers the relevance of the practice identified above as 'subsequent practice' for the purposes of applying the general rule of interpretation set out in Article 31 of the VCLT.[50] Implications for relevant customary rules are considered in Chapter 8.

5.3.1 Baseline change in existing scholarship: is there a legal duty to update established baselines?

For scholars taking the view that baselines ambulate with the relevant low-water line, the idea of examining baseline change might initially seem redundant. From this point of view, an ambulatory view of baselines supplies a complete answer to the question of how, when, and why a baseline changes. For example, Caron argued that 'the baseline[s] . . . [. . .] adjust themselves to a changing coastline';[51] and similarly, Schofield extends the same idea to the outer limits of maritime zones, explaining that:

> the direct relationship between the position of normal baselines and the limits of maritime jurisdiction is potentially and increasingly problematic,

[50] VCLT (opened for signature 23 May 1969, entered into force 27 January 1980) 1155 UNTS 331.

[51] David D Caron, 'Climate Change, Sea Level Rise and the Coming Uncertainty in Oceanic Boundaries: A Proposal to Avoid Conflict' in Jon M Van Dyke (ed), *Maritime Boundary Disputes, Settlement Processes, and the Law of the Sea* (Brill Nijhoff 2009) 2.

> however. This is the case because, just as the coast is dynamic and susceptible to change over time, so too, inevitably, is the location of the low-water line. The implication of this is that as normal baselines change or 'ambulate' over time, so too will the maritime jurisdictional limits measured from them should the critical basepoints along that baseline upon which the outer limits of maritime claims depend be affected.[52]

Arguably, this view of a 'direct relationship' between baseline and coastline aligns well with those coastal States identified in Chapter 4 which define the normal baseline as the low-water line along the coast.[53] However, more prevalent are normal baseline definitions that establish a more nuanced relationship between baseline and coastline, mediated in varying ways by the use of charts and/or coordinates.[54] Where such legislative methods are used to establish a baseline, changes in a coastline will not of themselves result in changes to the baseline unless there is coastal State action to do so. If we also consider that straight and archipelagic baselines are most commonly established by reference to coordinates,[55] this further increases the number of instances in which baselines would not automatically change in response to coastal change.

In an earlier work, Caron acknowledged that the way in which baseline changes might differ depends on how the coastal State has defined the baseline in its legislation. While recognizing that a charted line can remain in place unless changed by the coastal State, irrespective of coastal changes, Caron nevertheless regarded this as a '*practical* matter' which 'does not alter the legal question'.[56] But if the use of charts and coordinates is commonplace in coastal States' baselines, how might this logically connect with the widely held view that baselines are ambulatory, in 'direct relationship' with the relevant coastline? The connection rests on making a normative shift from describing the

[52] Clive Schofield, 'Departures from the Coast: Trends in the Application of Territorial Sea Baselines under the Law of the Sea Convention' (2012) 27 The International Journal of Marine and Coastal Law 723, 725.

[53] Type 1 definitions represent forty-eight of 118 observed definitions (approximately 41 per cent): see Section 4.2.1.2.

[54] Type 2 definitions (coordinates) represent thirty-seven out of 118 observed definitions (approximately 31 per cent), and Type 3 definitions (charts) represent twenty-nine out of 118 surveyed definitions (approximately 25 per cent): see Sections 4.2.1.4–4.2.1.5. Taken together, approximately 56 per cent of surveyed definitions fall into these two groupings.

[55] Noting that some coastal States use place names as terminal points for straight baselines, see eg Decree of 28 August 1968 delimiting the Mexican Territorial Sea within the Gulf of California. The ILA Baselines Committee has found that ninety coastal States use straight baselines; ILA (Committee on International Law and Sea Level Rise), 'Report (Sydney Conference)' (2018) [18] (2018 ILA SLR Report). Twenty-two coastal States have claimed archipelagic status: see ibid [77].

[56] David D Caron, 'When Law Makes Climate Change Worse: Rethinking the Law of Baselines in Light of a Rising Sea Level' (1990) 17 Ecology Law Quarterly 621, 634 (note 76, original emphasis).

practical matter (the way in which a baseline is established) to a legal state of affairs (the baseline *should* adjust in response to a changing coastline) on the basis of a duty to update established baselines. In other words, where a coastal State has established its baseline by reference to a charted line or through co-ordinates, the proposition is that the coastal State is under a duty to effect changes to that baseline in response to coastal change.

Much of the existing literature often glosses over the coastal State action of baseline change in the context of a general statement about the ambulatory character of baselines,[57] or dismisses it as a practical matter that is to be distinguished from questions of law.[58] This may in part be due to an assumption that most coastal States establish their baselines in a way that, more or less, identifies that baseline with the coastline, with the consequence that the baseline changes by operation of law, and without coastal State intervention on each occasion. However, Chapter 4 has demonstrated that global State practice is more diverse than such an assumption; instead, in most cases, positive coastal State action is necessary to effect baseline change. In these cases, are coastal States under a duty to effect baseline change in response to coastal change? What is the source of that duty, and its content? A handful of scholars have sketched potential justifications for such a duty, and these are discussed in the following section.

5.3.2 An implied duty to update established baselines: justifications and critiques

Justifications for a duty to update established baselines fall into three broad groupings. The first, and most straightforward, is that a duty to update baselines is a logical consequence of ambulatory baselines. Stoutenberg states that '[t]he law of the sea requires coastal states to adjust their baselines when the maritime features on which the baselines are anchored disappear [. . .] due to sea level rise'.[59] Hayashi explains that:

> When the sea level rises, *it follows* that the low-water line will normally move landwards, and since the low-water line must be marked on charts in

[57] Some scholars take the view that baselines are ambulatory but do not discuss the role of coastal State action or inaction in relation to that conclusion: see eg AHA Soons, 'The Effects of a Rising Sea Level on Maritime Limits and Boundaries' (1990) 37 Netherlands International Law Review 207.

[58] See eg Stoutenberg's caution not to blur 'the factual existence and the legal consecration of a situation': Jenny Grote Stoutenburg, *Disappearing Island States in International Law* (Brill 2015) 202.

[59] ibid 134.

> accordance with Article 5, the coastal State *is required to replace* the older line with the new one on its nautical charting.[60]

Hayashi applies the same reasoning in relation to straight and archipelagic baselines.

Árnadóttir offers a second line of justification, which is that there is a duty to update baselines to ensure their continued enforceability:

> Unilateral limits are only enforceable as long as they meet legal requirements concerning maritime entitlements. States have an obligation to adjust unilateral limits to changing circumstances. The only exception to that statement relates to continental shelf limits described as final and binding under UNCLOS Article 76(8) because even UNCLOS Article 7(2) (which affords provisional stability to straight baselines) assumes that such limits are adjusted at some point, by the coastal state. Therefore, maritime limits fluctuate in accordance with chartered [sic] lines and those limits are not enforceable unless they conform to the relevant law.[61]

A third justification is that such a duty is supported by the historical development of baseline rules, particularly that of Article 5, which envisaged the possibility of challenge to a baseline on the basis of certain discrepancies with the chart.[62] Lathrop describes what he calls the 'temporarily fixed approach',[63] under which baselines may be fixed by charts or coordinates 'with an obligation to update in the event of significant geographic change'.[64] From this perspective, the fact that the drafters envisaged the possibility of protest where there was either bad faith, fraud, or where a baseline 'depart[s] appreciably'[65] from the low-water line, supports the existence of a duty to maintain a certain correspondence between the baseline and the coastline.

Purcell argues against the existence of any duty to update established baselines, challenging in particular 'what may be the most influential assumption underpinning the ambulatory thesis—the assumption that the conditions set

[60] Moritaka Hayashi, 'Sea Level Rise and the Law of the Sea: How Can the Affected States Be Better Protected?' in Clive H Schofield, Seokwoo Lee, and Moon-Sang Kwon (eds), *The Limits of Maritime Jurisdiction* (Brill Nijhoff 2014) 611 (emphasis added).

[61] Snjólaug Árnadóttir, 'Fluctuating Boundaries in a Changing Marine Environment' (2021) 34 Leiden Journal of International Law 471, 472.

[62] See detailed discussion of the development of art 5 in Section 3.3.

[63] Coalter G Lathrop, 'Baselines' in Donald R Rothwell and others (eds), *The Oxford Handbook of the Law of the Sea* (Oxford University Press 2015) 78.

[64] ibid 77.

[65] See discussion of the proviso in Section 3.3.2.

out in the baselines provisions require satisfaction on a continuing basis'.[66] This assumption may clearly be seen at work in the context of all three justifications mentioned above. Drawing on Judge Huber's reasoning in the *Island of Palmas* case, Purcell argues that there are 'temporal dimensions of the law relating to maritime limits and boundaries'[67] that mean 'the creation of a right and its continuing existence may be subject to different legal conditions'.[68] Where there have been changes to a coast, Purcell contends that it need not necessarily follow that an established baseline should be reassessed to reflect changed coastal conditions. Paying due attention to temporality in this context entails recognizing that the LOSC baseline provisions are directed to a particular moment in time: the time of establishment.[69] Moreover, such provisions are 'largely unconcerned with the question of continuing entitlement to maritime space or the persistence of maritime limits'.[70] From this perspective, the particular geographic characteristics of the coast have legal significance at the time of the establishment of the baseline, and once baselines have been lawfully established, 'the coastal State is not legally required to redraw them in response to subsequent geographical change'.[71]

The suggested justifications for a duty to update baselines are certainly weakened if we do not assume that the geographic conditions set out in the LOSC baseline rules apply on a continuing basis. First, it challenges the overall logic of the ambulatory theory that a baseline must necessarily ambulate in 'direct relationship' with the coast. Secondly, it counters the idea that enforceability is contingent on continued satisfaction of the baseline rules at all times, rather proposing that validity should be assessed according to the law and geographic conditions at the time of a baseline's establishment. Thirdly, it invites us to acknowledge that in the development of Article 5 on the normal baseline, interventions on the possibility of challenge or protest to the baseline did not make clear whether such protest might relate to the baseline's establishment, or more generally.[72] For example, Amado stated that 'if the low-water mark in official charts departed appreciably from the line of

[66] Kate Purcell, *Geographical Change and the Law of the Sea* (Oxford University Press 2019) 216.
[67] ibid 216.
[68] ibid 230.
[69] ibid 248–49. Purcell uses the term 'delimitation' of maritime limits in this context, but it is apparent from the discussion that the situation envisaged is the establishment of unilateral maritime zones by the coastal State. To avoid confusion with third-party delimitation or delimitation by means of maritime boundary treaties, this book continues to use the term 'establishment'.
[70] ibid 258.
[71] ibid 261.
[72] See Section 3.3.2.

mean low-water spring tides, those charts would not be accurate and their validity would be questioned by any legal tribunal'.[73] These and similar comments are ambiguous as to whether they are directed to a specific point in time, and do not clarify whether drafters envisaged that an established baseline should be open to challenge on the basis of geographic circumstances different from those existing at its establishment.

5.3.3 Treaty silence: applying the general rule of interpretation, with caution

In addition to Purcell's challenge to the existence of a duty to update baselines by reason of the temporality of the LOSC baseline provisions, this chapter argues that treaty law presents a further challenge. Since the terms of the LOSC do not themselves articulate that coastal States have a duty to update established baselines, the existence of such a duty must be implied. While some scholars have offered theoretical justifications for the existence of such a duty, insufficient attention has been given to the fact that this invokes a particular understanding of the terms of the LOSC.[74] As such, the existence of an implied duty should be approached as a matter of treaty interpretation, governed by the law of treaties.

Treaty law scholars have offered different views about how to approach a treaty silence. Gardiner considers that the approach depends on the particular issue, 'the nature of the treaty and the interaction of the various elements of the Vienna rules'.[75] In this way, Gardiner considers that the interpretation of a treaty's silence should be treated as a (perhaps particularly difficult) case of treaty interpretation, applying the usual rules (such as context, and object and purpose of the treaty). Linderfalk articulates a 'rule of necessary implication',[76] under which an implied meaning may be reached 'if it can be shown that according to linguistics a meaning can be read into a treaty provision by implication',[77] and that such an implication is necessary to avoid a state of affairs

[73] Gilberto Amado, ILC, 'Summary Record of the 169th Meeting', Fourth Session (1952) UN Doc A/CN.4/SR.169, 172 [33].

[74] As explained by Oliver Dörr, in this situation 'interpretation is always required': Oliver Dörr, 'Article 31—General Rule of Interpretation' in Oliver Dörr and Kirsten Schmalenbach (eds), *Vienna Convention on the Law of Treaties: A Commentary* (Springer 2012) 529.

[75] Richard Gardiner, *Treaty Interpretation* (Oxford University Press 2015) 165.

[76] Ulf Linderfalk, *On the Interpretation of Treaties: The Modern International Law as Expressed in the 1969 Vienna Convention on the Law of Treaties*, vol 83 (Springer 2010) 287.

[77] ibid 291.

not envisaged by the Parties. And some scholars identify a rule of 'implied powers' relevant to the interpretation of treaties constituting international organizations.[78] Others query whether the 'rule of necessary implication' and doctrine of implied powers are so closely connected to the principle of effectiveness in treaty interpretation that it is difficult to clearly discern their separate operation.[79]

Although the principle of effectiveness is not mentioned in the wording of the VCLT, the ILC explained that this was because it considered the principle to be fully captured within the general rule of interpretation, now reflected in Article 31. The commentary accompanying the (then draft) general rule explained that '[w]hen a treaty is open to two interpretations one of which does and the other does not enable the treaty to have appropriate effects, good faith and the objects and purposes of the treaty demand that the former interpretation should be adopted'.[80] This brings us back to Gardiner's impression that interpretation in this context should be regarded principally as a species of treaty interpretation,[81] perhaps warranting special consideration of the principle of effectiveness as embraced within the general rule of interpretation.

However, in dealing with a treaty silence, caution is also needed in recognition of the consensual basis of the treaty text, where inclusions and omissions should be presumed to be the product of negotiation by States Parties. For this reason, Sinclair makes clear that the interpreter should approach an absence of terms with some caution, since it is 'not for the interpreter, under the guise of interpretation, to impose upon the parties obligations which were never in their contemplation at the time they concluded the treaty'.[82] This was also the warning given in the *Aerial Incident* case:

> Undoubtedly, the task of interpretation must not be confined to a literal interpretation of the bare letter of a provision. When a treaty is not clear the

[78] See eg Irina Buga, *Modification of Treaties by Subsequent Practice* (Oxford University Press 2018) 103ff.

[79] Andrew D Mitchell and Tania Voon, 'The Rule of Necessary Implication' in Joseph Klingler, Yuri Parkhomenko, and Constantinos Salonidis (eds), *Between the Lines of the Vienna Convention? Canons and Other Principles of Interpretation in Public International Law* (Wolters Kluwer 2019) 356.

[80] ILC, Draft Articles on the Law of Treaties, with Commentaries, UN Doc A/CN.4/SER.A/1966/Add.l (Draft Articles on the Law of Treaties, with Commentaries).

[81] The fact that some scholarly authorities on treaty interpretation (eg Mark E Villiger, *Commentary on the 1969 Vienna Convention on the Law of Treaties* (Brill 2008)) do not expressly deal with treaty silence tends to suggest that it is appropriate to approach the exercise within the frame of general treaty interpretation.

[82] Ian McTaggart Sinclair, *The Vienna Convention on the Law of Treaties* (2nd edn, Manchester University Press 1984) 140.

> Court is entitled and bound to take into consideration the circumstances surrounding its adoption. However, we consider that it is not within the province of interpretation to re-write a treaty, by inserting into it extraneous conditions, in reliance on realities of which, it is asserted, the parties were fully cognizant and to which they were in the position to give effect by a form of words of utmost brevity if in fact that had been their intention.[83]

This was also recognized in the development of the VCLT, where the ILC explained that 'it is not the function of interpretation to revise treaties or to read into them what they do not expressly or by necessary implication contain.'[84] Indeed, such caution may be seen at work in *Sovereignty over Pulau Litigan and Pulau Sipadan*, when the ICJ was called upon to interpret the 1891 Convention between Great Britain and the Netherlands to determine whether a land boundary provided for in that treaty extended into adjacent waters. Indonesia argued that there was nothing in the treaty to suggest that the boundary line terminated at the coast, and that the treaty 'instead requires a prolongation of the line so far as was necessary to achieve the Convention's purposes';[85] Malaysia argued that 'the plain and ordinary meaning of the words "across the Island of Sebittik" [sic] is to describe, "in English and in Dutch, a line that crosses Sebititk [sic] from the west coast to the east coast and goes no further".'[86] On this matter, the ICJ concluded:

> that any ambiguity could have been avoided had the Convention expressly stipulated that the 4° 10' N parallel constituted, beyond the east coast of Sebatik, the line separating the islands under British sovereignty from those under Dutch sovereignty. In these circumstances, the silence in the text cannot be ignored. It supports the position of Malaysia.[87]

If we take this approach to the LOSC baseline rules—applying the general rule of interpretation with appropriate caution—is there support for the implication of a duty for coastal States to update established baselines?

[83] *Case concerning the Aerial Incident of July 27th, 1955 (Israel v Bulgaria)* (Preliminary Objections) [1959] ICJ Rep 127, 60 (Joint Diss. Op. Lauterpacht, Koo, and Spender) (*Case concerning the Aerial Incident of July 27th, 1955*).

[84] Draft Articles on the Law of Treaties, with Commentaries (n 80) 220–21.

[85] *Sovereignty over Pulau Litigan and Pulau Sipadan (Indonesia/Malaysia)* (Judgment) [2002] ICJ Rep 625 [39] (*Sovereignty over Pulau Litigan and Pulau Sipadan*).

[86] ibid [40].

[87] ibid [42].

5.3.4 Revisiting ordinary meaning, context, and object and purpose

In considering first the 'ordinary meaning to be given to the terms of the treaty',[88] we recall that many scholars have taken the view that the ordinary meaning of Article 5 is that the normal baseline 'is the actual low-water line along the coast at the vertical datum, also known as the chart datum, indicated on charts officially recognized by the coastal State',[89] resulting in the conclusion that 'the normal baseline is ambulatory, moving seaward to reflect changes to the coast caused by accretion, land rise, and the construction of human-made structures associated with harbour systems, coastal protection and land reclamation projects, and also landward to reflect changes caused by erosion and sea level rise'.[90] While such scholars do not elaborate a duty to update baselines as a matter of treaty interpretation (and so do not themselves invoke the terms of the VCLT in their discussion), it might be possible to argue that if baselines are ambulatory, good faith performance of the LOSC baseline rules might require that established baselines be updated. That is, the duty to update established baselines might be seen as a 'necessary implication' to give effect to the obligation in Article 26 of the VCLT to perform treaties in good faith.

However, this book has argued that there are clear signs that the ambulatory theory of baselines should now be understood as outdated,[91] making it problematic to rest any particular requirements of good faith performance upon it. In addition, the ambulatory theory also itself rests on a 'negative implication',[92] positing a broader conclusion about baselines and maritime zones under the LOSC by connecting a silence (in Article 5, for example), with the express terms in Article 7(2) and 76. To establish an implied duty (to update established baselines) on an implied conclusion (that baselines are ambulatory) risks placing excessive weight on matters of implication, especially if not appropriately considered together with other factors relevant to the interpretation of the LOSC (including subsequent practice, considered later in this chapter).

Rather than commencing with an implied ordinary meaning, if we follow Malaysia's argument in *Sovereignty over Pulau Litigan and Pulau Sipadan* that was accepted by the Court, 'the ordinary meaning given to the terms of the

[88] VCLT, art 31(1).

[89] ILA (Committee on Baselines under the International Law of the Sea), 'Baselines under the International Law of the Sea (Sofia Conference)' 31 (2012 ILA Baselines Committee Report).

[90] ibid. See also detailed discussion of similar views in Section 2.3.1.

[91] See discussion in Section 2.3.3.

[92] See Caron, 'When Law Makes Climate Change Worse' (n 56). Purcell has critiqued this particular line of reasoning: see Purcell, *Geographical Change and the Law of the Sea* (n 66).

treaty' is that Article 5 provides that the normal baseline is 'the low-water line along the coast as marked on large-scale charts officially recognized by the coastal State'. Neither these, nor any other terms of the LOSC, specify a duty for coastal States to update established baselines. When considering whether the ordinary meaning of the LOSC baseline rules imposes a duty to update established baselines, the correct starting point is that the LOSC is silent.

Turning now to the second element referred to in Article 31(1) of the VCLT: context. The context of the LOSC as a whole frequently signals the existence of legal duties in express terms. For example, Article 192 provides that 'States have the obligation to protect and preserve the marine environment', Article 100 articulates the '[d]uty to cooperate in the repression of piracy', and Article 56 stipulates that in the exercise of its sovereign rights in the EEZ, 'the coastal State shall have due regard to the rights and duties of other States'. In the context of the LOSC baseline provisions more specifically, there is only one type of duty specified in this way: the obligation of due publicity. In relation to charts or coordinates ascertaining the location of straight baselines and closing lines for bays and rivers, coastal States 'shall give due publicity to such charts or lists of geographical coordinates and shall deposit a copy of each such chart or list with the Secretary-General of the United Nations'.[93] An analogous duty is prescribed in nearly identical terms in relation to archipelagic baselines.[94] In this context, it is perhaps unsurprising that no international courts or tribunals have yet determined the existence of an implied duty in the LOSC in the absence of express linguistic signals ('duty', 'obligation', or 'shall').[95]

On the contrary, even though the ICJ in *Obligations of States in Respect of Climate Change* did not expressly refer to the obligations of due publicity as a matter of context in its interpretative exercise, it did point to relevant provisions as examples in which the LOSC *does* place obligations on States to undertake certain actions in relation to the publication of established baselines and outer limits,[96] concluding that 'the Court observes that UNCLOS does not contain provisions requiring States parties to update normal baselines that have been

[93] LOSC, art 16(2).
[94] LOSC, art 47(9).
[95] The International Tribunal for the Law of the Sea (ITLOS) has extended the previously understood scope of flag State duties under art 94(2) to also include fisheries matters: *Request for an Advisory Opinion submitted by the Sub-Regional Fisheries Commission (SRFC)* (Advisory Opinion) (2015) Case no 21 [119] (*Request for an Advisory Opinion submitted by the SRFC*). In reaching this conclusion, ITLOS acknowledged that 'the issue of flag State responsibility for IUU fishing activities is not directly addressed in the Convention', [110].
[96] *Obligations of States in respect of Climate Change* (n 1) [358]–[359].

marked (Article 5), or to update charts or lists of geographical coordinates showing straight (Article 16) or archipelagic baselines, once they have been marked, published and deposited in accordance with the Convention (Article 47, paragraphs 8 and 9).'[97]

Thirdly, might the LOSC's object and purpose support the implication of a duty? The several objects and purposes of the LOSC (also mentioned in Chapter 4) offer mixed guidance. While also not expressly couched in 'object and purpose' terms, some scholars have advanced strong arguments that ambulatory baselines—underpinned by an implied duty to update established baselines—would promote the aims of the LOSC. Perhaps the strongest line of argument stems from the centrality of the principle that the 'land dominates the sea' to the establishment of the LOSC 'legal order for the seas and oceans'. A further, related argument is that the LOSC baseline rules speak not only of entitlement but also conditions for such entitlement (such as specifying particular geographic criteria). In this way, the LOSC baseline rules also constrain excessive claims, limiting the availability of baselines to circumstances which continue to meet the specified criteria.[98] Both these arguments might be marshalled to support the implication of a duty in that they highlight the close relationship between land and sea at the heart of the treaty's jurisdictional aims. A duty to update established baselines might be argued to be necessary to maintain this close relationship.

At the same time, a duty to update established baselines sits uneasily with the centrality of stability within the LOSC framework, made clear in the views of States during UNCLOS III and affirmed in States' contemporary interventions relating to sea-level rise.[99] If States were required to update baselines to match changes in the coast, this would result in a constantly moving allocation of rights and responsibilities, frustrating the stability and certainty of a global framework of maritime zones. It is also questionable whether a duty to adjust established baselines would promote the goal of the LOSC to 'contribute to the realization of a just and equitable international economic order which takes into account the interests and needs of mankind as a whole and, in particular, the special interests and needs of developing countries, whether coastal or land-locked'.[100] Updating an established baseline involves access to up-to-date surveys of the coastline to detect and measure coastal change, as well as

[97] ibid [359].
[98] See Árnadóttir, 'Fluctuating Boundaries in a Changing Marine Environment' (n 61).
[99] Such views are set out in Section 3.4.
[100] LOSC, Preamble.

requiring resources to reflect that change in the relevant domestic legal system (eg through changes to a chart or coordinates). Resources to undertake these activities vary dramatically between States,[101] and in other situations where there is likely to be a disparity between the ability of developing and developed States to access or secure rights under the LOSC, either the LOSC makes special provision for the interests of developing States,[102] or other mechanisms have been developed to support equitable participation.[103] To imply a legal duty to update established baselines—with the result that out-of-date baselines and maritime zones might become invalid or unenforceable—would frustrate a stable and certain allocation of ocean rights and also be a potential source of inequity among coastal States. These difficulties show that the objects and purposes of the LOSC offer mixed support for the implication of a duty to update established baselines.

In conclusion, these first steps in applying the general rule of interpretation result in an unclear picture of the legal basis for implying a duty for coastal States to update established baselines. Further, proceeding with caution suggests that on balance, insufficient support is available in the ordinary meaning of the LOSC baseline rules, their context, and the object and purpose of the LOSC, to conclude that such a duty may be implied.

5.3.5 Baseline change as 'subsequent practice' for the purposes of Article 31(3)(b) of the VCLT

In applying Article 31(3)(b) of the VCLT in relation to the practice of LOSC Parties included in the case study, it is convenient to recall Gardiner's four elements (also applied in the discussion in Chapter 3): (1) the meaning of

[101] See eg Pacific Islands Forum, 'Submission to the International Law Commission on the sub-topics of Sea-Level Rise in Relation to Statehood and to the Protection of Persons Affected by Sea-Level Rise (Seventy-Second Session of the International Law Commission)' (2021).

[102] eg art 148 provides that 'the effective participation of developing States in activities in the Area shall be promoted as specifically provided for in this Part, having due regard to their special interests and needs, and in particular to the special need of the land-locked and geographically disadvantaged among them to overcome obstacles arising from their disadvantaged location, including remoteness from the Area and difficulty of access to and from it'.

[103] eg the process of preparing a submission to the Commission on the Limits of the Continental Shelf is very resource-intensive as well as requiring technical expertise and potential appearances before the Commission: see Ruth Davis and Quentin Hanich, 'Small Island States and the LOS Convention; 30 Years On: Have the Benefits Been Realized?' (2012) 26 Ocean Yearbook 49. A trust fund was established by the General Assembly to facilitate the participation of developing countries making such submissions: UN Division for Ocean Affairs and the Law of the Sea, 'Article 76 Trust Fund' <www.un.org/oceancapacity/A76>.

'subsequent practice'; (2) that it be in the application of the treaty; (3) which Parties need to participate in the practice; and (4) what is it that establishes interpretative agreement.[104] Elements 1 and 2 are readily satisfied here, since the baseline legislation by definition emanates from the State's legislative organ,[105] and such legislation is directed (either expressly or otherwise) to the implementation of the LOSC baseline provisions.[106]

Elements 3 and 4 are less straightforward. Does the practice of the eighteen coastal States which have updated their established baselines through legislative action satisfy Element 3 as to the number of Parties needed to engage in the practice? As noted in Chapter 4, not all LOSC Parties need to engage in the relevant practice.[107] Citing the example of the World Trade Organization—a multilateral treaty system comparable to the LOSC in its membership—Buga opines that it might be sufficient if 'only some of the parties actively partake in the practice while the rest remain passive and may be taken to have accepted through acquiescence'.[108] Even so, the practice needs to have a degree of representativeness, particularly important for the LOSC because its membership reflects 'opposing interests and views among the parties, categories of which include, inter alia, coastal versus landlocked States, maritime versus non-maritime powers, and developed versus developing States'.[109] Arguably, the requirement of representativeness is met here, so the practice of eighteen coastal States which have undertaken legislative baseline change could be taken into account as potentially relevant subsequent practice for the purposes of Article 31(3)(b).

However, the weight that can be given to this practice is not clear. This is because a group of twenty coastal States displays inconsistent practice (ie twenty coastal States have not updated their established baselines in legislation, compared to the eighteen which have). The ILC suggests that the weight of subsequent practice can depend on the consistency of such practice;[110] indeed, '[i]nconsistent practice may prevent the concretization of the meaning of a rule

[104] Gardiner, *Treaty Interpretation* (n 75) 254.

[105] ILC, Draft Conclusions on Subsequent Agreements and Subsequent Practice in relation to the Interpretation of Treaties, with Commentaries, UN Doc A/73/10, Draft Conclusion 5 (ILC Draft Conclusions on Subsequent Agreements and Subsequent Practice).

[106] As Gardiner clarifies, 'subsequent practice' should be considered after the conclusion of the treaty (rather than after its entry into force): Gardiner, *Treaty Interpretation* (n 75) 261–62.

[107] ILC Draft Conclusions on Subsequent Agreements and Subsequent Practice (n 105) Commentary to Draft Conclusion 10.

[108] Buga, *Modification of Treaties by Subsequent Practice* (n 78) 61.

[109] ibid 74.

[110] ILC Draft Conclusions on Subsequent Agreements and Subsequent Practice (n 105) Commentary to Draft Conclusion 9.

or term'.[111] The existence of at least two groupings of variant practice in relation to updating established baselines means that it is difficult to give great interpretative weight to either set of practice. In contrast to the diversity of practice identified in the legislative study in Chapter 4, here the two groupings of variant practice are not only different from each other but demonstrate opposed, conflicting practice. For this reason, it is not possible to say that practice relating to baseline change demonstrates any 'discernible pattern'[112] of practice overall.

Even if Element 3 could be made out, a greater difficulty arises in relation to Element 4, requiring that the subsequent practice establish the Parties' agreement. The ILC clarifies that this requires evidence of a 'common understanding regarding the interpretation of a treaty which the parties are aware of and accept'.[113] In eighteen coastal States which have updated their baselines, there is little evidence to support the existence of a 'common understanding' that such practice was connected to an interpretation that the LOSC required such updates. The strongest case for such a position might arise in relation to those coastal States that have taken legislative action directed to improving the accuracy of their baselines (eg Denmark, Suriname). The United States and Netherlands might also be included here, on the basis of their policy of updating charts in relation to coastal changes. However, such evidence relates to the practice of only a handful of coastal States, and this seems insufficient to conclude that there is a 'common understanding' (even taken at its highest: among these eighteen States) of the need to update established baselines if coastlines change.

Moving beyond the parameters of the baseline change study, if we consider the LOSC Parties as a whole, it is even more difficult to sustain the claim that there is any 'common understanding' amongst LOSC Parties that there is a duty to update established baselines. This is because an increasing number of States express the opposite understanding: that there is no duty in the LOSC to update established baselines in the face of climate change-related sea-level rise. We recall that the Pacific Islands Forum (PIF) Declaration framed the position of its Member States as an interpretation of the LOSC and relevantly declared that 'the Convention imposes no affirmative obligation to keep baselines and

[111] Buga, *Modification of Treaties by Subsequent Practice* (n 78) 29.

[112] *Japan—Alcoholic Beverages II*, WT/DS8/AB/R, WT/DS10/AB/R, and WT/DS11/AB/R (1 November 1996) (Appellate Body Report) 13 (*Japan—Alcoholic Beverages II*). See also discussion in Section 4.3.3.

[113] ILC Draft Conclusions on Subsequent Agreements and Subsequent Practice (n 105) Draft Conclusion 10(1).

outer limits of maritime zones under review nor to update charts or lists of geographical coordinates once deposited with the Secretary-General of the United Nations'.[114] In similar language, the 2021 Alliance of Small Island States (AOSIS) Declaration affirmed that 'there is no obligation under the United Nations Convention on the Law of the Sea to keep baselines and outer limits of maritime zones under review nor to update charts or lists of geographical coordinates once deposited with the Secretary-General of the United Nations'. The Commonwealth Ocean Declaration expressed the view in similar terms.[115] Taken together, these three declarations represent the views of seventy LOSC Parties[116] on the question of the (non-)existence of a duty to update established baselines.

Moreover, this position has received the support of other LOSC Parties outside the PIF and AOSIS. In 2023, Aurescu and Oral observed that many States across all UN regions have expressed support for the preservation of maritime zones 'with various nuances, both explicitly and implicitly—stressing the absence of an obligation set forth by the United Nations Convention on the Law of the Sea to update the baselines'.[117] As explained by France, the LOSC 'does not provide for an obligation, for coastal States, to re-evaluate and update their baselines. States may update their baselines and their national maritime zone notifications, but they are not obliged to do so ... [...] France does not have any examples of past or recent practice relating to the updating of its baselines because of geographical factors.'[118] In a similar vein, Germany takes the view that there is 'a high level of convergence that UNCLOS does not impose any obligation on coastal States to regularly review or update their baselines, delimitation lines or the outer limits of their maritime zones. [...] Consequently, such baselines, delimitation lines and outer limits remain stable unless and until the coastal State voluntarily decides to update them.'[119] These views can be seen

[114] Declaration on Preserving Maritime Zones in the Face of Climate Change-Related Sea-Level Rise (signed 6 August 2021) <www.forumsec.org/2021/08/11/declaration-on-preserving-maritime-zones-in-the-face-of-climate-change-related-sea-level-rise/> (2021 PIF Declaration).

[115] Apia Commonwealth Ocean Declaration (signed 26 October 2024) <https://thecommonwealth.org/news/chogm2024/commonwealth-nations-adopt-ocean-declaration> (Commonwealth Ocean Declaration).

[116] See Appendix 1.1 for the current membership of the PIF, AOSIS, and Commonwealth.

[117] Bogdan Aurescu and Nilüfer Oral, Co-Chairs of the Study Group on Sea-Level Rise in relation to International Law, *Additional paper to the first issues paper* (Seventy-Fourth Session of the ILC, 13 February 2023) UN Doc A/CN.4/761 [85] (*Additional paper to the first issues paper*).

[118] France, 'Comments and Observations of the French Republic relating to the Subtopic of Sea-Level Rise in relation to the Law of the Sea' (29 November 2022) (2022 France ILC Submission).

[119] Germany, 'Comments and Observations by the Federal Republic of Germany on the Issue of Sea-Level Rise, International Law and its Impact on Statehood' (December 2024) (2024 Germany ILC Submission).

in a significant number of States Parties to the LOSC, including, for example, others of the twenty-seven members of the European Union.[120] No State has yet taken the view that the LOSC places a legal duty on coastal States to update their established baselines. If there is any 'common understanding' to be found amongst LOSC Parties, a much clearer argument may be made for the absence of any such duty, rather than for its existence.

Accordingly, while the case study identified eighteen coastal States' legislative actions that resulted in baseline change of some kind, and those actions should be considered as 'subsequent practice' relevant to the application of Article 31(3)(b) of the VLCT to the LOSC's interpretation, it is unclear whether the practice can be given great weight. Nor are those legislative actions capable of establishing the agreement of LOSC Parties as to the existence of a duty to update established baselines.

Section 5.3.4 concluded that there is an unclear picture of the legal basis for implying a duty on coastal States to update established baselines, and that if appropriate caution is exercised, insufficient support is available in the ordinary meaning of the LOSC baseline rules, their context, and the object and purpose of the LOSC, to conclude that such a duty may be implied. If we now throw subsequent practice into the 'crucible'[121] of the general rule of interpretation, this conclusion is reinforced.

In its reasoning in *Responsibilities of States in Respect of Climate Change*, the ICJ considered that the LOSC did not place any further obligations on States in respect of established baselines and outer limits beyond the obligations of due publicity, and in reaching that conclusion, considered Articles 16, 75(2), and 84(2), and State practice in the form of 'regional and cross-regional declarations, such as, among others, the 2021 Declaration of the Pacific Islands Forum on Preserving Maritime Zones in the Face of Climate Change-Related Sea-Level Rise, supported in 2022 by the Member States of the Organization of African, Caribbean and Pacific States',[122] together with the conclusion of the ILC that there is 'a convergence of views among States across all regions in support of the absence of an obligation of States parties to UNCLOS to update charts or lists of geographical co-ordinates relating to their maritime zones once they have been duly established, in conformity with UNCLOS'.[123] Placed within the framework of treaty interpretation, these might be considered

[120] European Union, 'Summary Record of the 23rd Meeting', UN GAOR Sixth Committee Seventy-Eighth Session (23 October 2023) UN Doc A/C.6/78/SR.23.

[121] ILC Draft Conclusions on Subsequent Agreements and Subsequent Practice (n 105) 22.

[122] *Obligations of States in respect of Climate Change* (n 1) [360].

[123] ibid [361].

evidence of context and interpretative agreement, respectively. When considered together with the findings of the baseline change study presented here, taken as subsequent practice for the purposes of Article 31(3)(b), a robust evidence base exists for the conclusion that a contemporary interpretation of the LOSC does not oblige States to update established baselines and maritime zones in circumstances of sea-level rise.

5.4 Implications for temporal stability under the LOSC

This chapter has examined the *temporal* dimension to an inquiry about the stability of baselines: once a baseline is established, do coastal States take action to change that baseline change over time? If so, under what circumstances?

The answers to these questions play out on two levels. First, the case study observing the baselines of thirty-eight coastal States over time yielded findings on the prevalence of baseline change effected by legislative action. These are observations of fact relating to a particular coastal State's baseline over the period 1982–2025. While no particular trends emerged to fully explain the circumstances in which such baseline change would occur, some of the findings build on those highlighted in the global legislative case study in Chapter 4, insofar as certain legislative choices to implement the baseline (eg through coordinates) have a stabilizing effect in terms of the baseline's position on the Earth (spatial) and over time (able to maintain that position over time, if left unamended by the coastal State).

Secondly, to address the 'international aspect'[124] of baselines over time, this chapter revisited the proposition put forward by some scholars that the LOSC places a duty upon coastal States to update baselines once established. The existence and potential content of such a duty directly bears on the extent to which existing international law may or may not accommodate the maintenance of established baselines over time. This chapter has argued that there is insufficient support for such a duty: as a factual matter, as seen in the practice of States examined in the case study, and as an interpretative matter relating to the LOSC, as examined through the lens of the VCLT's general rule of interpretation.

Making this argument has also demonstrated the likelihood that there is instead increasing positive support for the opposite proposition that legal

[124] *Fisheries (United Kingdom v Norway)* [1951] ICJ Rep 116 [132].

stability is available under international law on the basis that a particular baseline is able to be maintained in the same location over time; or, to use the language of the PIF Declaration, that because there is 'no obligation under the United Nations Convention on the Law of the Sea to keep baselines and outer limits of maritime zones under review nor to update charts or lists of geographical coordinates once deposited', this means that 'maritime zones, as established and notified to the Secretary-General of the United Nations in accordance with the Convention, and the rights and entitlements that flow from them, shall continue to apply, without reduction, notwithstanding any physical changes connected to climate change-related sea-level rise'.

Considering the views of States in what it calls a 'consolidation phase' in relation to the development of State practice relating to the preservation of maritime zones,[125] the International Law Association Committee on International Law and Sea Level Rise (ILA SLR Committee) noted the

> increasingly wide and strong support among States [. . .] that as a matter of interpretation of the LOSC there is no legal requirement for a coastal State to update its national charts to reflect changes in their coastlines brought about by sea level rise. It is however at present still arguable whether this support amounts to sufficient evidence to amount to 'subsequent practice in the application' of the LOSC which establishes the agreement of the parties regarding its interpretation. [. . .] The Committee was agreed that, while there is a broad consensus that the potential negative effects resulting from sea level rise on the maritime entitlements of coastal States, and in particular the low-lying island States, should be avoided, on the basis of the evidence available to the Committee so far, it seems that to date no such agreement has been reached.[126]

The ILA SLR Committee did not elaborate what further evidence it considered might be required to establish such agreement under Article 31(3)(b) of the VCLT (though presumably, the supportive views of a larger number of LOSC Parties would greatly assist). This chapter has argued that evidence of whether or not States take action to update their established baselines—as tested in the baseline change study—is also highly relevant to this interpretative question. Indeed, the approach advanced in this chapter has been to focus on evidence

[125] ILA (Committee on International Law and Sea Level Rise), 'Report (Lisbon Conference)' 7 (2022 ILA SLR Report).

[126] ibid 21.

of baseline change as subsequent practice, and to look to evidence about the views of States for the purposes of assessing the existence of 'agreement' as to interpretation. If this approach is followed, a convergence may be seen between the lack of evidence that coastal States routinely update baselines in response to coastal change ('subsequent practice in the application of the treaty') and the common understanding of well over seventy LOSC Parties which have interpreted the LOSC to mean that there is no requirement to update established baselines ('agreement of the parties regarding its interpretation').

Since this chapter has conducted a baseline change study of only selected coastal States, it cannot of course form the basis for firm conclusions about the practice of all LOSC Parties. However, given the representativeness of the coastal States selected—representing all geographic regions, including developing and developed States, using all baseline types—the findings and conclusions in this chapter clearly indicate the direction of international law on this issue. Namely, that there is insufficient evidence for the implication of a duty to update established baselines, with the result that established baselines enjoy a temporal stability if a coastal State opts to preserve them once established. With the exception of the outer limits of the continental shelf, a coastal State may revise or update its baselines, but not because it is required to do so under the LOSC.

Finally, it remains to consider the scope of the conclusions of this chapter, in particular the extent to which they are conclusions about the absence of any duty to update established baselines in general, or specifically in circumstances of sea-level rise. In selecting the thirty-eight coastal States on the basis of being in the LECZ, it can be assumed that those coastal States have experienced some degree of coastal change, likely for a range of factors that may include climate change-related sea-level rise. However, within that study, there was no evidence to show that baselines were updated for some reasons and not for others; indeed, there was no particular pattern of reasons for a coastal State's choices to update or not, lending support to the explanation offered by France that the LOSC grants coastal States 'room for manoeuvre when it comes to taking the initiative to modify, or maintain declared data regarding baseline and limits of their maritime zones'.[127] This 'room to manoeuvre' would seem to include a discretion not only whether to take the initiative to change established baselines but also for what reason. At the same time, most comments made by States supporting the absence of a duty to update established baselines were

[127] 2022 France ILC Submission (n 118).

made in the context of seeking the preservation of maritime zones notwithstanding sea-level rise.

Accordingly, in contrast to this book's assertion that the LOSC accommodates a degree of spatial stability for all baselines as a general proposition, it is necessary to take a slightly more nuanced position in relation to the temporal stability of such baselines. Certainly, this chapter has argued that there is a strong case to interpret the LOSC as providing for the maintenance of established baselines over time notwithstanding sea-level rise, as this is where evidence of State practice is converging most strongly. However, it is also important to keep sight of the fact that the legal propositions are potentially of broader application too: that the LOSC does not oblige States to update established baselines and that the LOSC gives coastal States 'room to manoeuvre' as to when and why it might opt to revise established baselines.

Appendix 5.1

Baseline change study—selection of coastal States[128]

	Country	Included in Neumann et al (Table 4)	Included in McGranahan et al (Table 3b – population share)	McGrahanan et al (Table 4b – land area)
1	Argentina	X		
2	Bahamas		X	X
3	Bangladesh	X		X
4	Belize		X	
5	Brazil	X		
6	Cambodia	X		
7	Cayman Islands*		X	
8	China	X		
9	Cuba			X
10	Denmark			X
11	Djibouti		X	
12	Egypt	X	X	
13	French Polynesia*			X

[128] In this Appendix, * indicates excluded from the baseline change study because neither a UN Member State nor a LOSC Party.

	Country	Included in Neumann et al (Table 4)	Included in McGranahan et al (Table 3b – population share)	McGrahanan et al (Table 4b – land area)
14	The Gambia		X	X
15	Germany	X		
16	Guinea-Bissau			X
17	Guyana		X	
18	India	X	X	
19	Indonesia	X		
20	Italy	X		
21	Japan	X		
22	Republic of Korea	X		
23	Malaysia	X		
24	Maldives		X	
25	Marshall Islands		X	
26	Mexico	X		
27	Myanmar	X		
28	Netherlands	X	X	X
29	Nigeria	X		
30	Pakistan	X		
31	Philippines	X		
32	Qatar			X
33	Russian Federation	X		
34	Spain	X		
35	Suriname		X	
36	Thailand	X		
37	Turks & Caicos*		X	
38	Tuvalu		X	
39	UK	X		
40	USA	X	X	
41	Viet Nam	X		X

Appendix 5.2

Baseline change study—representativeness of included coastal States

	Coastal State included in the baseline change study	UN Regional Group[129]	Appears in DAC list[130]	Uses the normal baseline	Uses straight baselines	Uses archi-pelagic baselines
		(LOSC non-Parties indicated in italics)				
1	Argentina	Latin American and Caribbean Group	X	X	X	
2	Bahamas	Latin American and Caribbean Group				X
3	Bangladesh	Asia-Pacific Group	X	X	X	
4	Belize	Latin American and Caribbean Group	X	X	X	
5	Brazil	Latin American and Caribbean Group	X	X	X	
6	*Cambodia*	Asia-Pacific Group	X		X	
7	China	Asia-Pacific Group	X		X	
8	Cuba	Latin American and Caribbean Group	X		X	
9	Denmark	Western European and others Group		X	X	
10	Djibouti	African Group	X	X	X	
11	Egypt	African Group	X		X	
12	The Gambia	African Group	X	X		
13	Germany	Western European and others Group		X	X	
14	Guinea-Bissau	African Group	X		X	
15	Guyana	Latin American and Caribbean Group	X	X		
16	India	Asia-Pacific Group	X	X	X	

[129] United Nations, 'Regional Groups of Member States' <www.un.org/dgacm/en/content/regional-groups>.

[130] <www.oecd.org/dac/financing-sustainable-development/development-finance-standards/DAC-List-of-ODA-Recipients-for-reporting-2022-23-flows.pdf>. A country has been treated as a 'developing country' for the purposes of this case study if it appears in any of the categories listed in this Development Assistance Committee (DAC) list.

	Coastal State included in the baseline change study	UN Regional Group[129]	Appears in DAC list[130]	Uses the normal baseline	Uses straight baselines	Uses archi-pelagic baselines
		(LOSC non-Parties indicated in italics)				
17	Indonesia	Asia-Pacific Group	X	X		X
18	Italy	Western European and others Group		X	X	
19	Japan	Asia-Pacific Group		X	X	
20	Republic of Korea	Asia-Pacific Group		X	X	
21	Malaysia	Asia-Pacific Group	X	X	X	
22	Maldives	Asia-Pacific Group	X			X
23	Marshall Islands	Asia-Pacific Group	X	X		X
24	Mexico	Latin American and Caribbean Group	X	X	X	
25	Myanmar	Asia-Pacific Group	X		X	
26	Netherlands	Western European and others Group		X	X	
27	Nigeria	African Group	X	X		
28	Pakistan	Asia-Pacific Group	X		X	
29	Philippines	Asia-Pacific Group	X			X
30	Qatar	Asia-Pacific Group		X		
31	Russian Federation	Eastern European		X	X	
32	Spain	Western European and others Group		X	X	
33	Suriname	Latin American and Caribbean Group	X	X	X	
34	Thailand	Asia-Pacific Group	X		X	
35	Tuvalu	Asia-Pacific Group	X	X		X
36	UK	Western European and others Group		X	X	
37	*USA*	Western European and others Group		X		
38	Viet Nam	Asia-Pacific Group	X		X	

Appendix 5.3

Baseline change study—legislative actions effecting baseline change[131]

	Coastal State	Establishment (type of baseline and legislation)	Legislation effecting baseline change (1982–2025)	Summary of baseline change/s
1	Brazil	Normal baseline – Law No 8.617 of 4 January 1993 Straight baseline coordinates – Decree No 1,290 (21 October 1994)^	a) Decree No 4,983 (10 February 2004)^ b) Decree No 8,400 (4 February 2015)	a) and b): Straight baseline coordinates revised
2	Denmark (mainland)	Normal baseline and straight baseline coordinates – Royal Decree of December 21, 1966	a) Decree No 189 of 19 April, 1978 b) Executive Order No 242 of 21 April 1999 c) Executive Order No 680 of 18 July 2003	a), b) and c): Coordinates revised
3	China	Straight baseline - Law on the Territorial Sea and the Contiguous Zone of 25 February 1992 Straight baseline coordinates (mainland and Xisha islands) - Declaration of the Government of the People's Republic of China on the baselines of the territorial sea, 15 May 1996	a) Statement of the Government of the People's Republic of China on the Baselines of the Territorial Sea Adjacent to the North Part of the Beibu Gulf b) The Chart of Baselines of Territorial Sea of Huangyan Dao (Minzhu Jiao) of the People's Republic of China	a) and b): new straight baselines coordinates declared
4	Guinea-Bissau	Straight baseline coordinates – Act No 2/85 of 17 May 1985	c) Law No 13/2013 on the Maritime Zones Limits of the Republic of Guinea Bissau	a) Straight baseline coordinates revised
5	Guyana	Normal baseline – Maritime Boundaries Act, 1977, Act No 10 of 30 June 1977 (description of river closing lines but no coordinates given)	a) Maritime Zones Act 2010 b) Maritime Zones (Internal Waters and River Closing Baselines) Regulations of 22 July 2015	a) 2010 Act replaced 1977 Act b) First prescription of coordinates for river closing lines

(continued)

[131] In this Appendix, ^ indicates that Google Translate was used to review the legislation.

	Coastal State	Establishment (type of baseline and legislation)	Legislation effecting baseline change (1982–2025)	Summary of baseline change/s
6	Indonesia	Normal baseline – Act No 6 of 8 August 1996 regarding Indonesian Waters (and including enabling legislation for archipelagic baselines) Archipelagic baseline coordinates - List of Geographical Coordinates of Baseline Points of the Indonesian Archipelago (28 June 2002)^	a) Government Regulation of the Republic of Indonesia Number 37 of 2008	a) Archipelagic baselines revised
7	Japan	Normal baseline and straight baselines in Seto Naikai – Law on the Territorial Sea (Law No 30 of 2 May 1977) and Enforcement Order of the Law on the Territorial Sea (Cabinet Order No 210 of 17 June, 1977)	a) Cabinet Order No 383 of 1993[132] b) Law No 30 of 1977, as amended by Law No 73 of 1996 c) Cabinet Order No 206 of 1996 d) Cabinet Order No 434 of 2001^	a) No baseline change (relates to date of enforcement) b) Express implementation of Art 7 LOSC c) Establishment of more extensive system of straight baselines d) No baseline change (amendment relates to effective date)
8	Republic of Korea	Normal baseline – Territorial Sea Law No 3037 of 31 December 1977 Straight baseline coordinates – Enforcement Decree of the Territorial Seas Act, promulgated by Presidential Decree No 9162, 20 September 1978	a) Presidential Decree No 13463, 7 September 1991 b) Presidential Decree No 15133, 31 July 1996 c) Presidential Decree No 17803, 18 December 2002 d) Presidential Decree No 24424, 23 March 2013	a) No baseline change (relates to application of pollution provisions) b) New table of straight baseline coordinates c) Table of coordinates replaced d) Addition of new coordinates for part of the limits of the territorial sea

[132] The full text of this legislation could not be located. For the purposes of this study, its existence and effect were discerned from the legislation in paragraph c).

	Coastal State	Establishment (type of baseline and legislation)	Legislation effecting baseline change (1982–2025)	Summary of baseline change/s
9	Malaysia	Straight baselines[133] – Baselines of Maritime Zones Act 2006 (Act No 660)	a) Baselines of Maritime Zones (Declaration of Geographical Coordinates of Base Points) Order 2022	a) Declares baseline coordinates
10	Mexico	Normal and straight baselines – Decree of 28 August 1968 delimiting the Mexican Territorial Sea within the Gulf of California	a) Federal Act relating to the Sea, 8 January 1986	a) Normal baseline now defined by reference to official charts; straight baselines mentioned but no coordinates listed
11	Myanmar	Normal and straight baselines – Territorial Sea and Maritime Zones Law, 1977, Pyithu Hluttaw Law No 3 of 9 April 1977	a) Law Amending the Territorial Sea and Maritime Zones Law of 5 December 2008 b) Myanmar Territorial Sea and Maritime Zones Law 2017	a) Straight baseline claim for Preparis and Co Co islands b) Consolidation of baseline claims – use of straight baselines only (normal baseline no longer used)
12	Philippines	Straight baselines – Republic Act No 3046 of 1961	a) Republic Act No 5446 of 1968 b) Republic Act No 9522 of 2009	a) Corrects typographical errors b) Declares archipelagic baselines (revoking previous inconsistent laws)
13	Qatar	Normal baseline – Decree No 40 of 1992 defining the Breadth of the Territorial Sea and Contiguous Zone of the State of Qatar, 16 April 1992	a) 2016 Coordinates for bay closing lines	a) New coordinates for closing lines
14	Republic of the Marshall Islands	Normal baseline – Marine Zones (Declaration) Act 1984 (also refers to archipelagic waters, but no archipelagic baselines declared)	a) Republic of the Marshall Islands Maritime Zones Declaration Act 2016 b) Baselines and Maritime Zones Outer Limits Declaration 2016	a) Repeals 1984 legislation b) Declares coordinates for normal and archipelagic baselines; and outer limits of maritime zones

(continued)

[133] The 2006 legislation does not make explicit what kind of baseline Malaysia adopts, but it was widely inferred from the 1979 *Peta Baru* that Malaysia adopted straight baselines; see Clive Schofield and Robert van de Poll, 'Claims to Straight Baselines in the Asia-Pacific: Contrary to Customary International Law?' 7 Asia-Pacific Journal of Ocean Law and Policy 313.

	Coastal State	Establishment (type of baseline and legislation)	Legislation effecting baseline change (1982–2025)	Summary of baseline change/s
15	Suriname	Normal baseline – Law concerning the extension of the Territorial Sea and the establishment of a Contiguous Economic Zone of 14 April 1978	a) Maritime Zones Act 2017	a) Normal baseline now defined by reference to charts; coordinates given for river closing lines
16	Thailand	Straight baseline – Announcement of the Office of the Prime Minister, 12 June 1970	a) Announcement of the Office of the Prime Minister, 11 August 1992 b) Announcement of the Office of the Prime Minister, 17 August 1992	a) Amendments to reflect change in geographic names b) Straight baselines established in an additional area
17	Tuvalu	Normal baseline – Maritime Zones Declaration Act 1983 (also refers to archipelagic baselines but none prescribed)	a) Maritime Zones Act 2012 b) Declaration of Territorial Sea Baselines 2012 c) Declaration of Archipelagic Baselines 2012	a) Replaces 1983 laws b) and c) specify coordinates for normal and archipelagic baselines
18	United Kingdom (mainland, Channel Islands, Isle of Man)	Normal and straight baselines for Cape Wrath and Mull of Kintyre – Territorial Waters Order in Council 1964	a) Territorial Sea (Amendment) Orders in Council 1979 b) Territorial Sea Amendment Order 1996 c) Territorial Sea (Amendment Order) 1998 d) Territorial Sea (Baselines) Order 2014	a) Revises straight baselines (eg Mull of Kintyre) b) Specifies straight baselines for part of southern coast (Southampton/ Isle of Wight) c) Revises straight baselines (eg Mull of Kintyre) d) Revokes and replaces 1964 and 1998 Orders in Council (affecting normal and straight baselines)

Appendix 5.4

Baseline change study—legislation in relation to which there were no legislative actions effecting baseline change[134]

	Coastal State	Legislation establishing baseline (including proclamation of coordinates)
1	Argentina	*Act No 23.968 of 14 August 1991*
2	Bahamas	*Archipelagic Waters and Maritime Jurisdiction Act 1993* *Bahamas' Archipelagic Waters and Maritime Jurisdiction (Archipelagic Baselines) Order, 2008*
3	Bangladesh	*Territorial Waters and Maritime Zones Act 1974* *SRO No 328-Law/2015/MOFA/UNCLOS/113/2/15* (declaring the baseline) Territorial Waters and Maritime Zones (Amendment) Act, 2021.
4	Belize	*Maritime Areas Act 1992*
5	Cambodia*	*Decree of the Council of State of 13 July 1982*
6	Cuba	*Decreto Ley Nº 1 – Establece las líneas de base para medir el mar territorial^*
7	Djibouti	*Law No 52/AN/78 concerning the territorial sea, the contiguous zone, the exclusive economic zone, the maritime frontiers and fishing*
8	Egypt	*Decree of the President of the Arab Republic of Egypt No 27 (1990) Concerning the baselines of the maritime areas of the Arab Republic of Egypt, 9 January 1990*
9	The Gambia	*Territorial Sea and Contiguous Zone Act 1968*
10	Germany	*Proclamation of 11 November 1994 by the Government of the Federal Republic of Germany concerning the extension of the breadth of the German territorial sea*
11	India	*Notifications of the Government of India dated 11 May 2009 and 20 November 2009*
12	Italy	*Presidential Decree No 816 implementing Act of 8 December 1961, No 1658*
13	Maldives	*Maritime Zones of Maldives Act 1996*
14	Netherlands	*Netherlands Territorial Sea (Demarcation) Act of 9 January 1985*
15	Nigeria	*Territorial Waters Act 1967*
16	Pakistan	*Territorial Waters and Maritime Zones Act 1976* *Statutory Notification of 29 August 1996, specifying the baseline from which the limits of the Territorial Waters, the Contiguous Zone, the Exclusive Economic Zone and the Continental Shelf shall be measured*

(continued)

[134] In this Appendix, * indicates a LOSC non-Party and ^ indicates that Google Translate was used to review the legislation.

	Coastal State	Legislation establishing baseline (including proclamation of coordinates)
17	Russian Federation	*Federal Act on the internal maritime waters, territorial sea and contiguous zone of the Russian Federation 1998* *1984 Decree of the Council of Ministers* *1985 Decree of the Council of Ministers*
18	Spain	*Act No 10/1977 of 4 January 1977* *Royal Decree No 2510/1977 of 5 August 1977*
19	USA*	*Territorial Sea of the United States of America by the President of the United States of America, Proclamation of 27 December 1988*
20	Viet Nam	*Statement of 12 November 1982 by the Government of the Socialist Republic of Viet Nam on the Territorial Sea Baseline of Viet Nam*

6

Stability of Legal Status? The Effect of Sea-Level Rise on Maritime Entitlements

6.1 Introduction

This chapter[1] addresses the final element of the legal stability identified in this book, considering whether stability might be available in relation to the status of features under the international law of the sea, and, as a result, also for the maritime entitlements flowing from such status. At a macro scale, questions of legal status arise at a State level: maritime entitlement flows from sovereignty over land territory,[2] which presupposes the existence of a 'State' as the bearer of such sovereignty. Only a coastal State is entitled to maritime zones,[3] while a landlocked State merely has a right of participation 'on an equitable basis, in the exploitation of an appropriate part of the surplus of the living resources of the exclusive economic zones of coastal States of the same subregion or region'.[4] And only an 'archipelagic State'[5] is entitled to 'archipelagic

[1] This chapter develops some arguments that were initially presented in Frances Anggadi, 'The Relevance of Habitability (and its Loss) for the Status of "Islands"' (*Opinio Juris*, 24 April 2023) <http://opiniojuris.org/2023/04/24/the-relevance-of-habitability-and-its-loss-for-the-status-of-islands/>.

[2] This is reflected in the oft-cited principle that 'the land dominates the sea': *North Sea Continental Shelf (Federal Republic of Germany/Denmark; Federal Republic of Germany/Netherlands)* (Judgment) [1969] ICJ Rep 3 [96] (*North Sea Continental Shelf*). More specifically, the ICJ has stated that '[i]t is solely by virtue of the coastal State's sovereignty over the land that rights of exploration and exploitation in the continental shelf can attach to it': *Aegean Sea Continental Shelf Case (Greece v Turkey)* (Judgment) [1978] ICJ Rep 3 [86] (*Aegean Sea*).

[3] This issue arose in the context of various proceedings between Mauritius and the United Kingdom in respect of the Chagos Archipelago, in which Mauritius challenged the UK's declaration of a marine protected area around the Chagos Archipelago on the basis that the UK was not the relevant coastal State which could exercise such rights over those waters: in 2021, the International Tribunal for the Law of the Sea found that 'Mauritius can be regarded as the coastal State in respect of the Chagos Archipelago for the purpose of the delimitation of a maritime boundary': *Dispute concerning the Delimitation of the Maritime Boundary between Mauritius and Maldives in the Indian Ocean (Mauritius/Maldives)* (Preliminary Objections) (2021) (ITLOS, Case no 28, 28 January 2021) [250] (*Dispute concerning the Delimitation of the Maritime Boundary between Mauritius and Maldives in the Indian Ocean*).

[4] LOSC, art 69.

[5] LOSC, art 46.

Sea-Level Rise and the Legal Stability of Maritime Zones. Frances Anggadi, Oxford University Press.
 DOI: 10.1093/9780198973515.003.0006

waters'.[6] At a micro scale, baseline rules specify that only certain geographic features can be used for the establishment of specified types of baselines. For example, a baseline may be drawn on the seaward outer edge of the reef for 'islands situated on atolls or of islands having fringing reefs'.[7] Similarly, straight baselines may be used to join 'appropriate points', but generally not 'to and from low-tide elevations'.[8] In this way, a geographic feature must satisfy the requirements of the relevant legal status (eg 'island situated on atolls') in order to support the use of a particular baseline.

This chapter focuses its inquiry at an intermediate scale, examining how the international law of the sea allocates certain maritime zones to particular categories of geographic features. For example, under Article 121 of the United Nations Convention on the Law of the Sea (LOSC), an 'island' is entitled to the full suite of maritime zones in the same way as 'other land territory', but '[r]ocks which cannot sustain human habitation or economic life of their own shall have no exclusive economic zone or continental shelf'.[9] A 'low-tide elevation', being a 'naturally formed area of land which is surrounded by and above water at low tide but submerged at high tide', has no territorial sea of its own if it is located beyond 12 nm of the mainland coast or island.[10] In this way, the classification of geographic features into certain categories of legal status (eg island, rock, low-tide elevation) is a critical part of determining whether the coastal State has an entitlement to particular maritime zones on the basis of that feature.

As discussed in this chapter, scholars have raised concerns that sea-level rise impacts on islands will destabilize their legal status, causing a loss or diminution of maritime entitlements. These scholars identify two potential causes of such destabilization due to sea-level rise (or climate change effects more broadly): partial or full submergence (resulting in a change in the feature's elevation in relation to the low-water line) and a decline in 'habitability'. However, as is also the case in relation to potential sea-level rise implications for baselines, several States have highlighted that a dimension of stability might also operate here.

[6] LOSC, art 49. There are many more possibilities in the LOSC more broadly, such as 'flag State' and 'port State': see Philip Allott, 'Power Sharing in the Law of the Sea' (1983) 77 American Journal of International Law 1, Annex A.

[7] LOSC, art 6.

[8] LOSC, art 7(1) and (4).

[9] LOSC, art 121(3).

[10] LOSC, art 13; but a low-tide elevation may contribute to the baseline if it is located within the coastal State's territorial sea.

This chapter will assess whether the international law of the sea can accommodate such stability when it comes to the legal status of features. To do this, Section 6.2 examines the justifications offered by scholars for the two causes of destabilization: habitability loss and submergence of features. The chapter argues that such justifications are problematic because, in the case of habitability loss, they overlook the significance of debates on the interpretation of Article 121 arising in relation to the *Philippines v China* Award. Section 6.2.1 connects these debates with scholarship on sea-level rise to demonstrate that alternative conclusions about the legal implications of habitability loss are not only possible but preferable. Section 6.2.2 outlines concerns about the effect of submergence on maritime entitlement, arguing that while the role of elevation is clear in terms of differentiating maritime entitlement between an 'island' and a 'low-tide elevation', this line of justification fails to articulate how the destabilization of legal status occurs. Section 6.3 takes a closer look at what it means to destabilize the legal status of features, arguing that the physical transformation of features does not necessarily entail the legal transformation of status. Crucially, whether such a legal transformation takes place is likely to depend on how a coastal State implements maritime zones in its domestic framework. For completeness, Section 6.4 also briefly discusses sea-level rise and 'archipelagic status', another kind of legal status for which sea-level rise might potentially have implications.

6.2 Interrogating the causes of destabilization: the relevance of habitability and elevation for the legal status of features

Many scholars taking an 'ambulatory' view of baselines[11] have also expressed the concern that sea-level rise will not only cause baselines to shift but also destabilize the legal status of features, resulting in the loss of entitlement to significant maritime zones. Caron succinctly captured both aspects of this concern in relation to islands:

> A rising sea level could taint the freshwater reservoir of an island potentially rendering it uninhabitable, submerge enough of it to leave only an uninhabitable rock, or submerge it entirely. In any of these circumstances, the island

[11] See overview in Section 2.3.1.

state potentially would lose the right to use that part of its island group to extend its exclusive economic zone.[12]

The following discussion contends that although these views (like those in relation to ambulatory baselines) are widely held, it is necessary to interrogate the conclusions they suggest for two reasons. First, fears of a loss of entitlement to an exclusive economic zone (EEZ) and continental shelf on the basis of a loss of habitability are predicated on a contested interpretation of Article 121 of the LOSC. The legal significance of the loss of habitability for maritime zone entitlement must be assessed against the backdrop of this legal uncertainty. Secondly, although elevation has a clear role in differentiating the maritime entitlements of different features, little justification is offered for the proposition that the destabilization of legal status is the necessary legal consequence of sea-level rise impacts in all cases. Each of these matters is discussed in turn below.

6.2.1 Habitability and maritime entitlement: competing views on the interpretation of Article 121

Article 121—the sole provision in the LOSC's 'Regime of Islands'—is central to providing for the differential allocation of maritime zone types in relation to different geographic features. An 'island', defined as 'a naturally formed area of land, surrounded by water, which is above water at high tide'[13] has the same entitlement to a territorial sea, contiguous zone, EEZ, and continental shelf as other land territory.[14] An exception to this is that '[r]ocks which cannot sustain human habitation or economic life of their own shall have no exclusive economic zone or continental shelf'.[15] Such rocks implicitly retain their entitlement to a territorial sea and contiguous zone.[16] Low-tide elevations and 'artificial islands' are not of themselves entitled to a territorial sea (nor a contiguous zone, EEZ, or continental shelf).[17] Despite Article 121 being 'an

[12] David D Caron, 'When Law Makes Climate Change Worse: Rethinking the Law of Baselines in Light of a Rising Sea Level' (1990) 17 Ecology Law Quarterly 621, 638.

[13] LOSC, art 121(1).

[14] LOSC, art 121(2).

[15] LOSC, art 121(3).

[16] Satya N Nandan, Myron H Nordquist, and Shabtai Rosenne, *United Nations Convention on the Law of the Sea 1982: A Commentary* (Brill 2013) 338.

[17] Although a low-tide elevation may contribute to the construction of a baseline if it is located within the breadth of the territorial sea (art 13(1)), and a coastal State may establish a safety zone around artificial islands, installations, and structures in its EEZ (art 60) and continental shelf (art 80).

imperfect compromise with deliberate ambiguity',[18] Symmons explains that the 'general drift' of discussions at the third United Nations Conference on the Law of the Sea (UNCLOS III) is reasonably clear:

> to prevent tiny (and particularly remote) insular features from generating either an EEZ or continental shelf—whether in terms of use in maritime delimitation of overlapping zones of same as basepoints or in terms of independent generation of such zones in their own right, that is, 'entitlement' per se (particularly if uninhabited)—from inequitably limiting or encroaching on such zones generated from mainlands and islands; or, more globally, on the international seabed (the 'common heritage of mankind') where they are far out to sea.[19]

As a result, the legal status of a feature as an island, rock, low-tide elevation, or artificial island is an essential part of determining that feature's entitlement to maritime zones.

Within this framework, the question of habitability arises from the wording of Article 121(3). This chapter uses the term 'habitability' to mean the capacity of a feature to sustain human habitation, as distinct from 'actual habitation'.[20] Habitability loss means the loss of such capacity. Strictly speaking, Article 121(3) only requires the satisfaction of either capacity to sustain human habitation *or* capacity to sustain economic life, although these factors are often interlinked.[21]

Sea-level rise can cause saltwater intrusion (as mentioned by Caron), and its impacts can also be compounded through interactions with other climate change effects, such as increased storms and other extreme weather events. In this more complex (but more likely) scenario,

> the timeline for sustainable human habitation on these low-lying atoll islands shortens considerably. Not only will such flooding affect terrestrial

[18] Myron H Nordquist, 'UNCLOS Article 121 and Itu Aba in the South China Sea Final Award: A Correct Interpretation?' in S Jayakumar and others (eds), *The South China Sea Arbitration* (Edward Elgar 2018) 202.

[19] Clive R Symmons, 'Maritime Zones of Islands and Rocks' in Shunmugam Jayakumar, Tommy Koh, and Robert Beckman (eds), *The South China Sea Disputes and Law of the Sea* (Edward Elgar 2014) 95.

[20] Stefan Talmon, 'Article 121—Regime of Islands' in Alexander Proelss (ed), *United Nations Convention on the Law of the Sea: A Commentary* (1st edn, CH Beck 2017) 874.

[21] See *Philippines v China* (Award) (2016) (PCA Case no 2013–19) [544] (*Philippines v China*). The Tribunal took the view that, in practice, the criterion of 'economic life' rarely (if ever) has an independent role; so if habitability is absent, it is very unlikely that the requirement for 'economic life' would be made out. This reasoning has been criticized by some scholars: see Myron H Nordquist and William G Phalen, 'Interpretation of UNCLOS Article 121 and Itu Aba (Taiping) in the South China Sea Arbitration Award' in Myron H. Nordquist, John Norton Moore and Ronán Long (eds), International Marine Economy: Law and Policy (Brill 2017) 1.

> infrastructure and habitats, but also, more importantly, it will make the limited freshwater resources nonpotable and, therefore, directly threaten the sustainability of human populations.[22]

Storlazzi et al predict that islands with no other source of fresh water will be 'uninhabitable by the middle of the 21st century—not by the end of the 21st century or the middle of the 22nd century as previously suggested'.[23] Sea-level rise and other climate change effects raise a wide range of practical issues for the life of a community,[24] such as how to maintain adequate food security in the face of changing ocean conditions affecting the health and availability of fish, as well as changing crop-growing conditions on land. There are also important social and cultural considerations, including how to ensure physical access to schools and hospitals, and considering whether sacred burial grounds may need to be relocated from traditional coastal locations.[25] Some or all of these factors may contribute to a loss of island habitability as a matter of *fact*, a phenomenon that has immediate humanitarian dimensions and, in the most extreme cases, raise the prospect of community dislocation. Some communities, such as those in the Carteret Islands, have already relocated elsewhere in Papua New Guinea on account of sea-level rise;[26] and the broader legal architecture applicable to the protection of persons affected by sea-level rise is a key focus of the *Second issues paper* of the International Law Commission's (ILC) Study Group on Sea-Level Rise in International Law.[27]

How do these factual risks of habitability loss relate to the legal requirements of Article 121(3)? Some scholars such as Caron suggest a straightforward

[22] Curt D Storlazzi and others, 'Most Atolls Will Be Uninhabitable by the Mid-21st Century because of Sea-Level Rise Exacerbating Wave-Driven Flooding' (2018) 4 Science Advances 1, 5.

[23] ibid.

[24] These examples are drawn from L'Université de la Nouvelle-Calédonie, *Nations of Water* (documentary directed by Géraldine Giraudeau) (2022).

[25] Many of these factors were considered by the Human Rights Committee in relation to conditions in certain Torres Strait islands affected by climate change: Views adopted by the Committee under article 5(4) of the Optional Protocol, concerning Communication no 3624/2019, UN Doc CCPR/C/135/D/3624/2019 (Billy Communication).

[26] Pacific Islands Forum (PIF), 'Submission to the International Law Commission on the sub-topics of Sea-Level Rise in Relation to Statehood and to the Protection of Persons Affected by Sea-Level Rise' (Seventy-Second Session of the International Law Commission) (2021); see also John Connell, 'Nothing There Atoll? "Farewell to the Carteret Islands"' in Tony Crook and Peter Rudiak-Gould (eds), *Pacific Climate Cultures* (De Gruyter Open Poland 2019). Fiji is also making similar plans for community relocation: Kate Lyons, 'How to Move a Country: Fiji's Radical Plan to Escape Rising Sea Levels' *The Guardian* (8 November 2022) <www.theguardian.com/environment/2022/nov/08/how-to-move-a-country-fiji-radical-plan-escape-rising-seas-climate-crisis>.

[27] Patricia Galvão Teles and Juan José Ruda Santolaria, Co-Chairs of the Study Group on Sea-Level Rise in relation to International Law, *Second issues paper* (Seventy-Third Session of the International Law Commission) (19 April 2022) UN Doc A/CN.4/752 (*Second issues paper*).

approach to this legal question: that realization of the factual risk of habitability loss means that the requirement in Article 121(3) is no longer satisfied, resulting in a loss of entitlement to an EEZ and continental shelf. Taking a similar approach, Rayfuse considers that '[p]rima facie, once rendered uninhabitable, an island will lose its exclusive economic zone and its continental shelf';[28] and Rothwell considers the potential conversion of legal status whereby 'a juridical island [becomes] a juridical rock because the feature is no longer capable of sustaining human habitation or an economic life of its own'.[29] Murphy clearly ascribes a causal connection between loss of habitability, change of legal status, and loss of maritime zones:

> A further issue is that with rising sea levels or other events such as increased storms, it is possible that over time an island that is habitable will become uninhabitable. [. . .] When this happens, an island that is not a 'rock' within the meaning of the LOS Convention Article 121, paragraph 3, might become such a rock. If so, then the rock would no longer support either an exclusive economic zone or a continental shelf.[30]

In its 2021 Report, the ILC also pointed to the 'potential significant consequences' of the reclassification of an island to a rock by reason of loss of habitability.[31]

However, this chapter argues that this reasoning—drawing a necessary and causal connection between the factual loss of habitability and loss of legal status and maritime entitlement—rests on a contested interpretation of Article 121(3). Rather than venturing a comprehensive re-evaluation of Article 121(3),[32] the following discussion focuses on a key area of contestation in the

[28] Rosemary Rayfuse, 'Sea Level Rise and Maritime Zones: Preserving the Maritime Entitlements of "Disappearing" States' in Michael B Gerrard and Gregory E Wannier (eds), *Threatened Island Nations* (Cambridge University Press 2013) 174.

[29] Donald R Rothwell, *Islands and International Law* (Bloomsbury 2022) 242.

[30] Sean D Murphy, *International Law Relating to Islands* (Brill 2017) 289.

[31] ILC, 'Report of the International Law Commission covering the Work of its Seventy-Second Session' (26 April–4 June and 5 July–6 August 2021) UN Doc A/76/10 [258] (2021 ILC Report).

[32] There is an expansive scholarship dealing with the interpretation of art 121(3), which has generated debate from 1982 to the present: for a selection of key works, see Barbara Kwiatkowska and Alfred HA Soons, 'Entitlement to Maritime Areas of Rocks Which Cannot Sustain Human Habitation or Economic Life of Their Own' (1990) 21 Netherlands Yearbook of International Law 139; Jonathan I Charney, 'Rocks That Cannot Sustain Human Habitation' (1999) 93 American Journal of International Law 863; Jon M Van Dyke and Robert A Brooks, 'Uninhabited Islands: Their Impact on the Ownership of the Oceans' Resources' (1983) 12 Ocean Development & International Law 265; Erik Franckx, 'The Regime of Islands and Rocks' in David Attard, Malgosia Fitzmaurice, and Norman Martinez (eds), *The IMLI Manual on International Maritime Law*, vol I: *The Law of the Sea* (Oxford University Press 2014); Clive Schofield, 'The Trouble with Islands: The Definition and Role of Islands

literature that is relevant here: in considering the legal categories of features envisaged in the regime of islands in the LOSC, are there two legal categories into which land features should be classified, or three? Or, put another way, does Article 121 set up a two-part model for classifying the legal status of features (island + rock) or a three-part one (island + two kinds of rock-island)? This chapter demonstrates that there is a plausible alternative interpretation of Article 121 supporting a three-part model, and that, crucially, the relevance of habitability for maritime entitlement varies under each model.

6.2.1.1 The two-part model under Article 121: the Tribunal's approach in *Philippines v China*

In the first sustained judicial examination of the meaning of Article 121(3) in *Philippines v China*,[33] the Arbitral Tribunal made clear its view on the relevance of habitability for legal status: '[d]oes the feature in its natural form have the capability of sustaining human habitation or an economic life? If not, it is a rock.'[34] Underpinning this reasoning is the view that there are two kinds of legal status provided for under Article 121 (as illustrated in Figure 6.1): the capacity to sustain human habitation or economic life (HHEL) is what differentiates between a high-tide feature that is entitled to all maritime zones (an island), and a high-tide feature that is only entitled to a territorial sea and contiguous zone (a rock).

Evident in the work of scholars writing both before and after the Award, the conclusions of Caron, Rayfuse, Murphy, and Rothwell on the consequences of habitability loss in the event of sea-level rise are underpinned by the same two-part understanding of Article 121 that we see in the Award: since capacity to sustain HHEL is a precondition for entitlement of an island to all maritime zones, its absence is taken to indicate that the high-tide feature can only have the legal status of a rock, attracting lesser maritime entitlements. Under a two-part model of Article 121, capacity to sustain HHEL functions as the sole fulcrum for the maritime entitlement of all naturally formed high-tide features; its presence (or absence) determines which of the two categories of legal status applies.

and Rocks in Maritime Boundary Delimitation' in Seoung-Yong Hong and Jon M Van Dyke (eds), *Maritime Boundary Disputes, Settlement Processes and the Law of the Sea*, vol 65 (Martinus Nijhoff 2009); Clive Schofield, *The Regime of Islands Reframed: Developments in the Definition of Islands under the International Law of the Sea* (Brill 2021); Karen N Scott, 'Review Essay: Islands in International Law' (2024) 42 The Australian Year Book of International Law 169.

[33] *Philippines v China* (n 21).
[34] ibid [483].

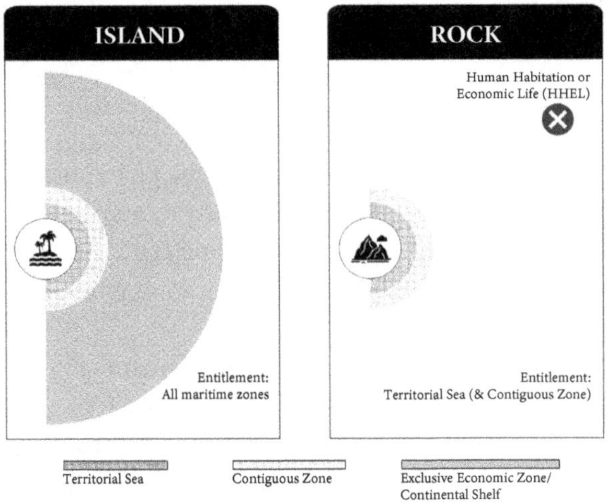

Figure 6.1 Two-part model of the regime of islands under Article 121 (Illustration credit: Lucky Wuwung)

6.2.1.2 Three-part model under Article 121: a critique on the basis of State practice

Klein writes that the Tribunal's adoption of a two-part model of high-tide features—differentiated on the basis of HHEL—appears to be driven by 'the policy of not granting extensive maritime zones, and hence exclusive rights to a coastal state, on the basis of a small feature lacking sufficient human life and activity'.[35] In this regard, the Tribunal referred to the remarks of Koh (then President of UNCLOS III):

> The rationale for the proposal that coastal States should have the right to establish an economic zone was essentially based upon the interests of the people and the desire to marshal the resources of ocean space for their development . . . However, it would be unjust, and the common heritage of mankind would be further diminished, if every island, irrespective of its characteristics, was automatically entitled to claim a uniform economic zone. Such an approach would give inequitable benefits to coastal States with small or uninhabited islands scattered over a wide expanse of the ocean. The economic zone of a barren rock would be larger than the land

[35] Natalie Klein, 'Islands and Rocks after the South China Sea Arbitration' (2017) 34 Australian Year Book of International Law 21, 24.

territory of many States and larger than the economic zones of many coastal States.[36]

But *which* characteristics of an island operate to disentitle an otherwise fully entitled feature to a claim for an economic zone and continental shelf? The answer under a two-part model is clear: inability to sustain HHEL. This aspect of the Tribunal's reasoning has attracted strong criticism on the basis that it incorrectly substitutes the word 'island' for 'rock' in Article 121(3), and that it insufficiently accounts for State practice.

Judge Guillaume has criticized the Tribunal's treatment of the relationship of the two terms in Article 121, pointing out that as a matter of textual construction, the LOSC 'uses the word "island" in Article 121(1) and (2) and the word "rock" in (3), and on the face of it, it is difficult to see how the same scope can be given to the two words'.[37] Challenging the Tribunal's reading of the drafting history, Oude Elferink writes that although it is true that the drafters rejected proposals to refer expressly to size in the language of Article 121, 'the negotiating record makes clear that the term "rock" was used to refer to one specific type of island and was not intended to be a synonym of the term "island"'.[38] Further, Talmon explains that in giving up any geological distinction between an island and a rock, the Tribunal in fact interpreted Article 121(3) to read '*islands* which cannot sustain human habitation or economic life of their own shall have no exclusive economic zone or continental shelf'—which should be seen as adopting 'a legislative role rewriting the text of Article 121(1)'.[39]

This line of critique is reinforced by concerns that the Tribunal's interpretation of Article 121(3) fails to take into account relevant State practice. The Tribunal recognized the potential relevance of State practice in the implementation of Article 121(3) for treaty interpretation, pointing to Article 31(3)(b)

[36] Singapore, 'Summary Record of the 39th Meeting', Official Records of the Third United Nations Conference on the Law of the Sea, Second Committee, Second Session (14 August 1974) UN Doc A/CONF.62/C.2/SR.39 (Summary Record of the 39th Meeting).

[37] Gilbert Guillaume, 'Rocks in the Law of the Sea: Some Comments on the South China Sea Arbitration Award' (*EJIL:Talk!*, 6 August 2021) <www.ejiltalk.org/ricks-in-the-law-of-the-sea-some-comments-on-the-south-china-sea-arbitration-award/>.

[38] AG Oude Elferink, 'The South China Sea Arbitration's Interpretation of Article 121(3) of the LOSC: A Disquieting First' (*The NCLOS Blog: The blog of the Norwegian Centre for the Law of the Sea*, 7 September 2016) <https://site.uit.no/nclos/2016/09/07/the-south-china-sea-arbitrations-interpretation-of-article-1213-of-the-losc-a-disquieting-first/>.

[39] Talmon, 'Article 121—Regime of Islands' (n 20) 868 (emphasis added). Another way to imagine how a two-part model 'rewrites' art 121(3) might be that it treats the paragraph to read 'Rocks—*those islands which* cannot sustain human habitation or economic life of their own—shall have no exclusive economic zone or continental shelf'. Both this version and Talmon's suggested wording (quoted above) necessitate a variation of the language of art 121(3).

of the Vienna Convention on the Law of Treaties (VCLT). However, without discussion of any evidence of State practice, the Tribunal concluded that 'as far as the case before it is concerned, there is no evidence for an agreement based upon State practice on the interpretation of Article 121(3) which differs from the interpretation of the Tribunal'.[40]

Certainly, commentators have acknowledged that the varying ways in which Article 121(3) has been implemented by States in diverse geographical circumstances might pose difficulties in demonstrating the 'common understanding' that is required for the element of 'agreement' under Article 31(3)(b) of the VCLT.[41] But there is also abundant evidence that States have claimed an EEZ and continental shelf in relation to features that fall within the interpretation of Article 121(3) rocks put forward by the Tribunal.

Numerous scholars have identified many examples of State practice in which States have claimed an EEZ and/or continental shelf in circumstances at odds with the Tribunal's approach:[42] Australia (Ashmore and Cartier Islands, Heard Island, McDonald Islands, Elizabeth and Middleton Reefs, Macquarie Island); Brazil (Penedos de São Pedro e São Paulo, Trindade e Martin Vaz); Chile (Isla Sala y Gómez, Islas Desventuradas); Costa Rica (Isla del Coco); Fiji (Ceva-i-Ra); France (Clipperton, Îles Chesterfield, Crozet, Îles Eparses in the Mozambique Channel, Îles Matthew et Hunter, Îles Saint Paul et Amsterdam, Tromelin); Iceland (Kolbeinsey); Japan (Okinotorishima, Minamitorishima); Kiribati (McKean Island, Christmas Island); Mexico (Isla Clarión and Roca Partida); New Zealand (Antipodes Islands, Auckland Islands, Bounty Islands, Campbell Island, Kermadec Islands, Snares Islands); Norway (Bouvet, Jan Mayen); Portugal (Ilhas Selvagens); South Africa (Prince Edward Islands); Russian Federation (Henrietta and Jeanetta); the United States (Maro Reef,

[40] *Philippines v China* (n 21) [553].

[41] See eg RR Churchill, 'Rocks', *Max Planck Encyclopedia of International Law* (2019) [30].

[42] This list is a consolidation of the State practice on the implementation of art 121 identified by these writers: Guillaume, 'Rocks in the Law of the Sea: Some Comments on the South China Sea Arbitration Award' (n 37); Yann-Huei Song, 'Okinotorishima: A Rock or an Island? Recent Maritime Boundary Controversy Between Japan and Taiwan/China' in Seoung-Yong Hong and Jon M Van Dyke (eds), *Maritime Boundary Disputes, Settlement Processes, and the Law of the Sea*, vol 65 (Martinus Nijhoff 2009); Oude Elferink, 'The South China Sea Arbitration's Interpretation of Article 121(3) of the LOSC' (n 38), Talmon, 'Article 121—Regime of Islands' (n 20); Chinese Society of International Law, 'The South China Sea Arbitration Awards: A Critical Study' (2018) 17 Chinese Journal of International Law 207, 538; Joanna Mossop, 'The South China Sea Arbitration and New Zealand's Maritime Claims' (2017) 15 New Zealand Journal of Public and International Law 265; Nordquist and Phalen, 'Interpretation of UNCLOS Article 121 and Itu Aba (Taiping) in the South China Sea Arbitration Award' (n 21); RR Churchill, AV Lowe, and Amy Sander, *The Law of the Sea* (4th edn, Manchester University Press 2022) 98; Malcolm D Evans and Reece Lewis, *Islands, Law and Context: The Treatment of Islands in International Law* (Edward Elgar 2023).

Howland and Baker Islands, Johnston Atoll, Jarvis Island, Kingman Reef, Palmyra Atoll, Wake Island); Venezuela (Aves Island); and Yemen (Jabal al-Yayr).

Protests have followed the establishment of an EEZ around some of these features (such as Aves Island and Okinotorishima).[43] Mossop suggests that the reasoning of the Tribunal in *Philippines v China* might also form the basis for challenge in either domestic or international litigation concerning features such as these:[44] for example, a domestic fisheries prosecution might be challenged on the basis that the relevant EEZ was established around an uninhabitable island, inconsistently with the LOSC; or similar arguments might arise in international litigation, along the lines of Judge Vukas' (obiter) declarations in the *Monte Confurco* and *Volga* cases (which accepted the Tribunal's findings on prompt release but expressed concerns about the validity of France's EEZ around the Kerguelen Islands, and Australia's EEZ around Heard and McDonald Islands).[45] However, in the years following the Award, such challenges have not eventuated. Rather than sparking increased protest over the status of features following the ruling in *Philippines v China*, Bateman predicted that Australia, France, Japan, and the United States—having also established EEZs around small isolated features—might simply ignore it.[46] No States have reclassified land features following the Award.[47] Rather, Japan has distanced itself from the implications of the ruling, making clear its view that the decision is binding only on the Philippines and China, and therefore does not apply to Okinotorishima (which is, in its view, an island entitled to an EEZ).[48]

This State practice as a whole shows that 'States almost invariably have claimed a continental shelf and exclusive economic zone for all the islands under their sovereignty',[49] and that, in most cases, such claims have not been

[43] See Yoshifumi Tanaka, 'Reflections on the Interpretation and Application of Article 121 (3) in the South China Sea Arbitration (Merits)' (2017) 48 Ocean Development & International Law 365, 373, and Churchill, 'Rocks' (n 41) [28].

[44] Mossop, 'The South China Sea Arbitration and New Zealand's Maritime Claims' (n 42).

[45] *Monte Confurco Case (Seychelles v France)* (Judgment) (2000) 125 ILR 203 (*Monte Confurco Case*); *Volga Case (Russian Federation v Australia)* (Judgment) (2003) 42 ILM 159.

[46] Sam Bateman, 'The South China Sea Arbitration: Challenges and Opportunities' (*Strategic Insights*, 2 August 2016) <www.aspistrategist.org.au/south-china-sea-arbitration-challenges-opportunities/>.

[47] Stefan Talmon, *The South China Sea Arbitration: Jurisdiction, Admissibility, Procedure* (Brill Nijhoff 2022) 375.

[48] Ayako Mie, 'Japan Steps up Rhetoric over Okinotorishima in Wake of Hague Ruling' *Japan Times* (15 July 2016).

[49] Oude Elferink, 'The South China Sea Arbitration's Interpretation of Article 121(3) of the LOSC' (n 38). As Oude Elferink here points out, a well-known exception to this is the UK's 'non-claim' of an EEZ around Rockall: see discussion in Section 6.3.

the subject of protest, either before or after the *Philippines v China* Award. Symmons expresses a similar view, stating that 'in general States have tended to attribute an EEZ or continental shelf to all their insular possessions, even if they clearly fall into the "Article 121(3) category"'.[50] Contrary to the Tribunal's conclusion on State practice on the implementation of Article 121(3), there is evidence that many States adopt an interpretation that differs from that of the Tribunal in relation to the significance of HHEL for the maritime zone entitlements of insular features.

For instance, Norway has proclaimed a 200 nm fishery zone and continental shelf around Jan Mayen,[51] a volcanic island of approximately 377 km^2 without fresh water or vegetation. The feature has no permanent population but is inhabited by personnel connected with its meteorological station.[52] Tanaka has remarked that '[a]pplying the Tribunal's interpretation in the South China Sea Arbitration, it is difficult to consider that Jan Mayen is a fully entitled island since there is no stable community of population and the life of people working on Jan Mayen is entirely dependent on external resources'.[53] However, the International Court of Justice (ICJ) implicitly treated Jan Mayen as generating an EEZ and continental shelf for the purposes of the delimitation of those zones with Greenland, an approach also taken by the Conciliation Commission in the delimitation of the continental shelves of Norway and Iceland.[54] Australia has established an EEZ and continental shelf around Heard and McDonald Islands, volcanic islands of approximately 368 km^2 and 2.45 km^2 respectively.[55] Those islands have no permanent population and little vegetation (Heard Island has some isolated vegetated headlands between glaciers); the limited human activities are for terrestrial and marine research.[56] Song notes that while eight States protested Australia's claim to a continental shelf beyond 200 nm from the Antarctic coastline, no States protested the EEZ or continental shelf

[50] Symmons, 'Maritime Zones of Islands and Rocks' (n 19) 107.

[51] Regulation no 4 on establishing the fishery zone around Jan Mayen (1980) (Norway), and Act no 89 on Norway's continental shelf (2021): certain sections of the outer limits of each of these zones are influenced by relevant delimitation agreements with Denmark and Iceland.

[52] CIA, 'Jan Mayen', *The World Factbook* <www.cia.gov/the-world-factbook/countries/jan-mayen/>.

[53] Tanaka, 'Reflections on the Interpretation and Application of Article 121(3) in the South China Sea Arbitration (Merits)' (n 43) 374.

[54] See discussion in ibid and Ulf Linderfalk, 'The Jan Mayen Case (Iceland/Norway): An Example of Successful Conciliation' in Christian Tomuschat, Riccardo Pisillo Mazzeschi, and Daniel Thürer (eds), *Conciliation in International Law: The OSCE Court of Conciliation and Arbitration* (Brill Nijhoff 2017).

[55] Geoscience Australia, 'Heard and McDonald Islands' <www.ga.gov.au/scientific-topics/national-location-information/dimensions/remote-offshore-territories/heard-and-mcdonald-islands>.

[56] Australian Antarctic Division, 'Location and Geography' <www.antarctica.gov.au/antarctic-operations/stations/other-locations/heard-island/location-geography/> and Australian Antarctic Division, 'Human Activities' <www.antarctica.gov.au/antarctic-operations/stations/other-locations/heard-island/human-activities/>.

around Heard and McDonald Islands[57] (even though Australia made its submission to the Commission on the Limits on the Continental Shelf in 2004, the year after Judge Vukas' remarks about Heard and McDonald Islands in the *Volga*).

While Jan Mayen and Heard Island are relatively large in size, States have also established EEZs and/or continental shelves around small insular features that would seem to fail the Tribunal's requirement for HHEL. For example, New Zealand has proclaimed an EEZ and continental shelf around the Bounty Islands.[58] The Bounty Islands comprise about twenty-two rocky and uninhabited outcrops, totalling approximately 1.35 km^2, and being without vegetation, fresh water, or extractive activity of any kind, Mossop suggests the features would struggle to meet the Tribunal's criteria for full maritime zone entitlement.[59] The United States has established an EEZ around similar small features,[60] such as Johnston Atoll, a barren coral atoll of around 2.8 km^2, with no permanent population or indigenous inhabitants.[61] There is no arable land or fresh water, and all supplies must be imported to support occasional visits by United States defence personnel.[62] For these reasons, Nordquist and Phalen suggest that Johnston Atoll would not satisfy the Tribunal's requirement of HHEL.[63]

As correctly observed by Oude Elferink, 'there is an abyss between the tribunal's approach and the practice of many States'.[64] Talmon suggests that Article 121 should be interpreted to provide for 'three categories of islands: (1) rocks that cannot sustain human habitation or economic life of their own; (2) rocks that can sustain human habitation or economic life of their own; and (3) all other islands [illustrated in Figure 6.2]. Only the first category of islands does not have an EEZ or continental shelf'.[65] This approach accords with State

[57] Song, 'Okinotorishima: A Rock or an Island?' (n 42) 251.

[58] Territorial Sea, Contiguous Zone, and Exclusive Economic Zone Act 1977 (New Zealand) and Continental Shelf Order 2018 (New Zealand).

[59] See Mossop, 'The South China Sea Arbitration and New Zealand's Maritime Claims' (n 42) 279.

[60] *Federal Register*, vol 60, no 163 (23 August 1995) 'Exclusive Economic Zone and Maritime Boundaries: Notice of Limits' (United States) <www.un.org/depts/los/LEGISLATIONANDTREATIES/PDFFILES/USA_1995_eez_public_notice.pdf>.

[61] CIA, 'Johnston Atoll', *The World Factbook* <https://user.iiasa.ac.at/~marek/fbook/03/geos/jq.html>.

[62] ibid.

[63] Nordquist and Phalen, 'Interpretation of UNCLOS Article 121 and Itu Aba (Taiping) in the South China Sea Arbitration Award' (n 21) 34.

[64] Oude Elferink, 'The South China Sea Arbitration's Interpretation of Article 121(3) of the LOSC' (n 38). Schofield comes to a similar view, pointing to the 'gulf between the Tribunal's standard for a fully entitled island and State practice': Schofield, *The Regime of Islands Reframed* (n 32) 84.

[65] Talmon, 'Article 121—Regime of Islands' (n 20) 871. This is also consistent with the views of some scholars writing prior to the Award: see Charney, 'Rocks That Cannot Sustain Human Habitation' (n 32) 866, and Symmons, 'Maritime Zones of Islands and Rocks' (n 19) 97; as well as those writing after the Award, such as Evans and Lewis, *Islands, Law and Context* (n 42) 52.

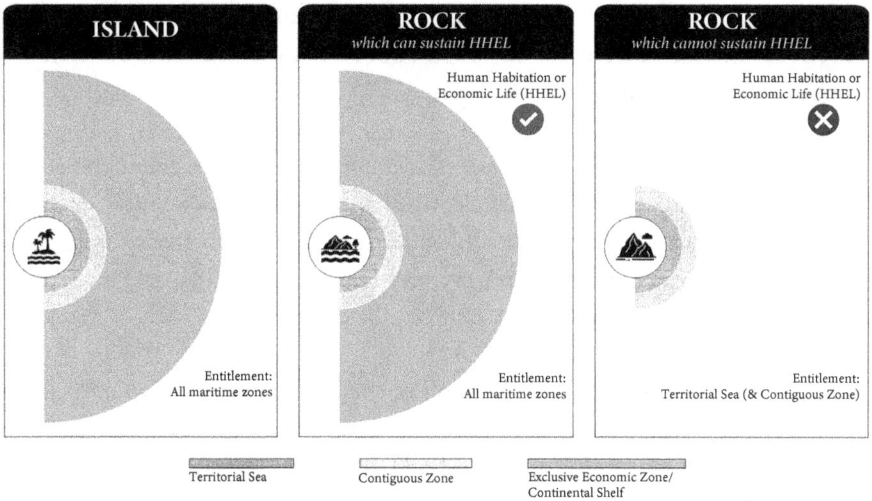

Figure 6.2 Three-part model of the regime of islands under Article 121 (Illustration credit: Lucky Wuwung)

practice, giving a restrictive application to the exception in Article 121(3) by applying the requirement for HHEL only to those islands which are rocks, not to all islands.

What can be made of this State practice—and the three-part model of features it suggests—for the purposes of the interpretation of Article 121? First, the three-part model of Article 121 has advantages over the two-part model in terms of the 'ordinary meaning'[66] of the provision, because the three-part model gives the term 'rock' a meaningful role in the differentiation of maritime entitlement. An interpretation that substitutes 'island' for 'rock' in the context of Article 121(3)—as the two-part model does—goes against the principle of effectiveness.[67] As many scholars have pointed out—and as recognized by the Tribunal in the *Philippines v China*, drafters considered various differentiating criteria between features (including size) and no agreement was reached. The Tribunal's response to this difficulty was to interpret 'rocks' to mean those islands which cannot sustain HHEL, with the result that the maritime entitlements of 'rocks' and 'islands' should be solely differentiated by reference to the presence or absence of HHEL. However, applying the exceptional requirement for HHEL to all islands gives the exception a very broad effect. The relevant

[66] VCLT, art 31(1).
[67] See discussion of the principle of effectiveness in Section 4.3.2 and Section 5.3.3.

preparatory materials[68] do not lend support to such breadth. Ambassador Satya N Nandan, who led the development of what was to become Article 121 at UNCLOS III, argued that:

> [the] attempt to exclude uninhabited islands from the concept of the economic zone ran counter to article 10 of the Geneva Convention on the Territorial Sea and the Contiguous Zone. To adopt any such proposals would be to impose an unjustifiable penalty on island States, particularly the small island territories of the South Pacific.[69]

Ambassador Nandan was also the head of the Fiji delegation, and noting that Fiji (together with many other Pacific countries) claims an EEZ and continental shelf from small, uninhabited features (in Fiji's case, Ceva-i-Ra or Conway Reef), Nandan reflected that '[w]ith respect to rocks which cannot sustain human habitation or economic life, Fiji accepted that apart from a territorial sea jurisdiction, it was difficult to justify an exclusive economic zone or continental shelf jurisdiction. The proposal for islands as contained in the Single Negotiating Text accorded with Fiji's views.'[70] Nandan's careful use of the terms 'rock' and 'island' in explaining what was to become Article 121 accords with Talmon's observation that it would be 'difficult to comprehend that Ambassador Nandan was drafting a provision that would have deprived all "islands" which cannot sustain human habitation or economic life of their own of an EEZ and continental shelf—an outcome that would have been contrary to the interests of his own country'.[71]

Accordingly, while the Tribunal was correct to point out that the LOSC does not specify any 'geological or geomorphological criteria' for 'rocks',[72] it does not follow that rocks are therefore indistinguishable from 'islands'. Notwithstanding the absence of agreed text on the maximum size of islands to be excluded from the operation of Article 121(2),[73] it is clear that drafters

[68] Relevant as a supplementary means of interpretation under VCLT, art 32.

[69] Fiji, 'Summary Record of the 39th Meeting' (n 36) 283.

[70] Satya N Nandan and Kristine Dalaker Kraabel, *Reflections on the Making of the Modern Law of the Sea* (NUS Press 2021) 102.

[71] Talmon, 'Article 121—Regime of Islands' (n 20) 870. Nordquist and Phalen also discuss Nandan's role on this issue: see Nordquist and Phalen, 'Interpretation of UNCLOS Article 121 and Itu Aba (Taiping) in the South China Sea Arbitration Award' (n 21) 37.

[72] See *Philippines v China* (n 21) [479].

[73] While no agreement was reached on a size criterion, the potential for size to differentiate between the maritime entitlement of a range of insular features was a clear concern for many delegations at UNCLOS III: details of various proposals are clearly outlined in Kwiatkowska and Soons, 'Entitlement to Maritime Areas of Rocks Which Cannot Sustain Human Habitation or Economic Life' (n 32).

intended Article 121(3) to apply the requirement of HHEL to only certain insular features, not all of them. As Judge Guillaume puts it, 'Rockall is a rock; Tromelin is not':[74] the effect of applying this distinction is that Rockall would only be entitled to full maritime zones if it could sustain HHEL. But Tromelin—not being a rock—would not be caught within the exception in Article 121(3) and is entitled to full maritime zones irrespective of its capacity to sustain HHEL. This reasoning comports with the State practice directly related to those two features: in order to bring itself into compliance with the LOSC ahead of ratification,[75] the United Kingdom rolled back its fishery zone around Rockall, a 'granite oceanic crag' of 754 m^2;[76] France has established an EEZ around Tromelin,[77] an uninhabited island of approximately 1.0 km^2 with no arable land or fresh water.[78]

Even though the three-part model gives effect to the term 'rock' in the context of Article 121, it remains the case that it is difficult to articulate what precise criteria differentiate rocks from islands generally. Churchill explains that there are few examples of a coastal State expressly applying Article 121(3) with the effect of denying or not claiming an EEZ and continental shelf: in addition to Rockall, the United Kingdom has not claimed any zone beyond the territorial sea in relation to Shag Rocks, 'six isolated, uninhabited rocks, 20 hectares in area, lying in the Southern Ocean some 135 nautical miles west of South Georgia'.[79] Similarly, Churchill cites Mexico's non-claim in respect of 'Rocas Alijos, a group of tiny islets with a total surface area of less than 0.001 square km lying about 160 nautical miles off Mexico's Pacific mainland coast'.[80] This handful of examples indicate that even though the LOSC is silent as to geological or size criteria, size remains a common theme in State practice in

[74] Guillaume, 'Rocks in the Law of the Sea: Some Comments on the South China Sea Arbitration Award' (n 37).

[75] RR Churchill, 'Accession to the UN Convention on the Law of the Sea' (1998) 13 International Journal of Marine and Coastal Law 263, 271: see discussion in Section 6.3.1.

[76] Rothwell, *Islands and International Law* (n 29) 8.

[77] Decree no 78-146 of 3 February 1978, establishing, pursuant to the Act of 16 July 1976, an economic zone off the coasts of the islands of Tromelin, Glorieuses, Juan de Nova, Europa, and Bassas da India (France). Mauritius also claims sovereignty over Tromelin and has protested the 1978 French Decree and 2009 deposit of coordinates for EEZ outer limits: see diplomatic notes recorded at UN Division for Ocean Affairs and the Law of the Sea, 'Mauritius' <www.un.org/depts/los/LEGISLATIONANDTREATIES/STATEFILES/MUS.htm>. Mauritius has also proclaimed baselines for its own maritime zones adjacent to Tromelin: see Maritime Zones (Baselines and Delineating Lines) Regulations 2005, First Schedule.

[78] CIA, 'Tromelin Island', *The World Factbook* <https://user.iiasa.ac.at/~marek/fbook/04/geos/te.html>.

[79] Churchill, 'Rocks' (n 41) [27].

[80] ibid.

relation to Article 121(3):[81] these examples suggest that States have interpreted 'rock' narrowly, encompassing small, rocky features, often at some distance from the mainland or other (larger) islands.

In addition to considering the treaty's ordinary meaning on this issue, the second aspect to consider in relation to the interpretation of Article 121 is whether there is 'subsequent practice in the application of the treaty which establishes the agreement of the parties regarding its interpretation'.[82] The examples given in this chapter represents the practice of sixteen LOSC Parties (and two non-Parties) that supports a three-part model of features. The lack of protest in relation to these examples of State practice—both before and after the *Philippines v China*—suggests tacit 'agreement' as to such interpretation. At the very least, this evidence indicates that the two-part model of features should be applied with caution. Indeed, this chapter argues that the evidence supports a more ambitious claim: that the three-part model of features is the preferred interpretation of Article 121, because it gives effect to all of its terms, is supported by State practice in the implementation of extended maritime zones from insular features, and is consistent with the drafting history.

6.2.1.3 Avoiding path dependency: the potential irrelevance of habitability for the status of an island (which is not a rock)

Whether Article 121 is interpreted to provide for a two- or three-part model of features has significant implications for assessing what legal consequences might result from sea-level rise impacts on island habitability. Interpreting Article 121 as a two-part model of features creates a logical path dependency: because HHEL is needed as a precondition for status as an 'island', absence of HHEL calls that status into question. However, this chapter has argued that scholars critiquing this model as articulated in the *Philippines v China* have drawn attention to the 'abyss' between this view and extensive State practice. So far, following the Award, States have not revisited established maritime zones that deviate from the Tribunal's approach; nor has the Tribunal's reasoning been marshalled in protests or challenges between States. Furthermore, 'it remains to be seen whether the approach of the tribunal will have traction with other international courts and tribunals',[83] particularly

[81] In the view of Evans and Lewis, size should be viewed as an important aspect of distinguishing islands from rocks: see Evans and Lewis, *Islands, Law and Context* (n 42) 53ff.

[82] VCLT, art 31(3)(b).

[83] Malcolm D Evans and Reece Lewis, 'The Regime of Islands' in Øystein Jensen (ed), *The Development of the Law of the Sea Convention: The Role of International Courts and Tribunals* (Edward Elgar 2020) 33.

noting that the Award has 'procedural finality' rather than 'substantive finality', meaning that 'it is the last award rendered on the issues in dispute between the parties; [but] it is not necessarily the last word on the legal questions at issue'.[84] Against this backdrop, the Tribunal's interpretation of Article 121—including the two-part model of features underpinning it—remains fragile.[85]

If Article 121 is instead interpreted to provide for a three-part model of features—which this chapter argues is the better view—then a different conclusion becomes available as to the legal consequences of habitability loss. If capacity to sustain HHEL is not required to qualify for status as an island in the first place, then the loss of such capacity to sustain HHEL should have no relevance to island status. Rather, loss of capacity to sustain HHEL might only logically affect the maritime entitlement of a rock. A potential difficulty might be that a State will seldom expressly articulate whether it is proclaiming full maritime zones because it considers the feature to be an 'island' within the meaning of Article 121(1), or because it considers the feature to be a rock capable of sustaining HHEL. But the many instances of coastal States establishing full maritime zones in circumstances that are unlikely to satisfy the HHEL test strongly suggest the former approach, favouring a generous interpretation of 'island' and a narrow interpretation of 'rock'. If this is the case, then loss of capacity to sustain HHEL is only likely to affect a very small number of features, if any at all.[86]

Under a three-part model of features suggested by State practice, capacity to sustain HHEL is an exceptional requirement that pertains only to the maritime zone entitlements of rocks, not all islands. This understanding—coupled with the likelihood that few States proclaim an EEZ and/or continental shelf

[84] Talmon, *The South China Sea Arbitration: Jurisdiction, Admissibility, Procedure* (n 47) 357. See also Clive Schofield and David Freestone, 'The Legal Regime of Islands after the South China Sea Award—Orphaned or Influential? An Essay in Honor of Ted L. McDorman' (2024) 55 Ocean Development & International Law 565.

[85] Tanaka refers to the fragility of the Tribunal's conclusions on this issue: Tanaka, 'Reflections on the Interpretation and Application of Article 121 (3) in the South China Sea Arbitration (Merits)' (n 43) 374.

[86] Outside of a delimitation context, the only example known to the author where a coastal State has expressly claimed an EEZ and continental shelf on the basis of a rock having the capacity to sustain HHEL is that of St Peter and Paul Islands (Brazil): see Alexandre Pereira da Silva, 'From Rocks to an Archipelago: The Brazilian Interpretation and Application of Article 121 of the United Nations Convention on the Law of the Sea with Respect to the St. Peter and St. Paul Insular Features' (2020) 51 Ocean Development and International Law 330. The apparent scarcity of this result also raises the broader question of whether—despite the intentions of the drafters at UNCLOS III—subsequent State practice has rendered art 121(3) to be of little practical use, since States do not tend to rely upon it to justify claims to an EEZ and/or continental shelf. If future practice confirms the current indications that 'island' status can be maintained notwithstanding factual habitability loss, this would potentially signal the decreasing relevance of art 121(3) as a basis for extended maritime zone entitlement.

for rocks capable of sustaining HHEL—means that the status of many features as 'islands' might be unaffected by habitability loss.

6.2.2 Elevation and maritime entitlement: submergence of features

This section now considers the second factor that might have the potential to destabilize the legal status of a feature, causing the loss or diminution of its maritime entitlements: the submergence of features. A key component of the definition of features relevant to such maritime entitlement is their elevation in relation to the high- or low-water line. For example, an 'island' must be 'above water at high tide'[87] while a 'low-tide elevation' may be submerged at low tide but must be above water at high tide.[88] This chapter uses the term 'fully submerged feature' to mean a feature that is submerged at all times (although the LOSC does not use a specific term for this circumstance).

It is immediately apparent that the prospect of sea-level rise raises questions relating to a feature's elevation relative to particular tidal heights. Rothwell highlights one potential scenario, in which an 'island' might become a 'low-tide elevation' due to rising sea levels:

> The first issue that therefore arises with respect to the consequence of SLR [sea-level rise] is whether an island becomes so awash that it is no longer above water at high tide and becomes an LTE [low-tide elevation]. [. . .] Low-lying islands, because of SLR, may therefore see their status converted from being an Article 121 island to an Article 13 LTE with consequential impacts upon the maritime entitlement of the feature.[89]

Noting that '[d]ue to their marginal height, low-tide elevations will be the first maritime features to be affected by sea-level rise', Stoutenberg also identifies the scenario in which a low-tide elevation might become a fully submerged feature.[90] Caron,[91] Murphy,[92] and Rayfuse[93] raise concerns in terms similar

[87] LOSC, art 121(1).
[88] LOSC, art 13.
[89] Rothwell, *Islands and International Law* (n 29) 242.
[90] Jenny Grote Stoutenburg, *Disappearing Island States in International Law* (Brill 2015) 143.
[91] David D Caron, 'Climate Change, Sea Level Rise and the Coming Uncertainty in Oceanic Boundaries: A Proposal to Avoid Conflict' in Seoung-Yong Hong and Jon M Van Dyke *Maritime Boundary Disputes, Settlement Processes, and the Law of the Sea* (Brill Nijhoff 2009) 11.
[92] Murphy, *International Law Relating to Islands* (n 30) 289.
[93] Rayfuse, 'Sea Level Rise and Maritime Zones' (n 28) 273–74.

to Rothwell and Stoutenberg. The ILA SLR Committee considered both scenarios,[94] and the ILC also considered 'whether "rocks" that become submerged should continue to enjoy maritime entitlements'.[95] Lisztwan draws attention to the effect of submergence on maritime claims, taking the view that '[i]f the entire island is submerged, presumably all maritime claims will be extinguished'.[96]

Distinguishing between an 'island' and a 'low-tide elevation' is relevant to the related issues of maritime entitlement and baselines. For example, an 'island' is treated like 'other land territory', and is generally entitled to the full suite of maritime zones.[97] A 'low-tide elevation' is not capable of appropriation[98] and does not have a territorial sea (or any other maritime zone) of its own; depending on its location, it might be able to contribute to the baseline and therefore expand the territorial sea.[99] Although the previous section has outlined competing interpretative approaches to understanding the relationship between an 'island' and a 'rock' (and the role of HHEL in distinguishing the two), in principle it is clear that an 'island', a 'low-tide elevation', and a fully submerged feature may be differentiated solely on the basis of elevation.[100] Less clear is what it means for a feature's status to be 'converted'[101] from an 'island' to a 'low-tide elevation'. Is the same or a different process implied in the question of 'whether "rocks" that become submerged should continue to enjoy maritime entitlements'?[102] Or if an 'island' is partially submerged

[94] ILA (Committee on International Law and Sea Level Rise), 'Report (Sydney Conference)' (2018) 13 (2018 ILA SLR Report).

[95] 2021 ILC Report (n 31) [282]; although the later work of the ILC did not pursue this issue in detail.

[96] Julia Lisztwan, 'Stability of Maritime Boundary Agreements' (2012) 37 Yale Journal of International Law 153, 175.

[97] LOSC, art 121. The maritime entitlements of 'rocks' is contested: as described in Section 6.2.1, this depends on whether a two- or three-part model of art 121 is applied.

[98] *Territorial and Maritime Dispute (Nicaragua v Colombia)* (Judgment) [2012] ICJ Rep 624, [26] (*Territorial and Maritime Dispute*).

[99] LOSC, art 13. The status of a feature as either an 'island' or 'low-tide elevation' may also be important for maritime entitlement in other ways: for example, the presence of islands is essential to qualify as an 'archipelagic state' and entitlement to 'archipelagic waters' (LOSC, arts 46 and 47); where an island has a 'fringing reef'—a type of low-tide elevation—it may establish the baseline on the seaward low-water line of that reef (LOSC, art 6), permitting the coastal State to enclose the lagoon waters between the reef and the island as internal waters.

[100] There remain some ambiguities in relation to the treatment of transient features such as cays and mudflats, and which tidal datum should be used to measure a feature's elevation: Clive R Symmons, 'Article 13—Low-Tide Elevations' in Alexander Proelss (ed), *United Nations Convention on the Law of the Sea: A Commentary* (1st edn, CH Beck 2017). These practical matters are not relevant to the in-principle distinction between an 'island' and 'low-tide elevation' on the basis of elevation, so they are not explored in this chapter.

[101] Rothwell, *Islands and International Law* (n 29) 242.

[102] 2021 ILC Report (n 31) [282].

so as to render it an unhabitable 'rock', is it that 'the EEZ may no longer be claimed'?[103]

Concerns that rising sea levels will result in a change in the legal status of features (resulting in diminished or lost maritime entitlements) imply a process of legal transformation that is not well understood. The vagueness with which scholars gesture to this legal transformation illustrates a deep uncertainty about the conditions under which the feared destabilization of legal status of features might be realized. Informed by insights from State practice that were identified in Chapters 4 and 5, Section 6.3 takes a closer look at what it might mean to destabilize the legal status of features.

6.3 What does it mean to destabilize the legal status of features?

This chapter refers to *destabilizing* the legal status of features to capture the concerns scholars articulate about the disruptive effects of climate change impacts—chiefly habitability loss and submergence—on the status of features under the international law of the sea. Destabilization therefore describes a legal process of transformation, whereby a feature that once had a particular legal status (eg 'island') comes to have another legal status (eg 'low-tide elevation') following certain changed circumstances (eg partial submergence resulting in the feature being above water at low tide). The *destabilization* of the legal status of a feature also entails undesirable consequences: being a 'low-tide elevation' means a diminution or loss of maritime entitlement (no entitlement to maritime zones of its own, but might influence the extent of the territorial sea).

But how does this legal transformation come about? If baseline change is little understood as a concept and in practice,[104] changes to the legal status of features have received even less attention. One practical reason for this is that unlike baselines (which are usually expressly established in legislation), a coastal State will generally not specify whether it considers a particular feature to be an 'island' or some other feature for the purposes of the establishment of its maritime zones. Rather, the status of the feature might only be implied by the maritime zone extending from it, or possibly also the type of baseline

[103] Moritaka Hayashi, 'Sea Level Rise and the Law of the Sea: How Can the Affected States Be Better Protected?' in Clive H Schofield, Seokwoo Lee, and Moon-Sang Kwon (eds), *The Limits of Maritime Jurisdiction* (Brill Nijhoff 2014) 614.

[104] See discussion in Section 5.2.

established upon it. Given the difficulty with gaining visibility on the legal status of features in the first place, it is unsurprising that it might be difficult to study whether there is any change to such status.

Against this backdrop, Section 6.3.1 examines the very few known examples of State practice demonstrating a change (or purported change) in the legal status of a feature. It revisits the United Kingdom's actions in relation to Rockall, and also examples where States have undertaken the artificial modification of natural features, to consider what these examples illuminate about the process of legal transformation. Section 6.3.2 then considers different approaches to conceptualizing the process of legal transformation, arguing that State practice, scholarship, and jurisprudence suggest that there need not always be a direct correlation between physical transformations of a feature and their legal transformation.

6.3.1 Transformation and non-transformation of legal status: the distinction between physical and legal processes

Much has been written,[105] and controversy continues,[106] about Rockall:

> Uninhabited (except by molluscs, periwinkles and, weather permitting, various species of nesting seabirds) and essentially uninhabitable, this small chunk of granite rock, the sole-remaining peak of a submerged volcanic plateau, is located around 167 nm (309 km) west of the Scottish island of St Kilda—itself now an uninhabited island—and about 230 nm northwest of the Irish (Donegal) coast, making it probably the most isolated uninhabited islet of its kind in the world.[107]

Our interest lies in the United Kingdom's actions in relation to Rockall preceding its accession to the LOSC in 1997. Churchill explains that twenty years

[105] eg Charney, 'Rocks That Cannot Sustain Human Habitation' (n 32), Kwiatkowska and Soons, 'Entitlement to Maritime Areas of Rocks Which Cannot Sustain Human Habitation or Economic Life' (n 32).

[106] See eg Sarah Burns, 'Irish Fishermen to Defy Scotland's "Bombshell" Warning on Rockall' *Irish Times* (8 June 2019) <www.irishtimes.com/news/ireland/irish-news/irish-fishermen-to-defy-scotland-s-bombshell-warning-on-rockall-1.3919670> and Ríán Derrig, 'An Irish Claim to Rockall' (*EJIL: Talk!*, 14 January 2021) <ejiltalk.org/an-irish-claim-to-rockall/>.

[107] Richard Collins, 'Sovereignty Has "Rock-all" to Do with it . . . or Has it? What's at Stake in the Recent Diplomatic Spat between Scotland and Ireland?' (*EJIL: Talk!*, 8 July 2019) <www.ejiltalk.org/sovereignty-has-rock-all-to-do-with-it-or-has-it-whats-at-stake-in-the-recent-diplomatic-spat-between-scotland-and-ireland/>.

earlier, the United Kingdom had applied its 200-nm fishery limits around Rockall.[108] However, to bring itself into compliance with the LOSC, the United Kingdom abandoned those claims, stating that 'the United Kingdom's fishery limits will need to be redefined based on St Kilda, since Rockall is not a valid base point for such limits under article 121(3) of the convention'.[109] This redefinition was achieved by the making of the Fishery Limits Order 1997.[110] The result of the abandonment of Rockall as a basepoint for the purposes of the United Kingdom's EEZ resulted in the loss of a sizeable area of its former fishery zone.[111]

This is the only known example of a coastal State expressly abandoning a claim to existing maritime entitlements on the basis of a feature's status in relation to Article 121.[112] However, the circumstances here differ from the scenario of potential EEZ loss contemplated in relation to sea-level rise. The reason for the United Kingdom's change of position in relation to the status of Rockall did not have anything to do with changes to Rockall's physical characteristics. As Purcell explains, the change of the United Kingdom's position on Rockall's status has to do with a change in the applicable law: that is, 'that the UK did not consider customary international law to preclude entitlement to the full complement of maritime zones around an island in the circumstances detailed in Article 121(3), at least not prior to 1997',[113] but that this was no longer the case in relation to the LOSC, to which it intended to accede.

Examples where States have undertaken construction activities in relation to natural features offer a different setting in which to examine possible change in the status of features. Indeed, when considering the status of disputed features in the South China Sea, the Tribunal in *Philippines v China* expressly used the terminology of transformation:

> Just as a low-tide elevation or area of seabed cannot be legally transformed into an island through human efforts, the Tribunal considers that a rock cannot be transformed into a fully entitled island through land reclamation. The status of a feature must be assessed on the basis of its natural condition.[114]

[108] See Churchill, 'Rocks' (n 41) [27].
[109] Mr Robin Cook, UK Foreign Secretary, quoted in Churchill, 'Accession to the UN Convention on the Law of the Sea' (n 75) 263.
[110] SI 1997/1750 (United Kingdom).
[111] There is some debate as to the exact size of the area; Churchill suggests approximately 60,000 square statute miles: Churchill, 'Accession to the UN Convention on the Law of the Sea' (n 75) note 32.
[112] Churchill, 'Rocks' (n 41) [27].
[113] Kate Purcell, *Geographical Change and the Law of the Sea* (Oxford University Press 2019) 278.
[114] *Philippines v China* (n 21) [508].

Here, the Tribunal draws attention to legal transformations in the context of human efforts purporting to change the status of a feature from one with relatively little or no maritime entitlement, to a feature with greater entitlement. This aspect of the Tribunal's reasoning follows logically from the requirement that an island be a 'naturally formed area of land'.[115] Applying this reasoning, the Tribunal concluded that construction activities undertaken by China did not have the effect of transforming any feature into an 'island' when the feature would not otherwise have had that status 'on the basis of its natural condition'. Rather, such activities transformed Gaven Reef (North) from a rock[116] to an artificial island;[117] and the atolls at Subi Reef[118] and Mischief Reef[119] from being low-tide elevations to 'artificial islands'.

If we look a little more closely at how these transformations into artificial islands have influenced the maritime entitlements of these features, some puzzling aspects emerge. If China's construction activities have transformed Gaven Reef (North) into an artificial island, one possible conclusion is that by virtue of Article 60(8), those artificial islands 'have no territorial sea of their own'. However, the Tribunal did not reach this conclusion, deciding instead that Gaven Reef (North) is entitled to a territorial sea, on the basis of its natural condition as rock.[120] So it appears that the effect of the 'natural state doctrine'[121] in this instance is that even though the features were, at a physical level, transformed into an artificial island, this did not affect the legal assessment of that feature's maritime entitlement. That legal assessment is undisturbed by the fact of China's construction activities; the Tribunal seems to be suggesting that it is a matter of 'once a rock, always a rock': no legal transformation has occurred. So in the same way that a rock or low-tide elevation cannot be legally transformed into an island, a rock or low-tide elevation also cannot be legally transformed into an artificial island.

Scholars have reasoned along similar lines in relation to construction activities aimed at coastal protection or reinforcement, emphasizing that legal status is to be assessed on the basis of a feature's natural condition. Song states

115 Imogen Saunders, 'Artificial Islands and Territory in International Law' (2019) 52 Vanderbilt Journal of Transnational Law 643, 665.

116 That is, a 'rock' in the Tribunal's interpretation of the term: see Section 6.2.1.

117 *Philippines v China* (n 21) [871]–[873].

118 ibid [368] and [886].

119 ibid [890].

120 ibid [1203].

121 See general discussion in Imogen Saunders, 'The Limits of the Natural State Doctrine: Rocks, Islands and Artificial Intervention in a Changing World' in Donald Rothwell and David Letts (eds), *Law of the Sea in South East Asia: Environmental, Navigational and Security Challenges* (Routledge 2019).

that naturally formed areas of land could undergo reinforcing works to prevent erosion and not transform into an artificial island.[122] Similarly, Oude Elferink considers that 'an island that is reinforced with coastal defences in principle remains an island and, conversely, an artificial island does not become an island if there is an accretion of land even if natural in origin.'[123] Soons takes a similar view that the 'artificial conservation of an island once formed by nature does not result in its losing its international legal status of "island." [...] Also the artificial conservation of an island exclusively for the purpose of preventing it from degenerating, as a result of sea level rise, to the status of "rock" [...] should be regarded as permissible.'[124]

Some have queried whether artificial interventions aimed at preservation might give rise to the possibility of transforming a naturally formed area of land into an 'artificial island',[125] particularly if the construction efforts are at a significant scale. In contrast to the type of transformations considered in *Philippines v China* (ie a purported 'upgrading' of status to an 'island'), this form of transformation might have the effect of 'downgrading' the ability of a feature to generate maritime zones. Aurescu and Oral ask: 'to what degree can the status of an island entitled to the entire panoply of maritime entitlements be conserved through artificial means and still maintain its character of being "naturally formed" as per paragraph 1 of article 121 of the Convention and international law.'[126] However, in these contexts, a consistent principle underlying potential legal transformations in any direction—that is, acquiring or losing insular status—is that while artificial interventions might physically transform a feature, they do not legally transform its status.

The above discussion of State practice, jurisprudence, and scholarship suggests that a distinction may be drawn between physical and legal processes of transformation as they relate to the status of a feature. Artificial interventions that physically transform a feature do not of themselves effect a legal transformation for the purposes of determining maritime zone entitlement. The example of Rockall can also be seen to illustrate this disjunction between

[122] Song, 'Okinotorishima: A Rock or an Island?' (n 42), discussing the concrete layer surrounding the rocky features, intended as protection from wave damage: 175.

[123] Alex G Oude Elferink, 'Artificial Islands, Installations and Structures', *Max Planck Encyclopedia of International Law* (2013) [4].

[124] AHA Soons, 'An Ocean under Stress: Climate Change and the Law of the Sea' in Ellen Hey and others (eds), *Climate Change: Options and Duties under International Law*, vol 145 (Koninklijke Nederlandse Vereniging voor Internationaal Recht 2018) 108.

[125] Bogdan Aurescu and Nilüfer Oral, Co-Chairs of the Study Group on Sea-Level Rise in relation to International Law, *First issues paper by Bogdan Aurescu and Nilüfer Oral* (28 February 2020) UN Doc A/CN.4/740 [215] (*First issues paper*).

[126] ibid [212].

legal and physical transformations relating to status: because of the United Kingdom's change of position on the applicable international law, an Executive Order transformed the legal status of Rockall from an 'island' to a 'rock not capable of sustaining human habitation and economic life', despite no physical transformations to Rockall itself. However, none of these examples deal with the scenario of 'natural' physical changes[127] affecting features (ie sea-level rise resulting in habitability loss and submergence). The following discussion considers how the distinction between physical and legal transformations might also play out here.

6.3.2 The legal transformation of features: the role of State practice relating to baseline legislation and baseline change

Rothwell's depiction of the scenario in which sea-level rise causes an island to become 'so awash that it is no longer above water at high tide and *becomes* an LTE'[128] implies a direct correlation between the legal transformation of an island into a low-tide elevation and the feature's submergence.[129] Relatedly, this correlation may also manifest in the consequences of a legal transformation, implied in concerns that an EEZ might be lost.[130] However, since there is a distinction between physical and legal transformations in the other scenarios discussed above (relating to Rockall, construction activities in the South China Sea, and the artificial preservation of coastlines), is it possible that such a distinction might also be present here, with the consequence that legal transformations might not always be the consequence of a feature's submergence?

Informed by the conclusions of Chapter 4 on the spatial stability of the normal baseline, this chapter argues that the answer to this question about the legal transformation of features also depends on how a coastal State has implemented its maritime zones. This book has demonstrated that coastal States

[127] Although Kaye suggests that there is some nuance in characterizing climate change effects as 'natural', given its anthropogenic causes: see Stuart Kaye, 'The Law of the Sea Convention and Sea Level Rise after the *South China Sea Arbitration*' (2017) 93 International Law Studies 423.

[128] Rothwell, *Islands and International Law* (n 29) 242 (emphasis added).

[129] It is also conceivable that a natural feature that was once classified as an 'island' might, following climate change impacts, be considered a 'rock'. Even if—as this chapter has argued—such a legal transformation is unlikely to be caused by habitability loss, it is still possible that a range of climate change effects could physically transform a feature to be less like Tromelin and more like Rockall. However, given the ongoing difficulties in interpreting the term 'rock' (including under a three-part model of features), this section focuses on the potential legal transformations that might occur as a result of sea-level-rise induced submergence: whether an 'island' becomes a 'low-tide elevation' or a fully submerged feature.

[130] See Rayfuse, 'Sea Level Rise and Maritime Zones' (n 28) 174–75.

implement their baselines in different ways: some coastal States' legislation identifies the baseline with the low-water line along the coast (a Type 1 definition of the normal baseline, eg Australia), and such domestic frameworks may be seen as having an 'ambulatory character'. Some coastal States pursue a greater degree of legal stability (such as those using a Type 2 or 3 normal baseline, eg Mauritius or Tuvalu), and these may be seen as adopting a more stable or 'fixed' means of implementation. The following section will consider each of these approaches, showing how choices about the legislative implementation of the baseline might affect questions of legal status (and its transformation or non-transformation).

Rothwell's description of an automatic legal transformation resulting from submergence most closely aligns with the situation of a coastal State which implements a Type 1 definition of the normal baseline. For example, Canada defines its baseline as 'the low-water line along the coast or on a low-tide elevation that is situated wholly or partly at a distance not exceeding the breadth of the territorial sea of Canada from the mainland or an island',[131] and the outer limit of its EEZ as 'the line every point of which is at a distance of 200 nautical miles from the nearest point of the baselines of the territorial sea of Canada'.[132] If, as a result of sea-level rise, there is no longer a low-water line along the coast (ie because the feature is submerged at high tide) or no longer any low-tide elevation within the breadth of the territorial sea (because it has become fully submerged), then the law's reference points for the location of the baseline and EEZ outer limits also no longer exist. Conceivably, this might be how an automatic transformation of features might occur: as a product of the 'direct relationship'[133] expressly created by a Type 1 definition between the existence of a particular physical feature and the location of a baseline and associated maritime zones.

However, many coastal States take a different approach to implementing their normal baselines. Chapter 4 found that 56 per cent of coastal States using the normal baseline use either coordinates (Type 2) or charts (Type 3) to define the location of the baseline.[134] For example, the Marine Zones (Declaration) Act 2011 provides that the 'Minister shall prescribe the baseline of Kiribati, from which the breadth of the territorial sea, the contiguous zone, the exclusive

[131] Oceans Act 1996 (Canada) s 5.

[132] ibid s 13(1).

[133] Clive Schofield, 'Departures from the Coast: Trends in the Application of Territorial Sea Baselines under the Law of the Sea Convention' (2012) 27 The International Journal of Marine and Coastal Law 723, 725.

[134] Section 4.2.1. Coastal States which exclusively use straight or archipelagic baselines might also be included in this group, since these types of baselines also use coordinates.

economic zone and the continental shelf of Kiribati shall be measured'.[135] Coordinates are then prescribed in various regulations, such as the Territorial Sea Baselines of Kiribati 2014 and the Exclusive Economic Zone Outer Limits Regulations 2014. Where a coastal State has implemented its baselines and associated maritime zones using this approach, if sea-level rise were to impact the elevation of an island or low-tide elevation (or other low-lying feature, such as a drying reef for the purposes of archipelagic baselines), this physical transformation would not directly affect the spatial definition of the baselines or maritime zones under the legislation: the location defined by coordinates or charts can only be changed by coastal State action. This suggests that in circumstances where the coastal State has defined the baseline (and maritime zones) using a fixed or stable approach, a physical transformation of the island or low-tide elevation due to its submergence need not lead to the destabilization of 'island' status (or loss of its EEZ).

Against this suggestion, it might be argued that 'States have an obligation to adjust unilateral limits to changing circumstances',[136] and that this obligation might extend to making adjustments as to the legal status of features. However, the proposition for such a duty to update—or indeed, abandon—an established maritime zone is inconsistent with the conclusion in Chapter 5 that there is no similar duty to update established baselines.[137] Indeed, the preservation of the status of features is implicit in the views expressed by many States[138] that there is no duty to update established baselines, notwithstanding the effects of sea-level rise.

This position is supported by the lack of evidence that States reclassify features or roll back their EEZ claims as a result of changed physical circumstances. There is also a lack of protest concerning the maintenance of maritime entitlements in relation to features which might have already experienced the effects of sea-level rise. In general, there are very few instances in which a State has protested the legal status of a feature in circumstances where it has undergone some kind of physical transformation. Okinotorishima is a well-known exception. In 1989, the Japanese government placed concrete and steel[139] around the small islets,[140] and, in 2007, planted tiny samples of laboratory-cultivated coral

[135] s 4(1).

[136] Snjólaug Árnadóttir, 'Fluctuating Boundaries in a Changing Marine Environment' (2021) 34 Leiden Journal of International Law 471, 472.

[137] See discussion in Section 5.4.

[138] See Section 5.3.

[139] Yoshifumi Tanaka, *The International Law of the Sea* (3rd edn, Cambridge University Press 2019) 78.

[140] For a description of the history and geography of the islets, see Song, 'Okinotorishima: A Rock or an Island?' (n 42).

around them with the aim of increasing the size of the coral reef, protecting the reef environment from risks of climate change (such as submergence), and, more generally, protecting 'national land'.[141] China, Taiwan, and the Republic of Korea have protested Japan's assertion of an EEZ and/or continental shelf around Okinotorishima,[142] implicitly rejecting any purported reliance on the physically transformative effects of concrete reinforcement or coral growth to satisfy the requirements of Article 121(3) for full maritime zones. But no States have yet protested an established EEZ or continental shelf on the basis that it is no longer supported by a feature that has been physically transformed, including through sea-level rise.

This section has argued that an inquiry about the legal transformation of features as a result of sea-level rise is enriched by bringing into view relevant State practice on the implementation of the baseline and on the non-existence of a duty to update baselines. This perspective highlights that the choice to adopt a Type 1 definition of the normal baseline creates a 'direct relationship' between the legislation and the physical features from which maritime zones are established, resulting in the creation of an equally direct relationship between the physical transformation of features and their legal transformation. However, where coastal States define their baselines using coordinates or charts, it is arguable that those baselines and maritime zones—and the legal status of the 'island' underpinning them—remain stable because no legal transformation has occurred.

6.4 Sea-level rise and 'archipelagic status'

In addition to the question of whether sea-level rise might potentially destabilize the legal status of features—the principal focus of this chapter—questions have also been raised about whether sea-level rise poses risks for 'archipelagic status', and these are now discussed briefly here. For example, in considering the scenario of widely scattered archipelagos and the requirement that archipelagic baselines enclose an 'area in which the ratio of the area of the water to the area of the land, including atolls, is between 1 to 1 and 9

[141] See Japanese fisheries officials quoted in various media reports: Chris Hogg, 'Japan Uses Coral to "Grow" Islets' *BBC News* (15 June 2007) <http://news.bbc.co.uk/2/hi/asia-pacific/6758271.stm>; 'Japan Plants Coral Islets to Bolster Territorial Claim' *New York Times* (15 July 2007) <www.nytimes.com/2007/06/15/world/asia/15iht-coral.1.6151693.html>; Agence France-Presse (Tokyo), 'Japan Plants Coral to Save Sinking Territory' *Terradaily* (18 June 2007) <www.terradaily.com/reports/Japan_Plants_Coral_To_Save_Sinking_Territory_999.html>.

[142] See Song, 'Okinotorishima: A Rock or an Island?' (n 42) 146.

to 1',[143] Kaye writes that '[a] rise in sea level might remove drying reefs from the archipelagic State's calculation in relation to land, and therefore it might struggle to retain its archipelagic status'.[144] Schofield and Freestone point out that the first impacts of inundation by a rising sea level will affect low-lying islands and other maritime features, which 'may potentially have disproportional impacts on the ability of an archipelagic State to which they belong to maintain its compliance with the detailed requirements for archipelagic status set out by UNCLOS, possibly even compromising its ability to maintain its claim to archipelagic status'.[145] In a similar vein, Aurescu and Oral also draw attention to this issue, writing that:

> [s]ea-level rise also poses a risk to an archipelagic State's baselines. As a result of the inundation of small islands or drying reefs, the existing archipelagic baseline could be impacted, resulting in the loss of archipelagic State status of baselines if the water to the area of land ratio exceeds 9:1. In addition, it could result in an appreciable departure from the general configuration of the archipelago and affect the distance/percentage criterion for the archipelagic baselines.[146]

Although the LOSC itself does not use the term 'archipelagic status', these concerns engage two key concepts under Part IV of the LOSC on 'Archipelagic States':[147] the 'archipelagic State' and the 'archipelagic baseline'. An 'archipelagic State' is defined to mean 'a State constituted wholly by one or more archipelagos and may include other islands', and 'archipelago' is further defined to mean 'group of islands, including parts of islands, interconnecting waters and other natural features which are so closely interrelated that such islands, waters and other natural features form an intrinsic geographical, economic and political entity, or which historically have been regarded as such'.[148] Archipelagic

[143] LOSC, art 47(1).

[144] Kaye, 'The Law of the Sea Convention and Sea Level Rise after the *South China Sea Arbitration*' (n 127) 435.

[145] David Freestone and Clive Schofield, 'Sea Level Rise and Archipelagic States: A Preliminary Risk Assessment' (2021) 35 Ocean Yearbook 340, 344.

[146] *First issues paper* (n 125) [76].

[147] For a comprehensive discussion of UNCLOS pt IV, including the concept of the 'archipelagic state', see Rothwell, *Islands and International Law* (n 29); Alex P de la Cruz, 'Making History, Making Archipelagos: A Parallel South China Sea Dispute' (2024) Blue Security 4; Till Markus, 'Article 46—Archipelagic States' in Alexander Proelss (ed), *United Nations Convention on the Law of the Sea: A Commentary* (1st edn, CH Beck 2017); Kevin Baumert and Brian Melchior, 'The Practice of Archipelagic States: A Study of Studies' (2015) 46 Ocean Development & International Law 60; ILA (Committee on Baselines under the International Law of the Sea), 'Baselines under the International Law of the Sea (Sydney Conference)' (2018 ILA Baselines Committee Report).

[148] LOSC, art 46.

baselines are defined to be straight baselines that join 'the outermost points of the outermost islands and drying reefs of the archipelago', provided that specific technical requirements on the drawing of such baselines are also satisfied.[149] Both of these concepts are significant for the maritime entitlements of archipelagic States, in that only an archipelagic State is entitled to establish archipelagic baselines,[150] and that in so doing, the archipelagic State has sovereignty over the waters enclosed by those baselines as its archipelagic waters:[151] these are the most significant entitlements enjoyed by an archipelagic State.[152]

If we consider first the extent to which concerns about the loss of 'archipelagic status' relate to the ability of a State to continue to meet the definition of an 'archipelagic State' in Article 46, the question might be asked whether sea-level rise might affect the satisfaction of geographical criteria (such as the State being comprised wholly by one or more archipelagos, where islands, waters, and other features form an intrinsic geographical entity) or non-geographical criteria (such as political or economic unity, or historical regard as such). It is possible to speculate, for example, that sea-level rise could submerge the low-lying islands of a State with the result that the State comprises a single island; in that scenario, the single island would not meet the 'primary factor in the definition of an archipelago',[153] which requires 'a group of islands'. Submergence of some islands in a group could also affect the overall configuration of an archipelago, and if this were to result in the remaining islands being very widely scattered, this could affect whether those islands continue to comprise an intrinsic geographical entity of an 'archipelago' for the purposes of Article 46(b). Stoutenburg also mentions that an uninhabitable archipelago might raise questions about the political or economic elements of an 'archipelago', and considers that if 'the island state acquire[s] new territory from a continental state—should the Maldives for example buy territory from India, as contemplated by its president—, it would therefore no longer qualify as an archipelagic state under Art 46(a) UNCLOS'.[154]

149 LOSC, art 47.

150 LOSC, art 47(1); this requirement was also discussed in *Maritime Delimitation and Territorial Questions between Qatar and Bahrain (Qatar/Bahrain)* (Judgment) [2001] ICJ Rep 40 [214] (*Qatar/Bahrain*) and *Philippines v China* (n 21) [573].

151 LOSC, art 49(1).

152 Rothwell, *Islands and International Law* (n 29) 120.

153 T Davenport, 'The Archipelagic Regime' in Donald R Rothwell and others (eds), *The Oxford Handbook of the Law of the Sea* (Oxford University Press 2015) 142.

154 Grote Stoutenburg, *Disappearing Island States in International Law* (n 90) 178–79, and note 425 in relation to Maldives and India. However, it is not clear whether Maldives continues to consider this as an option, since the potential purchase of territory from other States is not mentioned in Maldives' more recent engagements on the effects of sea-level rise (eg Maldives, 'Information and Examples of State Practice on "Sea-Level Rise in relation to International Law": A Submission by the Republic of Maldives' (31 December 2019) (2019 Maldives ILC Submission)).

However, even though the physical effects of sea-level rise relate to several aspects of the concept of an 'archipelagic State', does it necessarily follow that sea-level rise could automatically result in the disqualification of an 'archipelagic State', that is, a loss of its status as such? This chapter suggests that it is unlikely that loss of status as an 'archipelagic State' is either a necessary or an automatic product of such circumstances. This flows from the observation that there are some States which appear to meet the requirements of Article 46, but which do not consider themselves to be archipelagic States for the purposes of the establishment of their baselines and maritime zones: Japan, New Zealand, and the United Kingdom are often-cited examples.[155] To these could also be added Micronesia, which refers to its territory as being comprised of the 'Micronesian archipelago'[156] but has not proclaimed itself to be an archipelagic State for the purposes of its maritime zones, instead making clear that it exclusively uses the normal baseline for its territorial sea baseline.[157]

These examples suggest that there is some degree of discretion[158] on the part of a State in terms of bringing itself within the concept of an 'archipelagic State', at least in terms of its maritime entitlements. Relatedly, the ICJ expressed the view that archipelagic baselines are only available 'if the State has declared itself to be an archipelagic State under Part IV of the 1982 Convention on the Law of the Sea',[159] which reinforces the idea that a State is not automatically an archipelagic State for the purposes of Part IV of the LOSC but instead must claim such status. If being an archipelagic State for the purposes of the LOSC is not achieved through satisfaction of the Article 46 criteria alone, this suggests that sea-level-rise-induced changes to the geographical and non-geographical factors relevant to those criteria might not necessarily correlate to loss of status as an 'archipelagic State'. Bahamas makes explicit this view, stating that, '[d]uring the negotiations leading to the Convention, The Bahamas, along with a group of small island states and supported by others, ensured that the unique characteristics of archipelagic states, such as ours, were reflected in the Convention. This status is integral to our political, cultural and social identity and is not altered, changed or lost due to the impacts of sea-level rise.'[160]

[155] Markus, 'Article 46—Archipelagic States' (n 147) 348; Davenport, 'The Archipelagic Regime' (n 153).

[156] Constitution of the Federated States of Micronesia, art I.

[157] Title 18, chap 1 of the Code of the Federated States of Micronesia (Annotated), as amended by Public Law no 19-172 (28 April 2017) pt I, Annex I.

[158] Markus, 'Article 46—Archipelagic States' (n 147) 348.

[159] *Qatar/Bahrain* (n 150) [214].

[160] The Bahamas, 'Submission to the International Law Commission in regard to "Sea-Level Rise in relation to International Law"' (18 November 2024) 1 (2024 Bahamas ILC Submission).

This stability in the status of an 'archipelagic State' is also implicit in the views of other archipelagic States, as will be discussed later.

Let us consider now the extent to which concerns about 'archipelagic status' might relate to the requirements for archipelagic baselines set out in Article 47. The different ways in which this could potentially arise have been mentioned, such as the submergence of low-lying features (in particular, the outermost 'drying reefs of the archipelago'), or in relation to satisfying the land to water ratio and baseline length requirements.[161] Here, the question is whether established archipelagic baselines might be disrupted by sea-level rise, causing consequential changes to the location and extent of maritime zones.

In their preliminary assessment of the potential for sea-level rise to affect features currently contributing to an established archipelagic baseline system, Freestone and Schofield conclude that 'every single one of the twenty-two States that have claimed archipelagic status [. . .] have utilized the quite legitimate but high risk features of low-lying islands, coral reef features or low-tide elevations as archipelagic basepoints'.[162] Taking the example of Jamaica, a State comprising one large main island flanked to the south by low-lying features, Schofield and Freestone raise the concern that 'the loss of low elevation coral features such as Jamaica's southern cays would have major impacts and put the Jamaican archipelagic status at serious risk'.[163] Freestone and Schofield appear to take an expansive view of 'archipelagic status' not only to mean the satisfaction of Article 46—here, the question of Jamaica's status as an 'archipelagic State'—but encompassing also whether Jamaica's entitlement to archipelagic baselines for the purposes of Article 47. Rothwell takes a similar approach, explaining that 'even if a State meets all the generic criteria of Article 46, if the State is unable to comply with the specific requirements of the archipelagic baseline regime, its ability to proclaim itself as an archipelagic State will be compromised'.[164] While there is a distinction between the concepts of 'archipelagic State' and 'archipelagic baseline',[165] this expansive view of 'archipelagic status'

[161] See also Nilufer Oral, 'UNCLOS and Sea Level Rise' (2023) 149 Marine Policy 1, 2.

[162] Freestone and Schofield, 'Sea Level Rise and Archipelagic States' (n 145) 383. For a detailed analysis of the twenty-two archipelagic States, see also Rothwell, *Islands and International Law* (n 29) Table 5.1.

[163] Freestone and Schofield, 'Sea Level Rise and Archipelagic States' (n 145) 381.

[164] Rothwell, *Islands and International Law* (n 29) 121.

[165] This is well explained in the *Virginia Commentaries*: 'The effect is that a group of islands will come within the definition of an archipelago if it fits the criteria listed in article 46, subparagraph (b), but a State may not apply the concept of archipelagic waters to those islands unless it draws straight archipelagic baselines in accordance with the requirements of article 47. Conversely, a State is not entitled to draw archipelagic baselines unless it meets the criteria of article 46, subparagraphs (a) and (b)': Nandan, Nordquist, and Rosenne, *United Nations Convention on the Law of the Sea 1982: A Commentary* (n 16) [46.6(b)].

makes clear that in practical terms the two concepts are closely connected: this is because the key archipelagic State entitlements hinge on the establishment of archipelagic baselines to enclose archipelagic waters and from which to measure the territorial sea and other maritime zones.

Importantly, Rothwell, Freestone, and Schofield identify that questions about the potential legal effects of sea-level rise on archipelagic baselines engage the broader debate about whether baselines are ambulatory or fixed.[166] In particular, Freestone and Schofield observe that:

> these risks to the archipelagic status, baselines and maritime claims of archipelagic States can be tackled through a progressive interpretation of the international law of the sea. In particular, if the international community were to accept the recommendation made by the ILA in 2018, and voiced by the South Pacific Forum Leaders in Tuvalu in 2019, that baselines and maritime zone claims that have been established in accordance with provisions of UNCLOS should be regarded as being 'sea level rise proof,' then the claims of archipelagic States would be protected once defined and declared in communications to the United Nations Secretary-General.[167]

Articulating and evaluating the legal basis for such a 'progressive interpretation' is a core aim of this book, and it is now possible to elaborate how arguments presented earlier in the book apply particularly to archipelagic baselines, thereby also connecting to questions raised about sea-level rise and archipelagic status. First, the book drew attention to the use of coordinates in States' baseline legislation as 'a spatially stable method of defining a line on the surface of the earth, capable of expressing absolute location', and that 'implementing a spatially-stable baseline is a crucial first step in the pursuit of stable maritime zones that are capable of preservation'.[168] Archipelagic baselines, since they are always defined using coordinates,[169] inherently have such spatial stability and are accordingly capable of forming the basis of stable maritime zones. Secondly, the

[166] Rothwell, *Islands and International Law* (n 29) 243; Freestone and Schofield, 'Sea Level Rise and Archipelagic States' (n 145) 383.

[167] Freestone and Schofield, 'Sea Level Rise and Archipelagic States' (n 145) 383.

[168] Section 4.4.

[169] For a comprehensive list of legislation implementing archipelagic baselines, see Rothwell, *Islands and International Law* (n 29) Table 5.1, from p 116. All listed legislation specifies coordinates defining the location of the archipelagic baseline, with the exception of the Maritime Areas Act 1982 (Antigua and Barbuda). However, it is reasonably clear that such coordinates exist, as explained in Antigua and Barbuda, 'Submission on the Effects of Sea Level Rise on the Law of the Sea' (Seventy-Second Session of the International Law Commission) (2021), and as listed in US Department of State, 'Antigua and Barbuda: Archipelagic and Other Maritime Claims and Boundaries' *Limits in the Seas* no 133 (28 March 2014) (Antigua and Barbuda: Archipelagic and Other Maritime Claims and Boundaries).

book demonstrated that 'there is insufficient evidence for the implication of a duty to update established baselines, with the result that established baselines enjoy a temporal stability if a coastal State opts to preserve them once established.'[170] Against the backdrop of an increasing number of States that have 'explicitly taken the view that duly established baselines and maritime zones are not subject to any coastal State duty to update them',[171] it is particularly significant that archipelagic States are extremely well represented among these. In fact, all archipelagic States have expressed the view that international law permits the preservation of established maritime zones notwithstanding sea-level rise: this may be seen in statements made as members of the PIF or AOSIS (or both, as indicated in Table 6.1),[172] or because they have expressed this position elsewhere.[173]

Accordingly, there is a strong foundation for a contemporary interpretation of Article 47 of the LOSC that supports the preservation of archipelagic baselines notwithstanding sea-level rise. Furthermore, since only archipelagic States are entitled to use archipelagic baselines, this position implies that the status of an archipelagic State pursuant to Article 46 will also remain undisturbed by the effects of sea-level rise. The stability of status as an archipelagic State is consistent with views of States in relation to a different legal status—that

[170] Section 5.4.

[171] Section 5.3.5.

[172] Declaration on Preserving Maritime Zones in the Face of Climate Change-Related Sea-Level Rise (signed 6 August 2021) <www.forumsec.org/2021/08/11/declaration-on-preserving-maritime-zones-in-the-face-of-climate-change-related-sea-level-rise/> (2021 PIF Declaration); Leaders' Declaration of the Alliance of Small Island States (signed 22 September 2021) <www.aosis.org/launch-of-the-alliance-of-small-island-states-leaders-declaration/> (2021 AOSIS Declaration). To be clear, this position should be distinguished from the fact that from time to time, archipelagic States have updated their maritime zones legislation for different reasons, primarily in connection with bringing them into conformity with the LOSC: eg Indonesia and the Philippines, as discussed in Section 5.2.1. Another example is that of Papua New Guinea, which updated its baseline through the Maritime Zones Act 2015 because its previous baselines and maritime zones were 'not compliant with the requirements of the 1982 United Nations Convention of the Law of the Sea, which Papua New Guinea is a State party to having ratified it on the 14 January, 1997': Mr Ano Pala (Minister for Justice and Attorney-General), *Parliamentary Hansard from Second Reading and Passing of the Maritime Zones Act* (3 June 2015), 56.

[173] Indonesia has stated that 'the principles of legal stability, certainty, and predictability, as well as the preservation of the balance of rights and obligations under UNCLOS should be maintained. Stability of baselines and outer limits of maritime zones in accordance with UNCLOS should be upheld regardless of sea-level rise. Existing maritime boundary agreements shall be respected and that the law of treaties shall prevail. Charts or lists of geographical coordinates of baselines that have been deposited with the Secretary General pursuant to Article 16(2) and 47(9) of UNCLOS shall also continue to be relevant': 'Statement of Indonesia at the 27th Meeting of the Sixth Committee', Seventy-Eighth Session (25 October 2023) <www.un.org/en/ga/sixth/78/pdfs/statements/ilc/27mtg_indonesia_1.pdf?>, an official summary is recorded at UN Doc A/C.6/78/SR.27; Philippines stated that '[e]rosion of coastlines and inundation of features as a result of sea level rise, for example, should not affect the baselines that the State has established': Republic of the Philippines, 'Inputs on the International Law Commission's Subtopic of "Sea-Level Rise in relation to International Law"' (18 July 2022) (2022 Philippines ILC Submission).

Table 6.1 Archipelagic States and their membership of PIF and/or AOSIS

	Archipelagic State	Membership of PIF and/or AOSIS
1.	Antigua & Barbuda	AOSIS
2.	Bahamas	AOSIS
3.	Cape Verde	AOSIS
4.	Comoros	AOSIS
5.	Dominican Republic	AOSIS
6.	Fiji	PIF & AOSIS
7.	Grenada	AOSIS
8.	Indonesia	-
9.	Jamaica	AOSIS
10.	Kiribati	PIF & AOSIS
11.	Maldives	AOSIS
12.	Marshall Islands	PIF & AOSIS
13.	Mauritius	AOSIS
14.	Papua New Guinea	PIF & AOSIS
15.	Philippines	-
16.	Saint Vincent and the Grenadines	AOSIS
17.	São Tomé and Principe	AOSIS
18.	Seychelles	AOSIS
19.	Solomon Islands	PIF & AOSIS
20.	Trinidad and Tobago	AOSIS
21.	Tuvalu	PIF & AOSIS
22.	Vanuatu	PIF & AOSIS

of statehood—where the emerging consensus is that, '[w]ith regard to States particularly affected by climate change-related sea-level rise, there is strong support among States for the continuity of statehood and sovereignty'.[174] In parallel to the idea of distinguishing between the criteria required for the creation of a State and conditions for its extinguishment as an aspect of State continuity,[175] here, too, the stability of status as an archipelagic State makes clear that satisfaction of the requirements of Article 46 is required at the time such

[174] Study Group on Sea-Level Rise in Relation to International Law, 'Final Report of the Study Group on Sea-Level Rise in Relation to International Law', UN Doc A/80/10, Annex I [35] (2025 ILC Study Group Final Report). See further discussion on statehood issues in Section 8.3.2.

[175] Patrícia Galvão Teles, Nilüfer Oral, and Juan José Ruda Santolaria, 'Final Consolidated Report of the Co-Chairs of the Study Group on Sea-Level Rise in Relation to International Law' (3 February 2025) UN Doc A/CN.4/783 (Final Consolidated Report of the Co-Chairs), see [148]ff. This also recalls Purcell's discussion of the temporal dimensions of maritime entitlement, discussed in Section 5.3.2.

status is claimed. The LOSC does not require that such requirements be satisfied on an ongoing basis in the face of sea-level rise impacts.

6.5 Stability for the legal status of features under the LOSC

This chapter has argued that the destabilization of the legal status of features as a result of sea-level rise, bringing with it the loss of maritime zones such as the EEZ and continental shelf, is not necessarily a fait accompli. If we bring into view relevant State practice—relatively abundant in the case of the implementation of Article 121 yet scant in the case of the roll-back of extended maritime zones—more nuanced propositions can be advanced. First, the number of 'islands' potentially affected by habitability loss may not be as numerous as feared because State practice suggests that the better interpretation of Article 121 is that it envisages a three-part model of features. Habitability plays a second-order role under this model, since HHEL only potentially constrains the maritime entitlements of islands which are rocks. However, for islands which are not rocks, habitability loss is potentially irrelevant because capacity to sustain HHEL is not a requirement for 'island' status in the first place. In this way, many (if not most) 'islands' are likely to enjoy stability in relation to the full complement of maritime zones as a consequence of the interpretation of Article 121 advanced in this chapter, notwithstanding habitability loss.

Secondly, this chapter has shown that choices in domestic implementation affect whether or not the legal status of a feature will be destabilized as a result of submergence: in particular, whether a coastal State opts to implement a baseline by methods securing more or less spatial stability. As a result, if any coastal State which adopts a Type 1 definition of the normal baseline[176] wishes to avoid such an automatic legal transformation, one option might be to amend its implementing legislation to remove the 'direct relationship' between the physical feature and the baseline, and to instead move to a Type 2 or 3 definition. This chapter has argued that, under these conditions, the legal status of

[176] While there are forty-eight coastal States which adopt a Type 1 definition of the normal baseline (forty-two LOSC Parties and six LOSC non-Parties) (Section 4.3; Appendix 4.1), it is notable that none of these are identified by McGranahan et al as having a substantial portion of land in the LECZ: Gordon McGranahan, Deborah Balk, and Bridget Anderson, 'The Rising Tide: Assessing the Risks of Climate Change and Human Settlements in Low Elevation Coastal Zones' (2007) 19 Environment and Urbanization 17. For this reason, it may be that for these Type 1 coastal States, a physical transformation of territory from a high-tide elevation to a low-tide elevation is unlikely at a country level. However, some Type 1 coastal States do have low-lying islands (eg Australia, Tonga). Depending on the local projected risks of submergence in these specific locales, perhaps it is these coastal States that may wish to consider legislative reforms.

features has a degree of stability notwithstanding the physical transformation of a feature by submergence.

The 'international aspect'[177] of such domestic choices might be conceptualized as a form of acquiescence under international law. In the context of the maintenance of States' claims to an EEZ and/or continental shelf in circumstances not conforming with the Tribunal's approach in *Philippines v China*, Mossop points out the possibility that:

> the maritime zone has been confirmed due to the uncontested exercise of rights. Where a state has claimed an EEZ and continental shelf from a small off-shore feature for a long period of time and it has consistently exercised its rights accordingly without any objection from other states, it can be argued that the international community has acquiesced in the coastal state's interpretation of art 121 to the effect that the feature can generate an EEZ and continental shelf.[178]

This reasoning is equally applicable in the case of the maintenance of an established EEZ or continental shelf in circumstances where the feature has been impacted by sea-level rise. Mossop's reasoning also gestures to the potential for a broader implication. At a global scale, it is possible that a trend may emerge amongst Parties to the LOSC pointing to the emergence of a 'common understanding' as to the stability of the legal status of features affected by sea-level rise. Continued maintenance of established maritime zones in relation to features affected by submergence, coupled with increasing acquiescence amongst LOSC Parties, will provide a strong foundation to advance the stability of the status of features as a matter of the LOSC's interpretation.

[177] *Fisheries (United Kingdom v Norway)* [1951] ICJ Rep 116, [132].

[178] Mossop, 'The South China Sea Arbitration and New Zealand's Maritime Claims' (n 42) 286. On acquiescence generally, including as an element of interpretation, see IC MacGibbon, 'The Scope of Acquiescence in International Law' (1954) 2 British Yearbook of International Law 143.

7

Achieving Stable Maritime Zones

Options for Domestic and International Actions

7.1 Introduction

This book has demonstrated that there is a sound legal foundation for the preservation of maritime zones notwithstanding sea-level rise. Nevertheless, there remain some areas in which action to achieve stable maritime zones might still be needed or desired, at both the domestic and international levels, including in relation to bringing sea-level rise and maritime zones before international courts and tribunals.

7.2 Domestic action: implementing spatially stable baselines in legislation

At the domestic level, it must be recalled that there are a large number of coastal States which use a Type 1 normal baseline in their legislation;[1] as explained in Chapter 4, this is, in effect, the implementation in their national systems of a baseline which has an ambulatory character, in which legislation creates a 'direct relationship'[2] with the coast. State practice, however, supplies a clear answer to the potential problem of 'how to fix baselines formed by the low-water line along the coast',[3] which is to implement domestically a spatially stable form of normal baseline principally by the use of coordinates. This is an approach adopted by thirty-seven coastal States, which have selected this form of normal baseline from within the generally accepted

[1] Forty-two LOSC Parties and six non-Parties use a Type 1 definition: see Chapter 4, Figure 4.2.

[2] Clive Schofield, 'Departures from the Coast: Trends in the Application of Territorial Sea Baselines under the Law of the Sea Convention' (2012) 27 The International Journal of Marine and Coastal Law 723, 725.

[3] Ireland, 'International Law Commission's Study Group in relation to International Law' (January 2025) (Ireland 2025 ILC Submission); see discussion in Section 4.4.

Sea-Level Rise and the Legal Stability of Maritime Zones. Frances Anggadi, Oxford University Press.
 DOI: 10.1093/9780198973515.003.0007

'menu' of implementation types that exists for this baseline type.[4] A normal baseline marked on an officially recognized electronic chart—depicting the location of the baseline, underpinned by coordinates—could serve a similar purpose.[5]

In terms of unilateral actions to achieve legal stability, coastal States which do not currently use such spatially stable methods to implement their normal baselines would have a sound international law basis to take that course of action. It may be that such legislative reforms are not a priority for all coastal States currently using a Type 1 definition of their normal baseline. For example, a coastal State which enjoys a relatively stable coastline would have stable maritime zones as a direct product of its stable coastline, and, as a result, perhaps have less of a need to pursue legal stability through the use of coordinates. However, those coastal States that appear to have low-lying coastlines, and which also currently use a Type 1 definition, may wish to consider such reforms.[6] The implementation of a spatially stable baseline is an essential requirement for the achievement of stable maritime zones because, as a practical matter, a mobile maritime zone is impossible to preserve.

7.3 International action: solidifying the legal stability of maritime zones among States

At the international level, continued diplomatic and political statements explicitly supporting stable maritime zones at the international level—and making clear the understanding that this view is founded on an interpretation of the United Nations Convention on the Law of the Sea (LOSC) (as the PIF Declaration does)—will continue to solidify the convergence of views on this issue.[7] While no States have yet spoken against the PIF Declaration or the legal positions within it, some States have yet to express any view, including amongst LOSC Parties.[8] For States still developing views on this matter, it may be useful to have regard to the body of evidence identified in this book, pointing to a

[4] See Section 4.2.1.3.

[5] See discussions on the use of electronic navigational chart (ENCs) in relation to the normal baseline in Section 4.2.1.

[6] For a list of such States using a Type 1 definition, see Chapter 4, Figure 4.2.

[7] As discussed later in this chapter, this number stands at 104 States (n 43).

[8] Noting that many of those yet to speak are landlocked States Parties, such as Bolivia, Laos, and Zambia.

convergence between what States say and do about legal stability and maritime zones. Such a convergence not only carries political force but also has legal significance for all States.

It must also be recognized that pursuing legal stability as matter of the interpretation and application of the LOSC—supported by State practice and with the agreement of LOSC Parties—represents an incremental approach to the preservation of maritime zones. Its success relies on the convergence at a global scale between what States say and what States do about legal stability and maritime zones. The contestability of such an interpretative claim means that absolute legal certainty cannot be assumed, nor can it in the future be guaranteed; the matter continues to lie in the hands of States.

Of course, such certainty could be achieved by express provision in the LOSC, but this would require formal amendment and, especially given its procedural and political difficulties, there seems little benefit now in pursuing such a course of action, particularly as it may risk unravelling the significant degree of agreement that has already been reached on this issue through subsequent practice. More promising is the recommendation of the International Law Association Committee on International Law and Sea Level Rise (ILA SLR Committee) for an 'explicit recognition' of the interpretation of the LOSC advanced in the PIF Declaration, to

> significantly contribute to facilitating legal certainty concerning the stability of baselines, maritime limits, and maritime boundaries in the context of sea level rise, so that there would be considerable benefit from the adoption of a globally agreed instrument enabling wide participation—such as an UNGA resolution or whatever other format or forum might be agreed upon for this purpose—that confirms international law as reflected in the Convention, clarifying its contemporary interpretation.[9]

Similarly, the Final Report of the ILC Study Group recommended, as part of suggested ways forward, the consideration of an approach 'that allows for the interpretation and application of existing instruments and rules of international law to take into account the adverse impact of sea-level rise', including 'an interpretative statement or a subsequent agreement, as appropriate, [which] may be adopted by the States Parties to the United Nations Convention on the Law of the Sea or by the General Assembly regarding the preservation of

[9] ILA (Committee on International Law and Sea Level Rise) Res 1/2024 (ILA 2024 Resolution).

baselines and maritime zones under the Convention and other rules of international law'.[10]

It remains to be seen whether States take up such suggestions for clarification in these fora. It may be that the Opinion of the International Court of Justice (ICJ) in *Obligations of States in Respect of Climate Change* provides a basis for increased momentum to take further steps towards clarification. If that is the case, there are some matters on which there is already significant consensus which could readily be incorporated in a potential interpretative statement. For example (and adapting some of the language from the 2021 PIF Declaration), such a statement could provide:

- That maintaining maritime zones established in accordance with the Convention, and rights and entitlements that flow from them, notwithstanding climate change-related sea-level rise, is supported by a contemporary interpretation of Articles 5, 7, 47, and 121 of the LOSC; and
- That the legal stability of maritime zones is practically achieved by establishing spatially stable baselines and maritime zones in legislation, the maintenance of the legal status of features supporting full maritime zone entitlement, and the maintenance (non-update) of established baselines and maritime zones over time.

Addressing these matters would have the benefit of making clear *which* provisions of the LOSC are contemplated in this contemporary interpretation, and by articulating the three elements of legal stability, also clarifying *how* such an interpretation is practically applied to result in the preservation of maritime zones notwithstanding sea-level rise.

There are also further matters which could be addressed in an interpretative statement, but on which agreement remains outstanding within the international community. These matters pertain to notification, the treatment of contested or overlapping maritime claims, the point in time at which a baseline and maritime zone are preserved, and the overall scope of the interpretation. Perhaps the most straightforward of these is the question of whether notification should also be a requirement or condition for the preservation of maritime zones. The 2021 Pacific Islands Forum (PIF) Declaration, Alliance of Small Island States (AOSIS) Declaration, and Commonwealth Ocean Declaration all

[10] Study Group on Sea-Level Rise In relation to International Law, 'Final Report of the Study Group on Sea-Level Rise in relation to International Law' UN Doc A/80/10, Annex I [58] (2025 ILC Study Group Final Report).

refer to the requirement to notify or deposit maritime zones information with the UN Secretary-General. This reflects due publicity obligations already in the LOSC in relation to straight[11] and archipelagic baselines,[12] and although no such duty is provided for in the LOSC in relation to normal baselines, there is evidence that Pacific States, for example, have already demonstrated a strong trend in depositing all baseline and maritime zones information with the UN Secretary-General.[13]

In its 2025 Report, the International Law Commission (ILC) recognizes that '[t]here is no provision in the United Nations Convention on the Law of the Sea that imposes an obligation on States to update baselines, geographical coordinates or the outer limits of maritime zones once duly deposited with the Secretary-General in accordance with the Convention',[14] and this aspect has also been noted by States more broadly, such as the members of the European Union, Indonesia, and Malaysia.[15] However, it is not yet clear whether there should be a requirement to simply notify baselines and maritime zones information to the international community (as is currently the case in relation to straight and archipelagic baselines, as noted also by the ICJ),[16] or whether there might be a stronger requirement to notify a State's intention or policy to preserve those established baselines (as Micronesia and Cook Islands have done at the time of deposit).[17] On balance, there are sound reasons for suggesting that the requirement for notification could potentially be a fourth element in

[11] LOSC, art 16(1).

[12] LOSC, art 47(9).

[13] See Frances Anggadi, 'Establishment, Notification, and Maintenance: The Package of State Practice at the Heart of the Pacific Islands Forum Declaration on Preserving Maritime Zones' (2022) 53 Ocean Development & International Law 19.

[14] ILC, 'Report of the International Law Commission covering the Work of its Seventy-Sixth Session' (28 April–30 May 2025) UN Doc A/80/10 [29] (2025 ILC Report).

[15] See statements made in the Sixth Committee of the UN General Assembly, Seventy-Eighth Session <www.un.org/en/ga/sixth/78/ilc.shtml> and discussion in Section 5.3.5.

[16] *Obligations of States in Respect of Climate Change* (Advisory Opinion) [2025], [358] (*Obligations of States in Respect of Climate Change*) <https://www.icj-cij.org/case/187>.

[17] Micronesia, Observations made on 24 December 2019, and revised on 15 January 2020, by the Federated States of Micronesia in connection with the official deposit of lists of geographical coordinates of points, accompanied by illustrative maps, for maritime baselines and maritime zones in accordance with the 1982 United Nations Convention on the Law of the Sea (2019); and Cook Islands, Observations made on 12 August 2021 by the Cook Islands in connection with the official deposit of lists of geographical coordinates of points, accompanied by illustrative maps, for maritime baselines and maritime zones in accordance with the 1982 United Nations Convention on the Law of the Sea (2021). Other States have signalled such a policy through legislation: see eg Climate Change Act 2021 (Fiji) s 80; Republic of the Marshall Islands Maritime Zones Declaration (Amendment) Act 2025; Constitution of Tuvalu Act 2023, s 2(3). Micronesia is reported to have taken a similar approach: Mar-Vic Cagurangan, 'FSM Renews Claim over Mineral-Rich Territories in the High Seas' *Pacific Island Times* (15 January 2024) <www.pacificislandtimes.com/post/fsm-renews-claim-over-mineral-rich-territories-in-the-high-seas>.

the legal stability of maritime zones. If this were the case, it would represent a development in the interpretation and application of the Article 16 obligations of due publicity,[18] extending the obligation of notification to apply for all baseline types as a precondition for their preservation.

An additional reason in favour of a requirement of notification to the international community is that it could address situations where there are disputed or overlapping maritime claims. For example, Davenport and Benosa explain that:

> [f]or Southeast Asian states whose baselines have been the subject of objections and protests from other states, the preservation of baselines and outer limits raises even more complex questions on what it means for those 'to be made in accordance with UNCLOS'. Southeast Asian states whose straight baselines have been protested by other states due to noncompliance with Article 7 of UNCLOS may not be able to preserve them.[19]

The United Kingdom might have had similar concerns in mind when it clarified its view that preservation 'can only apply to baselines or outer limits which are initially established in accordance with UNCLOS. It remains the UK Government position that UNCLOS provides the complete and definitive rules on the drawing of baselines from which maritime zones are measured'.[20] If notification of baselines and maritime zones to the international community is a precondition for their preservation, this would give an opportunity for reaction from other States.

If notification is to be addressed in an interpretative statement, there could also be merit in considering the relevant point in time from which the baseline and maritime zones could be considered to be preserved: the PIF Declaration (and similar declarations) imply that preservation could occur from the time of the establishment of maritime zones. Ireland has also suggested that the relevant date could be the date of a decision of States Parties to the LOSC,[21] or perhaps the date of the interpretative statement. However, it may be that allowing the passage of a certain period of time after notification (say, one year) might

[18] Sean D Murphy, 'Durability, Flexibility and Plasticity in the UN Convention on the Law of the Sea' (2024) 39 International Journal of Marine and Coastal Law 225, 237.

[19] Tara Davenport and Maria Pia Benosa, 'Sea Level Rise and Implications for Maritime Security in South Ease Asia' (2023) 2 Blue Security 4, 22.

[20] United Kingdom of Great Britain and Northern Ireland, 'Response to the International Law Commission's Request for Information Concerning Sea-Level Rise in relation to International Law' (30 December 2024) (2024 UK ILC Submission).

[21] Ireland 2025 ILC Submission (n 3).

strike a better balance, allowing for certainty of coastal States' maritime entitlements as well as a prior opportunity for reactions from other States.

The final and perhaps most difficult matter requiring further consideration relates to whether any potential statement should clarify an interpretation of the LOSC *only* in relation to its application in circumstances of sea-level rise, or irrespective of the reason for coastal change. Certainly, the basis most likely to attain consensus would be to confine any statement to an interpretation of the LOSC as it applies in the context of sea-level rise. However, as Lando articulates, limiting the preservation of baselines to situations of sea-level rise raises the question of how to determine whether any particular instance of coastal change is a result of climate change-related sea-level rise, leading also to the potential for disputes 'between states acting to preserve their baselines and states objecting that sea-level rise is not the cause of coastal change and, therefore, baseline preservation is unlawful in the circumstances'.[22] Lando suggests that a 'blanket sanction of baseline prevention'[23] would serve well to avoid such disputes, and indeed this book has argued that there would be a sound legal foundation to support that broader view.

7.4 Bringing the legal stability of maritime zones before international courts and tribunals

Lando's example is a reminder that it remains possible (if unlikely) that States might seek clarification from international courts and tribunals about questions of sea-level rise and maritime zones. One way in which this might occur is through contentious proceedings, engaging the dispute settlement framework set out in Part XV of the LOSC to settle disputes between LOSC Parties 'concerning the interpretation or application'[24] of the LOSC's baseline provisions. Where a coastal State has experienced inundation of certain land features supporting critical basepoints for straight or archipelagic baselines, or significant shoreline erosion affecting the location of the low-water line along the coast from which a coordinates-based normal baseline has been established, one could imagine that an inter-State dispute about the continued lawfulness of such baselines could arise in several ways. For example, a State could directly challenge the lawfulness of the coastal State's baselines. International courts

[22] Massimo Lando, 'Baseline Preservation as a Response to Sea-Level Rise' (2025) 56 Ocean Development and International Law 100, 124.
[23] ibid.
[24] LOSC, art 279.

and tribunals have seldom directly addressed the conformity of a coastal State's baselines with international law. Normal and archipelagic baselines have never been so addressed, and straight baselines only on one occasion since the LOSC's entry into force.[25] It is possible to speculate that a challenge to a coastal State's baselines could take a similar form to Colombia's contention that Nicaragua's straight baselines did not meet the international law requirements for straight baselines, as reflected in Article 7 of the LOSC. Or it could arise in proceedings related to the arrest and detention of a vessel in a particular maritime zone, as suggested in prompt release proceedings relating to the *Volga*,[26] where one judge questioned whether there was a valid basis for the coastal State's arrest and detention of a vessel. Questions could be raised in relation to whether the coastal State's maritime zone was validly declared at the time of arrest if, for example, its baseline (and perhaps outer limits) were defined using coordinates, and if the coastal configuration had changed substantially since the establishment of the zone. While such questions could not be addressed in prompt release proceedings per se,[27] they could be addressed in a separate merits proceeding.[28]

Another scenario in which the baseline and outer limits of an established exclusive economic zone (EEZ) might be challenged following coastal change could be in relation to fishing activity:[29] a coastal State might seek to rely on its established EEZ to exclude foreign fishing vessels from a particular area. If however sea-level rise has shifted the low-water line along the coast from

[25] Colombia challenged the conformity of Nicaragua's straight baselines in *Alleged Violations of Sovereign Rights and Maritime Spaces in the Caribbean Sea (Nicaragua v Colombia)* (Judgment) [2022] ICJ General List no 2022/14. This was the only occasion since the *Fisheries* case on which a court or tribunal has ruled on the validity of baselines. It has however considered related issues of entitlement and/or delimitation many times, occasionally with baselines in mind: *Territorial and Maritime Dispute (Nicaragua v Colombia)* (Judgment) [2012] ICJ Rep 624; *Maritime Delimitation and Territorial Questions between Qatar and Bahrain (Qatar/Bahrain)* (Judgment) [2001] ICJ Rep 40; *Philippines v China* (Award) (2016) (PCA Case no 2013-19); *Maritime Delimitation (Eritrea/Yemen)* (Second Phase (Award)) (1999) 119 ILR 417. However, while some of these latter cases call into doubt the legality of certain baselines (such as the straight baselines claimed by Eritrea in respect of the Dahlak Islands), there is a clear distinction between those concerns and the delimitation task before the court or tribunal (this distinction was expressly recognized by the Tribunal in *Eritrea/Yemen* [142]).

[26] See obiter comments of Judge Vukas in *Volga Case (Russian Federation v Australia)* (Judgment) (2003) 42 ILM 159.

[27] Prompt release proceedings initiated under art 292 'shall deal only with the question of release'. Klein and Parlett point out that 'Australia's pursuit of the Volga raised questions about the legality of the hot pursuit, but this matter could not be addressed by ITLOS under Art 292': Natalie S Klein and Kate Parlett, *Judging the Law of the Sea: Judicial Contributions to the UN Convention on the Law of the Sea* (Oxford University Press 2022) 95.

[28] The sole example of such a merits phase following a prompt release proceeding under art 282 can be found in *MV Saiga (No 2) (St Vincent and the Grenadines v Guinea)* (Judgment) ITLOS Reports 1999, 10.

[29] Such a scenario was suggested in the 2025 Jessup Problem, 'The Case Concerning the Naegea Sea' <www.ilsa.org/jessup-history/jessup-2025/>.

which the EEZ outer limits were originally measured, the flag State of such vessels might argue that the area no longer lies in the coastal State's EEZ, such that the area should now be characterized as high seas. In such a circumstance, the flag State might argue that it is entitled to fish in that area of high seas in exercise of the freedom of fishing.[30] In the latter two scenarios, the key question before the court would be whether the coastal State remains entitled to rely on the declared coordinates for the purposes of asserting rights associated with the relevant maritime zones, where there has been a change to the coastline or particular maritime features after the establishment of the maritime zones. In all of these hypothetical challenges, a court would need to interpret the LOSC provisions on baselines and maritime zones to answer the questions presented.

Another way that questions of sea-level rise and maritime zones can come before international courts and tribunals is through advisory proceedings. So far, States have opted not to formally include questions of sea-level rise and maritime zones in recent requests for advisory opinions to the International Tribunal for the Law of the Sea (ITLOS)[31] and the ICJ.[32] However, in both proceedings such issues have nevertheless arisen. The questions put to ITLOS focused on the obligations of LOSC Parties in relation to pollution of the marine environment, and protection of the environment more broadly, resulting from the 'the deleterious effects that result or are likely to result from climate change'.[33] A number of States connected these questions to the preservation of maritime zones. For example, in its oral submissions, Mauritius invited the Tribunal to

> [c]onfirm in this advisory opinion that sea-level rise, a consequence of pollution that is not permitted by reference to the requirements of Part XII, will not affect existing maritime claims or entitlements. This should be so whether a State has claimed maritime entitlements on the basis of maritime features prior to sea-level rise, or where claims or boundaries have been agreed by States, or where they have been determined by an international court or tribunal. There is, in other words, no obligation under the convention or Part XII as a consequence of rising sea levels caused by pollution for a coastal State

[30] Reflected in LOSC, art 87(1)(e).

[31] *Request for an Advisory Opinion submitted by the Commission of Small Island States on Climate Change and International Law* (2023) ITLOS Case no 31 (*Request for an Advisory Opinion submitted by the Commission of Small Island States*).

[32] *Request for an Advisory Opinion of the International Court of Justice on the Obligations of States in respect of Climate Change* (GA Res 77/276, adopted 29 March 2023) UN Doc A/RES/77/276 (*Request for an Advisory Opinion of the International Court of Justice on the Obligations of States*).

[33] *Request for an Advisory Opinion submitted by the Commission of Small Island States* (n 31).

> to revisit its maritime boundaries. This is intimately connected to issues of obligations in relation to Part XII.[34]

Relatedly, the Federated States of Micronesia submitted that the Tribunal should effectively reject an ambulatory approach to baselines and maritime zones, urging the Tribunal instead to

> refrain from concluding in its advisory opinion in the present Case No. 31 that one of the 'deleterious effects' caused by sea-level rise as a result of anthropogenic greenhouse gas emissions is the landward shifting of maritime zones and the concomitant undermining of rights and entitlements to marine activities and other lawful uses of the sea in the maritime areas, as well as enjoyment of amenities, that are supposedly 'lost' for coastal States as a result of that landward shifting. [. . .] On the contrary, if the Tribunal is to opine on this particular issue, then the Tribunal should find that the international community as a whole—and particularly States that are major emitters of anthropogenic greenhouse gas emissions—has an obligation to support the above-mentioned Declarations by the Pacific Islands Forum and Alliance of Small Island States as accurate reflections of the Convention.[35]

Despite these invitations, the Tribunal took a strict approach to answering the questions placed before it, declining to express its opinion on these matters beyond the Request.[36] In so doing, the Tribunal did however acknowledge the preamble of the COSIS Agreement, in which the Parties affirm that 'maritime zones, as established and notified to the Secretary-General of the United Nations in accordance with the 1982 United Nations Convention on the Law of the Sea, and the rights and entitlements that flow from them, shall continue to apply, without reduction, notwithstanding any physical changes connected to climate change-related sea-level rise'.[37] This is a significant recognition because the Agreement—with a membership of nine Parties[38]—is the first plurilateral legally binding instrument that explicitly recognizes the preservation of maritime zones notwithstanding sea-level rise.

[34] ibid Verbatim Records (15 September 2023) ITLOS/PV.23/C31/9/Rev.1, Mauritius (Sands) 31.
[35] Written Statement of the Federated States of Micronesia, ibid [55].
[36] ibid [150].
[37] Agreement for the Establishment of the Commission of Small Island States on Climate Change and International Law (signed and entered into force 31 October 2021) 3444 UNTS (COSIS Agreement).
[38] Antigua and Barbuda, Tuvalu, Palau, Niue, Vanuatu, Saint Lucia, Saint Vincent and the Grenadines, Saint Kitts and Nevis, the Bahamas: <www.cosis-ccil.org/>.

Similarly, the questions presented in the ICJ climate change advisory proceedings do not on their face seek the Court's opinion on sea-level rise and maritime zones, focusing instead on 'obligations of States under international law to ensure the protection of the climate system and other parts of the environment from anthropogenic emissions of greenhouse gases for States and for present and future generations' and the 'legal consequences under these obligations for States where they, by their acts and omissions, have caused significant harm to the climate system and other parts of the environment'.[39] It is notable, then, that at least twenty-six[40] out of the ninety-one written statements filed with the Court,[41] and also numerous written comments and oral submissions of States and international organizations,[42] have nevertheless drawn the Court's attention to the impacts of sea-level rise on maritime zones. Some States took the opportunity to emphasize before the Court the high level of support demonstrated globally on the issue: for example, COSIS submitted that 'at least 104 States—representing a strong majority of island and coastal States—acknowledge that maritime baselines remain fixed at their current coordinates notwithstanding physical coastline changes brought about by sea level rise'.[43] Tuvalu added that 'Albania and El Salvador added their support in their written statements, taking the consensus to at least 106 States'.[44] Some States have gone further, calling on the Court to affirm this legal position in the context of these particular advisory proceedings. Standing with '25 States and international organizations',[45] Tonga invited the Court to 'affirm the presumption of continuity of statehood and preservation of maritime zones in the face

[39] *Request for Advisory Opinion transmitted to the Court pursuant to General Assembly resolution 77/276 of 29 March 2023; Obligations of States in Respect of Climate Change* (n 16).

[40] Tonga, Sierra Leone, Federated States of Micronesia, Forum Fisheries Agency (FFA), Vanuatu, Albania, Parties to the Nauru Agreement, Melanesian Spearhead Group (MSG), Bahamas, Tuvalu, United States, COSIS, PIF Secretariat, Kiribati, Organisation of African Caribbean and Pacific States (OACPS), Marshall Islands, Republic of Korea, El Salvador, Solomon Islands, Liechtenstein, Nauru, New Zealand, Dominican Republic, Australia, Costa Rica, Burkina Faso; written statements are available at <www.icj-cij.org/case/187/written-proceedings>.

[41] ICJ Press Release (12 April 2024) <www.icj-cij.org/sites/default/files/case-related/187/187-20240412-pre-01-00-en.pdf>.

[42] See eg the Written Comments of Colombia and Timor-Leste; and see Côte d'Ivoire and Romania in oral submissions; available at <www.icj-cij.org/case/187/written-proceedings>.

[43] Written Statement of COSIS (references are omitted, but the 104 States relied upon are listed in note 209 of the Written Statement) <www.ic<j-cij.org/sites/default/files/case-related/187/187-20240322-wri-09-00-en.pdf> [72].

[44] Written Comments of Tuvalu <www.icj-cij.org/sites/default/files/case-related/187/187-20240816-pre-01-00-en.pdf> [12].

[45] The States and international organizations identified by Tonga are: African Union, Albania, Australia, Bahamas, Colombia, COSIS, Cook Islands, Costa Rica, Dominican Republic, El Salvador, Kiribati, Liechtenstein, Mauritius, Micronesia, Nauru, Pacific Islands Forum, PNAO, Saint Vincent and the Grenadines, Sierra Leone, Solomon Islands, Sri Lanka, Timor-Leste, Tonga, Tuvalu, Vanuatu: Verbatim Record 2024/51 (12 December 2024) Tonga (Bajaj) [16].

of climate change-related sea-level rise'.[46] Solomon Islands distinguished these proceedings from the earlier matter before ITLOS, submitting that 'while it may have been proper for ITLOS to defer consideration of maritime entitlements, Solomons invites this Court to adopt a different course'.[47]

Relatedly, some States presented this issue to the Court as a matter of State responsibility, making a direct connection to paragraph (b) of the questions presented. In elaborating the obligation of reparation under the general international law of State responsibility[48]—one of the legal consequences of an internationally wrongful act—Vanuatu's Written Statement argued that although it was 'not possible for a State or a group of States to either restore the climate system to its previous state or undo the associated loss and damage [...] there are some impacts of climate change caused by the Relevant Conduct of a specific group of States which can be addressed by means of restitution'.[49] One such impact is the harm experienced by Vanuatu and other small island developing States in terms of 'loss of territory and maritime spaces, and a threat to their peoples' self-determination and continued survival. For such harm, restitution can take the form of declaratory relief whereby the official territorial and maritime limits of the State are recognized.'[50] Referring to the interpretation of the LOSC expressed in the PIF Declaration, Vanuatu submitted that:

> This position is the correct interpretation of the UNCLOS and its underlying principles, shared by most States. In Vanuatu's submission, States having engaged in the Relevant Conduct must expressly support this position to fulfil their obligation to provide restitution to small island developing States like Vanuatu.[51]

Furthermore, noting that the argued breaches of international law encompass serious breaches of obligations of an *erga omnes* nature[52] (such as the obligation to respect the right to self-determination), Vanuatu further submitted that 'the obligation of non-recognition of the situation resulting from the illicit

[46] ibid [20].
[47] Written Comments of Solomon Islands <www.icj-cij.org/sites/default/files/case-related/187/187-20240815-wri-27-00-en.pdf> [14].
[48] Draft Articles on Responsibility of States for Internationally Wrongful Acts, with Commentaries, in *Yearbook of the International Law Commission* (2001) vol II, pt Two, A/56/10 (ARSIWA) Draft Article 31.
[49] Written Statement of Vanuatu <www.icj-cij.org/sites/default/files/case-related/187/187-20240321-wri-06-00-en.pdf> [581].
[50] ibid [588].
[51] ibid [588], references omitted.
[52] ARSIWA, draft art 40.

conduct displayed by specific States and by a specific group of States requires the express recognition by all States of small island developing States' maritime zones established in accordance with the UNCLOS and the rights and entitlements that flow from them, notwithstanding climate change-related sea-level rise.'[53] This application of the obligation of non-recognition[54] is also referred to in several other States' submissions. Fiji explains that 'States and international organizations must not recognize the unlawful situation resulting from the breach. A corollary of that is the obligation to recognize the territory and maritime spaces of small island developing States, as established under the law of the sea, and of their continued sovereignty and statehood despite the effects of climate change.'[55] Similarly, Jamaica submitted that 'there are measures which could amount to restitution by the responsible States [. . .] These measures, which have been suggested by other States, should include [. . .] recognizing the existing sovereignty and maritime spaces of SIDS who may lose their territory because of sea level rise.'[56] The Bahamas also identified a connection between reparation and duties of cooperation:

> The Bahamas submits that States have an obligation to cooperate in establishing a clear, predictable, and fair legal framework that preserves maritime entitlements from the potential effects of sea level rise and addresses issues of continued statehood. This obligation flows from, among other sources, UNCLOS—which requires that States cooperate to prevent harm to the marine environment by adopting and harmonising laws and policies . . . The obligation also flows from States' duty to cooperate with a view to mitigating the effects of transboundary harm. Indeed, in circumstances where the erosion of the marine entitlements of Small Island States is primarily attributable to the actions of other States (particularly major emitters of GHGs), the duty of international cooperation takes on reparative significance.[57]

[53] Vanuatu (n 49) [205].

[54] ARSIWA, draft art 41(2).

[55] Verbatim Record 2024/40 (4 December 2024) Fiji (Leung) [30].

[56] Verbatim Record 2024/43 (6 December 2024) Jamaica (Walker) [10]. See also Written Statements of Sierra Leone, Saint Vincent and the Grenadines, Tuvalu, COSIS, OACPS, Federated States of Micronesia, Albania, Costa Rica, MSG, Cook Islands, Papua New Guinea, African Union, and Written Comments of Bahamas, available at <www.icj-cij.org/case/187/written-proceedings>; Federated States of Micronesia (while not expressly in terms of reparation, submitted that the Court 'should find that the international community as a whole—and particularly States that are major anthropogenic emitters of greenhouse gases—has an obligation to support the above-mentioned Declarations by the Pacific Islands Forum and Alliance of Small Island States as accurate reflections of the UNCLOS': Written Statement of the Federated States of Micronesia [117].

[57] Written Statement of Bahamas <www.icj-cij.org/sites/default/files/case-related/187/187-20240322-wri-04-00-en.pdf> [224].

Ultimately, the ICJ did address some of these matters in its Opinion. Notwithstanding the arguments made by participants linking the preservation of maritime zones to the consequences of an internationally wrongful act—relevant to paragraph (b) of the questions raised—the Court preferred instead to view the matter as relating to the obligations of States, therefore pertinent to paragraph (a) of the questions.[58] The Court placed emphasis on the obligations of due publicity in the LOSC in relation to straight and archipelagic baselines, outer limits, and lines of delimitation, and concluded that LOSC did not place any further obligations on States in this respect.[59] This is a welcome clarification of the importance of this element of the legal stability of maritime zones, affirming that the temporal element of the stability of maritime zones is secured by the ability for established zones to be maintained over time, without review.

It should also be noted, however, that some judges considered that the Opinion might have gone even further to address this issue in response to paragraph (a) of the question. For example, Vice President Judge Sebutinde considered that 'the Advisory Opinion could have more clearly highlighted the presumption that the loss by a State of its territory due to climate-related sea level rise shall not lead to the loss of its statehood or maritime entitlements'.[60] Similarly, Judge Aurescu found the unanimous Opinion 'excessively and unnecessarily cautious and minimalist',[61] pointing out that 'one most notable absence is the principle of legal stability, security, certainty and predictability',[62] and that the Court fell short in omitting to recognize 'that "fixed baselines" in the context of sea-level rise has already become part of the customary international law'.[63]

Both the ITLOS and ICJ advisory proceedings demonstrate that a significant number of States seek greater certainty on the preservation of their maritime zones, and even more States show their readiness to take the opportunity of such proceedings to affirm and consolidate this area of the law. The ICJ in its Advisory Opinion has indeed offered welcome clarification on certain aspects, though, as pointed out by Judges Sebutinde and Aurescu, perhaps not as much as might have been hoped. Regardless, the Advisory Opinion is likely to be highly influential in playing 'a critical role in the clarification and development

[58] *Obligations of States in Respect of Climate Change* (n 16).
[59] ibid [362]; see also discussion in Section 5.3.
[60] ibid Sep. Op. Sebutinde [8].
[61] ibid Sep. Op. Aurescu [1].
[62] ibid [4].
[63] ibid [5]; see further discussion of customary international law in Section 8.2.1.

of international law relating to climate change [including] as an invaluable resource for climate litigation at the domestic, regional, and international levels'.[64] If questions of sea-level rise and maritime zones are brought before an international court or tribunal in relation to a contentious matter, for example, a contemporary interpretation of all relevant provisions of the LOSC—fully informed by relevant State practice—would give the court or tribunal a sound basis to give a more comprehensive confirmation of the legal stability of maritime zones.

64 Margaretha Wewerinke-Singh, Ayan Garg, and Jacques Hartmann, 'The Advisory Proceedings on Climate Change before the International Court of Justice' (2023) 102 Questions of International Law: Zoom-in 23, 40.

8
Advancing a Contemporary Interpretation of the LOSC

8.1 Introduction

This book has documented how a significant number of States have in recent decades expressed the view that their baselines and maritime zones will be preserved notwithstanding climate change-induced sea-level rise impacts to their coastlines. The Pacific Islands Forum (PIF) Declaration—the leading example of this position—makes clear that this is a claim about the interpretation and application of the United Nations Convention on the Law of the Sea (LOSC) in the context of sea-level rise, and the relevance of 'principles of legal stability, security, certainty and predictability that underpin the Convention'.[1] However, this view is at odds with the view of many scholars (particularly those writing in the period up to 2018) that, in general, baselines and maritime zones are 'ambulatory', so that if a coastline recedes as the sea-level rises, the baseline recedes with it.

In light of this tension between old and new understandings of the law, and the disconnect between the views of States and scholars, the book asked: to what extent does a contemporary interpretation of the LOSC provide for the legal stability of maritime zones? To answer this question, the book identified the relevant provisions of the LOSC to be interpreted, and collected widespread State practice relevant to their interpretation. By applying the analytical framework of the Vienna Convention on the Law of Treaties (VCLT), the book then analysed such State practice and offered conclusions on the interpretation of the relevant rules and their application to questions of sea-level rise. These conclusions show that an ambulatory theory of baselines offers only a partly accurate account of the law and that a contemporary understanding of the law of the sea accommodates a greater degree of stability than had previously been appreciated.

[1] Declaration on Preserving Maritime Zones in the Face of Climate Change-Related Sea-Level Rise (signed 6 August 2021) <www.forumsec.org/2021/08/11/declaration-on-preserving-maritime-zones-in-the-face-of-climate-change-related-sea-level-rise/> (2021 PIF Declaration).

Sea-Level Rise and the Legal Stability of Maritime Zones. Frances Anggadi, Oxford University Press.
 DOI: 10.1093/9780198973515.003.0008

8.2 The legal stability of maritime zones and the interpretation of the LOSC

A key contribution of the book was to dig deeper into the 'legal stability of maritime zones', not only to recognize its conceptual connections with international peace and security, predictability, and certainty but, more importantly, to articulate its 'concrete and pragmatic'[2] expression in relation to maritime zones themselves. The book identified three key elements of such legal stability revealed in the concerns of States: the first element pertaining to the spatial stability of the baseline, the second element to the baseline's temporal stability, and the third element relating to the status of features.

Chapters 4 to 6 identified State practice relevant to each of these elements of legal stability: legislation implementing Article 5 on the normal baseline (relating to spatial stability), legislative actions effecting baseline change (relating to temporal stability), and State practice on the implementation of Article 121 (relating to legal status). Each type of practice was assessed as a matter of 'subsequent practice in the application of the relevant provisions of the LOSC', and considered together with the question of whether such practice 'establishes the agreement of the parties [to the LOSC] regarding its interpretation'.[3] Consistent with the general rule of interpretation reflected in the VCLT, this analysis formed part of a holistic exercise of interpretation, considering all relevant elements in the 'crucible of interpretation'.[4]

In respect of each element of legal stability, the associated State practice was found to play a slightly different role in the resulting interpretation. State practice revealed in the legislative study on the normal baseline (examined in Chapter 4) contributed to an expanded and modernized interpretation of Article 5, recognizing the potential for spatial stability within a margin of appreciation not well understood previously. State practice in the baseline change study (examined in Chapter 5) confirmed that indeed, no duty to update established baselines ought to be implied in the LOSC's silence on such a duty; here State practice served to confirm the LOSC's ordinary meaning. Finally, State practice in the implementation of Article 121 (considered in Chapter 6) problematizes the influential two-part model of features that underpins certain

[2] Bogdan Aurescu and Nilüfer Oral, Co-Chairs of the Study Group on Sea-Level Rise in relation to International Law, *Additional paper to the first issues paper* (Seventy-Fourth Session of the International Law Commission (ILC)) (13 February 2023) UN Doc A/CN.4/761 [84] (*Additional paper to the first issues paper*).

[3] VCLT, art 31(3)(b).

[4] Richard Gardiner, *Treaty Interpretation* (Oxford University Press 2015) 230. See discussion in Section 4.3.

interpretations of that Article, suggesting that the interpretation of this provision should be regarded as unsettled (or, at the very least, contested).

In a forward-looking account of what might still be done to promote the achievement of stable maritime zones, Chapter 7 suggested potential actions that could be taken at the domestic and international levels to confirm a contemporary interpretation of the LOSC, including clarifying some outstanding matters.

Below follows a synthesis of the conclusions reached by the book.

8.2.1 The contemporary interpretation of the LOSC

Chapter 4 identified a 'discernible pattern'[5] of State practice in the implementation of the normal baseline, in which the 108 definitions used by 100 coastal States (which are LOSC Parties)[6] are capable of being understood as a typology of four definition types. Significantly, these definition types differ in the amount of spatial stability offered: Type 2 definitions (a normal baseline defined by reference to coordinates) offer a high degree of stability because coordinates express absolute, rather than relative, location on the Earth's surface. Similarly, Type 3 definitions (a normal baseline defined by reference to charts) may share the same quality of stability, especially if a coastal State uses an electronic navigational chart, which relies on embedded coordinates.

It is clear that some coastal States opt for ambulatory baselines in their domestic frameworks, either because those domestic systems envisage baseline change (eg Romania), or because their laws identify the baseline with the coastline (eg Ireland). Such baselines were classified as Type 1 baselines (the normal baseline is the low-water line along the coast). It is equally clear that many coastal States opt for definitions of their normal baseline that afford a greater degree of spatial stability, either through coordinates (eg Mauritius) or charts (eg Republic of Korea). This pattern of diverse practice and its acceptance amongst LOSC Parties demonstrate that a coastal State has a margin of appreciation in how it implements Article 5, included in which is a discretion to opt for a more or less spatially stable method of defining the normal baseline. The use of coordinates was also identified as a point of commonality that these types of normal baselines share with straight and archipelagic baselines.

[5] *Japan—Alcoholic Beverages II*, WT/DS8/AB/R, WT/DS10/AB/R, and WT/DS11/AB/R (1 November 1996) (Appellate Body Report) 13 (*Japan—Alcoholic Beverages II*). See discussion in Section 4.3.3.

[6] See Chapter 4; see also Section 4.3.3.

A coastal State must still establish its normal baseline in good faith: that is, it may use a representation of the low-water line to establish its normal baseline (such as a chart or coordinates), which must be a good faith representation of the low-water line along the coast at the time it is established. Good faith would also preclude (for instance) maritime claims based on fraudulent information on the location of the coast. However, a coastal State's choice of a more or less spatially stabilizing method is not of itself determinative of conformity with Article 5.

In addition, Chapter 5 confirmed that a coastal State is not under a legal duty to update its baseline once established. This means that baselines which have been established by means of spatially stable methods (such as a normal baseline using coordinates, and also straight and archipelagic baselines) may be maintained after their establishment. Again, a coastal State may opt to revise coordinates (eg Denmark's revisions to take technical improvements into account). Equally, a coastal State may opt to preserve its established baselines, resulting in their stability over time.

In relation to the regime of islands, the book argued in Chapter 6 that Article 121 of the LOSC should be interpreted to provide for a three-part model of features, under which the question of a feature's capacity to sustain human habitation is relevant only to the maritime entitlements of an island which is a rock, not all islands. Because it is likely that very few States proclaim an exclusive economic zone (EEZ) and/or continental shelf on this basis, many (if not most) 'islands' are likely to enjoy stability in relation to the full complement of maritime zones, notwithstanding habitability loss.

Finally, the book argued that the prospect of the destabilization of a feature's legal status (eg losing the status of an 'island' and becoming a 'low-tide elevation') should be understood as a process of legal transformation. Chapter 6 demonstrated how the physical transformation of a feature does not necessarily lead to its legal transformation: if validly established baselines and maritime zones of an island are implemented using 'fixed' means (eg their location is legislatively described using coordinates), such means of implementation make possible the preservation of those baselines and maritime zones notwithstanding the feature's physical transformation. Such preservation requires the coastal State to first opt for stabilizing means of implementation. In consideration of the inherent 'international aspect'[7] of maritime zones, it is also necessary to satisfy the additional condition that there is acquiescence to the maintenance of such zones notwithstanding the physical transformation

[7] *Fisheries (United Kingdom v Norway)* [1951] ICJ Rep 116 [132].

of relevant features. If a trend develops amongst LOSC Parties at a sufficient scale, such case-by-case acquiescence might also form the basis for an interpretation of the LOSC regarding the stability of the status of an 'island'—and its maritime zones—notwithstanding the feature's submergence.

These conclusions confirm the robustness of the recognition by the International Court of Justice (ICJ) in *Obligation of States in Respect of Climate Change* that there is no obligation to update established baselines. Building on that confirmation, these conclusions also answer outstanding questions not directly addressed by the ICJ in relation to other elements of the legal stability of maritime zones that require the interpretation of the LOSC: in particular, the element of spatial stability under Article 5, and stability in relation to the legal status of features under Article 121. The book offers a holistic account of the legal stability of maritime zones, the connection between its constituent elements, and the interpretation of particular provisions of the LOSC, and how, taken together, such findings constitute a comprehensive, well-reasoned, and well-substantiated contemporary interpretation of the LOSC.

8.2.2 Customary international law

The evidence of State practice examined in the book includes that of both Parties and non-Parties to the LOSC. For example, the legislative study (Chapter 4) found that of the fourteen coastal States which are non-Parties to the LOSC, eight use the normal baseline. The full range of normal baseline definition types may be seen in this small sample, with a roughly similar distribution to that among LOSC Parties: five uses of Type 1, followed by one use of each of the other definition types. Of itself, it is difficult to assess the legal significance of this practice because there is simply so little of it. Nolte explains that this is largely a function of the now almost universal membership of the LOSC, which means that '[p]ractice which has formerly mainly contributed to the formation of customary international law must now be evaluated under the rules of UNCLOS and can influence the interpretation of the Convention'.[8]

However, some observations may still be made regarding the customary international law of the normal baseline, reflective of Article 5. First, the small

[8] Georg Nolte, 'Jurisprudence under Special Regimes relating to Subsequent Agreements and Subsequent Practice: Second Report for the ILC Study Group on Treaties over Time' in Georg Nolte (ed), *Treaties and Subsequent Practice* (Oxford University Press 2013) 285.

sample of State practice of non-Parties reflects a distribution of normal baseline definition types that is similar to that adopted by LOSC Parties. At the very least, the practice of non-Parties does not contradict the general acceptance among LOSC Parties of a range of ways to implement the normal baseline, including methods that secure a degree of spatial stability. Secondly, at least one non-Party has signalled its awareness of these matters of implementation. For example, as part of the United States' long-standing practice of reviewing baselines and maritime boundaries, *Limits in the Seas No 146* considers Kiribati's normal baselines and observes:

> For the 20 islands not included within its archipelagic baselines, Kiribati's Territorial Sea Baselines of Kiribati Regulations 2014 (Territorial Sea Baselines Regulations) set forth geographic coordinates for baseline points. [. . .] Neither Kiribati's Territorial Sea Baselines Regulations nor the Act of 2011 refer to the normal baseline or reefs, which are addressed in Articles 5 and 6 of the LOS Convention. However, the geographic coordinates set forth in the Territorial Sea Baselines Regulations appear to be normal baseline points located on the low-water line along the coast (Convention, Article 5) or on the seaward low-water line of a reef (Convention, Article 6).[9]

Recognizing the use of coordinates for the normal baseline around these features, *Limits in the Seas No 146* concludes that such normal baselines are consistent with Article 5 of the LOSC.[10] *Limits in the Seas No 139* comes to a similar conclusion about the use of coordinates for Tuvalu's normal baseline.[11] This is notable since these views indicate an acceptance of Kiribati's and Tuvalu's adoption of a Type 2 definition for their normal baselines, coming from the perspective of a (non-Party) adopting a Type 4 definition. Of course, this is the view of a single non-Party and does not represent those of all non-Parties, let alone the international community as a whole. However, the United States' view is consistent with the trend across LOSC Parties supporting a margin of appreciation in the implementation of the normal baseline, and, to the author's knowledge, no other non-Party has yet expressed a different view on this issue.

[9] US Department of State, 'Republic of Kiribati: Archipelagic and other Maritime Claims and Boundaries', *Limits in the Seas No 146* (5 March 2020) 4 (Republic of Kiribati: Archipelagic and other Maritime Claims and Boundaries).

[10] ibid 8.

[11] US Department of State, 'Tuvalu: Archipelagic and other Maritime Claims and Boundaries', *Limits in the Seas No 139* (23 May 2014) 3 (Tuvalu: Archipelagic and other Maritime Claims and Boundaries).

Furthermore, it might be argued that the wide membership of the LOSC, coupled with the substantial body of State practice of LOSC Parties on the normal baseline, might have an impact on the customary rule. Goodman, drawing on Crawford, explains that:

> if there is no alternative rule in play and the rule in the LOSC has not attracted criticism from third States, it is arguable that the LOSC rule should be considered to reflect a general practice accepted as law, applying equally to Parties and non-Parties. In this respect, widespread participation in the LOSC could be considered to generate a presumption of opinio juris leading to the formation of a customary rule.[12]

It is doubtful that there are any present contenders for an 'alternative rule' relating to the normal baseline rule in Article 5. The rule reflected in Article 5 is 'the only rule on offer, and it is not articulated as a rule limited to Parties to UNCLOS'.[13] Accordingly, it is reasonable to conclude that the customary international law rule on the normal baseline continues to reflect Article 5, and that its content may be discerned consistently with the interpretation of Article 5 advanced in this book.

In addition, some non-Parties have expressed support for the preservation of maritime zones more generally. The United States has indicated that it

> recognizes that new trends are developing in the practices and views of States on the need for stable maritime zones in the face of sea-level rise, [and that] the United States will work with other countries toward the goal of lawfully establishing and maintaining baselines and maritime zone limits and will not challenge such baselines and maritime zone limits that are not subsequently updated despite sea-level rise caused by climate change.[14]

Colombia has expressed a similar position, stating that:

[12] Camille Goodman, *Coastal State Jurisdiction over Living Resources in the Exclusive Economic Zone* (Oxford University Press 2021) 19 (references omitted). This section draws briefly on a similar point previously published in Frances Anggadi, 'Establishment, Notification, and Maintenance: The Package of State Practice at the Heart of the Pacific Islands Forum Declaration on Preserving Maritime Zones' (2022) 53 Ocean Development & International Law 19.

[13] James Crawford, *Chance, Order, Change: The Course of International Law, General Course on Public International Law* (Brill 2014) 134.

[14] United States, full statement at <www.un.org/en/ga/sixth/77/ilc.shtml>; an official summary is recorded at 'Summary Record of the 27th Meeting' UN GAOR Sixth Committee 77th Session (27 October 2022) UN Doc A/C.6/77/SR.27.

> baselines, although they are of a variable nature insofar as they change in accordance with changes in the coastline and variations in the low-water line, have to be set out on maps, and there is no express obligation to modify or update them. In the view of Colombia, there would be no legal impediment to updating or revising registered and publicized maps or coordinates, but nor is there a positive obligation to do so.[15]

Indeed, Colombia has gone further, explaining that 'its low-lying coastal areas are in danger, as particularly evidenced in the Archipelago of San Andrés, Providencia and Santa Catalina, home to a distinct ethnic and cultural community with a strong connection to their land. When addressing its legal effects, Colombia believes that the existing baselines and the resulting maritime rights should be preserved.'[16]

El Salvador has framed its view specifically in terms of customary international law, pointing to the 2021 PIF Declaration and the growing support of other States to assert that such 'practice is sufficiently widespread and representative to ground a rule of customary international law on this point',[17] a perspective which 'make[s] sense also of the position of States that are not party to UNCLOS, such as El Salvador'.[18] At this stage, no LOSC non-Parties have yet opposed the proposition that there is no legal duty to update established baselines and maritime zones, nor the preservation of maritime zones generally. These are indications that customary international law appears, at least at this stage, to align with the contemporary interpretation of the LOSC proposed by this book. This was the view advanced in the 2025 Final Consolidated Report of the Co-Chairs,[19] as well as by Judge Aurescu in his Separate Opinion in *Obligations of States in respect of Climate Change*.[20]

[15] Colombia, 'Comments by the Republic of Colombia with regard to the Report of the International Law Commission on the Work of its Seventy-Second Session (A/76/10)' on the topic of sea-level rise in relation to international law, submitted pursuant to UNGA Res 76/111 of 9 December 2021 (30 June 2022).

[16] Written Comments of Colombia, *Request for an Advisory Opinion of the International Court of Justice on the Obligations of States in respect of Climate Change*, UNGA Res 77/276 (adopted 29 March 2023) UN Doc A/RES/77/276 (*Request for an Advisory Opinion of the International Court of Justice on the Obligations of States in respect of Climate Change*) [1.21].

[17] Written Comments of El Salvador, ibid [8].

[18] Written Statement of El Salvador, ibid note 24.

[19] Patrícia Galvão Teles, Nilüfer Oral, and Juan José Ruda Santolaria, 'Final Consolidated Report of the Co-Chairs of the Study Group on Sea-Level Rise in relation to International Law' (3 February 2025) UN Doc A/CN.4/783 [483] (Final Consolidated Report of the Co-Chairs).

[20] *Obligations of States in Respect of Climate Change* (Advisory Opinion, Sep. Op. Aurescu) [2025] [12] (*Obligations of States in Respect of Climate Change*) <https://www.icj-cij.org/case/187>.

8.3 Addressing questions of sea-level rise

This section applies the conclusions of the book to address questions arising from the effects of sea-level rise on coastlines and features, and also considers situations *in extremis* in which there might be the complete inundation of a feature (or even the entire land territory of a State).

8.3.1 Applying a contemporary interpretation of the LOSC

Just as the 'ambulatory theory' of baselines is not expressed as a theory limited to baselines under conditions of sea-level rise, but baselines generally, so too are the conclusions of this book advanced as general propositions about the interpretation of the LOSC and customary international law. Such propositions are agnostic as to potential causes of coastal change, but of course may be applied to particular circumstances. The legal inquiry of the book is prompted by concerns related to sea-level rise, and this chapter now moves to consider those circumstances.

Applying the conclusions of the book to issues arising from the effects of sea-level rise, a key insight of the book is that a coastal State's approach to the implementation of its baselines and maritime zones is pivotal across all three elements of legal stability. Whether or not a coastal State uses 'fixed' methods in its implementing legislation will dictate the likely legal consequences for its maritime zones if its coastline is impacted by sea-level rise. Broadly speaking, if a coastal State defines its baseline as the low-water line along the coast (Type 1), this creates a 'direct relationship'[21] between the coastline and the baseline. Accordingly, recession of the coast due to sea-level rise, or submergence of the low-water line entirely, automatically translates to corresponding legal impacts which may include a decrease in the area of an EEZ, or its loss entirely if a feature becomes submerged at high tide. Furthermore, for baselines and maritime zones defined in this way, the question whether there is a duty to update established baselines becomes moot, since changes to the location of the baseline occur by operation of law, as a result of the 'direct relationship' between the baseline and the coastline. This scenario indeed follows the 'ambulatory'

[21] Clive Schofield, 'Departures from the Coast: Trends in the Application of Territorial Sea Baselines under the Law of the Sea Convention' (2012) 27 The International Journal of Marine and Coastal Law 723, 725.

paradigm envisaged by many scholars, but it must be recognized as the consequence in just one type of permissible scenario under international law.

If a coastal State does opt to use 'fixed' methods in its implementing legislation—such as coordinates (Type 2) or charts (Type 3)—there is no 'direct relationship' between the coastline and the baseline. Rather, baselines and maritime zone outer limits defined in this way have a spatial stability due to having an objective, absolute location: a location so described will be unaffected by sea-level rise impacts to the coast. This same characteristic means that such baselines and maritime zones can remain in place once established: maritime zones that are unamended by a coastal State will therefore have a temporal stability. Furthermore, the unilateral choices by a coastal State to rely on 'fixed' methods should not merely be seen as domestic actions but rather have legitimacy under international law. This is because they conform to a robust interpretation of the LOSC, as advanced in this book, and are also consistent with custom. Unless the direction of State practice changes significantly in the future, it is likely that such a conclusion will also solidify in relation to the stability of a feature's legal status under the law of the sea, bringing with it the preservation of an island's established maritime zones.

Furthermore (and irrespective of a coastal State's choices in domestic implementation) the work argues that legal status of an 'island', and any EEZ and/or continental shelf established therefrom, is likely to be unaffected by a loss of that island's habitability brought about by sea-level rise. Habitability loss might—under the three-part model of features—conceivably affect the maritime entitlements of an island which is a rock, but there are very few known examples where States have expressed maritime claims on the basis of a rock being capable of sustaining human habitation.[22] Much more common are maritime claims based on an expansive interpretation of 'island', which means that the number of 'islands' potentially affected by habitability loss may not be as numerous as feared.

In relation to concerns raised about sea-level rise and 'archipelagic status', the book clarified that while the LOSC does not itself use the term, the idea of 'archipelagic status' engages other key concepts in Part IV of the LOSC, being 'archipelagic State'[23] and 'archipelagic baseline'.[24] The book argued that sea-level rise is unlikely to automatically result in loss of status as an 'archipelagic State', or to disrupt established archipelagic baselines. This conclusion is

[22] The author is only aware of one example (St Peter and Paul Islands (Brazil)): see Section 6.2.2.
[23] LOSC, art 46.
[24] LOSC, art 47.

reinforced by the fact that all archipelagic States have expressed the view that international law permits the preservation of established maritime zones notwithstanding sea-level rise.[25]

8.3.2 How much legal stability is available?

A question remains as to how much legal stability is or might be available for maritime zones. As summarized above, this book argues that compelling conclusions can be reached that the existing law of the sea does accommodate a degree of stability in a spatial and temporal sense, and that this also likely provides for the stability of the legal status of features. However, given the projected scale of sea-level rise impacts to the coast described in Chapter 1,[26] the question necessarily arises as to how far these conclusions can hold. Is legal stability available for a baseline in circumstances where there has been a significant landward shift of the low-water line along the coast? Where an island has become completely submerged? Or where the entire land territory of a State has become submerged? These *in extremis* scenarios range in their projected timescales, but when they eventuate they are likely to test the limits of legal stability. Each of these scenarios raises slightly different considerations.

In relation to significant coastline change, there are already some clues as to how much legal stability might be presently available. For example, if we recall debates on the proviso in the development of what was to become Article 5 of the LOSC, it was clear that potential challenge was envisaged in relation to situations where there was a physical discrepancy of a certain magnitude between the baseline and the coastline ('departed appreciably', or 'differed to any great extent'), or where there was an element of bad faith or unreasonableness ('clearly fraudulent' or shifting the charted line 'unreasonably').[27] State practice also supplies some guidance to quantify what this might mean in terms of the scale of coastline change. For example, the United States' policy is to consider baseline review on the basis of coastline changes of +/- 500 m.[28] The Netherlands adopts a slightly different measure, implementing changes to its charted baseline where there has been a coastline change of +/- 0.1 nm

25 See Section 6.4.
26 Section 8.3.
27 See discussion in Section 2.3.2.
28 United States, 'Comments of the United States regarding Sea-Level Rise in Relation to the Law of the Sea' (14 February 2020) (2020 US ILC Submission).

(approximately 182 m).[29] This might be seen as an indicator of a measure of legal stability vis-à-vis coastline changes, suggesting the baseline may reasonably tolerate up to 500 m of coastline change.

Recognizing this degree of legal stability can provide some reassurance with respect to the security and legitimacy of many established maritime claims. While not free from doubt, it is likely that this degree of tolerance might increase further in response to developing State practice in the face of increasingly severe coastal impacts. This is especially so since PIF members have declared that they 'do not intend to review and update the baselines and outer limits of our maritime zones as a consequence of climate change-related sea-level rise'.[30]

In relation to the complete submergence of an island, the picture is less certain. Some writers are concerned that maintenance of maritime zones would be untenable in this scenario on the basis that there would no longer be any land appurtenant to the claimed ocean space.[31] However, in principle it is arguable that legal stability might also be available in this situation, resulting in the preservation of established baselines and maritime zones even if low-lying features had become submerged at a later date. This reasoning would also support the preservation of established archipelagic baselines if other low-lying features (such as drying reefs) were submerged.

However, in the event that the entire land territory of a State is submerged, questions of maritime entitlement become intertwined with those around continued statehood, a matter which was also considered by ILC on the topic of sea-level rise and international law. In terms of the law of the sea, the question is whether the submergence of a State's entire land territory might result in that State no longer being a 'coastal State' (because it is no longer a State).

One idea that has been suggested is the notion of a '*sui generis* status for territories submerged owing to sea-level rise, in particular because sea-level rise was not a natural phenomenon, but was human-caused'.[32] Liechtenstein supported exploration of this idea,[33] and Malta explained its related view that 'territory constitutes a prerequisite for the establishment of a state, sovereignty

[29] Kingdom of the Netherlands, 'Submission of the Netherlands to the International Law Commission' (27 December 2019) (2019 Netherlands ILC Submission).

[30] 2021 PIF Declaration (n 1).

[31] eg Snjólaug Árnadóttir, 'The Impact of Sea Level Rise on Maritime Limits: A Grotian Moment in the Law of the Sea?' (2021) 42 Grotiana 277, 300.

[32] ILC, 'Report of the International Law Commission covering the Work of its Seventy-Fifth Session' (29 April–31 May and 1 July–2 August 2024) UN Doc A/79/10 [153] (2024 ILC Report).

[33] Liechtenstein, full statement at <www.un.org/en/ga/sixth/78/ilc.shtml>; an official summary is recorded at 'Summary Record of the 23rd Meeting' UN GAOR Sixth Committee Seventy-Eighth Session (23 October 2023) UN Doc A/C.6/78/SR.23.

refers to the whole territory under the State's control and not solely to the land territory. Therefore, a territory that becomes partially inundated or fully submerged due to sea-level rise should not be considered a non-existent territory.'[34] Considering these views, the International Law Association Committee on Sea Level Rise and International Law reflected that this line of argument seemed to propose that 'the concept of "territory" might be extended *de lege ferenda* to include submerged lands which have become inundated by sea level rise. The development of this argument would mean that the presence of submerged lands might be used to justify the maintenance of marine resources zones—such as the EEZ or the continental shelf',[35] and that accordingly the Committee considered it may be 'premature to be proposing legal solutions *de lege ferenda* regarding the issue of persistence of maritime entitlements following the *full* submergence of the entire land territory of some of the present-day States in a rather long-term (end of the century, or beyond) perspective'.[36] Ultimately, the Committee's conclusion on this proposal seems to have been borne out, as there has been little further pursuit of the substance of such a *sui generis* status as a legal solution, or how it might be realized.

More promising, however, are the implications for maritime zones that may be drawn from the body of increasing support for the continuity of statehood. As observed in the Final Report of the ILC's Study Group on sea-level rise in relation to international law, '[w]ith regard to States particularly affected by climate change-related sea-level rise, there is strong support among States for the continuity of statehood and sovereignty and the maintenance of international legal personality and membership of international organizations'.[37] This view is given expression in the 2023 PIF Declaration on the Continuity of Statehood and the Protection of Persons in the Face of Climate Change-Related Sea-Level Rise[38] and the 2024 Alliance of Small Island States (AOSIS) Leaders

[34] Malta, full statement at <www.un.org/en/ga/sixth/78/ilc.shtml>; an official summary is recorded at 'Summary Record of the 27th Meeting' UN GAOR Sixth Committee Seventy-Eighth Session (27 October 2023) UN Doc A/C.6/78/SR.27.

[35] ILA (Committee on International Law and Sea Level Rise), 'Report (Athens Conference)' 47 (2024 ILA SLR Report).

[36] ibid.

[37] Study Group on Sea-Level Rise in relation to International Law, 'Final Report of the Study Group on Sea-Level Rise in relation to International Law', UN Doc A/80/10, Annex I [35] (2025 ILC Study Group Final Report). See also ILC, 'Report of the International Law Commission covering the Work of its Seventy-Sixth Session' (28 April–30 May 2025) UN Doc A/80/10 [61] (2025 ILC Report).

[38] Declaration on the Continuity of Statehood and the Protection of Persons in the Face of Climate Change-Related Sea-Level Rise, Pacific Islands Forum (signed 20 November 2023) <https://forumsec.org/publications/2023-declaration-continuity-statehood-and-protection-persons-face-climate-change> (2023 PIF Declaration).

Declaration on Sea-Level Rise and Statehood,[39] which have received broad support from other States and international organizations.[40] The continuity of statehood has also been articulated in the specific bilateral context of the Australia-Tuvalu Falepili Union Treaty, under which Parties undertake to recognize that the statehood and sovereignty of Tuvalu will continue, and the rights and duties inherent thereto will be maintained, notwithstanding the impact of climate change-related sea-level rise.[41] As is recognized in the Treaty's Explanatory Memorandum, this is significant in 'recognising for the first time in a legally binding treaty Tuvalu's continuing statehood in the face of climate change'.[42] The view of the ICJ in *Obligations of States in Respect of Climate Change* that the complete loss of land territory or displacement of population 'would not necessarily entail the loss of its statehood'[43]—while cautious—takes steps in a similar direction.

Increasingly, positions on the preservation of maritime entitlements and continued statehood are being expressed together, signalling an emerging view that the preservation of maritime zones is—at the very least—implicit in the recognition of continued statehood. For example, Tuvalu explains that 'respect for sovereignty and territorial integrity requires recognition that maritime baselines remain fixed despite physical changes to the coastline due to sea-level rise. This encompasses the recognition of statehood in perpetuity, as set out in Tuvalu's Constitution.'[44] Similarly, Kiribati considers that 'all States must continue to recognize the sovereignty, statehood, territory and maritime spaces of Kiribati and other small island developing States',[45] and Vanuatu refers to 'the obligation to recognize the territory and maritime spaces of small island developing States, as established under the law of the sea, and of their continued

[39] Declaration on Sea Level Rise and Statehood, Alliance of Small Island States (signed 25 September 2024) <www.aosis.org/aosis-leaders-declaration-on-sea-level-rise-and-statehood/> (2024 AOSIS Statehood Declaration).

[40] 2025 ILC Study Group Final Report (n 37) [36].

[41] Australia-Tuvalu Falepili Union Treaty (signed 11 September 2023, entered into force 28 August 2024) [2024] ATS 10, art 2(2)(b) (Falepili Union Treaty).

[42] Explanatory Memorandum <www.dfat.gov.au/geo/tuvalu/australia-tuvalu-falepili-union-treaty/treaty-text-falepili-union>. Scholars have pointed out that, in terms of the international law of statehood, this is also significant because it 'represents the first publicly binding rejection by any State of the traditional view that inhabitable land is necessary for State continuity': see Alex Green and Douglas Guilfoyle, 'The Australia-Tuvalu Falepili Union Treaty: Statehood and Security in the Face of Anthropogenic Climate Change' (2024) 118 American Journal of International Law 684.

[43] *Obligations of States in Respect of Climate Change* (n 20) [363].

[44] Verbatim Record 2024/51, *Request for an Advisory Opinion of the International Court of Justice on the Obligations of States in respect of Climate Change* (n 16) Tuvalu (Webb) [13]. Notably, Tuvalu's constitution addresses the permanence of its maritime zones in the provision entitled 'Tuvalu Statehood': Constitution of Tuvalu Act 2023.

[45] Written Statement of Kiribati, *Request for an Advisory Opinion of the International Court of Justice on the Obligations of States in respect of Climate Change* (n 16) [190].

sovereignty and statehood despite the effects of climate change'.[46] More pointedly, the Commission of Small Island States (COSIS) points to 'the emerging customary international law norm under which States are required to respect existing maritime spaces and the continued sovereignty of those States that lose territory as a result of sea-level rise'.[47]

Further discussions will be required on this issue, including to consider practical issues in relation to the continuity of statehood, and its contours in the law of statehood. For now, however, in linking implications for maritime areas with the continued recognition of statehood, there appears to be a relatively clear trajectory for the preservation of maritime zones together with statehood in the *in extremis* circumstance where there is a complete submergence of land territory.

8.4 The significance of State practice for international law scholarship

The State practice identified in the book, and resulting conclusions on the interpretation of the LOSC, have implications for international law scholarship in a fundamental area of the law of the sea. If the conclusions of this study are correct, it means that 'fixed baselines'—usually framed as a proposal to amend or create existing laws to address the problem of ambulatory baselines—should no longer be seen as a matter *de lege ferenda*. Instead, this book makes its claims regarding the law as a matter *de lege lata*. The proponents of both old and new understandings of the LOSC have had before them the same text, then and now; however, a convergence of States' views and practice on legal stability in the present is what makes these interpretative conclusions available at the time of writing, compared to the relative paucity of such evidence visible to those scholars first tackling sea-level rise and maritime zones three decades ago. These conclusions demonstrate the capacity of the LOSC to evolve through interpretation, making visible the quality of the LOSC as a 'living instrument', with capacity to grow and adapt to changing circumstances.[48]

[46] Verbatim Record 2024/35, ibid Vanuatu/Melanesian Spearhead Group (Wewerinke-Singh) [13].

[47] COSIS Written Comment, ibid [111]. See also Written Comments of African Union and Sierra Leone, Verbatim Records 2024/40 Fiji (Leung), and Verbatim Records 2024/43 Jamaica (Walker).

[48] This idea was most clearly given expression by Judge Lucky, who stated that '[t]he 1982 Convention and the Statute of the Tribunal are "living instruments". This means that they "grow" and adapt to changing circumstances. [. . .] The law of the sea is not static': *Request for an Advisory Opinion submitted by the Sub-Regional Fisheries Commission (SRFC)* (Advisory Opinion) (2015) ITLOS Case no 21 [18] (Lucky). Considering the different ways in which the LOSC may be understood to 'live and grow', Barrett explains that, '[d]ue to the very design of UNCLOS, unilateral acts of individual States play an even more important and specific role, to the point that certain national laws and regulations are

To paraphrase Allott, the book demonstrates the capacity of interpretation to be 'an act of power across time and space', as we interpret the LOSC today, a text that was created in another time and space.[49]

What does this mean for how we should conceptualize baselines and maritime zones in legal research and scholarship? The conclusions of this book invite us to revisit, contextualize, and where necessary challenge and overhaul the dominant scholarly narrative that baselines are 'naturally ambulatory'. This book has identified that State practice embraces both ambulatory and fixed approaches to baselines, both of which may be embraced within the margin of appreciation afforded to a coastal State in how it opts to establish its baseline. On the basis of this insight, we should cast aside the bipolar framing of earlier debates on the nature of the normal baseline, in which the 'ambulatory' and 'fixed' approaches were seen as mutually exclusive theoretical alternatives.

Rather, the better explanatory narrative, consistent with the contemporary interpretation of the LOSC advanced in this book, focuses on a permissible pattern of practice in the implementation of the normal baseline. That pattern embraces a margin of appreciation, within which a coastal State may opt for various approaches differing in the degree of stability they afford; seen in this way, the terms 'ambulatory' and 'fixed' lie on a spectrum of less or more spatial stability. A coastal State's choice to adopt fixed methods in implementing its maritime zones is necessary for the realization of legal stability in relation to all three elements: spatial, temporal, and in relation to the status of features.

The conclusions of the book also invite us to revisit the two-part model of Article 121 of the LOSC that underlies concerns that loss of an island's conditions of habitability will result in the loss of its 'island' status and full maritime zone entitlement. Again, the book has highlighted a gap between prevailing interpretations and State practice, arguing that the better interpretation of Article 121, consistent with such State practice, is a three-part model of features under which habitability has only a second-order role in the differentiation of maritime entitlements.

said to form part of the "legal order for the seas and oceans" established by UNCLOS': Jill Barrett, 'The UN Convention on the Law of the Sea: A "Living" Treaty?' in Jill Barrett and Richard Barnes (eds), *Law of the Sea: UNCLOS as a Living Treaty* (British Institute of International and Comparative Law 2016) 3, 30. The argument made in this book for the significance of State practice for the interpretation of the LOSC shows another way in which the unilateral acts of individual States—at a global scale—may contribute to the dynamism of the LOSC. See also Reece Lewis, 'The "Constitution for the Oceans"? The Law of the Sea Convention as a Living Treaty' (2025) 74 International and Comparative Law Quarterly 1.

[49] Philip Allott, 'Interpretation: An Exact Art' in Andrea Bianchi, Daniel Peat, and Matthew Windsor (eds), *Interpretation in International Law* (Oxford University Press 2015) 374.

Crucially, the identification and legal evaluation of State practice in the book provides a clear illustration of how alternative legal conclusions might become available on the basis of a full account of relevant State practice. This book has demonstrated how the identification and analysis of State practice in international law scholarship can significantly influence understandings of treaty and customary rules. Furthermore, the application of such rules to questions of sea-level rise casts concerns about the prospect of jurisdictional loss in a very different light: such a result is not necessarily automatic, and coastal States may take permissible unilateral actions to pursue stability for maritime zones. If, as foreshadowed here, a coastal State is challenged in its reliance on such rights, any international court or tribunal should have close regard to relevant State practice in assessing the substance of the applicable law. Especially in relation to baselines, maritime zones, and the regime of islands—foundational aspects of the law of the sea—a full account of State practice is essential not only because it is a required part of international law method for the interpretation of treaties and the identification of custom but also to ensure the ongoing relevance and legitimacy of the law of the sea as it applies to contemporary challenges.

Selected Bibliography

Alexander LM, 'Baseline Delimitations and Maritime Boundaries' (1983) 23 Virginia Journal of International Law 503

Allott P, 'Power Sharing in the Law of the Sea' (1983) 77 American Journal of International Law 1

Allott P, 'Interpretation: An Exact Art' in A Bianchi, D Peat, and M Windsor (eds), *Interpretation in International Law* (Oxford University Press 2015)

Anderson D, 'Negotiating Maritime Boundary Agreements: A Personal View' in R Lagoni and D Vignes (eds), *Maritime Delimitation* (Brill Nijhoff 2006)

Anderson DH, 'Baselines in the Modern Law of the Sea' in M Lodge and MH Nordquist (eds), *Peaceful Order in the World's Oceans* (Brill Nijhoff 2014)

Anggadi F, 'Reconceptualising the "Ambulatory Character" of Baselines: The International Law Commission's Work on Sea-Level Rise and International Law' (2021) 22(2) Melbourne Journal of International Law 163

Anggadi F, 'Establishment, Notification, and Maintenance: The Package of State Practice at the Heart of the Pacific Islands Forum Declaration on Preserving Maritime Zones' (2022) 53 Ocean Development & International Law 19

Anggadi F, 'The Meaning and Legal Significance of "Fringing Reefs" in the LOSC, and Importance for Contemporary Challenges in the Law of the Sea' in P Leucci and I Vianello (eds), *ASCOMARE Yearbook on the Law of the Sea 2021: Law of the Sea, Interpretation and Definitions* (vol 1, Luglio Editore 2022)

Anggadi F, 'What States Say and Do about Legal Stability and Maritime Zones, and Why it Matters' (2022) 71 International & Comparative Law Quarterly 767

Árnadóttir S, 'Termination of Maritime Boundaries Due to a Fundamental Change of Circumstances' (2016) 32 Utrecht Journal of International and European Law 94

Árnadóttir S, 'Fluctuating Boundaries in a Changing Marine Environment' (2021) 34 Leiden Journal of International Law 471

Árnadóttir S, 'The Impact of Sea Level Rise on Maritime Limits: A Grotian Moment in the Law of the Sea?' (2021) 42 Grotiana 277

Árnadóttir S, *Climate Change and Maritime Boundaries: Legal Consequences of Sea Level Rise* (Cambridge University Press 2022)

Aust A, *Modern Treaty Law and Practice* (3rd edn, Cambridge University Press 2013)

Azaria D, '"Codification by Interpretation": The International Law Commission as an Interpreter of International Law' (2021) 31 European Journal of International Law 171

Barrett J, 'The UN Convention on the Law of the Sea: A "Living" Treaty?' in J Barrett and R Barnes (eds), *Law of the Sea: UNCLOS as a Living Treaty* (British Institute of International and Comparative Law 2016)

Batongbacal JL, 'The Maritime Territories and Jurisdictions of the Philippines and the United Nations Convention on the Law of the Sea' (2021) 76 Philippines Law Journal 123

Baumert K and Melchior B, 'The Practice of Archipelagic States: A Study of Studies' (2015) 46 Ocean Development & International Law 60

Bell JD and others, 'Pathways to Sustaining Tuna-Dependent Pacific Island Economies during Climate Change' (2021) 4 Nature Sustainability 900

Bernard L and others, 'Securing the Limits of Large Ocean States in the Pacific: Defining Baselines Limits and Boundaries amidst Changing Coastlines and Sea Level Rise' (2021) 11 Geosciences 394

Bethlehem D, 'The End of Geography: The Changing Nature of the International System and the Challenge to International Law' (2014) 25 European Journal of International Law 9

Bird E, *Coastal Geomorphology: An Introduction* (2nd edn, Wiley 2008)

Bird E and Prescott V, 'Rising Global Sea Levels and National Maritime Claims' (1989) 1 Marine Policy Reports 177

Boyle A, 'Law of the Sea Perspectives on Climate Change' in D Freestone (ed), *The 1982 Law of the Sea Convention At 30: Successes, Challenges and New Agendas* (Brill 2013)

Brilmayer L and Klein N, 'Land and Sea: Two Sovereignty Regimes in Search of a Common Denominator' (2001) 33 New York University Journal of International Law and Politics 703

Buga I, *Modification of Treaties by Subsequent Practice* (Oxford University Press 2018)

Carleton C, 'Problems Relating to Non-Natural and Man-Made Basepoints Under UNCLOS' in CR Symmons (ed), *Selected Contemporary Issues in the Law of the Sea* (Brill Nijhoff 2011)

Carleton C and Schofield CH, *Developments in the Technical Determination of Maritime Space: Charts, Datums, Baselines, Maritime Zones and Limits* (vol 3, International Boundaries Research Unit 2001)

Caron DD, 'When Law Makes Climate Change Worse: Rethinking the Law of Baselines in Light of a Rising Sea Level' (1990) 17 Ecology Law Quarterly 621

Caron DD, 'Climate Change, Sea Level Rise and the Coming Uncertainty in Oceanic Boundaries: A Proposal to Avoid Conflict' in S-Y Hong and JM Van Dyke (eds), *Maritime Boundary Disputes, Settlement Processes, and the Law of the Sea* (Brill 2009)

Cass D, 'The Quiet Revolution: The Development of the Exclusive Economic Zone and Implications for Foreign Fishing Access in the Pacific' in K Rubenstein (ed), *Traversing the Divide: Honouring Deborah Cass's Contributions to Public and International Law* (ANU Press 2021)

Charney JI, 'Rocks That Cannot Sustain Human Habitation' (1999) 93 American Journal of International Law 863

Chinese Society of International Law, 'The South China Sea Arbitration Awards: A Critical Study' (2018) 17 Chinese Journal of International Law 207

Churchill R, 'Accession to the UN Convention on the Law of the Sea' (1998) 13 International Journal of Marine and Coastal Law 263

Churchill R, 'Rocks' (last updated February 2019) in A Peters (ed.), *The Max Planck Encyclopedia of Public International Law* (OUP 2008–) <www.mpepil.com>

Churchill R, Lowe A, and Sander A, *The Law of the Sea* (4th edn, Manchester University Press 2022)

Cogliati-Bantz V, 'Sea-Level Rise and Coastal States' Maritime Entitlements' (2020) 7 Journal of Territorial and Maritime Studies 86

Cogliati-Bantz V, 'The Way Forward is not Fast-Forward: Sea-Level Rise, Maritime Zones and Back to Basics' in LAT Nguyen and HD Vu (eds), *Viability of UNCLOS amid Emerging Global Maritime Challenges* (Springer 2024)

Connell J, 'Nothing There Atoll? "Farewell to the Carteret Islands"' in T Crook and P Rudiak-Gould (eds), *Pacific Climate Cultures* (De Gruyter Open Poland 2019)

Cot J-P, 'Margin of Appreciation' (last updated June 2007) in A Peters (ed.), *The Max Planck Encyclopedia of Public International Law* (OUP 2008–) <www.mpepil.com>

Cot J-P, 'The Dual Function of Base Points' in H Hestermeyer (ed), *Coexistence, Cooperation and Solidarity: Liber Amicorum Rüdiger Wolfrum* (Brill Nijhoff 2012)

Crawford J, *Chance, Order, Change: The Course of International Law, General Course on Public International Law* (Brill 2014)

Crawford J, *Brownlie's Principles of Public International Law* (9th edn, Oxford University Press 2019)

da Silva AP, 'From Rocks to an Archipelago: The Brazilian Interpretation and Application of Article 121 of the United Nations Convention on the Law of the Sea with Respect to the St. Peter and St. Paul Insular Features' (2020) 51 Ocean Development and International Law 330

Davenport T, 'The Archipelagic Regime' in DR Rothwell and others (eds), *The Oxford Handbook of the Law of the Sea* (Oxford University Press 2015)

Davenport T and Pia Benosa M, 'Sea Level Rise and Implications for Maritime Security in South East Asia' (2023) 2 Blue Security 4

Davis R and Hanich Q, 'Small Island States and the LOS Convention; 30 Years On: Have the Benefits Been Realized?' (2012) 26 Ocean Yearbook 49

de la Cruz AP, 'Making History, Making Archipelagos: A Parallel South China Sea Dispute' (2024) 12 Blue Security 4

DeMers MN, *Fundamentals of Geographic Information Systems* (4th edn, Wiley 2009)

Denny M, *The Science of Navigation: From Dead Reckoning to GPS* (Johns Hopkins University Press 2012)

Dörr O, 'Article 31—General Rule of Interpretation' in O Dörr and K Schmalenbach (eds), *Vienna Convention on the Law of Treaties: A Commentary* (Springer 2012)

Dryzek JS and Pickering J, *The Politics of the Anthropocene* (Oxford University Press 2019)

Elferink AGO, 'Artificial Islands, Installations and Structures' (last updated July 2024) in A Peters (ed.), *The Max Planck Encyclopedia of Public International Law* (OUP 2008–) <www.mpepil.com>

Evans M, 'Maritime Boundary Delimitation' in D Rothwell and others (eds), *The Oxford Handbook of the Law of the Sea* (Oxford University Press 2015)

Evans MD and Lewis R, 'The Regime of Islands' in Ø Jensen (ed), *The Development of the Law of the Sea Convention: The Role of International Courts and Tribunals* (Edward Elgar 2020)

Evans MD and Lewis R, *Islands, Law and Context: The Treatment of Islands in International Law* (Edward Elgar 2023)

Fellowes TE and others, 'Stability of Coral Reef Islands and Associated Legal Maritime Zones in a Changing Ocean' (2022) 17 Environmental Research Letters 17

Fietta S and Cleverly R, *A Practitioner's Guide to Maritime Boundary Delimitation* (Oxford University Press 2016)

Franckx E, 'The Regime of Islands and Rocks' in *The IMLI Manual on International Maritime Law: Vol I: The Law of the Sea* (Oxford University Press 2014)

Freestone D, 'Sea Level Rise and Archipelagic States: A Preliminary Risk Assessment' (2021) 35 Ocean Yearbook 340

Freestone D, 'International Law and Sea Level Rise' in R Churchill and D Freestone (eds), *International Law and Global Climate Change* (Graham & Trotman 1991)

Freestone D and Schofield C, '2016 Maritime Zones Declaration Act: Drawing Lines in the Sea' (2016) 31 International Journal of Marine and Coastal Law 732

Frost R and others, 'Redrawing the Map of the Pacific' (2018) 95 Marine Policy 302

Gardiner R, *Treaty Interpretation* (Oxford University Press 2015)

Gaspar JA and Leitão H, 'Early Modern Nautical Charts and Maps: Working Through Different Cartographic Paradigms' (2019) 23 Journal of Early Modern History 1

Goodman C, *Coastal State Jurisdiction over Living Resources in the Exclusive Economic Zone* (Oxford University Press 2021)

Green A and Guilfoyle D, 'The Australia-Tuvalu Falepili Union Treaty: Statehood and Security in the Face of Anthropogenic Climate Change' (2024) 118 American Journal of International Law 684

Grima A, *Sea Level Change and Maritime Boundaries* (Routledge 2023)

Grote Stoutenburg J, *Disappearing Island States in International Law* (Brill 2015)

Hayashi M, 'Sea Level Rise and the Law of the Sea: How Can the Affected States Be Better Protected?' in CH Schofield, S Lee, and M-S Kwon (eds), *The Limits of Maritime Jurisdiction* (Brill Nijhoff 2014)

Intergovernmental Panel on Climate Change, *Climate Change: The 1990 and 1992 IPCC Assessments* (1992)

Intergovernmental Panel on Climate Change, *Climate Change 2021: The Physical Science Basis. Working Group I Contribution to the Sixth Assessment Report of the Intergovernmental Panel on Climate Change* (2021)

International Hydrographic Organization, *Hydrographic Dictionary: IHO Publication S-32* (5th edn, 1994)

International Hydrographic Organization, *S-66: Facts about Electronic Charts and Carriage Requirements* (2010)

International Hydrographic Organization, *The Future of the Paper Nautical Chart - Final Report* (Nautical Cartography Working Group 2020)

International Hydrographic Organization, *C-55: Status of Hydrographic Surveying and Charting Worldwide* (2023)

Kapoor D and Kerr AJ, *A Guide to Maritime Boundary Delimitation* (Carswell 1986)

Kaye S, 'The Law of the Sea Convention and Sea Level Rise after the South China Sea Arbitration' (2017) 93 International Law Studies 423

Klein N, 'Islands and Rocks after the "South China Sea Arbitration"' (2017) 34 Australian Year Book of International Law 21

Klein N, 'Land and Sea: Resolving Contested Land and Disappearing Land Disputes under the UN Convention on the Law of the Sea' in C Giogetti and N Klein (eds), *Resolving Conflicts in the Law* (Brill Nijhoff 2018)

Klein NS and Parlett K, *Judging the Law of the Sea: Judicial Contributions to the UN Convention on the Law of the Sea* (Oxford University Press 2022)

Koh T, *Building a New Legal Order for the Oceans* (NUS Press 2020)

Kwiatkowska B and Soons AH, 'Entitlement to Maritime Areas of Rocks Which Cannot Sustain Human Habitation or Economic Life of their Own' (1990) 21 Netherlands Yearbook of International Law 139

Lando M, *Maritime Delimitation as a Judicial Process* (Cambridge University Press 2019)

Lando M, 'Baseline Preservation as a Response to Sea-Level Rise' (2025) 56 Ocean Development and International Law 100

Lathrop CG, 'Baselines' in DR Rothwell and others (eds), *The Oxford Handbook of the Law of the Sea* (Oxford University Press 2015)

Lewis R, 'The "Constitution for the Oceans"? The Law of the Sea Convention as a Living Treaty' (2025) 74 International and Comparative Law Quarterly 1

Liao X, 'The LOSC as a Package Deal and Its Implications for Determination of Customary International Law' (2020) 35 International Journal of Marine and Coastal Law 704

Linderfalk U, *On the Interpretation of Treaties: The Modern International Law as Expressed in the 1969 Vienna Convention on the Law of Treaties* (Springer 2010)

Linderfalk U, 'The Jan Mayen Case (Iceland/Norway): An Example of Successful Conciliation' in C Tomuschat, R Pisillo Mazzeschi, and D Thürer (eds), *Conciliation in International Law: The OSCE Court of Conciliation and Arbitration* (Brill Nijhoff 2017)

Lisztwan J, 'Stability of Maritime Boundary Agreements' (2012) 37 Yale Journal of International Law 153

Lumba SF, 'The Philippines—The Philippines Archipelagic Baselines Law' (2009) 2 Journal of East Asia and International Law 296

Lusthaus J, 'Shifting Sands: Sea Level Rise, Maritime Boundaries and Inter-State Conflict' (2010) 30 Politics 113

MacGibbon I, 'The Scope of Acquiescence in International Law' (1954) 2 British Yearbook of International Law 143

Magnan A and others, 'Cross-Chapter Box 9: Integrative Cross-Chapter Box on Low-Lying Islands and Coasts' in H-O Pörtner and others (eds), *IPCC Special Report on the Ocean and Cryosphere in a Changing Climate* (2019)

Markus T, 'Article 46—Archipelagic States' in A Proelss (ed), *United Nations Convention on the Law of the Sea: A Commentary* (1st edn, CH Beck 2017)

McDougal MS and Burke WT, *The Public Order of the Oceans: A Contemporary International Law of the Sea* (New Haven Press 1987)

McGranahan G, Balk D, and Anderson B, 'The Rising Tide: Assessing the Risks of Climate Change and Human Settlements in Low Elevation Coastal Zones' (2007) 19 Environment and Urbanization 17

Merkouris P, *Interpretation of Customary International Law: Of Methods and Limits* (Brill 2024)

Mitchell AD and Voon T, 'The Rule of Necessary Implication' in J Klingler, Y Parkhomenko, and C Salonidis (eds), *Between the Lines of the Vienna Convention? Canons and Other Principles of Interpretation in Public International Law* (Wolters Kluwer 2019)

Morgan W, 'Large Ocean States: Pacific Regionalism and Climate Security in a New Era of Geostrategic Competition' (2022) 39(1) East Asia 45

Mossop J, 'The South China Sea Arbitration and New Zealand's Maritime Claims' (2017) 15 New Zealand Journal of Public and International Law 265

Murphy S, *International Law Relating to Islands* (Brill 2017)

Murphy S, 'Ambulatory Versus Fixed Baselines Under the Law of the Sea' (2023) 38 American University Law Review 721

Murphy S, 'Durability, Flexibility and Plasticity in the UN Convention on the Law of the Sea' (2024) 39 International Journal of Marine and Coastal Law 225

Mycoo M and others, 'Small Islands' in H-O Pörtner and others (eds), *Climate Change 2022: Impacts, Adaptation and Vulnerability Contribution of Working Group II to the Sixth Assessment Report of the Intergovernmental Panel on Climate Change* (Cambridge University Press 2022)

Nandan SN and Kraabel KD, *Reflections on the Making of the Modern Law of the Sea* (NUS Press 2021)

Nandan SN, Nordquist MH, and Rosenne S, *United Nations Convention on the Law of the Sea 1982: A Commentary* (Brill 2013)

Neumann B and others, 'Future Coastal Population Growth and Exposure to Sea-Level Rise and Coastal Flooding—A Global Assessment' (2015) 10 PloS one e0118571
Nolte G, 'Jurisprudence under Special Regimes Relating to Subsequent Agreements and Subsequent Practice: Second Report for the ILC Study Group on Treaties over Time' in G Nolte (ed), *Treaties and Subsequent Practice* (Oxford 2013)
Nordquist MH, 'UNCLOS Article 121 and Itu Aba in the South China Sea Final Award: A Correct Interpretation?' in S Jayakumar and others (eds), *The South China Sea Arbitration* (Edward Elgar 2018)
Nordquist MH and Phalen WG, 'Interpretation of UNCLOS Article 121 and Itu Aba (Taiping) in the South China Sea Arbitration Award' in MH Nordquist, JN Moore, and R Long (eds), *International Marine Economy: Law and Policy* (Brill 2017) 1
Nurbintoro G, 'International Tribunals Approach Toward Maritime Boundaries Delimitation of an Archipelagic State' (2024) 21 Indonesian Journal of International Law 2
O'Connell D, *The International Law of the Sea* (vol I, Shearer I ed, Clarendon Press 1984)
Oral N, 'UNCLOS and Sea Level Rise' (2023) 149 Marine Policy 1
Orford A, *International Law and the Politics of History* (Cambridge University Press Cambridge 2021)
Oxman BH, 'The Rule of Law and the United Nations Convention on the Law of the Sea' (1996) 7 European Journal of International Law 353
Papanicolopulu I, 'The Land Dominates the Sea (Dominates the Land Dominates the Sea)' (2018) 47 Questions of International Law: Zoom-in 39
Pörtner H-O and others, *IPCC Special Report on the Ocean and Cryosphere in a Changing Climate* (2019)
Purcell K, *Geographical Change and the Law of the Sea* (Oxford University Press 2019)
Rayfuse R, 'Sea Level Rise and Maritime Zones: Preserving the Maritime Entitlements of "Disappearing" States' in MB Gerrard and GE Wannier (eds), *Threatened Island Nations* (Cambridge University Press 2013)
Reed MW, *Shore and Sea Boundaries: The Development of International Maritime Boundary Principles through United States Practice* (vol 3, Shalowitz AL ed, US Government Printing Office 2000)
Roach JA, 'Today's Customary International Law of the Sea' (2014) 45 Ocean Development & International Law 239
Roach JA, *Excessive Maritime Claims* (4th edn, Brill 2021)
Roberts A, *Is International Law International?* (Oxford University Press 2017)
Roland Holst RJ, *Change in the Law of the Sea: Context, Mechanisms and Practice* (Brill 2022)
Rothwell DR, *Islands and International Law* (Bloomsbury 2022)
Rothwell DR and Stephens T, *The International Law of the Sea* (3rd edn, Bloomsbury 2023)
Saunders I, 'Artificial Islands and Territory in International Law' (2019) 52 Vanderbilt Journal of Transnational Law 643
Saunders I, 'The Limits of the Natural State Doctrine: Rocks, Islands and Artificial Intervention in a Changing World' in D Rothwell and D Letts (eds), *Law of the Sea in South East Asia: Environmental, Navigational and Security Challenges* (Routledge 2019)
Schofield C, 'The Trouble with Islands: The Definition and Role of Islands and Rocks in Maritime Boundary Delimitation' in S-Y Hong and JM Van Dyke (eds), *Maritime Boundary Disputes, Settlement Processes and the Law of the Sea* (vol 65, Martinus Nijhoff 2009)
Schofield C, 'Departures from the Coast: Trends in the Application of Territorial Sea Baselines under the Law of the Sea Convention' (2012) 27 International Journal of Marine and Coastal Law 723

Schofield C, *The Regime of Islands Reframed: Developments in the Definition of Islands under the International Law of the Sea* (Brill 2021)
Schofield C, 'Sea Level Rise: Implications for Baselines, Limits and Boundaries' in LAT Nguyen and HD Vu (eds), *Viability of UNCLOS amid Emerging Global Maritime Challenges* (Springer 2024)
Schofield C and Arsana IMA, 'Closing the Loop: Indonesia's Revised Archipelagic Baselines System' (2009) 1 Australian Journal of Maritime & Ocean Affairs 57
Schofield C and Freestone D, 'The Legal Regime of Islands after the South China Sea Award—Orphaned or Influential? An Essay in Honor of Ted L. McDorman' (2024) 55 Ocean Development & International Law 565
Schofield C and van de Poll R, 'Claims to Straight Baselines in the Asia-Pacific: Contrary to Customary International Law?' (2022) 7 Asia-Pacific Journal of Ocean Law and Policy 313
Scott KN, 'Review Essay: Islands in International Law' (2024) 42 Australian Year Book of International Law 169
Scott KN, 'International Law in the Anthropocene: Responding to the Geoengineering Challenge' (2012) 34 Michigan Journal of International Law 309
Sefrioui S, 'Adapting to Sea Level Rise: A Law of the Sea Perspective' in G Andreone (ed), *The Future of the Law of the Sea* (Springer 2017)
Sengupta M, Ford MR, and Kench PS, 'Shoreline Changes in Coral Reef Islands of the Federated States of Micronesia since the Mid-20th Century' (2021) 377 Geomorphology 107584
Sinclair IM, *The Vienna Convention on the Law of Treaties* (2nd edn, Manchester University Press 1984)
Song Y-H, 'Okinotorishima: A Rock or an Island? Recent Maritime Boundary Controversy Between Japan and Taiwan/China' in Hong S-Y and Van Dyke JM (eds), *Maritime Boundary Disputes, Settlement Processes, and the Law of the Sea* (vol 65, Martinus Nijhoff 2009)
Soons A, 'The Effects of a Rising Sea Level on Maritime Limits and Boundaries' (1990) 37 Netherlands International Law Review 207
Soons A, 'An Ocean under Stress: Climate Change and the Law of the Sea' in *Climate Change: Options and Duties under International Law* (vol 145, Koninklijke Nederlandse Vereniging voor Internationaal Recht 2018)
Stevenson JR and Oxman BH, 'The Future of the United Nations Convention on the Law of the Sea' (1994) 88 American Journal of International Law 488
Storlazzi CD and others, 'Most Atolls Will Be Uninhabitable by the Mid-21st Century Because of Sea-Level Rise Exacerbating Wave-Driven Flooding' (2018) 4 Science Advances 1
Symmons CR, 'Maritime Zones of Islands and Rocks' in S Jayakumar, T Koh, and R Beckman (eds), *The South China Sea Disputes and Law of the Sea* (Edward Elgar 2014)
Symmons CR, 'Article 13—Low-Tide Elevations' in A Proelss (ed), *United Nations Convention on the Law of the Sea: A Commentary* (1st edn, CH Beck 2017)
Talmon S, 'Article 121—Regime of Islands' in A Proelss (ed), *United Nations Convention on the Law of the Sea: A Commentary* (1st edn, CH Beck 2017)
Talmon S, *The South China Sea Arbitration: Jurisdiction, Admissibility, Procedure* (Brill Nijhoff 2022)
Tanaka Y, 'Reflections on the Interpretation and Application of Article 121(3) in the South China Sea Arbitration (Merits)' (2017) 48 Ocean Development & International Law 365
Tanaka Y, *The International Law of the Sea* (3rd edn, Cambridge University Press 2019)

Tanaka Y, *Predictability and Flexibility in the Law of Maritime Delimitation* (2nd edn, Hart 2019)
Tassinis OC, 'Customary International Law: Interpretation from Beginning to End' (2020) 31 European Journal of International Law 235
Trümpler K, 'Article 5—Normal Baseline' in A Proelss (ed), *United Nations Convention on the Law of the Sea: A Commentary* (1st edn, CH Beck 2017)
Tseng H-S and Ou C-H, 'The Evolution and Trend of the Traditional Fishing Rights' (2020) 53 Ocean & Coastal Management 270
UN Division for Ocean Affairs and Law of the Sea, *Handbook on the Delimitation of Maritime Boundaries* (United Nations 2000)
UN Office for Ocean Affairs and the Law of the Sea, *Baselines: An Examination of the Relevant Provisions of the United Nations Convention on the Law of the Sea* (United Nations 1989)
Van Dyke JM and Brooks RA, 'Uninhabited Islands: Their Impact on the Ownership of the Oceans' Resources' (1983) 12 Ocean Development & International Law 265
Vidas D, 'Sea-Level Rise and International Law: At the Convergence of Two Epochs' (2014) 9 Climate Law 70
Vidas D and Freestone D, 'Legal Certainty and Stability in the Face of Sea Level Rise: Trends in the Development of State Practice and International Law Scholarship on Maritime Limits and Boundaries' (2022) 37 International Journal of Marine and Coastal Law 1
Vidas D and others, 'International Law for the Anthropocene? Shifting Perspectives in Regulation of the Oceans, Environment and Genetic Resources' (2015) 9 Anthropocene 1
Villiger ME, *Commentary on the 1969 Vienna Convention on the Law of Treaties* (Brill 2008)
Walker GK, *Definitions for the Law of the Sea: Terms Not Defined by the 1982 Convention* (Martinus Nijhoff 2012)
Weil P, *The Law of Maritime Delimitation: Reflections* (Grotius 1989)

Documents Relating to the Work of the International Law Commission

Aurescu B and Oral N, *First issues paper by Bogdan Aurescu and Nilüfer Oral* (Co-Chairs of the Study Group on sea-level rise in relation to international law, 2020)
Aurescu B and Oral N, *Additional paper to the first issues paper* (Co-Chairs of the Study Group on sea-level rise in relation to international law, 2023)
Draft Articles on the Law of Treaties, with commentaries (1966)
Draft Articles on Responsibility of States for Internationally Wrongful Acts, with commentaries (2001)
Draft conclusions on identification of customary international law, with commentaries (2018)
Draft conclusions on subsequent agreements and subsequent practice in relation to the interpretation of treaties, with commentaries (2018)
Galvão Teles P and Ruda Santolaria JJ, *Second issues paper* (Co-Chairs of the Study Group on sea-level rise in relation to international law, 2022)
Galvão Teles P, Oral N, and Ruda Santolaria JJ, *Final consolidated report of the Co-Chairs of the Study Group on sea-level rise in relation to international law*, UN Doc A/CN.4/783 (3 February 2025)
Report of the International Law Commission covering the work of its seventieth session (2018)
Report of the International Law Commission covering the work of its seventy-second session (2021)

Report of the International Law Commission covering the work of its seventy-fourth session (2023)
Report of the International Law Commission covering the work of its seventy-fifth session (2024)
Report of the International Law Commission covering the work of its seventy-sixth session (2025)
Study Group on sea-level rise in relation to international law, *Final Report of the Study Group on sea-level rise in relation to international law* (2025)

Documents of the International Law Association

International Law Association (Committee on Baselines under the International Law of the Sea), Baselines under the International Law of the Sea (Sofia Conference) (2012)
International Law Association (Committee on Baselines under the International Law of the Sea, Baselines under the International Law of the Sea (Sydney Conference) (2018)
International Law Association (Committee on International Law and Sea Level Rise), Report (Sydney Conference) (2018)
International Law Association (Committee on International Law and Sea Level Rise), Resolution 5/2018
International Law Association (Committee on International Law and Sea Level Rise), Report (Lisbon Conference) (2022)
International Law Association (Committee on International Law and Sea Level Rise), Report (Athens Conference) (2024)
International Law Association (Committee on International Law and Sea Level Rise), Resolution 1/2024

Index

For the benefit of digital users, indexed terms that span two pages (e.g., 52–53) may, on occasion, appear on only one of those pages.

Tables and figures are indicated by an italic *t* and *f* following the page number

A

Alliance of Small Island States (AOSIS)
  Leaders' Declaration of the Alliance of Small Island States, 1–2, 4–5, 62, 135–36, 185, 193–94
  Leaders' Declaration on Sea-Level Rise and Statehood, 217–18
  membership, *24*
ambulatory baselines
  critiques of, 43–46, 72, 110, 126–27, 130, 205
  development in scholarship, 34–46
  unsatisfactory consequences of, 38–39
Angola, 77*t*, 79–80, 86*t*
Antigua and Barbuda, 65–67, 86*t*, 187*t*
archipelagic baseline(s)
  due publicity, 131–32, 193–94, 203
  interpretation of Article 47, 180–82, 186–88, 214–15
  meaning and usage, 27, 28–29, 100, 116n.18, 118, 181–82
  spatial stability of, 103, 185–86, 216
  use of coordinates, 81, 101–2, 123, 178–79, 185–86, 207–8
archipelagic State, 66–67, 151–52, 181–84, 186–88
archipelagic status, 180–88, 214–15
Argentina, 77*t*, 79–80, 86*t*, 114*t*, 115*t*
Australia, 77*t*, 83–84, 86*t*, 161–62, 163–64

B

Bahamas, The, 65–66, 86*t*, 114*t*, 115*t*, 187*t*, 201–2
Bangladesh, 77*t*, 79–80, 86*t*, 115*t*
Barbados, 77*t*, 86*t*
baseline(s)
  ambulatory theory of *see* ambulatory baselines
  archipelagic *see* archipelagic baseline
  duty to update, 124–27, 208
  'fixed' theory of *see* fixed baselines
  legal significance of, 3, 27
  legal stability of *see* legal stability
  normal *see* normal baseline
  role in delimitation, 29–34
  straight *see* straight baseline
basepoints, 29–31, 184–85, 196–97 *see also* baselines, role in delimitation
Belgium, 77*t*, 86*t*
Belize, 64, 77*t*, 86*t*, 114*t*, 115*t*
Benin, 77*t*, 86*t*
Brazil, 77*t*, 79–80, 86*t*, 114*t*, 115*t*, 118, 161–62, 169n.86
Bulgaria, 77*t*, 86*t*

C

Cambodia, 114*t*, 115*t*
Cameroon, 77*t*, 86*t*
Canada, 77*t*, 78–79, 86*t*, 178
Cape Verde, 187*t*
charts
  types of, 82–83
  use in the definition of the normal baseline, 81–83
Chile, 49–50, 161–62
China, 114*t*, 115*t*
climate change impacts, 1–2, 11–12, 112–13, 153–54, 156
Colombia, 77*t*, 86*t*, 211–12
Commission of Small Island States (COSIS), 199–201, 218–19
Commonwealth, the
  membership, *24*
  Ocean Declaration, 4–5, 98n.145, 135–36, 193–94
Comoros, 187*t*

Congo, 77*t*, 86*t*
Cook Islands, 77*t*, 80, 86*t*, 194–95
coordinates (geographical)
  meaning, 81
  use in the definition of the normal baseline (see *normal baseline, use of coordinates*)
Costa Rica, 77*t*, 78–79, 86*t*, 161–62
Cote d'Ivoire, 77*t*, 86*t*
Croatia, 77*t*, 86*t*
Cuba, 114*t*, 115*t*

D
delimitation *see* maritime boundary delimitation
Democratic Republic of Congo, 77*t*, 78–79, 86*t*
Denmark, 77*t*, 78–79, 86*t*, 114*t*, 115*t*, 116–17
Djibouti, 77*t*, 86*t*, 114*t*, 115*t*
Dominican Republic, 187*t*
due publicity, obligations of, 71–72, 131–32, 137–38, 193–95, 203

E
Egypt, 114*t*, 115*t*
El Salvador, 77*t*, 86*t*, 212
Equatorial Guinea, 77*t*, 86*t*
Eritrea, 77*t*, 86*t*
Estonia, 77*t*, 78–79, 86*t*

F
features, legal status of
  relevance of capacity to sustain human habitation, 154–55 *see also* habitability
  relevance of elevation and submergence, 170–72
  transformation of legal status, 172–80, 208–9
Fiji, 63, 65–66, 77*t*, 80, 86*t*, 161–62, 166, 187*t*, 201–2
fixed baseline(s)
  discussion in scholarship, 34, 36–37, 99
  as a form of spatially stable baseline, 38–39, 41–42, 71n.1, 97–98, 99, 190–91, 219–20
France, 77*t*, 78, 86*t*, 136–37, 161–62, 166–67
fundamental change of circumstances, 32–34

G
Gabon, 77*t*, 86*t*
Gambia, The, 77*t*, 86*t*, 114*t*, 115*t*
Georgia, 77*t*, 86*t*
Germany, 65–67, 77*t*, 86*t*, 114*t*, 115*t*, 136–37
Ghana, 77*t*, 86*t*
Greece, 77*t*, 86*t*
Grenada, 77*t*, 86*t*, 187*t*
Guatemala, 77*t*, 86*t*
Guinea, 76–78, 77*t*, 86*t*
Guinea-Bissau, 114*t*, 115*t*
Guyana, 77*t*, 86*t*, 114*t*, 115*t*

H
habitability
  legal significance for maritime entitlement, 153–72
  loss of, 155–56
  meaning, 155
Haiti, 77*t*, 86*t*
Honduras, 76–78, 77*t*, 86*t*

I
Iceland, 77*t*, 78–79, 86*t*, 161–62
India, 77*t*, 79–80, 86*t*, 114*t*, 115*t*
Indonesia, 77*t*, 78–79, 86*t*, 114*t*, 115*t*, 115–16, 187*t*
International Law Association, Committee on Baselines
  consideration of the normal baseline, 37–38, 73
International Law Association, Committee on Sea-Level Rise
  2018 Report and Resolution, 5, 42–43, 44
  2024 Resolution, 192
International Law Commission (ILC), Study Group on sea-level rise
    Additional Paper to the First Issues Paper, 43–44, 46, 62, 69, 136–37, 206
    First Issues Paper (2020), 39–42, 61, 65–66, 181
    Final Report (2025), 5, 15, 32–34, 43–44, 186–88, 192–93, 217–18
  2025 ILC Report, 6, 12–14, 44, 47, 194–95, 217–18

interpretation *see* treaty interpretation
Iran, 77*t*, 86*t*
Ireland, 77*t*, 86*t*, 195–96
Island
  artificial, 154–55, 175–76
  definition in the LOSC *see* LOSC Article 121
  status (of a land feature), 23, 66–67, 68, 70, 151–89, 208–9, 214, 215, 216, 220
Israel, 77*t*, 86*t*
Italy, 77*t*, 86*t*, 114*t*, 115*t*

J
Jamaica, 184–85, 187*t*, 201–2
Japan, 77*t*, 86*t*, 114*t*, 115*t*, 115–16, 161–62

K
Kenya, 77*t*, 86*t*
Kiribati, 77*t*, 80, 86*t*, 161–62, 178–79, 187*t*, 209–10, 218–19
Korea, Republic of, 77*t*, 81–82, 86*t*, 114*t*, 115*t*
Kuwait, 77*t*, 86*t*

L
'land dominates the sea' principle, 26–27, 92–93, 132, 151–52
League of Nations Conference for the Codification of International Law (the Hague Conference), 49–50, 53–58, 60, 90
Lebanon, 77*t*, 86*t*
legal stability
  definition and elements, 7 *see also* spatial stability; temporal stability
  emergence in scholarship, 43–46
  in extremis, 215–19
  relating to the status of features, 7, 65–66
  relevance to UNCLOS interpretation, 43–44
  use of term by States, 61–68
Liberia, 77*t*, 86*t*
Lithuania, 77*t*, 78–79, 86*t*
low-tide elevation, 22–23, 28, 35–36, 151–89
low-water line
  discussion in drafting history of Article 5, 56–58
  vertical datum(s), 89–90, 89*f*

M
Madagascar, 77*t*, 86*t*
Malaysia, 114*t*, 115*t*
Maldives, 64, 86*t*, 114*t*, 115*t*, 187*t*
maritime boundary/boundaries
  delimitation, 29–31
  maritime boundary treaties
    effect of sea-level rise, 32–34
    stability under treaty law, 32–34
    role of baselines, 29–34
Marshall Islands, Republic of, 77*t*, 80, 86*t*, 114*t*, 115*t*, 187*t*
Mauritania, 77*t*, 86*t*
Mauritius, 77*t*, 78–79, 80, 86*t*, 187*t*, 198–99
Mexico, 77*t*, 86*t*, 114*t*, 115*t*, 117, 161–62
Micronesia, Federates States of, 3–4, 64, 77*t*, 80, 86*t*, 194–95, 199
Monaco, 77*t*, 86*t*
Mozambique, 77*t*, 86*t*
Myanmar, 114*t*, 115*t*

N
Namibia, 77*t*, 86*t*
Nauru, 77*t*, 80, 86*t*
Netherlands, The, 77*t*, 81–82, 86*t*, 111–12, 114*t*, 115*t*, 120
New Zealand, 77*t*, 86*t*, 161–62, 164
Nicaragua, 77*t*, 86*t*
Nigeria, 77*t*, 86*t*, 114*t*, 115*t*
Niue, 77*t*, 80, 86*t*
normal baseline(s)
  drafting history of Article 5, 52–61
  interpretation of Article 5, 87–99, 207–8
  meaning, 27
  spatial stability of, 99–103, 177–78, 185–86, 188–89, 206–8, 209–10, 214
  use of coordinates, 78–81, 85, 87*f*, 96, 98–99
Norway, 77*t*, 78–79, 86*t*, 161–62, 163–64

O
Okinotorishima, 161–62, 179–80

P
Pacific Islands Forum (PIF)
  Declaration on Preserving Maritime Zones in the Face of Climate Change-Related Sea-Level Rise, 1–2, 4, 8–9, 12–13, 19–20, 62, 65–66, 135–36, 138–39, 191–92, 193–94, 195–96, 205, 212

Pacific Islands Forum (PIF) (*cont.*)
  Declaration on the Continuity of Statehood and the Protection of Persons in the Face of Climate Change-Related Sea-Level Rise, 217–18
  membership, *24*
Pakistan, 114*t*, 115*t*
Palau, 77*t*, 80, 86*t*
Palestine, State of, 77*t*, 80, 86*t*
Papua New Guinea, 66–67, 77*t*, 80, 86*t*, 187*t*
Peru, 77*t*, 78–79, 86*t*
Philippines, 114*t*, 115*t*, 115–16, 187*t*
Poland, 77*t*, 86*t*
Portugal, 77*t*, 86*t*, 161–62

Q
Qatar, 77*t*, 86*t*, 114*t*, 115*t*

R
Rebus sic stantibus see fundamental change of circumstances
Rock, 35, 151–89, 208, 214
Rockall, 173–74
Romania, 39–40, 77*t*, 86*t*
Russian Federation, 77*t*, 86*t*, 114*t*, 115*t*, 161–62

S
Saint Kitts and Nevis, 77*t*, 86*t*
Saint Lucia, 77*t*, 86*t*
Saint Vincent and the Grenadines, 187*t*
Samoa, 12–13, 77*t*, 80, 86*t*
Sao Tome and Principe, 187*t*
Saudi Arabia, 77*t*, 86*t*
sea-level rise
  coastal erosion and inundation, 1–2
  legal implications, 213–15
  scientific projections, 1–2
Senegal, 77*t*, 86*t*
Seychelles, 77*t*, 80, 86*t*, 187*t*
Sierra Leone, 77*t*, 86*t*
Slovenia, 76–78, 77*t*, 86*t*
Solomon Islands, 77*t*, 86*t*, 187*t*, 200–1
Somalia, 77*t*, 86*t*
South Africa, 77*t*, 86*t*, 161–62
Spain, 77*t*, 86*t*, 114*t*, 115*t*
spatial stability, 7, 14n.60, 17, 21–22, 48, 70, 71–109, 188–89, 206–7, 214, *see also* normal baseline, spatial stability of
Sri Lanka, 77*t*, 86*t*
straight baseline(s)
  comparison with normal baselines, 96, 97, 99–100, 101–2
  interpretation of Article 7, 95–96
  meaning, 27
  spatial stability of, 100, 101–2
  state practice, 95–96
state practice
  meaning of, 14
  legislation as a form of, 15
  relevant to the interpretation of UNCLOS *see* Treaty interpretation, subsequent practice
  relevant to customary international law, 20–21, 209–12
Sudan, 77*t*, 86*t*
Suriname, 77*t*, 86*t*, 114*t*, 115*t*, 116–17
Sweden, 77*t*, 86*t*
Syria, 77*t*, 86*t*

T
Tanzania, 77*t*, 86*t*
temporal stability, 7, 48, 65–66, 70, 110–49, 185–86, 206, 214
Thailand, 114*t*, 115*t*
Third UN Conference on the Law of the Sea (UNCLOS III), 49–53, 132–33, 154–55, 159, 165–66
Timor-Leste, 77*t*, 81–82, 86*t*
Togo, 77*t*, 86*t*
Tonga, 77*t*, 86*t*, 200–1
treaty interpretation
  compared with modification, 19–20
  general rule of interpretation, 88–89, 122, 128
  interpretative agreement, 96–98, 135–37
  subsequent practice, 9, 93–99, 133–38
  treaty silence, 127–29
  Vienna Convention on the Law of Treaties (VCLT), 17–18, 44–45, 88–89, 93–94, 96, 100, 110, 129, 130, 131
Trinidad and Tobago, 187*t*
Tunisia, 77*t*, 86*t*
Türkiye, 77*t*, 86*t*
Tuvalu, 77*t*, 80, 86*t*, 114*t*, 115*t*, 117, 187*t*, 200–1, 217–19

U
Ukraine, 77*t*, 78–79, 86*t*
United Kingdom, 39–40, 77*t*, 83–84, 86*t*, 114*t*, 115*t*, 115–16, 117, 166–67, 195
United Nations Convention on the Law of the Sea (LOSC)
  Article 5 *see* normal baseline
  Article 7 *see* straight baseline
  Article 47 *see* archipelagic baseline
  Article 121
    two-part model of features, 158, 159*f*
    three-part model of features, 159–68, 165*f*
    interpretation of, 208
  evolution of, 7, 8–9, 10–11, 43, 44–46, 219–20, 221
  negotiation of *see* Third UN Conference on the Law of the Sea
United States, 39–40, 77*t*, 83–84, 86*t*, 111–12, 114*t*, 115*t*, 120–21, 161–62, 164, 209–10, 211
Uruguay, 77*t*, 78–79, 86*t*

V
Vanuatu, 77*t*, 80, 86*t*, 187*t*, 201–2, 218–19
Venezuela, 77*t*, 86*t*, 161–62
Viet Nam, 114*t*, 115*t*

Y
Yemen, 161–62